Helping Relationships
With Older Adults

SAGE was founded in 1965 by Sara Miller McCune to support the dissemination of usable knowledge by publishing innovative and high-quality research and teaching content. Today, we publish over 900 journals, including those of more than 400 learned societies, more than 800 new books per year, and a growing range of library products including archives, data, case studies, reports, and video. SAGE remains majority-owned by our founder, and after Sara's lifetime will become owned by a charitable trust that secures our continued independence.

Los Angeles | London | New Delhi | Singapore | Washington DC | Melbourne

Helping Relationships With Older Adults

From Theory to Practice

Adelle M. Williams
Slippery Rock University of Pennsylvania

Los Angeles | London | New Delhi
Singapore | Washington DC | Melbourne

FOR INFORMATION:

SAGE Publications, Inc.
2455 Teller Road
Thousand Oaks, California 91320
E-mail: order@sagepub.com

SAGE Publications Ltd.
1 Oliver's Yard
55 City Road
London, EC1Y 1SP
United Kingdom

SAGE Publications India Pvt. Ltd.
B 1/I 1 Mohan Cooperative Industrial Area
Mathura Road, New Delhi 110 044
India

SAGE Publications Asia-Pacific Pte. Ltd.
3 Church Street
#10-04 Samsung Hub
Singapore 049483

Acquisitions Editor: Nathan Davidson
Development Editor: Abbie Rickard
Production Editor: Kelly DeRosa
Copy Editor: Lana Todorovic-Arndt
Typesetter: C&M Digitals (P) Ltd
Proofreader: Dennis W. Webb
Indexer: Maria Sosnowski
Cover Designer: Candice Harman
Marketing Manager: Shari Countryman

Printed in the United States of America

Library of Congress Cataloging-in-Publication Data

Names: Williams, Adelle M., author.

Title: Helping relationships with older adults : from theory to practice / Adelle M. Williams.

Description: First Edition. | Thousand Oaks : SAGE Publications, Inc., 2017. | Includes bibliographical references and index.

Identifiers: LCCN 2016005370 | ISBN 9781483344584 (pbk. : alk. paper)

Subjects: LCSH: Older people. | Social work with older people. | Older people—Services for. | Older people—Medical care.

Classification: LCC HQ1061 .W495 2016 | DDC 362.6—dc23
LC record available at http://lccn.loc.gov/2016005370

This book is printed on acid-free paper.

16 17 18 19 20 10 9 8 7 6 5 4 3 2 1

Brief Contents

Detailed Contents

SECTION II   COMMON ISSUES AND PROBLEMATIC BEHAVIORS EXPERIENCED BY OLDER ADULTS

4   Health Challenges That Impact the Well-Being of Older Adults

5 Challenging Conditions Experienced by Older Adults   142

6 Family Issues and Support Systems   169

7 Loss and Its Effect on Older Adults 199

12   Future Trends 367

Index **373**

About the Author **386**

Series Editors' Preface

In 2014, the Census Bureau noted that the number of Americans aged 65 and older was expected to nearly double by the middle of the century, when they will make up more than a fifth of the nation's population. This same report projected that by 2050, 83.7 million American will be 65 or older, which is noteworthy given the 43.1 million cited in 2012. The stresses and life challenges confronting those 65 and older, while reflecting those experienced by all adults, are oftentimes quite unique to this population. And, just as the challenges are unique, so too must be the services provided in support of these individuals as they continue to journey through life.

The specific knowledge, skills, and professional disposition required of those serving the psychological and emotional needs of an aging population are brilliantly articulated in *Fundamentals of Helping Relationships With Older Adults: From Theory to Practice* written by Dr. Adelle M. Williams. In this text, Dr. Williams employs her extensive expertise and clinical experience in working with the older adults to provide counselors-in-training with a guide to adult normative development as well as ways of recognizing and responding to that which is non-normative.

The material found in *Fundamentals of Helping Relationships With Older Adults: From Theory to Practice* reflects the latest research findings on issues of older adult development, as well as the best practice employed by those serving that population. In this text, readers will not only be provided an overview to the aging process, both as a gift and a challenge, but also will be guided in their development of those competencies essential to providing ethical, best-practice counseling to this older population. *Fundamentals of Helping Relationships With Older Adults: From Theory to Practice* provides the reader with insight into assessing, diagnosing, and treatment planning, including both general interventions and specialized counseling interventions, that constitute best practice for those working with today's older adults. The text, with its extensive use of case illustrations, is designed to not only develop the reader's understanding of the older adult experience, but also to develop those competencies necessary for professionally engaging with the older adult client. Unique to Dr. Williams's approach is that she not only focuses on the reader's development of essential knowledge and skill, but also on the dispositions and attitudes essential to the effective delivery of counseling service to older adults.

As is obvious, one text, one learning experience will not be sufficient for mastery of the processes of case conceptualization, or for the successful formation of your professional identity and practice. The formation of both your professional identity and practice will be a lifelong process, a process that we hope to facilitate through the presentation of this text and the creation of our series: *Counseling and Professional Identity in the 21st Century*.

Counseling and Professional Identity in the 21st Century is a new, fresh, pedagogically sound series of texts targeting counselors in training. This series is not simply a compilation of isolated books matching those already in the market. Rather, each book, with its targeted knowledge and skills, will be presented as but a part of a larger whole. The focus and content of each text serves as a single lens through which a counselor can view his or her clients, engage in his or her practice, and articulate his or her own professional identity.

Counseling and Professional Identity in the 21st Century is unique not because it "packaged" a series of traditional text, but because it provides an *integrated* curriculum targeting the formation of the readers' professional identity and efficient, ethical practice. Each book within the series is structured to facilitate the ongoing professional formation of the reader. The materials found within each text are organized in order to move the reader to higher levels of cognitive, affective, and psychomotor functioning, resulting in readers' assimilation of the materials presented into both their professional identity and approach to professional practice. While each text targets a specific set of core competencies (cognates and skills) essential to the practice of counseling, each book in the series emphasizes each of the following:

1. The assimilation of concepts and constructs provided across the text found within the series, thus fostering the reader's ongoing development as a competent professional

2. The blending of contemporary theory with current research and empirical support

3. A focus on the development of procedural knowledge with each text employing case illustrations and guided practice exercises to facilitate the reader's ability to translate the theory and research discussed into professional decision making and application

4. The emphasis on the need for and means of demonstrating accountability

5. The fostering of the reader's professional identity and with it the assimilation of the ethics and standards of practice guiding the counseling profession.

We are proud to have served as coeditors of this series; feeling sure that text, just like *Fundamentals of Helping Relationships With Older Adults: From Theory to Practice,* will serve as a significant resource to you and your development as a professional counselor.

Richard Parsons, PhD
Naijian Zhang, PhD

The Author's Purpose

Gerontology is an exciting integration of many disciplines. Students preparing for careers in the counseling and related professions who plan to work with older adults are in need of theoretical and practical experiences to be prepared to work effectively. They need to understand the complexities of the aging process and appreciate the challenges and opportunities that the process entails. With the dramatic increase in the current older adult population and the large projected increase in the future, many opportunities will be available for students in counseling and related professions to help older adults realize their strengths and assets and empower them to manage life's inconsistent terrain. Older adults are a very heterogeneous population, and they require helping professionals who have the knowledge, skills, and positive attitude to work effectively with their issues.

This textbook entails fundamental theoretical perspectives of the aging process and societal influences. It reinforces the strength and resiliency of this older population throughout the textbook. Common changes experienced by elders and problematic conditions are examined. The significance of the relationship of the helping professional in the therapeutic encounter is also examined. The standards and competencies required of gerontological counselors and unique attributes of the helping professional are highlighted. Various therapeutic modalities and the effectiveness for older adults are explored. Throughout the textbook, case illustrations and guided practice exercises allow the reader to experience the various issues that are challenging in the lives of older clients. Instructors can stimulate critical thinking skills and sensitize students to the uniqueness of their older clients. It is my hope that through a concerted effort, we will be able to improve and enhance the overall health of older adults because the later years are just as significant as the early and middle years of the life span. I hope that *Fundamentals of Helping Relationships With Older Adults* is a text that students, faculty, and helping professionals enjoy.

Adelle M. Williams, PhD
Slippery Rock University of Pennsylvania

Acknowledgments

A special thank you is extended to Ms. Patti Pink, who has worked tirelessly and consistently by my side in the preparation of this manuscript. I'd also like to extend my appreciation to Dr. Joan Rogers, who has been a source of inspiration during this process and throughout my professional career. A final thank you is extended for the personal assistance obtained in the manuscript preparation process.

I'd also like to thank the following reviewers:

Amy Gray-Graves, Webster University

Jeanne L. Thomas, Eastern Michigan University

Kyle H. O'Brien, Gateway Community College

Lee Slivinske, Youngstown State University

Nancy A. Orel, Bowling Green State University

Patricia Kolar, University of Pittsburgh

Polly McMahon, Spokane Falls Community College

Robert A. Jecklin, University of Wisconsin – La Crosse

Ronica N. Rooks, University of Colorado – Denver

J. Steven Fulks, Barton College

Denice Goodrich Liley, Boise State University

Geri M. Lotze, Virginia Commonwealth University

Liz Stevens, City University of Seattle

Adrienne L. Cohen, Georgia Southern University

Dianne Oakes, Excelsior College

Tim Chandler, Hardin-Simmons University

From the Author's Chair

A genuine respect and appreciation for older adults is a value that I have adhered to since childhood. Providing assistance without compensation was taught from a very early age, and it is a rewarding experience. Therefore, it was not surprising to me that I chose a helping profession to continue to emphasize rendering services to older persons. I earned a master's and a doctoral degree in rehabilitation counseling from the University of Pittsburgh and continued my focus on the aging population. The rehabilitation philosophy encompasses maximizing the functional capacity of individuals in all spheres of life. This philosophy is eclectic in its orientation, and it emphasizes doing whatever is appropriate to maximize the capabilities of clients. My personal philosophy and experiences are consistent with rehabilitating persons to their maximum level of functioning.

Clinical, administrative, and research experiences were obtained in a variety of formats and various organizations. However, my clinical skills were enhanced at the Western Psychiatric Institute and Clinic (W.P.I.C.) where I had the opportunity to develop my skills in individual, group, and family counseling while simultaneously working with a multidisciplinary team. It should be noted that very few inpatient psychogeriatric units existed at this time, and I was fortunate to become one of the clinicians to work on the psychogeriatric units that focused exclusively on a comprehensive approach to the treatment of older adults with mental health issues. I had a unique opportunity to co-develop, recruit, and monitor the geropsychiatry admission process and to facilitate the admissions process for older adults and their families. Additionally, research opportunities were an integral component of my employment at W.P.I.C. Interacting with various therapists in the team proved valuable in the therapeutic process with older adults. Furthermore, I managed research grants that focused on improving and enhancing the well-being of older adults in the community. Throughout all of my professional experiences, I stayed committed to working with older adults. I had the opportunity to work on inpatient and outpatient units, long-term care systems, health care systems, and in educational and consultant positions. The Benedum Geriatric Outpatient Center provided numerous opportunities for assessment and treatment for older adults and excellent supervision by personnel who specialized in gerontology, geriatrics, and geropsychiatry. This breadth of experience facilitated my completion of a master's degree in business administration to better prepare me to understand the business aspects of the health care industry and its impact on aging services.

Currently as a professor and Gerontology Coordinator at Slippery Rock University, I have developed courses, revised curricula, managed academic programs, developed and supervised internship placements, advised students, conducted research, published articles, engaged in university governance, and provided community service. Positions included Director of a Health Services Administration program, Assistant to the Dean of the College of Health, Environment, and Science, and Gerontology Coordinator, while maintaining faculty responsibilities. Courses taught in administration included the organization, delivery, management, and financing of the health care delivery system. Courses in health included personal health, community health, and international health. Aging courses include the aging process, death and dying process, senior aging seminar, women and aging, foundations of aging, counseling older adults, career development counseling, and internship supervision.

In all of the various transitions within the university, I continue to focus on increasing awareness of aging issues and promoting the counseling and related health professions to enhance their ability to serve older clients. Elevating the status of aging as a specialty and increasing the numbers of gerontological specialists remains a high priority.

Overview of the Aging Process, Aging Theories, Positive Aging, and the Helping Process

CHAPTER 1

Introduction

"There is a fountain of youth: it is your mind, your talents, the creativity you bring to your life and the lives of people you love. When you learn to tap this source, you will truly have defeated age."

—Sophia Loren

Learning Objectives

After reading this chapter, you will be able to

1. Describe the basic changes that occur in the aging process
2. Analyze the various biological theories that explain aging
3. Examine the normative physical changes that accompany the aging process
4. Explain the cognitive changes that accompany aging

The aging of the population is one of the most profound and far-reaching changes affecting contemporary society. Between 2014 and 2060, the U.S. population is projected to increase from 319 million to 417 million, reaching 400 million in 2051 (Colby & Ortman, 2014). By 2030, one in five Americans is projected to be 65 and over (Colby & Ortman, 2014). In 2014, the 65 plus population is expected to grow from 15% gradually upwards to 24% by 2060 (Colby & Ortman, 2014). The baby boomers (individuals born between 1946 and 1964) largely account for the increase in this demographic, as they began turning 65 in 2011. By 2050, the surviving baby boomers will be over the age of 85.

The aging of the population has wide-ranging implications for the country. By *aging,* demographers often mean that the proportion of the population in the older age range increases. As the United States ages over the next several decades, its older population will become more racially and ethnically diverse. The projected growth of the older U.S.

population will present challenges to policymakers and programs. It will also affect families, businesses, and health care providers (Ortman, Velkoff, & Hogan, 2014). There is a clear need for health professionals with a thorough understanding and appreciation for the experiences of this older population. With so many individuals over age 65, mental health professionals with the expertise to assess and treat the problems of later life are sorely needed (Zarit & Zarit, 2011).

People are not just living longer, but they are living better longer than ever before. Improvements in disease prevention and health promotion, the widespread availability of public and private pensions and other financial benefits, and increased educational opportunities for each successive generation have dramatically improved the lives of today's society. The next generation of older people will have had better education and have taken better care of their health across the life span, so their prospects for successful old age are even greater (Zarit & Zarit, 2011).

These demographic and social changes mean that an increasing number of older people are in need of psychological services. The mental health field, however, has been slow to respond with adequate numbers of trained professionals who have specialized training in geriatrics. For many years, geriatric practice was a backwater, a minor field viewed condescendingly by clinicians who felt that little could be done for anyone over age 50 (Zarit & Zarit, 2011). That viewpoint was a luxury of a society that had relatively few older people. The dramatic expansion of life expectancy and growth in the proportion of people over age 65, coupled with empirical findings of the effectiveness of treatment for many problems of later life, provides a solid foundation for geriatric mental health practice. The number of clinicians with geriatric expertise, however, falls far short of the need (Zarit & Zarit, 2011).

Aging is a natural and inevitable process and a very complex one. Many changes occur in this process; however, no two persons experience these changes at the same time or at the same rate. It is a variable experience. Some elders accept the natural changes that occur as a positive experience, while others view these changes with disgust and frustration. The process of aging is also a time to explore hidden talents, engage in new activities, commit to new relationships, and express oneself in novel and creative ways. Aging is more than the physical, social, psychological, and environmental changes. It involves a renewed energy and appreciation for life, opportunities to explore, and an inner transformation that is unique to every aging individual.

AGING

Aging is characterized by a variety of changes. These changes can be social, physical, or cognitive. Constant adjustments and readjustments are required to maintain some sense of normalcy.

Socially, a number of adjustments may occur, such as a change in the quantity and quality of relationships one has, a change in role from a caregiver to a care receiver, becoming single after being married for 50 years, and transitioning from utilizing informal supports (e.g., family, friends) to formal support systems (e.g., long-term care facilities, respite care services). Society's perception of aging persons can change as well, with many perceiving older persons as less valued. Environmental modifications can be required if older adults live in environments that are inconsistent with their functional abilities. Changes in their residence, proximity to significant others, and driving status will impact their social situation.

Physical changes are an inevitable consequence of the aging process. Gradual changes will occur in an older adult's senses, appearance, balance, strength, and cognition, though most conditions can be addressed and corrected in the earlier stages. Sense of taste and smell will decline with age; however, there may exist other causes for impaired taste and smell that are treatable (e.g., dental problems, nasal/sinus problems). Vision will decline, but it can be corrected at earlier stages. Hearing will become impaired, though simple modifications can correct this issue. Balance, flexibility, and muscle strength will decrease, but with adequate exercise, including cardio, strength training, and yoga, these changes do not necessarily impair one's routine activities.

Cognition depends on a healthy, well-functioning brain. While the ability to learn, store, and retrieve information may require more time than for a younger person, barring any major disorders, older persons adapt well to changes in cognitive status. Older adults continue to have the capacity to learn new information; however, it may take longer and may require the use of more mnemonic devices to assist them.

Healthy, highly functioning older adults have high self-esteem, are internally controlled, maintain balance in their lives, minimize stressful situations, and are actively engaged in a variety of activities. They have a belief system that allows them to handle life's ups and downs. When confronted with losses, such as that of a spouse, residence, physical and cognitive health, or relationships, they grieve but readjust to the loss and continue pursuing their goals and aspirations. However, even under the best circumstances, there are older persons who respond to losses in such a manner that necessitates the interventions of a professional. Their self-esteem and self-worth may be jeopardized, and therefore, outside support is required. This constant cycle of adjustment and re-establishment is an ongoing process for older adults and can affect their psychological well-being.

Older adults are wise, resilient, and spend most of their lives free of disabilities. However, many physical and mental conditions can accompany the aging process. With a comprehensive geriatric assessment and maintenance of a healthy lifestyle, these conditions are managed so that older persons can continue with their daily activities. Later life provides many opportunities for social interaction, participation in activities, continued employment, volunteerism, and leisure pursuits. These opportunities are different for each person because resources vary. There are older persons who will have the ability to retire, while others will continue to work. Time, income, interest, and health will determine the extent to which each older person is able to take advantage of various opportunities. Promotion and adherence to a healthy lifestyle that includes a good diet, adequate rest, exercise, engagement in meaningful activities, and a connection to others is critical at all stages of the life cycle.

Many transitions occur throughout the life course. Most are managed with little effort, while others require the assistance of professionals. Professional counselors have an opportunity to position themselves to provide advocacy, referral, counseling, and educational services to a growing older population.

BIOLOGICAL THEORIES ASSOCIATED WITH AGING

Numerous theories have been identified to explain why the human body ages, as there is no single theory that can do so. Each theory provides insight into certain aspects of aging, and a firm grasp of these concepts will help mental health professionals better understand their older clients and the aging process.

Neuroendocrine Theory

The neuroendocrine theory of aging focuses on the neuroendocrine system, which is a complicated network of biochemicals that govern the release of hormones altered by the hypothalamus located in the brain. The hypothalamus controls various chain reactions to instruct other organs and glands to release their hormones. The hypothalamus also responds to the body hormone levels as a guide to the overall normal activity, and as we grow older, the hypothalamus loses its precision regulatory ability, and the receptors that uptake individual hormones become less sensitive to them. Additionally, as we age, the secretion of many hormones decline, and their effectiveness is also reduced (Ramaswamy, 2012). As the body ages, it produces lower levels of hormones that are vital for well-being. Dehydroepiandrosterone (DHEA) is a hormone that comes from the adrenal gland and also made in the brain. DHEA leads to the production of male and female sex hormones. DHEA levels begin to decrease after age 30 and levels decrease more quickly in women. Lower DHEA levels are found in people with hormonal disorders, HIV/AIDS, Alzheimer's disease, heart disease, depression, diabetes inflammation, immune disorders, and osteoporosis (Mayo Clinic, 2015). DHEA may cause side effects related to other hormones, and women may experience symptoms such as increased unnatural hair growth and deep voice, and men may experience urinary urgency and aggression, among other symptoms. Other side effects that may occur in either sex include sleep problems, headache, nausea, skin itching, and mood changes; and DHEA may affect levels of other hormones such as insulin (hormone that controls the glucose levels in the blood) (Mayo Clinic, 2015). Melatonin is another hormone and has been called the antistress hormone due to its ability to regulate rhythms of other hormones and its ability to blunt the negative effects of cortisol. Cortisol is a hormone that regulates a wide range of processes throughout the body including metabolism and the immune response. It also has a very important role in helping the body respond to stress; however, when cortisol levels are elevated longer than normal, it contributes to illnesses and diseases because cortisol is considered the stress hormone when it is elevated. A decline in human growth hormone results in changes in body composition. Lean body mass shrinks, and there is an increase in adipose (fatty) tissue. This loss of lean body mass leads to atrophy, or wasting away, of skin, skeletal muscle, and bone. Decreased levels of human growth hormone can also lead to elevated cholesterol levels (Park et al., 2011).

The neuroendocrine theory proposes that the most effective approaches to delay (and even reverse) the aging process and ameliorate the diseases of aging is to restore hypothalamic (and peripheral) receptor sensitivity, restore hormone levels to more youthful values by hormone replacement therapy, prevent damage effects of hormones, and restore intracellular bioenergetics (energy transfers in living cells). This theory explains the cause of major diseases of aging, which contribute to over 85% of deaths and disabilities of middle-aged and elderly individuals. These diseases include obesity, atherosclerosis, hypertension, diabetes, and cancer among others (Dean, 2012).

Autoimmune Theory of Aging

The autoimmune theory of aging proposes that protective immune reactions decline with age, as the body becomes less capable of producing sufficient antibodies (Bengtson, Putney, & Johnson, 2005). According to this theory, aging is attributed to the decline of the body's immunological system. Studies indicate that as individuals age, the body's ability to produce necessary antibodies declines and immune systems become less effective in fighting disease (Bengtson et al., 2005). At the same time, the white blood cells active in immune response become less able to recognize foreign invaders and are more likely to mistakenly attack the body's own proteins. For example, one hypothesis proposes that cancer rates are higher in older people because the immune system's surveillance mechanism may not recognize and destroy precancerous cells as it does in younger individuals (Bengtson et al., 2005).

Additionally, the aging immune system mistakenly produces antibodies against normal body proteins, leading to a loss of self-recognition. An example of this is rheumatoid arthritis, in which the immune system attacks the joints, particularly the hands, wrists, feet, ankles, and knees. While a decline in immune system functioning causes disease, there is no evidence to suggest that a less efficient immune system causes aging (Hayflick, 1996). This theory is unable to account for the mechanism of biological aging, the progressive generalized impairment of functioning that occurs as people grow older. However, the autoimmune theory is another theory that attempts to explain why diseases occur. Its basic premise is that immune reactions normally directed against disease-producing organisms as well as foreign proteins or tissue begin to attack cells of the individual's own body.

Free Radical Theory of Aging

The free radical theory of aging explains the basic chemical process underlying aging. The reaction of active free radicals, normally produced in the organisms, with cellular constituents initiates the changes associated with aging (Herman, 2006). The free radical theory of aging suggests that free radicals, or unstable molecules, are produced when the body transforms food into chemical energy, creating damage that causes aging. This transformation occurs at the individual cell level. Free radicals also may be generated in the body due to cigarette smoke, drugs, and radiation (Dietrich & Horvath, 2010) and are a by-product of normal cells. Most changes associated with aging result from damage caused by free radicals (Bengtson et al., 2005). Free radicals disrupt the normal production of DNA and RNA and alter the lipids, or fats, in cell membranes. They also damage cells lining blood vessels and interfere with the production of prostaglandins, which are derived from essential fatty acids and regulate many physiological functions. Partly as a result of free radical damage, aging leads to alteration of proteins (cross-linking). The prematurely aged, wrinkled skin of smokers is caused by free radical-induced damage that smoking engenders, and cataracts have been linked to free-radical exposure (de Magalhaes, 2014). Free radicals have also been associated with dementia, cancer, and heart disease. Combating free radicals requires the consumption of antioxidants, which can be obtained through food.

This theory helps to explain why some individuals are at a greater risk of certain diseases than others, and it attempts to explain why aging occurs. Aging occurs when cells become permanently damaged from the life-long and unrelenting attack of charged molecular fragments, known as free radicals. The cellular damage inflicted by this uncontrolled oxidative stress inexorably spreads outward to the level of tissues and organs, where it eventually manifests itself as some form of degenerative disease. Over 80 degenerative diseases are now known to be linked to free radicals. Some of these diseases include heart disease, cancer, diabetes, arthritis, senile dementia, and Alzheimer's disease. It is now believed that when people age, their ability to make sufficient amounts of antioxidants (substances that fight free radicals) declines, and then free radicals begin to accumulate and damage the cells. This is how the aging process ensues (MacWilliam, 2002).

Cross-Linkage Theory of Aging

The cross-linkage theory of aging proposes that the physical changes seen on the body result from the accumulation of cross-linking compounds in the collagen, which gradually become more numerous. Cross-linking is side-by-side (lateral) linking in which two or more adjacent molecules of a polymer (substance made up of a large number of smaller molecules) join to form a bigger molecule. Collagen is the most abundant protein in the human body and is the substance that holds the whole body together. The piling up of harmful molecules is thought to eventually impair cell function (Moody & Sasser, 2012). The accumulation of cross-linked collagen is responsible for such changes as the loss of skin elasticity, hardening of the arteries of the circulatory system, and stiffness of joints throughout the body. This accumulation also plays a role in the formation of cataracts and is connected to the decline of kidney function (Mitteldorf, 2010).

This theory contributes to our understanding of aging, but it does not explain the totality of the process. It explains that it is the binding of glucose (simple sugars) to protein (a process that occurs under the presence of oxygen) that causes various problems. Once this binding has occurred, the protein becomes impaired, and it is unable to perform as efficiently. Living a longer life is going to lead to the increased possibility of oxygen meeting glucose and protein. Also, in persons with diabetes, 2–3 the times the numbers of cross-linked proteins when compared to their healthy counterparts has been observed (Anti-Aging Today, 2013). This theory proposes that reducing the risk of cross-linking by reducing sugar (and also simple carbohydrates) in one's diet would be helpful in the aging process.

Genetic Control Theory of Aging

The genetic control theory of aging suggests that the genetic information in our cells provides a blueprint for the aging process and that different cells may be programmed to divide a set number of times. This theory of aging assumes that the life span of a cell or organism is genetically determined—that the genes of an animal contain a program that determines its life span, just as eye color is determined genetically (*Encyclopaedia Britannica,* 2015). This theory finds support in the fact that people with parents who have lived long lives are likely to live long themselves. Also, identical twins have life spans more similar in length than do nontwin siblings (*Encyclopaedia Britannica,* 2015). For example, the cells from an embryo will divide approximately 50 times before dying, but similar cells from an adult will divide only 20 times (Cristofalo, 1988). Genes influence life expectancy and place some people at risk for certain diseases, but despite the fact that some older persons are more susceptible to diseases than others, it is not definite that they will develop the disease.

The genetic theory of aging centers on telomeres, which are repeated segments of DNA (deoxyribonucleic acid) occurring at the ends of chromosomes. The number of repeats in a telomere determines the maximum life span of a cell, since each time a cell divides, multiple repeats are lost. Once telomeres have been reduced to a certain size, the cell reaches a crisis point and is prevented from dividing further. As a consequence, the cell dies. This may be an important mechanism of aging in tissues like bone marrow and the arterial lining where active cell division is necessary (Block, 2015). This theory contributes to our understanding of aging by attempting to explain a genetic foundation for why individuals live as long as they do. However, other factors may be operating in the aging process, so it cannot be explained purely by genetics.

Somatic Mutation Theory of Aging

The somatic mutation theory of aging proposes that harmful or deleterious mutations (genes that are incorrectly copied) will accumulate with advancing age, leading to an increase in pathological changes (disease altering) in body systems (Bengtson et al., 2005). Over a lifetime, a person's body is exposed to many external insults from air pollution, chemicals in food and water, and radiation, which cause mutations or genetic damage to somatic (body) cells. Air pollution has been linked to respiratory illnesses (bronchitis, emphysema, asthma), chemicals in food and water have been linked to gastrointestinal disorders (stomach and liver problems), and radiation has been linked to cancer.

This theory is helpful in understanding variations between body systems in the aging process, but fails to explain basic processes of normal change. As cells grow and divide, a small proportion of them undergo mutations. This change in the genetic code is then reproduced when the cells again divide. The somatic mutation theory of aging assumes that aging is due to the gradual accumulation of mutated cells that do not perform normally. Genetic mutations occur and accumulate with increasing age, causing cells to deteriorate and malfunction (Jin, 2010). This leads to cellular dysfunction such as cancer. Different organs may develop diseases and some may be spared; however, these mutations are uncontrolled.

Wear and Tear Theory of Aging

The wear and tear theory of aging is an early theory that proposes that the body wears out (Cristofalo, 1988). This theory is difficult to test, as normal wear and tear has not been defined, and the breakdown of various body systems cannot be predicted (Hayflick, 1996). The wear and tear theory postulates that the daily grind of life, in particular abuse or overuse, literally wears the body out, leading to disease states. This theory proposes that

Table 1.1   Major Biological Theories of Aging

Theory	Significance in the Aging Process
Neuroendocrine theory	Loss of neurons and hormones influences the aging process
Autoimmune theory of aging	Compromised immune system associated with aging
Free radical theory of aging	Free radical production creates damage that causes aging
Cross-linkage theory of aging	Cross-links impair cell function and cause physical signs of aging
Genetic control theory of aging	Genes are programmed for a set number of divisions from birth
Somatic mutation theory of aging	Harmful mistakes occur in the body and may lead to diseases associated with aging
Wear and tear theory of aging	Initial theory postulates that the body simply wears out and aging occurs

vital parts of our cells and tissues wear out resulting in aging (Jin, 2010). Wear and tear is an accumulation of errors and damage due to natural use (MacWilliam, 2002). The degeneration of cartilage and eventual grinding of bone on bone is an example of the aging process on body joints, as wear and tear exceeds the body's ability to repair. This theory was the first theory that attempted to explain aging as a result of damage accumulated over time and laid the foundation for other scientists to explore additional explanation as to why and how the body ages.

Though none of these major biological theories encapsulate the aging process on its own, they are each an important piece of the aging puzzle. Table 1.1 provides a brief overview of the theories and what they contribute to the knowledge of aging.

The various theories identified are an attempt to explain why the body ages from the biological perspective and causes the physical changes that older persons experience.

PHYSICAL CHANGES THAT ACCOMPANY AGING

Adulthood is a time of life characterized mostly by personal growth and stability, but over the adult life span, loss and decline begins (Heckhausen, 2001). Age-related declines in physical function are observed from midlife onward, even in the absence of disease, as a result of normal age-related changes in the musculoskeletal system and other body systems (Cooper, Kuh, & Cooper, 2011). It is important to remember that no two people age at the same rate. Levels of stability or decline differ greatly in areas of physical, sensory, and cognitive functioning.

Physically, some of the most noticeable signs of aging include the loss of pigmentation leading to the graying of hair, thinning of hair caused by hair germination center destruction, rigidity of the skin's dermal layer leading to wrinkling, and changes in the strength and tone of voice (Whitbourne, 2001). Less noticeable signs of aging, which may affect most individuals in adulthood, include a decrease in bone density, decline in muscle mass, visual and auditory deterioration, changes in cardiovascular fitness and respiratory functioning, and changes in body regulation (e.g., decreased basal metabolism rates, endocrine and immune function, and sexual changes) (Masoro & Austad, 2001).

Typically, older people walk more slowly, have less muscle strength, have poorer memory and reasoning abilities, and are slower to respond on cognitive tasks relative to younger adults and to themselves when they were younger. Physical and cognitive functioning are both indicators of biologic aging. The aging process is often characterized by a loss of adaptive response to life challenges and an increasing vulnerability to pathology (i.e., aging-associated diseases) and functional limitations. However, biological aging is not tied absolutely to chronological aging. It may be possible to slow biological aging and even reduce the possibility of suffering from age-related diseases such as dementia (Peters, 2006). Many natural changes occur in the aging process, and the central nervous system is the major mechanism behind all changes.

Central Nervous System

The nervous system is the body's control center. It controls the body's movements, senses, thoughts, and memories. It also controls the organs such as the heart and bowels. There are two parts to the nervous system: the central nervous system, which is made up of the brain and spinal cord, and the peripheral nervous system, which is mainly comprised of nerves. The spinal cord is the bundle of nerves that runs from the brain down the center of the back. Nerves extend out from the spinal cord to every part of the body (Dugdale, 2012) and are the pathways that carry signals between the brain and the rest of the body.

As the body ages, the central and peripheral nervous systems go through natural changes. The brain and spinal cord lose nerve cells and weight (atrophy). Nerve cells may begin to pass messages more slowly. Waste products can collect in the brain tissue as nerve cells break down, causing abnormal changes in the brain called plaques and tangles to form. A fatty brown pigment (lipofuscin) can also build up in nerve tissue, which can impair the functioning of seemingly unrelated cellular systems. Lipofuscin has also been associated with dementia and severe memory loss. Breakdown of nerves affect the senses, causing reduced or lost reflexes or sensation, which can lead to problems with movement and safety.

The slowing of thought, memory, and thinking is a normal part of aging. This is caused by changes to the brain's size, blood vessels, and cognition. As it ages, the brain shrinks in volume, particularly in the frontal cortex. As we age, the blood vessels may stiffen and blood pressure rises, and may result in inadequate oxygen to the heart muscle (ischemia), and a narrowing or blockage of one or more arteries may lead to a stroke and subsequent lesion (area of tissue that has been damaged through injury or disease). As a person's vasculature ages and blood pressure rises, the possibility of stroke and ischemia increases, and the brain's white matter develops lesions. Memory decline also occurs, and brain activation becomes more bilateral (use of left and right prefrontal cortex) for memory tasks because older brains tend to show more symmetrical activation (using both the left and right hemispheres). This may be an attempt to compensate and use additional networks or because specific areas are no longer easily accessed. These anatomical changes are linked to a number of functional alterations. In general, neural processing becomes less efficient. For example, memory consolidation often becomes more difficult, and sensory systems of the elderly, notably hearing, balance, vision, smell and taste, become less acute. Light must be brighter, sounds louder, and smells stronger before they are perceived (American Academy of Health and Fitness [AAHF], 2015). Genetics, neurotransmitters, hormones, and experience all play a role in how quickly the brain ages.

Sensory Perception

Some sensory changes begin in early middle age. They are progressive and are apt to cause limitation of activity in later years. All sensory organs show some degree of altered function by the age of 70. In general, the changes in sensory function due to aging include a higher sensory threshold (level of strength a stimulus must reach to be detected) and a decrease in sensory acuity (actual physical ability of the sensory organs to receive input). Natural changes in vision, hearing, taste, and smell occur as one ages.

Vision

A reduction in vision can have a negative psychological impact on many aspects of functioning in older adults. Older adults may not be able to enjoy leisure activities such as reading, watching television, playing chess/checkers, finishing crossword puzzles, and a host of other activities. A loss of vision may impede social activities and physical activities, which will eventually negatively impact their emotional and physical health. Loss of vision will impact their ability to remain independent in their homes and also negatively impact their ability to drive. Older adults may suffer unnecessary falls due to their decreased vision. Self-esteem will be adversely affected, interaction with significant others will be challenging and their overall quality of life is diminished. Counselors can help older adults adjust to their vision loss. They can support them with resolving any issues resulting from the visual impairments. Counselors can also encourage or make referrals for optical devices (e.g., eye glasses, larger numbers on their phones). Counselors can provide strategies to live independently with redesigning their environment, and they can also monitor their compliance with any treatment regimes. Loss of independence will be a concern for many older adults who are visually impaired, and counselors are positioned to facilitate the relocation to another environment (if necessary) and to offer resources as alternatives for loss of ability to drive. Counselors will provide support, encouragement, coping strategies, referrals, and resources to make the transition easier for older adults, while maintaining a focus on strengths and capabilities versus disabilities with older clients.

Vision is affected in various ways due to aging. Changes occur in the components of the eye itself and in central processing in the brain. These changes affect reading, balance, and driving, but compensatory glasses and behavior can maintain safety. As the eyes age, it is normal for older adults to have a reduced visual field. Pure aging makes clear that no disease, environmental, lifestyle, or behavioral risk factor plays a role in the change. It includes a decline in accommodation, which is the increase in optical power by the eye in order to maintain a clear image (focus) as objects are moved closer (e.g., presbyopia or farsightedness). Low-contrast acuity refers to the sharpness or keenness of vision. Glare tolerance declines, as does adaptation (adjustment to environmental conditions) and color discrimination. Also, there is a decreased attentional visual field that describes a person's ability to divide attention and extract visual information from the visual field within a glance. The common eye diseases in old age (e.g., glaucoma, macular degeneration, cataracts, diabetic retinopathy) are superimposed upon these pure aging changes (Besdine & Wu, 2008).

Older individuals may begin to have difficulties with contrast sensitivity, in which the difference between an object and its background is reduced. This reduction in sensitivity is gradual because of progressive eye problems that can lead to scarring or clouding of the cornea, which decreases vision. Decreased contrast sensitivity also diminishes an elderly person's ability to perceive depth. Reduced depth perception makes steps or street curves difficult to manage. Additionally, seeing at night can become difficult. A person with early nuclear sclerosis (cloudiness of the eye lens) may complain of glare especially during night driving, due to light scattering, which is light directed in many different directions. At the same time, older people need more lighting in their surroundings than a younger person. Beginning in the early mid-40s, most adults start to experience problems with their ability to see clearly at close distances, especially for reading and computer tasks.

A reduction in number of cones at the fovea causes generalized reduction in color vision. Fovea is the central focal point on the retina (lines the back of the eye) around which cones cluster. Cones are photoreceptors located near the center of the retina that are responsible for your ability to see during the day, in color, and in detail. For people of all ages, it is harder to distinguish blues and greens than it is to differentiate reds and yellows. This becomes even more pronounced with age. Using more warm contrasting colors (e.g., yellow, orange, and red) in the home can improve the ability to determine where things are and make it easier to perform activities of daily living. Many older people find that keeping a red light on in darkened rooms (such as the hallway or bathroom) makes it easier to see than a regular night light (white/yellow in color) (Salvi, Currie, &Akhtar, 2005). Another common visual change in older adults is the increase of floaters or tiny black specks moving across their field of vision. These specks are bits of normal fluid in the eye that have solidified. Floaters do not significantly interfere with vision and are not a cause for concern unless they suddenly increase in number. Additionally, the eyes tend to become dry. This change occurs due to a decrease in the number of cells that produce fluids to lubricate and a decrease in tear production (Porter, 2009). Vision loss has profound effects on the quality of life of older adults, as does the loss of hearing.

Hearing

Conductive and sensory hearing losses occur with age. Individuals with hearing loss may be unable to hear higher tones, making consonants in speech difficult to differentiate. Other consequences of hearing loss include difficulty in localizing sound and understanding speech, usually accompanied by hypersensitivity to loudness. Common conditions in old age (ruptured eardrum, wax buildup, infection) are superimposed upon these changes, often resulting in worsening hearing impairment (Besdine & Wu, 2008).

Hearing loss can create a psychological solitary confinement, yet many older adults with hearing loss deny the disability or the impact it exerts on their quality of life. A practitioner working with older adults experiencing hearing loss may need to ascertain the individual's stage of acceptance. Family members who attribute hearing loss as mild or moderate inadvertently bolster the individual's denial (Dewane, 2010).

Older adults who are hard of hearing often report that when their hearing loss causes communication problems, it can result in difficulty thinking or concentrating. This results in inattentiveness, distraction, and boredom. The most serious consequence is withdrawal or abandoning participation in conversations. Older adults with hearing loss face many of the same fears that anyone with a disability encounters: They worry about loss of significant relationships or jobs or about being perceived as incompetent. Communication breakdown problems may show up in physical symptoms such as tension, exhaustion, and psychological symptoms (Dewane, 2010).

Sometimes hearing loss exerts a direct impact on mental health. Depression and adjustment disorder can occur as a natural response to hearing loss and its subsequent impact on the quality of life. On the other hand, some people have premorbid mental health issues and hearing loss simply compounds the problem. Inability to hear and discern messages and their meaning can result in feelings of shame, humiliation, and inadequacy. It can be highly embarrassing to be unable to behave according to applicable social rules. The feeling of shame linked to hearing loss stems from older adults inadvertently reacting in inappropriate and socially unacceptable ways, such as responding to a misunderstood question in an inaccurate fashion (Dewane, 2010).

Most changes in hearing are likely due as much to noise exposure as to aging. Exposure to loud noise over time damages the ear's ability to hear. Nonetheless, some changes in hearing occur as people age, regardless of their exposure to loud noise. As people age, hearing high-pitched sounds becomes more difficult. This change is considered age-associated hearing loss (presbycusis). For example, violin music may sound less bright. The most frustrating consequence of presbycusis is that words become harder to understand. As a result, older people may think that other people are mumbling. Individuals need to articulate consonants more clearly, rather than speak louder. Many older people have more trouble hearing in loud places or in groups because of the background noise. Also, earwax, which interferes with hearing, tends to accumulate more (Porter, 2009; Talbot & Hogstel, 2001). Changes in the ability to hear impacts older adults in many ways, and the change in taste also interferes with personal well-being.

Taste

Taste helps all of us recognize when food is good or bad. When an elderly person loses taste, it can cause a loss of appetite, weight loss, poor nutrition, weakened immunity, and even death (Sollitto, 2015). When older persons lose the ability to taste certain foods, they may also lose interest in eating them, which could affect the amount of nutrients they consume, and they could accidentally consume food that has gone bad or contains harmful ingredients (Orenstein & Marcellin, 2015). Mental health professionals can refer older adults to a nutritionist. They can also provide ways to make meals more enjoyable by eating with others, teaching the use of herbs and spices, experimenting with new foods. Mental health professionals are able to develop programs with older persons to educate and monitor progress toward healthier dietary habits.

Older adults will experience a reduction in their taste sensation. Taste buds diminish; perception of salty and sweet tastes decrease first, followed by bitter and sour tastes. The volume and quality of saliva diminish. Such changes combine to make eating less interesting. These aging changes are compounded by common diseases (periodontal) and medications (Besdine & Wu, 2008).

This decreased taste sensation leads to a change in the type of foods that older people prefer. They generally like highly seasoned foods or simply more sugar or salt in food so it can be tasted. The ability to taste and smell starts to diminish when individuals are in their 50s. Both senses are needed to enjoy the full range of flavors in food. The tongue can identify only five basic tastes: sweet, sour, bitter, salty, and umami (commonly described as meaty or savory). Also, the mouth tends to feel dry more often, partly because less saliva is produced, and dry mouth further reduces the ability to taste food.

Guided Practice Exercise 1.1 provides an opportunity to obtain the perception of taste sensation and its effect on adequate nutrition from an older adult. Adequate nutrition is critical to maintaining one's health at all points in life.

Guided Practice Exercise 1.1

Visit an assisted living facility and interview an older adult regarding the changes in his or her sense of taste over time. Inquire as to what effect it has had on his or her nutritional intake and satisfaction with meals.

Smell

As individuals age, the olfactory (smell) function declines. Not only is there a loss of sense of smell, but also a loss of ability to discriminate between smells (Boyce & Shone, 2006). More than 75% of people over the age of 80 years have evidence of major impairment in ability to smell, and smell declines considerably after the seventh decade (Boyce & Shone, 2006). A major consequence of the loss of smell could pose a threat to the health and well-being of the older persons and other individuals within the environment. For example, if an older adult does not know that the pot is burning on the stove, a fire could develop. An older person who is unable to smell a gas leak places himself or herself in danger and potentially others in close proximity. If the elder cannot smell the freshness of food in the refrigerator, which has now spoiled, they will consume harmful foods, which may lead to hospitalization for an illness. Older persons may become depressed at the changes they are experiencing, and a mental health professional can provide counseling and referral services to manage the depression. Mental health practitioners can also provide education and support services to facilitate a continued good quality of life for their clients while facilitating coping and adaptation to their environment.

Smell activity declines with aging. There is atrophy of olfactory bulb neurons, and central processing is altered. The result is decreased perception and less interest in food. Again, these age-related changes are compounded by disease. For example, Alzheimer's disease (AD) and Parkinson's disease (PD) are related to diminution and alteration of smell (Besdine & Wu, 2008). The ability to smell diminishes because the lining of the nose becomes thinner and drier and the nerve endings in the nose deteriorate. However, the change is slight, usually affecting only subtle and complex smells. Because of these changes, many foods tend to taste bitter, and foods with subtle smells may taste bland.

The olfactory nerves are also thought to have fewer cells functioning in older adults. Because the odor of foods stimulates salivation and hunger, a diminished sense of smell often contributes to a decreased appetite. A decreased sense of smell also leads to the inability to smell danger in the environment, such as leaking gas stove burners that are not completely turned off, and spoiled food. Older adults who live alone should develop the habits of checking all burners after use to be certain they are turned completely off and marking the date food is placed in the refrigerator to prevent eating spoiled food (Talbot & Hogstel, 2001). Changes in the ability to smell negatively impacts quality of life for older adults as does changes in sensation with aging.

Sensation

Changes in sensation common to older adults include the peripheral nerve function that controls the sense of touch declines slightly with age and the ability to perceive painful stimuli is preserved in aging; however, there may be a slowed reaction time for pulling away from painful stimuli with aging (Cacchione, 2005). Consequences of decreased sensations include the possibility of falls due to inability to recognize position sense or inability to ascertain where feet are on the floor and development of calluses or serious foot lesions. Older adults who fall may develop a fear of falling, which will negatively impact all activities of daily living and social endeavors. Older adults may become anxious and depressed, which may warrant psychological interventions. Mental health practitioners can facilitate coping mechanisms with their older clients, coordinate service providers, provide psychosocial interventions, and facilitate social interaction, which is essential if the older client has become withdrawn.

Sensations may be diminished or changed in older adults. Peripheral nerve function that controls the sense of touch declines slightly with age. Two-point discrimination and vibrating sense both decrease with age. The ability to perceive painful stimuli is preserved in aging; however, there may be a slowed reaction time for pulling away from painful stimuli with aging (Cacchione, 2012). The sense of touch may decrease, and a firmer touch may be needed to elicit a response. Many older adults respond positively to touch; perhaps it indicates a special sense of caring by another person. However, sensations are also compounded by disease, and most older adults will have at least one or more chronic diseases. Diabetic patients will have difficulties in the area of pain sensation. Osteoporosis can produce a sense of being off-balance when ambulating.

The sensation of pain varies considerably in older adults. It may be more difficult to evaluate acute pain because of an older adult's reduced ability to locate the source of pain. The autonomic response to pain, such as rapid pulse, elevated blood pressure, pallor, and nausea, may not occur in older adults. Every person exhibits learned behaviors in response to pain, and older adults may have experienced chronic discomfort for such a long time that they fail to respond to a new stimulus. Also, the inflammatory response is often reduced or delayed, resulting in a decreased stimulus for pain. A combination of assessment skills to detect the presence of pain is necessary. It is essential to differentiate acute from chronic pain because the cause and treatment may be quite different.

Typically, painful disorders are often less or not at all painful in elders. In the cortex, populations of neurons continuously receive input from upstream neurons, integrate it with their own ongoing activities, and generate output destined for downstream neurons. Such cortical information processing and transmission is limited, and pain sensation appears to decline with age. The brain has a neural (relating to the nervous system) circuit and endogenous (developing from within) substances to modulate pain and as individuals age endogenous pain inhibition is reduced with aging. Some pain thresholds show age-related changes. Although sensitivity to heat pain decreases with age, sensitivity to pressure pain is enhanced. Sensory nerves lose myelin, which is a layer of tissue that surrounds the nerve fibers (axons) selectively, and perhaps predisposing individuals to neuropathy (problem with the nerves). Vibration sensation perception diminishes with aging, especially in the legs (Besdine & Wu, 2008). Changes in sensation may negatively impact older adults and create an unsafe environment, while issues with balance pose similar safety issues within the environment.

Balance

Having good balance means being able to control and maintain your body's position, whether you are moving or remaining still. An intact sense of balance helps you walk without staggering, get up from a chair without falling, climb stairs without tripping, and bend without falling (NIH Senior Health, 2014). Good balance is important to help elders move around, maintain independent functioning and carry out daily activities. As individuals get older, many people experience problems with their sense of balance. They feel dizzy or unsteady, or feel that their surroundings are in motion, and usually disturbances of the inner ear are a common cause (NIH Senior Health, 2014).

Balance problems in older persons can result in falls. Falls and fall-related injuries, such as hip fracture, can have a serious impact on an older person's life. If the older person falls, it could limit his or her activities or make it impossible to live independently. Many persons often become more isolated after a fall. Additional consequences of balance are disruptions in normal sleep patterns, a cause for excessive fatigue, and balance disturbances can shorten your attention span and cause major disruptions in routine activities, social activities, and work and/or leisure activities. These limitations diminish the quality of life for older adults, and mental health practitioners can provide education, referral, and counseling to older clients. They can encourage older clients to obtain a comprehensive physical examination from their primary care provider, refer client for services as needed (e.g., occupational therapist), educate clients on their condition, conduct an assessment of the environment (identify potential environmental hazards), and support their clients in their efforts to cope with their condition.

Balance function declines with increasing age, but it is rarely the sole cause of falls in older persons. A person's sense of balance is controlled by the vestibular (sensory) system that is affected by many diseases (e.g., diabetes, stroke, Parkinson's disease) and is also sensitive to various combinations of medications, both prescription and over the counter (Besdine & Wu, 2008). In a normal healthy individual, our senses of touch (feet, ankles, and joints), sight (eyes), and inner ear motion sensors work together in harmony with the brain. A person with a balance disorder, however, may have a problem in any one of these systems or in multiple systems. The risk of developing one or more of these problems increases with age as our senses or brain centers are exposed to degenerative or infectious diseases or the effects of injuries accumulated over a lifetime. The natural aging process produces changes in our bodies as we grow older, but these changes do not necessarily result in a loss of balance control or mobility (Natus Balance & Mobility, 2015).

The response to both vestibular and kinesthetic stimuli (sensation of muscle contraction) is reduced in very old people. Vestibular sense receptors are located in muscles and tendons and relay signals to the central nervous system concerning joint motion and body position in space. Because both of these senses help maintain equilibrium, coordination, and body position, a diminution in their effectiveness produces a general unsteadiness, a lack of coordination in movements, and an increase in the amount of body sway. Because a longer time is required for stimuli to reach the central nervous system and be interpreted, and for messages then to be sent to the periphery, there is a great need for older adults to move slowly, have a wide stance, refrain from rapid body or head turning to maintain balance and prevent falls, and perhaps use a cane for support when walking. Older people should be instructed not to make quick changes in direction because such movements may cause loss of balance (Talbot & Hogstel, 2001). Maintaining good balance is critical for all older adults, and no living organism can exist without a fully functioning respiratory system.

Respiratory System

The major function of the respiratory system is the delivery of air to sites in the lungs where gas exchange can occur between the air and circulating blood (AAHF, 2015). The lungs have two main functions. One function is to get oxygen from the air into the body, and the other function is to remove carbon dioxide from the body. The body needs oxygen to work properly, and carbon dioxide is a gas the body produces when it uses oxygen (Martin, 2014). During breathing, air enters and exits the lungs. When you breathe in (inhale), air flows through the airways into the lungs. The airways are made of stretchy tissue and bands of muscle, and other support tissue wraps around each airway to help keep it open. Air keeps flowing into the lungs until it fills tiny air sacs, and blood circulates around these sacs through tiny blood vessels. Oxygen crosses into the bloodstream at the place where the vessels and air sacs meet, and this is also where carbon dioxide crosses the bloodstream into the lungs to be breathed out (exhaled) (Martin, 2014).

As a result of aging changes in the body, older people are at increased risk for lung infections (i.e., pneumonia, bronchitis), shortness of breath, low oxygen level, and abnormal breathing patterns resulting in problems such as sleep apnea (episodes of stopped breathing during sleep) (Martin, 2014). Mental health professionals can create a supportive environment to provide health education to encourage the older client to decrease or eliminate smoking (if appropriate) and to encourage an exercise to improve lung function. Lying around for long periods of time allows mucus to collect in the lungs and places the older adult at risk for lung infections. Mental health practitioners will address concerns, fears, and psychological issues, which may impede the recovery process. Coordination of services and arranging access to obtain needed equipment (if required) will be an essential component of the therapeutic process.

Aging changes in the body that affect the lungs include changes to the bones and muscles of the chest and spine. Bones become thinner and change shape, and this can change the shape of your ribcage, and as a result, the ribcage cannot expand and contract as well during breathing. The muscle that supports your breathing (diaphragm) becomes weakened and may prevent the older adult from breathing enough air in or out. These changes in your bones and muscles may lower the oxygen level in the body, and less carbon dioxide may be removed from the body. Symptoms such as tiredness and shortness of breath can result (Martin, 2014). Changes to lung tissue include muscles and other tissues that are near the airways, which may lose their ability to keep the airways completely open, and this causes the airways to close easily. Aging also causes the air sacs to lose their shape, and these changes in lung tissue can allow air to get trapped in the lungs. Too little oxygen may enter the blood vessels and less carbon dioxide may be removed, which makes it hard to breathe (Martin, 2014). Changes to the nervous system involve the part of the brain that controls breathing, which may lose some of its function. When this happens the lungs are not able to get enough oxygen, and not enough carbon dioxide may leave the lungs, which makes breathing more difficult. Nerves in the airways that trigger coughing become less sensitive, and large amounts of particles (smoke/germs) may collect in the lungs and may be hard to cough up (Martin, 2014). Changes to the immune system include weakening of the immune system, which means the body is less able to fight lung infections and other diseases, and the lungs are also less able to recover after exposure to smoke or other harmful particles (Martin, 2014).

The respiratory system becomes more restrictive with age (Whitbourne, 2000). As a person ages, the elastic component in the lungs becomes smaller, resulting in the collapse of the peripheral airways while a person breathes out intensively. This is intensified due to a reduction in the maximum vital capacity of the lungs. The maximum breathing capacity is believed to reduce by 40% in older people. It can progress to the extent that this problem can arise during normal breathing. This leaves an older person feeling tired or results in shortness of breath caused by exertion. Furthermore, coughing becomes weaker with age, which is very problematic for older people, who are more susceptible to illness. Without the proper strength to cough, secretions in the lungs build up, and this can lead to aspiratory pneumonia (Weber, 2010).

It is very important that older people quit smoking because smoking greatly increases the chances of developing a respiratory disease. Diseases such as emphysema and chronic obstructive pulmonary disease are sometimes the natural effects of aging on the lungs. This is intensified in smokers, and these diseases impair respiratory functioning. Exposure to environmental pollutants is also linked to these diseases associated to the elderly because the effects are cumulative.

Older people who exercise consistently have less decrease in lung function. The major decrease in lung function occurs when the older adult requires maximal breathing for a period of time. The respiratory system is usually able to meet the needs of a normal older adult, but when illness or stress precipitates a need for increased respiratory function, the reserve capacity may be inadequate to meet the need. For most people, the reserve capacity is greater if they have remained active throughout life. Alterations in the respiratory system may require adjustments as one ages, as does changes to the cardiovascular system.

Cardiovascular System

Issues related to the cardiovascular system in older adults may negatively impact their psychological well-being. They may become depressed and anxious if they have been diagnosed with any accompanied heart disorders (e.g., angina, congestive heart failure, high blood pressure). The heart works harder due to medications, emotional stress, physical exertion, illness, infections and injuries (Hurd, 2014). These factors might interfere with daily activities, engaging in social relationships and activities, employment and a host of routine activities that bring meaning to the lives of older persons. Mental health professionals are in a position to educate their older clients on their condition and the impact it has had on their lives, provide support in their adjustment to their condition, and empower them to make decisions that will support a healthy lifestyle. Mental health professionals will need to encourage their older clients to eat a heart-healthy diet, encourage physical exercise, maintain appointments with health care providers, and comply with their identified treatment regimen as prescribed by their primary care physician. Mental health practitioners will need to address the cardiovascular issues as they impact daily activities and be certain to conduct sessions with the older patient and available family members. Encouraging family support or initiating new supports is essential in this treatment process.

Changes and diseases associated with the cardiovascular system can be attributed to aging, genetics, and also lifestyle choices. The cardiovascular system is responsible for having the heart pump an adequate amount of blood to the cells throughout the body. Aging, however, limits the heart's functionality (Whitbourne, 2010). The heart has more difficulty pumping out blood so, in older adults, strenuous activities can become problematic at times. It is difficult to pinpoint the exact cause of the decline in functionality because major studies are not able to control the amount of a person's physical activity throughout their life as well as other lifestyle choices such as drinking and smoking that have profound effects on the system (Whitbourne, 2010). For example, disease rates in older adults are significantly higher for people who smoke. Studies also show that change in body compositions in seniors are probably caused both by the process of aging and those external factors like physical inactivity (Weber, 2010).

A person's age cannot be accurately defined by examining a heart; however, studies show a strong correlation between a person's age and an increase in coronary artery disease (Arking, 2006). This is a severe problem because about half of the elderly population shows symptoms of cardiovascular disease, which is the leading cause of death. There is approximately a 30% increase in the thickness of the left ventricle wall among older adults (Arking, 2006).

Some of the problems associated with the cardiovascular system result from the loss in mass of muscle cells within the heart due to aging (Whitbourne, 2000). The left ventricle wall becomes thicker because of an increase in fat and connective tissue buildup caused by muscle mass decreasing. This makes the heart produce fewer functional contractions that pump the blood. During the diastolic phase (relaxation and dilation of the ventricles), the heart muscle stretches and the ventricles fill up with blood. Pressure builds in the blood as it is released into the aorta. During a condition known as diastolic dysfunction, the capacity of the walls of the heart is decreased, which reduces and delays filling up the left ventricle with blood. This impairs blood flow to various arteries throughout the body.

Another problem for older adults is that the cardiac muscle becomes less responsive to neural stimulation (activation/energizing of a nerve). The "pacemaker" cells in the heart are responsible for starting each contraction but become less responsive as a person ages. In addition, the heart muscles become less flexible, and the buildup of plaque forms in the inner linings of the arteries. This causes the arteries to become narrower, impeding the flow of blood through them. There is a natural age-related change that stiffens and narrows these arteries called vasculopathology of aging. The walls of the aorta are less flexible, which causes resistance for blood trying to travel far into the arteries. The main way to stave off these various cardiovascular problems is a healthy diet with exercise (Whitbourne, 2000). The purpose of Guided Practice Exercise 1.2 is to provide the opportunity to view the aging process from the perspective of an older family member.

Guided Practice Exercise 1.2

Interview your grandparent or other older adult in your family and inquire regarding the changes they noticed as they aged. Ask them how they felt regarding the changes and how they adjusted to them. Share this information with peers and colleagues.

Integumentary System

Older adults may be negatively affected by the changes to the integumentary system. They may have difficulties with adjusting to the aging process and the outward changes that affect their physical appearance. In a youth-oriented culture within the United States, many elders might adjust to the changes; however, others may suffer from low self-esteem, being depressed, and may result to alterations to their bodies to communicate a more youthful appearance. Mental health practitioners are positioned to counsel older adults to help facilitate an adjustment to the outward changes, which may be inconsistent with how they feel inside. They may need to teach coping strategies, educate them on the natural and inevitable processes of aging, and they may need to advocate for them if they feel they have been discriminated against based on their appearance. Empowering older adults to learn to embrace themselves, which might include some wrinkles and gray hair, is important. Counselors will need to remain open and receptive to older adults who have always given a great deal of attention to their physical appearance. However, all changes must be kept in a perspective as just one component of the aging process. Getting the older person to focus on intrinsic factors versus extrinsic factors will be helpful. Educating older adults on the benefits and risks associated with procedures that modify one's appearance may prove beneficial, if presented objectively. Counselors working with older clients are in an excellent position to assist with the emotional and psychological adjustments to the physical manifestations of the aging process.

Several changes occur in the integumentary system, which consists of skin, hair, and nails, with aging. Obvious changes are the graying of hair and wrinkling of the skin that lead to the loss of self-esteem in many Americans as these changes are noticeable to others and are not respected in our culture (Cash, 2001; Yaar & Gilchrest, 2001). As melanocyte (pigment-producing cell) activity declines, this causes the hair to turn gray or white. Hair loss (alopecia) in men begins between the late teens and the late 20s, and by the time they reach their 60s, 80% of men are substantially bald (Stough, Stenn, & Haber, 2005). There are two types of male hair loss: bitemperol hair loss is universal, constant, gradual, and does not respond to treatment. Male pattern baldness (androgenetic alopecia) accounts for the majority of all hair loss and can be treated with oral medications (Scheinfeld, 2012). Inherited or pattern baldness affects many more men than women, and male pattern baldness is the most common type of baldness in men, especially older men, and the hair loss is gradual. In men, the hair loss usually starts with a receding hairline, while in women, it manifests a diffuse thinning of hair on the crown (Scheinfeld, 2012). Female baldness tends to be associated with more diffuse hair loss than it occurs in men. Most women develop widening partings and thinning of the hair all over the scalp with age, and this process starts in the teens or early 20s, and it affects 50% of women by the age of 50 (Price, 1999). After menopause, thinning of the hair is more pronounced. Guided Practice Exercise 1.3 examines feelings regarding premature graying of the hair.

Guided Practice Exercise 1.3

Imagine you are 23 years old and just noticed your first gray hair. Over the next year, your entire head has turned gray. What are your feelings regarding your premature change in hair color? How are you perceived by others? Do you feel you look older with gray hair and will you accept the change or dye your hair? Explain your response in detail.

Changes in the skin are the most obvious, especially on the top layer, known as the epidermis. This layer thins with age (Aging Changes in the Skin, 2014). As the body ages, the effects of nutrition, environment, genetics, and especially sun exposure begin to manifest through this system. The overall number of melanocytes, or pigmented cells, decreases. However, heavily sun-exposed areas, such as the hands, arms, and face, will show an increase in pigment called lentigo senilis. These areas are sometimes called liver spots, although they have no relationship to the liver, or age spots. They are harmless but may result in feelings of self-consciousness. Additionally, skin will droop and sag with age, which is due to the loss of elasticity, also known as elastosis (Aging Changes in the Skin, 2014).

The middle layer of the skin, known as the dermis, is the site of blood vessels and oil glands. In younger years, the blood vessels here are strong, but as one gets older, they weaken and may occasionally break, causing bleeding within; cherry angiomas are commonly what result (benign blood vessel skin growths). Sebaceous glands decrease oil production with time, making it more difficult for the skin to stay hydrated. This can cause problems, including dryness, itchiness, and peeling. This condition can be partially overcome by using tepid rather than hot water when bathing, using less soap or an oily soap, eliminating the use of powder, and applying an emollient lotion after the bath.

Below the dermis is the subcutaneous fat layer, containing fat and sweat glands. This layer thins just as the epidermis does, resulting in difficulty maintaining a reasonable body temperature (homeostasis). This may explain why older adults chill easily and are at an increased risk for hypothermia in cold weather. However, in the warmer months, older adults are at risk for heat-associated conditions due to decreased functioning of sweat glands. The thinning of this subcutaneous layer also limits the normal functioning of nerve receptors associated with touch, pain, and pressure (Aging Changes in the Skin, 2014).

Wrinkling is caused by the loss of subcutaneous fat and water in epidermal layers and exposure to the sun over many years. Highly pigmented skin is less prone to wrinkling and sun damage, which causes thinning of the epidermis. With the thinning of the epidermis, the skin is easily injured and healing is slow if the blood flow to the dermis is impaired. Because of the changes in the skin, prolonged bed rest can cause major problems such as pressure ulcers. Special beds, mattresses, and lotions should be used to help prevent skin breakdown.

Changes in the thickness, shape, color, and growth rate of the nails occur with age. Vascular supply to the nail bed decreases resulting in dull, brittle, hard, and thick nails, with a slowed growth rate. The fingernails may flake and become brittle or develop ridges. The toenails may become discolored or abnormally thickened. The nails of older adults may be thick and easily split. It is imperative that nails be soaked in warm water before being cut or shaped to prevent splintering and to avoid possible trauma leading to infection. The condition of an older person's toenails may help to indicate whether the person is capable of living alone and caring for personal hygiene needs. Older persons may develop bunions, which are misaligned bone at the base of the big toe, and eventually the big toe may bend abnormally toward the small toes. They may develop calluses and corns, which are dead, yellowish, thickened skin on toes. Hammertoes may develop, which are toe joints that curl up or under, either rigidly or with some flexibility, often resulting in a permanently dislocated joint (Health in Aging, 2012). Finally, ingrown toenails may develop. These foot problems may impede mobility and may necessitate admission to a supervised living facility. Also these problems will make it difficult for these older adults to ambulate to take care of their activities of daily living and instrumental activities of daily living. An older adult client should be encouraged to seek professional care for their feet from a podiatrist at periodic intervals to prevent trauma, especially if the client has a severe visual deficit, vascular problems, and diabetes, or if the client's body is no longer flexible enough to allow them to care for their feet. It is essential to address all changes in the integumentary system of older adults and also the gastrointestinal system, which undergoes changes as one ages.

Gastrointestinal System

Gastrointestinal issues can have a negative effect on the psychological well-being of older adults. Problems in this area can also adversely affect the ability of older adults to maintain good nutritional habits, which might lead to malnourishment that can precipitate a host of other problems (e.g., susceptibility to illnesses/diseases, hospitalizations, increased use of medications). Another example is problem with the absorption of calcium required for bone growth and maintenance can be disrupted, which may lead to osteoporosis that may precipitate falls, injuries, and subsequent hospitalizations. Mental health practitioners may serve the role of a coach to encourage older adults to maintain their health, maintain appointments with health providers, and recommended tests and encourage healthy behaviors. They can teach coping strategies for dealing with stress and the consequences associated with any abnormalities within the digestive system. Mental health practitioners must also assist in the coordination of care and provide appropriate referrals. They must also encourage older adults to separate their personal experience of the aging process from the disease or illness that they may be experiencing. Mental health practitioners may also need to address issues of social withdrawal, isolation, fear, and depression. These psychological issues will definitely decrease the overall functioning for older adults. The psychological well-being of older adults can be enhanced by the supportive and trusting relationship with the mental health practitioner.

The gastrointestinal (GI) system is the digestive system of the human body. The major functions of this system are the processing of food and the absorption of nutrients, minerals, vitamins, and water (AAHF, 2015). Aging has relatively little effect on GI functioning because of the large functional reserve capacity of most of the GI tract. The digestive system is made up of the mouth, teeth, tongue, salivary glands, pharynx, esophagus, stomach, pancreas, liver, gall bladder, and both the large and small intestines. Essentially normal digestion and absorption occur in the elderly; however, there are many changes in the digestive system that parallel age-related changes seen in the other systems. Like other systems, the rate of new cell growth declines and tissues become more susceptible to damage (AAHF, 2015).

The elderly face changes to their digestive systems. Though the digestive system suffers little from changes related directly to aging, psychological and social strains threaten the system's functionality (Whitbourne, 2000). The digestive system is a series of tubes and glands that run all the way from the mouth to the rectum. It is responsible for extracting nutrients from food and then eliminating the remaining waste. Anxiety and stress are key components to problems linked to the digestive system. Stress inhibits saliva and gastric juice secretion, which makes swallowing foods and eliminating waste difficult. Saliva secretion is important for lubricating food, making it easier to move down the esophagus (p. 127).

One change associated with aging and the digestive system is known as presbyesophagus. This particular condition is characterized by a weakening of the esophagus muscles. It reduces food movement down the esophagus and leads to difficulty swallowing. Another challenge for older people is maintaining a healthy appetite. A condition known as anorexia of aging is when older adults fail to eat a sufficient amount to satisfy his or her nutritional needs. This can be made worse by poor teeth and taking multiple prescription medications that reduce appetite. Psychological changes, such as anxiety, also affect this system. Anxiety and stress can lead to a loss of sensory functioning such as taste and smell, further ruining a person's appetite and causing disturbances to the digestive system (Whitbourne, 2000).

Aging causes a slight decrease in the amount of pancreatic enzymes, which further decreases digestion and the absorption of nutrients. Thus digestion is slowed but remains fairly adequate until an advanced age. Slowed peristalsis (involuntary contraction and relaxation of the muscles of the intestine or another canal), reduced abdominal muscular strength, inadequate exercise, and reduced food and fluid intake are responsible for a high prevalence of constipation. Some older adults may have problems related to relaxation of the anal sphincter because of cold environments or ulcers or hemorrhoids that lead to constipation (Talbot & Hogstel, 2001).

The digestive system remains a cause of concern among older adults. They fear that they may lose control of or not be able to have bowel movements. Constipation is problematic because they cannot eliminate waste, which could build up in the system to toxic levels and has been linked to cancer of the gastrointestinal tract. The loss of control of defecation is often linked to more advanced stages of Alzheimer's disease, which is becoming an increasing problem for older people (Whitbourne, 2000). Changes in the digestive system of older adults can negatively affect their overall well-being, as does changes in the musculoskeletal system.

Musculoskeletal System

Psychological changes will accompany the natural changes in the musculoskeletal system of older adults. The changes will affect their emotional well-being, sense of security, living environments, self-esteem, and ability to function in all aspects of daily life. Older adults may fear falling due to loss of muscle mass and difficulty ambulating as a result. They may become isolated and fearful of having to move to an unfamiliar environment, which facilitates dependence on others. Older adults may perceive themselves in a negative manner because of any limitations imposed by the changes in the muscles and bones. Self-care and activities such as grocery shopping, driving, and handling financial transactions may not be managed by older adults. Fearfulness, anxiety, depression, social isolation, and low self-esteem are just some of the issues counselors will need to address to improve the quality of life for elders. Counselors must also evaluate the environment or make a referral for a home assessment to decrease any possibility of falls or other injuries. They must teach older adults how to cope with the consequences and/or diseases that they have developed. They must always focus on the strengths and abilities while providing the required resources to improve their quality of life.

There are three types of muscles in the musculoskeletal system: skeletal, cardiac, and smooth muscles. Skeletal muscle is a collection of striated muscle fibers connected at either or both extremities with the bony framework of the body. Cardiac muscle is an extremely specialized form of muscle tissue that has evolved to pump blood throughout the body. Smooth muscle fibers form the supporting tissues of blood vessels and hollow internal organs, such as the stomach, intestine, and bladder. The skeletal muscles make up most of the muscle content in the body and lose the most mass with aging. Muscle tissue and strength begin to decrease around the age of 30 and continue throughout the life span

(Arking, 2006). With proper precautions, most older people retain enough muscle mass and strength to carry out everyday tasks. Lean muscle is the amount of weight you carry on your body that isn't fat. When lean muscle mass decreases, it is caused by muscle atrophy. The decrease in hormones and testosterone that stimulate muscle development is a reason why muscle mass declines with age. Disuse and disease, as in many systems, are major confounders of age effect. One hypothesis is that disuse atrophy occurs, arguing for a "use it or lose it" construct. Age-related changes include loss of muscle mass, though strength loss can be relatively preserved by exercise (Besdine & Wu, 2008).

The size and number of muscle fibers decreases with age, which causes the muscle to respond more slowly. The muscles cannot contract as quickly because there are more muscle fibers in fast-contracting muscles than compared to the slow-contracting muscles. Sprinters require short but intense bursts of energy and therefore need more fast-contracting muscles, while postural muscles of the back are composed of slow-contracting muscles, and long-distance runners require more slow-contracting muscles (Aging Changes in the Bones, Muscles, and Joints, 2012). As the muscle mass decreases, fat content increases, which affects the body's metabolic rate. This can make it harder to maintain a healthy weight and good cholesterol level (Arking, 2006). The change in the metabolic rate is the reason why older people do not metabolize medications as well.

The human body is a complex network of symbiotic systems. The skeletal system and the muscular system work together as the framework for the body as well as providing the pieces that allow for movement. The human skeleton consists of 206 separate bones that provide a solid frame to support the body, as well as protection for internal organs. The bones come together at joints, which allow for movement of individual limbs as well as movement of the entire body in conjunction with skeletal tissue and the muscular system. The muscular system is composed of over 600 muscles, which include involuntary muscles of the heart and the smooth muscle of the internal organs. The skeletal muscles connect to the bones and work with connective tissue at the joints to allow for movement. The muscles connect to the nervous system and allow initiation of movement through nerve signals to and from the brain (Hurd, 2014). The skeletal system gives strength and support to the body. It is also affected by age. As a person ages, the amount of cells present in cartilage decreases, and it loses its translucence. One of the most notable changes with the skeletal system is that of calcification and calcium deposits in joints and tendons, which sometimes contributes to inflammation, causing pain and limiting movement and sometimes causes soft tissues to harden. Calcium crystals can also contribute to the erosion of cartilage (Aging Changes in the Bones, Muscles, and Joints, 2012). The replacement of tissues like collagen decreases with age (Arking, 2006). Lipofuscin (an age-related pigment) and fat are deposited in muscle tissue. The muscle fibers shrink. Muscle tissues are replaced more slowly, and lost muscle tissue may be replaced with a tough fibrous tissue. This is most noticeable in the hands, which may look thin and bony (Hurd, 2014). Bone mass or density is lost as part of the aging process, and it is especially significant for women after menopause. The bones lose calcium and other minerals. The disks gradually lose fluid and become thinner in the spine, and vertebrae lose mineral content, which results in thinner bones. Foot arches become less pronounced contributing to a slight loss of height. Hip and knee joints, as well as finger joints, may begin to lose cartilage. Lean muscle mass decreases due partly to loss of muscle tissue (atrophy) (Hurd, 2014). Aging brings about changes in the musculoskeletal system that is essential for all movement, while the immune system is critical to fight against infections.

Lymphatic System

The major function of the immune system is defense against infection and disease. With advancing age, the lymphatic system becomes less effective at combating disease and fighting off infections. A compromised immune system leaves older persons vulnerable. Illnesses or diseases negatively impact the lives of older adults due to the potential social inactivity, isolation, decreased ability to perform activities of daily living, and increased financial expenses due to the need to purchase equipment supplies and medication and pay for any health care services. Older persons may become depressed and/or anxious. Mental health professionals can assist older persons by encouraging them to obtain flu vaccinations, eat nutritious meals, comply with their treatment regimen, and engage in physical activity. Mental health professionals can provide counseling around issues of stress and loss and medical issues that have arisen from the suppressed immune system. Mental health professionals can also encourage social interaction, teach stress reduction techniques, and educate older persons on various issues pertaining to their illness. A compromised immune system with any associated conditions does not need to impede the quality of life for older persons. Mental health practitioners are in an excellent position to assist older persons in developing coping mechanisms.

As a person ages, the ability to fight off infections declines, and the risk of becoming ill increases. The cells within the immune system react more slowly. Specifically, T and B cells are associated with fighting off disease. The T cells, white blood cells that coordinate immune defenses, are responsible for cell immunity. They coordinate and regulate the immune system to allow it to fight off diseases. With age, the T cells become less responsive and make it harder to respond to pathogens. The B cells are responsible for producing antibodies. The antibody levels do not rise quickly enough after an infection enters the body with age (Aging Changes in Immunity, 2012).

The decline in immune system functioning can explain several findings that are associated with aging (Whitbourne, 2000). The cancer rate increases with age because the cells of the immune system are not able to recognize the malfunctioning cells that cause cancer. Vaccines are less protective for older people because the body is not able to produce the antibodies needed. Older adults are more susceptible to common infections, such as pneumonia and influenza, which become more prominent and can cause death. Additionally, open wounds will not heal as fast because the cells responsible for healing act slower and are reduced in number. The lymphatic system provides protection for all human beings and without it, illness and death may occur. The emotional state of an older adult can either promote a healthy outcome or become detrimental to the recovery process.

Emotions

Emotions change with age; however, aging adults can improve in the area of emotional regulation (Kensinger, 2009). Healing emotions (serenity, gratitude, and reverence) bolster the immune system. They have been long understood in alternative medicine and are slowly coming to be accepted by the mainstream medical community as well. Since decreased immune function is common in later life, whatever can be done to strengthen it is good. Positive emotions boost two kinds of immune system cells: T cells and natural killer cells, large white blood cells that attack cancer cells and infected cells (Cohen, 1998). Immune function varies greatly, but people over 75 or 80 usually need longer to recover from a cold or from wounds, and their infections tend to be more serious than those of younger people.

Older adults can develop healing emotions. Practitioners can teach stress reduction techniques to encourage relaxation. They can also encourage older persons to develop a spiritual connection (if one does not already exist), and they can empower elders to be assertive and take control of their health. Practitioners can also encourage older adults to embrace the aging process, focus on their strengths and abilities, and give of themselves (talents, knowledge, experience) to others. A common way serenity is cultivated is gardening. Nurturing new growth is calming, and gardeners seem to thrive in old age. The ability to feel and express gratitude is an important part of healthy aging. In the lives of most people, there are at least a few things to be grateful for. Sometimes this is just a matter of mindfulness, for example, promoting thinking like "I'm grateful that it is a clear night and I can see the stars." Gratitude does not depend on external circumstances, and it helps to counter the message from industrial societies that we need more of everything (Macy, 2007). Reverence is more abstract than gratitude or serenity. The hard breathing that accompanies strenuous exertion or exercise can induce feelings of reverence. This emotion acknowledges the life force greater than our individual spark. It may make us feel small or exalted. A group experience may evoke it, or it may be solitary. People who see the northern lights report feelings of reverence. This emotion may come from a flash of understanding that all things are interconnected. Looking over one's life may inspire reverence for the sheer doggedness of humans who live to be old (Cruikshank, 2009).

Case Illustration 1.1 shows the natural physical changes that may accompany aging and the manner in which older persons can adapt to their environments with an adequate support system and stay actively engaged. The changes demonstrated include mobility issues, development of osteoporosis, decreased activities of daily living, loss of vision and hearing acuity, and digestive challenges.

CASE ILLUSTRATION 1.1

A 98-year-old elderly woman lives in her three-bedroom home with her adult daughter who is 75 years old. She drove until her early 80s, at which time she had an accident and was hospitalized. She ambulates with the assistance of a walker and an occasional arm to hold onto and is fearful of falling because of her recent diagnosis of osteoporosis. She attends church services regularly, watches television daily, and enjoys conversing with family and friends in her home and via telephone. Her daughter prepares her meals, washes her laundry, and manages her finances. She has one outside provider, a registered nurse, who comes to her home on a monthly basis and conducts a physical assessment. Overall, she is in good health and is thankful for every day she is alive. She doesn't know if she will see age 99; however, she leaves it up to the "man upstairs."

This individual is living in her home, has the assistance of a loving daughter, and is visited regularly by friends and neighbors. She is able to attend church (which is very important to her) and engage in a few activities that bring her joy. Despite her limited mobility and slowness in ambulating, she is overall very satisfied with life. She is able to live at home because she has an excellent support system. Though she has difficulty with her vision, she wears bifocal glasses to help her see; her hearing is impaired, but she wears a hearing aid, which enhances her ability to hear. Her biggest complaint is that of constipation, which is not uncommon due to the slowing of the digestive system and more sedentary lifestyle, along with decreased daily fluid intake.

COGNITIVE CHANGES THAT ACCOMPANY AGING

In general, cognitive changes are much more subtle than physical changes. Cognitive abilities peak in young adulthood (Ericsson, 2000). Losses in midlife occur primarily during peak performances; in other words, declines in developmental reserve capacity are apparent when performance is pushed to its limits (Lindenberger, Marsiske, & Baltes, 2000). Differences in cognitive developmental change can be seen when distinguishing between fluid and crystallized intelligence. Crystallized intelligence refers to general knowledge developed through a lifetime of experiences (accumulated knowledge) (Sternberg, Grigorenko, & Oh, 2001). In contrast, fluid intelligence refers to the "creative and flexible thinking" required to solve novel problems (e.g., anagrams, memory tests).

Generally, fluid intelligence declines with age, but crystallized intelligence remains stable or even increases (such as when one becomes specialized in a career, hobby, etc.) across the life span. It is important to distinguish between fluid intelligence pertaining to the solving of more practical problems versus more traditional (academic) problem-solving tasks. Performance on traditional problem-solving tasks peaks around the age of 20 and then declines, whereas performance on practical problem-solving tasks peaks in midlife, suggesting that it is at this time that individuals are best at practical problem solving (Sternberg et al., 2001).

Fluid cognition or fluid reasoning, the capacity to think logically and solve problems in novel situations, independent of acquired knowledge, has been shown to decline from midlife onward as a result of normal aging (Richards, Shipley, & Fuhrer, 2004; Singh-Manoux, Kivimaki, & Glymour, 2012), while cognitive decline of functional or clinical significances is generally not detected until much later in life, often as a result of significant neurologic morbidity such as cerebrovascular disease (Richards et al., 2004). Given that changes in cognitive and physical functioning probably result from interactions between aging and disease, their effects may not be fully distinguishable (Blumenthal, 2003).

As people age, some individuals experience normal declines in physical and cognitive functioning that increase their risk of dependence on others and premature death (Cooper, Kuh, & Cooper, 2011; Cooper, Kuh, & Hardy, 2010; Dewey & Saz, 2001; Studenski, Perera, & Patel, 2011). There are, however, remarkable individual differences in rates of age-associated decline in the age at which these declines begin to accelerate.

In their related dual-processing model, Baltes and colleagues (1999) distinguish between the mechanics of intelligence that generally refer to processing abilities (information-processing strategies and problem-solving functions) independent of specific content and the pragmatics of intelligence that typically refer to knowledge about facts and procedures, including practical thinking, expertise, wisdom, and knowledge accumulated across the life span.

While the pragmatics of intelligence are expected to grow into adulthood and then remain stable into old age, there is abundant evidence of age-related decline in the mechanics of intelligence (Salthouse, 2003). This decline compromises individual capacities beginning in midlife only under conditions of multitasking and time pressure (Lindenberger et al., 2000). Thus, the implications of these declines for everyday functioning in midlife are constrained to time-sensitive multitasking in everyday behavior (e.g., talking on the phone while merging into freeway traffic) and select professions (e.g., air traffic controllers). Strategies that are part of the pragmatics of intelligence (e.g., sequence activities to avoid multitask overload) in midlife can compensate for the weaknesses in the mechanics of intelligence. Such strategies may become increasingly insufficient as cognitive decline progresses in advanced old age. Guided Practice Exercise 1.4 provides the opportunity to examine physiological changes and one's personal adaptation to inevitable changes.

Guided Practice Exercise 1.4

Numerous physiological changes occur as people age. Identify two of the major systems that change as one ages and discuss ways to adjust to these changes. What modifications in your current behavior will enable you to adjust more positively to these natural and inevitable changes?

Attention

Healthy aging is associated with relatively little cognitive decline. An examination of cognition in aging includes attention, learning and memory, language, and intelligence. Sustained attention is very good in healthy older adults, and there is a mild decline in overall accuracy beginning in the 60s that progresses slowly. Older adults are more easily distracted, especially if irrelevant information is presented with important material. A good suggestion is to give instructions directly and simply, encourage encoding strategies, and refer them to reputable memory training (Besdine & Wu, 2008). When counselors provide critical information to older patients, they should stick to core data, repeat it, and write it down (Besdine & Wu, 2008).

Cid-Fernandez, Lindin, and Diaz (2014) tested attentional performance in three age groups: young (21–29 years old), middle-aged (51–64 years old), and older adults (65–84 years old). The task used in this study involved presenting both visual and auditory cues to the participants, who were required to focus on the visual cues while ignoring the auditory cues. The results showed that there was an increase in distractibility and changes in motor selection in the middle-aged and older groups compared to the younger groups. It is thus suggested that these cognitive working memory changes in aging lead to the slowing of motor response selection. This study also has implications for understanding motor and cognitive problems associated with age-related neurodegenerative disorders, including Parkinson's and Alzheimer's diseases. This study helps us understand the changes that occur in neurodegenerative disorders by increasing our knowledge of what happens in the brain as symptoms are manifested in diseases such as Parkinson's and Alzheimer's disease. These diseases are characterized by slow reaction time to stimuli, slowed working memory, and slowed movements. Attention in later life remains an important function for older adults, and learning and memory are important concerns for adults as they age.

Learning and Memory

Learning and memory involve the encoding, storage, and retrieval of information. Sensory memory is the earliest stage (i.e., visual, auditory, tactile), which is inherently unstable and decays rapidly. There is no age-related change. Primary (short-term) memory occurs after transfer of sensory memory. There is no loss with age. Secondary (long-term) memory persists for hours, days, and years. There is a decline with age, mostly in free recall; however, recognition is well preserved. The universal temporary decline in the ability to retrieve names generally begins early in middle age and worsens over time. The lost name is almost always retrieved soon after the episode. The phenomenon does not predict any neurodegenerative disorder, such as Alzheimer's disease. Encoding strategies such as mnemonics, mental hierarchies, and clusters help with retrieval; however, older adults use them less frequently. Training provides long-lasting improvements.

The most widely seen cognitive change associated with aging is that of memory. Memory function can be divided into four sections: episodic memory, semantic memory, procedural memory, and working memory. Episodic and semantic memories are most important with regard to aging. Episodic memory is a unique memory of a specific event or a personal memory of an experience. An example of an episodic memory would be a memory of the first day at school, last week's important meeting, or learning that Paris is the capital of France. Episodic memory is thought to decline from middle age onward. This is particularly true for recall in normal aging and less so for recognition (Nyberg & Blackman, 2004).

Semantic memory refers to general facts and knowledge. Examples of this type of memory include knowing that Paris is the capital of France, that 10 millimeters make up a centimeter, or that Mozart composed *The Magic Flute*. Semantic memory increases gradually from middle age (30–45 years) to the young elderly (46–60 years) but then declines in the very elderly (61–75 and 76–90 years) (Nyberg & Blackman, 2004). It is unclear why these changes occur, and it has been hypothesized that the very elderly have fewer resources to draw from and that their performance may be affected in some tasks by slower reaction times, lower attention levels, slower processing speeds, detriments in sensory and/or perceptual functions, or potentially a lesser ability to use strategies (Cabeza, 2004; Cabeza, Daselaar, & Dolcos, 2004; Lustig & Buckner, 2004; Nyberg & Blackman, 2004).

Davis and colleagues (2003) examined memory performance in four age groups (30–45 years, 46–60 years, 61–75 years, and 76–90 years) on a multitrial verbal recall task with 20-minute and 1-day delay free recall and recognition trials. The rate of acquisition across five learning trials was similar for all ages except the youngest group. Despite the similarities, the level of acquisition achieved was lower in the two oldest groups. Subjective organization decreased with age (tendency for individuals to impose greater organization of words, either no improvement or a decrease in sequential organization) but remained strongly related to the number of words during acquisition for all age groups. The two oldest groups demonstrated significant declines in words recalled on the 20-minute and 1-day delay trials. Thus, it was concluded that many aspects of free recall are impaired with age, and variance measurement of recall showed greater interindividual differences with increasing age. This increase in individual differences could reflect a single form of age-related memory impairment, or it could indicate that memory impairment in the elderly is due to multiple processes (Davis et al., 2003).

Physically, the function of the prefrontal cortex is altered with aging. There is evidence of atrophy in gray and white matter within the prefrontal cortex, which results in slowed neurotransmissions, which causes slowed reactions, thinking, and signaling among other functions (Head et al., 2004). The brain of older adults works harder and uses both the right and left hemispheres (bilateral recruitment) for functions that young adults can perform unilaterally. These activities include the initiation of goal-related task strategies, and with age the brain will recruit additional prefrontal regions to help perform the task (Kensinger, 2009). The hippocampus (part of the brain involved in emotions, memory, learning, and the autonomic nervous system) is the other region of the brain that shows large decline with age and affects the encoding and retrieval phases of recollective and associate memory, which tend to be underused in aging adults. Recollective memory is recall in memory, which is the retrieval of events or information from the past, whereas associate memory is the ability to learn or remember the relationship between unrelated items (e.g., name of someone you just met or aroma of a particular perfume). The changes within the hippocampus correlate with reduced performance on memory tasks.

As adults progress through their later years, many note the decline in their ability to recall bits of information and perform mental calculations. Though reflections about cognitive aging are expected to grow more pessimistic with the passage of chronological time, people's life courses elapse in ways besides objective days, months, calendar, and years. Therefore, age identity may be a more telling indicator of dispositions toward cognitive aging than chronological age. Subjective evaluations of age are an important aspect of the self with implications for well-being (Westerhof & Barrett, 2005).

Language

Normal aging causes widespread changes in the brain, many of which could be expected to impact language functions. However, in the absence of disease (such as Alzheimer's dementia) or stroke, which can have serious consequences for language, it is generally found that older adults perform much like younger adults on language comprehension tasks, and indeed, that vocabulary and other kinds of knowledge can increase throughout the life span (Cognition and Brain Lab, 2015). Vocabulary increases well into the 50s and 60s and shows no decline with age in those who continue to be engaged in complex language use. Similarly, syntactic skills, the ability to combine words in meaningful sequences, show no decline with pure aging. Subtle differences in performance on language tasks occur after middle age. Some of these changes such as poorer speech processing and less accuracy is related to the loss of auditory (hearing) acuity. Older people have more difficulty finding specific words and making inferences from complicated discourse. However, knowledge of words and the understanding of real-world expectations, as well as storytelling skills, appear to remain unimpaired (Clark-Cotton, Williams, Goral, & Obler, 2007).

Declining language skills have been associated with diminishing cognition, overall health, factors of fatigue, and a variety of social variables (level of education, gender, culture, and socioeconomic status), behavioral factors (motivation and interest), and comfort of the assessment environment. Disease can compound any language usage. For example, a transient ischemic attack (TIA), also referred to as a mini stroke, will interfere with the ability to speak. Also, a childhood language disorder (stuttering) if left undiagnosed and untreated, will lead to problems with disordered language production in older adulthood (Clark-Cotton et al., 2007). However, most older adults communicate successfully throughout most of their lives.

Intelligence

Intelligence, as measured by the Wechsler Adult Intelligence Scale, declines with age, but the biggest, earliest losses were reported in flawed studies. Cohort differences undermined these cross-sectional studies, causing selection bias regarding education, gender, race, occupation, and income. However, measuring specific intellectual functions has become typical. Crystallized intelligence (learning and experience) remains stable or improves with age until the late 70s or beyond, especially in those who remain healthy and engaged in cognitively demanding activities. Fluid intelligence declines rapidly after adolescence. Perceptual motor skills (timed tasks) decline with age (Besdine & Wu, 2008).

Individuals may experience a wide array of physical and cognitive shifts as they go through the aging process. Such changes can include issues with vision to problems with cardiovascular or integumentary systems to losses in episodic memory to attention deficiencies. The degrees to which these changes occur differ from person to person. Older adults' health and well-being are dependent on the professionals who are available to help them through these new stages of life. In particular, counselors should acknowledge any diminished capacities that a client is experiencing and provide him or her support in those areas, while also reinforcing the person's strengths and emphasizing his or her ability to lead a happy life.

KEYSTONES

- Natural physiological and psychological changes occur as one ages.
- Older adults are able to adapt to these physiological and psychological changes.
- Declines in functioning and strengths can and do coexist within elders.
- Professional counselors are encouraged to acknowledge diminished capacity while reinforcing the older client's strengths.

ADDITIONAL RESOURCES

Print Based

Aldwin, C. M., & Gilmer, D. F. (2004). *Health, illness, and optimal aging.* Thousand Oaks, CA: Sage.

Cutler, N. E. (2000, November 20). *Myths and realities of aging 2000.* Paper presented at the Annual Meeting of the Gerontological Society of America, Washington, DC.

Dalton, D. S., Cruickshanks, K. J., Klein, B. E. K., Wiley, T. L., & Wondahl, D. M. (2003). The impact of hearing loss on quality of life in older adults. *The Gerontologist, 43,* 661–668.

Desai, M., Pratt, L. A., Lentzner, H., & Robinson, K. N. (2001). Trends in vision and hearing among older Americans. *Aging Trends, 2,* 1–8.

Kemmet, D., & Brotherson, S. (2008). *Making sense of sensory losses as we age—Childhood, adulthood, elderhood.* Fargo: North Dakota State University.

Masoro, E. J. (2001). Dietary restriction: An experimental approach of the biology of aging. In E. J. Masoro & S. N. Austad (Eds.), *Handbook of the biology of aging* (5th ed.). San Diego, CA: Academic Press.

Olshansky, S. J., Hayflick, L., & Carnes, B. A. (2002). No truth to the fountain of youth. *Scientific American, 286,* 92–95.

Rattan, S. J. S., & Clark, B. F. C. (2005). Understanding and modulating ageing. *UBMB Life, 57,* 297–304.

U.S. National Library of Medicine and National Institutes of Health. (2009). Aging changes in the senses. *Medline Plus.* Retrieved from http://www.nlm.nih.gov/

Vijg, J. (2007). *Aging of the genome.* Oxford, UK: Oxford University Press.

Web Based

www.aarp.org
www.aghe.org
www.aoa.gov
www.geron.org
www.nih.gov

REFERENCES

Aging changes in the bones - muscles - joints. (2012, November 10). In *Medline Plus medical encyclopedia.* Bethesda, MD: U.S. National Library of Medicine. Retrieved from http://www.nlm.nih.gov/medlineplus/ency/article/004015.htm

Aging changes in immunity. (2012, November 10). In *Medline Plus medical encyclopedia.* Bethesda, MD: U.S. National Library of Medicine. Retrieved from http://www.nlm.nih.gov/medlineplus/ency/article/004008.htm

Aging changes in the skin. (2014, September 15). In *Medline Plus medical encyclopedia.* Bethesda, MD: U.S. National Library of Medicine. Retrieved from http://www.nlm.nih.gov/medlineplus/ency/article/004014.htm

American Academy of Health and Fitness (AAHF). (2015). *Respiratory system.* Retrieved from http://www.aahf.info/sec_exercise/section/respiratory.htm

Anti-Aging Today. (2013). *The cross-linking theory.* Retrieved from http://www.anti-aging-today-org/research/aging/theory/cross-linking.htm

Arking, R. (2006). *The biology of aging: Observations and principles* (3rd ed.). Oxford, UK: Oxford University.

Baltes, P. B., Staudinger, U. M., & Lindenberger, U. (1999). Lifespan psychology: Theory and application to intellectual functioning. *Annual Review of Psychology, 50,* 471–501.

Bengtson, V., Putney, N., & Johnson, M. (2005). The problem of theory in gerontology today. In M. Johnson (Ed.), *The Cambridge handbook of age and aging* (pp. 3–20, 117). New York, NY: Cambridge University Press.

Besdine, R. W., & Wu, D. (2008). Aging of the human nervous system: What do we know? *Geriatrics, 91*(5), 129–131.

Block, W. (2015, February). How effective are aging theories? *Life Enhancement.* Retrieved from http://www.life-enhancement.com/magazine/article/2379-how-effective-are-aging-theories

Blumenthal, H. T. (2003). The aging-disease dichotomy: True or false? *Journal of Gerontology A: Biological Sciences and Medical Sciences, 58*(2), 138–145.

Boyce, J., & Shone, G. (2006). Effects of ageing on smell and taste. *Post-graduate Medical Journal, 82*(966), 239–241.

Cabeza, R. (2004). Commentary: Neuroscience frontiers of cognitive aging: Approaches to cognitive neuroscience of ageing. In R. Dixon, L. Blackman, & L. Nilsson (Eds.), *New frontiers in cognitive ageing* (pp. 179–198). Oxford, UK: Oxford University Press.

Cabeza, R., Daselaar, S., & Dolcos, F. (2004). Task-independent and task-specific age effects on brain activity during working memory, visual attention and episodic retrieval. *Cerebral Cortex, 14,* 364–375.

Cacchione, P. (2005). Tools and tips for evaluating the senses of older adults. The 16th Annual Saint Louis University Summer Geriatric Institute. *Staying Focused on Quality.* St. Louis, MO: Department of Veterans Affairs.

Cacchione, P. (2012). Sensory changes. *Evidence-based geriatric nursing protocols for best practice* (4th ed.). New York, NY: Springer.

Cash, T. (2001). The psychology of hair loss and its implications for patient care. *Clinics in Dermatology, 19*(2), 161–166.

Cid-Fernandez, S., Lindin, M., & Diaz, F. (2014). Effects of aging and involuntary capture of attention on event-related potentials associated with the processing of and the response to a target stimulus. *Frontiers in Human Neuroscience, 8,* 745.

Clark-Cotton, M., Williams, R., Goral, M., & Obler, L. (2007). *Language and communication in aging.* Boston, MA: Elsevier, Inc.

Cognition and Brain Lab. (2015). *Aging and sematic memory.* Retrieved from http://internal.psychology.illinois.edu/ ~ kfederme/aging.html

Cohen, L. (1998). *No aging in India: Alzheimer's, the bad family, and other modern things.* Berkeley: University of California Press.

Colby, S., & Ortman, J. (2014). Projections of the size and composition of the U.S. population: 2014 to 2060. *Current Population Reports* (pp. 1–13). Washington, DC: U.S. Census Bureau.

Cooper, R., Kuh, D., & Cooper, C. (2011). Objective measures of physical capability and subsequent health: A systematic review. *Age Ageing, 40*(1), 14–23.

Cooper, R., Kuh, D., & Hardy, R. (2010). Objectively measured physical capability levels and mortality: Systematic review and meta-analyses. *British Medical Journal, 341,* 44–67.

Cristofalo, V. (1988). An overview of the theories of biological aging. In J. Birken & V. Bengtson (Eds.), *Emergent theories of aging* (pp. 118–128). New York, NY: Springer.

Cristofalo, V. (1996). Ten years later: What have we learned about human aging from studies of cell cultures? *The Gerontologist, 36*(6), 737–741.

Cruikshank, M. (2009). *Learning to be old: Gender, culture, and aging* (2nd ed.). Washington, DC: Rowman & Littlefield.

Davis, H. P., Small, S. A., Stern, Y., Mayeux, R., Feldstein, S. N., & Keller, F. R. (2003). Acquisition, recall, and forgetting of verbal information in long term memory by young, middle-aged, and elderly individuals. *Cortex, 39*(4–5), 1063–1091.

Dean, W. (2012). *Neuroendocrine theory of aging.* Retrieved from http://warddeanmd.com/articles/neuroendocrine-theory-of-aging-chapter-1/

de Magalhaes, J. (2014). *Damage-based theories of aging.* Retrieved from http://www.senescence.info/causes-of-aging.html

Dewane, C. (2010). Hearing loss in older adults—Its effect on mental health. *Social Work Today, 10*(4), 18.

Dewey, M. E., & Saz, P. (2001). Dementia, cognitive impairment and mortality in persons aged 65 and over living in the community: A systematic review of the literature. *International Journal of Geriatric Psychiatry, 16*(8), 751–761.

Dietrich, M., & Horvath, T. (2010). The role of mitochondrial uncoupling proteins in lifespan. *European Journal of Physiology, 459,* 269–275.

Dugdale, D. (2012). *Aging changes in the nervous system.* Retrieved from http://www.nlm.nih.gov/medlineplus/ency/article/004023.htm

Encyclopaedia Britannica. (2015). Aging. Retrieved from http:///www.britanica.com/science/aging-life-process

Ericsson, K. A. (2000). How experts attain and maintain superior performance: Implications for the enhancement of skilled performance in older individuals. *Journal of Aging and Physical Activity, 8*(4) 366–372.

Hayflick, L. (1996). *How and why we age.* New York, NY: Ballantine Books.

Head, D., Buckner, R., Shimony, J., Williams, L., Akbudak, E., Conturo, T., . . . Snyder, A. (2004). Differential vulnerability of anterior white matter in nondemented aging with minimal acceleration in dementia of the Alzheimer type: Evidence from diffusion tensor imaging. *Cerebral Cortex, 14,* 410–423.

Health in Aging. (2012). *Foot problems: Basic facts and information.* Retrieved from http://www.healthinaging.org/aging-and-health-a-to-z/topic:foot-problems

Heckhausen, J. (2001). Adaptation and resilience in midlife. In M. E. Lachman (Ed.), *Handbook of midlife development* (pp. 345–394). New York, NY: John Wiley.

Herman, D. (2006). Free radical theory of aging: An update: Increasing the functional lifespan. *Annals New York Academy of Science, 1067,* 10–21.

Hurd, R. (2014). *Aging changes in the heart and blood vessels.* Retrieved from https://www.nlm.hih.gov/medlineplus/ency/article/004006.htm

Jin, K. (2010). Modern biological theories of aging. *Aging and Disease, 1*(2), 72–74.

Kensinger, E. (2009). Cognition in aging and age-related disease. In P. R. Hof & C. V. Mobbs (Eds.), *Handbook of the neuroscience of aging.* San Diego, CA: Academic Press.

Lindenberger, U., Marsiske, M., & Baltes, P. B. (2000). Memorizing while walking: Increase in dual-task costs from young adulthood to old age. *Psychology and Aging, 15,* 417–436.

Lustig, C., & Buckner, R. (2004). Preserved neural correlates of priming in old age and dementia. *Neuron, 42,* 865–875.

MacWilliam, L. (2002, April). *Modern theories of aging.* Retrieved from http://www.nutrisearch.ca/pdf/aging.pdf

Macy, J. (2007, November). Gratitude: Where healing the earth begins. *Shambhala Sun,* pp. 48–51.

Martin, L. (2014). Aging changes in the lungs. *Medline Plus medical encyclopedia.* Bethesda, MD: U.S. Department of Health and Human Services. Retrieved from https://nlm.nih.gov/medlineplus/ency/article/004011.htm

Masoro, E. J., & Austad, S. N. (2001). *The handbook of biology of aging.* San Diego, CA: Academic Press.

Mayo Clinic. (2015). *DHEA.* Retrieved from http://www.mayoclinic.org/drugs-supplements/dhea/background/hrh-20059173

Mitteldorf, J. (2010). Aging is not a process of wear and tear. *Rejuvenation Research, 13,* 322–326.

Moody, H. R., & Sasser, J. R. (2012). *Aging: Concepts and controversies* (7th ed.). Thousand Oaks, CA: Sage.

Natus Balance & Mobility. (2015). *How to control your balance.* Retrieved from http://balanceandmobility.com/for-patients/how-to-control-your-balance/

NIH Senior Health. (2014). *About balance problems.* Retrieved from http://nihseniorhealth.gov/balanceproblems/aboutbalanceproblems/01.html

Nyberg, L., & Blackman, L. (2004). Cognitive ageing: A view from brain imaging. In R. Dixon, L. Blackman, & L. Nilsson (Eds.), *New frontiers in cognitive ageing* (pp. 135–160). Oxford, UK: Oxford University Press.

Orenstein, B., & Marcellin, L. (2015). *When aging steals your sense of taste.* Retrieved from http://www.everydayhealth.com/senior_health/when-aging-steals-your-sense-of-taste.aspx

Ortman, J. M., Velkoff, V. A., & Hogan, H. (2014). An aging nation: The older population in the United States. Population estimates and projections. *Current Population Reports.* Washington, DC: U.S. Census Bureau.

Park, J., Hong, J., Kim, C., Chung, Y., Kim, S., & Lee, E. (2011). Sustained-released recombination human growth hormone improves body composition and quality of life in adults with somatopause. *Journal of the American Geriatrics Society, 59,* 944–947.

Peters, R. (2006). Ageing and the brain. *Postgraduate Medical Journal, 82*(964), 84–88.

Porter, R. S. (2009). *The Merck manual: Home health handbook* (pp. 1883–1934). Kenilworth, NJ: Merck & Co., Inc.

Price, V. (1999). Treatment of hair loss. *New England Journal of Medicine, 341,* 964–973.

Ramaswamy, B. (2012). *Theories of aging.* Retrieved from http://www.physio-pedia.com/Theories_of_Aging

Richards, M., Shipley, B., & Fuhrer, R. (2004). Cognitive ability in childhood and cognitive decline in midlife: Longitudinal birth cohort study. *British Medical Journal, 328*(7439), 552–557.

Salthouse, T. A. (2003). Interrelations of aging, knowledge, and cognitive performance. In U. M. Staudinger & U. Lindenberger (Eds.), *Understanding human development: Dialogues with lifespan psychology* (pp. 265–287). Dordrecht, The Netherlands: Kluwer Academic Publishers.

Salvi, S. M., Currie, Z., & Aktar, S. (2005). Ageing changes in the eye. *Postgraduate Medical Journal, 82*(971), 581–587.

Scheinfeld, N. (2012). *Skin disorders in older adults: Age-related changes to hair and nails.* Retrieved from http://www.consultant360.com/article/skin-disorders-older-adults-age-related-changes-hair

Singh-Manoux, A., Kivimaki, M., & Glymour, M. M. (2012). Timing of onset of cognitive decline: Results from Whitehall II prospective cohort study. *British Medical Journal, 344*(d7622), 1–8.

Sollitto, M. (2015). *Loss of taste in the elderly.* Retrieved from https://www.agingcare.com/articles/loss-of-taste-in-the Elderly—135240.htm

Sternberg, R. J., Grigorenko, E. L., & Oh, S. (2001). The development of intelligence at midlife. In M. E. Lachman (Ed.), *Handbook of midlife development* (pp. 217–247). New York, NY: John Wiley.

Stough, D., Stenn, K., & Haber, R. Psychological effect, patho-physiology, and management of androgenetic alopecia in men. *Mayo Clinic Procedures, 80,* 1316–1322.

Studenski, S., Perera, S., & Patel, K. (2011). Gait speed and survival in older adults. *Journal of American Medical Association, 305*(1), 50–58.

Talbot, L., & Hogstel, M. O. (2001). Biological and physiological aging. In M. O. Hogstel (Ed.), *Gerontology: Nursing care of the older adult* (pp. 66–82). Albany, NY: Delmar.

U.S. Census Bureau. (2012). *Population estimates and national projections.* Retrieved from http://www.census .gov/population/projections/data/national/2012.html

Weber, P. (2010). Organ systems in old age and their specifics. In *Aging issues, health and financial alternatives* (pp. 43–45). Hauppauge, NY: Nova Science Publishers.

Westerhof, G., & Barrett, A. (2005). Age identity and subjective age well-being: A comparison of the United States and Germany. *Journal of Gerontology: Social Sciences, 60,* S129–S136.

Whitbourne, S. K. (2000). *The aging individual: Physical and psychological perspectives* (2nd ed.). New York, NY: Springer.

Whitbourne, S. K. (2001). The physical aging process in midlife: Interactions with psychological and sociocultural factors. In M. E. Lachman (Ed.), *Handbook of midlife development* (pp. 109–155). New York, NY: John Wiley.

Whitbourne, S. K. (2010). *The search for fulfillment: Revolutionary new research that reveals the secret to long-term happiness.* New York, NY: Ballantine Books.

Yaar, M., & Gilchrest, B. (2001). Skin aging: Geriatric dermatology, part I. Postulated mechanisms and consequent changes in structure and function. *Clinics in Geriatric Medicine, 17,* 4.

Zarit, S. H., & Zarit, J. M. (2011). *Mental disorders in older adults: Fundamentals of assessment.* New York, NY: Guilford Press.

Historical Perspectives and Changing Attitudes Toward Older Adults

"Old age is not lost youth, but a new stage of opportunity and strength."

—Betty Friedan

Learning Objectives

After reading this chapter, you will be able to

1. Discuss society's perceptions of aging
2. Describe the major historical milestones that created support for older adults
3. Examine the impact of the baby boomer generation as these adults move throughout the life course
4. Analyze older adults' use of mental health services
5. Explain the shifts in society's perceptions of aging

INTRODUCTION

Older persons have made and continue to make numerous contributions to society. They are instrumental to their families, communities, work environment, and numerous other arenas. While on a personal level many families respect their elders, as a society, much more work is needed. American society values youth, beauty, and vitality, and these attributes are not viewed as representative of aging persons. These negative perceptions

39

impede their ability to live comfortably and engage successfully in all avenues of life. Change is needed to reengage and reinvigorate this large segment of our society, as myths, stereotypes, and discrimination abound. Helping professionals must work as advocates on behalf of older clients and display a willingness to train and educate the uninformed regarding the strengths that elders bring to different situations. Issues including ageism, impact of the baby boom generation, employment practices, and mental health services as part of the aging network will be examined in this chapter.

PERCEPTIONS OF GROWING OLDER AND SOCIETAL INFLUENCES

The media have a very powerful influence on the way society thinks, feels, and behaves. Mass media, particularly television and movies, define social roles in contemporary culture by presenting a steady and repetitive portrayal of images and a system of messages. The media emphasizes youth and beauty and overly simplistic portrayals of individuals. This emphasis exacerbates the negative image of aging and the elderly in American culture, because the stereotypes of aging are the antithesis of the attributes upon which television and movies thrive (Monsees, 2002).

The mass media play a powerful role in shaping American attitudes, and the media's portrayal of aging and older people can vary depending on its objective. In promotion of products, older people may be pictured in association with products such as medicine, including those to address incontinence and impotence, dental and digestive aids, and cosmetics to decrease signs of aging (Brownell, Mundorf, & Mundorf, 2006). When the media focus on general television programming or movies for the general public, older persons are typically cast in supporting roles versus leading roles (Hilt & Lipschultz, 2004), which promote stereotypes. Television programming has few older heroes. Older fashion models are rare, and advertising lacks the mature face (Dennis & Thomas, 2007). Repeated exposure to negative images of older adults, limited exposure to elders in more positive and leading roles may continue to lead to devaluing of older adults in society. Examination of the role of the media will highlight the portrayal of older persons and the need to alter this portrayal in Guided Practice Exercise 2.1.

Guided Practice Exercise 2.1

The media have a powerful influence on our viewpoints, and it permeates many aspects of our lives. How do the media portray older persons? Choose one form of media (television, radio, print) and identify both positive and negative images of older adults. Quantify the images and place in a positive or negative category. Now tabulate the columns and discuss the implications of these data with peers and colleagues. Identify ways to improve the representation of older persons in the media and ways to enhance the image of older persons.

Gender plays a role in societal perceptions, and many studies have found that people are more likely to view men as losing general competence or ability with age, yet they are more likely to judge women as needing more help with age (Kite, Stockdale, Whitley, & Johnson, 2005). Because of age stereotypes, the very same behavior in younger versus older individuals is perceived differently. When younger adults forget information, the cause is more likely to be seen as transient and external, such as "that's a hard thing to remember." When older people forget, the cause is more likely to be seen as something stable and internal, such as having a poor memory (Kite et al., 2005).

Aging can bring stereotypic reaction and expectations from others, which may interfere with satisfying social interactions. Researchers have found that when older individuals perceive themselves as the target of age discrimination, their sense of well-being is negatively affected (Gartska, Schmitt, Branscombe, & Hummert, 2004). This discrimination can come from anyone, as individuals of all ages tend to judge older people more negatively when compared to younger people (Hess, 2006).

Stereotypes

One of the problems with stereotyping is that people sometimes act on these oversimplified assumptions, which leads to age discrimination. Older workers have been discriminated against on the basis of the stereotypes that they are unable to learn new things, are less productive than younger workers, are more likely to miss work because of sickness, and are set in their ways. Even though all of these stereotypes have been disproven by research, they still persist.

Consequences of stereotyping have been examined. There is a new line of research showing that older people internalize negative stereotypes and that these aging self-stereotypes can influence cognitive and physical health (Levy, 2002). Hess, Hinson, and Stratham (2004) studied the ways in which positive and negative stereotypes influence older adults' performance on a memory task. Participants who were exposed to negative stereotypes performed more poorly than those who were primed with positive stereotypes. Additionally, the concept of "stereotype threat" is used to help explain the impact of stereotypes on memory, cognition, and health. It suggests that when individuals are afraid that their behavior will reinforce a negative stereotype about a group to which they belong, their performance is affected.

Age stereotypes are communicated in numerous ways. Television programs, advertisements, jokes, and birthday cards are often full of age stereotypes. Stereotypes stem from society's need to simplify the social world through the creation of categories, and they are related to age norms that suggest certain roles and behavior as appropriate at certain ages and not at others. From these benign or neutral starting points, age stereotypes can lead to age discrimination and aging self-stereotypes and can thus affect the psychological and social quality of life for older people.

Guided Practice Exercise 2.2 provides an opportunity to explore ways to replace stereotypes and myths regarding aging with factual information.

Many individuals fear growing older and there exists stereotypes and myths associated with aging. Identify ways you would dispel myths and stereotypes of aging. At what levels would you suggest target areas? How would you suggest integrating aging content into a curriculum at an early developmental stage?

Case Illustration 2.1 provides a glimpse of how preconceived ideas on the part of the professional counselor can impede the development of a trusting therapeutic relationship with an older client seeking services.

CASE ILLUSTRATION 2.1

Ageism is one of the negative consequences experienced by some elders in today's society. Differential treatment of older clients may occur in mental health settings, which lead to underutilization of mental health services. Ms. Timmons is a 75-year-old female who is self-referred to an outpatient mental health facility. Her presenting symptoms include difficulty sleeping, appetite disturbance, lack of interest in activities, and other symptoms related to a diagnosis of depression.

The professional counselor greets Ms. Timmons using her first name. She proceeds by speaking loudly to Ms. Timmons in a childlike manner. She then escorts Ms. Timmons to her office, placing her arm around Ms. Timmons' arm, despite the fact that Ms. Timmons is fully ambulatory. During the initial intake assessment, the counselor is interrupted several times with incoming phone calls. The counselor was very directive in her approach and used a depressive screening instrument to determine the extent of the symptoms and level of severity. This instrument was not normed on older adults, but one she typically uses with adult clients. Ms. Timmons did not complete the assessment, as she felt rushed and was given little opportunity to express other issues she was experiencing. Ms. Timmons had just experienced the loss of her pet of 12 years, foreclosure of her home, relocation of her major support system (her daughter moved out of state), and loss of her driver's license. These areas were not addressed, and Ms. Timmons did not return for her follow-up session.

Prejudice

Age prejudice is a human rights violation that is exhibited in health care, employment, and the media. Prejudice is a state of mind and entails feelings and attitudes, including stereotypes and discrimination, that lead to the unfair or unequal treatment of members of a minority group (*Oxford Dictionary,* 2015; *Merriam-Webster,* 2015). For instance, discrimination exists in the definition of who is considered poor in the United States, as people ages 65 and older must be poorer than younger adults in order to be counted as poor by the U.S. Census Bureau (Estrine, Nyberg, & Muller, 2001). There exists a great deal of misinformation and a lack of accurate facts about the aging process and older people, both in society as a whole and among practitioners. Some of the myths about older adults include that they cannot change; like to live in the past; cannot learn new information; are grouchy all of the time; are childish; are cute; live in nursing homes; lose interest in life; are sick most of the time; become children to their adult children; and are sick, senseless, and sexless (Hogstel, 2001). However, older adults are not only more mature, but also more independent and often more assertive in expressing their thoughts and ideas because they are not subject to peer pressure or employment status.

Guided Practice Exercise 2.3 provides the opportunity to explore personal perceptions of older adults.

Guided Practice Exercise 2.3

What are your views regarding older adults, and what experiences or events led to the views you currently hold? Remember to examine various aspects as they pertain to older adults, which include, but are not limited to, finances, relationships, values, religion/spirituality, and work. Do you perceive your views as promoting or impeding your ability to working constructively with older adults? Are any of your views modifiable, and how would you modify them?

Individuals may cling to these myths and stereotypes because they have not interacted with an older adult. Children and young people growing up today often do not have personal contact with an older family member such as a grandparent. They therefore may feel uncomfortable around older people. Increased contact with healthy, happy, and active older adults may change the perception of older adults as clients (Hogstel, 2001).

There are a number of common misconceptions about aging, as seen in Table 2.1. Some of the myths include lack of productivity, inflexibility, senility, and loss of sexuality (National Academy on an Aging Society, 2001). This is beginning to slowly change as more attention is being paid to the productive capabilities of older people and a better understanding that older persons have desires, capabilities, and satisfaction with regard to sexual activities. The "write-off" of older persons as senile because of memory problems, for example, is being replaced by an understanding of the profound and most common forms of what is popularly referred to as "senility," namely Alzheimer's disease. Senility is no longer seen as inevitable with age. Rather, it is understood to be a disease or group of diseases. When means of effectively treating dementia are available, ageism will also decline.

The underlying psychological mechanism of ageism makes it possible for individuals to avoid dealing with the realities of aging, at least for a time. It also becomes possible to ignore the social and economic plight of some older persons. Ageism is manifested in a wide range of phenomena (on both individual and institutional levels), including stereotypes and myths, outright disdain and dislike, or simply subtle avoidance of contact; discriminatory practices in housing, employment, and services of all kinds; and epithets, cartoons, and jokes. At times, ageism becomes an expedient method by which society

Table 2.1 Common Misconceptions (Myths) of Aging Older Adults

- Are resistant to change
- Are incapable of growth and engaging in new experiences
- Are isolated from family members
- Are sick and disabled most of their lives
- Mostly reside in nursing homes
- Are not interested in intimate activities
- Are forgetful and carry a diagnosis of Alzheimer's disease
- Are disagreeable and cantankerous
- Have high accident and absentee rates
- Are retired, which brings poor health and early death
- Are lonely and depressed
- Are all alike
- Prefer to live with their children
- Are more fearful of death than younger people

promotes viewpoints about the aged to relieve itself from the responsibility toward them, while other times it serves a highly personal objective, protecting younger (usually middle-aged individuals) from thinking about things they fear (aging, illness, and death).

Ageism can apply to stages of life other than old age. Older persons have prejudices against younger people and the attractiveness and vigor of youth. Angry and ambivalent feelings may flow, too, between older and middle-aged people. Middle-aged people often bear many of the pressures of both younger and older people, and they may experience anger toward both groups. Some older people refuse to identify with their peers and may dress and behave inappropriately in an attempt to appear young. Others may underestimate or deny their age.

Case Illustration 2.2 is representative of an older woman who is grieving over the loss of her spouse. This case provides the opportunity to reexamine perceptions of older clients and knowledge of the grieving process as well as explore ways in which a more favorable outcome could be achieved.

CASE ILLUSTRATION 2.2

Mrs. Denver is a highly functional 72-year-old female referred for counseling services at an outpatient mental health facility. Mrs. Denver is resistant, stating, "I'm not mentally ill." However, she made the appointment and attends her initial session. Mrs. Denver is assigned to a professional counselor who has been employed for approximately 5 years, but works primarily with young and middle-aged clients. This counselor has a license and certifications in numerous areas, which are displayed on her office walls. Mrs. Denver was referred for counseling services because her daughter feels that she is still grieving (6 months later) for her deceased spouse. Mrs. Denver has agreed to see a counselor to comply with her daughter's request.

Mrs. Denver was married for 45 years and really misses her husband. She describes her relationship as a good wholesome one—"not like the marriages of today." She tries to convey to the counselor the pain she has been experiencing that just sweeps over her unexpectedly when engaging in activities they once did together. She attempts to share her feelings for having cared for her husband for 5 years prior to his death. He died of end-stage renal disease, but prior to that, she escorted him to and from all dialysis treatments three times per week for several years. Mrs. Denver cries intermittently throughout the session and speaks of how lonely she is without him. Her counselor tries to console her by saying, "everything is going to be okay" and "unfortunately as we grow older, death becomes a part of life."

The counselor appears uncomfortable during the session, distances herself, and begins investigating another referral for Mrs. Denver. Mrs. Denver does not feel that her counselor understands what she has been experiencing, but accepts the referral to a psychiatrist and thanks her for her time. Her counselor expresses to Mrs. Denver that she is depressed and would benefit from an antidepressant and follow-up sessions. Mrs. Denver did not return for her follow-up sessions, nor did she follow through with the referral to the psychiatrist.

HISTORICAL ASPECTS OF AGING

National interest in aging and gerontology has resulted in major milestones and contributions to the well-being of older adults through a proliferation of research and dissemination of research findings. The federal government began in 1935 to acknowledge and support the needs of the older population, which served as an impetus to changing the landscape for older persons. Such milestones include the establishment of the Social Security Administration in 1935 and the National Institute on Aging (NIA) in 1974 as part of the National Institutes of Health. The establishment of the Social Security Administration was particularly significant, as there were very few officially recognized federal agencies on aging before 1935. At this time, the age 65 was chosen as a reflection of the age used by retirement, or pension, systems that were in place for private industry and state systems.

Several aging-related organizations developed between 1935 and 1950 and more were established after the Older Americans Act (OAA) of 1965 (Smith, 2014). The OAA established the Administration on Aging within the Department of Health, Education, and Welfare and called for the creation of State Units on Aging. State Units on Aging (SUAs) are agencies of state and territorial governments designated by governments and state legislatures to administer the Older Americans Act in their area. States coordinate and oversee the services through Area Agencies on Aging in their particular state (Day, 2014). Also in 1965, Title XVIII of the Social Security Act, a health insurance program for the elderly (also known as Medicare), was established as well as Title XIX, a health insurance program for low-income persons, known as Medicaid.

Additional amendments to the OAA authorized funding for nutrition programs for the elderly; grants for multipurpose senior centers and employment programs; and transportation, congregate housing services, home care, legal services, and home renovation/repair services. The OAA established a long-term ombudsman program to cover nursing homes and emphasized supportive services to help older persons remain independent in the community while expanding ombudsman coverage to board and care homes. The Long-Term Care Ombudsmen are advocates for residents of nursing homes, board and care homes, assisted living facilities, and similar adult care facilities. They work to resolve problems of individual residents and to bring about changes at the local, state, and national levels that will improve residents' care and quality of life (U.S. Department of Health and Human Services, 2015).

Many other notable events related to aging and gerontology have occurred to date, including resource centers, research, consortiums, additional amendments to the OAA, White House Conferences on Aging, enactment of the Medicare Prescription Drug Act, NIA activities, and the development of the Administration for Community Living (ACL). The ACL brings together the Administration on Aging, the Office on Disability, and the Administration on Developmental Disabilities to focus on reducing fragmentation in community living services (Smith, 2014). The Age Discrimination and Employment Act of 1967, amended in 1978, ended mandatory retirement in the federal government and advanced it to age 70 in the private sector. Mandatory retirement at all ages was abolished in the United States in 1986 (with a few exceptions), and the European Commission has mandated that members of the European Union have laws making age discrimination illegal in place by 2006.

Although the underlying dread, fear, and distaste for older persons remains for some individuals, several trends may reduce ageism in the future: (1) With the aging of baby boomers, old age is in the process of being redefined as a more robust and contributory stage of life. (2) Increasing interest in aging in the general public, mass media, government, and academia will support increasing knowledge and reducing misconceptions about older persons. (3) Increasing scientific research on aging has reduced and will continue to reduce ageism by providing a realistic picture of older persons. (4) Stereotypes are being challenged and disproven. For example, in 2009, for persons 65 and over, 77% had completed high school or more education, and 20% completed a bachelor's degree or higher education (U.S. Census Bureau, American Community Survey, 2009), challenging the stereotype that older men and women were illiterate or poorly educated. (5) As people become more aware of racism and sexism, they tend to become more aware of discrimination in general and will be less likely to approve of or practice ageism (Palmore, 2004). Numerous developments, both positive and negative, have evolved over time. However, a re-evaluation of pre-existing negative patterns of behavior is necessary to encourage greater participation of older adults in all aspects of society.

Aging of the Baby Boomer Generation

As the boomer generation moves through the life course, the projected growth of the 65 and older population, as seen in Table 2.3, will have big implications over the coming decades. The baby boomers will be influenced by age effects, period effects, and cohort effects. Aging effects are brought about by the physiological process of aging, along with responses to those effects by others. Period effects are those affecting all age groups in society at the same time. Finally, cohort effects are associated with events affecting groups of people during the same years (Moody & Sasser, 2012).

The baby boomers are an extremely large group because of higher fertility rates. They make up around a quarter of the entire U.S. population. There are a number of aspects that differentiate this segment of the population from the older and younger groups. First, more attention has been paid to this group as they crowded schools, became a target for marketers, and reached eligibility to vote. Second, boomers on average have higher levels of educational attainment than earlier generations. Third, in their childhood (1950s and 1960s), they experienced an extended period of post-war affluence and economic

Table 2.2   Classification of Older Adults According to Age

Age	Classification
65–74	Young-old
75–84	Old-old
85 +	Oldest-old

Source: U.S. Census Bureau (2014a).

Table 2.3   Projections and Distribution of the Total Population by Age for the United States 2015 to 2060

(Numbers in thousands)										
Age	2015	2020	2025	2030	2035	2040	2045	2050	2055	2060
65 +	47,830	56,441	65,920	74,107	79,233	82,344	84,712	87,996	92,470	98,164
85 +	6,304	6,727	7,482	9,132	11,909	14,634	17,259	18,972	19,454	19,724
100 +	72	89	119	138	154	193	267	387	493	604

Source: U.S. Census Bureau, Population Division (December, 2014b).

prosperity. Finally, the 1960s and 1970s were a time of dramatic upheaval, including the Vietnam War protests and campaigns for civil rights, feminism, and environmental advocacy. Some boomers protested, while others were more conservative, which is an example of the diversity within the cohort (Moody & Sasser, 2012). Baby boomers are a large and unique cohort who share common experiences and express their individual differences. They are expected to transform the way aging and older persons are viewed and treated in society.

Differences in the Baby Boomer Generation

A number of differences exist between the baby boomers and previous generations. Baby boomers are in better physical health than the generations preceding them (Zapolsky, 2003). They hold vastly different worldviews because they have been raised in a country at relative peace and have not faced a global war. Furthermore, unlike any prior generation, their worldviews have been expanded by mass media, technological advances, and world travel.

Fewer tragedies and family sacrifices were the goals set by their parents for the baby boomers, which were believed possible because their parents were America's Greatest Generation—strong, courageous, and self-reliant. The baby boomers grew up differently than their parents did. They are more affluent than their parents, perhaps because of their education, their courage, their ingenuity, or a combination of these (Vaillant, 2003). This group has not experienced the same struggles as their parents, such as the deprivations brought by the Great Depression. Although these differences make them unique, these same differences will affect the needs of those baby boomers who will reach their 60s in this decade and the future concerns of the baby boomers who are in their early 50s. Case Illustration 2.3 highlights some of the challenging aspects experienced by persons of the older generation.

CASE ILLUSTRATION 2.3

Mr. Jones grew up during the 1930s and experienced the Great Depression. Older persons today who grew up during this period are a distinct group and were shaped by the events and experiences in their youth. Mr. Jones was from a middle-class family and enjoyed the luxury of having nice clothes, a nice home, vacations, allowances, and several cars in their garage. They had family dinners, and he was able to attend a reasonable private school in his neighborhood. He recalled his life changing during the Great Depression because his family lost everything. They lost their jobs, their home, their cars, eliminated vacations, and Mr. Jones was enrolled in the public school within his neighborhood. His family did everything and sold everything to put food in his mouth, and while not nutritious by today's standards, it kept him from going hungry.

Mr. Jones's daughter is concerned because he is stockpiling canned goods, dry goods, newspapers, and a host of other items. He is what she calls "stingy," and while he has money from a pension and savings, he refuses to spend his money. He hides his money in mattresses, linings of curtains, shoeboxes, dresser drawers, tips of shoes, and is paranoid regarding banks. Other than this type of behavior, he does well in maintaining himself, but he has begun hoarding more items and refuses to sign living wills, advance directives, or any documents she feels would be beneficial due to his advanced age. She is accompanying him to his primary physician, whom he has been seeing for the past 30 years, for an evaluation.

Considering when Mr. Jones was born, do you feel he is exhibiting unusual behavior, or is this behavior appropriate for his cohort and life experiences? Conduct research on the life experiences of those persons born during the Great Depression and see if there are connections to Mr. Jones's current behavior. How would you, as a future practitioner, address the concerns that the daughter perceives as hoarding and refusal to spend money? How do you feel regarding his behavior, considering what you have learned from your research?

Baby boomers have been socially constructed in both positive and negative ways. They have been portrayed as aging hippies who "sold out" and became materialistic yuppies (Brooks, 2000) and as greedy and narcissistic (Okrent, 2000). Others challenge these portrayals (Freedman, 2002; Green, 2003; Steinhorn, 2006). Critics have pushed a distinctive ageism about boomers that links them to an unpatriotic image from the 1960s with traditional negative images of aging (Green, 2003). Steinhorn (2006) sees boomers as the greatest generation and rejects the notion that they are selfish; rather, he equates them with positive social change. Freedman (2002) paints an optimistic portrayal of boomers as favoring encore careers that bring idealism into extended working lives.

Regardless of the social construction of the baby boomer generation, one must always consider individual differences to avoid stereotyping and misrepresenting this group. The baby boomers are extremely conversant with many divergent ideas and dissenting values. This generation is characterized by not feeling old and, often, not looking or acting old. Nothing that was assumed about age in the past will fit this group. Just as their parents were shaped by the Great Depression of the 1930s, boomers were shaped by the great affluence of the post-war decades and later by the Great Recession of 2008.

Reconfiguring Work and Retirement

Many workers of all ages desire to be their own boss and chart their own path. According to research by the Ewing Marion Kauffman Foundation (2011), older baby boomers (aged 55–64) are driving a new entrepreneurship boom. The average age of the founders of high-tech companies is nearly 40, and there are twice as many founders over the age of 50 as there are under the age of 25 (Ewing Marion Kauffman Foundation, 2011). The Great Recession of 2008 brought about the highest unemployment levels since the Great Depression. Many of these older boomers are becoming part of the "second chance revolution" (Rogoff & Carroll, 2009).

Baby boomers are overturning long-standing assumptions about working until age 65, calling for dramatic changes in current employment practices, and proving that retirement and working are not mutually exclusive. The crux of their vision is born out of today's realities including the prolonged recovery from the Great Recession and retirement savings' shortfalls as well as the extraordinary gifts of increased longevity, active living, healthy aging, and opportunities to stay engaged and involved (Collinson, 2014). Sixty-five percent of baby boomer workers plan to work past age 65 or do not plan to retire. More than half (52%) plan to continue working after they retire. Given the current level of inadequate savings, it is not surprising that 62% of the baby boomer workers who plan to work in retirement and/or past age 65 indicate that their main reason is income or health benefits. One-third (34%) plan to continue working for enjoyment, including 18% who want to stay involved and 16% who enjoy what they do (Collinson, 2014).

For most baby boomer workers, retirement is no longer a point in time in which one immediately stops working. Sixty-eight percent of baby boomer workers envision a phased transition into retirement during which they will either continue working, reducing hours with more leisure time to enjoy life, or work in a different capacity that is less demanding and/or brings greater personal satisfaction. Only 21% expect to immediately stop working when they retire and 12% are "not sure" (Collinson, 2014). Boomers will likely remain taxpayers and part of the active economy for longer than most economists assume. If this occurs, millions of boomers will be income-producing assets, not liabilities, on society's balance sheet well into their 70s and beyond (Goldsmith, 2008).

Moreover, the boomers cannot always be replaced even if they do wish to retire. The United States faces a looming and potentially crippling shortage of skilled workers that affects its vital infrastructure—schools, the health care system, government at all levels, and even manufacturing. Forecasts suggest a costly shortage of skilled workers in the future with the retirement of the baby boomers. Knowledge-based enterprises will have a particularly difficult time replacing their older workers (Goldsmith, 2008). Retirement consultant and author Dave Bernard (2013) wrote, "age 54 is just another year in an ongoing career and retirement has no set time frame" (p. 1). This can give pause to those who have thought of aging and retirement in a traditional sense. With this delayed retirement can come challenges for baby boomers.

Challenges Facing Baby Boomers

A few of the challenges facing the baby boomers are similar to those facing the entire United States. Due to various events, the bulk of the boomers' retirement savings and investments have dwindled. This has resulted in a decision for some to continue to work past traditional retirement age. However, for others, businesses and other institutions give incentives to their highest paid employees to retire or resign—or ultimately force them to do so. The vacancies created by these forced retirements or resignations are often not filled and the responsibilities of the individuals, who held those jobs are assumed by younger, lower paid employees. This action is causing older adults to seek counseling for problems and concerns related to stress at work (Vaillant, 2003).

Personnel policies that push older workers out of the skilled positions will be re-examined by human resource professionals and organizations in the future. In some segments of the workforce, the cost of replacing experienced older workers could exceed the increased expenses of retaining them. Therefore, rather than encouraging boomers to retire, tax and pension policies may need to be revised, as well as Social Security and Medicare programs to encourage boomers to remain engaged and productive citizens (Goldsmith, 2008).

Problems can arise in the workplace when generations collide (Lancaster & Stillman, 2003). Employee productivity remains the key to success and that means ensuring the productivity of workers both young and old. Understanding multigenerational differences in the workplace will be a major factor in organizational life as aging boomers remain longer on the job. For example, working collaboratively might pose challenges for younger age cohorts as they attempt to work with older adults. Johnson and Johnson (2010) have offered practical suggestions regarding how younger workers can respond to aging baby boomers, such as "Don't ignore older workers" and "Don't give up on them." In other words, age-related stereotypes should be avoided. Younger workers are also encouraged to ask older workers to make continuing contributions, for example, by becoming mentors to young people. Complete Guided Practice Exercise 2.4 to better understand the characteristics and viewpoints of the baby boomer generation.

Guided Practice Exercise 2.4

Baby boomers were born between 1946 and 1964 and represent a very distinct cohort. What are some of the characteristics of this cohort? How do you think the baby boomers view the aging process? What are your views regarding baby boomers working for longer periods of time (well past 65 years of age)? Interview a person born between 1946 and 1964. Ask questions that will provide data to help you understand this age cohort. Ask questions regarding employment, retirement, cross-cultural experiences, sexuality/intimacy, living arrangements, health, family relationships, and their most significant accomplishment(s). Share this information with your peers and colleagues.

Older workers can show strong productivity because of greater life experience, but their skills may be outdated. Though they are likely to have lower rates of absenteeism, they may have more health problems than younger persons. A key to productivity over the life span will be whether employers can build on the positive attributes of older workers, while also providing training to ensure that their skills and knowledge remain up to date (Moody & Sasser, 2012). Attributes of older workers such as experience, reliability, work ethic, and loyalty are valued; however, some employers have doubts about older boomers' creativity, flexibility, and willingness to learn new things (Mermin, Johnson, & Toder, 2008). The baby boomer generation may seek counseling to address the challenges posed by delayed retirement, incentives to retire, remaining in the workforce, or reentry into the workplace.

Guided Practice Exercise 2.5 provides the opportunity to explore benefits and challenges that older workers perceive within the workplace and examine available mental health services and the extent to which these services are utilized.

Guided Practice Exercise 2.5

In this exercise, you will develop a personal list of the benefits and challenges (stressors) associated with work. Informally sample 10 older workers and ask them to create their own list of benefits and challenges. You will then compare the lists and identify areas that pose challenges for older workers. Next, you will explore services available within the work environment and mental health services available in the community to address workplace stressors. Finally, you will examine barriers that impede utilization of these services and develop strategies to minimize the impediments.

Mental health counselors are to use their knowledge of the baby boomer generation to increase their understanding of these older clients. Mental health professionals need to be well-versed in the aging process, leisure activities, career paths for nontraditional clients, loss and grief, retirement issues, financial planning, health insurance, health concerns, and environmental issues. These professionals are required to be advocates for their older clients and change agents. Mental health counselors will be in a position to provide better counseling services to older clients due to their enhanced appreciation for older adults' unique characteristics.

Work remains important to many older clients, which poses an opportunity for the mental health counselor to address issues that promote and/or impede participation in the labor force. Mental health counselors will also become a resource to connect their older clients with services in the community to assist with financial planning, obtaining insurance, and projecting lifestyle changes. The baby boomer generation will need mental health counselors to assist with emotional issues experienced as a result of continued employment, anxiety regarding retirement, uneasiness surrounding unanticipated expenses, and other issues that accompany major life transitions. Career counseling with older clients will become an integral component of the counseling process.

AGING AND MENTAL HEALTH

Older adults typically underutilize mental health services, which may be a result of interacting biases. One reason for this is older adults' denial of problems because of feared social stigma or the generational psyche (Ronch & Maizler, 1977) that casts a shaming and critical eye on the "mentally ill" as weak, crazy, or morally inferior. The stigma of mental difficulties reflects and is reflected in social attitudes and the way society relegates these problems to subordinate status in health coverage, a powerful synergy for mutual disincentive on the part of providers and prospective consumers. Additionally, older adults feel that they should not share private matters with others outside of the family. They are a very heterogeneous population, and many grew up in an era where personal events and unpleasant occurrences remained within the family environment. Sharing personal accounts was negatively viewed, and therefore counseling was not viewed favorably, because it occurred outside the realm of the family.

Guided Practice Exercise 2.6 challenges the mental health counselor to diminish some longstanding beliefs regarding sharing private matters to persons other than family members. Counselors will need to become astute in working with reluctant clients who may not believe in the mental health system or the effectiveness of counseling services.

Guided Practice Exercise 2.6

Elderly individuals have been taught to maintain private matters within their family systems. This belief interferes with their ability to access the services of mental health counselors. As a new professional, how would you address the reluctance to pursue counseling services? What specific strategies would you employ? What resources would you need to increase their level of involvement? What information, skills, or abilities would you need to cultivate to work effectively with elderly clients?

Other causes for the underutilization of mental health services fall on mental health professionals. Mental health providers may avoid the aging client partially because of ageist myths, gerontophobia, or ageist attitudes toward older people, and lack of expertise. Sometimes professionals need to identify the signs and symptoms of emotional and psychological problems when they are presented with older clients.

Finally, barriers to access of services may play a role, such as cost and location. Current systems are suboptimal due to inadequate coordination and competing priorities between primary care, mental health, and aging service providers; funding and reimbursement problems; health care models oriented to acute medical illnesses of younger people; the role of managed care; and a shortage of trained providers in the medical and mental health arenas. Additional contributions to barriers of appropriate service include gaps in service that reflect a view of people as disparate diagnoses or unrelated needs and the lack of an adequately powerful consumer voice (Ronch & Goldfield, 2003).

When these barriers are removed and older clients receive the help that they need, they can lead happy, healthy lives. Case Illustration 2.4 shows the benefits that occur when older adults overcome their fear of practitioners and the practitioners collaborate for the bettering of their client. In this case, the loss of a spouse caused a depressive episode that was effectively treated with a combination of an antidepressant and individual counseling sessions.

CASE ILLUSTRATION 2.4

In the 4 months since the unexpected death of her husband of 48 years (married at age 20), Mrs. Jones has lost interest in all the activities that she and her husband enjoyed together. She has lost weight and sleeps irregularly, complaining of early morning awakening and difficulty falling asleep. She has difficulty concentrating and has no energy to do even the most basic tasks at home. Her adult children are alarmed and take her to see Dr. Zoy, a geropsychiatrist. Once evaluated, Dr. Zoy diagnoses her with depression and prescribes a low-dose antidepressant to be taken at night, which would be titrated upward as necessary.

Mrs. Jones discontinues her medications after one week, complaining that she feels "funny" and dizzy and is thirsty all of the time. Dr. Zoy meets with her and educates her on the benefits and side effects of the antidepressant and encourages her to comply with her medication regimen. He also refers her to a counselor within his practice who is trained in issues related to older persons for individual counseling sessions. After several months, Mrs. Jones sees the benefits of the medication and counseling sessions. She feels back to her old self, with a little sadness from time to time. She is now actively involved in her local community, interacting positively with family and friends, and eating a well-balanced diet and exercising regularly. She feels as though a burden has been lifted from her shoulders and now does not delay doing anything she wants to do.

Mrs. Jones is a baby boomer who now feels that she has the time and resources to explore various cultures by traveling to different countries. She feels that age 68 is entirely too young to be unproductive and plans to pursue her bachelor's degree in psychology on a part-time basis. She's also interested in developing a career, fully understanding she is getting off to a late start. Her excitement and enthusiasm is contagious, and she is fully supported by her family and friends.

At present, managed care is the most prevalent payer model in the health care arena. Called "managed cost" by some of its critics, it has been troubled by managed Medicare debacles and a failure to deliver on preventive services that address the unique, interrelated health care (physical and mental) needs of the aging (Ronch & Goldfield, 2003). Limits on mental health benefits combine with an inadequate network of expert providers to limit access for those aging people in need of state-of-the-art care. As these models confront their economic and conceptual limits, the number of aging people continues to grow rapidly. The result is increasing pressure on the current system of care that appears to be unprepared to answer the call for the health- and wellness-oriented system that would likely be the most beneficial and least costly in the future (Ronch & Goldfield, 2003). Additionally, public policy in the coming decade will face tensions between cost containment and facilitation of integrated models of care (Karel, Gatz, & Smyer, 2012).

In the acute care arena, older people turn first to their primary care providers when they have a mental health problem. More than 50% of those who seek mental health care receive it from primary care physicians, because it carries fewer stigmas than going to a mental health provider, insurance plans encourage use of the primary care provider, and the care is usually more accessible (Karel et al., 2012; Ronch & Goldfield, 2003). However, many primary care providers are not adequately trained in mental health problems of the aging and tend to use psychotropic drugs as their first or only line of treatment. Pressures from managed care economics also result in briefer physician visits, often averaging 8 minutes in duration. Also because of their coexisting physical conditions, older adults are significantly more likely to seek and accept services in primary care versus specialty mental health care settings (Institute of Medicine [IOM], 2012). More desirable collaborative service models that coordinate mental and physical health services in primary care are being investigated (Ronch & Goldfield, 2003).

While the baby boomers were growing up, the needs of these young families were a high priority in community development, with particular concern for family-friendly housing, parks, and schools. Now, their needs are shifting. Most baby boomers would like to stay in their own homes, or at least in their own communities, as they age. Nearly three-quarters of all respondents of an AARP survey felt strongly that they want to stay in their current residence as long as possible (Bayer & Harper, 2009). The image that most elders will move to a retirement village away from their communities is the exception rather than the rule. Most people will not have the resources or the inclination to move to Florida or its equivalent (the Sunbelt states); therefore, communities cannot rely on "exporting" to meet the needs of an aging population. If communities want to be successful in caring for their aging population, they will have to make significant, yet feasible, changes in housing, health care, and human services (Knickman & Snell, 2002). These changes can create stronger communities with healthy, long-living seniors.

RETHINKING THE VALUE OF AGING

While it might be difficult to change culture and the way elders are viewed in society, there are practical steps that communities, employers, and individuals can begin to take to prepare for a society with greater numbers of healthy elders. First, it is worth reassessing the responsibilities and assets of elders. All ages need roles in life. According to Erik Erikson (1959), the hallmark of successful late-life development is the capacity to be generative and to pass on to future generations what one has learned from life. The elderly can be viewed as "America's one growing resource," and aging can be viewed as an opportunity to be seized (Freedman, 2002). More than half of all older adults volunteer their time, and more opportunities are available to contribute to their communities.

Firms are integrating workforces through programs of "unretirement" or by rehiring retirees as temps, consultants, and part-time workers. Surveys suggest that the 60-year trend of a decreasing number of elderly working has reversed itself as baby boomers reconsider their financial needs for retirement as well as how they want to spend more than a third of their adult life (Walsh, 2001). Most forecasters project this trend to continue as more elderly work longer for economic, social, and personal reasons; employers become more flexible and aware of the needs and benefits of older workers; and the labor market remains tight, with a smaller number of available younger workers.

The sheer size and energy of the baby boom generation has led to other dramatic social shifts, and experts hope that a new imagery for aging is possible. A growing interest in "age integration"—a process that takes advantage of the broadened range of accumulated life course experiences in society—has occurred over the last few decades. In an age-integrated society, changes made to bring older people into the mainstream could simultaneously enlarge personal opportunities and relieve many other people who are in their middle years of the work–family "crunch" (Uhlenberg, 2000). Actual physical integration can also take place. Although some towns have seen a trend toward senior-only housing, others are exploring options in integrated apartment buildings. Some older persons prefer a mixed-age neighborhood over one restricted to people their own age. Some community centers are integrating senior centers with childcare centers, facilitating cross-age interaction and conserving space and resources (Knickman & Snell, 2002). Cultural change is also possible with regards to one-on-one relationships. Baby boomers have made an art of enjoying and taking pride in caring for their children, even managing to pay for college tuition. The needed cultural shift is for children and communities to find more enjoyment and pride in providing for the care of parents and neighbors. The ultimate intangible goal is to recognize the reciprocity within all aspects of society. Everyone can benefit when the elderly are fully integrated into a caring society (Knickman & Snell, 2002).

It is clear that the process of aging, societal influences, organizational dynamics, and lack of adequately trained practitioners will influence the therapeutic work needed by older clients. Helping professionals and those in training have enormous opportunities to not only provide services to older adults, but to act as change agents within the larger society. Helping professionals will need to strongly advocate on behalf of their elderly clients and advocate against the institutional policies that impede full participation.

Many baby boomers express a desire and a need to continue with employment, though only a small number of employers are genuinely interested in utilizing their services. Helping professionals who understand and can promote the strengths, abilities, and competencies of the older worker to employers will prove extremely valuable in this process. Educating different constituents in society will dispel myths and erroneous information regarding the aging process and potentially open doors to various opportunities for older persons. Helping practitioners are in a good position to assist elderly clients with navigating personal, societal, and organizational barriers that might interfere with their well-being.

The real challenges of caring for the elderly in 2030 will involve (1) making sure society develops payment and insurance systems for long-term care that work better than existing ones, (2) taking advantage of advances in medicine and behavioral health to keep the elderly as healthy and active as possible, (3) changing the way society organizes community services so that care is more accessible, and (4) altering the cultural view of aging to make sure all ages are integrated into the fabric of community life (Knickman & Snell, 2002). If these challenges can be addressed, the quality of life of all individuals can be vastly improved.

KEYSTONES

- Negative perceptions that stereotype older adults pose barriers to their personal and professional development.
- Employers are challenged to address attitudes that limit the participation of older adults within the workplace.
- The baby boomer generation possesses unique characteristics and is projected to work past traditional retirement age.
- Underutilization of mental health services by older persons continues to exist, which is due to barriers such as the fear that individuals have of receiving mental health services, practitioners' lack of expertise, and individuals' inability to access mental health providers.
- Professional counselors are challenged to advocate within organizations on behalf of older workers.
- Knowledge of the unique challenges faced by older clients will enhance the effectiveness of the counselor–client relationship.

ADDITIONAL RESOURCES

Print Based

Brokaw, T. (2000). *The greatest generation.* New York, NY: Random House.

Cohen, G. D. (2000). *Creative age: Awakening human potential in the second half of life.* New York, NY: Avon Books.

Croker, R. (2009). *The boomer century 1946–2046: How America's most influential generation changed everything.* New York, NY: Grand Central Publishing.

Gullette, M. (2011). *Agewise: Fighting the new ageism in America.* Chicago, IL: University of Chicago Press.

Maples, M. F., & Agney, P. (2006). Baby-boomers mature and gerontological counseling comes of age. *Journal of Counseling and Development, 84*(1), 3–10.

Nelson, T. (2004). *Ageism: Stereotyping and prejudice against older persons.* Denver, CO: Bradford Books.

Palmore, E. B., Branch, L. G., & Harris, D. K. (Eds.). (2005). *Encyclopedia of ageism.* Binghamton, NY: Hayworth.

Web Based

www.aarpmagazine.org

www.agingnetwork.com/

www.agingsociety.org/agingsociety/links/links_ageism.html

www.aoa.gov/AoA_programs/OAA/Aging_Network/Index.aspx

www.aoa.gov/AoA_Root/AoA_Programs/HCLTC/ADRC_CareTransitions/toolkit/docs/

AgingNetwork_Structure_Program.pdf

www.asaging.org/ondex.cfm
www.cpa.ca/contents.html
www.hhs.gov/asl/testify/2012/02/t20120213a.html
www.log.wayne.edu/APADIV20/APADIV20.htm
www.thirdage.com

REFERENCES

Bayer, A., & Harper, L. (2009). *Fixing to stay: A national survey on housing and home modification issues.* Washington, DC: American Association of Retired Persons.

Bernard, D. (2013). The impact of baby boomers working past 65. Retrieved from http://money.usnews.com/money/on-retirement/2013/01/18/the-impact-of-baby-boom

Brooks, D. (2000). *Bobos in paradise: The new upper class and how they got there.* New York, NY: Touchstone.

Brownell, W., Mundorf, N., & Mundorf, J. (2006). Images of aging. In R. Schultz, N. Noelker, K. Rockwood, & R. Sproh (Eds.), *The encyclopedia of aging* (4th ed). New York, NY: Springer.

Collinson, C. (2014). Baby boomer workers are revolutionizing retirement: Are they and their employers ready? 15th Annual Transamerica Retirement Survey. New York, NY: Transamerica Center for Retirement.

Day, T. (2014). About the aging network. National Care Planning Council. Retrieved from www.longtermcarelink.net

Dennis, H., & Thomas, K. (2007). Ageism in the workplace. *Generations, 31,* 1.

Discrimination. (2015). In *Merriam-Webster.com*. Retrieved from http://www.merriam-webster.com/dictionary/discrimination

Erikson, E. H. (1959). The healthy personality. *Psychological Issues, 1,* 50–100.

Estrine, J., Nyberg, J., & Muller, C. (2001). *Old and poor in America.* New York, NY: International Longevity Center.

Ewing Marion Kauffman Foundation. (2011). The coming of entrepreneurship boom. Retrieved September 22, 2011, from http://www.Kaufman.org/research-and-policy/the-coming-entrepreneureal-boom.aspx

Freedman, M. (2002). *Prime time: How baby boomers will revolutionize retirement and transform America.* New York, NY: Public Affairs.

Gartska, T. A., Schmitt, M. T., Branscombe, N. R., & Hummert, M. L. (2004). How young and older adults differ in their responses to perceived age discrimination. *Psychology and Aging, 19,* 326–335.

Goldsmith, J. (2008). *The long baby boom: An optimistic vision for a graying generation.* Baltimore, MD: The Johns Hopkins University Press.

Green, B. (2003). *Marketing to leading-edge baby boomers.* New York, NY: Paramount Market.

Hess, T. M. (2006). Attitudes toward aging and their effects in behaviors. In J. E. Birken & K. W. Schaire (Eds.), *Handbook of the psychology of aging* (pp. 379–406). San Diego, CA: Academic Press.

Hess, T. M., Hinson, J. T., & Stratham, J. A. (2004). Explicit and implicit stereotype activation effects on memory: Do age and awareness moderate the impact of priming? *American Psychological Association, 19*(3), 495–505.

Hilt, M., & Lipschultz, J. (2004). Elderly Americans and the Internet. E-mail, television news, information and entertainment. *Educational Gerontology, 30,* 57–72.

Hogstel, M. O. (2001). *Gerontology: Nursing care of the older adult.* New York, NY: Delmar Cengage Learning.

Institute of Medicine. (2012). The mental health and substance use workforce for older adults: In whose hands? Retrieved from http://www.iom.edu/Reports/2012/The-Mental-Health-and-Substance-Use-Workforce-for-Older-Adults.aspx

Johnson, M., & Johnson, C. (2010). Generations, Inc.: From boomers to linksters—managing the friction between generations at work. Retrieved from AMA.com.

Karel, M. J., Gatz, M., & Smyer, M. A. (2012). Aging and mental health in the decade ahead: What psychologists need to know. *American Psychologist, 67*(3), 184–198.

Kite, M. E., Stockdale, G. D., Whitley, B. E., Jr., & Johnson, B. T. (2005). Attitudes toward younger and older adults: An updated meta-analytic review. *Journal of Social Issues, 61,* 241–266.

Knickman, J. R., & Snell, E. K. (2002). The 2030 problem: Caring for aging baby boomers. *Healthy Services Research, 37*(4), 849–884.

Lancaster, L., & Stillman, D. (2003). *When generations collide: Who they are: Why they clash. How to solve the generational puzzle at work*. New York, NY: Harper.

Levy, B. (2002). Longevity increased by positive self-perceptions of aging. *Journal of Personality and Social Psychology, 83*(2), 261–270.

Mermin, G., Johnson, R. W., & Toder, E. (2008). *Will employers want aging boomers?* Washington, DC: Urban Institute.

Monsees, C. V. (2002). Ageism. *Encyclopedia of aging.* Retrieved from http://www.encyclopedia.com/topic/Ageism.aspx

Moody, H. R., & Sasser, J. R. (2012). *Aging concepts and controversies* (7th ed.). Thousand Oaks, CA: Sage.

National Academy on an Aging Society. (2001, February). What are the attitudes of young retirees and older workers? Washington, DC: Author.

Okrent, D. (2000, June). Twilight of the boomers. *Times.* Retrieved from http://www.time.com/time/magazine/article10.9171, 997133.00.html

Prejudice. (2015). In *Oxford Dictionary* online. Retrieved from http://www.oxforddictionaries.com/us

Palmore, E. B. (2004). *The future of ageism.* New York, NY: International Longevity Center—USA.

Rogoff, E., & Carroll, D. (2009). *The second chance revolution: Becoming your own boss after 50.* New York, NY: Rowhouse.

Ronch, J. L., & Goldfield, J. A. (2003). *Mental wellness in aging: Strengths-based approaches.* Baltimore, MD: Health Professions Press.

Ronch, J. L., & Maizler, J. S. (1977). *Individual psychotherapy with the institutionalized aged.* Detroit, MI: American Orthopsychiatric Association.

Smith, P. R. (2014). A historical perspective in aging and gerontology. In H. F. O. Vakalahi (Ed.), *The collective spirit of aging across cultures, international perspectives on aging.* doi:1007/978-94-017-8594-5-2

Steinhorn, L. (2006). *The greater generation: In defense of the baby boom legacy.* New York, NY: St. Martin's Press.

Uhlenberg, P. (2000). Integrating of old and young. *Gerontologist, 40*(3), 276–279.

U.S. Census Bureau, American Community Survey. (2009). *Educational attainment in the United States: 2009 Population characteristics.* Current Population Reports, Washington, DC.

U.S. Census Bureau. (2014a). Current population survey. A profile of older Americans: 2014. Retrieved from http://www.aoa.acl.gov/aging_statistics/profile/2014/docs/2014-Profile.pdf

U.S. Census Bureau. (2014b). Population estimates and national projections. Retrieved from http://www.census.gov/population/projections/data/national/2014.html

U.S. Department of Health and Human Services. (2015). Administration on Aging (AOA): Long-term care ombudsman program. Retrieved from http://www.aoa.acl.gov/AOA_Programs/Elder-Rights/Ombudsman/index.aspx

Vaillant, G. E. (2003). *Aging well: Surprising guideposts to a happier life from the Landmark Harvard Study of Adult Development.* New York, NY: Little, Brown and Co.

Walsh, M. W. (2001, February 26). Reversing decades-long trend, Americans retiring later in life. *New York Times,* Section A, p. 1.

Zapolsky, S. (2003). American Association of Retired Persons. Retrieved from www.aarp.org

CHAPTER 3

Characteristics of Positive Older Adults and the Helping Process

"To all, I would say how mistaken they are when they think that they stop falling in love when they grow old, without knowing that they grow old when they stop falling in love."

—Gabriel Garcia Marquez

Learning Objectives

After reading this chapter, you will be able to

1. Explain the concept of successful aging
2. Describe the positive characteristics related to aging well
3. Analyze the ways that counselors can support the older population
4. Examine the attributes of successful practitioners

INTRODUCTION

As evidenced in Chapter 2, aging has been viewed as a negative experience fraught with problems, deterioration, and decline. This negativity has permeated throughout society and has altered the personal perceptions of many elders. However, perceptions of elders in society are changing. Many individuals are shedding light on the positive aspects of aging gracefully, productive aging, comfortable aging, and successful aging.

Identifying positive attributes and components of successful aging does not negate the fact that some elders will experience limitations that interfere with a comfortable aging experience. However, a thorough discussion of positive characteristics and components of a healthy lifestyle will replace myths and stereotypes that are prevalent in our society. Understandably, healthy elders will be traumatized by life events and may seek the services of a helping professional, while others will have similar experiences and manage without such assistance. Helping professionals need to understand the strengths and resiliency of their older clients and find ways to promote their use of mental health services. The therapeutic relationship between the elderly client and the practitioner may need to address roadblocks, but with persistence, change can be facilitated.

SUCCESSFUL AGING AND MENTAL WELLNESS

Aging is not merely a matter of accumulating years but also of "adding life to years, not years to life" (Kinsella & Phillips, 2005, p. 40). People grow old in a social and economic context that affects their psychosocial development: their feelings of self-esteem, value, and place in family and society. These factors have a combined effect on the morale of older people, and a number of models have been developed to explain why some people remain more active and healthier at older ages than others. These models can identify factors that favor healthy lifestyles and ways in which society can assist its members to grow old with dignity and comfort.

Defining Successful Aging

Successful aging has been empirically defined to include (1) a low probability of disease and disease-related disability, (2) a high level of physical and cognitive functioning, and (3) an active engagement in life (Rowe & Kahn, 1997). To some extent, these components represent a hierarchical relationship, as it is suggested that the absence of disease and disability leads to a prolonged maintenance of physical and cognitive functioning, which enables a higher level of engagement defined as the combination of social activity and productive activity (Tate, Lah, & Cuddy, 2003), participation in leisure activities (Bono, Sala, Hancock, Gunnell, & Parisi, 2007), and belonging to neighbor groups (Zunzunegui et al., 2004). Individuals who meet these hierarchical components during the aging process maintain the capacity to adequately function during daily living, leading to greater independence (Guralnik, Fried, & Salive, 1996). Continued independence is suggested to be an important factor throughout the aging process as it facilitates control and autonomy, both of which increase well-being and life satisfaction (Hertz & Anschutz, 2002). In addition to the psychosocial benefits associated with successful aging, the absence of chronic disease seen in older adults who have aged successfully has the potential to reduce health care costs required for an aging population (Thorpe & Philyaw, 2012). While there are older adults who are successfully aging, the majority of older adults are dealing with some kind of limitation (Carr, Weir, Azar, & Azar, 2013).

The concept of successful aging is related to the broad issues of coping and adaptation in later life. Successful aging is viewed as maximizing desired outcomes and minimizing undesired ones. Older adults can compensate for losses and declines and retain the potential for further growth. Successful aging can be viewed as the confluence of three functions: decreasing the risk of diseases and disease-related disabilities, maintaining physical and mental functioning, and being actively engaged with life (Kinsella & Phillips, 2005). This is evident today as growing numbers of older people do not exhibit the chronic health problems and declining cognitive skills that were once assumed to accompany aging. The concept of successful aging is illustrated in Guided Practice Exercise 3.1 from the viewpoint of older persons at a lower socioeconomic status (SES). The issues present challenges for the mental health counselor to examine successful aging from a completely different perspective.

Guided Practice Exercise 3.1

Successful aging is a subjective phenomenon that is comprised of various dimensions. Each elderly person experiences it differently, and it varies based on situational experiences. As a mental health practitioner, can an elderly person be seen as aging successfully if he or she has numerous health problems and limited income? Explore your feelings as to what constitutes successful aging. Visit a nearby senior center and examine how individuals with limited education, few financial resources, and multiple health challenges define successful aging. Share this information with your peers and examine if your definition of successful aging has changed.

Successful aging is a perspective that assumes that healthy functioning and even achievement of certain gains is possible in later life. A series of studies called the MacArthur Study explores these possibilities (Rowe & Kahn, 1998). The fruits of 10 years of intensive investigations involving thousands of participants, millions of dollars, and the combined expertise of biologists, neuropsychologists, sociologists, epidemiologists, geneticists, and gerontologists, among others, tell us a great deal about successful aging.

Most importantly, the MacArthur Study provides evidence for positively influencing the aging process and enhancing the quality of life in later years. The more physically and mentally fit older individuals are, the more likely they will age successfully. One's lifestyle prior to old age can have a tremendous influence on the quality of later life. A healthy diet and regular exercise, including aerobics and weight training, confers a real physical advantage. Although maintaining healthy habits provides protection from disease and should ideally be maintained consistently, the MacArthur Study revealed that positive changes in eating and exercise habits, even in old age, can help people live longer and healthier lives. Equally important to successful aging are social relationships. Older people benefit more from emotional rather than instrumental support in many cases.

Some potential gains in old age relate to the task of obtaining fulfillment in meeting social and civic obligations. For example, older people accumulate knowledge about life (e.g., wisdom) and can thus contribute to the development of other (younger) people and to society, providing wins for all. As the proportion of older people continues to increase, advancements in understanding the aging process will likely lead to identifying further developmental tasks associated with gains for and purposeful lives among older adults (Wrosch, 2006). In addition, the presence of meaning in life that refers to the extent to which people comprehend, make sense of, or see significance in their lives, accompanied by the degree to which they perceive themselves to have a purpose, mission, or overarching aim in life (Steger, Oishi, & Kashdan, 2009), was found to increase throughout the life span. Older adults reported the highest levels of meaning in their lives. Therefore, meaning thus emerges as an important resource for well-being, especially in later life (Steger et al., 2009).

Reichstadt Sengupta, Depp, Palinkas, and Jeste (2010) conducted qualitative interviews with 22 community-dwelling adults over 60 to obtain older adults' perspectives on what constitutes successful aging. Reichstadt and colleagues (2010) found that older adults viewed successful aging as a balance between self-acceptance and self-contentedness on one hand and engagement with life and self-growth in later life on the other. This perspective supports the concept of wisdom as a major contributor to successful aging.

Productive, Healthy, and Active Aging

In addition to successful aging, concepts such as productive aging (the ability to contribute directly and indirectly to society in older age) and healthy aging (the ability to remain physically and mentally fit) have been identified. Active aging has been identified as well. It refers to continuing participation in social, economic, cultural, spiritual, and civic affairs, not just being physically or economically active. This type of aging encompasses individuals who have retired as well as those who are frail, disabled, or in need of care, and it takes place within a broader social context of friends, family, neighbors, associates, and the workplace. Active aging recognizes principles of independence, participation, dignity, care, and self-fulfillment. A life course approach to active aging recognizes older people not as a homogeneous group, but as individuals who, collectively, are as diverse as younger members of a society (Kinsella & Phillips, 2005).

A sense of being productive appears to be a benchmark of healthy aging as well. Healthy men and women are three times more likely than those with physical or mental health problems to be engaged in paid work or volunteer activities. However, even people with physical limitations often manage, with some creativity, to engage in activities that keep them in touch with the world. Productive engagement with others, in whatever form it takes, is linked to a sense of mastery or personal self-efficacy. A "can-do" attitude contributes enormously to well-being.

Mental Wellness

The term *mental wellness* is used to reflect the belief that health and illness are not dichotomously arranged in nature or in life and because people can, in collaboration with knowledgeable helpers, move along the continuum toward optimal wellness at each stage of life by their own efforts. People have more options than to be sick or healthy. They do not have to be sick to improve wellness. This is an especially important outlook for aging as a process—people can have an array of illnesses as they age yet still enjoy wellness and a good quality of life.

Feinberg's (2001) work added another layer of richness to the analysis of how "the self," as a unifying perpetually created process of the brain, is a lifelong process. He shed importance on the intricate, fluid, lifelong nature in which the holistic nature of mind–body unity are demonstrated throughout the life span. Mental wellness is important, but it is not intended to be ignorant of the fact that frailties, problems, and dependencies may exist for some aging individuals. However, there exists a need to focus on the strengths of aging persons throughout their development.

Older adults are generally challenged to create a positive sense of their lives as a whole. The feeling that life has had order and meaning is expected to result in happiness (ego-integrity) (Erikson, 1986). Older adults must adjust to decreasing physical strength and health. Thus, older adults might be confronted with life situations that are characterized by not being in perfect health, serious illness, and dependency on other people's help. Moreover, older adults also have to adjust to the death of their spouses; this task arises more frequently for women than for men. After having lived with their spouses for several decades, widowhood might force older individuals to adjust to emotional states of loneliness, moving to smaller places, and learning about business matters. Having an optimistic outlook on life can help older adults cope with and compensate for these adjustments in healthy ways and continue on their path to successful aging. Guided Practice Exercise 3.2 will help counseling professionals identify factors integral to successful aging. These factors can be integrated into the therapeutic sessions to promote and improve the quality of life for older clients.

Guided Practice Exercise 3.2

Interview an older woman and investigate her perception of successful aging. Compare her responses to those factors identified in the chapter. What similarities and differences have been identified? What do you feel constitutes successful aging?

POSITIVE AGING CHARACTERISTICS

Many of today's older adults lead active, productive lives. For example, 83.6% of persons 65 and older in 2014 had completed high school or higher education, and 26.3% of these older adults earned a bachelor's degree or higher (U.S. Census Bureau, 2014). The majority of adults over 65 continue to work, volunteer for humanitarian causes, serve in public office, travel, and remain otherwise active (Centers for Disease Control and Prevention, 2009).

Typically, people who have aged successfully have the following characteristics:

- In general, they have managed to avoid serious debilitating diseases and disability.
- They function well physically, live independently, and engage in most normal activities of daily living.

- They have maintained cognitive function and are actively engaged in mentally challenging and stimulating activities and in social and productive pursuits.
- They are resilient and able to cope reasonably well with physical, social, and emotional changes.
- They feel a sense of control over circumstances in their lives. (Lachman, 2005)

The best way to experience a productive, full, and satisfying old age is to lead a productive, full, and satisfying life prior to old age. Establishing these qualities early on in life creates habits and beliefs that will continue into older adulthood. Tips for successful aging are shown in Table 3.1.

A number of attributes are vital to successful aging (Walker, 2001). Individuals who are oriented toward the future age successfully. This attribute is defined as the ability to anticipate, to plan, and to hope. Additionally, gratitude, forgiveness, and optimism are important and are described as the need to see the glass as half full, not half empty. Empathy is another key factor in successful aging, which is the ability to imagine the world from someone else's viewpoint. Finally, reaching out to others and having the desire to do things with people are important attributes (Walker, 2001). Individuals who possess a long-term perspective and engage in positive lifestyle behaviors increase their potential for successful aging.

Resiliency

Resilient people share some common qualities that can be cultivated to master any crisis. They stay connected with others, which improves their well-being and quality of life. Resilient people are optimistic and have a sunny outlook on life. They are often spiritual or actively involved in religious faith and know how to overcome negative thinking and difficult times. Resilient people enjoy themselves like children do. They wonder about things, experiment, and laugh. They also give back to others, and the benefit they receive is as great as the support that they are providing. People who help others live longer.

Table 3.1   Keys to Aging Well

Do not smoke, or quit smoking early.

Do not abuse alcohol, as this destroys physical and mental health.

Take life's ups and downs in stride.

Maintain a healthy weight, as obesity is a risk factor for poor health in later life.

Cultivate a solid marriage, which is important for physical and psychological health.

Establish an active lifestyle with regular exercise, as this positively affects physical and psychological well-being.

Persevere and have good self-care.

Source: Walker, L. A. (2001, September 16). We can control how we age. *Parade*, pp. 4–5.

Resilient people pick their battles and focus on things over which they have some influence and avoid spending time on things they can't control. They stay healthy by following a good diet and engaging in regular physical activity that tends to buffer stress. Exercise helps to repair neurons in brain areas that are particularly susceptible to stress. Resilient people convert misfortune into good luck and gain strength from adversity. They see negative events as opportunities to better themselves (Howard, 2009). Research conducted by Fry and Keyes (2010) emphasizes resilience. Successful aging and personality addresses the potential to maximize an individual's potential given particular personality traits or, conversely, the ability of an individual to modify pliable traits that are not compatible with successful aging.

Case Illustration 3.1 is an example of an older woman who demonstrates resiliency. She is actively engaged in life, financially prepared to manage her expenses, engages in healthy behaviors, and displays optimism.

CASE ILLUSTRATION 3.1

Mrs. Lesser is a retired attorney who is 85 years old. She is living comfortably in a retirement community and travels extensively. Her investments, assets, and pensions are more than adequate to meet her personal financial obligations. She plays golf during the summer and swims indoors during the winter. She runs a small business making flowers, eats a well-balanced diet, and has no medical problems. She takes a multivitamin, calcium supplement, vitamin C capsule, fish oil supplement, and vitamin D_3. She attributes her excellent cognitive skills and mental health to her work, healthy diet, active engagement with family and friends, and providing companionship to members of her church who need emotional support. She also believes that the decisions individuals make earlier in life can either help or hinder them later on. Therefore, making healthy lifestyle choices, managing her finances, and staying focused on what is important in life has enabled her to age comfortably.

Healthy Lifestyle

Much of what we call *aging* results from lack of exercise, smoking, other addictions, poor nutrition, falls, and stress. The challenge is to distinguish the late-life conditions that are truly unavoidable from those caused by disuse and lack of movement. However, this distinction is often lost in mainstream elders' health care, and age denial keeps many who are under 60 from realistically assessing their chances of reaching 80 intact.

Increased susceptibility to disease often accompanies aging. Age-dependent conditions (those that rise steadily with age) include vision and hearing loss, Type 2 diabetes, hip fracture, Parkinson's disease, dementia, pneumonia, incontinence, and constipation. Measurements of health and ability show gradual rather than precipitous changes with age, according to the Baltimore Longitudinal Study of Aging.

To keep older adults healthy, it is important to prevent chronic diseases. Chronic diseases are ongoing (usually lasting a year or more), generally incurable illnesses or conditions that require ongoing medical attention and affect a person's daily life. Some of the most prevalent and costly chronic diseases include arthritis, cancer, cardiovascular disease, depression, and others that lower the quality of life (Anderson & Horvath, 2004; Hwang, Weller, Ireys, & Anderson, 2004; National Center for Health Statistics, 2008). Approximately 80% of older adults have one chronic condition, and 50% have at least two (Agency for Healthcare Research and Quality, 2005). The Centers for Disease Control and the Merck Company Foundation (2007) have identified five priorities for improving older adults' health and quality of life: (1) promote healthy lifestyle behaviors, (2) increase older adults' use of clinical preventive services, (3) address cognitive impairment issues, (4) deal with issues related to mental health, and (5) provide education on planning for serious illness.

The increasing number of older Americans poses significant challenges for our nation's public health system. The current focus is to promote health and functional independence to help older adults stay healthy and remain in their homes. When older adults practice healthy behaviors, make use of clinical preventive services, and continue to engage with family and friends, they are more likely to remain healthy and to live independently (Centers for Disease Control and Prevention and the Merck Company Foundation, 2007).

Exercise

Exercise is extremely beneficial in all stages of life. Much of older adults' physical decline stems not from age but from disuse. When they sit all day, year after year, their bones, muscles, and organ systems atrophy, and their self-confidence wanes. However, the ability of exercise to revitalize and invigorate older adults' lives is now a proven fact (Manson et al., 2002). Reichstadt and colleagues (2010) found that 50% of assisted living community residents reported exercising regularly. Physiological (e.g., glucose level regulation, balance, and coordination), psychological, and social (empowerment, social and cultural integration) benefits of physical activity also foster successful aging (Chodzko-Zajko, Schwingel, & Park, 2009). Guided Practice Exercise 3.3 provides the opportunity to identify benefits associated with exercising and address modifications needed for exercise prescription for older persons.

Guided Practice Exercise 3.3

There are tremendous benefits associated with exercise. Guidelines exist that identify the type and frequency of exercises necessary for healthy functioning for older persons. List the types of exercises and benefits of exercises you are familiar with. Now examine how these exercises may need modification for older adults with chronic medical conditions. Share this information with your peers and professional colleagues.

Exercise regimens that build muscle produce a cascade of positive health effects. Rebuilding and maintaining strength helps to preserve aerobic capacity, keep blood pressure low, retain a healthy blood-sugar tolerance, maintain healthy cholesterol, sustain mineral density of the bones, and stabilize the body's ability to regulate its internal temperature. Guided Practice Exercise 3.4 illustrates the role of exercise in preventing the development of a chronic disease.

Guided Practice Exercise 3.4

An elderly woman maintained her appointment with her primary care physician (PCP) who reported that she had "osteopenia," a precursor to osteoporosis. Her PCP recommended strength training 3 times per week for 6 weeks. She complied, and upon examination, her PCP reported that she exhibited no signs of osteopenia. She was delighted and continued with her regular strength training sessions. Research other older persons with health conditions and examine how they used exercise to improve their health challenges.

Aerobic capacity (also called maximal oxygen intake or work capacity) is a fundamental measure of the cardiopulmonary system, made up of the heart, lungs, and circulatory mechanisms. Simply put, aerobic capacity is the body's ability to process oxygen. It includes the ability to breathe air into the lungs for aeration of the blood and the ability to transport oxygen effectively to all parts of the body through the bloodstream. By age 65, the average American has lost 30 to 40% of his or her aerobic capacity—and the health of his or her entire cardiovascular system.

Another biomarker for physiological aging that can be reversed by regular exercise is glucose tolerance and insulin sensitivity. For most people, the body's ability to use glucose in the bloodstream declines with age. As people develop more body fat and less muscle, their muscle tissue becomes less and less sensitive to insulin. As a consequence, it takes more and more insulin to have the desired effect. Increasing the muscle-to-fat ratio can reverse this deterioration, improve the blood-sugar tolerance, keep the insulin sensitivity high, and greatly reduce the chances of developing diabetes.

Improving fitness level, especially if one is sedentary, can enhance functional years. As the body ages, it loses muscle mass. The less muscle it has, the less energy it will burn even while resting. The lower a person's metabolic rate, the more likely he or she will gain weight. Regular strength training can increase muscle mass, boost metabolism, strengthen bones, prevent osteoporosis, and in general, make one feel better and function more efficiently (Nelson, Rejeski, Blair, Duncan, & Judge, 2007). Both aerobic and muscle strengthening activities are critical for healthy aging. Basic recommendations for aerobic and strength training exercises in older adults include moderately intense aerobic exercise for 30 minutes 5 days a week or vigorous intense aerobic exercise for 20 minutes 3 days a week as well as 8 to 10 strength training exercises with 10 to 15 repetitions of each exercise 2 to 3 times per week (Nelson et al., 2007). In addition, the American College of Sports Medicine (ACSM) and the American Heart Association (AHA) recommend that older adults or adults with chronic conditions develop an activity plan with a health professional to manage risks and take therapeutic needs into account. This will maximize the benefits of physical activity and ensure safety. Case Illustration 3.2 identifies the significance of exercise for an elderly woman with major health problems.

CASE ILLUSTRATION 3.2

Mrs. Morris is a happily married 67-year-old female who lives in a four-story home with her spouse. She has suffered from various forms of cancer, received treatment, and has been considered in remission. Her outlook is usually positive; however, she worries a great deal about her daughter, who has developed a rare disease of unknown etiology. She frequently accompanies her to her physician appointments and also assists with paying for these medical services.

Unfortunately, she has been unable to attend the "Silver Sneakers" classes that she enjoyed, and she is not taking adequate care of herself. Her cancer has re-emerged, and she is receiving chemotherapy treatment, which she is optimistic will help, as it has in the past. When she exercised, her mood improved, her body was toned, and she completed all activities of daily living with ease. Despite her recent recurrence of cancer, she appears to be more concerned with getting back to the health club. She reported that she developed relationships there, had something to look forward to, and felt good because she was able to stay mentally sharp. Exercise had become an integral component of her life.

Nutrition

Nutrition is an essential element not only in weight management and disease prevention, but additional considerations that are critical to older adults. Adequate calcium consumption is necessary to prevent bone loss. During perimenopause and menopause, bone loss accelerates rapidly, with an average of about 3% skeletal mass lost per year over a 5-year period. Vitamin D is necessary for adequate calcium absorption, yet as people age, particularly in their 50s and 60s, they do not absorb vitamin D from foods as readily as they did in their younger years. If vitamin D is unavailable, calcium levels are also likely to be lower. As older adults become more concerned about cholesterol and fatty foods, and as their budgets shrink, they often cut back on protein. Because protein is necessary for muscle mass, protein insufficiencies can spell trouble. Other nutrients, including folic acid (folate), vitamin E, iron, potassium, and vitamin B_{12}, are important to the aging process, and most of these are available in any diet that follows the nutrition guidelines for older adults (U.S. Department of Agriculture & U.S. Department of Health and Human Services, 2015).

The U.S. government's Dietary Guidelines for Americans 2015 includes the following recommendations for a healthy lifestyle and diet (U.S. Department of Agriculture & U.S.

Department of Health and Human Services, 2015). Individuals are encouraged to adhere to dietary patterns that emphasize the following items.

- Consume a variety of foods within and among the basic food groups while staying within energy needs.
- Consume dietary patterns that are higher in vegetables, fruits, and whole grains.
- Include seafood and legumes.
- Moderate intake of dairy products (with an emphasis on low and non-fat dairy).
- Moderate consumption of alcohol.
- Lower intake of meats (including red and processed meats).
- Lower intake of sugar-sweetened foods, beverages, and refined grains.
- Limit sodium and saturated fat.
- Tailor dietary patterns to individuals' biological, cultural, and individual food preferences.
- Control caloric intake to manage body weight.
- Be physically active every day.
- Keep food safe to eat.

The Older Americans 2012 report (Federal Interagency Forum on Aging-Related Statistics, 2012) identifies guidelines to improve the nutritional health of older Americans. Major improvements in the nutritional health of older Americans could be made by increasing intakes of whole grains, dark green and orange vegetables and legumes, and fat-free or low-fat milk products. Additionally, incorporating foods and beverages that are lower in sodium and have fewer calories from solid fats, alcoholic beverages, and added sugars is also recommended (Federal Interagency Forum on Aging-Related Statistics, 2012). A healthy diet for an older person must take into account the slowing of the system with age, the body's increased sensitivity to extremes (like hot, spicy, and rich foods), and the body's need for high-quality nutrients with minimal calories. Guided Practice Exercise 3.5 provides the opportunity to conduct a nutritional assessment of an elderly client and determine ways to enhance his or her nutritional intake to prevent and/or decrease health conditions.

Guided Practice Exercise 3.5

Identify an elderly man or woman and have him or her complete a 3-day nutritional intake diary. Take this data and give them to a nutritionist for a dietary analysis. Once analyzed, discuss with the nutritionist how you should relay this information to your client and any medical conditions associated with inadequate nutritional habits.

Calorie needs decline with age due to a slow-down in metabolism and physical activity, nutritional requirements may remain the same or in some cases increase. My Plate for Older Adults provides examples of foods that contain high levels of vitamins and minerals per serving and is consistent with the federal dietary guidelines (USDA Human Nutrition Research Center on Aging, 2011). These calories should be gained through a healthy diet, such as that shown in Table 3.2.

A healthy diet is essential to everyday life and prevention and controlling chronic disease. As people age, they need to obtain maximum nutrition with the fewest calories. Guided Practice Exercise 3.6 addresses how a person's diet plays a role in controlling the chronic medical condition, diabetes. If it is improperly managed, it poses serious long-term health risks. Practitioners will be confronted with clients with diabetes and will be challenged to address their noncompliance issues in a constructive manner.

Guided Practice Exercise 3.6

Diabetes is a chronic disease that affects many older persons. This disease is managed by altering one's diet, exercise, and/or medication. Many older persons live comfortable lives and manage this chronic disease effectively. Visit an assisted living facility and discuss your knowledge of diabetes with an elderly individual. Find ways to convince your resident of the necessity in following a diabetic diet to decrease his or her potential for insulin injections. Make sure you have thoroughly researched the topic and obtained data pertinent to diabetes management and older adults. What did you learn from this experience and how will it help you when working with older clients?

 Table 3.2 My Plate for Older Adults

Bright-colored vegetables such as carrots and broccoli
Deep-colored fruit such as berries and peaches
Whole, enriched, and fortified grains and cereals such as brown rice and 100% whole wheat bread
Low- and non-fat dairy products such as yogurt and low-lactose milk
Dry beans and nuts, fish, poultry, lean meat, and eggs
Liquid vegetable oils, soft spreads low in saturated trans-fat, and spices to replace salt
Fluids such as water and fat-free milk
Physical activity such as walking, resistance training, and light cleaning

Source: USDA Human Nutrition Research Center on Aging (2011).

Active Engagement

Many elements affect the quality of life for older adults. Developing and maintaining healthy relationships is one essential element. Social bonds lend vigor and energy to life. Giving to others and seeking a variety of relationships provides older adults with diverse acquaintances and experiences. Interacting with diverse persons brings different points of view and different perspectives on life. Enriching spirituality also enhances quality of life. Cultivating a relationship with nature, the environment, a higher being, and oneself is a key factor in personal growth and development. It is also important that older adults take time for thought and contemplation, enjoying the sunset, sounds, and energy of life. By engaging in these behaviors, elders will be better able to cope with the challenges posed by simply living, especially as the body undergoes many physiological changes in the aging process (Koenig, McCullough, & Larson, 2001). Guided Practice Exercise 3.7 provides the opportunity to identify and explore current activities and the extent to which they may be continued in later years of life.

Guided Practice Exercise 3.7

Examine the activities that you engage in regularly. Now specifically identify benefits that you derive from these activities. Is there a social component to any of your identified activities? If so, why is the social component important to you? Which of your activities do you expect to continue into your later years of development? Are there any activities you have deleted from your list? If so, discuss your reasoning.

Accumulated evidence suggests that better health and community engagement lead to greater well-being later in life. Successful aging has been defined as the absence of disease and disability, high levels of physical and cognitive functioning, and active engagement in life (Rowe & Khan, 1997). The literature on successful aging suggests that to comprehensively understand "living well" and "being well," one must attend to factors beyond the aging body, including the social and physical environment in which one lives. Researchers argue further that the subjective experiences related to the interaction between aging bodies and an ever-changing social and physical world exert a meaningful force on overall health and well-being (Cermin, Lysack, & Lichtenberg, 2011; Strawbridge, Wallhagen, & Cohen, 2002). Gerontology theorists and researchers also point to the complex relationships between the environment, both home and extended, and health and functioning in older adults (Stark, 2001; Wahl, Fange, Oswald, Gitlin, & Ivarsson, 2009; Yen, Michael, & Perdue, 2009). This research leaves little doubt that the physical location in which one lives shapes the activities that are possible to engage in and ultimately contributes to health (Yen, Shim, Martinez, & Barker, 2012). Case Illustration 3.3 demonstrates the capabilities of an elderly gentleman who, despite his advancing chronological years, remains actively engaged in life. Age is one point on the continuum, and numerous factors impact the aging experience.

CASE ILLUSTRATION 3.3

Mr. Simmons is an 85-year-old, happily married, retired university professor in physics. He has no chronic diseases and continues his longtime exercise routine: running 5 times a week and strength training 3 times per week. He also swims twice per week and gardens when the weather permits. His primary care physician tells him that he has the vital signs of a highly functioning 50-year-old.

Mr. Simmons keeps his mind sharp by learning new activities and has decided to try three new activities each year and retain the one activity he likes the most. He is taking violin lessons and is learning to speak Spanish. He learns this language through auditing courses within his former university environment. He socializes with family and friends regularly and takes long distance trips 3 times a year. He is very religious and very active within his synagogue. He is an optimistic, easily engaged individual who believes that every day is a new beginning.

Social Participation

According to data from the National Social Life, Health, and Aging Project (NSHAP), age is positively associated with increased participation in social activities (e.g., volunteering, religious events) in part because older adults have more time after they retire (Cornwell, Laumann, & Schumm, 2008). Participating in one's social world is seen to be a significant factor for maintaining overall health and well-being. African-American and white older adults have cited social activity as an important contributor to aging well (Corwin, Laditka, Laditka, Wilcox, & Liu, 2009). Greater community engagement and social participation, in turn, are associated with better health in old age and much reduced risk of mortality—as significant an effect as smoking, drinking, exercise, and diet (Holt-Lunstad, Smith, & Layton, 2010).

Perspective

Many adults reaching the age of 50 or 60 begin to free themselves from cultural constraints and express themselves in ways that they had not dared before. They become less defined by what others think of them and more by what they think of themselves. Increasingly freed from the burden of always having to fulfill other people's expectations, their lives start to reflect a new kind of willingness to be exactly who they are. They break free from histories of physical stress, neglect, and abuse. They become more alive (Robbins, 2007). Guided Practice Exercise 3.8 provides the opportunity to explore why and how older persons choose to reinvent themselves in their later years.

Guided Practice Exercise 3.8

Are you familiar with older persons who have decided to "live life to the fullest"? This newfound freedom is not unusual later in life. What activities does he or she now participate in? Examine why this behavior is different from his or her youth. What do you think motivates him or her to break free from past roles, responsibilities, and normative behavior? How do you feel when you hear an older person discussing that he or she just went skydiving at the age of 85?

Scientific studies have found that attitude is profoundly important to health. In 1984, the MacArthur Foundation Research Network on Successful Aging began one of the largest and most interesting aging studies ever undertaken. Recognizing that the field of gerontology had become preoccupied with studies of disability and disease, the Research Network began studying healthy elderly people. A central goal of the MacArthur study was to determine what factors enable some people to retain their mental faculties as they age. The researchers found that one of the most statistically significant predictors of maintaining cognitive functioning with age is the sense of self-efficacy. Elders who have a "can do" attitude are far more likely to retain intact mental abilities (Rowe & Kahn, 1998).

Instead of thinking of it as a tragedy when their bodies begin to slow down, happy older adults accept the limitations that arise and see the transitions they are going through as opportunities to ground themselves in a deeper sense of self and a greater wisdom. Their love for others and the world becomes more accepting. They increasingly let go of minutiae and the nonessentials of life. Their perspective shifts, details soften, and the larger panorama comes into focus. They are able to enjoy life more than when they were young because they have a deeper understanding of it (Robbins, 2007). These are people who do not conform to a youth-obsessed culture's expectations of what their later years will be like. Instead, their lives come to enact an entirely different vision of aging. No longer so driven by the desires that shaped the first part of their lives, their lives become more about meaning than about ambition, more about intimacy than about achieving. They experience the second half of their life as a time of deepening creativity and ripening of the soul (Robbins, 2007).

Leisure Activities

Participation in challenging programs has a positive effect on physical health, mental health, and social functioning in older adults. Cognitively fit older adults benefit from participation in leisure activities. Among cognitive activities, reading, playing board games, and playing musical instruments were associated with a lower risk of dementia.

Dancing is the only physical activity associated with a lower risk of dementia (Verghese et al., 2003). Senior participants in a Dancing Heart program reported better health, stating that the dance and movement improvisation activities improved their flexibility, coordination, balance, and endurance, and the shared reminiscence and discussion increased their memory and socialization skills (Tabourne & Lee, 2005–2006). Researchers found that long-term social dancing may be associated with better balance and gait in older adults

(Verghese, 2006), and dancers reported slightly more improvement in sleep, mood, and the ability to participate in hobbies, do housework, and have sex than the others.

Playing music, specifically taking group keyboard lessons, was found to increase human growth hormone (hGH) levels. Growth hormone levels decline during aging and contribute to unwelcomed effects of aging (Clements, 2010). Low hGH is implicated in such aging phenomena as osteoporosis, energy levels, wrinkling, sexual function, muscle mass, and aches and pains while controlling for differences in life events and social support. Boyer (2007) found that participants in music classes also showed a decrease in anxiety, depression, and perception of loneliness.

Participating in the arts improves older adults' quality of life as well, particularly for those who suffer from dementia. Participation in weekly sessions focused on objective and subjective indicators of affect, and self-esteem contributed to each individual's sense of well-being (Rentz, 2002). An increase in quality of life was measured following music performances and wall murals, which can be effective for cueing residents away from situations that may evoke agitation as well as potential harm and litigation (Kincaid & Peacock, 2003). In older adults without dementia, creating visual art was found to alleviate boredom, loneliness, helplessness, and distraction from physical pain and stimulated cognitive faculties (National Assembly of State Arts Agencies, 2005).

Research into the effects of exercising the body, mind, and social ability proves promising. Healthy adults who received 10 memory training sessions, reasoning training, and speed training did better than the control group (Willis et al., 2006). Researchers found that fitness training may also improve some mental processes, and physical exercise might slow the effects of aging and help people maintain cognitive abilities well into older age (Kramer, Colcombe, Erickson, & Paige, 2006). Such positive effects of leisure activities prove the importance of encouraging all older adults participate in them.

Intimacy

Older people desire and continue intimate relations, and they embrace the need for love, partnership, and physical intimacy (Aleman, 2005; Connidis, 2006). Sex, like love, is an important component of a close emotional relationship in old age (Connidis, 2006; Gott & Hinchliff, 2004; National Council on Aging, 2002). Most people with sexual partners consider sex at least somewhat important. Only those who face insurmountable barriers to sex, such as poor health, place no importance on it (Gott & Hinchliff, 2004).

Nearly half of all Americans over the age of 60 have sexual relations at least once a month, and 40% would like to do so more often (Cutler, 2001). Sexual relations taper off with age, with 71% of men and 51% of women in their 60s having sex once a month or more and 27% of men and 18% of women in their 80s saying they do (Cutler & NCOA, 2001). Those who had sex at least once a month said it was important to their relationship. Women had sex less often in part because they are more likely to be widowed.

Thirty-nine percent of people surveyed stated that they are happy with the amount of sexual relations they currently have—even if it is none—while another 39% would like to do so more often (Cutler & NCOA, 2001). Only 4% of people said that they would like to have sexual relations less frequently. The survey also found that 74% of men and 70% of women find their sex lives more emotionally satisfying now that they are older than when they were in their 40s. As to whether it is physically better, 43% say it is just as good, or better, than in their youth, while 43% say sex is less satisfying. When it comes to knowledge about sex, older people are not necessarily wiser than their children. A third of the respondents believed it was natural to lose interest in sex as they aged (Cutler & NCOA, 2001). Psychosocial factors have been identified as being very important determinants of sexual response. These factors include sexual attitudes and knowledge; previous sexual behavior and enjoyment; length and quality of relationship; physical and mental health; body image and self-esteem; stress; and partner availability, health, and sexual functioning (Avis & Stellato, 2001). However, women are much more likely to attribute declining sexual response to physical changes of menopause than to other factors. Case Illustration 3.4 is an example of intimacy between two older adults in a nursing facility. It demonstrates perceptions and reactions by staff and family members toward this subject. This case demonstrates that intimate acts do not cease to exist for all elders, and the subject of intimacy needs to be addressed at various levels (individual, family, and institutional).

CASE ILLUSTRATION 3.4

Ms. Jones and Mr. Waters are both in their 80s and have been residing in the local nursing home. They were admitted there from the hospital where it was decided that a nursing home would provide them with 24-hour care, including supervision of their medical problems, medication management, nutritious meals, and assistance with activities of daily living. Ms. Jones and Mr. Waters have developed an intimate relationship over time, which, at the outset, staff and family members thought was cute and harmless.

However, over the next several months, family members became disturbed when they exhibited public displays of affection, kissing each other on the lips, holding hands, and caressing. Mr. Waters's son also learned from his father that they had sex. His son was enraged and shared this information with Ms. Jones's family members and also with the nursing home administrator and staff of the facility. The staff and administrator remained calm, and the staff did not seem to have a problem with their relationship. It was reported that they genuinely enjoyed each other's company and were just happy to be with each other. This was unacceptable behavior for their adult children. Mr. Waters's son moved his father into another facility, which has devastated Ms. Jones. Ms. Jones has deteriorated, is depressed, refuses all activities, and spends most of her time in her room, picking at her food.

There are many life stressors facing older adults that challenge existing competencies. Their social networks will shrink and they must create new connections, they will lose loved ones and have to manage feelings of grief and chronic loneliness, and they must deal with declining health and financial resources. Each of these spheres (e.g., initiating social contacts, managing instrumental needs, coping with negative emotion, managing interpersonal conflict) requires various competencies. Counselors are in a pivotal position to assist older adults in acquiring and cultivating these competencies to continue to be effective and enjoy life. By developing resiliency, maintaining healthy lifestyles, remaining actively engaged, and having intimacy, older adults have the keys to successful aging.

COUNSELING OLDER ADULTS

As society continues to grow older, the issues concerning the elderly increasingly become issues for the community. There are already legislative changes being made that address Social Security, medical benefits, and retirement as the government is forced to address the needs of an aging society. Just as the government has been slow to act on behalf of senior citizens, so has the counseling community. Counselors have seemingly avoided actively seeking to help the elderly, possibly because of a lack of knowledge or experience (Karel, Gatz, & Smyer, 2012). For those not specializing in gerontological counseling, counselor training in working with older adults has relied on Erikson's final stage of development: integrity versus despair. However, developing interventions to successfully resolve this stage has not been a priority in the counseling field.

Developing New Perspectives, Attitudes, and Knowledge

Changing demographics are encouraging counselors to seek answers to support the older population. As a person ages, psychological issues increase in breadth and depth. They broaden to include physical health, economic factors, familial loss, decrease in independence, and many more. Issues deepen from the perspective that any psychological problems that remained unresolved earlier in the life span will increase in intensity when facing the issue of mortality. Working in the preventative mode, counselors are provided the opportunity to offer the older client a variety of intrapersonal and network interventions. Locating, exploring, and using available outside networks are perhaps the most essential interventions a counselor can offer to the older client.

Another component of the changing perspective of the counseling field is the growing age of counselors themselves. Not only are counselors presented with issues of the older client, but they are facing their own changing demographics. The majority of university counselor educators who joined the field in the early to mid-1960s and who currently train and lead the profession are growing older. In looking toward retirement, these counselors are developing a deeper empathy with the older generation and a vested interest in supporting their needs.

As members of the baby boomer generation move beyond 65, much of what mental health professionals know about how to treat their concerns become obsolete (American Psychological Association [APA], 2003; Langer, 2009). A survey by the American Psychological Association (2004) found that almost 70% of psychologists work with adults over 65, but only 30% received graduate training for this demographic, and only 20% worked with older adults in a practicum or internship setting. Therefore, these individuals as well as students and early-career professionals are urged to take the necessary steps to prepare themselves to work with this population. Mental health counselors have a responsibility to acknowledge stereotypes and validate older adults' experiences, but they must also be able to provide accurate information about normative development so that older adults can base their self-assessments on facts rather than myths or unrealistic expectations (Walters & Boyd, 2009).

When working with older adults, mental health counselors are in a unique position to foster positive expressions in their clients. Physiological, psychological, and social/relational factors are all important dimensions of the aging process. Lack of knowledge about normative physiological changes that accompany aging, combined with stereotypes may cause older adults to feel abnormal and internalize feelings of inferiority that will negatively impact the helping relationship. Helping professionals need to address clients in an unbiased and nondiscriminatory manner, allowing older adults a comfortable environment to express their concerns.

It is important for counselors to continue to develop their knowledge, attitude, and skills including self-awareness, so that they can counsel older adults on a variety of issues. Staying aware of the older adult client as a unique individual with a combination of racial, ethnic, gender, sexual orientation, cultural, religious, and socioeconomic identities will prevent professional and emerging practitioners from viewing the client primarily in terms of age (Zeiss & Kasl-Godley, 2001). This awareness will further develop the client–counselor relationship.

Many factors, such as coping mechanisms, influence how older persons address changes in later life. Coping has been defined as a person's "cognitive and behavioral efforts to manage (reduce, minimize, master, or tolerate) the internal and external demands of the person—environment transaction that is appraised as taxing or exceeding the resources of the person" (Folkman, Lazarus, Gruen, & DeLongis, 1986, p. 572). Adaptive coping, or managing the demands of life relatively well, is at the heart of achieving and maintaining optimal health and wellness. This is certainly true at any age, but perhaps even more so in old age, when the threat of overtaxed resources and the need to tolerate limitations become inevitable. Life involves gains and losses; it is naïve to assume that everyone can and will maintain a high quality of life right up to their death. On the other hand, unnecessarily pessimistic views of old age, fueled by negative stereotypes of the elderly, restrict the ways people choose to adapt to aging and limit their sense of control over their lives.

Helpers who are knowledgeable about and skilled in understanding coping mechanisms can promote healthy adaptation, regardless of client age. Sources of concrete information about how to cope with getting older, how to understand the perspective of elders (Pipher, 1999), and how to deal with dementia can help clinicians build their foundations of knowledge. Whitbourne (1989) summarizes the task:

> The main point that a clinician must keep foremost in mind, when working with an aging client, is the need to be flexible. The aging process involves multiple physical, psychological, and social demands that can all potentially impact on the individual's ability to function. Clinicians may be called upon to perform advocacy services, environmental interventions, and interdisciplinary consultations, which they would not ordinarily regard as falling within the domain of "psychotherapy." It is only by maintaining an open approach to the multiple needs of the aged client that the clinician can hope to bring about successful change. Helping professionals assume multiple roles when working with older clients and should remain open and flexible in their encounters. (p. 168)

Remaining Flexible and Open

Stereotypes, myths, and erroneous information regarding aging and the abilities of older adults is pervasive within the American culture. Henderson, Xiao, Siegloff, Kelton, and Peterson (2008) found that first year nursing students' attitudes toward aging tended to be positive; however, the students did not aspire to work with geriatric patients. The reasons for not wanting to work with older adults were difficulty in relating or communicating with older people, feelings of the work being boring, and inexperience in caring for older people. However, students who had previously worked with elderly patients reported more positive attitudes, suggesting that positive exposure to such persons diminished negative feelings about aging.

Similarly, social work students' negative attitudes toward older adults regarding their productivity, adaptation, independence, and optimism were a result of little previous contact with elderly individuals and minimal knowledge about aging prior to graduate school (Gellis, Sherman, & Lawrence, 2003). While Gellis and colleagues (2003) did not find experiences to predict attitudes toward older people among nursing, gerontology, and health science students, attitudes toward elderly adults changed as a result of ongoing exposure to and meaningful intergenerational exchanges with such persons (Butler & Baghi, 2008).

Older clients are capable of personal growth in the latter stage of life, unless there exists diseases that negatively impact their cognitions. While an individual's basic personality is usually formed by around age 30, personality traits of older men and women take on a different pattern. For example, in later life, women may become more assertive and aggressive (when needed), and older men may become more nurturing. Therefore, the idea of being inflexible and rigid is questionable, at best. Both the older client and helping professional need to maintain openness to what can be accomplished within the therapeutic encounter.

Counselors help people with issues of career and sexual development well before they are fully active in these areas. Similarly, work to promote successful aging must begin before old age. Successful aging can involve adjusting to life transitions (such as from work to retirement), which can be thought of as turning points that occur between periods of stability within one's life (Goodman, Schlossberg, & Anderson, 2006). Transitions often require a person to journey into the unknown, take risks, adapt, and cope with fears. They can therefore be challenging times in one's life, often experienced as a crisis. Transitions can also create opportunities for personal discovery, renewal, and transcendence to heightened levels of existence.

Promoting Successful Aging

The process of helping to promote successful aging can be implemented by counselors in individual counseling, group counseling, workshops, or courses. The underlying philosophy or theme for these endeavors has been stated by Bortz (1990):

Aging is a self-fulfilling prophecy. If we dread growing old, thinking it is a time of forgetfulness, and physical deterioration, then it is likely to be just that. On the other hand, if we expect to be full of energy and anticipate that their lives will be rich with more adventures and insights, then that is the likely reality. We prescribe what we are to become. (p. 55)

Three key concepts anchor the development and implementation of promoting successful aging work. The first concept assumes that older people can prescribe their future and that counselors can effectively help them with this process. The second concept assumes that although general knowledge of developmental stages and sociocultural background is helpful in formulating working or guiding hypotheses, it is no substitute for developing a comprehensive understanding of the client. Third, each person uniquely interacts with and creates his or her own environment. Different cultures might have distinct views on the aging process, but individuals vary in their awareness and interpretation of these views. It is likely, however, that almost all people have concerns regarding aging and can be helped to age more successfully. Guided Practice Exercise 3.9 provides the opportunity to examine cross-cultural aging, which will be valuable in understanding older clients who seek counseling services.

Guided Practice Exercise 3.9

Individuals from various cultures experience aging differently. It may be welcomed or viewed with disdain. Identify two older adults from different ethnicities and examine their views of aging, the ways older persons are treated in their society, and their use of professionals for personal problems. Share the similarities and differences with your colleagues. Are you surprised by your findings?

Optimizing the Vision for Aging

At varying levels of consciousness, people imagine what it means to grow older. These imaginings need to be evaluated in terms of their accuracy and whether they represent how the person wants to age. Discussion, art therapy, relevant print and audiovisual materials, and interviewing are ways of making older people more conscious of their own thoughts and feelings about aging, expanding their notions as to what is possible, and then enlightening them on what they could be doing to achieve it. Gerontological counselors should take some of the following concerns into account when working with older adults. These concerns include losing their health, their ability to care for themselves, and their mental capacity; running out of money; finding meaning in older age; managing loss and grief; navigating sex and impotency; and sustaining marriage in the later years. A key element is helping people realize what later life will be is highly contingent on current practices. Neugarten (1971) said, "Most of us have a half-conscious and irrational fear that one day we will find ourselves old, as if suddenly we will fall off a cliff, and that what we will be then has little to do with what we are now" (p. 45). Appreciating this—and after the investigation and evaluation of current wellness levels and practices in the areas of physical health, emotions, nutrition, play, spirituality, finances, family, and friends—clients should have an expanded vision of possibilities for successful aging and should know what wellness practices will help them have greater control over their future. People need to be empowered to prescribe a life course that best fits who they are and who they want to become. A sense of being in control is essential. Guided Practice Exercise 3.10 encourages counselors to examine their strengths and weaknesses as they relate to working with older clients. Developing the right knowledge, skills, and attitudes is critical to effectively provide services to an elderly client population.

Guided Practice Exercise 3.10

You have been trained to provide counseling services to clients from young adulthood through middle age. Your knowledge of older adults comes primarily from your experiences with your grandparents and their friends. You are now expected to provide counseling services to an older clientele (65+). How would you prepare yourself to work with this client population? Do you believe you can use the same strategies and interventions you have used previously with these older clients?

Change will occur as people control their lives and work to implement and optimize their vision for successful aging. It will also occur because living and aging means that the body changes, friends and relatives die, and many aspects of community and society are transformed. It is imperative to provide older adults with conceptual models and coping skills for handling change. These strategies should help them deal with the uncomfortable feelings that often accompany change and thus make them more effective with their change efforts. Competent counselors are already knowledgeable in these areas and need only to target their professional abilities to the area of promoting successful aging.

ATTRIBUTES OF SUCCESSFUL PRACTITIONERS

Counseling is a unique profession requiring a particular set of qualities. In order to be successful, all counselors need to have the following qualities: comfort with ambiguity, empathy, good boundaries, and belief in the capacity for change (LoFrisco, 2012). Counselors cannot always clearly see the results of their work and must learn to be comfortable in situations where they won't have all of the facts. They must also have a particular kind of empathy and balance it with accountability. A good counselor holds clients accountable for their actions. Counseling is a profession that has a higher risk for burnout, therefore counselors with good boundaries understand their limitations, know where their responsibility for the change process ends and where the client's begins, and establish policies and procedures and apply them consistently. Lastly, good counselors believe that people can and do change and provide optimism and hope when there is none. They are realistic about the change process and are able to help clients set attainable goals (LoFrisco, 2012).

General Attributes Needed for Success

The qualities and actions of effective therapists, based on theory, policy, and research evidence, can guide others toward continual improvement. Various therapists delivering different treatments in various contexts will emphasize some of these important qualities more than others (Wampold, 2011). Effective therapists have a sophisticated set of interpersonal skills. Clients of effective therapists feel understood, trust their therapist, and believe the therapist can help them. Effective therapists form working alliance with a broad range of clients and provide an acceptable and adaptive explanation for the client's distress. They provide a treatment plan that is consistent with the explanation provided to the client. The therapist is influential, persuasive, and convincing and continually monitors client progress in an authentic way. Additionally, this therapist is flexible, adjusting therapy if resistance to the treatment is apparent or the client is not making adequate progress. Difficult material in therapy is not avoided but is used therapeutically, and the therapist communicates hope and optimism.

Effective therapists are aware of the client's characteristics and context. They are aware of their personal psychological process and do not inject their own material into the therapy process unless such actions are deliberate and therapeutic. The effective therapist is also aware of the best research evidence related to the particular client in terms of treatment, problems, and social context and understands the biological, social, and psychological bases of the disorder or problem experienced by the patient. The effective therapist typically achieves expected or more than expected progress with his or her clients (Wampold, 2011). Finally, the effective therapist seeks to continually improve his or her skills and knowledge.

Attributes Needed for Success With Older Adults

Older Americans are not easily categorized. Their needs and preferences are varied and becoming more so. There are a number of personal attributes (Spar & LaRue, 1997) that practitioners should either amplify or adopt for success with older adults. Such attributes include the following:

- Comfort with broad-based rather than narrowly focused interventions
- Appreciation for the social factors in older people's health and well-being
- Remaining an activist in the face of degenerative or terminal disease
- Patience for the time required and complexity encountered with seniors
- Lack of embarrassment when confronted with one's youth and inexperience
- Comfort in collaboration with family and other providers (shared authority)
- Focus on function, rehabilitation, and quality of life rather than on survival
- Capacity to anticipate the older adult's needs and advocate for care
- Examining various causes of illness and disability
- Appreciation for cultural as well as physiological diversity

- Awareness of greater hetereogeneity among the aged (flexibility)
- Willingness to physically interact (touch) and give concrete health advice
- Capacity to tolerate dependency yet press for optimum autonomy
- Ability to lead as well as follow in the person's care and decisions
- Ongoing commitment to clinical education

Additionally, it should be noted that older clients may not wish to speak with a counselor. Older clients may approach the helping professionally independently of others, they may be accompanied or coerced by family members to meet with a helping practitioner, or a crisis may require a referral by another concerned professional. Reluctance by resistant clients can be overcome by creating an atmosphere of trust, openness, and respect for the older client, while simultaneously conveying knowledge of the issues that he or she faces.

It is clear from the earlier discussions of aging issues that age-related problems exist and will continue to exist. The probability of increased physical and mental health or emotional issues may occur with major life transitions. These age-related problems need not be viewed as impediments to the helping relationship; they should instead be viewed as opportunities to learn strategies to circumvent the challenges. Older adults are capable of successful aging. They are resilient and are able to maintain an exceptional quality of life with increased health and engagement with others. However, mental health practitioners may need to assist this group in developing these characteristics. This requires such attributes as being flexible and open, understanding, and collaborative and having an ongoing commitment to clinical education and the well-being of older clients. Together, older adults and their mental health practitioners can ensure a good relationship and realize the goal of successful aging.

KEYSTONES

- Older adults are capable, competent, and resilient.
- Maintaining one's health involves exercise, good nutrition, and active social engagement.
- Intimacy is important to older adults, despite unanticipated limitations.
- Aging successfully is a subjective experience and continues to be a goal that elders should strive for.
- Older adults experience stressors that require intervention, though they continue to underutilize the mental health system.
- Professional counselors are challenged to increase their knowledge and skills to effectively work with elderly clients.
- Successful counselors are those who build trust, create an atmosphere of warmth, and acknowledge both the challenges and strengths brought to the therapeutic relationship.

ADDITIONAL RESOURCES

Print Based

Charness, N., & Schaie, K. W. (2003). *Impact of technology on successful aging*. New York, NY: Springer.

Haber, D. (2010). *Health promotion and aging* (5th ed.). New York, NY: Springer.

Hill, R. D. (2005). *Positive aging: A guide for mental health professionals and consumers*. New York, NY: W.W. Norton.

Morrow-Howell, N., Hinterlong, J., & Sherrade M. (Eds.). (2001). *Productive aging: Concepts and challenges*. Baltimore, MD: Johns Hopkins University Press.

Wykle, M. L., Whitehouse, P. J., & Morris, D. L., (2005). *Successful aging throughout the lifespan: Intergenerational issues in health*. New York, NY: Springer.

Web Based

www.agingwithdignity.org/

www.cdc.gov/aging

www.geron.org

www.healthfinder.gov

www.healthinaging.org

www.ncoa.org

www.nihseniorhealth.gov

REFERENCES

Agency for Healthcare Research and Quality (AHRQ). (2005). *Medical expenditure panel survey household component*. Washington, DC: Author.

Aleman, M. (2005). Embracing and resisting romantic fantasies as the rhetorical vision on a senior-net discussion board. *Journal of Communication, 55*(1), 5–21.

American Psychological Association (APA). (2003). Guidelines on multicultural education, training, research, practice, and organizational change for psychologists [Electronic Version]. *American Psychologist, 58,* 377–402. doi: 10.1037/0003-066Y.58.5.377

American Psychological Association (APA). (2004). Report of the association: Guidelines for psychological practice with older adults [Electronic Version]. *American Psychologist, 59,* 236–260. doi: 10.1037/0003-066Y.59.4.236

Anderson, G., & Horvath, J. (2004). The growing burden of chronic disease in America. *Public Health Reports, 119,* 263–270.

Avis, N. E., & Stellato, M. A. (2001). Is there an association between menopause status and sexual functioning? *Patient Education and Counseling, 23,* 227–233.

Bono, E., Sala, E., Hancock, R., Gunnell, C., & Parisi, L. (2007). *Gender, older people and exclusion: A gendered review and secondary analysis of the data*. Essex, UK: Institute for Social and Economic Research.

Bortz, W. (1990). Use it or lose it. *Runner's World, 25,* 55–58.

Boyer, J. M. (2007). *Creativity matters: The arts and aging toolkit*. Retrieved http://artsandaging.org

Butler, F. R., & Baghi, H. (2008). Using the Internet to facilitate positive attitudes of college students toward aging and working with older adults. *Journal of Intergenerational Relationships, 6*(2), 175–189.

Carr, K., Weir, P., Azar, D., & Azar, N. (2013). Universal design: A step toward successful aging. *Journal of Aging Research*. Retrieved from http://dx.doi.org/10.1155/2013/324624

Centers for Disease Control and Prevention. (2009). *Healthy aging for older adults*. Retrieved from www.cdc .gov/aging

Centers for Disease Control and Prevention & the Merck Company Foundation. (2007). *The state of aging and health in America*. Whitehouse Station, NJ: The Merck Company Foundation.

Cermin, P. A., Lysack, C., & Lichtenberg, P. A. (2011). A comparison of self-rated and objectively measured successful aging constructs in an urban sample of African American older adults. *Clinical Gerontologist: The Journal of Aging and Mental Health, 34*(2), 89–102.

Chodzko-Zajko, W., Schwingel, A., & Park, C. (2009). Successful aging: The role of physical activity. *American Journal of Lifestyle Medicine, 3*(1), 20–28.

Clements, A. C. (2010). *Alternative approaches in music education: Case studies from the field*. Lanham, MD: Rowman & Littlefield Education.

Connidis, I. (2006). Intimate relationships: Learning from later life experience. In T. Calasanti & K. Slevin (Eds.), *Age Matters*. New York, NY: Routledge.

Cornwell, B., Laumann, E. O., & Schumm, L. P. (2008). The social connectedness of older adults: A national profile. *American Sociological Review, 73,* 183–203. PMCID: PMC 2583428

Corwin, S. J., Laditka, J. N., Laditka, S. B., Wilcox, S., & Liu, R. (2009). Attitudes on aging well among older African Americans and whites in South Carolina. *Preventing Chronic Disease, 6*(4), A 113. doi: 10.1093/geront/gnp084

Cutler, N. (2001). *SIECUS Report, 30,* 2. December 2001/January 2002, 509, SIECUS.

Cutler, N., & NCOA. (2001). Half of Americans over 60 have sexual relations at least once a month. *SIECUS Report, 30*(2), 5–9.

Erikson, E. H. (1986). *Identity: Youth and crisis*. New York, NY: Norton.

Federal Interagency Forum on Aging-Related Statistics. (2012). *Older Americans 2012: Key indicators of well-being*. Washington, DC: U.S. Government Printing Office.

Feinberg, T. (2001). *Altered egos: How the brain creates the self*. New York, NY: Oxford University Press.

Folkman, S., Lazarus, R., Gruen, R., & DeLongis, A. (1986). Appraisal, coping, health status, and psychological symptoms. *Journal of Personality and Social Psychology, 50*(3), 571–579.

Fry, P., & Keyes, C. (2010). *New frontiers in resilient aging: Life-strengths and well-being in late life*. New York, NY: Cambridge University Press.

Gellis, Z. D., Sherman, S., & Lawrence, F. (2003). First year graduate social work students' knowledge of an attitude toward older adults. *Educational Gerontology, 29,* 1–16.

Goodman, J., Sclossberg, N., & Anderson, M. (2006). *Counseling adults in transition: Linking practice with theory* (3rd ed.). New York, NY: Springer.

Gott, M., & Hinchlift, S. (2004). How important is sex in later life? The views of older people. *Social Science and Medicine, 56,* 117–128.

Guralnik, J., Fried, L., & Salive, M. (1996). Disability as a public health outcome in the aging population. *Annual Review of Public Health, 17,* 25–46.

Henderson, J., Xiao, L., Siegloff, L., Kelton, M., & Peterson, J. (2008). Older people have lived their lives: First year nursing students' attitudes towards older people. *Contemporary Nurse, 30,* 32–45.

Hertz, J., & Anschutz, C. (2002). Relationships among perceived enactment of autonomy, self-care, and holistic health in community-dwelling older adults. *Journal of Holistic Nursing, 20*(2), 166–186.

Holt-Lunstad, J., Smith, T. B., & Layton, J. B. (2010). Social relationships and mortality risk: A meta-analytic review. *PLOS Medicine, 7*(7), e1000316.

Howard, B. (2009, November/December). The secrets of resilient people. *AARP Magazine, 34,* 36–37.

Hwang, W., Weller, W., Ireys, H., & Anderson, G. (2004). Out-of-pocket medical spending for care of chronic conditions. *Health Affairs, 20*(6), 267–278.

Karel, M. J., Gatz, M., & Smyer, M. A. (2012). Aging and mental health in the decade ahead: What psychologists need to know. *American Psychologist, 67*(3), 184–185.

Kincaid, C., & Peacock, J. R. (2003). The effect of a wall mural on decreasing four types of door-testing behaviors. *Journal of Applied Gerontology, 22*(1), 76–88.

Kinsella, K., & Phillips, D. (2005, March). Successful aging. *Population Bulletin, 32–34.* Population Reference Bureau.

Koenig, H. G., McCullough, M. E., & Larson, D. B. (2001). *Handbook of religion and health.* New York, NY: Oxford University Press.

Kramer, A. F., Colcombe, S. J., Erickson, K. I., & Paige, P. (2006). *Fitness training and the brain from molecules to minds.* Presentation at the University of Illinois at Urbana Champaign.

Lachman, M. (2005). Aging under control. *Psychological Science Agenda.* Washington, DC: American Psychological Association.

Langer, N. (2009). Late life love and intimacy. *Educational Gerontology, 35,* 752–764. doi: 10.1080/03601270 802708459

LoFrisco, B. (2012). *4 qualities every successful counselor has.* Retrieved from https://www.mastersincounsel ing.org/4-qualities-every-successful-counselor-has.html

Manson, J. E., Greenland, P., LaCroix, A. Z., Stefanick, M. L., Mouton, C. P., Oberman, A., Perri, M. G., . . . Siscovick, D. S. (2002). Walking compared with vigorous exercise for the prevention of cardiovascular events in women. *New England Journal of Medicine, 347*(10), 716–725.

National Assembly of State Arts Agencies. (2005). *Creating art inspires wellness among North Dakota seniors.* State Spotlight. Washington, DC: Assembly of State Arts Agencies. Author. Retrieved from www.nasaa-arts .org/spotlight/stspot_0805.shtml.

National Center for Health Statistics. (2008). *Health, United States.* Retrieved http://www.cdc.gov/nchs/datawh/ nchsdefs/healthcondition.htm#chronic

National Council on Aging. (2002). Half of older Americans report they are sexually active. Washington, DC: NCOA.

Nelson, M., Rejeski, W., Blair, S., Duncan, P., & Judge, J. (2007). Physical activity and public health in older adults: Recommendation from the American College of Sports Medicine and the American Heart Association. *Circulation, 116*(9), 1094–1105.

Neugarten, B. L. (1971). Grow old along with me! The best is yet to be. *Psychology Today, 5,* 45–48.

Pipher, M. (1999). *Another country: Navigating the emotional terrain of our elders.* New York, NY: Ballantine Books.

Reichstadt, J., Sengupta, G., Depp, C., Palinkas, L. M., & Jeste, D. (2010). Older adults' perspectives on successful aging: Qualitative interviews. *American Journal of Geriatric Psychiatry, 18*(7), 567–575.

Rentz, C. A. (2002). Memories in the making: Outcome-based evaluation of an art program for individuals with dementing diseases. *American Journal of Alzheimer's Disease and Other Dementias, 17*(3), 175–181.

Robbins, J. (2007). *Healthy at 100.* New York, NY: Ballantine Books.

Rowe, J., & Kahn, R. (1987). Human aging: Usual and successful. *Science, 237*(4811), 143–149.

Rowe, J., & Kahn, R. (1998). *Successful aging.* New York, NY: Pantheon Books.

Spar, J. E., & LaRue, A. (1997). *Concise guide to geriatric psychiatry* (2nd ed.). Washington, DC: American Psychiatric Press.

Stark, S. (2001). Creating disability in the home: The role of environmental barriers in the United States. *Disability and Society, 16,* 37–49. doi: 10.1080/713662037

Strawbridge, W. J., Wallhagen, M. I., & Cohen, R. D. (2002). Successful aging and well-being: Self-rated compared with Rowe and Kahn. *The Gerontologist, 43*(5), 735–744.

Steger, M., Oishi, S., & Kashdan, T. (2009). Meaning in life across the life span: Levels and correlates of meaning in life from emerging adulthood to older adulthood. *The Journal of Positive Psychology, 4*(1), 43–52.

Tabourne, C. E. S., & Lee, Y. (2005–2006). *Study of Kairos dance theatre's dancing heart program*. University of Minnesota, Department of Kinesiology.

Tate, R., Lah, L., & Cuddy, T. (2003). Definition of successful aging by elderly Canadian males: The Manitoba follow-up study. *The Gerontologist, 43*(5), 735–744.

Thorpe, K., & Philyaw, M. (2012). The medicalization of chronic disease and costs. *Annual Review of Public Health, 33,* 409–423.

United States Department of Agriculture & United States Department of Health and Human Services. (2015). *The dietary guidelines for Americans: Good nutrition in later life*. Washington, DC: Author.

U.S. Census Bureau, Current Population Survey. (2014). *Annual social and economic supplement*. Washington, DC: Author.

USDA Human Nutrition Research Center on Aging (USDA HNCRCA). (2011). *My plate for older adults*. Boston, MA: Tufts University, Gerald J. & Dorothy R. Friedman School of Nutrition Science and Policy.

Verghese, J. (2006). Cognitive and mobility profile of older social dancers. *Journal of the American Geriatrics Society, 54,* 8.

Verghese, J., Lipton, R. B., Katz, M. J., Hall, C. B., Derby, C. A., Kuslansky, G., . . . Buschke, H. (2003). Leisure activities and the risk of dementia in the elderly. *New England Journal of Medicine, 348,* 2508–2516.

Wahl, H. W., Frange, A., Oswald, F., Gitlin, L. N., & Ivarsson, S. (2009). The home environment and disability-related outcomes in aging individuals: What is the empirical evidence? *The Gerontologist, 49,* 355–367. doi: 10.1093/geront/gnp056

Walker, L. A. (2001, September 16). We can control how we age. *Parade*, pp. 4–5.

Walters, Y., & Boyd, T. V. (2009). Sexuality in later life: Opportunity for reflections for healthcare providers. *Sexual and Relationship Therapy, 24,* 307–315. doi: 10.1080/14681990903398047

Wampold, B. E. (2011). *Qualities and actions of effective therapists*. Wilmington, DE: American Psychological Association.

Whitbourne, S. K. (1989). Psychological treatment of the aging individual. *Journal of Integrative and Eclectic Psychotherapy, 8,* 161–173.

Willis, S., Tennstedt, S., Marsiske, M., Ball, K., Elias, J., Koepke, K., . . . Wright, E. (2006). Long-term effects of cognitive training on everyday functional outcomes in older adults. *Journal of the American Medical Association, 296,* 2805–2814.

Wrosch, C. (2006). Adulthood and old age. In R. Schultz (Ed.), *Encyclopedia of aging* (4th ed., pp. 309–310). New York, NY: Springer.

Yen, I. H., Michael, Y. L., & Perdue, P. (2009). Neighborhood environment in studies of health of older adults: A systematic review. *American Journal of Preventive Medicine, 37*(5), 453–463. doi: 10.10160/02Fj.amepre. 2009.06.022PMCID: PMC 2785463

Yen, L., Shim, J., Martinez, A., & Barker, J. (2012). Older people and social connectedness: How place and activities keep people engaged. *Journal of Aging Research*. Article ID 139523, 10 pages, doi: 10.1155/2012/139523

Zeiss, A. M., & Kasl-Godley, J. (2001). Sexuality in older adults' relationships. *Generations, 25,* 18–25.

Zunzunegui, M., Koné, A., Johri, M., Beland, F., Wolfson, C., & Bergman, H. (2004). Social networks and self-rated health in two French speaking Canadian community dwelling populations over 65. *Social Science and Medicine, 58*(10), 2069–2081.

Common Issues and Problematic Behaviors Experienced by Older Adults

Health Challenges That Impact the Well-Being of Older Adults

"We are not victims of aging, sickness, and death. These are part of scenery, not the seer, who is immune to any form of change. This seer is the spirit, the expression of eternal being."

—Deepak Chopra

Learning Objectives

After reading this chapter, you will be able to

1. Analyze the impact of activities of daily living on functioning
2. Describe the cardiovascular diseases experienced by older adults and their effects on emotional health
3. Summarize the symptoms and treatment for diabetes, as well as consequences for mental well-being
4. Examine what cancer is and identify strategies for prevention, screening, and treatment, as it impacts overall health
5. Differentiate between the types of arthritis and their treatment and their influence on activities of daily living
6. Define osteoporosis, its treatment implications for older persons, and its effect on psychological well-being

(Continued)

(Continued)

7. Identify risk factors for falls and strategies for fall prevention, as well as implications on daily functioning
8. Explain vision disorders that interfere with activities of daily living and describe their treatments and influence on mental health
9. Analyze the different types of cerebrovascular disease and treatment recommendations
10. Discuss the incidence, prevalence, and treatment recommendations for HIV/AIDS, as well as implications for mental health

INTRODUCTION

Many older adults progress through life and all of its major and minor transitions extremely well. They manage minor and sometimes major illnesses in an effective manner. However, the reality is that it is highly probable that older adults will experience some diseases that require professional attention.

Unlike many younger persons who might see themselves as invincible, older persons, when ill, will experience uneasiness, uncertainty, and potential fear. Helping practitioners must understand the psychological impact on an elder who is diagnosed with a major disease because it impacts his or her emotional well-being, potential for rehabilitation, family dynamics, finances, and living arrangements. All of these areas and many others can be affected when older adults are diagnosed with a chronic health condition. It is essential that helping practitioners communicate effectively with health care practitioners to ensure the best quality of care for the older client and his or her family. Guided Practice Exercise 4.1 provides an opportunity to identify diseases in one's family to decrease the risk of developing the disease. Gaining knowledge of modifiable and nonmodifiable risk factors will assist the practitioner when counseling older clients.

Guided Practice Exercise 4.1

You are studying the acute and chronic diseases that affect persons within the United States and wish to identify what diseases (if any) you feel that you are at risk for developing. To respond to this question, ask your parents about their medical history, then determine the modifiable and non-modifiable risk factors. What information did you gain from this exercise, and how will your behavior change to avoid the diseases you identified?

Major health challenges can have a devastating effect on the quality of life of older adults. However, many chronic health conditions can be managed, which enables the older adult to live a satisfying life. Helping professionals and potential professionals are encouraged to understand the impact of these health conditions that challenges older adults daily. Cardiovascular disease, diabetes, cancer, arthritis, osteoporosis and falls, vision disorders, and cerebrovascular disease will be examined. These conditions are treatable and need not impair the practitioner–client relationship.

IMPACT OF AGE-RELATED DISEASES ON ACTIVITIES OF DAILY LIVING

Activities of daily living (ADLs) are basic self-care tasks that include feeding, toileting, selecting proper attire, grooming, maintaining continence, putting on clothes, bathing, and walking and transferring. Instrumental activities of daily living (IADLs) are the complex skills needed to successfully live independently. These skills are usually learned in earlier years and include managing finances, handling transportation, shopping, preparing meals, using the telephone and other communication devices, managing medications, and housework and basic home maintenance. Together, ADLs and IADLs represent the skills that people usually need to live as independent adults (Kernisan & Scott, 2015). Doctors, rehabilitation specialists, geriatric social workers, and other clinicians assess ADLs and IADLs as part of an older person's functional assessment.

A decline in IADLs can indicate any number of physiological changes. For instance, there is evidence that subtle changes in the performance of IADLs, which make greater demands on cognitive skills, precede conditions of dementia (Perez et al., 2008). The occurrence of a stroke, which can occur quickly, is a determinant of disability regarding IADL in men (Alexandre et al., 2012). Cross-sectional studies have found associations between difficulty in IADL and a poorer performance on the one-leg balance test as well as lesser grip strength (Drusini et al., 2007). A poorer perception of hearing is a risk factor for the development of disability in IADL in men and women (Cruickshanks et al., 2003). Patients with mild cognitive impairment (MCI) performed significantly worse than control groups on IADLs, such as the ability to use the telephone, prepare meals, take medication, manage belongings, keep appointments, discuss recent events, and perform leisure activities/hobbies (Ahn et al., 2009).

ADLs and IADLs provide an indication of the functional status of older adults. Impairments of these activities, whether due to cardiac limitations, cancer, arthritis, diabetes, sensory deficits, or cognitive deficits, have tremendous impact on the health and overall well-being of older adults. Diminished ability to perform ADLs and/or IADLs may lead to a loss of independence, decreased ability for social interaction, and a deteriorating emotional state. Counselors armed with the knowledge of various health conditions and their impacts on the lives of older adults can assist older persons to adapt to the changes in their functional abilities.

CARDIOVASCULAR DISEASES

The cardiovascular system includes all of the blood vessels throughout the body and the heart, which provides the force necessary to move blood through the system. The effects of aging on this system are often confused with diseases and the effects of inactivity or deconditioning. Diseases of the cardiovascular system are the leading cause of death for persons 65 years of age and older (Jackson & Wenger, 2011). Intense effort is focused on understanding cardiovascular diseases in an attempt to control illness and to preserve functioning of individuals until late in life. Prevention measures in older age are similar to those in younger persons: avoid smoking, increase physical activities, control blood pressure, control glucose intake, maintain a healthy weight, and reduce cholesterol. Eating a well-balanced, nutritious, heart-healthy diet also helps. These recommendations are suggested for all older adults regardless of cardiovascular status.

Atherosclerosis

Atherosclerosis is a disease in which plaque builds up inside the arteries and is called hardening of the arteries, which is a leading cause of heart attacks, stroke, and peripheral vascular disease (National Heart, Lung, and Blood Institute [NHLBI], 2015b). The effects of atherosclerosis differ depending upon which arteries in the body narrow and become clogged with plaque. If the arteries that bring oxygen-rich blood to your heart are affected, you may have coronary artery disease, chest pain, or a heart attack (NHLBI, 2015b). Atherosclerosis is a slow, progressive disease that may start in childhood; however for some people the disease progresses rapidly in their 30s, and in others it doesn't become dangerous until they reach their 50s or 60s. However, it is normal to have hardening of the arteries as you get older (NHLBI, 2015b).

Vessel narrowing effectively reduces blood flow capacity. Initially, no effect is evident because the flow rate may still equal peak demand. Later, in stressful situations, flow will be inadequate and symptoms develop. Late in the disease, symptoms will be evident at rest. A common clinical syndrome associated with atherosclerosis is leg pain when walking, the result of inadequate nutrient flow to leg muscles. Surgery can sometimes reopen narrowed vessels. On occasion, vessel replacement with grafts taken from elsewhere in the body or the use of synthetic materials may be necessary. When heart vessels are narrowed, chest pain (angina pectoris) may occur on exertion. Brief episodes of thinking problems, paralysis, or sensory disorders may be evident when brain circulation is compromised.

When blood clots form at the site of narrowing, complete blockage of the artery can occur. Occasionally, small clots will form on the surface of the plaques and break free and drift downstream, eventually lodging where the arterial system narrows and blocking circulation, which is known as an embolism. This may cause a toe to suddenly turn blue. Occasionally, a foot or leg may be deprived of circulation by such events. When blockage occurs in arteries supplying the heart, a heart attack (myocardial infarction) will occur. Blockage in brain circulation results in a stroke (cerebral infarction). Medications can sometimes reestablish flow (White & Sullivan, 2006).

Individuals at risk of developing atherosclerosis will be recommended to change their lifestyle and maintain a healthy weight, and in some cases treatment may include medication or surgery (Nordqvist, 2015). Recommended lifestyle changes will focus on weight management, physical activity, and a healthy diet. The physician may prescribe medications to prevent the build-up of plaque or to help prevent blood clots, and other medications may be prescribed to lower cholesterol and lower blood pressure. In severe cases of atherosclerosis, surgical procedures may be necessary, which include angioplasty or coronary bypass grafting (CABG) (Nordqvist, 2015). Angioplasty involves expanding the artery and opening the blockage, so that the blood can flow through properly again. CABG is another form of surgery that can improve blood flow to the heart by using arteries from other parts of the body to bypass a narrowed coronary artery (Nordqvist, 2015).

There are a number of factors that contribute to the occurrence of this disease. Certain factors that can damage the inner area of the artery (endothelium) and can trigger athero-sclerosis include high blood pressure, high levels of cholesterol, smoking and high levels of sugar in the blood. Patients with poorly controlled diabetes, who frequently have excess blood glucose levels, are much more likely to develop atherosclerosis. People with a parent or sibling who has/had atherosclerosis and cardiovascular disease have a much higher risk of developing atherosclerosis than others, and air pollution (exposure to diesel exhaust particles in the air) has been linked to a higher risk of bad cholesterol building in the arter-ies (Nordqvist, 2015; White & Sullivan, 2006).

Angina Pectoris

Angina pectoris, which is pain in the left chest or more commonly "chest tightness," especially if elicited by physical or emotional stress, is a very frequent symptom in the elderly and becomes more frequent with advancing age (Stern, Behar, & Gottlieb, 2003). Angina pectoris occurs when arterial narrowing prevents satisfactory flow to the heart muscle. The patient experiences chest pain or pressure, which spreads to the arms or jaw, commonly on the left side. Symptoms may be more vague in older adults, such as extreme fatigue or shortness of breath. Exercise aggravates the pain, and rest relieves it. Medications that limit cardiac response to exercise or alter blood circulation flow throughout the body can relieve symptoms. No heart muscle damage occurs, and each symptom episode is usually short lived (White & Sullivan, 2006). Re-vascularization therapies for angina pec-toris, such as angioplasty or bypass surgery, seem to be superior to treatment with medi-cines in improving quality of life and reducing angina severity. Episodes of angina occur when the heart's need for oxygen increases beyond the oxygen available from the blood nourishing the heart. Physical exertion is the most common trigger for angina. Other fac-tors include emotional stress, extreme cold or heat, heavy meals, alcohol, and cigarette smoking (NHLBI, 2015a).

Myocardial Infarction

Myocardial infarction, commonly known as a heart attack, is a more serious manifesta-tion of arterial narrowing that results in heart muscle death, when an atherosclerotic plaque ruptures and a clot forms. At the time of muscle injury, some individuals may be totally unaware that a problem exists. Diabetics are particularly susceptible to such silent events owing to changes in their nervous system. Some individuals may suspect that they are suffering from heartburn. Many elderly people will manifest confusion, stomach upset, or weakness as their only symptoms. When severe, crushing, and prolonged chest pain occurs associated with nausea, myocardial infarction is extremely likely. Presenting symptoms of a myocardial infarction in the elderly may differ from younger patients.

They are more likely to be termed "atypical" because the description differs from the classical one of pressure with exertion. When pain is the presenting complaint, it may be different in character or location, and sometimes appears as an upper abdomen pain rather than a crushing or squeezing sensation (Rittger et al., 2011). Symptoms may be described primarily as dyspnea syncope, shoulder or back pain, weakness, fatigue (in women), acute confusion, and epicardial discomfort and may be precipitated by concurrent illness (Carro & Kaski, 2011).

An electrocardiogram and measurement of enzymes within the bloodstream can provide definitive evidence of muscle damage. Treatment may involve thrombolytic agents, which are drugs that dissolve clots (thrombus) and reopen an artery or vein. Balloon angioplasty is a procedure in which a catheter equipped with a tiny balloon at the tip is inserted into an artery that has been narrowed by the accumulation of fatty deposits. The balloon is then inflated to clear the blockage and widen the artery (*Miller-Keane Encyclopedia,* 2003). A stent replacement is a wire mesh stainless steel tube that holds an artery open and keeps it from closing again, which allows blood to flow smoothly. Good blood flow reduces pain and risks of clots forming (Johns Hopkins Medicine, 2015). Coronary artery bypass graphing surgery is a type of surgery that improves blood flow to the heart by removing a blood vessel or redirecting it from one area of the body and placing it around the area or areas of narrowing to bypass the blockages and restore blood flow to the heart muscle (NHLBI, 2012). Early mobilization rather than bed rest is now advocated following myocardial infarction.

Heart attack or acute symptoms that warn of an impending heart attack are called acute coronary syndromes (ACS), which become more frequent with advancing age. Even with a decrease in mortality from this disease over recent years, many individuals die from coronary heart disease (CHD). Coronary heart disease alone caused approximately 1 of every 6 deaths in the United States in 2010. In 2010, 379,559 Americans died of CHD (American Heart Organization [AHA], 2014). Each year, an estimated 620,000 Americans have a new coronary attack (defined as first hospitalized myocardial infarction or coronary heart disease death) and 295,000 have a recurrent attack (AHA, 2014). It is estimated that an additional 150,000 silent myocardial infarctions occur each year. Approximately every 34 seconds, one American has a coronary event, and approximately every 1 minute 23 seconds, an American will die of one (AHA, 2014). In the elderly, ACS may go unnoticed unless the patient and the physician are aware of sudden shortness of breath, sudden fatigue, discomfort that may be confined to the abdomen more than to the chest, profound sweating, irregular heartbeat, or even fainting (syncope). Each of these symptoms alone or in combination may herald the development of ACS. With high alertness, the high rate of unrecognized heart attacks in the elderly may be significantly reduced (Stern et al., 2003).

Risk factors for a heart attack include age. Men ages 45 or older and women age 55 or older are more likely to have a heart attack than are younger men and women (Mayo Clinic, 2014). Smoking and long-term exposure to secondhand smoke increase the risk of a heart attack. High blood pressure can damage arteries that feed the heart by accelerating atherosclerosis, and high blood pressure that occurs with obesity, smoking, high cholesterol, or diabetes increases the risk even more. A high level of low-density lipoprotein (LDL) cholesterol (bad cholesterol) can narrow arteries. A high level of triglycerides, a type of blood fat related to your diet, increases the risk of a heart attack. Low levels of high-density lipoprotein (HDL) cholesterol (the good cholesterol) increases the risk of a heart attack (Mayo Clinic, 2014). Uncontrolled diabetes increases one's risk of a heart attack as well as a family history of heart attack. If siblings, parents, or grandparents have had early heart attacks (by age 55 for male relatives and by age 65 for female relatives), there exists increased risk for a heart attack (Mayo Clinic, 2014). An inactive lifestyle, obesity, stress, illegal drug use (stimulant drugs), and a history of an autoimmune disease (i.e., rheumatoid arthritis, lupus) can increase the risk of having a heart attack (Mayo Clinic, 2014).

Case Illustration 4.1 demonstrates the complexity in addressing issues with an elderly client who has been diagnosed with cardiovascular disease. Professional counselors will have the opportunity to explore the impact of this disease on various aspects of the elderly person's life and simultaneously advocate and promote a healthy lifestyle.

CASE ILLUSTRATION 4.1

Mrs. T. is an 85-year-old woman who had several myocardial infarctions over the past 8 years. A retired chief executive officer of a major Fortune 500 company, she lives with her 70-year-old nephew, who also has a serious cardiovascular disease, in a one-story house that she owns. Her only other relatives are the nephew's two adopted sons, both of whom are in their early 30s, who live 1,000 miles away and are unavailable.

Mrs. T. is 5 feet, 8 inches tall but weighs 90 pounds. She cooks at least one healthy, balanced meal per day. She snacks during the day and does not like her nephew's cooking. He describes her as becoming more rigid and less open to any ideas. Mrs. T. is mobile and occasionally attends church or goes to the store when her nephew drives her. She regularly attends office visits to her physician. She has given up tennis and volunteer work. She has hired persons to tend to her garden and for household maintenance activities. She is a lifelong smoker and refuses to quit. Her husband died many years ago. Her male companion died recently (within the last 6 months).

After attending a funeral she collapsed with crushing pain and was rushed to the hospital. A myocardial infarction (MI) was confirmed, and within two days she was sent home on a medication regimen. She was viewed as an inappropriate candidate for surgery. She did share with her nephew that prior to the funeral she experienced severe chest pain and took her sublingual nitroglycerin during this time.

Congestive Heart Failure

Congestive heart failure occurs when the heart cannot pump enough blood and oxygen to support other organs in the body. Heart failure is a serious condition, but it does not mean that the heart has stopped beating (Centers for Disease Control and Prevention [CDC], 2013). About 5.1 million people in the United States have heart failure (Go, Mozaffarian,

Roger, Benjamin, & Berry, 2013). Heart failure is most common in those who are 65 years and older and is the number one reason older people are hospitalized. Heart failure tends to be more common in men than in women, but because women usually live longer, the condition affects more women in their 70s and 80s (MedicineNet, 2015). One in nine deaths in 2010 included heart failure as a contributing cause (AHA, 2014). Almost half of people who develop congestive heart failure die within 5 years of diagnosis (Go et al., 2013).

Diseases that damage your heart also increase your risk for heart failure. Some of these diseases include coronary heart disease (the most common type of heart disease) and heart attacks. High blood pressure and diabetes also damage the heart. Unhealthy behaviors can also increase the risk for heart failure especially for persons who have one of the identified diseases. Unhealthy behaviors include smoking tobacco; eating foods high in fat, cholesterol, and sodium; not getting enough physical activity; and obesity (CDC, 2014b). Common symptoms of heart failure include shortness of breath during daily activities; having trouble breathing when lying down; weight gain with swelling in the feet, ankles, or stomach; and a general feeling of being tired or weak (CDC, 2014b).

There is no one specific test to diagnose congestive heart failure, because the symptoms are common for other conditions; therefore the physician will determine the diagnosis of heart failure by conducting a detailed medical history, an examination, and several tests. These tests will identify whether you have any diseases or conditions that can cause heart failure, and the test will rule out any other causes of your symptoms and determine the extent of damage to your heart (MedicineNet, 2015). Tests given to determine heart failure include an EKG or ECG (electrocardiogram), which measures the rate and regularity of the heartbeat, and the EKG shows if you have had a heart attack and whether the walls of the heart have thickened. A chest x-ray takes a picture of your heart and lungs and shows whether the heart is enlarged or if the lungs have fluid in them, both signs of heart disease. A BNP blood test measures the level of a hormone called B-type natriuretic peptide that increases in heart failure (MedicineNet, 2015). Once these initial tests have been performed, a referral to a cardiologist might entail additional tests of a halter monitor, which is a small box that is attached to patches placed on your chest, and this monitor is worn for 24 hours and provides a continuous recording of heart rhythm during normal activity. An exercise stress test reads your EKG and blood pressure before, during, or after exercise to see how your heart responds to exercise (MedicineNet, 2015).

There is no cure for heart failure, but it can be controlled by treating the underlying conditions that cause it. The goals for treatment are to improve symptoms, stop it from getting worse, and prolong the life span. Treatment includes lifestyle changes, medications, and specialized care for those who are in advanced stages (CDC, 2014b). Recommendations might include following a diet low in salt, because salt can cause extra fluid to build up in your body, making heart failure worse. Limiting fluids might be recommended, and you might need to lose weight, quit smoking, and limit alcohol intake. Medications to improve heart function and symptoms include diuretics, which are fluid pills that reduce fluid in your lungs and swelling in your feet and ankles. ACE inhibitors lower blood pressure and reduce strain on your heart, beta blockers slow your heart rate, which will also lower blood pressure to relieve some of the workload on your heart, and digoxin will help the heart beat stronger and pump more blood (MedicineNet, 2015). Persons with severe heart failure may also receive a mechanical heart pump that is placed inside the body to help pump blood, and others may be considered for a heart transplant. A transplant is an option when all other treatments fail to control symptoms.

Congestive heart failure occurs when the heart fails to perform its normal pumping function. Fatigue, shortness of breath, and swollen legs are the most common symptoms of this condition. The incidence of heart failure increases with age as the heart becomes more vulnerable to various injuries or begins to deteriorate as a pump as part of the aging process. The underlying causes of heart failure include impaired pumping function of the heart (contractibility) due to damage from decreased blood supply or a prior heart attack (systolic dysfunction) or an increase in pressure load or impaired relaxation (diastolic dysfunction), the ability of the heart to relax and fill passively with blood. With advancing age, the proportion of people with heart failure but normal systolic function approaches 50% or more (National Institutes of Health [NIH], 2014).

Cardiac Arrhythmias

Cardiac arrhythmias, problems with the rhythm or rate of heartbeats, constitute a serious chronic condition that may lead to fainting, heart attack, stroke, and sudden death. Arrhythmias are most common among older adults (Centers for Medicare and Medicaid Services [CMS], 2006). Alterations in the heartbeat are not necessarily perceived in the chest, and frequently patients experience them over the neck arteries or may become aware of their presence because of sudden sweating, pallor, weakness, occasional dizziness, and/or fainting. Sometimes such disturbances may be present without any symptoms. The most frequent but usually not too serious arrhythmia is atrial fibrillation, which becomes more prevalent with advancing age. An arrhythmia is when the heart beats too slowly, too fast, or in an irregular way. When a person has atrial fibrillation (AFib), the normal beating in the upper chambers of the heart is irregular, and blood doesn't flow as well as it should from the atria to the lower chambers of the heart. AFib may occur in brief episodes, or it may be a permanent condition (CDC, 2015f).

An estimated 2.7 to 6.1 million people in the United States have AFib, and with the aging of the U.S. population, this number is expected to increase (January et al., 2014). Nine percent of people aged 65 years or older have AFib, African Americans are less likely than those of European descent to have AFib, and because AFib cases increase with age and women generally live longer than men, more women than men experience AFib (January et al., 2014).

Slow heartbeat is effectively treated with the implantation of a pacemaker, a procedure that can be done at any age. The defibrillator (device to control heart fibrillation by application of an electric current to the chest wall or heart) is also used frequently in the elderly with considerable benefit (Stern et al., 2003). Drug therapies for the management of arrhythmias can be used in the elderly, but with consideration to other illnesses that the person may have. For people with arrhythmias, experts recommend a variety of patient education and self-management approaches to manage this chronic condition and reduce risk of complications, such as keeping a record of changes in pulse rate, attending all medical appointments, maintaining a list of current medications, reporting symptoms and side effects promptly, and following the provider's advice regarding treatment and healthy lifestyle (National Institutes of Health, National Heart, Lung, and Blood Institute, 2003).

The risk for AFib increases with age and high blood pressure, which also increases in risk with advancing age, accounts for 14% to 22% of AFib cases (Mozzafarian, Benjamin, & Go, 2015). Risk factors for AFib include advancing age, high blood pressure, obesity, European ancestry, diabetes, heart failure, ischemic heart disease, hyperthyroidism, chronic kidney disease, heavy alcohol use, and enlargement of the chambers of the left side of the heart (Mozzafarian et al., 2015).

Hypertension

Hypertension (high blood pressure) is a particularly widespread problem in older adults. About 70 million American adults (29%) have high blood pressure, which is 1 of every 3 adults (Nwankwo, Yoon, Burt, & Gu, 2013). Only about half (52%) of people with high blood pressure have their condition under control (Nwankwo et al., 2013). Nearly 1 of 3 American adults has prehypertension, which is blood pressure numbers that are higher than normal, but not yet in the high blood pressure range (Nwankwo et al., 2013). High blood pressure costs the nation $46 billion each year, and this total includes the cost of health care services, medications to treat high blood pressure, and missed days of work (Mozzafarian et al., 2015). For people 65 years of age and older, high blood pressure affects more women than men (ages 65–74, 64.0% men versus 69.3% women; and ages 75 and older, 66.7% men versus 78.5% women) (Mozzafarian et al., 2015).

High blood pressure risk factors include health conditions, lifestyle, and family history. Prehypertension, that is, blood pressure slightly higher than normal (e.g., 120/80 mmHg and 189/89 mmHg), increases the risk for developing chronic (long-lasting) high blood pressure in the future (CDC, 2014c). Diabetes also increases the risk for heart disease because diabetes causes sugars to build up in the blood, and many persons with diabetes also have high blood pressure (CDC, 2014c). Lifestyle choices can increase risk for high blood pressure that include unhealthy diet, physical inactivity, obesity, excessive alcohol intake, and tobacco use (CDC, 2014c). Family members share genes, behaviors, lifestyles, and environments that can influence their health and their risk for disease; high blood pressure can run in a family; and risk for high blood pressure can increase based upon your age and race or ethnicity (CDC, 2014c). Blood pressure tends to rise as one ages, therefore risk increases with age (Vasan, Beiser, & Seshadri, 2002). Women are more likely to develop high blood pressure at some point in their lives, and African Americans develop high blood pressure more often than any other race or ethnicity (Go et al., 2013). Clearly risk factors of age, gender, family history, and race/ethnicity cannot be modified; however, lifestyle changes and treatments are available to manage hypertension. Living a healthy lifestyle can help keep blood pressure in a healthy range and lower the risk for hypertension. A healthy lifestyle includes eating a healthy diet, maintaining a healthy weight, getting enough physical activity, not smoking, and limiting alcohol use (CDC, 2014c).

If lifestyle changes do not lower blood pressure enough to a safe level, then medications may be prescribed (National Institute on Aging [NIA], 2015). You may try several kinds or combinations of medicines before finding a plan that works best for you. Medicine can control your blood pressure, but it can't cure it (NIA, 2015). The major classes of drugs commonly used for treating hypertension are diuretics, calcium channel blockers, and renin-angiotensin system blockers, and each class has specific benefits and adverse side effects

(Council on Medical Education [COME], 2015). Diuretics are the initial drugs in the treatment of older persons with hypertension because these drugs have been demonstrated to reduce cardiovascular events and mortality in older adults (Aronow, 2008). Starting with the lowest dose, titrating upward slowly, and monitoring for adverse effects is recommended for older patients. Common side effects of some drugs include orthostatic hypotension (drop in blood pressure upon standing) and edema (swelling). Older adults with co-occurring medical conditions will require treatment for those conditions as well as for their hypertension (COME, 2015). Hypertension in the elderly is a condition that if left untreated poses harm to older adults; however, treatments are effective in managing this condition. Case Illustration 4.2 demonstrates issues that may be brought to the attention of mental health counselors by elderly clients. Medical issues, medication noncompliance, communication challenges, and decreased intimacy are significant issues that warrant further examination within the counseling sessions.

CASE ILLUSTRATION 4.2

Mr. and Mrs. Winters are in their late 70s. Mr. Winters is a retired truck driver, and Mrs. Winters is a retired registered nurse. They both visit the local senior adult center for Zumba classes for aerobic conditioning 3 days per week and to socialize with friends. They participate in the health fairs that are held monthly where they are able to get their weight, blood pressure, pulse, and blood work checked. They have six grandchildren, and they take many senior bus and train trips to exciting areas within the United States.

Mr. Winters was recently diagnosed with hypertension and was prescribed medication, dietary changes, and an exercise regimen. He feels fine on this prescribed therapeutic regimen. Mrs. Winters, on the other hand, was recently diagnosed with osteoporosis, based on results from bone mineral density studies showing loss of bone mass. She is slightly overweight and admits to eating excessively when under stress. She takes 1,200 milligrams (mg) of calcium daily and a vitamin D supplement. Mrs. Winters confides in one of her friends following one of their exercise classes that she is concerned about her husband. She worries that he does not take his hypertension seriously and might have a stroke. He is not following the regimen identified for him, and intimate activity between them has dramatically decreased. Mrs. Winters's friend refers her to a local outpatient agency that she felt could provide the counseling services needed to assist Mrs. Winters and her husband.

Cardiovascular Diseases and Mental Health

Cardiovascular disease consists of a variety of diseases related to the heart and blood vessels. There are a number of modalities used to treat these age-related diseases. All older adults will respond differently to treatment based on the severity of the diagnosis and their ability to cope with the effects of the disease. The psychological well-being of older adults may not be impaired, for example, with a diagnosis of hypertension. However, a diagnosis of congestive heart failure or angina pectoris may be perceived as a life-threatening situation.

Older persons may fear pain, the need for hospitalization, follow-up treatment, and potential death. Along with these fears they may become extremely worried about surgery and whether they'll survive it. Routine ADLs, social activities, and physical pursuits may diminish. Fear of dying may decrease elders' engagement in life's activities, and they may become hopeless, helpless, and exhibit other signs of depression. Based upon the specific diagnosis, medications, dietary changes, exercise program, relaxation for stress reduction, and/or surgery may be indicated. Psychological effects of physical diseases, if untreated, can significantly impact the overall well-being of older clients.

Cardiovascular Diseases and Mental Health Practice

Many older individuals adjust and make the necessary modifications when given a diagnosis of cardiovascular disease. However, counseling services are sought to assist older clients when they are experiencing difficulty adjusting or adapting to the changes related to the diagnosis. Counselors will intervene to enhance the adjustment process by examining clients' fears and anxieties. Counselors will also explore their concerns regarding hospitalization, rehabilitation, and surgical procedures. Exploring clients' perceived threat of dying requires careful and thorough examination. Promotion of a healthy lifestyle with a healthy diet, exercise, stress reduction, and eradication of smoking (if appropriate) is essential. Counseling professionals will address the mental health issues of their clients in a comprehensive manner, while allowing for input from family members and other health care professionals. Guided Practice Exercise 4.2 provides the mental health counselor the opportunity to address fears and stressors related to the fear of dying from the perspective of an elderly person with cardiac conditions.

Guided Practice Exercise 4.2

Older adults who have had previous myocardial infarctions and/or open heart surgeries may be fearful of dying. As a mental health counselor, how do you address the fears related to dying? How do you address the stressors that may contribute to this fear of dying? Are there assessment tools you'll administer or will you address these issues with your elderly client and/or within the extended family unit?

DIABETES

In 2012, 29.1 million people or 9.3% of the population had diabetes. 11.2% of this figure includes persons 65 years or older (CDC, 2014d). Diabetes is a group of diseases marked by high levels of blood glucose resulting from problems in how insulin is produced, how insulin works, or both. Type I diabetes was previously called insulin-dependent diabetes mellitus or juvenile-onset diabetes, and it develops when the cells that produce the hormone insulin, known as beta cells, in the pancreas are destroyed (CDC, 2015h). Type 2 diabetes was previously called non-insulin-dependent diabetes mellitus or adult-onset diabetes, and this is a disorder in which the cells primarily within the muscles, liver, and fat tissue do not use insulin properly (CDC, 2015h). Diabetes is a major cause of adverse health outcomes in older adults. Diabetes can affect many parts of the body and is associated with heart disease, stroke, blindness, kidney failure, and lower limb amputation (CDC, 2015h). The risk factors for developing Type 2 diabetes is associated with older age (40+), obesity, family history of diabetes, history of gestational (during pregnancy) diabetes, impaired glucose metabolism, physical inactivity, and race/ethnicity (African Americans, Hispanics/Latinos, American Indians, some Asians and Native Hawaiians or other Pacific Islanders) (CDC, 2014d). Older adults with diabetes may also suffer from devastating conditions such as depression, cognitive impairment, muscle weakness (sarcopenia), falls and fractures, and physical frailty (Kim, Kim, Sung, Cho, & Park, 2012).

In older adults with diabetes, risks of disabilities related to mobility and daily tasks increase twofold. Individuals experience accelerated loss of lower extremity strength and muscle quality, as well as skeletal muscle mass (Gregg et al., 2002; Sinclair, 2000; Sinclair & Meneilly, 2006). These impairments in muscle function are important contributors to physical limitations. For example, approximately 25% of older adults with diabetes are unable to walk one-quarter of a mile, climb 10 stairs, or do housework, and about 50% have difficulty performing these tasks (Ghosh & Sinclair, 2006). Older adults with diabetes are also particularly vulnerable to falls and related complications. Falls are common occurrences in elderly people that often result in serious injury and loss of independent living. In a study of osteoporotic fractures, older women with diabetes were reported to have an increased risk of recurrent falls (Gregg et al., 2000). Diabetes is also a powerful predictor of falls in older adults with a disability.

Both weight loss and improved fitness are significant mediators for the prevention of mobility limitations (Gregg et al., 2000). Apart from intensive lifestyle intervention, better control over glucose levels may improve short-term and long-term maintenance of lower extremity function (Volpato et al., 2002).

Diagnosis

While diabetes is common in the older population, it can be difficult to diagnose because individuals are often asymptomatic (Brown, Mangioine, Saliba, & Sakinsain, 2003). Diagnosis of diabetes may be just one piece of a bigger picture, the so-called metabolic syndrome. The components of this syndrome include impaired fasting glucose, hypertension, hyperlipidemia (elevated triglycerides and low high-density lipoprotein [HDL]), and abdominal obesity. Metabolic syndrome leads to diabetes and cardiac disease, is a serious condition in older adults, and is on the rise in overweight children. The importance of recognizing and treating this syndrome aggressively by treating insulin resistance, hyperglycemia, and cardiac risk factors is key in reducing the cardiac mortality and morbidity that these patients face (Isomaa, Almgren, & Tuomi, 2001; Saad, Cardoso, Martins, Vilarde, & Filho, 2014).

Diabetes in older adults often presents itself atypically in the form of falls, urinary incontinence, cognitive impairment, or functional decline. Late-stage presentations are also seen with such complications as visual problems, myocardial infarction, and infections such as gangrene. Older people tend not to manifest the classic symptoms of fatigue, nocturia (nighttime urination), blurred vision, polyuria (frequent urination), weight loss, infections, polydipsia (frequent thirst), and hunger. This is because elderly individuals have a high renal threshold, and therefore polyuria is less frequent, polydipsia is often absent due to no renal water loss and impaired thirst mechanism, and weight loss is often attributed to other illnesses.

The diagnosis of diabetes is accomplished using several tests. A random glucose test can be given at any time during the day (NIA, 2012). The fasting plasma glucose test measures fasting plasma glucose (PG) levels, the oral glucose tolerance test checks blood glucose levels before and 2 hours after consuming a sweet drink, and the A1C test measures an individual's average blood glucose for 2 to 3 months (Kirkman et al., 2012; McNamara, 2006).

Treatment

The goals of diabetes management should be set according to the motivation, combined diseases, presence of complications, resources, support system, and life expectancy of each individual patient (Valderrama-Gama, Damian, Ruigomez, & Martin-Moreno, 2002). The goals for therapy in older individuals are no different than for others with diabetes. It is important to keep blood sugar levels within the normal range, or individuals may become confused, disoriented, or despondent. For many elderly people with diabetes, there is a lack of adequate control of blood sugar levels. The aim is to prevent acute symptoms and complications, avoid hypoglycemia (low glucose levels in the blood), and prevent or delay chronic complications. In older adults, it is important to consider coexisting illness such as dementia, life expectancy, and quality of life. Individualized approaches may be necessary.

Treatments range from diet and physical activity to oral hypoglycemic agents and insulin. Most older persons have developed personal strategies (e.g., pill boxes) to assist them with managing their diabetes. Proper treatment can be challenging because of other comorbidities; social situations; or limited finances, such as if health insurance does not fully cover expenses, each of which can impair the ability to adhere to the treatment.

An interdisciplinary team approach is necessary, including a dietician/nutritionist to teach healthy eating and develop meal plans for individual patients. Often with Type 2 diabetes, a weight management program is necessary to attain acceptable glucose levels. An exercise regimen of resistance training and aerobic activity is recommended for improved glucose control, lipid levels, and blood pressure. Together, these approaches decrease the risk of cardiovascular disease, and some older adults have been able to effectively manage their diabetes with such exercise and dietary changes. Even the frail elderly will benefit from a modified, low-intensity exercise program that includes strength training, even if it is from a sitting position. Overall, exercise in older adults has been shown to improve balance and strength and benefit overall health (McNamara, 2006).

Diabetes and Mental Health

Progressive cognitive decline and dementia are commonly observed in older adults with diabetes. According to a comprehensive meta-analysis, results indicated that diabetes is a risk factor for incident dementia and mild cognitive impairment (Anderson, Freedland, Clouse, & Lustman, 2001). Cognitive impairment is known to affect diabetes self-management, as individuals may become confused regarding their medications and/or insulin dosages. Therefore, older adults are more likely to experience treatment-related complications.

Depression is highly prevalent in older adults with diabetes. Depression can strike anyone, but people with diabetes may be at a greater risk (National Institute of Mental Health [NIMH], 2013). Diabetes doubles the risk of depression compared to those without the disorder. The chances of becoming depressed increase as the diabetes complications worsen (NIMH, 2013). Depression leads to poorer physical and mental functioning, so a person is less likely to follow a required diet or medication plan (NIMH, 2013).

Diabetes and Mental Health Practice

The professional counselor's role is primarily to educate older clients, monitor their compliance, and explore any impact the diagnosis has had on their ability to function. The counselor must play a supportive role and provide a safe environment that allows the client to express his or her emotions. Older persons may need reassurance and guidance from their counselor. The counselor needs to be prepared to address the problems that may arise from having a diagnosis of diabetes for an extended period of time. Some of these issues include vision problems, nerve damage in extremities, kidney problems, and poor healing ulcers/sores. While each individual is unique, the counselor must have the knowledge to provide the necessary education regarding subsequent problems that they might experience. Guided Practice Exercise 4.3 provides an opportunity to examine issues related to the treatment plan for an elderly client diagnosed with diabetes.

Guided Practice Exercise 4.3

Your elder client has just completed his assessment, and you have discovered that diabetes is one of his many medical problems. As a mental health counselor, how do you proceed in examining the complications related to this diagnosis? Is there a need to coordinate services with health care providers, and if so, which providers will you contact? How does the diagnosis of diabetes and its complications affect the mental status and emotional health of your client?

CANCER

Cancer is a class of diseases characterized by out-of-control cell growth. There are over 100 different types of cancer, and each is classified by the type of cell that is initially affected. The most common sites of cancer among men are lung, prostate, colon, rectum, stomach, and liver. The most common sites of cancer among women are breast, colon, rectum, lung, cervix, and stomach (CDC, 2015g). Cancer most commonly develops in older people. Seventy-eight percent of all cancer diagnoses are in people 55 years of age or older

(American Cancer Society [ACA], 2015). People who smoke, eat an unhealthy diet, or are physically inactive also have a higher risk of cancer (ACA, 2015). Nearly 14.5 million Americans with a history of cancer were alive in January 1, 2014 (ACA, 2015). Approximately 1,658,370 new cancer cases are expected to be diagnosed in 2015 (ACA, 2015), and in 2015, approximately 589,430 Americans are expected to die of cancer, or about 1,620 persons per day (ACA, 2015). Cancer is the second most common cause of death in the United States, exceeded only by heart disease (ACA, 2015). The 5-year survival rate for all cancers diagnosed in 2004–2010 was 68%, which is up from 49% in 1975–1977 (ACA, 2015). Older adults experience the majority of cancer diagnoses and deaths and make up the majority of cancer survivors (nearly half are 70 years of age and older) (ACA, 2015).

The probability of developing cancer increases for men and women as they age for all sites. For men ages 60 to 69, 15.1% or 1 in 7 individuals versus 10.0 or 1 in 10 women will develop cancer. For ages 70 and older, 36.0% or 1 in 3 men and 26.4% or 1 in 4 women will develop cancer. It must be acknowledged that a percentage for different cancer sites varies for both men and women (ACA, 2015). Older cancer patients are physiologically, psychologically, socially, economically, and culturally heterogeneous. As a result, there is a complexity in the care of older cancer patients that deserves to be addressed through research on this growing segment of the population (Ries et al., 2000; Yancik et al., 2001; Yancik & Holmes, 2001).

Causes of cancer include genes (the DNA type), carcinogens, and genes (the family type). Cells can experience uncontrolled growth if there are mutations to DNA, and therefore alterations occur to the genes involved in cell division. Carcinogens are a class of substances that are directly responsible for damaging DNA and promoting or aiding cancer. Examples include tobacco, asbestos, arsenic, radiation such as gamma and x-rays, the sun, and compounds in car exhaust fumes. Cancer can also be the result of a genetic predisposition that is inherited from family members. It is possible to be born with certain genetic mutations or a fault in a gene that makes one statistically more likely to develop cancer later in life (Crosta, 2015).

Impact of Aging

As we age, there is an increase in the number of possible cancer-causing mutations in our DNA. This makes age an important risk factor for cancer. Several viruses have been linked to cancer such as hepatitis B and C (causes of liver cancer) and human papillomavirus (a cause of cervical cancer). Human immunodeficiency virus (HIV) and anything else that suppresses or weakens the immune system inhibits the body's ability to fight infections and increases the chance of developing cancer (Crosta, 2015). There are many correlations between cancer and aging, which relate not just to how long the individual has been exposed to cancer causing agents but also the importance of interaction factors. Cancer and aging are also linked intrinsically; there is considerable evidence showing that the introduction and accumulation of somatic mutations (alterations in DNA) caused by excessive stress and combined with age-related faulty repair mechanisms is of particular importance (Skinner & Turker, 2005).

Cancers that occur more often in older adults, such as lung, colon, breast, and prostate cancer, have been shown to require multiple events which changes the genetic material (DNA). Other evidence that cancer and age are connected comes from studies of calorie reduction, which inhibits the expression of biological age and increases longevity. Reduction of total calories consumed per day (30% to 40% reduction) has been shown to have dramatic effects on aging and cancer in several experimental animal models. Calorie restriction (CR) slows the rate of aging; delays the appearance of age-related pathologies, including cancer; and extends the life span of several animal species (Hursting, Lavinge, Berrigan, Perkins, & Barrett, 2003).

Older adults respond differently to cancer treatments than younger people. This is partly attributable to age-associated physiologic changes, such as alterations in organ function. It is also influenced by the higher incidence of accompanying chronic conditions and use of medications in older adults, which may interact with cancer treatments (Hurria et al., 2015). According to the Centers for Disease Control and Prevention (2015), approximately 80% of older adults have one chronic condition, and 50% have greater than or equal to two. These factors make older adults more sensitive to toxicity and adverse effects resulting from treatment. In addition, the treatment of older adults is complicated by the fact that there is great heterogeneity in their health (Hurria et al., 2015). The underrepresentation of older adults in clinical trials means that clinicians have less evidence on how to treat the majority of patients with cancer and uncertain as to whether all older adults are able to tolerate and benefit from cancer therapy (Juliusson, Antunovic, & Derolf, 2009). Older patients receive chemotherapy less frequently than recommended by clinical practice guidelines, which could contribute to suboptimal health outcomes (Berry, Worni, & Pietrobon, 2013; Mandelblatt, et al., 2010).

Prevention

Finding cancer at its earliest, most treatable stage gives patients the greatest chance of survival (ACA, 2015). To help the public and health care providers make informed decisions about cancer screening, the American Cancer Society (2015) publishes a variety of early detection guidelines for various cancers, and it has implemented a number of aggressive awareness campaigns for the public and health care professionals. Cancer control involves primary and secondary cancer prevention, with the goal of reducing cancer-related morbidity and mortality. Primary prevention includes elimination of environmental carcinogens and stopping or reversing carcinogenesis (Anisimov, 2005) with drugs (chemoprevention). Secondary prevention includes early detection of cancer by screening individuals at risk (Beghe & Balducci, 2005). Age is the major risk factor for all common cancers, and cancer is the major cause of mortality for the American population under age 86 (Jemal et al., 2005). However, reduced life expectancy (Carey, Walter, Lindquist, & Covinski, 2004), higher prevalence of more indolent (slow-growing) tumors, and increased susceptibility to the complications of surgery may lessen the benefits of cancer prevention. Thus, cancer control strategies should be individualized and focused on older individuals who are more likely to benefit from them according to life expectancy and treatment tolerance (Beghe & Balducci, 2005).

Treatment

When making decisions about treatment, older adults and their physicians need to consider their overall health and ability to keep up with daily activities, and they may have a different set of concerns than other adults with cancer, which may affect how they cope with their disease (Navigating Cancer Care, 2012). Disease and disability that may interfere with cancer treatment and recovery are more likely to occur in older adults. Older adults with cancer may express concerns regarding maintaining independence, feelings of social isolation, spiritual concerns, financial concerns, physical limitations, and transportation (Navigating Cancer Care, 2012). All of these issues need to be addressed in relationship to their treatment process.

Older cancer patients face both clinical and broader institutional barriers to appropriate treatment and are less likely to have their cancer staged (Uyar, Frasure, Markman, & von Gruenigen, 2005). They may receive less aggressive treatment (e.g., doses of drugs below the level of therapeutic effectiveness). Older breast cancer patients are less likely to receive auxiliary lymph node dissection, adjuvant radiation therapy, or chemotherapy or hormone therapy (Rose et al., 2000). Further, older patients may not be referred to comprehensive cancer centers or offered participation in clinical trials. Assessments can form the basis for determining eligibility for trials and open communication as to older patients' interest in trial participation and referral to larger centers for second opinions or treatment plans (Bouchardy, Rapiti, Blagojevic, Vlastos, & Vlastos, 2007; Wedding, Honecker, Bokemeyer, Pientka, & Hoffen, 2007). Older patients, when selected carefully, appear to tolerate and respond well to cancer treatments (Kemeny, 2004).

The treatment and management decisions for older cancer patients should be guided by treatments for comorbid conditions, organ function, frailty, and cognitive status. Older persons in good health can benefit from treatment, but some may require reduced dosing due to intolerance (Bokemeyer, Aapro, & Courdi, 2006; Burdette-Radoux & Muss, 2006; Repetto, Biganzoli, & Koehne, 2003). Older cancer patients who are not suited for therapeutic approaches due to health status should receive palliative care. Palliative care is an approach that improves the quality of life of patients and their families facing the problem associated with life-threatening illness. Palliative care offers pain and symptom management and emotional and spiritual support when one faces a chronic, debilitating disease or life-threatening illness (Mayo Clinic, 2011). It is essential that patients and families are guided to palliative care, where they are assisted with decisions, receive support and communication between providers and patients, and are encouraged so that goals of care can be reassessed (Berger et al., 2006). Education is needed to overcome the misconception that older individuals do not benefit from preventive interventions. Guided Practice Exercise 4.4 examines numerous questions posed that may go beyond the knowledge of some mental health practitioners. In some cases, a referral might be necessary if the counselor feels that another professional may be more effective due to specialized expertise.

Guided Practice Exercise 4.4

Your elderly client did not attend her weekly session, and you later learn that she has been diagnosed with breast cancer. As a mental health counselor, how do you view your role in her care? To what extent do you feel comfortable inquiring regarding her health condition? What goals do you anticipate working on upon her return? Are you familiar with support groups for persons diagnosed with cancer? These questions, along with other pertinent questions, require answers to work constructively with this elderly client.

Cancer and Mental Health

A diagnosis of cancer in an older adult is a frightening diagnosis and evokes an array of emotions. Older adults are fearful of dying, of hospitalizations, and of treatments that can alter their physical appearance and negatively impact other areas of functioning. They may become depressed, anxious, and isolated/withdrawn and require assistance with ADLs and IADLs (managing checkbook, transportation, etc.). Helplessness, hopelessness, and feelings of doom may be expressed. Worries regarding financial matters, such as absenteeism from work, paying bills, and hospital costs, may also be expressed.

Older patients are in a fragile, vulnerable state, and with a supportive network of family and friends, they may be able to effectively address the treatment challenges that they will need to endure. However, when family members and/or treating professionals refer the client for counseling, it is usually to address issues that go beyond the scope of their practice. Increasing the psychological well-being of the older client is an integral component of the healing process.

Cancer and Mental Health Practice

Mental health counselors who possess knowledge of the symptoms and treatment modalities of cancer are in a unique position to intervene on behalf of their older clients. Older clients may possess a fatalistic attitude once a diagnosis of cancer has been determined and feel that life is not worth living. Knowledge of death, dying, and bereavement will be helpful, as well as palliative care. If the cancer has been effectively treated and the older client is in a state of remission, then the counselor may need to address fears related to the potential recurrence of the cancer. Cancer and aging are multidimensional processes that pose challenges to older patients and their families and require a multidisciplinary team of professionals. As such, the mental health counselor is in a unique position to partner with other professionals to provide the best treatment for his or her client.

In practice, life will change radically for the older client for a period of time. It may be difficult to return to the life prior to the diagnosis of cancer; however, the professional counselor can develop strategies to facilitate this transition over a period of time. Counselors are encouraged to engage their older clients in pursuit of any and all activities that they have been delaying. They should also refer their clients to agencies that provide social support, if their social support network is limited. Counselors need to remain mindful that their older clients may have problems with memory, experience anger, and feel out of control. Coping strategies will need to be taught and employed and at times assertiveness training may be needed as well. In practice, mental health counselors will educate, provide referrals, utilize counseling interventions, hold family meetings, and coordinate the treatment process with other members of the treatment team.

ARTHRITIS

Arthritis is strictly defined as inflammation occurring within the confines of the joints. It is a complex family of musculoskeletal disorders with many causes that are not yet fully understood, and so far there are no cures. There are more than 100 different types of arthritis, which destroy joints, bones, muscles, cartilage, and other connective tissues, hampering or halting physical movement. In older adults, the most common types are osteoarthritis, rheumatoid arthritis, and gout. Arthritis is the leading cause of disability in the United States, striking over 50 million Americans (CDC, 2014e). By 2030, an estimated 67 million Americans will have arthritis, unless the trend is reversed. Arthritis is not just a disease of old age, as two-thirds of individuals with arthritis are under the age of 65 (Arthritis Foundation, 2011). Arthritis is more common among women (26%) than men (19%) in every age group, and it affects members of all racial and ethnic groups. Arthritis is also more common among obese adults than among those who are normal weight or underweight (CDC, 2015e).

The impact of arthritis is extensive. People with arthritis rate their health as fair to poor. They are more likely to stay in bed because of illness, use more health services, move to a nursing home, and require more help with ADLs than people unaffected by arthritis. Almost any type of arthritis is progressive with aging and increasing disability affects function, independence, and the need for additional resources (Luggen & Meiner, 2002). Assessment of ADLs and IADLs, specifically asking about using the telephone, taking medications, and doing housework, is essential. Nearly 10% of community-living elders older than 65 need help with one or more ADLs, and these needs grow with increasing age (Novak, 2012). Guided Practice Exercise 4.5 examines issues related to an elderly client diagnosed with severe arthritis. While this chronic disease is not fatal, it can negatively impact the performance of routine activities.

Guided Practice Exercise 4.5

Your older client was recently hospitalized and discharged to home with specific instructions for managing her severe arthritis. She arrives late to her appointment by means of senior citizens transit services. You have 20 minutes left of her appointment time until your next client arrives. How will you use this limited time? What assessments do you need to better understand her presenting problems? Are there other health care providers involved in her care, and how do you access their assessments? Will you contact family members to obtain a more comprehensive perspective on your client's issues? Will you make a referral for an occupational therapy assessment? In 20 minutes, how realistic are these issues, and how can they be addressed?

Osteoarthritis

Osteoarthritis (OA) is a degenerative joint disease (DJD) characterized by the breakdown of joint cartilage and is the most common form of arthritis. It is associated with risk factors such as being overweight, a history of joint injury, and age (Arthritis Foundation, 2011). It is a nearly universally active, destructive process (Birchfield, 2002; Luggen, 2002), and it may be inflammatory or noninflammatory. The clinical features of OA are insidious pain onset, stiffness, and a progressive loss of function (Luggen, 2002). OA preferentially affects the hips, knees, finger joints, feet, and spine.

The goals of osteoarthritis treatment include alleviation of pain and improvement of functional status. Osteoarthritis is the leading cause of chronic disability in those older than 70 years (Lozada, 2015). Management strategies for osteoarthritis include nonpharmacological therapy, analgesics (painkillers), intra-articular therapy (corticosteroids/steroids injected directly into the joint space of a painful inflamed joint), surgery, and medical therapies. The goals of treatment are pain relief, improved function, and prevention of disability. Nonpharmacological therapy includes psychological and physical support; moist heat or cold packs; assistive devices such as canes, crutches, splints, and walkers; rest, diet, and improved nutrition; joint taping; exercise; tai chi; and physical therapy. Psychosocial support includes identifying and treating depression, which is common in elderly arthritis patients. Counseling and education can help patients participate in their own care and providing support by telephone can help reduce symptoms (Lozada & Altman, 2001). Physical therapy is a useful treatment modality and joint unloading (removing weight from the affected area) can be important as well.

Rheumatoid Arthritis

Rheumatoid arthritis (RA) is the second most common rheumatic disease, and it is the most destructive. RA is a chronic, progressive, systemic, auto-immune inflammatory disease of bone and connective tissue. It manifests itself in multiple joints of the body and the inflammatory process primarily affects the lining of the joints, but can also affect other organs (CDC, 2014). The incidence of RA is typically 2 to 3 times higher in women than men and the onset of RA, in both women and men is highest among those in their 60s (Silman & Hochberg, 2001). The cause of RA is not known. The course of RA is variable and unpredictable with flares and remissions or a continuously progressive course. About half of patients are disabled within 10 years (Suarez-Ahmacor & Foster, 2001).

Two patterns of RA are encountered in older persons (Kerr, 2003). The first belongs to those with the long-standing disease, who developed RA in their late 20s or early 30s, and over time have had considerable damage to multiple joints and possibly toxicity from years of treatment. The second pattern of onset is the development of RA after age 65. Individuals with this pattern of disease may have marked disability from joint pain and swelling, but are less likely to have destruction of their joints.

The goals of RA treatment are to stop inflammation (put disease in remission), relieve symptoms, prevent joint damage, improve physical function and overall well-being and reduce long-term complications (Arthritis Foundation, 2015). Pharmacological, surgical, and nonpharmacological treatments are utilized in treating older persons with RA. Pharmacological treatments are medications used to ease the symptoms and others used to slow or stop the course of the disease and to inhibit structural damage. Examples of drugs are corticosteroids, disease-modifying antirheumatic drugs (DMARDs), biologics (subset of DMARDs that work more quickly) and JAK inhibitors (subcategory of DMARDs which block the pathways). Surgical intervenes may not be needed, but if needed, the surgery is joint replacement surgery. The procedure involves replacing damaged parts of a joint with metal and plastic parts that are effective in the relief of pain and restoration of function in badly damaged joints (Arthritis, 2015). Nonpharmacological therapy includes local rest of an inflamed joint and splinting with emphasis on weight reduction and the use of walking aids. An occupational therapist can determine the needed devices (Lozada & Altman, 2001a). Environmental modifications must meet the patient's specific needs. Rest and exercise are equally important. Regular physical activity is essential since it helps decrease dysfunction and disability. Physical therapists can design an appropriate program for treatment (Lozado & Altman, 2001b).

Gout

Gout is a type of inflammatory arthritis highly prevalent in older adults and is one of the most painful. It is an immune response that occurs when a buildup of uric acid in the body causes crystal-like deposits to travel to the joints, causing sudden, severe attacks of pain and tenderness, redness, warmth, and swelling (Arthritis Foundation, 2011). Gout increases substantially with age, starting at age 40 to 50 in men and over 60 in women (Wortman & Kelley, 2001). Risk factors for gout include being overweight or obese, having hypertension, alcohol intake (beer and spirits more than wine), diuretic use (drugs that increase urination), a diet rich in meat and seafood, and poor kidney function (Choi, Atkinson, Karlson, Willet, & Curhan, 2004; Choi, Atkinson, Karlson, & Curhan, 2005; Krishman, 2013). The goals of gout management are to terminate acute attacks quickly and gently; prevent recurrences; prevent or reverse complications of crystals in joints, kidneys, and other sites; and prevent or reverse associated issues such as obesity, high triglycerides, and hypertension (Wortman & Kelley, 2001). Cold packs and rest are useful for relieving pain, splints limit mobilization to minimize pain or movement, steroids may be used to decrease inflammation, and modification of diet to decrease alcohol intake is also beneficial (Pagana & Pagana, 2013). Drinking too much alcohol can lead to hyperuricemia (build-up of uric acid in the blood) because alcohol interferes with the removal of uric acid from the body. When the kidneys are unable to process all of the uric acid in the blood, levels become too high and crystal deposits are formed (National Institute of Arthritis and Musculoskeletal and Skin Diseases, 2015).

Arthritis and Mental Health

Arthritis is a chronic disease that may include pain, swelling, and in some cases, deformity. Mild cases of arthritis are effectively managed with medication, but in more severe cases an elderly person may have immense difficulty in engaging in activities that require a great deal of movement and will have trouble performing personal and IADLs. Therefore, older persons with arthritis are at an increased risk for depression. They may require assistance with opening a jar, lifting a piece of furniture, or walking for long distances. The constriction of activities, along with feelings of being a burden, negatively impacts the older person's psychological well-being. While many older adults adapt and learn to live with the intermittent pain, others seek the services of counseling professionals. Guided Practice Exercise 4.6 provides the opportunity to experience challenges that come with being confined to a wheelchair.

Guided Practice Exercise 4.6

Get permission to use a wheelchair for one afternoon. For the entire afternoon, you must conduct all activities from the wheelchair. What was this experience like for you? What activities did you have difficulty with? Did you experience any environmental barriers? How do you feel you were perceived by others in the environment? Now imagine an elderly person with severe arthritis and diabetic neuropathy having no ability to ambulate independently. What are your thoughts regarding their situation?

Arthritis and Mental Health Practice

Arthritis is not fatal, but it is a chronic, potentially debilitating disease. Counselors with older clients must understand the physical manifestations of this disease as well as the social and psychological effects that may accompany it. The negative effects of arthritis will be presented to the counselor for effective intervention strategies.

Professional counselors will increase their effectiveness if they are knowledgeable regarding arthritis and demonstrate a caring and optimistic attitude toward their clients. They must address the physical and social issues as well as feelings of dependency, being a burden, and sadness. The pain that older clients feel is extremely important to acknowledge because it can be experienced daily. Allowing more time for clients to complete assessments, move from one location to another, and take breaks as needed are also considerations within counseling sessions. Counselors will also need to pay close attention to verbal and nonverbal clues that the older client is experiencing pain. For example, facial grimaces, clenched fists, and tightening hands around armrests are nonverbal indications of discomfort. If a concern exists regarding pain medication, whether an over-the-counter or prescription medicine, communication with the client's primary physician is required.

Counselors will also need to assist older clients with learning ways to manage their arthritis, which will improve their quality of life. They should encourage clients to become physically active, despite any resistance they may have. Physical activity lessens pain and improves physical function, mental health, and overall well-being. Encouraging patients to maintain healthy weight and adhere to their treatment regimen are also important considerations.

OSTEOPOROSIS

Osteoporosis is a skeletal disorder characterized by compromised bone strength, predisposing an individual to an increased risk of fracture. Bone strength reflects the integration of two main features: bone density and bone quality (Hellekson, 2002). It is estimated that osteoporosis affects about 10 million Americans over age 50, and another 33.6 million have low bone mass. It is a silent disease until a fracture occurs. About one in two postmenopausal women and one in five men over 50 will have an osteoporosis-related fracture during their lifetime (National Osteoporosis Foundation, 2013). Because of increased bone loss after menopause in women and age-related bone loss in both women and men, the prevalence of osteoporosis increases markedly with age from 2% at 50 years to more than 25% at 80 years in women (National Institute for Health and Clinical Excellence [NICE], 2012). Fractures due to osteoporosis are most likely to occur in the hip, spine, and wrist, but any bone can be affected (National Osteoporosis Foundation, 2013). Long-term morbidity of osteoporotic fractures can include chronic pain, loss of ability to ambulate, and nursing home placement (Braithwaite, Col, & Wong, 2003; Huddleston & Whitford, 2001; Oleksik, Lips, & Dawson, 2000).

In the United States, 52.4 million people were estimated to have osteoporosis or low bone mass in 2010 (National Osteoporosis Foundation, 2013), resulting in more than 2 million fractures in that year alone. The estimated $18.7 billion in direct medical costs of these fractures was largely borne by the Medicare program. Population growth is projected to increase these costs to $25.3 billion in 2025, assuming constant rates of testing and treatment (Burge, Dawson-Hughes, & Solomon, 2007). Among Medicare beneficiaries over age 65, about 8% had a primary diagnosis of osteoporosis in 2006, up from 4% in 1997. It is unclear how much of this increase is related to greater incidence of disease and how much is related to more awareness and treatment. Seven percent of Medicare beneficiaries had osteoporosis, 8% of these beneficiaries were 65 years of age and over, and 2% were male and 11% were female (CMS, 2012). Over two-thirds of Medicare beneficiaries had two or more chronic conditions, and 14% had 6 or more chronic conditions (CMS, 2012). Sixty-three percent of 65- to 74-year-olds, 78% of 75- to 84-year-olds, and 83% of 85 and over had two or more chronic conditions (CMS, 2012). In addition, 72% of women and 65% of men had two or more chronic conditions.

At present, the only clinical index of bone quality is a history of fragility fracture. A fragility fracture is any fall from a standing height or less that results in a fracture (Goulet & Cumming, 2015). A fragility fracture occurs in the absence of major trauma, such as during coughing or as a result of a fall from standing height. The most common sites for fragility fractures are the wrist, hip, and spine. A prior fragility fracture is associated with a 1.5- to 9.5-fold increased risk of future fracture, depending on the person's age and the number and site of previous fractures (Klotzbuecher, Ross, Landsman, Abbot, & Berger, 2000). Hip fractures are 8.4 to 36% excess mortality within 1 year, with a higher mortality in men than in women (Abrahamsen, van Staa, Ariely, Olson, & Cooper, 2009), additionally hip fractures are followed by a 2.5-fold increased risk of future fractures (Colon-Emeric, Kuchibhatla, & Pieper, 2003). Approximately 20% of hip fracture patients require long-term nursing home care, and only 40% fully regain their pre-fracture level of independence (U.S. Department of Health and Human Services, 2004). Fragility fractures can also reduce quality of life and have been associated with fear of falling (Adachi et al., 2001; Papaioannou et al., 2002; Petrella, Payne, Meyers, Overend, & Chesworth, 2000). Approximately 50% of community-living individuals do not regain their pre-fracture level of mobility and are dependent on assistive devices post-hip fracture (Wiktorowicz, Goeree, Papaioannou, Adachi, & Papadimitropoulos, 2001).

A time trade-off study revealed that 80% of women aged 75 years and older would prefer death than experience the loss of independence and quality of life associated with a hip fracture and subsequent nursing home admission (Salkeld et al., 2000). The clinical consequences of vertebral fracture include acute and chronic pain, reduced quality of life, functional impairment, and increased risk of future hip and vertebral fracture (Papaioannou et al., 2002). According to the National Institutes of Health (NIH) (2015), genetics may determine up to 80% of the risk for osteoporosis. Genetic risk factors include gender (female), ethnicity (Caucasian and Asian), body size (small frame, low body weight-less than 125 pounds), and family history (maternal history of osteoporosis, hip fracture, smoking, tallness, thinness). Additionally after age 50, the rapid and severe decrease in estrogen production that occurs during and after menopause increases the risk for osteoporosis. Modifiable osteoporosis risk factors include changing diet and habits, decreasing or eliminating cigarette smoking, excessive alcohol use, and caffeine intake. Also inactivity/sedentary lifestyle, inadequate calcium and phosphorous intake and lack of vitamins are changes that can be modified to decrease risk of osteoporosis (Swierzewski, 2015).

Treatment

Older adults with osteoporosis use many health services. Experts have suggested that health professionals can take a number of steps to improve bone health, such as identifying and treating individuals at high risk for bone disorders and educating them about how to prevent and manage bone disease (Office of the Surgeon General, 2004). Nonpharmacologic interventions, such as diet, exercise, and fall prevention, are essential in prevention and management. Regular exercise may be one of the only ways to prevent fractures due to osteoporosis (Kamus, 2014). Being active is a proven way to help bone mass, density, and strength. Oral protein and energy supplementation after hip fracture may reduce the number of patients with complications and unfavorable outcomes (Avenell & Handoll, 2003). Adequate calcium and vitamin D are crucial in preventing bone loss. Calcium and vitamin D supplementation in combination have been shown to significantly reduce hip fractures in older women.

Osteoporosis and Mental Health

The physical consequences of osteoporosis can have a devastating impact on an older person's psychological and social well-being. Adults with severe osteoporosis often feel a sense of hopelessness, suffer a loss of self-esteem, and become depressed. They may curtail their activities for fear of falling. Working individuals may be forced to quit their jobs because they are unable to lift, carry, or bend. Others may experience a loss of familial roles. For example, grandparents who cannot carry their grandchildren for fear of fractures may be denied an important means of bonding. Individuals may be unable to do simple household chores and routine household maintenance.

Osteoporosis and Mental Health Practice

Professional counselors will be required to increase their knowledge of osteoporosis and its impact, as they will provide psycho-educational and counseling services to their older clients. They should support a healthy lifestyle by encouraging the inclusion of calcium and vitamin D into their client's daily diet. The hormone estrogen, which prevents bone loss, may be indicated and should be discussed with the older client and his or her physician. Addressing issues of low self-esteem, hopelessness, and depression during counseling sessions will require patience and an examination of the negative impact osteoporosis has had on fulfilling clients' routine responsibilities. Providing individual counseling and family counseling will reinforce that the disease has an impact on the entire family system, not just the older client.

FALLS

Millions of older adults fall each year, causing injuries and increasing the risk of death. Falls have many causes, including gait and balance problems, neurological and musculoskeletal problems, use of medications affecting balance, impaired thinking and memory, impaired vision, and environmental hazards (slippery floors, uneven surfaces, stairs, poor lighting, loose rugs). Additionally, many older adults fail to exercise regularly, resulting in poor muscle tone, decreased strength, and loss of bone mass and flexibility, which makes them more prone to falling (Chang, Lynm, & Glass, 2010).

Falls can be a consequence of osteoporosis because of the weakening, less dense bones. Fractures and breaks associated with osteoporosis often take much longer to heal and can really interfere with an older adult's ability to perform previous activities. They can cause permanent disability and, in some cases, even death. Fractures from falls are most common in the hip, wrist, and spine. Of all fractures, hip fractures are the most detrimental to a person's health. It is hard to recover from a hip fracture and afterward many people are not able to live on their own (CDC, 2015a). Each year at least 250,000 older people are hospitalized for hip fractures. More than 95% of hip fractures are caused by falling, and falls are the most common cause of traumatic brain injuries (CDC, 2015a). Treating fall injuries was $34 billion in 2013, and both the number of falls and the costs to treat fall injuries are likely to rise (CDC, 2015a). Anyone of any age can have osteoporosis, although it is most common in white and Asian women over the age of 50 (Admin, 2011). Guided Practice Exercise 4.7 provides the opportunity to conduct an environmental assessment and to make recommendations to decrease the risk for falls.

Guided Practice Exercise 4.7

Visit an elderly person and assess his or her environment to decrease the risk for falling. Identify areas that place this elder at risk for falls. Provide solutions to minimize the risks and share this information with the older adult and his or her family. What were your impressions of this experience and how can you incorporate this information in counseling sessions with clients?

Fall Prevention Strategies

One of the most important strategies to preventing falls is regular exercise and remaining active, which maintains bone mass, density, and strength. Some studies show that the best type of exercise for bone strength is impact type exercises (CDC, 2015a). However, both impact exercises (walking, running, aerobics) and nonimpact (resistance or strength training, weight lifting) exercises have a positive impact on bone in postmenopausal women at the lumbar spine and femoral neck. Other types of exercises can improve balance, coordination, and reaction time. Improving these things can reduce the risk of falling. Beginning exercise and being active before or at the start of puberty and continuing this through adulthood is the only proven way to improve bone strength and lessen the chance of falls (Kamus, 2014).

Multifactorial risk factor screening and intervention programs, muscle strengthening and balance training, and home hazard assessment and modification are a few interventions that have been proven to reduce falls in elderly people (Chang et al., 2004; Gillespie et al., 2003). Hip protectors have shown some promise in reducing hip fractures in individuals living in nursing homes who are at high risk of fracture; however, adherence with wearing the protectors can be a problem (Parker, Gillespie, & Gillespie, 2004). Strengthening of the back extensions and postural retraining are key elements of an osteoporosis rehabilitation program aimed at reducing falls and future fractures in individuals with vertebral fractures (Sinaki, 2003). Given the escalating risk of future fracture in individuals, it remains critical to assess patients who are at risk. Guided Practice Exercise 4.8 explores ways to manipulate the furniture in the home environment to minimize risk for falls. While this may be considered a minor issue, it must be remembered that older adults may bruise, become disfigured, or fracture a bone, which will severely impair their functioning and may require hospitalization.

Guided Practice Exercise 4.8

Older adults who have experienced falls may develop a fear of falling, which adversely affects their activities. From an environmental perspective, how would you rearrange the furniture in an older person's home to decrease the potential for falls? What home modifications would you suggest? What assistive devices can you foresee this older adult might need?

Falls and Mental Health

Loss of balance and coordination with age can cause a shuffling gait. A change in gait is not harmful in and of itself; however, it may limit an individual's activity. Restrictions in activity, in turn, may cause further declines in physical functioning and increase the risk of a fall. Half of falls result in minor injuries, but 5 to 10% result in serious injury such as a deep cut, broken bone, or head injury (Davison, Bond, Dawson, Steen, & Kenny, 2005). Older clients may lose their confidence in performing routine activities and become fearful of falling. They also might experience feelings of anxiety, social withdrawal, and depression. While these feelings may be situation specific, if they are prolonged and left unaddressed, they could develop into major psychiatric diagnoses.

Falls and Mental Health Practice

Mental health counselors working with older clients will educate them on strength and balance training for preventing falls. In order to provide effective counseling services, counselors must become aware of strategies to prevent falls by environmental monitoring. Counselors can survey the environment for obstacles, such as poor lighting, loose carpets, lack of handrails, and poorly constructed steps. Professional counselors can coordinate with the older client's primary care physician to request a home visit by an occupational therapist to evaluate and make recommendations to modify the home environment.

When older clients fall, some develop a fear of falling syndrome. They become afraid, and this fear further restricts their ADLs and enjoyment in social activities. They may exhibit symptoms of anxiety and depression that have resulted from falls requiring hospitalization and subsequent rehabilitation. The mental health counselor will provide intervention strategies to desensitize older clients to their fear of falling, provide cognitive restructuring to increase their self-esteem and activity level, and assess the extent of their anxiety and depressive symptoms. Coordination of treatment efforts may require communication with their primary care physician or a geriatric psychiatrist, if it is determined that medications are needed.

VISION DISORDERS

Vision loss is one of the health complications that older adults fear most. More than 2.9 million Americans have a visual impairment (CDC, 2011). By age 65, 1 in 3 Americans have some form of vision-impairing eye disease (Sollitto, 2015). There are four major age-related eye diseases that affect older adults, which include glaucoma, cataracts, macular degeneration, and diabetic retinopathy (Sollitto, 2015).

Adults with visual impairments may suffer from depression, social withdrawal, and isolation. These individuals are at a greater risk for falls as well as potential hospitalization due to self-administered medication errors (Pelletier & Thomas, 2009). Hallucinations can be associated with progressive vision loss. Though they are harmless, they can be frightening or disturbing to those who experience them. Guided Practice Exercise 4.9 examines challenges in negotiating one's environment with impaired vision.

Guided Practice Exercise 4.9

Go to a nearby convenience store and purchase a pair of eyeglasses. Take a bar of soap and rub against the lenses, which should leave a cloudy residue. Now place the glasses on in the comfort of your home. How does it feel to navigate around your environment? Are you experiencing any difficulty in performing your ADLs (e.g., dressing, bathing, combing your hair)? Can you imagine what older persons experience when they have severe visual impairment?

The following practices should be implemented with older adults and are highly recommended:

- Periodic screening for vision problems
- Dilated eye examination within a year of diagnosis of diabetes
- Tight control of glucose and blood pressure
- Smoking cessation counseling because it is linked to causes of progressive visual impairment
- Antioxidant and zinc supplements taken daily, which may delay the progression of age-related macular degeneration in some persons with advanced disease (Pelletier & Thomas, 2009).

Though these practices may not prevent vision loss altogether, they may help to delay its onset.

Cataracts

Cataracts, the disabling opacification, or clouding, of the lens, are the leading cause of visual impairment among older adults. In the United States, approximately 50% of people aged 65 or more have some degree of lens clouding (Nordqvist, 2014). Seventy percent of Americans aged 75 or more have their vision significantly impaired by cataracts (Nordqvist, 2014). The number of people in the United States affected by cataracts is estimated to rise to 30.1 million people in the next 20 years, an increase of 50% because people will live longer (Nordqvist, 2014). They affect nearly 20.5 million Americans age 40 and older. By age 80, more than half of all Americans have cataracts (National Eye Institute [NEI], 2010). Women are more likely to develop cataracts than men, and African Americans and Hispanic Americans are at particularly high risk. About 50% of adults manifest early cataracts by age 75, and by age 80 close to 70% of adults exhibit clinically significant cataracts (NEI, 2010). In 2013, visual limitations among persons 65 years and over were 14.3% (CDC, 2013). For persons 65–74 years of age, 11.5% had visual limitations and 18.0% were 75 years and over (CDC, 2013). By 2050, the number of people in the United States with cataracts is expected to double to about 50 million (NEI, 2010).

Risk factors for cataracts beyond aging include sunlight, steroid use, and smoking (Nordqvist, 2014). Cataracts reduce acuity (sharpness), color discrimination, and contrast sensitivity and increase susceptibility to disability glare. Fortunately, cataracts are readily treated by the replacement of the natural lens with a synthetic intraocular lens (Kline, 2003).

Macular Degeneration

Macular degeneration, often called age-related macular degeneration (AMD), is an eye disorder associated with aging and results in damaging sharp and initial vision (CDC, 2013). There are two types of macular degeneration. The "dry" or early form of the disease causes more impairment of acuity, as the center of the retina begins to deteriorate. The late form is accompanied by the growth of fragile new retinal blood vessels (neovascularization) that leak blood and fluid and is referred to as the exudative or "wet" form of the disease (CDC, 2013).

It destroys the macula, the part of the eye that provides sharp, central vision needed to see objects clearly (NEI, 2010). The risk of macular degeneration with age and the disease is most common among older white Americans, affecting more than 14% of white Americans age 80 and older (NEI, 2010). In 2010, 2.5 percent of white adults age 50 and older had macular degeneration and by comparison macular degeneration affected 0.9% each of blacks, Hispanics, and people of other races (NEI, 2010). Women generally have a longer life expectancy than men and are therefore more likely to develop age-related eye disease such as macular degeneration, and in 2010, 65% of cases were in women compared with 35% in men (NEI, 2010). By 2050, the estimated number of people with macular degeneration is expected to more than double from 2.07 million to 5.44 million, and white Americans will continue to account for the majority of cases (NEI, 2010).

Dry AMD is when the macula thins over time as part of the aging process, gradually blurring central vision. The dry form is more common and accounts for 70% to 90% of cases of AMD, and it progresses more slowly than the wet form (CDC, 2013). Over time, as less of the macula functions, central vision is gradually lost in the affected eye and dry AMD affects both eyes (CDC, 2013). While photodynamic and/or antioxidant therapy may slow the progression of neovascularization, no current treatments can reverse the vision loss. The severe loss of acuity, color perception, and contrast sensitivity with age-related macular degeneration (AMD) can impair the patient's ability to carry out even basic activities of daily life (Kline, 2003). Age is the biggest risk factor for developing macular degeneration. After age 75, up to 46% of people have some form of it (Sollitto, 2015). Family history, race (whites have a higher risk than blacks or Hispanics), and smoking are other risk factors (Sollitto, 2015).

Glaucoma

Glaucoma is a group of eye diseases that, when left untreated, damage the optic nerve and can lead to blindness. It is a progressive loss of peripheral vision due to damage to sensory neurons where they converge to form the optic nerve, which usually occurs in association with elevated intraocular pressure, or the fluid pressure in the eye. In addition to "tunnel vision," glaucoma can result in losses of contrast sensibility, night vision, motion perception, and color vision. Glaucoma usually produces no early warning signs and no symptoms until it has progressed to the point of stealing sight. Risk factors for glaucoma include age, family history of glaucoma, taking steroid medications, and being nearsighted (Sollitto, 2015). The risk of blindness is four times greater in African Americans than in Caucasians, and the risk is greater for African Americans over the age of 60 who have family members with glaucoma or who are diabetic or very nearsighted. Daily activities that demand good peripheral vision, such as walking, obstacle avoidance, and driving, can be impaired early in the disease (Aging Care, 2015; Coeckelbergh, Cornelissen, Brouwer, & Kooijman, 2002).

Glaucoma has no cure, but it can be controlled. Treatment may include medications and surgery, and although treatment focuses on reducing pressure in the eye, it is possible to have higher than normal eye pressure and not have glaucoma. Moderate glaucoma often responds well to drugs that reduce watery fluid in the front and rear chambers of the eye. There is no way to prevent glaucoma, but regular comprehensive eye examinations are the best way to identify disease before it affects vision. Guided Practice Exercise 4.10 increases awareness of visual problems and devices that allow older adults to continue with their responsibilities in life.

Guided Practice Exercise 4.10

Are you aware of the common visual problems experienced by older adults? Are these problems considered in the work that you do? What adaptive devices are you familiar with that will aid older adults with visual deficits?

Vision Disorders and Mental Health

Most visually impaired older adults have some degree of partial vision as opposed to being completely blind. Severe vision loss is a serious matter, for it can limit an individual's activities, lower self-esteem, and lead to a loss of independence (Pelletier & Thomas, 2009). Older people need more light to perceive depth and to see clearly. Diminishing depth perception can be dangerous, because it can cause an individual to trip over things or miss his or her footing on steps or curbs. Poor vision forces older people to limit their activities and give up pleasurable hobbies such as gardening, cooking, sewing, and traveling. Driving ability might also be affected when vision is impaired (Alma et al., 2011).

Loss of self-esteem and sadness over restriction of activities and decreased independence are some of the issues that affect the psychological well-being of older clients. A potential loss of driving privileges for many older persons could be viewed as the last sign of their independence and may result in isolation, withdrawal, sadness, and a perception of being a burden on family, friends, and neighbors. These feelings need to be assessed to enhance the quality of life for older adults.

Vision Disorders and Mental Health Practice

Professional counselors who are cognizant of natural changes in vision throughout the aging process and the major vision disorders will have the knowledge required to provide therapeutic interventions with older clients. Older clients will present with expressions of being a burden on others if they require assistance. They may question their self-worth due to their inability to engage in previous activities that brought them satisfaction. The emotional changes associated with the threat of losing or having lost their license will become a central issue within the counseling sessions. Counselors will be required to educate clients on modifications in their environment to compensate for vision problems. Counselors should obtain large print screening instruments or have available devices to enlarge fine print during sessions. Arranging counseling sessions with family members will provide the support the older client will need to attend to the challenges associated with vision loss. A supportive network of family and significant others is instrumental in enhancing satisfaction with life. Counselors will also encourage and reinforce all rehabilitative efforts that are a component of their client's treatment plan.

CEREBROVASCULAR DISEASE

Cerebrovascular diseases are conditions caused by problems that affect the blood supply to the brain. The four most common types are stroke, transient ischemic attack (TIA), subarachnoid hemorrhage, and vascular dementia. A stroke occurs when a clot blocks the blood supply to the brain or when a blood vessel in the brain bursts (CDC, 2015f). TIA is a temporary ball in the blood supply to one part of the brain resulting in brief symptoms similar to stroke (CDC, 2015f). Subarachnoid hemorrhage is a type of stroke where blood leaks out of the brain's blood vessels on the surface of the brain (CDC, 2015f). Finally, vascular dementia is persistent impairment in mental ability resulting from stroke or other problems with blood circulation to the brain (CDC, 2015f). Stroke is the fifth leading cause of death in the United States, killing nearly 130,000 Americans each year, which equates to 1 of every 20 deaths (CDC, 2015f). Every year, about 800,000 people in the United States have a stroke, and approximately 610,000 of these are first or new strokes, and 185,000 are recurrent strokes (Mozzafarian et al., 2015). Disruption of circulation results in tissue death, as shown by persistent clinical signs and abnormalities on neuroimaging that are characteristic of infarction (tissue death due to lack of oxygen) (Albers, Clark, Madden, & Hamilton, 2002). Depending on the extent and location of damage to brain tissue, a stroke may profoundly affect an individual's physical, mental, and social functioning (Clark, Black, & Colantonio, 2002; Michael & Shraughnessy, 2006; Sturm, Donovan, Macdonell, McNeil, & Thrift, 2000).

Age is the single most important risk factor for stroke, and clinical and functional consequences may be compounded by other conditions associated with aging, such as cardiovascular and metabolic disease. For each successive 10 years after 55, the stroke rate more than doubles for men and women (Control, 2006). Nearly three-quarters of all strokes occur in people older than 65 years. Stroke incidence rates are 1.25 times greater in men, but because women tend to live longer than men, more women die of strokes each year (Thom, Haase, & Rosamond, 2006).

However, stroke is not an inevitable consequence of aging. By identifying and modifying risk factors which include hypertension, dyslipidemia (characterized by elevated total or LDL cholesterol levels, or low levels of HDL cholesterol), smoking, diabetes, obesity, physical inactivity, excessive alcohol intake, and diets high in saturated fats and low in fruits and vegetables, there are opportunities to reduce the incidence and mortality of the condition (MacKay & Mensah, 2004; Michael & Straughnessy, 2006; Rodgers et al., 2004). Guided Practice Exercise 4.11 explores challenges faced by victims of strokes, assessments utilized in examining functional ability, and rehabilitation professionals required on this multidisciplinary team.

Guided Practice Exercise 4.11

Cerebrovascular disease poses challenges to older adults in their daily functioning. Go online and collect data regarding the treatment modalities to assist victims of stroke regain their premorbid functioning. Identify rehabilitation professionals who are critical to his or her recovery and the various types of functional assessments used.

Stroke Prevention and Treatment

Eighty percent of all strokes are preventable (American Stroke Association, 2015). It starts with managing key risk factors, including high blood pressure, cigarette smoking, atrial fibrillation, and physical inactivity (American Stroke Association, 2015). More than half of all strokes are caused by uncontrolled hypertension, making it the most important risk factor to control (American Stroke Association, 2015). Medical treatments may be used to control blood pressure and/or manage atrial fibrillation, and these medicines include anticoagulants or antiplatelets and antihypertensives. Antiplatelet agents such as aspirin and anticoagulants such as warfarin interfere with the blood's ability to clot and can play a role in preventing stroke (American Stroke Association, 2015). Antihypertensives are medications that treat high blood pressure, and depending on the type of medication, they can lower blood pressure by opening the vessels, decreasing blood volume, or decreasing the rate and/or force of heart contraction (American Stroke Association, 2015). Additionally, when arteries show plaque buildup or blockage, medical procedures may be needed such as carotid endarterectomy and angioplasty or stents. Carotid endarterectomy is also called carotid artery surgery and is a procedure in which blood vessel blockage is surgically removed from the carotid artery. Doctors sometimes use balloon angioplasty and implantable steel screens called stents to treat cardiovascular disease and can help open up the blocked bold vessel (American Stroke Association, 2015).

The major goals of treatment include minimizing brain damage, preventing complications, and reducing the possibility of stroke recurrence. All strategies of demonstrated value in stroke prevention are pertinent in the care of older adults. Control of hypertension, resolution of dyslipidemia, management of diabetes mellitus, anticoagulation therapy (drugs to reduce the body's ability to form clots in the blood), promotion of exercise and healthy diet, and cessation of smoking are obligatory at all ages but are of particular importance in older adults (Barnett, 2002).

An acute stroke is a medical emergency, and the sooner treatment is given in a hospital, the less damage is likely to occur (NHS, 2015). The goals of acute stroke management include minimizing brain damage and restoration of perfusion (delivering blood to a capillary bed in its biological tissue). These goals may be reached by utilizing several different approaches. Thrombolytic therapy with recombinant tissue plasminogen activator (rt-PA) (drugs administered to break up or dissolve blood clots) administered intravenously within 3 hours of stroke onset for patients who meet strict eligibility criteria has been shown to save lives and reduce disability despite an early risk of intracerebral hemorrhage, in which blood leaks in the brain (Society of Neuro Interventional Surgery, 2014; Wardlaw, del Zoppo, Yamaguchi, & Berge, 2003). Administering aspirin (75 to 150 milligrams [mg] per day) within the first few days after stroke will reduce the relative risk of stroke (and other adverse vascular accidents) by about 20% (Antithrombotic Trialists' Collaboration, 2002). However, the use of anticoagulants in acute stroke has not been proven to be of net benefit (Gubitz, Sandercock, & Counsell, 2004). Restoration of functional independence is critical, and reliable evidence from reviews of randomized trials strongly supports a policy of caring for all patients with acute stroke on a geographically defined stroke unit with a coordinated multidisciplinary team (Stroke Unit Trialists' Collaboration, 2001). Such an approach will result in less death and dependency than thrombolytic therapy because far more patients are eligible for stroke unit care.

Primary stroke prevention refers to the treatment of individuals with no history of stroke, while secondary stroke refers to the treatment of individuals who have already had a stroke or transient ischemic attack (Silver, 2015). New guidelines on the primary prevention of stroke include use of new oral anticoagulants, home self-monitoring of blood pressure in hypertensive patients, and all patients should follow the Mediterranean diet supplemented with nuts and reduce sodium intake and smoking cessation (Silver, 2015). Risk reduction measures in primary stroke prevention include the use of antihypertensive medications, smoking cessation, dietary intervention, weight loss, and exercise (Silver, 2015). Modifiable risk factors include the following: hypertension, cigarette smoking, diabetes, dyslipidemia, atrial fibrillation, sickle cell disease, postmenopausal HRT, depression, diet and activity, and weight and body fat (Silver, 2015). Secondary prevention of stroke can be summarized by the following: use antiaggregants (e.g., aspirin) and anticoagulants (e.g., warfarin), prescribe blood pressure-lowering medication, cease cigarette smoking, prescribe cholesterol-lowering medications and perform carotid revascularization, and finally adhere to a healthy diet and incorporate exercise into one's life (Silver, 2015).

Prevention of complications is another goal of acute stroke management because people with acute stroke are at a higher risk of complications such as infection, pneumonia, skin breakdown, and deep venous thrombosis (blood clot that forms in a deep vein). Reducing the risk of stroke recurrence is another major goal. Secondary prevention is accomplished by careful attention to risk factor modification. Hypertension must be treated aggressively and blood pressure maintained at acceptable standards (Canadian Hypertension Society, 2005; Progress Collaborative Group, 2001). There is convincing evidence for the use of statins (cholesterol lowering medication) in people with stroke and TIA (similar to a stroke but usually lasts a few minutes and causes no permanent damage), even if their LDL cholesterol level is not significantly elevated (Progress Collaborative Group, 2001). Regular monitoring of blood glucose levels in diabetics is essential, and smoking cessation strategies should be employed whenever possible.

Cerebrovascular Disease and Mental Health

Cerebrovascular disease is a leading cause of serious long-term disability, and its effects can have enormous psychological effects on older adults. Some strokes are major, and some older persons experience "mini strokes" or TIAs that can occur several years before the onset of a major stroke. Older adults and their families need to seek treatment quickly to potentially minimize the negative consequences of the stroke. Older clients may experience weakness, fatigue, numbness, difficulty speaking or understanding, dizziness, and other symptoms following a stroke. They may become depressed, have difficulty with ambulation or performing basic activities, and may have difficulty with communication and comprehension. Feelings of hopelessness, helplessness, and sadness may be experienced because the effects of the stroke have permeated all aspects of the older person's life. Clients will have to endure comprehensive rehabilitation efforts in an attempt to regain functioning. Frustration, anger, resentment, and depression may be manifested; however, professionals need to remain patient and diligent throughout the rehabilitative process.

Cerebrovascular Disease and Mental Health Practice

Mental health professionals will be challenged to address the psychological issues that accompany physical and cognitive impairment resulting from a stroke. Counselors will need to be aware of all health care providers providing treatment for their older client. They may, at times, need to coordinate the treatment efforts, make referrals as needed, consult with the treatment team, and advocate on behalf of their client. Within the counseling session modifications, the use of assessment instruments may be necessary, varying modes of communication may be required, abbreviating sessions should be a consideration, and a family systems approach should be emphasized. Counselors will intervene at an appropriate time when his or her client's primary physician indicates the client is ready for treatment intervention. Careful listening, patience, and an optimistic outlook on the part of the counselor may increase the effectiveness of any interventions employed. Counselors need to come to an understanding that the lives of their older client and their family might be changed forever as a result of the stroke.

HIV/AIDS

Few people think of the elderly when they hear about human immunodeficiency virus (HIV) or acquired immunodeficiency syndrome (AIDS). HIV is a specific virus that destroys the T cells (specifically CD4) that are widespread in the body's internal immune system. The T cells are responsible for "fighting off" diseases and infections. Therefore, individuals who have HIV will become more vulnerable to diseases that their bodies should be able to fight off, including pneumonia, common colds, and other viruses. AIDS occurs when HIV has weakened the immune system to the point at which a person can get life-threatening infections and cancers. Adults ages 65 to 74, compared with the total population, have about one-half the death rates due to HIV (National Center for Health Statistics, 2010). The National Institute on Aging (NIA) (2008) goes on to say that women and people of color run a higher than average risk of getting AIDS.

In addition to the physical issues and ailments associated with contracting HIV, there are various psychosocial issues to address regarding HIV, especially among the elderly population. The stigma, or negative and discriminatory beliefs, associated with HIV is frightening. The term *invisible* has been used to describe many groups affected by the AIDS epidemic, including the elderly. Relatively little attention has been paid to the present and future aspects of HIV in the older adult. Although the average age of a first diagnosis of HIV/AIDS is rising, many aspects of these conditions, such as response to therapy, drug interactions, and updated epidemiological and clinical data, have not been studied in controlled trials with older adults (Manfredi, 2004). People ages 55 years and older accounted for approximately one quarter (24% or 288,700) of the estimated 1.2 million people living with HIV infection in the United States in 2012 (Centers for Disease Control and Prevention, 2015c). In 2013, there were an estimated 8,575 new HIV diagnoses among people aged 50 and over. Most (44% or 3,747) were among those aged 50–54 (CDC, 2015c).

A growing number of people ages 50 years and older in the United States is living with HIV infection (CDC, 2015d). This is due to several factors. Better clinical care and increasingly effective regimens of antiretroviral therapy (ART) have extended the lives of HIV-positive persons, transforming what was once considered to be a death sentence into a chronic, albeit manageable, illness. Treatment with antiretroviral medications lowers the level of HIV in the blood, reduces HIV-related illness, and reduces the spread of HIV to others (CDC, 2015d). As a result, people who were first diagnosed with HIV in their 20s, 30s, and 40s are now living into their 50s, 60s, 70s, and beyond. Second, the proportions of newly infected people who are 50 years or older have risen in recent years due to high-risk sexual behaviors that account for 90% of new HIV infections (Lovejoy, 2014).

AARP reported that about 62% of males and 51% of females ranging from 60 to 69 years old have a strong belief that sexual activity is a good component of maintaining health (Bradford & Meston, 2010). Women in their 60s experiencing sexual activity were estimated at 51% and those in their 70s were estimated at 30% (Bradford & Meston, 2010). Survey results revealed that 33% of sexually active men in their 70s and 19% of sexually active men in their 80s were having sex at least twice a month (Oerman, 2015). The study also found that 36% of sexually active women in their 70s and 32% of sexually active women in their 80s reported having sex at least twice a month (Oerman, 2015). These data show that sexual activity is prevalent in the older population. This can be a problem in regards to their sexuality because society's perceptions have been distorted by a lack of discussion about it in the media. While the elderly population is engaging in sexual activity beyond the "normative" age, society is lacking in various forms of protection for them. These include sexual health education involving physicians and their aging patients, protecting elderly adults from sexually transmitted infections (STIs), and even providing support for them to express their sexuality. Since older adults are engaging in sexual activity, they can be at risk for contracting HIV/AIDS. Guided Practice Exercise 4.12 provides the opportunity to examine these issues with older clients to assist them with managing the disease while continuing to live a full life.

Guided Practice Exercise 4.12

There is a growing number of older people who have AIDS or HIV. Transmission of the virus among older people takes the same routes as among younger people. However, rates of the disease among people 65 and older are probably underestimated because of the common misperception that sexual activity ends with age. People are living longer and continue to be sexually active in their later years.

Few physicians and other health care providers think about the sex lives of older patients, and many other diseases can mimic the symptoms of early AIDS. For example, the mental confusion of AIDS may be mistaken for Alzheimer's disease. How comfortable are you with addressing sexual issues with your older clients? Are you familiar with community resources that would provide your clients with the support they may need? What do you think your older clients are experiencing when given a diagnosis of HIV/AIDS? How can you best address their sadness, dismay, shock, disapproval from family members, and the stigma attached to this disease? Design a support group for older persons with HIV/AIDS and include involvement at the personal, family, and community levels. How would you facilitate such an emotionally charged support group?

The need for medical professionals to become more sensitive and knowledgeable of the issue of HIV in older adults is greatly needed. Hughes (2011) examined attitudes and knowledge regarding HIV and older adults. Results indicated that all medical personnel scored or reported sufficient results to demonstrate their knowledge of HIV. Although general knowledge was fairly high, knowledge specific to HIV in older adults was relatively low. Almost half of the participating physicians could not properly rank the four most common risk factors for HIV in older adults. The most common risk factors include having unprotected sex; having many sexual partners; having sex with a sex worker or an intravenous (IV) drug user; sharing needles, syringes, or equipment used to prepare or inject drugs with someone who is infected; and using needles for piercing or tattooing that are not sterile (Derrer, 2014). Other factors may also increase your HIV risk; which include having another sexually transmitted disease (STD); having sex after drinking alcohol or taking drugs; having a mother who was infected with HIV before you were born; having a blood transfusion or received blood products before 1985; and having fewer copies of a gene that helps fight HIV (Derrer, 2014). There was alarming information that physicians were not aware of. For example, the majority of medical providers were not aware that dementia caused by contraction of HIV could be reversed. This piece of information is highly important and needed to be emphasized among all medical professionals who come into contact with HIV-positive older adults (Hughes, 2011). Though specific knowledge was low, attitudes with working and interacting with older adults with HIV were generally positive across all medical personnel. This shows that medical professionals working with HIV positive older adults will bring a more calming and comfortable demeanor, allowing these individuals to feel accepted and supported by their providers (Hughes, 2011).

In addition to medical professionals expanding their knowledge of HIV and the older generations, older adults themselves need to understand the serious and risky behaviors that could result in contraction of HIV. This group has adopted a sense of invincibility when it comes to sexual health concerns. Researchers have found that older adults are increasingly engaging in high-risk sexual behaviors; most are involved in at least one activity that constitutes as a risk factor for HIV (Adekeye, Heiman, Onyeabor, & Hyacinth, 2012). In fact, older adults were about six times less likely to use condoms during sexual intercourse and about five times less likely to be screened and tested for STIs and HIV, compared to their younger generational cohorts (Adekeye et al., 2012).

Many older adults believe that because of their old age, they are "immune" or "too old to get STIs or HIV." This reckless thinking has caused a misconception and misunderstanding of sexual concerns among the older adult community. In fact, many postmenopausal women with low levels of estrogen are more vulnerable for vaginal tears and scarring, which could lead to the contraction of STIs and HIV (Adekeye et al., 2012). For older men, the introduction of erectile dysfunction medications has allowed them to not only achieve an erection, but to act upon their desires for promiscuity. These types of behaviors require interventions on the part of counselors and society in general.

Interventions

Interventions are required at all levels of the system to positively impact older adults. Many researchers believe an ecological model can be utilized that affects the entire complex system (Jacobson, 2011). The ecological model involves the use of intrapersonal or individual factors, interpersonal factors, institutional or organizational factors, community factors, and policy factors to provide awareness and help to the older HIV community (Jacobson, 2011).

First, prevention must start at the lowest level possible—the intrapersonal level. The intrapersonal level involves individual traits that affect behavior such as knowledge and beliefs (Jacobson, 2011). This step is vital in order for older adults to understand that HIV and STIs are still a problem among their population. At this level, a health belief model is typically used to eliminate barriers to understanding the issues surrounding HIV and older adults. Educational programming at senior centers, retirement homes, or even at geriatric wellness sites will help disperse information about preventing HIV and promoting safe sex practices among the elderly (Jacobson, 2011). Guided Practice Exercise 4.13 provides professional counselors the opportunity to explore personal feelings regarding HIV and older adults, develop strategies to address the subject, and create an educational program for older clients.

Guided Practice Exercise 4.13

Many individuals in society refuse to accept that older persons engage in meaningful sexual activity. Unfortunately, some elders contract HIV and are devastated. How would you approach the subject of safe sex practices? Develop a program with specific subcomponents to address this issue.

Next, there is prevention at the interpersonal level. The interpersonal level involves the processes between a person and a community or group. By promoting consistent condom usage to the older adult community, there will be a serious increase in psychological well-being among all orientations and gender. These practices are meant to help individuals enjoy their times with their partners/spouses and not have to worry about the consequences. The safe sex practice of using condoms challenges older adults to become more responsible when engaging in sexual activity; nonetheless, the idea of not having to worry about contracting an STI or HIV is the positive trade-off. The need for improving the communication and relationship between older adults and their doctors regarding sexuality and HIV/AIDS is significant (Jacobson, 2011). Therefore, a program known as the Senior HIV Intervention Program (SHIP) was created to raise doctor awareness of HIV in older adults. This program encourages physicians to complete a full sexual risk assessment for all patients (Jacobson, 2011).

Following the interpersonal level, the next level is prevention at the institutional or organizational level. These factors include policies, informal structures, and regulations that promote or restrain behaviors (Jacobson, 2011). There are many organizations that consistently fail at providing or encouraging HIV testing among older adults. Since there are such delays in testing, researchers have provided guidelines for older adults to be proactive with their STI/HIV testing. Older adults over the age of 50 should have annual testing for HIV; however, as this may become too costly and Medicare may not cover these tests, an older adult should have an initial test performed and records should be kept with their doctors/affiliated hospital or clinic in order to monitor throughout future years (Jacobson, 2011).

Once other organizations and institutions are involved with these prevention measures, the communities must become involved. At the community level, social networks (both informal and formal) are involved, which affect individuals' behaviors. Community level intervention allows social practices and behaviors to spread through its members, allowing behavioral changes to be reinforced. Therefore, disseminating preventative information will allow these social networks to adopt a reinforced behavior change (Jacobson, 2011).

Finally, prevention at the policy level is one of the most impactful methods for interventions with HIV and older adults. Factors include local, state, and federal policies that support disease prevention (Jacobson, 2011). Unfortunately, there are disparities that exist even among state health department policies regarding older adults. Public Health Departments in all 50 states have provided literature on HIV, but only 15 of those 50 departments targeted older adults (Jacobson, 2011). The inadequacy of these public health policies toward older adults is threatening their health and well-being. Overall, all of these interventions provide specific plans to help create a safe environment. In order to improve the awareness of HIV among older adults, a combination of all interventions would be most beneficial. Case Illustration 4.3 examines the impact of a diagnosis of HIV in a sexually active and fully functional older woman. It demonstrates the myriad of issues that the professional counselor will need to address in the counseling sessions.

CASE ILLUSTRATION 4.3

Alicia is a 65-year-old happily married woman of 30 years. She has a supportive family and an excellent career as a regional pharmaceutical sales director. Her husband, who had always been supportive, feels neglected and decides that a divorce is best for the couple. He leaves the home abruptly and initiates

(Continued)

(Continued)

divorce proceedings. Several years later she begins dating Johnathan, whom she has known most of her adult life. She trusts him immensely, and they soon become intimate partners. She has never used a condom or any form of birth control because she is past childbearing age. It never occurred to her to inquire regarding Johnathan's sexual history because she has known him for so many years.

After a routine yearly gynecological examination with blood work to rule out sexually transmitted diseases, Alicia finds out that she has tested positive for HIV. It must be noted that HIV is routinely tested for in her home state. Johnathan, whom she has fallen in love with, has infected her. She confronts him regarding this, and he denies that she became infected from him. Neither Alicia nor Johnathan exhibited any symptoms of the infection. Alicia now worries constantly about any potential symptoms that may arise, the cost of hospital bills, and whom she should share this devastating news with. She is fearful that someone at her job will find out and her job might be in jeopardy. The conscientious, well-organized, highly motivated Alicia is becoming distraught, disorganized, and depressed.

HIV/AIDS and Mental Health

Stigma is a particular concern among older Americans because they may already face isolation due to illness or loss of family and friends. Stigma negatively affects people's quality of life, self-image, and behaviors and may prevent them from seeking HIV care and disclosing their HIV status (CDC, 2012). Diagnosis of HIV infection later in the course of their disease will mean a late start to treatment and potential damage to their immune system that could lead to a poorer prognosis and shorter survival after an HIV diagnosis (CDC, 2012). Lack of testing for HIV among older adults by health care professionals and lack of discussion regarding older adults' sexual practices places older adults in a vulnerable position that may cause them harm, disruption in their lives, and potentially devastating consequences (CDC, 2012).

Numerous concerns arise with older persons diagnosed with HIV infection. These concerns may negatively impact their relationships with peers, family members, coworkers, and health care providers. Older persons will be concerned regarding treatment options, insurance coverage, fear of disapproval from others, transportation to appointments, potential alienation from loved ones, thoughts of dying, and a host of other issues that may impede their recovery. Fearfulness, lowered self-esteem, depression, and anxiety may be exhibited and must be addressed along with any co-occurring physical conditions.

HIV/AIDS and Mental Health Practice

Mental health practitioners will assume numerous roles and responsibilities when counseling older adults who have been diagnosed with HIV/AIDS. Mental health practitioners are to educate themselves on the etiology, treatment, and prognosis of the disease to better educate their elderly clients. Discussions may be challenging due to reluctance to discuss intimate issues revolving around sexual interactions. These practitioners must persevere in a nonthreatening and supportive environment to facilitate the trust required to engage in these delicate discussions. This role as educator will be a continuous responsibility throughout all encounters as clients continue to experience various conditions that may accompany the HIV/AIDS.

Advocacy will be an important role of mental health practitioners. Advocacy may be manifested in employment situations, securing housing, navigating the insurance arena, obtaining support services, applying for financial or disability benefits and many others. The practitioner may need to become the voice for his or her elderly clients who feel unprepared or ill-equipped to advocate for themselves, maybe due to their deteriorating status. For those older clients who are earlier in their disease process, mental health practitioners can teach them assertiveness skills and empower them to speak for themselves.

Mental health practitioners will assume roles of resource and referral specialists that will be critical needed throughout the therapeutic encounters with older persons diagnosed with HIV/AIDS. Practitioners will need to be knowledgeable of a range of services to meet the social, emotional, financial, and physical needs for their clients. Knowledge of the community services and building relationships with various providers will prove extremely beneficial in working with older clients. Referral to various agencies and assistance with completion of documents will be an asset for older clients who may be frustrated with the rules, procedures, and administrative details inherent in many agencies.

To effectively facilitate any process with one's client, it is imperative that the mental health practitioner acknowledge any personal biases regarding different conditions. Should the mental health practitioner feel uneasy regarding the fact that older persons engage in sexual acts, the therapist must find a way to address his or her biases so that he or she can effectively assist their client with all of the changes they are experiencing as a result of the diagnosis of HIV/AIDS. If the mental health practitioner has difficulty addressing his or her personal issues, then a referral to another practitioner may be more appropriate.

Coordinating of services will be a major role in working with older adults with a diagnosis of HIV/AIDS. The mental health practitioner will be one member of a multidisciplinary team who is concerned regarding their client. Addressing fears, stigmas, side effects of the various treatments, depression, concerns regarding finances, sexual activity, medications, family perceptions, and services will require a collaborative approach for the practitioner's older client. The stigma of HIV/AIDS continues to persist in today's society and mental health practitioners are in a position to assist older clients living with the HIV/AIDS diagnosis while continuing to remain as engaged in meaningful activity as they can. They can also educate various constituents, including health care providers and places for employment to extend the work lives of their clients and advocate and remain members of interdisciplinary teams to manage the disease progression and its impact on the psychological well-being of their older clients.

It is well established that people are living longer than at any previous point in history. This longevity has occurred and is occurring as a result of advanced technology, public health measures, health care institutions, and the personal commitment of many to pursue healthier behaviors. However, with this longevity, older persons continue to live with numerous chronic diseases. Many acute diseases are a remnant of the past; however, chronic diseases are here today and projected for the future of most older adults. Despite these projections, most of these diseases are not only preventable but are managed with the assistance of various health care providers.

Older adults face many challenges as they age. Some of the major health challenges have been identified, along with mental health implications. Counseling professionals who understand the health conditions that older clients experience are in a better position to assist them with various life transitions. Some elders will experience limitations in their ADLs, while others will not. Professional counselors must never lose sight of the heterogeneity of this age cohort and must call upon the expertise of geriatric practitioners to assist in their work with older clients. Despite the health challenges that older clients endure, they continue to live productive lives and make valuable contributions to society.

KEYSTONES

- Selected chronic diseases have been identified that pose challenges to older adults.
- Ineffective management of these chronic conditions can be detrimental for older adults.
- A comprehensive assessment requires an examination of the symptoms, treatments, and outcomes for each elderly client.
- Knowledgeable professional counselors are needed to provide effective services to elderly clients.
- Adherence to treatment regimens and counseling sessions are impacted by the medical condition of elderly clients.

ADDITIONAL RESOURCES

Print Based

Aronow, W., Fleg, J., & Rich, M. (2013). Cardiovascular disease in the elderly. *Fundamental and Clinical Cardiology* (5th ed.). Boca Raton, FL: CRC Press.

Barker, B., & Dorien, P. (2000). *Recovering from heart disease in body and mind: Medical and psychological strategies for living with coronary artery disease.* Los Angeles, CA: Lowell House.

Gawande, A. (2007, April 30). The way we age now. *The New Yorker,* pp. 50–59.

Guns, B. (2008). *Rewire your brain, rewire your life: A handbook for stroke survivors and their caregivers.* Livermore, CA: Wingspan Press.

Levine, P. (2012). *Stronger after stroke: Your roadmap to recovery* (2nd ed.). New York, NY: Demos Health Publishing.

National Institute on Aging. (2009). *Glaucoma.* Retrieved January 19, 2001, from http://nihseniorhealth.gov/glaucoma/toc.html

Schieber, F. (2003). Human factors and aging: Identifying and compensating for age-related deficits in sensory and cognitive function. In N. Charness & K. W. Schaie (Eds.), *Impact of technology on successful aging* (pp. 42–77). New York, NY: Springer.

Schieber, F. (2006). Vision and aging. In J. E. Birren & K. W. Schaie (Eds.), *Handbook of the psychology of aging* (6th ed., pp. 129–161). Burlington, MA: Elsevier Academic Press.

Stein, J., Silver, J., & Frates, E. (2006). *Life after stroke: The guide to recovering your health and preventing another stroke.* Baltimore, MD: Johns Hopkins University Press.

Taylor, J. (2009). *My stroke of insight: A brain scientist's personal journal.* New York, NY: Plume Publishing.

Web Based

www.agingaidsnet.psc.isr.umich.edu/

www.agingcare.com/Arthritis

www.agingcare.com/Articles/cancer-treatments-for-the-elderly-136535.htm

www.agingsociety.org/agingsociety/pdf/heart.pdf

www.aids.gov/hiv-aids-basics/just-diagnosed-with-hiv-aids/overview/aging-population/

www.americangeriatrics.org/health_care_professionals/clinical_practice/clinical_guidelines_recommenda
tions/prevention_of_falls_summary_of_recommendations

www.arthritis.com

www.arthritis.org

www.cancer.gov

www.cancer.net/navigating-cancer-care/older-adults

www.cancer.org

www.cancercare.org/questions/tagged/elderly

www.cardiosource.org/ACC/ACC-Membership/Sections-Segments-Councils/Cardiovascular-Care-for-Older-
Adults.aspx

www.care.com/senior-care-helping-seniors-recover-from-stroke-p1143-q275845.html

www.cdc.gov/hiv/risk/age/olderamericans/

www.diabetes.org

www.healthinaging.org/aging-and-health-a-to-z/topic:stroke/info:unique-to-older-adults/

www.niddk.nih.gov

www.nlm.nih.gov/medlineplus/arthritis.html

www.nlm.nih.gov/medlineplus/ency/article/004006.htm

www.nof.org

www.stopfalls.org

www.strokeassociation.org/STROKEORG/LifeAfterStroke/Life-After-Stroke_UCM_308546_SubHomePage.jsp

REFERENCES

Abrahamsen, B., van Staa, T., Ariely, R., Olson, M., & Cooper, C. (2009). Excess mortality following hip fracture: A systematic epidemiological review. *Osteoporosis International, 20*(10), 1633–1650.

Adachi, J. D., Ioannidis, G., Berger, C., Joseph, L., Papaioannou, A., Pickard, L., . . . Tenenhouse, A. (2001). The influence of osteoporotic fractures on health-related quality of life in community-dwelling men and women across Canada. *Osteoporosis International, 12,* 903–908.

Adekeye, O. M., Heiman, H. J., Onyeabor, O. S., & Hyacinth, H. I. (2012). The new invincible: HIV screening among older adults in the United States. *Public Library of Science, 7*(8), 1–9.

Admin. (2011, January). *Fall prevention and osteoporosis.* ASOP. Retrieved April 9, 2014, from http://www.asop
.org/fall-prevention-and-osteoporosis/

Aging Care. (2015). *What is glaucoma and why does it affect the elderly?* Retrieved from http://www.agingcare.com/Articles/Glaucoma-and-elderly-people-133337.htm

Ahn, I. S., Kim, J. H., Kim, S., Chung, J. W., Kim, H., Kang, H. S., & Kim, D. K. (2009). Impairment of instrumental activities of daily living in patients with mild cognitive impairment. *Psychiatry Investigation, 6*(3), 180–184.

Albers, G. W., Clark, W. M., Madden, K. P., & Hamilton, S. A. (2002). Atlantis trial: Results for patients treated within 3 hours of stroke onset. Alteplase thrombolysis for acute noninterventional therapy in ischemic stroke. *Stroke, 33,* 493–495.

Alexandre, T. S., Corona, L. P., Nunes, D. P., Santos, J. L. F., Duarte, Y. A. O., & Lebrao, M. L. (2012). Gender differences in incidence and determinants of disability in activities of daily living among elderly individuals: SABE Study. *Archives of Gerontology and Geriatrics, 55*(2), 431–437.

Alma, M., Van Der Mei, S., Melis-Dankers, B., Van Tilburg, T., Groothoff, J., & Suurmeijer, T. (2011). Participation of the elderly after vision loss. *Disability and Rehabilitation, 33,* 63–72.

American Cancer Society (ACA). (2015). *Cancer treatment and survivorships facts & figures: 2014–2015.* Atlanta, GA: Author.

American Heart Association. (2014). *Heart disease and stroke statistics—*2014 update: A report from the American Heart Association. Retrieved from http://www.circ.ahajournals.org/cgi/content/short/113/6/e85

American Stroke Association. (2015). *Stroke treatments.* Retrieved from http://www.strokeassociation.org/STROKEORG/About Stroke/Treatment/Stroke-Treatment

Anderson, R. J., Freedland, K. E., Clouse, R. E., & Lustman, P. J. (2001). The prevalence of comorbid depression in adults with diabetes: A meta-analysis. *Diabetes Care, 24,* 1069–1078.

Anisimov, M. (2005). Biologic interactions of aging and carcinogenesis. In L. Balducci & M. Extermann (Eds.), *Biological basis of geriatric oncology* (pp. 17–50). New York, NY: Springer.

Antithrombotic Trialists' Collaboration. (2002). Collaborative meta-analysis of randomized trials of antiplatelet therapy for the prevention of death, myocardial infarction, and stroke in high-risk patients. *British Medical Journal, 324,* 71–86.

Aronow, W. (2008). Treatment of hypertension in older adults. *Geriatrics and Aging, 11*(8), 457–463.

Arthritis Foundation. (2011). *News from the arthritis foundation: The heavy burden of arthritis in the United States.* Atlanta, GA: Author.

Arthritis Foundation. (2015). *Rheumatoid arthritis treatment.* Retrieved from http://www.arthritis.org/about-arthritis/types/rheumatoid-arthritis/treatment.php

Avenell, A., & Handoll, H. H. (2003). A systematic review of protein and energy supplementation for hip fracture aftercare in older people. *European Journal of Clinical Nutrition, 57,* 895–903.

Barnett, H. J. (2002). Stroke prevention in the elderly. *Clinical Experimental Hypertension, 24,* 563–571.

Beghe, C., & Balducci, L. (2005). Biological basis of cancer in the older person. In L. Balducci & M. Extermann (Eds.), *Biological basis of geriatric oncology* (pp. 189–221). New York, NY: Springer.

Berger, N. A., Savvides, P., Koroukian, S. M., Kahana, E. F., Deimling, G. T., Rose, J. H., . . . Miller, R. H. (2006). Cancer in the elderly. *Transactions of the American Clinical and Climatological Association, 117,* 174–156.

Berry, M., Worni, M., & Pietrobon, R. (2013). Variability in the treatment of elderly patients with stage 111A (N2) non-small-cell lung cancer. *Journal of Thoracic Oncology, 8,* 744–752.

Birchfield, P. (2002). Osteoarthritis. In A. Luggen & S. Meiner (Eds.), *Care of the older adult with arthritis* (pp. 9–22). New York, NY: Springer.

Bokemeyer, C., Aapro, M., & Courdi, A. (2006). EORTC guidelines for the use of erythropoietic proteins in anaemic patients with cancer: 2000 update. *European Journal of Cancer, 40,* 926–938.

Bouchardy, C., Rapiti, E., Blagojevic, S., Vlastos, A., & Vlastos, G. (2007). Older female cancer patients: Importance, causes, and consequences of undertreatment. *Journal of Clinical Oncology, 25,* 1858–1869.

Bradford, A., & Meston, C. (2010). Senior sexual health: The effects of aging. *Innovations in Clinical Practices: Focus on Sexual Health,* 35–45.

Braithwaite, R. S., Col, N. F., & Wong, J. B. (2003). Estimating hip fractures morbidity, mortality, and costs. *Journal of American Geriatrics Society, 51,* 364–370.

Brown, A. F., Mangioine, C. M., Saliba, D., & Sakinsain, C. (2003). Foundation/American Geriatrics Society panel on improving care for elders with diabetes. Guidelines for improving the care of the older person with diabetes mellitus. *Journal of the American Geriatrics Society, 51*(Suppl. 5), S265–S280.

Burdette-Radoux, S., & Muss, H. (2006). Adjuvant chemotherapy in the elderly: Whom to treat, what regimen? *Oncologist, 11,* 234–242.

Burge, R., Dawson-Hughes, B., & Solomon, D. H. (2007). Incidence and economic burden of osteoporosis-related fractures in the United States, 2005–2025. *Journal of Bone Mineral Research, 22,* 465–475.

Canadian Hypertension Society. (2005). *Canadian hypertension education program (CHEP) 2005 guidelines.* Retrieved from http://www.hypertension.ca/

Carey, E. C., Walter, L. C., & Lindquist, K., & Covinski, K. E. (2004). Development and validation of a functional morbidity index to predict mortality in community-dwelling elders. *Journal of General Internal Medicine, 19,* 1027–1033.

Carro, A., & Kaski, J. (2011). Myocardial infarction in the elderly. *Aging Disease, 2*(2), 116–137.

Centers for Disease Control and Prevention (CDC). (2011). *The state of vision, aging, and public health in America.* Retrieved from http://www.cdc.gov/visionhealth/pdf/vision_brief.pdf

Centers for Disease Control and Prevention (CDC). (2012). *HIV among people aged 50 and over.* Retrieved http://www.cdc.gov/hiv/group/age/olderamericans/index.html

Centers for Disease Control and Prevention (CDC). (2013). *Common eye disorders.* Retrieved from www.cdc.gov/

Centers for Disease Control and Prevention (CDC). (2014a). *Division of Diabetes Translation.* National diabetes statistics report, 2014. Atlanta, GA: National Center for Chronic Disease Prevention and Health Promotion.

Centers for Disease Control and Prevention (CDC). (2014b). *Heart failure fact sheet.* Retrieved from http://www.cdc.gov/dhdsp/data_statistics/fact_sheet

Centers for Disease Control and Prevention (CDC). (2014c). *High blood pressure facts.* Retrieved from http://www.cdc.gov/bloodpressure/htm

Centers for Disease Control and Prevention (CDC). (2014d). National diabetes statistics report: Estimates of diabetes and its burden in the United States, 2014. Atlanta, GA: U.S. Department of Health and Human Services.

Centers for Disease Control and Prevention (CDC). (2014e). *Rheumatoid arthritis.* Retrieved from http://www.cdc.gov/arthritis/basics/rheumatoid.htm

Centers for Disease Control and Prevention (CDC). (2015a). *Falls.* Retrieved from http://www.cdc.gov/homeandrecreationalsafety/falls.html

Centers for Disease Control and Prevention (CDC). (2015b). *Healthy aging: Helping people to live long and productive lives and enjoy a good quality of life.* Retrieved from http://stacks.cdc.gov/view/cdc/6114

Centers for Disease Control and Prevention (CDC). (2015c). *HIV.* Retrieved from http://www.cdc.gov/hiv/index.html

Centers for Disease Control and Prevention (CDC). (2015d). *HIV among people aged 50 and over.* Retrieved from http://www.cdc.gov/hiv/group/age/olderamericans/index.html

Centers for Disease Control and Prevention (CDC). (2015e). *Meeting the challenge of living well at a glance.* Retrieved from http://www.cdc.gov/chronicdisease/resources/publicatioins/aag/arthritis.htm

Centers for Disease Control and Prevention (CDC). (2015f). *Other conditions related to heart disease.* Retrieved from http://www.cdc.gov/heartdisease/other_conditions.htm

Centers for Disease Control and Prevention (CDC). (2015g). *What is cancer?* Retrieved from http://www.cdc.gov/cancer/dcpc/prevention/index.htm

Centers for Disease Control and Prevention (CDC). (2015h). *What is diabetes?* Retrieved from http://www.cdc.gov/diabetes/living/index.html

Centers for Medicare and Medicaid Services (CMS). (2006). *Medicare claims file five percent sample.* Washington, DC: Department of Health and Human Services.

Centers for Medicare and Medicaid Services (CMS). (2012). *Chronic conditions among Medicare beneficiaries, chartbook, 2012 edition.* Baltimore, MD: U.S. Department of Health and Human Services.

Chang, H. J., Lynm, C., & Glass, R. M. (2010). Falls and older adults. *Journal of American Medical Association, 303*(3), 288.

Chang, J. T., Morton, S. C., Rubenstein, L. Z., Mojica, W. A., Maglione, M., Suttorp, M. J., . . . Shekelle, P. G. (2004). Interventions for the prevention of falls in older adults: Systematic review and meta-analysis of randomized clinical trials. *British Medical Journal, 328,* 680.

Choi, H., Atkinson, K., Karlson, E., & Curhan, G. (2005). Obesity, weight change, hypertension, diuretic use, and risk of gout in men. *Archives of Internal Medicine, 165,* 742–748.

Choi, H. Atkinson, K., Karlson, E., Willet, W., & Curhan, G. (2004). Alcohol intake and risk of incident gout in men: A prospective study. *Lancet, 363,* 1277–1281.

Clark, V., Black, S. E., & Colantonio, A. (2002). Well-being after stroke in Canadian seniors: Findings from the Canadian Study of Health and Aging. *Stroke, 33,* 1016–1021.

Coeckelbergh, T. R. M., Cornelissen, F. W., Brouwer, W. H., & Kooijman, A. C. (2002). The effect of visual field defects on eye movements and practical fitness to drive. *Vision Research, 42,* 667–669.

Colon-Emeric, C., Kuchibhatla, M., & Pieper, C. (2003). The contribution of hip fracture to risk of subsequent fracture: Data from two longitudinal studies. *Osteoporosis International, 14,* 879–883.

Control, C. D. (2006). Stroke facts and statistics. In Centers for Disease Control (Ed.), *Heart Disease and Stroke Prevention.* Atlanta, GA: U.S. Department of Health and Human Services.

Council on Medical Education (COME). (2015). *Hypertension in the elderly: Some practical considerations.* Family Medicine Board Review Course. Las Vegas, Nevada: Author.

Crosta, P. (2015). Cancer: Facts, types and causes. *Medical News Today.* Retrieved from http://www.medicalnewstoday.com/info/cancer-oncology/

Cruickshanks, K. J., Tweed, T. S., Wiley, T. L., Klein, B. E., Klein, R., & Chappell, R. (2003). The 5-year incidence and progression of hearing loss: The epidemiology of hearing loss study. *Archives of Otolaryngology Head Neck Surgery, 129*(10), 1041–1060.

Davison, J., Bond, J., Dawson, P., Steen, I., & Kenny, R. (2005). Patients with recurrent falls attending Accident & Emergency benefit from multifactorial intervention—a randomized controlled trial. *Age Ageing, 34*(2), 162–168.

Derrer, D. (2014). *HIV/AIDS risk factors.* Retrieved from http://www.webmd.com/hiv-aids/guide/hiv-risk-factors-are-you-risking-your-life

Drusini, A. G., Eleazer, G. P., Caiazzo, M., Veroncese, E., Carrara, N., & Ranzato, C. (2002). One-leg standing balance and functional status in an elderly community-dwelling population in northeast Italy. *Aging Clinical Experimental Research, 14*(1), 42–46.

Ghosh, K., & Sinclair, A. (2006). Diabetes in older people: Defining the issues and evidence-based management strategies. *Aging Health, 2,* 171–174.

Gillespie, L. D., Gillespie, W. J., Robertson, M. C., Lamb, S. E., Cumming, R. G., & Rowe, B. H. (2003). Interventions for preventing falls in elderly people. *Cochrane Database of Systematic Reviews,* CD000340.

Go, A., Mozaffarian, D., Roger, V., Benjamin E., & Berry, J. (2013). Heart disease and stroke statistics—2013 update: A report from the American Heart Association. Circulation, 127, e6-e245.

Goulet, J., & Cummings, K. (2015). Fragility fracture clinic. Retrieved from http://medicine.umich.edu/dept/orthopaedic-surgery/patient-care-services/trauma/fragility

Gregg, E. W., Mangione, C. M., Cauley, J. A., Thompson, T. J., Schwartz, A. V., Ensrud, K. E., & Nevitt, M. C. (2002). Study of osteoporotic fractures research group: Diabetes and incidence of functional disability in older women. *Diabetes Care, 25,* 61–67.

Gregg, E. W., Yaffe, K., Cauley, J. A., Rolka, D. B., Blackwell, T. L., Narayan, K. M., & Cummings, S. R. (2000). Is diabetes associated with cognitive impairment and cognitive decline among older women? *Archives of Internal Medicine, 160,* 174–180.

Gubitz, G., Sandercock, P., & Counsell, C. (2004). Anticoagulants for acute ischemic stroke. *Cochrane Database of Systematic Reviews, 2,* CD000024.

Hellekson, K. L. (2002). NIH releases statement on osteoporosis prevention, diagnosis, and therapy. *American Family Physician, 66,* 161–162.

Huddleston, J. M., & Whitford, K. J. (2001). Medical care of elderly patients with hip fractures. *Mayo Clinic Procedures, 76,* 295–298.

Hughes, A. K. (2011). HIV knowledge and attitudes among providers in aging: Results from a national survey. *AIDS Patient Care and Standards, 25*(9), 539–545.

Hurria, A., Levit, L., Dale, W., Mohile, S., Muss, H., Fehrenbacher, L., . . . Cohen, H. (2015). Improving the evidence base for treating older adults with cancer: American Society of Clinical Oncology Statement. *Journal of Clinical Oncology, 33*(27).

Hursting, S. D., Lavigne, J. A., Berrigan, D., Perkins, S. N., & Barrett, J. C. (2003). Calorie restriction, aging and cancer prevention: Mechanisms of action and applicability to humans. *Annual Review of Medicine, 54,* 131–152.

Isomaa, B., Almgren, P., & Tuomi, T. (2001). Cardiovascular morbidity and mortality associated with the metabolic syndrome. *Diabetes Care, 24,* 683–689.

Jackson, C., & Wenger, N. (2011). Cardiovascular disease in the elderly. *Revista Española de Cardiologia, 64*(8), 697–712.

Jacobson, S. A. (2011). HIV/AIDS interventions in an aging United States population. *Health and Social Work, 36*(2), 149–156.

January, C., Wann, L., Alpert, J., Calkins, H., Cigarroa, J., & Cleveland, J. (2014). AHA/ACC/HRS guideline for the management of patients with atrial fibrillation. *Journal of the American College of Cardiology, 21,* 2246–2280.

Jemal, A., Murray, T., Ward, E., Samuels, A., Tiwari, R. C., Ghafoor, A., . . . Thun, M. J. (2005). Cancer statistics, 2005ca. *Cancer Journal for Clinicians, 55*(1), 10–30.

Johns Hopkins Medicine. (2015). *Stent replacement.* Retrieved from http://www.hopkins.medicine.org/. . ./stents

Juliusson, G., Antunovic, D., & Derolf, A. (2009). Age and acute myeloid leukemia: Real world data on decision to treat and outcomes from the Swedish Acute Leukemia Registry. *Blood, 113,* 4179–4187.

Kamus (2014, April). Preventing osteoporosis. *PMC.* Retrieved from http://www.nchi.nlm.nih.gov/pmc/articles/PMCIII4702/

Kemeny, M. (2004). Surgery in older patients. *Seminal Oncology, 31,* 175–184.

Kernisan, L., & Scott, P. S. (2015). Activities of daily living: What are ADLs and IADLs? Retrieved from http://.www.caring.com/articles/activities-of-daily-living-what-are-adls-and-iadls

Kerr, L. D. (2003). Inflammatory arthritis in the elderly. *Mount Sinai Journal of Medicine, 70,* 23–26.

Kim, K. S., Kim, S. K., Sung, K. M., Cho, Y. W., & Park, S. W. (2012). Management of Type 2 diabetes mellitus in older adults. *Diabetes Metabolism, 36*(5), 336–344.

Kirkman, S., Briscoe, V., Clark, N., Florez, H., Haas, L., Halter, J., . . . Swift, C. (2012). Diabetes in older adults. *Diabetes Care, 35*(12), 2650–2664.

Kline, D. (2003). Aging effects on vision: Impairments, variability, self-report and compensatory change. *Impact of technology on successful aging.* New York, NY: Springer.

Klotzbuecher, C. M., Ross, P. D., Landsman, P. B., Abbott, T. A., III, & Berger, M. (2000). Patients with prior fractures have an increased risk of future fractures: A summary of the literature and statistical synthesis. *Journal of Bone Mineral Research, 15,* 721–739.

Krishman, E. (2013). Chronic kidney disease and the risk of incident gout among middle-aged men. *Arthritis Rheumatism, 65*(12), 3271–3278.

Lovejoy, T. (2014). Sexual risk behavior in HIV-positive older adults. *American Psychological Association.* Retrieved from http://www.apa.org/pr/aids/resources/exchange/2014/01/sexual-risk.aspy

Lozada, C. (2015). Osteoarthritis: Practice essentials. Retrieved from http://emedicine.medscape.com/article/330487-overview

Lozada, C., & Altman, R. (2001a). Osteoarthritis. In L. Robbins (Ed.), *Clinical care in the rheumatic diseases* (2nd ed., pp. 113–119). Atlanta, GA: Atlanta American College of Rheumatology.

Lozada, C., & Altman, R. (2001b). New and investigational therapies for osteoarthritis. In R. W. Moskowit, D. S. Howell, R. D. Altman, J. A. Buckwalter, & V. M. Goldberg (Eds.), *Osteoarthritis. Diagnosis and medical/surgical management* (3rd ed., pp. 447–456). Philadelphia, PA: Saunders.

Luggen, A., & Meiner, S. (2002). Introduction and demographics of older adults with arthritis. In A. Luggen & S. Meiner (Eds.), *Care of the older adult with arthritis.* New York, NY: Springer.

Luggen, M. L. (2002). *Advances in the assessment and treatment of arthritis.* Greater Cincinnati Gerontological Nursing Association presentation.

MacKay, J., & Mensah, G. (2004) *The atlas of heart disease and stroke.* Geneva, Switzerland: World Health Organization. Retrieved from http://www.who.int/cardiovascular.diseases/resources/atlas/en/

Mandelblatt, J., Sheppard, V., Hurria, A., Kimmick, G., Isaacs, C., Taylor, K., . . . Muss, H. (2010). Breast cancer adjuvant chemotherapy decisions in older women: The role of patient preference and interactions with physicians. *Journal of Clinical Oncology, 28*(19), 3146–3153.

Manfredi, R. (2004). HIV infection and advanced age: Emerging epidemiological clinical, and management issues. *Aging Research Reviews, 3,* 31–54.

Mayo Clinic. (2011). *Definition of palliative care.* Retrieved http://www.mayoclinic.org/tests-procedures/palliative-care

Mayo Clinic. (2014). *Diseases and conditions: Heart attack.* Mayo Foundation for Medical Education and Research. Retrieved www.mayoclinic.org.

McNamara, C. (2006). Management of hypertension and dyslipidemia. In R. Schultz, L. S. Noelker, K. Rockwood, & R. L. Sprott (Eds.), *The encyclopedia of aging* (pp. 315–316). New York, NY: Springer.

MedicineNet (2015). *Definition of ischemia.* Retrieved from http://www.medicinenet.com/script/main/art.asp?articlekey = 4052

Michael, K., & Shaughnessy, M. (2006). Stroke prevention and management in older adults. *Journal of Cardiovascular Nursing, 21*(5), S21–S26.

Miller-Keane Encyclopedia and Dictionary of Medicine, Nursing, and Allied Health. (2003). Balloon angioplasty. St. Louis, MO: Saunders.

Mozzafarian, D., Benjamin, E., & Go, A. (2015). Heart disease and stroke statistics—2015. Circulation, 131, e29–e322.

National Center for Health Statistics. (2010). *Faststats: Deaths and mortality.* Retrieved from www.cdc.gov/nchs/fastats/deaths.html

National Eye Institute (NEI). (2010). *Cataracts.* Retrieved from https://nei.nhi.bov/eyedata/cataract

National Heart, Lung, and Blood Institute (NHBLI). (2012). *Myocardial infarctions.* Retrieved from http://222.nhlbi.nih.gov/health/health-topics/I

National Heart, Lung, and Blood Institute (NHLBI). (2015a). *Angina facts.* Retrieved from http://www.elder-issues.com/library/index.cfm?fu

National Heart, Lung, and Blood Institute. (NHLBI). (2015b). *What is atherosclerosis?* Retrieved from www.nhibi.nih.gov/health/health-topics/topics/atherosclerosis/

National Institute for Health and Clinical Excellence (NICE). (2012). *Osteoporosis: Assessing the risks of fragility fracture.* Retrieved from http://patient.info/doctor/osteoporosis-pro

National Institute of Arthritis and Musculoskeletal and Skin Diseases (NIAMS). (2015). *Gout.* Retrieved from http://www.niams.nih.gov/Health_Info/Gout/

National Institutes of Health (NIH). (2014). *Aging changes in the heart and blood vessels.* Retrieved from https://www.nlm.nih.gov/medlineplus/ency/article/004006.htm

National Institutes of Health (NIH). (2015). *Osteoporosis: Peak bone mass in women.* Retrieved from http://www.niams.nih.gov/Health_Info/Bone/Osteoporosis/bone-mass.asp

National Institutes of Health, National Heart, Lung, and Blood Institute. (2003). *The seventh national report of the joint national committee on prevention, detection, evaluation, and treatment of high blood pressure.* Washington, DC: United States Department of Health and Human Services.

National Institute of Mental Health (NIMH). (2013). *Diabetes and depression.* Retrieved from http://psychcentral.com/lib/diabetes-and-depression

National Institute on Aging (NIA). (2008). HIV, AIDS, and older people. *Age page.* Retrieved from www.nia.nih.gov/HealthInformation/Publications/hiv-aids.html

National Institute on Aging (NIA). (2012). *Age page: Diabetes in older people: A disease you can manage.* Retrieved from https://www.nia.nih.gov/health/publication/diabetes

National Institute on Aging (NIA). (2015). *Age page: High blood pressure.* Retrieved from http://www.nia.nih.gov/health/publication/high-blood-pressure

National Osteoporosis Foundation (NOF). (2013). *Osteoporosis.* Retrieved from http://www.nof.org

Navigating Cancer Care. (2012). *Aging and Cancer.* Retrieved from http://www.cancer.net/navigating-cancer-care/older-adults/aging-and-cancer

NHS. (2015). *Cerebrovascular disease.* Retrieved from http://www.nhs.uk/conditions/cerebrovascular-disease/Pages/Definition.aspx

Nordqvist, C. (2014). *What are cataracts? What causes cataracts?* Retrieved from http://www.medicalnewstoday.com/articles/157510.php

Nordqvist, J. (2015, August 13). Atherosclerosis: Causes, symptoms and treatments. *Medical News Today.* Retrieved from http://www.medicalnewstoday.com/articles/247837.php

Novak, M. (2012). *Issues in aging.* Boston, MA: Allyn & Bacon.

Nwankwo, T., Yoon, S., Burt, V., & Gu, Q. (2013). Hypertension among adults in the U.S. National Health and Nutrition Survey, 2011–2012. NCHS Data Brief, No. 133. Hyattsville, MD: National Center for Health Statistics, Centers for Disease Control and Prevention, U.S. Department of Health and Human Services.

Oerman, A. (2015). *How much you'll have sex in your 70s and 80s.* Retrieved from http://www.womenshealthmag.com/sex-and-love/how-much-sex-old-people-have

Office of the Surgeon General. (2004). *Bone health and osteoporosis: A report of the surgeon general.* Washington, DC: United States Department of Health and Human Services.

Oleksik, A., Lips, P., & Dawson, A. (2000). Health-related quality of life in postmenopausal women with low BMD with or without vertebral fractures. *Journal of Bone Mineral Research, 15,* 1384–1392.

Pagana, K. D., & Pagana, T. J. (2013). *Mosby's diagnosis and laboratory test reference* (11th ed.). St. Louis, MO: Mosby.

Papaioannou, A., Watts, N. B., Kendler, D. L., Yuen, C. K., Adachi, J. D., & Ferko, N. (2002). Diagnosis and management of vertebral fractures in elderly adults. *American Journal of Medicine, 113,* 220–228.

Parker, M. J., Gillespie, L. D., & Gillespie, W. J. (2004). Hip protectors for preventing hip fractures in the elderly. *Cochrane Database of Systematic Reviews,* CD001255.

Pelletier, A. L., & Thomas, J. (2009). Vision loss in older persons. *American Family Physician, 79*(11), 963–970.

Perez, K., Helmer, C., Amieva, H., Orgogozo, J. M., Rouch, I., & Dartigues, J. F. (2008). Natural history of decline in instrumental activities of daily living performance over the 10 years preceding the clinical diagnosis of dementia: A prospective population-based study. *Journal of American Geriatrics Society, 56*(1), 37–44.

Petrella, R. J., Payne, M., Meyers, A., Overend, T., & Chesworth, B. (2000). Physical function and fear of falling after hip fracture rehabilitation in the elderly. *American Journal of Physical Medicine and Rehabilitation, 79,* 154–160.

Progress Collaborative Group. (2001). Randomized trial of a perindopril-based blood-pressure lowering regimen among 6,105 individuals with previous stroke or transient ischemic attack. *Lancet, 358,* 1033–1041.

Repetto, L., Biganzoli, L., & Koehne, C. (2003). Cancer in the Elderly Task Force Guidelines for the use of colony-stimulating factors in elder patients with cancer. *European Journal of Cancer, 39,* 2264–2272.

Ries, L. A. G., Eisner, M. P., Kosary, C. L., Hankey, B. F., Miller, B. A., & Clegg, L. X., (2000). *Cancer Statistics Review*, 1973–1998. National Institute of Health, NIH publication 00-2789.

Rittger, H., Rieber, J., Breithardt, O., Ducker, M., Schmidt, M., Abbara, S., . . . Brachmann, J. (2011). Influence of age on pain perception in acute myocardial ischemia: A possible cause for delayed treatment in elderly patients. *International Journal of Cardiology, 149*(1), 63–67.

Rodgers, H., Greenaway, J., Davies, T., Wood, R., Steen, N., & Thomson, R. (2004). Risk factors for first-ever stroke in older people in the northeast of England: A population-based study. *Stroke, 35,* 7–11.

Rose, J. H., O'Toole, E. E., Dawson, N. V., Thomas, C., Conners, A. F., Wenger, N., . . . Lynn, J. (2000). Age differences in care practices and outcomes for hospitalized patients with cancer. *Journal of American Geriatrics Society, 48,* S25–S32.

Saad, M., Cardoso, G., Martins, W., Velarde, L., & Filho, R. (2014). Prevalence of metabolic syndrome in elderly and agreement among four diagnostic criteria. *Arquivos Brasileiros de Cardiologia, 102*(3), 263–269.

Salkeld, G., Cameron, I. D., Cumming, K. G., Easter, S., Seymour, J., Kurrle, S. E., & Quine, S. (2000). Quality of life related to fear of falling and hip fracture in older women: A time trade off study. *British Medical Journal, 320,* 341–346.

Silman, A., & Hochberg, M. (2001). *Epidemiology of the rheumatic diseases.* New York, NY: Oxford University Press.

Silver, B. (2015). *Stroke prevention: Practice essentials.* Retrieved from http://emedicine.medscape.co/article/323662-overview#a3

Sinaki, M. (2003). Critical appraisal of physical rehabilitation measures after osteoporotic vertebrae fracture. *Osteoporosis International, 14,* 773–779.

Sinclair, A. (2000). Diabetes in old age: Changing concepts in the secondary care arena. *Journal of Royal College of Physicians London, 34*(3), 240–244.

Sinclair, A. J. (1999). Diabetes in the elderly. *Clinical Geriatric Medicine, 15*(2), 225–235.

Sinclair, A. J., & Meneilly, G. S. (2006). Type 2 diabetes mellitus in senior citizens. In M. S. J. Pathy, A. J. Sinclair, & J. E. Morley (Eds.), *Principles and practice of geriatric medicine* (4th ed.). Chichester, UK: John Wiley & Sons.

Skinner, A. M., & Turker, M. S. (2005). Oxidative mutagenesis, mismatch repair, and aging. *Science of Aging Knowledge Environment, 9,* 3.

Society of Neuro Interventional Surgery. (2014). *Acute stroke.* Retrieved from http://www.snisonline.org/stroke

Sollitto, M. (2015). *The 4 most common age-related eye diseases.* Retrieved from http://www.agingcare.com

Stern, S., Behar, S., & Gottlieb, S. (2003). Cardiology patient page: Aging and diseases of the heart. *Circulation, 108,* e99–e101.

Stroke Unit Trialists' Collaboration (2001). Organized inpatient (stroke unit) care for stroke. *Cochrane Database of Systematic Reviews, 3,* CD000197.

Sturm, H. M., Donovan, G. A., Macdonell, R., McNeil, J. J., & Thrift, A. G. (2000). Handicap after stroke: How does it relate to disability, perception of recovery, and stroke subtype? The North East Melbourne Stroke Incidence Study (NEMESIS). *Stroke, 17,* 12–35.

Suarez-Ahmacor, M., & Foster, W. (2001). *Rheumatoid arthritis. Clinical Evidence, 6,* 927–944.

Swierzewski, S. (2015). *Osteoporosis.* Retrieved from http://www.healthcommunities.com/osteoporosis

Thom, T., Haase, N., & Rosamond, W. (2006). Heart disease and stroke statistics—2006 update: A report from the American Heart Association Statistics Committee and Stroke Subcommittee. Circulation, 113, e85–e151.

U.S. Department of Health and Human Services. (2004). *Bone health and osteoporosis: A report of the surgeon general.* Rockville, MD: U.S. Department of Health and Human Services Office of the Surgeon General.

Uyar, D., Frasure, H. E., Markman, M., & von Gruenigen, V. E. (2005). Treatment patterns by decade of life in elderly women (≥ 70 years of age) with ovarian cancer. *Gynecology Oncology, 98,* 403–408.

Valderrama-Gama, E., Damian, J., Ruigomez, A., & Martin-Moreno, J. M. (2002). Chronic disease, functional status, and self-ascribed causes of disabilities among noninstitutionalized older people in Spain. *Journal of Gerontology A: Biological Sciences, 57,* M716–M721.

Vasan, R., Beiser, A., & Seshadri, S. (2002). Residual lifetime risk for developing hypertension I middle-aged women and men: The Framingham Heart Study. *Journal of American Medical Association, 287*(10), 1003–1010.

Volpato, S., Blaum, C., Resnick, H., Ferrucci, L., Fried, L. P., & Guralnik, J. M. (2002). Comorbidities and impairments explaining the association between diabetes and lower extremity disability: The Women's Health and Aging Study. *Diabetes Care, 25,* 678–683.

Wardlaw, J. M., del Zoppo, G., Yamaguchi, T., & Berge, E. (2003). Thrombolysis for acute ischemic stroke. *Cochrane Database of Systematic Reviews* 3CD000213.

Wedding, U., Honecker, F., Bokemeyer, C., Pientka, L., & Hoffken, K. (2007). Tolerance to chemotherapy in elderly patients with cancer. *Cancer Control, 14,* 44–56.

West, L., Goodkind, D., & He, W. (2014). American Community Survey 2010: 65+ in the United States: 2010: Special Studies Current Population Reports. U.S. Census Bureau: U.S. Department of Health and Human Services.

White, H., & Sullivan, R. (2006). Cardiovascular system: Overview. In R. Schulz, N. Noelker, K. Rockwood, & R. Sprott (Eds.), *The encyclopedia of aging* (4th ed.). New York, NY: Springer.

Wiktorowicz, M. E., Goeree, R., Papaioannou, A., Adachi, J. D., & Papadimitropoulos, E. (2001). Economic implications of hip fracture: Health service use, institutional care and cost in Canada. *Osteoporosis International, 12,* 271–278.

Wortman, R. L., & Kelley, W. N. (2001). Gout and hyperuricemia. In S. Ruddy, E. D. Harris, & C. B. Sledge (Eds.), *Kelly's textbook of rheumatology* (6th ed., pp. 1339–1352). Philadelphia, PA: W. B. Saunders.

Yancik, R., & Holmes, M. E. (2001, June 13–15). NIA/NCI Report of the Cancer Center Workshop. *Exploring the Role of Cancer Centers for Integrating Aging and Cancer Research.* Retrieved from http://www.nia.nih.gov/ResearchInformation/ConferencesAndMeetings/WorkshopReport

Yancik, R., Wesley, M. N., Ries, L. G. Havlik, R. J., Edwards, B. K., & Yates, J. W. (2001). Effect of age and comorbidity on treatment and early mortality in post-menopausal breast cancer patients aged 55 years and older. *Journal of American Medical Association, 7,* 885–892.

Challenging Conditions Experienced by Older Adults

"If I'd known I was going to live this long, I'd have taken better care of myself."

—Eubie Blake

Learning Objectives

After reading this chapter, you will be able to

1. Describe the incidence, prevalence, and treatment recommendations for persons diagnosed with Alzheimer's disease
2. Examine the challenges in the diagnosis of depression in older adults and discuss its treatment
3. Explain the symptoms and treatment modalities for anxiety disorders
4. Analyze the causes for substance abuse in later life and its treatment and prevention
5. Summarize the types of elder abuse and intervention strategies

INTRODUCTION

Many individuals believe that they have control over their bodies and that promoting and engaging in a healthy lifestyle will prevent or delay the onset of many diseases. While older adults may avoid risky behaviors that predispose them to certain diseases (e.g., hypertension, diabetes), many challenging conditions may be beyond their control. Such challenging conditions experienced by many older adults will be explored in this chapter, including Alzheimer's disease and dementia, depression, anxiety disorders, substance abuse, and elder abuse. While not all older adults may experience these problematic encounters, a careful examination is warranted because they occur with increasing frequency in today's society. Practitioners and counselors-in-training must be able to identify these conditions and explore potential treatments or interventions to better address the needs of the aging client.

ALZHEIMER'S DISEASE

Alzheimer's disease is the most common type of dementia. *Dementia* is an umbrella term describing a variety of diseases and conditions that develop when nerve cells in the brain (called neurons) die or no longer function normally. The death or malfunction of neurons causes changes in one's memory, behavior, and ability to think clearly. In Alzheimer's disease, these brain changes eventually impair an individual's ability to carry out such basic bodily functions as walking and swallowing. This is ultimately fatal (Alzheimer's Association, 2013). Case Illustration 5.1 highlights changes in the progression of dementia and the impact on loved ones and the elder experiencing the inevitable loss of functioning.

CASE ILLUSTRATION 5.1

Ms. Dennison is a 73-year-old widow who lives alone in her home of 50 years. She is comfortable in her environment where she spent many happy days with her husband, raising their family. She is ambulatory and enjoys "going down memory lane" as her daughter recalls it. Her daughter is concerned about her mother so she accompanies her to her primary care physician's (PCP's) office for an evaluation. The daughter shares with the PCP that her mother has become increasingly forgetful to the point where she forgets to turn off the stove, cannot find her way home when driving, neglects to pay her bills, and does not change her clothing. Ms. Dennison's daughter describes her mother as meticulous regarding her appearance, and her home was always clean and well organized with everything in its place. However, Ms. Dennison insists that nothing is wrong and that her daughter just "wants to put me away to get my money." Upon physical examination, there are no physical findings that would account for her change in behavior. The PCP performs a mini-mental state exam where Ms. Dennison scores 10 points, which is considered low and is an indication of her deteriorating cognitive status.

How do you think Ms. Dennison feels regarding her daughter sharing the aforementioned information with her PCP? How do you think Ms. Dennison's daughter feels regarding the accusations made by her mother toward her? How does the daughter continue to allow her mother a sense of autonomy and control with a deteriorating mental condition? How does she adjust to a parent who infrequently recognizes her as her daughter and instead views her as a stranger?

Alzheimer's disease affects people in different ways. The most common symptom pattern begins with a gradually worsening ability to remember new information. This occurs because the first neurons to die and malfunction are usually neurons in brain regions involved in forming new memories. As neurons in other parts of the brain malfunction and die, individuals experience other difficulties. Common symptoms of Alzheimer's disease include memory loss that disrupts daily life; challenges in planning or solving problems; difficulty completing familiar tasks at home, at work, or at leisure; confusion with time or place; trouble understanding visual images and spatial relationships; new problems with words, speaking, or writing; misplacing things and losing the ability to retrace steps; decreased or poor judgment; withdrawal from work or social activities; and changes in mood and personality (Alzheimer's Association, 2013).

Individuals progress from mild Alzheimer's disease to moderate to severe disease at different rates. As the disease progresses, the individual's cognitive and functional abilities decline. In advanced Alzheimer's, people need help with basic activities of daily living (ADLs), such as bathing, dressing, eating, and using the bathroom. Those in the final stages of the disease lose their ability to communicate, fail to recognize loved ones, and become bed-bound and reliant on around-the-clock care (Alzheimer's Association, 2013).

The most important risk factors for Alzheimer's disease include age, family history, and heredity, which cannot be changed (Alzheimer's Association, 2015). The greatest known risk factor of Alzheimer's is advancing age. Most individuals with the disease are age 65 or older. The likelihood of developing Alzheimer's doubles every 5 years after age 65. After age 85, the risk reaches nearly 50%. Scientists are unsure as to why this occurs (Alzheimer's Association, 2015). Individuals who have a parent, brother, sister, or child with Alzheimer's are more likely to develop the disease. There exist two types of genes that can play a role in affecting whether a person develops Alzheimer's, which are risk genes and deterministic genes. Risk genes increase the likelihood of developing a disease, but do not guarantee it will happen (Alzheimer's Association, 2015). Deterministic genes directly cause a disease, guaranteeing that anyone who inherits them will develop the disorder (Alzheimer's Association, 2015). Risk factors we may be able to influence are through general lifestyle and wellness choices and effective management of other health conditions. There may be a strong link between serious head injury and future risk of Alzheimer's, especially when trauma occurs repeatedly or involves loss of consciousness. The risk of developing Alzheimer's appears to be increased by many conditions that damage the heart or blood vessels, which include high blood pressure, heart disease, stroke, diabetes, and high cholesterol. Overall healthy aging strategies may offer protection against developing Alzheimer's or related disorders, which include avoiding tobacco and excess alcohol, staying socially connected, and exercising the body and mind (Alzheimer's Association, 2015). Guided Practice Exercise 5.1 is an experiential exercise to enhance knowledge and appreciation of Alzheimer's disease and its impact on the lives of those affected.

Guided Practice Exercise 5.1

Visit an Alzheimer's disease unit of a local nursing home. What are your observations regarding the behavior of the residents and the environmental modifications to ensure their safety? What is unique regarding the environment and what qualifications are needed to work there? How were the residents treated? How did you feel entering the unit and what were your perceptions of this experience?

Prevalence of Alzheimer's

An estimated 5.3 million Americans of all ages had Alzheimer's disease in 2015. This number includes an estimated 5.1 million people age 65 and older (Chicago Health and Aging Project [CHAP], 2010; Hebert, Weuve, Scherr, & Evans, 2013) and approximately 200,000 individuals under age 65 who have younger onset Alzheimer's (Alzheimer's Association, 2006). Table 5.1 shows the age breakdown of those who have been diagnosed with the disease.

Almost two-thirds of Americans with Alzheimer's disease are women. Of the 5.1 million people age 65 and older who have the disease, 3.2 million are women and 1.9 million are men (CHAP, 2010; Hebert et al., 2013). Sixteen percent of women age 71 and older has Alzheimer's disease compared with 11 % of men (Plassman et al., 2007). The larger proportion of older women with Alzheimer's is primarily explained by the fact that women live longer, on average, than men (Hebert, Scherr, McCann, Beckett, & Evans, 2001).

While most people in the United States living with Alzheimer's are non-Hispanic whites, older African Americans and Hispanics are proportionately more likely than older whites to have Alzheimer's disease (Alzheimer's Association, 2015; Dilworth-Anderson, Hendrie, Manly, Khachaturian, & Fazio, 2008; Manly & Mayeuv, 2004). Older African Americans are about twice as likely to have Alzheimer's as older whites, and Hispanics are about one and one-half times as likely to have Alzheimer's as older whites (Potter et al., 2009).

The prevalence of Alzheimer's is expected to increase as the number of individuals surviving into their 80s, 90s, and beyond grow dramatically due to advances in medicine and medical technology, as well as social and environmental conditions (Vincent & Velkof, 2010). By 2050, the number of people age 65 and older with Alzheimer's disease may nearly triple, from 5.1 million to a projected 13.8 million barring the development of medical breakthroughs to prevent or cure the disease (Alzheimer's Association, 2015). Additionally, a large segment of the population—the baby boomer generation—has begun to reach the age range of elevated risk for Alzheimer's and other dementias. In the future, many people may be faced with caring for someone with Alzheimer's disease. Guided Practice Exercise 5.2 provides the opportunity to examine feelings regarding transforming the home environment to care for an aging family member with Alzheimer's disease.

Table 5.1 Age of Adults With Alzheimer's Disease

Under age 65	65–74 years old	75–84 years old	Over age 85
4%	15%	43%	38%

Source: Alzheimer's Association. (2015). 2015 Alzheimer's disease facts and figures. *Alzheimer's & Dementia, 11*(3), 332.

Guided Practice Exercise 5.2

Are you familiar with any persons diagnosed with Alzheimer's disease? If so, what symptoms of the disease have you observed? Are these individuals living at home with monitoring from family members, or are they institutionalized? What modifications to the home environment would be indicated to allow the elder to age in the comfort of his or her home? Would you be willing to make the necessary adaptations to allow your grandparent to remain at home? Please elaborate on your response.

Longer life expectancies and aging baby boomers will also increase the number and percentage of Americans who will be among the oldest-old (85+). Between 2010 and 2050, the oldest-old are expected to increase from 14% of all people age 65 and older to 20% of all people age 65 and older (Vincent & Velkof, 2010). This will result in an additional 13 million oldest-old people for a total of 21 million, who will have the highest risk for developing Alzheimer's (Vincent & Velkof, 2010). In 2013, the 85 years and older population includes about 2 million people with Alzheimer's disease, or 40% of all people with Alzheimer's age 65 and older (Hebert et al., 2013). When the first wave of baby boomers reaches age 85 (in 2031), it is projected that more than 3 million people age 85 and older are likely to have Alzheimer's (Hebert et al., 2013).

Treatment and Prevention

Alzheimer's disease is very difficult to treat. There are medications that may allow the patient to function for an extra few months. However, these are only palliatives that do nothing to slow the progressive neurodegeneration that ultimately leads to dementia and death. While there are many risk factors for developing Alzheimer's, there are ways to postpone, but not prevent its onset. Puzzles and mentally stimulating leisure activities can assist in delaying the onset of the disease for a short amount of time (Pillai et al., 2014).

Regular physical exercise may play an essential role in preventing Alzheimer's disease. The value of exercise in sustaining healthy cognitive function was demonstrated in a 5-year study revealing that persons with the highest activity level were half as likely as inactive people to develop Alzheimer's disease and were also substantially less likely to suffer any other form of dementia or mental impairment (Laurin, Verreault, Lindsay, MacPherson, & Rockwood, 2001). Weuve et al. (2004) found that women aged 70 and older who had higher levels of physical activity scored better on cognitive performance tests and showed less cognitive decline than women who were less active. Abbott and colleagues (2004) found that older men who walked 2 miles a day had only half the rate of dementia found among men who walked less than a quarter-mile a day.

Exercise produces a multitude of positive changes in the brain. It enhances memory, improves learning, and boosts attention, as well as increases abilities like multitasking and decision making. Exercise makes the brain more adaptive, efficient, and capable of reorganizing neural pathways based on new experiences (Roan, 2006). It increases the flow of oxygen to the brain, producing a larger number of capillaries and possibly the production of new brain cells. It also boosts brain neurotransmitters, including dopamine, serotonin, and norepinephrine, that play critical roles in cognition.

Diet is also important in the prevention of Alzheimer's disease. Antioxidants are substances that keep individuals young and healthy by increasing immune function, decreasing the risk of infection and cancer, and most importantly, by protecting against free-radical damage. Free radicals are unstable organic compounds that play a pivotal role in the aging process, and their damage takes a toll on virtually every organ and system in the aging human body. This sets the stage for a host of degenerative diseases, including Alzheimer's and other forms of dementia. Antioxidants neutralize free radicals and prevent some of the damage to cell structures (Zandi et al., 2004). Antioxidants are found in fresh vegetables, whole grains, fresh fruits, and legumes such as soy. Carotenoids, the substances that give fruits and vegetables their deep, rich colors, are antioxidants. Vitamins C and B are also antioxidants, as are the minerals magnesium and zinc. A diet high in antioxidants lowers the risk of many age-associated diseases, including cancer, heart disease, macular degeneration, and cataracts.

Alzheimer's is so common today that many people have come to view it as an inevitable adjunct of aging. Most people in nursing homes are there because of Alzheimer's. But as widespread as it is, Alzheimer's is a disease. It is not normal aging. Case Illustration 5.2 demonstrates how early identification of cognitive decline can precipitate a referral for a comprehensive geriatric assessment. This case also demonstrates the collaboration between the geropsychiatrist and an outpatient mental health facility to address issues, feelings, and decisions related to the diagnosis of Alzheimer's disease.

CASE ILLUSTRATION 5.2

Mr. Watson has always been a distinguished gentleman who does not look his chronological age of 90. He prides himself on his professional attire and well-groomed hair and nails, and most of all, his polished shoes. He is well spoken, articulate, and speaks with a voice that is quite authoritarian. Mr. Watson lives alone in a two-bedroom condominium with numerous amenities. His income consists of interest from his investments, pension, and Social Security benefits. He is proud of his accomplishments and the quality of life that he has worked hard to achieve.

Mr. Watson's daughter visits him regularly and begins to see a serious change in his attire (from neat to unkempt) and hygiene. Additionally, she has observed that he is becoming forgetful even when told the information several times. He has walked around his neighborhood and forgotten how to return home. He has also forgotten how to turn on the television, set his alarm clock, and cannot remember the names of common household items. His daughter is scared that one day he might forget to turn the stove off and burn the condominium down or fall and forget how to call 911 for assistance.

(Continued)

(Continued)

His daughter makes an appointment with a geropsychiatrist who conducts a full geriatric assessment with lab work and a computerized tomography (CT) scan and diagnoses Mr. Watson with dementia of the Alzheimer's type. The geropsychiatrist refers him to a mental health outpatient clinic for counseling services to educate both Mr. Watson and his daughter on the stages in the progress of Alzheimer's disease, medications that may manage behavioral symptoms, and placement arrangements (if the daughter is unable to take care of her father). The daughter also needs help in addressing issues related to the loss of the father she knew.

DEPRESSION

Depression, feelings of sadness often associated with hopelessness and inadequacy, is among the most common complaints of older adults and is the leading cause of suicide in late life. Depression can be caused by, but is not limited to, the changing of social roles or functions, bereavement of loved ones, movement to assisted facilities, loss of control over one's life, unaccomplished goals, or fear of death. Depression can manifest as withdrawal, lack of interest, and loss of energy and put people at risk for weakness, falls, and broken bones (Novak, 2012). Depression that goes untreated may lead to thoughts of suicide or reduced functioning rates in individuals. Depressive disorders therefore should be considered disorders of major concern to all persons caring for older adults. Guided Practice Exercise 5.3 gives the counseling student an opportunity to interact with an older adult in a community setting. Student will be able to become familiar with depressive symptoms, activities of daily living, and importance of social engagement.

Guided Practice Exercise 5.3

Visit your local senior citizen center and obtain permission to interview one older adult who attends the center on a regular basis. Develop a brief interview of no more than 10–20 open-ended questions. These questions need to address symptoms of depression, activities of daily living, and social interaction. Once administered, analyze your results and see if there is a relationship between the identified symptoms and performance of activities of daily living and involvement in activities in the center. Share your findings with your peers and, if appropriate, with your interviewee.

Of greater importance are those major depressive disorders that may occur for the first time after the age of 60 or that recur in later life. Such "clinical depressions" are characterized by severe symptoms and a prolonged duration of a profound depressed mood.

Clinicians and other health care providers must learn to recognize these depressive disorders, for they can potentially precipitate a suicide attempt or even a successful suicide (Conwell, Duberstein, & Carne, 2002). Suicide remains 1 of the 10 most frequent causes of death in late life and may be preventable if the symptoms of major depression are recognized (National Center for Health Statistics, 2000). Severe depression is also associated with nonsuicidal mortality, though the association of less severe depression and mortality may be confounded by factors associated with both depression and aging, such as functional impairment (Blazer, Hybels, & Pieper, 2001; Schulz, Drayer, & Rollman, 2002). Unfortunately, severe depressive episodes often remain undetected, and older adults suffer unnecessarily from the burden of depressive illness. Numerous causes and risk factors contribute to depression in older adults. Predisposing risk factors for depression include: female sex, widowed or divorced status, previous depression, brain changes due to vascular problems, major physical and chronic disabling illnesses, polypharmacy, excessive alcohol use, social disadvantage and low social support, caregiving responsibilities for person with a major disease (e.g., dementia), and personality type (e.g., relationship or dependence problems). Precipitating risk factors for depression include: recent bereavement, move from home to another place (e.g., nursing home), adverse life events (e.g., loss, separation, financial crisis), chronic stress caused by declining health, family, or marital problems, social isolation, and persistent sleep difficulties (Wiese, 2011).

Diagnosis

Clinical depression is not easily diagnosed in late life because many symptoms are expectations of changes commonly associated with normal aging. For example, older persons have more difficulty sleeping and often complain of broken sleep patterns and early morning awakening—cardinal symptoms of major depression at any stage of the life cycle. Lethargy, a frequent physical symptom that accompanies depression, can be overlooked for physical illness in older individuals, and even aging may lead to decreased energy and activity. Late-life depression is frequently associated with physical illness, which is usually chronic but not life threatening.

Some older adults with depressive symptoms complain that they cannot concentrate and notice problems with memory. Such persons may be diagnosed as suffering from an irreversible dementing process and be denied appropriate treatment, yet most cases of depression and memory loss in older adults reflect a comorbid process of dementia (even mild forms) and depression (Rubin, Veiel, Kinscherf, Morris, & Storandt, 2001). The unfortunate circumstance of not treating a depression associated with memory loss may lead to long-term institutionalization for an individual who is suffering from a treatable illness.

Treatment

Depression is a treatable disorder. The treatment of depression in the elderly involves biological, psychosocial, and spiritual interventions (Khouzam, 2009). The combination of biological and psychosocial intervention is more effective than either of these interventions alone, especially in the prevention of relapse (Hollon, 2011). Treatment should take into account the patient's preferences and treatment history (focusing on treatments that have been helpful in the past), and it should address coexisting medical and psychiatric conditions (Khouzam, 2012). Before treatment is initiated, it is important to clarify common patient concerns about side effects, and to reassure patients that dependence is not a realistic concern with antidepressants and that these medications will not inhibit normal emotional reactions such as bereavement (Zisook & Shear, 2009). When severe late-life clinical depression is identified, the use of appropriate medications, such as selective serotonin reuptake inhibitors (SSRIs) and tricyclic antidepressants (TCAs), can reverse symptomatology in elderly patients (Coupland, Dhiman, & Barton, 2011; Fava, Rush, & Trivedi, 2003; Kelsey, 2002). However, the physician who prescribes medications to older adults must always be aware of the potential of adverse side effects from these medications. The SSRIs are the first-line treatment of choice for some patients because side effects are much less frequent (Alexopoulos, Katz, Reynolds, Carpenter, & Docherty, 2001; Coupland et al., 2011; Fava et al., 2003; Kelsey, 2002). By adjusting the medications carefully, therapists can assist most depressed older adults to tolerate medications without difficulty. When medications fail and depression is accompanied by psychosis, then electroconvulsive therapy (ECT) has proven to be effective. ECT is a procedure in which electric currents are passed through the brain, intentionally triggering a brief seizure. ECT seems to cause changes in brain chemistry that can quickly reverse symptoms of certain mental illnesses. It often works when other treatments are unsuccessful (Mayo Clinic, 2012). ECT is a relatively safe, well-tolerated, and effective treatment for depression.

ECT is only one of the nonpharmacological treatments for late life resistant depression. Transcranial magnet stimulation, which is a type of focal brain stimulation, has shown promising outcomes for treatment-resistant depression (Allan, Hermann, & Ebmeier, 2011). Deep brain stimulation is a surgical treatment that involves the implantation of a medical device called a brain pacemaker, which sends electrical impulses to specific parts of the brain, is used in rare cases with the treatment of Parkinson's disease and co-occurring treatment-resistant depression (Hirschfield, 2011). Light exposure therapy (Flory, Ametepe, & Bowers, 2010), acupuncture that involves the insertion of needles to different parts of the body (Nahas & Sheikh, 2011), and complementary/alternative treatments (i.e., St. John's Wort) (Flory et al., 2010) are additional nonpharmacological treatments that are being investigated.

The effectiveness of biologic treatments for severe depression in late life has overshadowed the use of psychotherapy. Nevertheless, investigators have reported that individuals suffering from major depression with fewer "biological signs" (e.g., sleep problems) can be treated effectively with short-term psychotherapy (Gallagher & Thompson, 1982). These psychotherapies are generally cognitive and behaviorally oriented and may serve, at the least, as useful adjuncts to biological treatments. Studies of the young-old (65–74) have shown that a combination of interpersonal therapy (a variant of cognitive-behavioral therapy) and antidepressant medications is more effective than either treatment alone, both in producing a remission and in preventing a recurrence of an episode of major depression (Reynolds et al., 1999). When psychotherapeutic medication and/or ECT are not effective, the clinician must rely exclusively on psychotherapy. For severe depression, there is always the hope that remission will occur spontaneously, because depression, by definition, is a self-limiting illness.

Methods of treatment of depression are varied on an individual basis, whether drug therapy or psychotherapy or a combination of the two. Patients should consider nutrition, exercise, sleep, and stress reduction tactics as well as focusing on the depression itself. While the most common forms of treatment are psychotherapy and drug therapy, alternative treatments come in the form of acupuncture and relaxation techniques, such as yoga.

Overcoming depression often involves finding new things to enjoy, learning to adapt to change, staying physically and socially active, and feeling connected to the community and loved ones. Physical activity has powerful mood-boosting effects. Additionally, receiving the support needed from others, preferably face-to-face, plays a huge role in lifting depression. Older adults should bring their lives into balance if they are feeling overwhelmed by stress and pressures. Learning new emotional management skills is also helpful (Robinson, Smith, & Segal, 2015). Counselors can assist older clients by educating them, supporting them, and encouraging engagement in activities.

ANXIETY

Anxiety is a state of unpleasantness that is accompanied by nervous behavior and often leads into depression. Some risk factors that are associated with older adults and anxiety are recurring physical problems, cognitive impairment, and emotional stress, which often worsen functionality in individuals (Lang & Stein, 2001). The fear of falling is a common example of anxiety in older people. For older adults, this fear causes severe anxiety whether they have experienced falls previously or not and with rates of fear between 35% and 55% (Allison et al., 2012). This phenomenon has been associated with the intensity of depression and anxiety and, in turn, has a direct effect on activity engagement (Allison et al., 2012). Guided Practice Exercise 5.4 gives students the opportunity to become familiar with anxiety in older adults.

Guided Practice Exercise 5.4

Identify symptoms of anxiety in older adults and discuss how these symptoms might negatively impact their daily functioning. Next, identify nonpharmacological interventions that have been shown to decrease anxiety in older adults. How comfortable are you with using the various interventions? Explain what additional knowledge and experiences would be required to enhance your ability to effectively use the different psychosocial interventions you have identified.

Diagnosis

Older adults may experience anxiety that does not meet criteria for diagnosis; however, even these levels of anxiety consequently lead to significant functional impairment.

Most anxiety disorders do not solely begin at an older age, but they are a recurrence or worsening of a pre-existing condition (Lang & Stein, 2001). Several biological, psychological, and social risk factors for anxiety disorders have been identified for older adults. Biological risk factors include: chronic health conditions (Schoevers, Beekman, Deeg, Jonker, & Tilburg, 2003), poor self-perception of health (van Zelst, deBeurs, & Beckman, 2003), and functional limitation (Schoevers et al., 2003). Psychological risk factors include external focus of control, poor coping strategies, neuroticism, and psychopathology (Schoevers et al., 2003; van Zelst et al., 2003). Social risk factors include: low frequency of contact (Forsell, Palmer, & Fratglioni, 2003), smaller network (Beekman et al., 1998), lack of social support (Beekman, van Balkom, Deeg, van Dyck, & van Tilburg, 2000; Forsell, 2000), loneliness (van Zelst et al., 2003), stressful life events (van Zelst et al., 2003), lower educational level (Beekman et al., 1998), and being female (Schoevers et al., 2003; van Zelst et al., 2003). The diagnosis of anxiety can be difficult to determine due to the intertwined physical symptoms. Misconceptions with anxiety are common because the symptoms are prevalent in both depression and normal with aging. Anxiety commonly coexists with depression, and aggressive treatment of both types of symptoms appears to result in the most favorable clinical outcome (Lang & Stein, 2001). Older adults with anxiety and depression use more services, experience reduced quality of life and increased disability, and have more severe symptoms and greater suicidal ideation (Steffens & McQuoid, 2005). Therefore, recognition of anxiety and its cause is important so treatment can follow.

Treatment

Education is a form of treatment that builds relaxation behaviors and understanding of the causes of anxiety. Much like depression, anxiety is often treatable by medication, psychotherapy, and in some circumstances a combination of both. A Community-Based Survey of Older Adults Preference for Treatment of Anxiety (Mohlman, 2012) revealed that older adults tend to choose psychotherapy over medication as well as using the primary care office for their preferred settings for discussing and obtaining treatment. Since this population visits the doctor frequently, they tend to rely on the doctor's professional expertise and referrals for help. Doctors recommend alternative therapy so their patients focus on their body, community influence, and nutrition to help reduce their anxiety.

Treatment for anxiety disorders may include a supportive intervention, which is a relationship with a caring person who directly addresses isolation and inactivity—a byproduct of anxiety. This can be a family member, friend, social worker at an older adult center, clergyman or chaplain, or others. Engaging people with anxiety in social, creative, or other activities they find interesting is also helpful (Friedman, Fursty, Gellis, & Williams, 2013). Psychotherapeutic interventions include cognitive-behavioral problem solving and interpersonal therapy, which are effective in the treatment of anxiety disorders. Teaching progressive muscle relaxation, deep breathing, and the importance of adequate sleep habits is also effective (Friedman et al., 2013).

There is a growing dispute about the use of pharmacologic interventions for older adults, particularly those with chronic health conditions, because of the physical health risks associated with psychiatric medications, including antianxiety agents, antidepressants, and antipsychotics (Center for Disease Control and Prevention, 2011). Nevertheless, psychiatric medications can be used to treat older adults with anxiety disorders, and they can be successful either alone or in combination with psychotherapy.

SUBSTANCE ABUSE

Substance abuse, the harmful and excessive use of substances like alcohol and drugs, is growing in older adults. The number of Americans aged 50 and over with a substance use disorder is projected to reach 5.7 million in 2020 (Wu & Blazer, 2011). The increase reflects known predictors of substance abuse and the growth of the baby boom cohort and the post–baby boom cohort born between 1965 and 1970. It is estimated that older adults in need of substance abuse treatment services will increase to 4.4 million in 2020, an increase from 1.7 million in 2000 (Rothrauff, Abraham, Bride, & Roman, 2011). Guided Practice Exercise 5.5 gives the counseling student the opportunity to become familiar with substance abuse in an older adult.

Guided Practice Exercise 5.5

You are to conduct extensive research on substance abuse in older adults. You will then narrow your research to one particular substance abused by older adults. Identify difficulties in functioning into different categories (i.e., psychological, cognitive, social, occupational, physical). Once categorized, review different psychotherapeutic approaches to address the challenges identified from your research. Share your findings with your peers and agency or academic professionals.

It is not unusual for individuals to lose social and emotional support systems as they age. The aging process often results in social isolation due to the death of a spouse or partner, other family members, and close friends. Similarly, retirement, altered activity levels, disability, relocation of family and friends, and family dissonance may produce feelings of isolation and depression that exacerbate substance use and abuse in older adults (Myers, Dice, & Dew, 2000; Williams, Bullard, & Alessi, 2005). Most people adjust to these changes without abusing substances. They discover new joys in everyday living, create new friendships in retirement communities, or explore new personal aspects in this phase of life. But unfortunately older adults who do struggle with substance abuse or dependence are often overlooked or misdiagnosed (Blow, Oslin, & Barry, 2002; Collier, Compton, Gfroerer, & Conlon, 2006; Epstein, Fischer-Elber, & Al-Otaiba, 2007; Han, Gfroerer, Gulliver, & Penne, 2009). It is imperative that helping practitioners understand the aging process, the vulnerability of older adults, and recognition and treatment for older adults with a substance abuse problem that diminishes quality of life. The use and misuse of alcohol and other substances place older adults at risk for detrimental physical, psychological, and social consequences that are often undetected in many health care settings. These substances exacerbate functional impairment and hamper an elder's ability to perform basic ADLs. Estimates of the current prevalence of alcohol and drug use in the older population vary, but the result of the aging baby boomers, who have a history of alcohol and drug abuse, will impact health care (Boyle & Davis, 2006). The 2012–2013 National Epidemiologic Survey on Alcohol and Related Conditions 111 (NESARC 111) found that 55.2% of adults age 65 and over drink alcohol (National Institute on Alcohol Abuse and Alcoholism, 2015).

Prescription Drug Abuse

Prescription drug use is rising in the United States. Among adults aged 65 and over, 70.2% took at least one cardiovascular agent and 46.7% took a cholesterol-lowering drug in the past 30 days in 2007–2010. Other commonly used classes for this age group include anti-acid reflux, antidiabetics, anticoagulants, and analgesics. The use of antidepressants, anticoagulants, and anti-acid reflux drugs substantially increased between 2007 and 2010 (U.S. Department of Health and Human Services, 2014). As Americans rely more on prescription drugs, some are taking multiple drugs each month, which is considered polypharmacy. Polypharmacy increased the likelihood of drug interactions, adverse effects, and dosing and compliance issues. Patients taking multiple drugs are more likely to confuse medication dose and timing (Bushardt, Massey, Simpson, Ariail, & Simpson, 2008). Polypharmacy is of particular concern for the elderly, who may be more at risk for significant side effects with some commonly prescribed medicines (National Committee for Quality Assurance, 2013).

The rise in older adults' prescription drug use has been accompanied by an increase in patterns of abuse where prescription drugs that are not medically necessary are taken intentionally. Older adults are particularly vulnerable to misuse and abuse of prescription medications. Persons ages 65 and over make up less than 15% of the population, but they consume about one-third of all prescription medications (National Council on Patient Information and Education [NCPIE], 2015). Older adults take more potentially addictive medications than any other age group (Johns Hopkins Health Alerts, 2010). One in four older adults has used psychoactive medications with abuse potential, and such use is likely to grow as the population ages (Simoni-Wastila & Yang, 2006). Although illicit drug use is relatively rare among older adults compared to younger adults and adolescents, there is increasing evidence that prescription drug misuse and abuse is a growing problem in the older population (Simon-Wastila & Yang, 2006). The prevalence of prescription drug abuse in older adults may be as high as 11% (Culberson & Ziska, 2008).

Abuse places a financial toll on health care systems and on individuals and their families. Experts estimate that the issue is underdiagnosed in seniors; although 60% of substance abuse is recognized in patients younger than 60, only 37% is recognized in patients over the age of 60 (Meyer, 2005). Abuse or misuse of prescription drugs is second only to alcohol abuse in the over-65 demographic, and the most commonly abused prescription medications include opiates, central nervous system depressants, and stimulants due to their addictive qualities (NIH Senior Health, 2014). Drug misuse and abuse in the elderly is of special concern because it can cause cognitive and physical impairment, putting them at greater risk for falls and motor vehicle accidents and making them generally less able to care for their daily needs.

The life changes that occur as one reaches his or her twilight years are significant. Elderly patients can experience a mixture of social-emotional, physical, and functional changes that may encourage addiction (Simonson & Feinberg, 2005). Physiological contributors include high rates of co-morbid illnesses, changes in metabolism (that affect drug potency), and shifting hormone levels. Mental health concerns also arise, especially with those experiencing major health problems. Though not considered a part of aging, depression is a specific concern that can initiate or exacerbate a decline in function and overall health. Physically, some seniors slow down and become compromised in their mobility and dexterity. If unable to engage socially or participate in activities of daily living as they are accustomed to, seniors may turn to medications that ease this reality or that appear to make life easier. Often, doctors prescribe "coping" drugs to help patients with anxiety, depression, or sleeplessness, many of which are addictive. Medical care providers do not always coordinate their care and treatment, which can confuse the patient and cause potential adverse drug interactions. Often the elderly, their families, and their service providers are uninformed about the potential for misuse and abuse of prescription drugs (NIH Medline Plus, 2015).

Risk Factors for Alcohol Abuse

A number of risk factors have been identified for late onset drinking problems. Often, the presence of chronic medical disorders and sleep disturbances may place the elderly at risk to self-medicate with alcohol to control pain or to induce sleep (Amosko, Richardson-Campbell, & Kennedy-Malone, 2003; Oslin & Blow, 2000). There is evidence to suggest that women in this age group are more vulnerable to late onset alcoholism than men (Blow, 2000). Additionally, older adults who are isolated or have excess leisure time may drink to stave off boredom or loneliness.

Elderly persons also have physiological characteristics that predispose them to problems with alcohol. A clear understanding of the significant consequences of its misuse may help clinicians to identify potential problems exhibited by these individuals. Elders have a decreased biological ability to process alcohol and other such substances, are susceptible to psychiatric illnesses co-morbid with substance abuse such as dementia and depression, and are prone to increased morbidity and suicide when substance abuse is present (Fingerhood, 2000). As the population continues to age, helping professionals will increasingly confront the needs of elders with alcohol abuse problems and need effective strategies to work with this population.

Risk Factors for Prescription Drug/Other Substance Misuse and Abuse

Factors that increase the risk for substance use among older adults include a previous history of substance abuse, comorbid psychiatric illness, and cognitive impairment (Blazer & Wu, 2009; Voyer, Preville, Cohen, Berbiche, & Beland, 2010). Female gender, social isolation, history of substance abuse, history of mental illness, and medical exposure to prescription drugs with abuse potential are factors associated with drug abuse in older adults (Simoni-Wastila & Yang, 2006).

Most prescription drug misuse by older adults is unintentional, and there are many factors that contribute to or increase the risk of misuse (Basca, 2008). Prescription drug misuse is the use of a medication other than as directed or indicated, including taking too little or too much of a drug, taking it too often, or taking it too long, whether harm results or not (Katz, Adams, & Chilcoat, 2007). Numerous factors for prescription drug misuse include use of numerous medications for chronic conditions frequently with uncoordinated care between multiple prescribers, inappropriate prescribing, small print instructions and package inserts, limited English language proficiency, and low health literacy (Basca, 2008). Memory problems, hearing or vision problems, failure to inform the physician about over-the-counter medications, vitamins and herbals, and finally willingness of doctors to prescribe drugs for sleeplessness, anxiety, and depression without investigating and treating the root cause of these problems are additional factors (Basca, 2008).

Prescription drug abuse is the intentional taking of prescription drugs that are not medically necessary or for the experience or feeling a drug causes (Basca, 2008). Older women have been found to be at greater risk for prescription drug abuse than older men or younger women. Compared with older men, older women take more psychoactive drugs, especially benzodiazepines, and are more likely to be long-term users of these medications (Center for Substance Abuse Treatment [CSAT], 2006). Social isolation or loss of social supports, factors related to the provider and health care system, depression, and history of mental health problems or substance abuse may increase vulnerability for abusing prescribing medications (Simoni-Wastila & Yang, 2006). Exposure or access to prescribed medications with abuse potential may be the single greatest risk factor for prescription drug abuse by older adults (Simoni-Wastila & Yang, 2006).

Treatment

Treatment strategies and screening methods used for substance abuse in older adults occur on three levels. Primary prevention includes age-appropriate screening instruments, increased media attention, and public health initiatives. Secondary prevention entails early detection of risk factors and assessment using geriatric assessment instruments. Tertiary prevention includes inpatient programs; outpatient individual, group, and family counseling; and support groups. Any combination of these approaches is used with older adults with substance abuse problems, and Table 5.2 illustrates these approaches.

Treatment approaches are being developed for older clients. A primary assumption of an age-specific approach is that treatment is most effective when the issues dealt with are congruent with the life stage of the client. Older substance abusers face different issues than their younger counterparts, including loss, isolation, serious physical health problems, and other aging-related experiences (Blow, Walton, Chermack, Mudd, & Brower, 2000). Social isolation, depression, and health problems may be more central to the substance use of older persons (Lemke & Moos, 2002). Therefore, elder-specific programs are designed to address such associated challenges and how they impact substance use (Blow et al., 2000). Further, older persons with alcohol use disorders may have somewhat lesser problems than younger patients in terms of severity of alcohol use problems, psychosocial functioning, and social consequences. Elder-specific programs often embrace a supportive,

---

Table 5.2 Screening Methods and Treatment Strategies Used for Substance Abuse in Older Adults

- Comprehensive assessment of medications, substance use/abuse history, major life changes, cognition, and medical problems
- Utilize screening instruments designed for older adults (e.g., Geriatric Version of the Michigan Alcohol Screening Test—MAST-G) (Blow, 1991)
- Individualized treatment plan based on the older adult, individual conditions, and situations
- Detoxification inpatient programs to monitor complications
- Aftercare support services in outpatient rehabilitation facilities
- Individual and group therapy sessions including brief therapy, psychoeducation, counseling, and motivation interviewing
- Family therapy sessions using the systems approach
- Support groups (e.g., Alcoholics Anonymous [AA] or Narcotics Anonymous [NA])

non-confrontational approach under the belief that confrontation may dissuade aging substance abusers from entering into or remaining in treatment.

In addition to age-specific treatment, cognitive-behavioral approaches are generally recommended for the effective treatment of older substance abusers (CSAT, 1998). These cognitive-behavioral approaches are typically based on Marlatt and Gordon's (1985) relapse prevention model, identified by the National Institute on Drug Abuse (1999) as an efficacious, scientifically based treatment approach for substance use disorders. The relapse prevention model views addictive behaviors as over-learned habits that can be analyzed and modified. As such, cognitive-behavioral treatment typically consists of a functional analysis of the antecedents to substance use and the short- and long-range consequences of substance use. Treatment is designed to modify the client's association between substance use antecedents and consequences through cognitive-behavioral restructuring (Rice, Longabaugh, Beattie, & Noel, 1993). Treatment programs utilizing the cognitive-behavioral approach usually employ approaches to teach clients the skills necessary to avoid relapse, such as cognitive restructuring, thought-stopping, problem-solving, self-monitoring, and self-reinforcement techniques (Schonfeld & Dupree, 2002). Cognitive-behavioral and age-specific approaches are not mutually exclusive and may be combined in a single treatment program.

Prescription Drug Abuse Prevention

Strategies to address prescription drug misuse and abuse require a collaborative approach. Strategies include educating the elderly, enhancing screening and brief intervention skills of health care clinicians, and forming community coalitions. One educational strategy is to create and disseminate promotional materials, in large print, targeting older adults. Media coverage regarding specific drug abuse should be accurately reported, and pharmacists should be encouraged to provide clear information and advice on how to take medications properly. The development of consumer education programs that specifically target older adult concerns is important. Recruitment of older adults as spokespersons and ensuring that substance abuse prevention and treatment professionals are included in the preparation and launching of all educational activities is also important. Collaborating with existing senior services, such as Home Support Services, senior centers, Meals on Wheels, and City Parks and Recreation programs, is also valuable to increase opportunities to disseminate information on prescription drug misuse and abuse to inform consumers.

Screening and brief intervention skills for health care clinicians can be enhanced. Clinicians can properly assess their patients by determining their risk of abuse, diagnosing them, and keeping proper records. Clinicians can also screen for any type of substance abuse using standardized screening tools and inquiring about what prescriptions and over-the-counter medications patients are taking and why. Clinicians are in a unique position to implement brief intervention skills to identify prescription drug abuse when it exists and help patients recognize the problem, set goals for recovery, and seek appropriate treatment when necessary (NIH, 2005).

Another strategy is to form community coalitions, which serves to create alliances with various organizations to work toward a common goal and share responsibility for addressing the prescription drug misuse and abuse problem in the elderly population. Partnerships can be made with local Retired Senior Volunteer Programs, AARP, Area Agencies on Aging, Departments of Health, community centers, retirement homes, and the faith community. The importance of collaboration should be reinforced in all of the activities. A memorandum of understanding (MOU) among state and local agencies should be established to better ensure their commitment to this issue that involves pharmaceutical companies, pharmacies, and medical professionals (Basca, 2008).

Training and education is provided to consumers within the communities through the American Society on Aging (ASA) and the American Society of Consultant Pharmacists (ASCP). Programs and services have been provided through the IMPACT Program; the Gatekeeper Program; and Screening, Brief Intervention, Referral and Treatment (SBIRT). The IMPACT program is one in which a depression care manager works closely with the patient's primary care physician (PCP) and a consulting psychiatrist to treat depression in the patient's regular primary care clinics. The Gatekeeper Program seeks to identify isolated older adults who are at risk for developing substance abuse and mental health problems. The SBIRT program is a federally funded program that involves implementation of a system within community and/or medical settings that screens for and identifies individuals who are at risk for substance use-related problems. For older adults, addressing the factors related to willful and inadvertent misuse of prescription medication and other substances is a necessary part of prevention and early intervention (Basca, 2008).

ELDER ABUSE

Elder abuse is a serious concern, and it involves any knowing, intentional, or negligent act by a caregiver or any other person that causes harm or a serious risk of harm to a vulnerable adult and warrants intervention by all concerned individuals (Administration on

Aging, 2013). Contrary to popular belief, perpetrators of elder abuse are not always nursing home staff members. Family members can be just as guilty, and a perpetrator of elder abuse can be anyone from an acquaintance to children and grandchildren. This abuse is a growing problem in society. It can be broken down into further categories, including, but not limited to, physical abuse and domestic violence, sexual abuse, emotional abuse, neglect, and exploitation (Administration on Aging, 2013). There are a number of signs pointing to these types of abuse. Physical abuse is the most obvious, with visible bruises, pressure marks, broken bones, and burns. The signs of emotional or sexual abuse are less obvious. More often than not the victim will "suffer in silence," with only slight signs of emotional or temperament changes that could be easily overlooked. If abuse is suspected, other family members and official agency personnel should be alerted and the situation should be questioned (Administration on Aging, 2013).

Physical Abuse

Physical abuse is inflicting physical pain or injury on a senior, e.g., slapping, bruising, or restraining by physical or chemical means (Administration on Aging, 2013). Signs that this type of abuse is happening include broken bones, unexplained bruises, welts and scarring, broken eye glasses, and unusual markings on wrists and ankles, as if the individual had been physically restrained (Elder Abuse & Neglect, 2014). Another situation that should indicate a red flag is if a caregiver will not allow family members or another caregiver, such as a doctor or nurse, to see the elder. Further signs of abuse are if a person runs out of medication before they should or has more left over than they should.

Domestic violence against the elderly can generally be put into categories: "domestic violence grown old" and "late-onset domestic violence." Domestic violence grown old is violence that began earlier in life and has continued with age, while late-onset domestic violence occurs when the violence begins in old age. Late onset could result from a strained past and the changes of aging, such as retirement, disability, roles, and sexual changes, or entering into a new but abusive relationship (National Committee for Prevention of Elder Abuse [NCPEA], 2008b). Victims are usually women and display the same signs and symptoms of those experiencing general physical abuse. Domestic violence and physical abuse can often lead to or couple with sexual abuse. Sexual abuse, is the nonconsensual sexual contact of any kind (Administration on Aging, 2013), and this can include can include rape, molestation, or any sexual conduct with a person who lacks the mental capacity to give consent (NCPEA, 2008b).

Emotional Abuse

Abuse doesn't always mean physical harm to an elder; emotional abuse can be just as dangerous. Emotional abuse is inflicting mental pain, anguish, or distress on an elderly person through verbal or nonverbal acts, for example, humiliating, intimidating, or threatening, and any person can fall subject to emotional abuse (Administration on Aging, 2013). Factors which place elders at risk include isolation and lack of social or emotional support (NCPEA, 2008b). A person may show signs of stress-related conditions such as unexplained weight-loss and high blood pressure, nervousness, and depression. The victim will have trouble sleeping, will fear being around or seeing the abuser, will be unusually upset and withdrawn, and will demonstrate behaviors like sucking, biting, or rocking, and the perpetrator will often isolate the elder (NCPEA, 2008b).

Emotional abuse and neglect can usually go hand-in-hand, but there are some distinct differences. The failure by those responsible to provide food, shelter, health care, or protection for a vulnerable elder defines neglect (Administration on Aging, 2013). It can be classified into two categories: passive and active neglect. Active neglect is intentional; a caregiver will purposefully withhold care or necessities. Passive neglect is when situational specific restrictions cause a caregiver to be unable to fulfill his or her duties as a result of any of the following: illness, disability, stress, ignorance, lack of maturity, or lack of resources (NCPEA, 2008b). Neglect is not always a problem with a caregiver; self-neglect is also a problem among the elderly population. Self-neglect occurs when the elder is unable to perform self-care tasks and this failure poses a threat to his or her safety (Administration on Aging, 2013).

Financial Abuse

With regards to social and economic challenges, elders face another type of abuse—financial abuse. Financial abuse can take many forms and might include exploitation: the illegal taking, misuse, or concealment of funds, property, or assets of a senior for someone else's benefit (Administration on Aging, 2013). In this case, perpetrators are usually family members, children, grandchildren, and in some cases, spouses. While most perpetrators have a sense of entitlement, exploitation may also be a result of a dependence and desperation, such as alcoholism or a gambling problem, or it could be a result of poor relationships among family members (NCPEA, 2008a). The most likely to be victimized are those who are alone and isolated, recently widowed, or suffering from mental and physical limitations. Ways to tell if financial abuse is occurring is if the elder starts to have unpaid bills, notices to shut off utilities, eviction from the home notices, or unexplained bank transactions. The elderly are often a target for scams because they will sign things they do not understand.

Elder abuse is a problem all across the world in both rich and developing countries and no race or ethnicity is more likely to be abused than another. Case Illustration 5.3 provides a glimpse of financial exploitation by a family member toward his mother and the mother's reluctance to take any action against her son.

CASE ILLUSTRATION 5.3

Many types of elder abuse exist and the perpetrators of abuse are oftentimes family members. This family member is reluctant to share what is happening because she is dependent on her son and does not want him to get into trouble, and she dearly loves him. Kevin is a middle-aged adult who has moved back into his mother's home to assist with her care. His mother has had difficulty ambulating, has severe back pain, and stays primarily in a recliner for most of the day and sometimes at night.

Kevin prepares her meals, cleans her home once per week, does the laundry, goes grocery shopping, pays the bills, and from the outside, appears as a loving and devoted son.

His mother owns her home, which has a market value of approximately $150,000, and Kevin's older brother is the beneficiary. His mother also receives a pension of $2,000 per month and a Social Security check of $1,800 per month. Her husband left her 75 acres of land near the local airport, which currently is in negotiations to be sold. She does not have any outstanding bills, except for food, utilities, and life insurance payments. She has accumulated $50,000 in her savings account, which took her years to do.

One day she asked Kevin to withdraw $10,000 from this account so she could help her grand-daughter's tuition. Kevin scolded her saying, "that's not your responsibility." He appeared angry that she asked for some of her money. She conceded and stated, "Just get $5,000 out of the account." Kevin scolded her once again. When Kevin left the house to purchase groceries, she began rummaging through her desk to obtain records of her accounts. She learned that her $50,000 was gone.

Additionally, Kevin changed the beneficiary on her house to himself, added his name to her checking account, and routinely spends all of the money that she receives monthly. She learned she has a total of $400 to her name.

She confronted Kevin, who became angry and left the house for several days. Upon his return, he scolded her once again. He threatened to leave and never return. His mother suffers in silence, fearful of her son, and scared of losing the only caregiver she has. She has been afraid of saying anything because she is dependent on her son and does not want to see him in trouble. Her ultimate fear is being placed in a facility.

Protecting Against Elder Abuse

Adult Protective Services (APS) is the agency responsible for protection of vulnerable adults by investigating allegations of elder abuse, including abuse, neglect, abandonment, and financial exploitation. Based on the outcome of an investigation, APS may offer legal and/or social services. Older adults who need APS tend to have physical or mental impairments that put them at risk for self-neglect or being harmed by others.

Factors placing older adults at risk for mistreatment include the presence of a brittle support system, loneliness, family conflict, alcohol abuse, psychiatric problems, social awkwardness, and short-term memory problems (Shugarman, Fries, Wolf, & Morris, 2003). In cases where elder abuse occurs in institutional settings, there are mechanisms set in place to identify the abuse and manage the consequences. Such resources include institutional review processes and the State Ombudsman program adopted after the passage of the Omnibus Budget Reconciliation Act of 1987. When elder abuse occurs in the community, recourse is available through the APS program in each state.

APS workers are frequently called on to make critical life changing decisions in complex situations. Statutes typically require APS investigations to be initiated within 24 hours of receiving a report with the appropriate actions taken as quickly as possible to ensure the safety of the victim. Many cases involve life and death medical problems, difficult issues surrounding the older adult's mental capacity to consent to or refuse services, undue influence, guardianship, powers of attorney, and the rights of victims to self-determination versus the state's parens patriae duty to protect citizens who cannot protect themselves (National Association of Adult Protective Services Administrators, 2003).

To protect and serve older adults subject to abuse, APS receives reports, conducts investigations, evaluates risks to clients, assesses clients' ability to give consent, develops and implements case plans, counsels clients, arranges for a variety of services and benefits, and monitors ongoing service delivery (Otto, 2000). Services most likely to be recommended by APS for abuse of older adults include medical and social services, guardianship, psychological and/or family counseling, legal counsel, and institutional placement when necessary.

Elder abuse takes many forms, and unfortunately the victims are older persons who are dependent upon their caretakers. Helping professionals are in a position to advocate on behalf of their older clients and refer them to protective services for investigations of alleged abuse. Practitioners can provide counseling services to assist older clients in altering their current situation that is adversely affecting their health and overall well-being. Guided Practice Exercise 5.6 provides an opportunity to gain knowledge of an aging organization designed to protect victims of elder abuse and examine personal feelings regarding intervening in abusive situations.

Guided Practice Exercise 5.6

Visit your nearest Area Agency on Aging and identify the services being offered for older adults. Discuss with agency staff any changes they have experienced in the last 5–10 years regarding the profile and needs of their clients. Protective Services exist to protect older adults from abusive situations. Identify the types of elder abuse, perpetrators of elder abuse, and ways to intervene to protect older adults from their abusers. How comfortable are you with intervening on behalf of elders in an abusive situation?

Helping professionals and emerging professionals are in a pivotal position to identify challenging conditions and intervene at different stages when addressing issues posed by the older client. While these conditions pose particular challenges to the older client, the family is also challenged to help their aging members cope successfully. Clinicians must be cognizant of the lack of awareness on behalf of many older clients and the reluctance to address some of these issues outside of the family system. An understanding of these challenging conditions and their adverse impact on older clients and their families enhances the ability of helping practitioners to help all involved navigate this difficult terrain.

KEYSTONES

- Alzheimer's disease is a degenerative disease that adversely affects the functional ability of elders in their later years.
- Depression is a treatable disorder that is experienced by many older persons.
- Anxiety disorders occur in older adults and can lead to depression.
- Alcohol abuse and prescription drug abuse are underreported problems within the elderly population.
- Common types of elder abuse include physical abuse, emotional abuse and neglect, and financial abuse.
- Comprehensive examination of problematic conditions is critical in the treatment of older adults.

ADDITIONAL RESOURCES

Print Based

Abdel-Rahman, E. (2012). *Depression in the elderly*. Hauppauge, NY: Nova Science Publishers.

Barry, K., Blow, F., & Oslin, D. (2001). *Alcohol problems in older adults. Prevention and management*. New York, NY: Springer.

Bourgeois, M., & Hickey, E. (2009). *Dementia: From diagnosis to management—a functional approach*. East Sussex, UK: Psychology Press.

Colleran, C., & Jay, D. (2002). *Aging and addiction: Helping older adults overcome alcohol or medication dependence*. Center City, MN: Hazelden Publishing.

Dickerson, B., & Atri, A. (2014). *Dementia: Comprehensive principles and practices*. New York, NY: Oxford University Press.

Griswold, J. (2013). *Fears of the elderly*. Seattle, WA: Create Space Independent Publishing Platform.

Gurnack, A., Atkinson, R., & Osgood, N. (2002). *Treating alcohol and drug abuse in the elderly*. New York, NY: Springer.

Mellor, J., & Brownell, P. (2006). *Elder abuse and mistreatment*. New York, NY, Routledge.

Runcan, P. (2013). *Depression in the elderly*. Newcastle upon Tyne, UK: Cambridge Scholars Publishing.

Seme, A. (2009). *Elderly abuse is alive and well*. Pittsburgh, PA: Dorrance Publishing.

Web Based

www.adaa.org/living-with-anxiety/older-adults

www.agingcare.com/elderly-alcohol-abuse

www.alz.org

www.aoa.gov/AoA_programs/elder_rights/EA_prevention/whatisEA.aspx

www.apa.org/helpcenter/aging-depression.aspx

www.drugabuse.gov/publications/research-reports/prescription-drugs/trends-in-prescription-drug-abuse/older-adults

www.helpguide.org/mental/depression_elderly.htm

www.mentalhealthamerica.net/conditions/depression-older-adults

www.ncadd.org/learn-about-alcohol/seniors-vets-and-women/196-alcohol-and-senior

www.ncea.aoa.gov/index.aspx

www.nia.nih.gov/alzheimers/publication/alzheimers-disease-fact-sheet

www.nihseniorhealth.gov/anxietydisorders/medication/01.html

www.tandfonline.com/toc/wean20/current

REFERENCES

Abbott, R. D., White, L. R., Ross, G. W., Masaki, K. H., & Curb, J. D. (2004). Walking and dementia in physically capable elderly men. *Journal of the American Medical Association, 292*(12), 1447–1453.

Administration on Aging. (2013, December). *What is elder abuse?* Retrieved from http://www.aoa.gov/AOA_programs/ElderRights/EA_Prevention/whatisEA.aspy

Alexopoulos, G., Katz, I., Reynolds, C., Carpenter, D., & Docherty, J. (2001). The expert consensus guideline serves: Pharmacotherapy of depressive disorders in older patients. *Postgraduate Medicine, Special Issue October*, 1–86.

Allan, C., Hermann, L., & Ebmeier, K. (2011). Transcranial magnetic stimulation in the management of mood disorders. *Neuropsychobiology, 64*(3), 163–169.

Allison, L., Cogdill, K., Daughtery, J., Dhingro, P., Painter, J. A., & Trujillo, L. G. (2012). Fear of falling and its relationship with anxiety, depression, and activity engagement among community-dwelling older adults. *American Journal of Occupational Therapy, 66*(2), 169.

Alzheimer's Association. (2006). *Early-onset dementia: A national challenge, a future crisis.* Washington, DC: Alzheimer's Association.

Alzheimer's Association. (2013). Alzheimer's disease facts and figures. *Alzheimer's & Dementia, 9*, 2.

Alzheimer's Association. (2015). 2015 Alzheimer's disease facts and figures. *Alzheimer's & Dementia, 11*(3), 332.

Amosko, E. P., Richardson-Campbell, L., & Kennedy-Malone, L. (2003). Self-medication with over-the-counter drugs among elderly adults. *Journal of Gerontological Nursing, 29*(8), 10–15.

Basca, B. (2008). The elderly and prescription drug use and abuse. *Prevention Tactics*, Edition 9, 2. Retrieved from http://www.cars.rp.org/publications/Prevention%20Tactics/PT09.02.08.pdf

Beekman, A., Bremmer, M., Deeg, D., van Balkom, A., Smit, J., de Beurs, E., & van Tilburg, W. (1998). Anxiety disorders in later life: A report from the longitudinal aging study Amsterdam. *International Journal of Geriatric Psychiatry, 13*(10), 717–726.

Beekman, A., van Balkom, A., Deeg, D., van Dyck, R., & van Tilburg, W. (2000). Anxiety and depression in later life: Co-occurrence and communability of risk factors. *American Journal of Psychiatry, 157*(1), 89–95.

Blazer, D., Hybels, C., & Pieper, C. (2001). The association of depression and mortality in elderly persons: A case for multiple independent pathways. *Journal of Gerontology: Medical Science, 56A*, M505–M509.

Blazer, D., & Wu, L. (2009). Non-prescription use of pain relievers by middle-aged and elderly community-living adults: National Survey on Drug Use and Health. *Journal of American Geriatrics Society, 57*(7), 1252–1257.

Blow, F. (1991). *Michigan Alcoholism Screening Test-Geriatric Version (MAST-G)*. Ann Arbor, MI: University of Michigan Alcohol Research Center.

Blow, F. (2000). Treatment of women with alcohol problems: Meeting the challenge for a special population. *Alcohol Clinical Experience Research, 24*(8), 1257.

Blow, F. C., Oslin, D. W., & Barry, K. J. (2002). Misuse and abuse of alcohol, illicit drugs, and psychoactive medication among older people. *Generations, 26,* 50–54.

Blow, F. C., Walton, M. A., Chermack, S. T., Mudd, S. A., & Brower, K. J. (2000). Older adult treatment outcome following elder-specific inpatient alcoholism treatment. *Journal of Substance Abuse Treatment, 19,* 67–75.

Boyle, A. R., & Davis, H. (2006). Screening and assessment of alcohol and substance abuse in the elderly: Clinical implications. *Journal of Addiction Nursing, 17,* 95–103.

Bushardt, R., Massey, E., Simpson, T., Ariail, J., & Simpson, K. (2008). Polypharmacy: Misleading, but manageable. *Clinical Interventions in Aging, 3*(2), 383–389.

Centers for Disease Control and Prevention. (2011). Vital signs overdoses of prescription opioid pain relievers—United States: 1999–2008. *MMWR Morbidity and Mortality Weekly Report, 60*(43), 1487–1492.

Center for Substance Abuse Treatment (CSAT). (1998). Substance abuse among older adults. Rockville, MD: Substance Abuse and Mental Health Sources Administration. *Treatment Improvement Protocol (TIP) Series, no 26.*

Center for Substance Abuse Treatment (CSAT). (2006). Prescription medications: Misuse, abuse, dependence, and addiction. *Substance Abuse Treatment Advisory, 5*(2).

Chicago Health and Aging Project (CHAP). (2010). Prevalence of Alzheimer's disease and other dementias. *Alzheimer's & Dementia, 9,* 2.

Collier, J. C., Compton, W. M., Gfroerer, J. C., & Condron, T. (2006). Projecting drug use among aging baby boomers in 2020. *Annals of Epidemiology, 16,* 257–265.

Conwell, Y., Duberstein, P., & Carne, E. (2002). Risk factors for suicide in later life. *Biological Psychiatry, 52,* 193–204.

Coupland, C., Dhiman, P., & Barton, G. (2011). A study of the safety and harms of antidepressant drugs for older people: A cohort study using a large primary care database. *Health Technology Assessment, 15*(28), 1–202.

Culberson, J., & Ziska, M. (2008). Prescription drug misuse/abuse in the elderly. *Geriatrics, 63*(9), 22–31.

Dilworth-Anderson, P., Hendrie, H. C., Manly, J. J., Khachaturian, A. S., & Fazio, S. (2008). Diagnosis and assessment of Alzheimer's disease in diverse populations. *Alzheimer's Dementia, 4*(4), 305–309.

Elder Abuse & Neglect. (2014, February). Warning signs, risk factors, prevention, and reporting abuse. In Help guide. Retrieved from http://www.helpguide.org/mental/elder_abuse_physical_emotional_sexual_neglect.html

Epstein, E. E., Fischer-Elber, K., & Al-Otaiba, Z. (2007). Women, aging, and alcohol use disorders. *Journal of Women and Aging, 19,* 31–48.

Fava, M., Rush, A., & Trivedi, M. (2003). Background and rationale for the sequenced treatment alternatives to relieve depression (STAR*D) study. *Psychiatric Clinical North America, 26*(2), 457–494.

Fingerhood, M. (2000). Substance abuse in older people. *Journal of the American Geriatrics Society, 48,* 985–995.

Flory, R., Ametepe, J., & Bowers, B. (2010). A randomized, placebo-controlled trial of bright light and high-density negative air ions for treatment of seasonal affective disorder. *Psychiatry Research, 177*(2), 101–108.

Forsell, Y., Palmer, K., & Fratglioni, L. (2003). Psychiatric symptoms/syndromes in elderly persons with mild cognitive impairment. Data from a cross-sectional study. *Acta Neurologica Scandavica Supplementum, 179,* 25–28.

Friedman, M. B., Fursty, L., Gellis, Z. D., & Williams, K. (2013). Anxiety disorders in older adults. *Social Work Today, 13,* 10.

Gallagher, D., & Thompson, L. (1982). Treatment of major depressive disorder in older outpatients with brief psychotherapies. *Psychotherapy: Theory, Research, and Practice, 19,* 482–490.

Han, B, Gfroerer, J. C., Colliver, J. D., & Penne, M. A. (2009). Substance use disorder among older adults in the United States in 2020. *Addiction, 104,* 88–96.

Hebert, L. E., Scherr, P. A., McCann, J. J., Beckett, L. A., & Evans, D. A. (2001). Is the risk of developing Alzheimer's disease greater for women than for men? *American Journal of Epidemiology, 153*(2), 132–136.

Hebert, L. E., Weuve, J., Scherr, P. A., & Evans, D. A. (2013). Alzheimer's disease in the United States (2010–2050) estimated using the 2010 Census. *Neurology, 80*(19), 1778–1783.

Hirschfield, R. (2011). Deep brain stimulation for treatment-resistant depression. *American Journal of Psychiatry, 168*(5), 455–456.

Hollon, S. (2011). Cognitive and behavior therapy in the treatment and prevention of depression. *Depression Anxiety, 28*(4), 263–266.

Johns Hopkins Health Alerts. (2010). *Drug abuse and the elderly*. Retrieved from http://www.johnshopkin shealthalerts.com/reports/prescription_drugs/3363-1.html?zKPrintable=true

Katz, N., Adams, E., & Chilcoat, H. (2007). Challenges in the development of prescription opioid abuse-deterrent formulations. *Clinical Journal of Pain, 23*(8), 648–660.

Kelsey, J. E. (2002). Treatment strategies in achieving remission in major depressive disorder. *Acta Psychiatrica Scandinavica, Supplement, 106*(415), 18–23.

Khouzam, H. (2012). Depression in the elderly: How to treat. *Consultant, 22,* 4.

Khouzam, H. R. (2009). The diagnosis and treatment of depression in the geriatric population. *Comprehensive Therapy, 35*(2), 103–114.

Lang, A. J., & Stein, M. B. (2001). Anxiety disorders. *Geriatrics, 56*(5), 24–38.

Laurin, D., Verreault, R., Lindsay, J., MacPherson, K., & Rockwood, K. (2001). Physical activity and risk of cognitive impairment and dementia in elderly persons. *Archives of Neurology, 58*(3), 498–504.

Lemke, S., & Moos, R. H. (2002). Prognosis of older patients in mixed-age alcoholism treatment programs. *Journal of Substance Abuse Treatment, 22,* 33–43.

Manly, J., & Mayeuv, R. (2004). Ethnic differences in dementia and Alzheimer's disease. In N. Anderson, R. Buffalo, & B. Cohen (Eds.), *Critical perspectives on racial and ethnic differentials in health in late life* (pp. 95–141). Washington, DC: National Academics Press.

Marlatt, G. A., & Gordon, J. R. (Eds.). (1985). *Relapse prevention: Maintenance strategies in the treatment of addictive behaviors*. New York, NY: Guilford Press.

Mayo Clinic. (2012). *Electroconvulsive therapy: Definition*. Rochester, MN: Mayo Foundation for Medical Education and Research.

Meyer, C. (2005). Prescription drug abuse in the elderly: How the elderly become addicted to their medications. *The People's Media Company*. Retrieved from http://www.associatedcontent.com/article/5731/prescriptiondrugabuseintheelderly.html

Mohlman, J. (2012). A community-based survey of older adults' preferences for treatment of anxiety. *Psychology and Aging, 27*(4), 1182–1190. doi: 10. 1037/a0023 (CSAT)

Myers, J. E., Dice, C. E., & Dew, B. J. (2000). Alcohol abuse in later life: Issues and interventions for counselors. *Adultspan, 2,* 2–13.

Nahas, R., & Sheikh, O. (2011). Complementary and alternative medicine for the treatment of major depressive disorder. *Canadian Family Physician, 57*(6), 659–663.

National Association of Adult Protective Services Administrators. (2003). *Problems facing the state adult protective services programs and the resources needed to resolve them*. Washington, DC: Author.

National Center for Health Statistics, C. F. D. C. A. P. (2000). *Death Rates for Suicide, 1950–1998*.

National Committee for Prevention of Elder Abuse (NCPEA). (2008a). *Financial abuse*. Retrieved from http://www.preventelderabuse.org/elderabuse/fin_abuse.html

National Committee for Prevention of Elder Abuse (NCPEA). (2008b). *Neglect and self-neglect*. Retrieved from http://www.preventelderabuse.org/elderabuse/neglect.html

National Committee for Quality Assurance. (2013). HEDIS 2013: Healthcare effectiveness data and information set. Vol 1, Narrative. Washington, DC: Author. Retrieved from http://www.ncqa.org/HEDIS QualityMeasurement/HEDISMeasures/HED15S013.aspx

National Council on Patient Information and Education (NCPIE). (2015). *Educate before you medicate*. Retrieved from http://www.talkaboutrx.org/select_groups.isp

National Institute on Alcohol Abuse and Alcoholism. (2015). *Alcohol and aging*. Retrieved from http://nihse niorhealth.gov/alcoholuse/alcohol andaging/01.html

National Institute on Drug Abuse. (1999). *Principles of drug addiction treatment: A research-based guide* (NIH Publication No. 99-4180). Washington, DC: Author.

NIH Medline Plus. (2015). *Prescription drug abuse*. Retrieved from https://www.nlm.nih.gov/medlineplus/pre-scription drugabuse.html

NIH Senior Health. (2014). *Improper use of medications*. Retrieved from http://www.nihseniorhealth.gov/dru-gabuse/improperuse101.html

Novak, M. (2012). *Issues in aging*. Boston, MA: Allyn & Bacon.

Oslin, D. W., & Blow, F. C. (2000). Substance use disorders in late life. In I. Katz & D. Oslin (Eds.), *Annual review of gerontology and geriatrics: Focus on psychopharmacologic intervention in late life* (Vol. 19, pp. 213–224). New York, NY: Springer.

Otto, J. (2000, Summer). The role of Adult Protective Services in addressing abuse. *Generations*, 33–38.

Pillai, J. A., Hall, C. B., Dickson, D. W., Buschke, H., Lipton, R. B., & Verghese, J. (2014). Association of crossword puzzle participation with memory decline in persons who develop dementia. *Journal of International Neurological Society, 17*(6), 1–13. doi:10.1017/S1355617711001111

Plassman, B. L., Langa, K. M., Fisher, G. G., Heeringa, S. G., Weir, D. R., & Ofstendal, M. B. (2007). Prevalence of dementia in the United States: The aging, demographics, and memory study. *Neuroepidemiology, 29*(1–2), 125–132.

Potter, G. G., Plassman, B. L., Burke, J. R., Kabette, M. U., Langa, K. M., & Llewellyn, D. J. (2009). Cognitive per-formance and informant reports in the diagnosis of cognitive impairment and dementia in African-Americans and whites. *Alzheimers Dementia, 5*(6), 445–453.

Reynolds, C. F. III, Frank, E., Perel, J. M., Imber, S. D., Cornes, C., Miller, M. D., . . . Kupfer, D. J. (1999). Nortriptyline and interpersonal psychotherapy as maintenance therapies for recurrent major depression: A randomized controlled trial in patients older than 59 years. *Journal of American Medical Association, 281,* 39–45.

Rice, C., Longabaugh, R., Beattie, M., & Noel, M. (1993). Age group differences in response to treatment for problematic alcohol use. *Addiction, 88,* 1369–1375.

Roan, S. (2006, January 9). "To sharpen the brain, first hone the body: Mental benefits include better memory and learning; dementia may be slowed," *Los Angeles Times*.

Robinson, L., Smith, M., & Segal, J. (2015). *Depression in older adults and the elderly*. Retrieved from http://www.helpguide.org/articles/depression/depression-in-older-adults-and-the-elderly.htm

Rothrauff, T., Abraham, A., Bride, B., & Roman, P. (2011). Substance abuse treatment for older adults in private centers. *Substance Abuse, 32*(1), 7–15.

Rubin, E., Veiel, L., Kinscherf, D., Morris, J., & Storandt, M. (2001). Clinically significant depression symptoms and very mild to mild dementia of Alzheimer type. *International Journal of Geriatric Psychiatry, 16,* 694–701.

Schoevers, R. A., Beekman, A., Deeg, D., Jonker, C., & Tilburg, W. (2003). Comorbidity and risk patterns of depression, generalized anxiety disorder and mixed anxiety-depression in later life: Results from the longitudinal aging study Amsterdam. *International Journal of Geriatric Psychiatry, 18,* 994–1001.

Schonfeld, L., & Dupree, L. W. (2002). Age-specific cognitive behavioral and self-management treatment approaches. In A. M. Gurnack, R. Atkinson, & N. J. Osgood (Eds.), *Treating alcohol and drug abuse in the elderly* (pp. 109–130). New York, NY: Springer.

Schulz, R., Drayer, R., & Rollman, B. (2002). Depression as a risk factor for non-suicide mortality in the elderly. *Biological Psychiatry, 52,* 205–225.

Shugarman, L. R., Fries, B. E., Wolf, R. S., & Morris, J. N. (2003). Identifying older people at risk of abuse during routine screening practices. *Journal of the American Geriatrics Society, 51*, 24–31.

Simoni-Wastila, L., & Yang, H. (2006). Psychoactive drug abuse in older adults. *American Journal of Geriatric Pharmacotherapy, 4*(4), 380–394.

Simonson, W., & Feinberg, J. (2005). Medication-related problems in the elderly: Defining the issues and identifying solutions. *Drugs and Aging, 22*(7), 559–569.

Steffens, D., & McQuoid, D. (2005). Impact of symptoms of generalized anxiety disorder on the course of late-life depression. *American Journal of Geriatric Psychiatry, 13,* 40–47.

United States Department of Health and Human Services (U.S. DHHS). (2014). *Health, United States, 2013: With special feature on prescription drugs.* Hyattsville, MD: Centers for Disease Control and Prevention, National Center for Health Statistics.

van Zelst, W., deBeurs, E., & Beckman, A. (2003). Prevalence and risk factors of posttraumatic stress disorder in older adults. *Psychotherapy Psychosomatic, 72,* 333–342.

Vincent, G. K., & Velkof, V. A. (2010). *The next four decades: The older population in the United States: 2010 to 2050.* Washington, DC: U.S. Census Bureau.

Voyer, P., Preville, M., Cohen, D., Berbiche, D., & Beland, S. (2010). The prevalence of benzodiazepine dependence among community-dwelling older adult users in Quebec according to typical and atypical criteria. *Canadian Journal of Aging, 29*(2), 205–213.

Weuve, J., Kang, J. H., Manson, J. E., Breteler, M. M., Ware, J. H., & Grodstein, F. (2004). Physical activity, including walking, and cognitive function in older women. *Journal of American Medical Association, 292*(12), 1454–1461.

Wiese, B. S. (2011). Geriatric depression: The use of anti-depressants in the elderly. *British Columbia Medical Journal, 53*(7), 341–347.

Williams, J. M., Ballard, M. B., & Alessi, H. (2005). Aging and alcohol abuse: Increasing counselor awareness. *Adultspan, 4,* 7–18.

Wu, L., & Blazer, D. (2011). Illicit and nonmedical drug use among older adults: A review. *Journal of Aging Health, 23*(3), 481–504.

Zandi, P., Sparks, L., Khachaturian, A., Tschanz, J., Norton, M., & Steinberg, M. (2004). Do statins reduce risk of incident dementia and AD? The cache county study. *Archives of General Psychiatry, 62,* 217–224.

Zisook, S., & Shear, K. (2009). Grief and bereavement: What psychiatrists need to know. *World Psychiatry, 8*(2), 67–74.

Family Issues
and Support Systems

"The most romantic story isn't Romeo and Juliet, who died together, but Grandma and Grandpa who grew old together."

—Anonymous

Learning Objectives

After reading this chapter, you will be able to

1. Examine the opportunities and challenges posed within the caregiving relationship and psychosocial interventions that can be implemented for the family
2. Describe the impacts of caring for a grandchild in the later stages of life
3. Analyze the benefits of formal support systems and informal support

INTRODUCTION

Elders do not function in isolation; therefore, family issues and support systems must be examined. The family is the primary informal support system available to older adults, and when they are not available, the formal support network is accessed. Caregiving is a major necessity for older adults who experience difficulties in the activities of daily living (ADLs). While caregiving is a vital component for aging members to remain in their communities, this responsibility poses challenges to many working family members.

Grandparenting is examined to highlight the increasing role of many elders in today's society. Some older adults see grandparenting as an opportunity to parent a second time, and it is welcomed. However, others take on the responsibility due to negative events that have occurred with their children. This grandparent role has health, mental health, and economic implications.

Formal support networks are utilized to assist in providing services and environments that can allow older adults to remain in their communities. For those persons requiring additional supervision, living arrangements that provide personnel and other necessities are available. Helping professionals must have a working knowledge of the significance of the family as a support system, the complexities of assuming responsibility for young persons in the later years, and the services available within the community.

CAREGIVING

Caregivers provide assistance to someone who is, in some degree, incapacitated and needs help (Family Caregiver Alliance, 2005). The recipients of care reside in both residential and institutional settings and range from children to older adults. Typically, they have a chronic illness or disabling condition and need ongoing assistance with everyday tasks to function on a daily basis (Family Caregiver Alliance, 2006).

Prior to the development of residential care facilities, the family was the primary source of care for their aging family members. As more of the elderly population is living longer because of advances in health care and medical technology, more resources are needed to provide longer and better care. Caregiver demand is partially driven by the increase in the older population; therefore, as the number of older Americans rises, so does the number of needed caregivers (Talley & Crews, 2007). In 2030, when all baby boomers will be at least 65 years old, the population of adults in this age group is projected to be 71 million (Administration on Aging [AOA], 2007). The population 65 and over has increased from 44.7 million in 2013 and is projected to more than double to 98 million in 2060 (AOA, 2014). However, the majority of family caregivers (60%) caring for adults in 2014 were employed either full-time or part-time, placing competing demands on the caregivers' time (Reinhard, Feinberg, Choula, & Houser, 2015).

Individuals experience a variety of transitions throughout the life course. One later-life transition that is particularly important is the transition to the caregiver role, whether it is for a spouse, parent, or both. Informal care is a burden that many family members will experience in their lifetime, with spousal caregiving being one of the most common forms of informal long-term care (Lima, Allen, Goldscheider, & Intrator, 2008). Caregiving takes a tremendous toll on caregivers' health and well-being and accounts for significant costs to families and society as well. Studies suggest that as a result of providing assistance due to physical, cognitive, or emotional impairments, caregivers often compromise and sacrifice their own well-being, leading to adverse health outcomes. Across a variety of outcomes, caregivers seem to exhibit a greater risk of health problems compared to non-caregivers (Vitaliano, Zhang, & Scanlan, 2003). Studies indicate that caring for an ill family member is associated with higher levels of depressive symptoms (Hahn, Kim, & Chirboga, 2011; Turner, Killian, & Cain, 2004) and anxiety as well as higher use of psychoactive medications, poorer self-reported physical health, compromised immune function, a higher number of health risk behaviors (Burton,

Zdaniuk, Shulz, Jackson, & Hirsch, 2003), and increased mortality (Kiecolt-Glaser & Glaser, 2001). Caregivers also indicate that their decline in health compromises their ability to provide care.

However, some studies suggest that older caregivers, compared to non-caregivers, actually experience better health outcomes (Bertrand et al., 2012; O'Reilly, Connolly, Rosato, & Patterson, 2008), perhaps due to caregivers being more physically active than non-caregivers (Fredman, Bertrand, Martire, Hochberg, & Harris, 2006; Fredman et al., 2008) as well as continuously engaging in cognitive tasks (Colcombe & Kramer, 2003; Lachman, Neupert, Bertrand, & Jette, 2006). Other research has found that the relationship between caregiving and declines in health is mediated, or at least partially accounted for, when controlling for socio-demographic characteristics and health factors, including age, education, income, and functional limitations (Jenkins, Kabeto, & Langa, 2009).

When multiple health problems and long-term care needs begin to occur, especially for those people in their late 80s, 90s, and 100s, independent living and functioning is not possible for physical, safety, psychological, and/or financial reasons. Family members often need to take on more and more caregiving responsibilities such as shopping, housekeeping, help in paying bills, transportation for medical appointments, and important socialization. With progression of a disease or disability, more direct care may be needed, such as assistance with bathing, dressing, feeding, taking medications, and toileting. Help with these tasks requires a competent, willing caregiver, either an employee (reliable 24-hour help is difficult to find and expensive) or a family member or friend. Guided Practice Exercise 6.1 provides the opportunity to identify advantages and disadvantages of caregiving and perceptions of the caregiver role.

Guided Practice Exercise 6.1

Caregiving can be viewed as an opportunity or a burden. There are many advantages and challenges in providing care to a loved one. Interview your grandparent and examine his or her role in providing care to his or her children and his or her views on receiving care from his or her adult children. What type of services did your grandparent receive and how did he or she view his or her role as a caregiver? Finally, identify a time in which you were placed in the role of caregiver. Was caregiving provided to a sibling, parent, grandparent, or friend? What services did you provide and how did you feel about your involvement?

Informal Caregiving

Informal caregiving is a broad term that implies providing a variety of services and assistance to a family member or close friend, generally without payment. Informal caregivers may be family members, neighbors, or close friends. The most typical family caregivers are spouse, daughter, sister, daughter-in-law, grandchild, son, or brother.

When the care recipient becomes immobile, incontinent, and confused or disoriented, the person often is unable to leave home except for essential trips for medical care. When this situation occurs, the caregiver usually cannot leave the home either because it is not safe for the care recipient to be alone. Sometimes there are adequate financial resources for paid assistance or other family members who are available and willing to be part-time caregivers (sometimes causing family conflicts in deciding a shared responsibility plan). Caregiving ranges from occasional social visits to full-time 24-hour care for a dependent, ill older adult in the home with many needs.

Many options exist in today's society, giving families more opportunities to gain the assistance needed in this caregiving role. When an elderly person becomes unable to take care of himself or herself and sustain the basic needs for living, the family generally takes responsibility. This type of care is considered informal because outside establishments are not needed. The care of the elderly by their spouse and/or adult children is a universal phenomenon seen across cultures and has been in practice for centuries. Both good and bad experiences of family-based care have been reported in different cultures and parts of the world (Bhattarai, 2013). Quality of care is an important aspect that comes into play when deciding what option is best for an older individual. When those resources are not found or economic struggles limit the quality of care the family wants, the family dynamic sometimes has to take the leading role.

Benefits of Caregiving

There are numerous benefits associated with caregiving. Benefits of caregiving include, but are not limited to, developing a closer bond with the loved one; getting to know the loved one better; knowing the person is safe, comfortable, and well cared for; learning about aging and the normal aging process; receiving appreciation and thanks from family members for what you do; and feeling personal satisfaction for a job well done.

The family knows the individual on an emotional and personal level and feels the need to care for him or her and pay back the favor, especially if that elderly person took care of the family for most of their younger life. Relational dynamics may outweigh perceptions of burden in family care, and family members may feel motivated to provide services to older members (Bhattarai, 2013). The benefits of this type of caring can provide a way to grow better, more sympathetic, and stronger relationships within the family.

The role of caregiving can be divided so every family member's life does not need to be interrupted, and they can still partake in helping out. Most family members today have working careers, and it can be overwhelming having a member who needs help while being so busy with other obligations. Being capable of managing both roles grants a sense of satisfaction, supporting one's sense of balance in life. The balance can be supported by sharing the responsibility of caring for the aging parent with others (Eldh & Carlsson, 2011). It can also be economically helpful because outside resources are not needed. Guided Practice Exercise 6.2 illustrates how neighbors can provide needed services to an elder to improve his or her quality of life during a brief crisis period.

Guided Practice Exercise 6.2

Your next-door neighbor is an elderly gentleman who was recently discharged from the hospital. He does not have any family nearby, and the harsh weather has interfered with the home health services he would normally receive. Identify activities and/or services you can provide to him. Would any of these services require resources that are unavailable to you? Please identify and describe.

Challenges of Caregiving

With every decision, there are negative attributes that accompany it. In idealizing the family for its role in caring for older people, the disadvantages of the family as the primary care structure could be overlooked. Some families' circumstances may not be suitable for those who are growing older. For example, a family in poverty or holding a low socioeconomic status or one with terminally ill members, children, and/or disabled members or those who have recently immigrated may not be ideal for the care of older people (Bhattarai, 2013). These types of disadvantages can become burdens to those who are in the position of taking care of the family.

As the baby boomers move toward retirement, almost a third of the population in the United States is already engaged in some form of elder care, spending an average of 20 hours per week helping their loved one over a span of roughly 5 to 18 years (Calvano, 2013). This burden falls most heavily on women, but responsibilities are increasing for men (Calvano, 2013). More and more families are being put into the position of caring for their loved ones that might not be possible for their schedules. These situations can become burdens and lead to more problems within the family care system.

Women as Caregivers

Women have traditionally been the family caregivers, perhaps because of their historical nurturing nature, their role as homemaker, and/or their personal and emotional feelings of commitment to older family members. With the large majority of working-age women away from the home during the day and with younger family members in school or at work, there are fewer family members in the home to provide essential supervision and care to older members. It is not likely that this trend will change because of the financial need to work and the personal satisfaction of an active rewarding career.

American Association of Retired Persons (AARP; 2012) provides an example of the "average" caregiver in the United States: a 49-year-old woman who works full-time outside of the home, who also spends nearly 20 hours per week providing unpaid care to an elderly family member. In the United States, 42% of full-time workers have provided care for an aging adult (Feinberg & Choula, 2012). As the role of caregiving progresses, it can become difficult to juggle work-related responsibilities, family responsibilities, and caregiver responsibilities. Many women in the workforce must adjust their work schedules to accommodate for their caregiving role. Adjustments include leaving work early or arriving late, taking time off, cutting back work hours, changing careers, or quitting work entirely (Feinberg & Choula, 2012).

Lee and Tang (2013) examined the role of women in the labor force and changes due to caregiving roles for their spouses, parents, and grandchildren. Results indicated that women caregivers were less likely to be in the labor force than non-caregivers. Another finding was that women try to balance work and caregiving commitments. Additionally, for most middle-aged people, caregiving is not a choice. Most middle-aged Americans have a young family to provide for along with older dependents (Lee & Tang, 2013).

Caregiver Burden

There are cases where families experience caregiver burden when caring for older loved ones. Challenges or perceived burdens include lack of time, anxiety, fear, worry, fatigue, guilt, depression, increased expenses, family conflicts, decreased social contacts, and loss of other relationships (Hogstel, 2001). Caregivers face a great deal of distress at home and at work. When the elder experiences health issues and deaths of friends and other persons they are close to, this increases the need for family members to provide caregiving.

It is essential that the adult family caregiver, who may range in age from 30 to 70 years or more, does not talk to or treat the older adult like a child. Disrespectful and demeaning terms such as childish and childlike should never be used to refer to a person who is becoming more dependent because of a medical condition such as a stroke or dementia. An adult child never becomes a parent to his or her parent. While the caregiving role may be one voluntarily chosen, it may also become a problematic role and interfere with the provision of needed care. Guided Practice Exercise 6.3 illustrates this phenomenon.

Guided Practice Exercise 6.3

Oftentimes caregivers may neglect themselves because there is so much of a demand on their personal time when providing care to a loved one. This personal neglect can become problematic and interfere with their ability to take care of others and themselves. Identify challenges or burdens associated with caregiving. How would you address these challenges to provide support to the caregiver?

Decline in Health

Many caregivers experience a decline in their health when caring for their elderly loved ones. Though normally willingly undertaken, caregiving at the end of life entails considerable cost for family caregivers and the wider family, incurring emotional, social, physical, and financial costs (Stajduhar, 2013). While taking care of a loved one, many caregivers often forget about their own health and well-being. Emotional stress is one of the main components that caregivers seem to suffer from. Family caregivers may experience levels of depression similar to patients and greater than the general population (Stajduhar, 2013).

Caregivers do not look after themselves, do not eat properly, often cease activities outside of the home, and postpone their own medical appointments (Coristine, Crooks, & Grunfeld, 2003). Many family members who are caregivers experience anxiety and depression (Grunfeld, Janz, & Glossop, 2004), and these psychosocial and mental health challenges are accompanied by physical burdens. Long hours of care provision are often associated with significant fatigue and sleep deprivation (Aoun & Kristjanson, 2005; Strang, Koop, & Peden, 2002). The physical demands are often a result of the excessive work involved in the caregiving process. An examination revealed that caregivers reported poorer health and took more medications for physical problems compared to non-caregivers. They had 23% higher level of stress hormones and a 15% lower level of antibody responses (Schulz & Beach, 1999). These findings are important because elevated stress hormones can increase the risk for hypertension and diabetes. Caregivers can also have a harder time fighting viruses due to their poor antibody production. Older caregivers are especially vulnerable, so being placed in these circumstances may increase their risk of health problems and mortality (Schulz & Beach, 1999). Interventions to assist caregivers include night respite service aimed at reducing family caregiver fatigue and promoting sleep, a three-session psycho-educational group program that increases perceived family caregiver competence and preparedness to care, and a program designed to increase a family caregiver's sense of hope (Stajduhar, 2013).

Competing Priorities

Being employed while caring for an aging parent can be difficult to manage, as both roles take time and effort, and caregivers can feel guilty for not providing enough support to the aging parent (Eldh & Carlsson, 2010). When focusing on the aging patient, work and family life become less central and when the opposite situation occurs, the aging patient is left alone. Oftentimes, caregivers can feel like their work and home lives are competing against each other. Elder care produces more strain than childcare (Calvano, 2013).

Different coping mechanisms to help address strain in the workplace have been identified. One way of coping is creating relationships at work. This creates opportunities to offload frustration and provide a forum that serves to remind caregivers that there are other parts to life outside their caregiving responsibilities (Eldh & Carlsson, 2010). Being at work is sometimes seen as a positive factor where it prevents family members from engaging further in care, thus keeping a balance between their lives and the aging patient (Eldh & Carlsson, 2010). The purpose of Guided Practice Exercise 6.4 is to allow for an examination of the impact of caregiving when the family member is also employed. The mental health counselor can explore employer strategies to alleviate caregiver burden, which may subsequently improve the employee's productivity.

Guided Practice Exercise 6.4

Caregiving poses opportunities and challenges. Identify and address concerns of caregivers who are employed full-time. Can you identify strategies or approaches that will alleviate the stress associated with caregiving? How can the employer provide options to decrease some of the perceived burden associated with caring for an aging family member? What support do employers currently provide for their employees?

Living Situation

Deciding where the care recipient will live can be difficult. Health problems and changes in condition are usually the reasons for a change in living arrangements. These issues may cause fear, anxiety, fatigue, and depression for the caregiver. If the older adult does not have adequate financial resources to pay for needed housing and care, the caregiver must pay those costs and plan for how the needs are to be met. If there is a critical and/or dementing illness, the caregiver will likely need legal assistance regarding financial and health care decisions and the preparation of documents to allow the caregiver to make decisions on behalf of their loved one.

Most older adults would prefer to live in their own home or apartment as long as they can, but sometimes it becomes unsafe and simply impossible. Ideally, the elder will be able to make or participate in the decision about where to live before a move has to be made due to his or her changing physical conditions or mental status. There are many alternative types of facilities today, so the older adult should be able to provide input. If family members will be providing care, the caregiver may decide to live in the elder's home, but that may not be feasible if the caregiver's other family members are involved. More often the older adult will move into the home of a family member, perhaps a daughter, son, sister, or brother. If this occurs, it is best if the older adult has individual private space where he or she can use some favorite furniture and other furnishings from a previous home.

The helping professional needs to be aware of caregiver conflicts and attempt to intervene and assist families in obtaining essential facts and information so they can make wise choices. Examples of conflicts that caregivers might experience include stress in managing caregiver duties and balancing work responsibilities, emotional distress over ambivalence in relocating elder to an unfamiliar environment, and family tensions over what course of action is best for their loved one. Increased knowledge of the aging process and sources for personal and family assistance in the community are extremely valuable to increase awareness of services for adult caregivers. If living with a caregiver is not an option, the family may consider assisted living. Assisted living is designed for individuals who require assistance with everyday activities such as meals, medication management or assistance, bathing, dressing, and transportation (Assisted Living Federation of America [ALFA], 2013).

Many elders like the thought of living in a community surrounded by people of the same age and interests, similar to an assisted living facility. This subpopulation of older adults is likely to have chronic health conditions, limitations in ADLs, and functional limitations as they require supervision or assistance with these activities, but not the intensive level of skilled care that a nursing home provides (Kozar-Westman, Troutman-Jordan, & Nies, 2013). These older adults are an ideal group to target with preventative and health promotion interventions, which may delay the need for costly skilled nursing care. As aging family members grow older, physical exercise is one of the main concerns regarding sustaining optimal health. Assisted living community residents could be supported with opportunities to engage in physical activity, which might contribute to successful aging and other established benefits (Kozar-Westman et al., 2013).

Another option for families to consider for their aging loved ones is help within the community. This can be beneficial to the older adults who are still able to maintain living in their own homes but require some help. Community programs are in place for elders who may need assistance with activities such as eating or who need transportation. There are food programs set in place for older adults funded by the Older Americans Act. This allows for meals at community sites and home delivered meals, which may be delivered or served by volunteers through nonprofit entities (Collins, Wacker, & Roberto, 2013). Another community food program is the Supplemental Nutrition Assistance program (SNAP). This helps lower income elders who receive about $113 or less in benefits each month (Collins et al., 2013).

Transportation is also available for aging adults living at home. Older adults are potential consumers of public transportation in cities where it is available, and most municipalities offer a discount for elders (Collins et al., 2013). These transportation systems can involve buses or special pick-up routes. These programs help older adults get to the common necessities such as the grocery store or doctor appointments.

There are times when older adults need care 24 hours per day, 7 days a week. Nursing homes are alternatives to caregiving, but some families may only consider them as a last resort. Society has made nursing homes seem like a negative place to live where residents do nothing but sit in wheelchairs and watch television all day with no social involvement. Many older adults do not want to go to nursing homes because of horror stories or they think they are being abandoned and will die in the facility. They often do not see the benefits of living in this type of facility. Care is provided around-the-clock and personnel are always available. Nursing homes offer many specialized services such as physical therapists, occupational therapists, dental and eye care, as well as many other services. There are medical doctors and registered nurses available. Oftentimes, as elders age, nursing homes are safer alternatives to remaining at home. Additionally, social interaction is enhanced, as there are many activities for residents to participate in. Families are relieved of the primary caregiver role, allowing them to stay in their jobs and decreasing stress.

Case Illustration 6.1 demonstrates the distress experienced by an adult child in managing her daily activities, providing care to her mom, and the difficulty with contemplating nursing home placement. Case Illustration 6.2 demonstrates the ultimate confinement of an older woman to a nursing home. Despite all attempts to remain independent and function within the community, her health challenges and lack of 24-hour supervision necessitated the nursing home admission. This situation poses multiple issues that need to be addressed by professional counselors.

CASE ILLUSTRATION 6.1

Delores is a 45-year-old senior underwriter for a large insurance company. She is considered part of the sandwich generation, defined as individuals who raise their children while simultaneously caring for their aging parents. In this case, Delores provides care for her mother who has Alzheimer's disease. Delores's mother attends an adult day program 5 days a week and has a paid caregiver who assists with her care 2 days per week. Delores sold her mother's house and built an addition onto her house to enable her mother to move in with her family. For the past 5 years, Delores leaves work promptly to pick her mother up from adult day care. Prior to her mother moving in, Delores extended her work day to get caught up on her daily responsibilities. In the evenings, Delores does the housework, prepares the meals, cares for her mom, and assists her teenage children with their homework assignments. Delores's mother is fearful at night, so Delores now sleeps in the room with her mom, and she does not want her to wander off unnoticed.

Family members have encouraged Delores to consider placement in a facility, but she refuses. She feels distressed by the changes she is witnessing in her mother and feels guilty over the changes she has had to make at work. Delores is leaving promptly to pick her mother up from adult day care, which leaves work unfinished. She has to leave work early on other days and arrives to work late, if she has difficulty getting her mom ready for adult day care. Delores is unable to travel long distances for her job, which does not please her supervisor because they may be losing clients as a result of the lack of travel to their companies. She has begun making costly mistakes when her sleep has been disrupted during the night. Delores is also accepting more calls during the day, when she should otherwise be working. She feels alone, guilty, sad, and is worried about losing her job, but also feels guilty at the thought of having to place her mother in a facility. Delores's family is very supportive, but Delores remains the primary caregiver.

CASE ILLUSTRATION 6.2

Ms. Beverly is a 78-year-old widowed female who lived independently in her small home in the inner city of Washington, D.C. She has five children who are very supportive. Her children finished high school and hold good, steady jobs. She has four grandchildren who visit her regularly. Her medical conditions include diabetes, glaucoma, hypertension, and she is obese for her 5-foot height (weighing 160 pounds). All medical problems were under control, and Ms. Beverly was capable of performing all ADLs and instrumental activities of daily living (IADLs).

However, one Sunday in the fall, Ms. Beverly was cooking dinner and fell to the floor. She was not injured, but from that day forward, she was unable to stand, even with assistance. She was diagnosed with severe diabetic neuropathy and prescribed physical therapy; however, she was unable to ambulate. Her physician recommended increasing her upper body strength to assist with transferring herself from her bed to a wheelchair and the reverse. While disappointed, fearful at times, and reluctant to attend public gatherings, overall she has adjusted well with assistance of her family and friends.

Ms. Beverly moved from her independent home to a subsidized apartment complex for seniors, which was located within a reasonable distance from family and friends. She received Meals-on-Wheels, and there was a social worker within the building if she needed additional referrals. She also received services from a home health aide for several hours 5 days per week. With the assistance of these limited services, Ms. Beverly was pleased to be able to live independently. Unfortunately, she mixed up her medications and began having visual hallucinations and became confused. Family members called the paramedics, and she was admitted to a nearby medical center where she stayed for approximately 5 days. It was determined that she needed to be transferred to a nearby nursing home until there was a family member who was available 24 hours per day to monitor her medications and address her daily needs.

At the nursing home, Ms. Beverly became depressed and asked her family daily why she couldn't return home. They replied that all family members worked full-time and worked different shifts throughout the day and weekends. So therefore, it was best that she remain in a supervised environment until other arrangements could be made. Ms. Beverly was placed on a low-dose antidepressant and responded well. After approximately one year, she has adjusted to the nursing home environment. Her family visits regularly, and she participates in activities such as bingo. Family members see that she receives medical follow-up appointments and take her out often for family outings.

A more current trend is the alternative to a nursing home, called a green house (Crary, 2011). Ten or so residents live together and receive ultra-individualized care from nursing staff who knows them well and cooks their meals in an open country-style kitchen. The price for this type of living is the same as for a normal nursing home. The purpose of this new style nursing home is to provide residents with private bedrooms and bathrooms that surround a living and dining room, which looks like it could be in a single-family home.

With more opportunities such as assisted living communities and new styled nursing homes, aging adults and their families can have more options than just family caregiving to help make the older adult years the most comfortable of their loved one's life. Over the life course of older persons, they have accumulated what is termed *social credits.* Social credits are resources built up over a lifetime that may be available later in life. Most older adults prefer to live independently, and only when necessary, they will rely on family and friends. Older adults comprise a generation of persons who do not want to be perceived as a burden on others. Therefore, they forge ahead and manage to the best of their ability, until they are completely incapable of caring for themselves. They feel as though they should be the providers, not the individuals receiving care. There is a great need to better educate families about what they can do to help promote mental health and to prevent and treat mental health problems in their older family members.

Psychosocial Interventions

Ensuring caregivers' mental and physical health is vital for not only their well-being, but also for the older people in their care. Support groups and services aimed at caregivers can improve their health and quality of life, improve management of elders in their care, and can delay elders' institutionalization.

Interventions that promote social role functioning include support and psychoeducational groups that effectively facilitate role transitions and performance. Outcome data indicate that individuals, care providers, and family members who participated in such groups experienced decreased grief and loss issues, decreased feelings of isolation and alienation, and enhanced coping ability and skill performance (Kropf & Cummings, 2008). Additional benefits include decreased depression and anxiety of caregivers, decreased behavior problems for care recipients, improved caregiver affect, and increased caregiver knowledge of resources. Psychotherapy approaches also effectively increase individuals', families', and groups' well-being and future planning ability, and improve role functioning. Individual or family psychotherapy decreases or delays institutionalization of the care recipient (Kropf & Cummings, 2008).

Evidence-based psychological treatments (EBTs) for reducing distress and improving the well-being of family members caring for an older relative with significant cognitive and/or physical impairment have been identified (Gallagher-Thompson & Coon, 2007). Three categories of psychologically derived treatments met EBT criteria: psychoeducational programs, psychotherapy, and multicomponent interventions. Specifically, support within the psychoeducational category was found for skill-training programs focused on behavior management, depression management, and anger management. Within the psychotherapy category, cognitive-behavioral therapy receives strong empirical support. Within the multicomponent category, programs using a combination of at least two distinct theoretical approaches (e.g., individual counseling and support group attendance) were also found to be effective (Gallagher-Thompson & Coon, 2007). Interventions such as these enable great improvements within family structures that allow for a better quality of life for older adults, caregivers, and their families.

GRANDPARENTING

When parents are absent or unable to raise their children, grandparents often step in. Raising a second generation brings many rewards, including the fulfillment of providing their grandkids a sense of security, developing deeper relationships, and keeping the family together. It also comes with many challenges. No matter how much grandparents love their grandkids, taking them into the home requires major adjustments (Smith & Segal, 2015). Grandparents are an important resource for both parents and children. They habitually provide child care, financial assistance, and emotional support for their families. Occasionally, they are called upon to offer more than the average care. More than 2.5 million grandparents are taking on the responsibility for raising grandchildren. Often they assume this responsibility with neither of the children's parents present in the home, and nearly 1 million children are living in these homes (AARP, 2015). Delivering full-time care and assuming responsibility for grandchildren gives grandparents a second chance to use their parenting skills.

The number of grandparents has increased over the past few decades. Recent data suggest that approximately 5.6 million grandparents maintain households that include children younger than the age of 18 (Williams, 2011). Many of the grandparents taking on the role as the primary caregiver are not able to meet the standards of parenting due to health problems. When these grandparents take on the major role, they may feel overwhelmed with negotiating their own physical needs in addition to the needs of their grandchildren. The grandparent has to be able to coordinate legal, medical, and educational care for their grandchildren. Case Illustration 6.3 illustrates the challenges in parenting a second time around.

CASE ILLUSTRATION 6.3

Ms. Thomas is a proud woman of 70 years and feels her greatest accomplishment was raising six children alone in the inner city of Chicago. She managed to educate all of her children, and they have a minimum of an associate's degree, and several of her children have a master's degree. They are independent, strong, and doing well in their respective fields. Once her children were grown and on their own, she looked forward to retirement. Unfortunately, things did not go as she had planned. Ms. Thomas is raising her 12-year-old grandson because her daughter was incarcerated for possessing drugs with intent to sell them. Her grandson's father has never been in the picture and does not acknowledge his son.

Ms. Thomas did not want her grandson to become a ward of the State, and no one else in the family was able to take care of him. As a good, loving person, she accepted full responsibility for parenting her grandson. She does the best that she can for him. His mother is still serving time (10 years) and chooses not to communicate with him. Ms. Thomas tries to help him with his homework, attends parent–teacher conferences, and encourages him to become active in various school activities. She feels really good that she's providing a good home atmosphere for her grandson, but she misses her friends and former life. Many of her friends choose not to invite her on outings because she does not have the freedom as she once did. She also feels guilty that maybe she contributed to her daughter's incarceration in some way. Her grandson is not a problem; however, he is getting teased at school, and it is affecting his grades. Ms. Thomas is tired, has not been not taking care of herself, and struggles financially as well.

Effects of Caregiving by Grandparents

It is generally expected that parents will assume direct responsibility for raising their own children, and although grandparents play a role—either as buffers, family historians, occasional caretakers, or as fun-loving, unambivalent stabilizers—they are not seen as the primary caretakers and socializers. When grandparents are viewed as the primary caregivers and socializers of their grandchildren, this is an example of an "off-time" transition (Neugarten, 1979). It is off-time for the grandparents to be raising infants, young children, and adolescents, and this unexpected transition can be stressful. Everything about the grandparents' lives changes (leisure, friendships, work, health, and finances). The psychological consequences of this transition are enormous. Often, grandparents are gaining a grandchild but losing their own child. In addition, grandparents are facing double jeopardy as they question their own sense of inadequacy: What have they done wrong to have children who cannot care for their own children, and are they competent enough to deal with raising children again? The emotional response is often grief—grief for the loss of their children and grief for the loss of freedom to realize their own dreams.

Increase in Stress

When grandparents take on the status of primary caregiver, they do not know how long they will have to care for the child. Their stress levels increase as time passes, which makes it difficult for them to fulfill demands. In addition, some grandparents may not be able to meet the physical demands of parenting due to prior health problems and aging. This elderly group may already feel overwhelmed with their own health as well as having to deal with the well-being of their grandchildren (Williams, 2011). The studies about stress and burnout associated with grandparent caregivers emphasize a strong correlation with physical and emotional health and only secondary effects on work roles. Minkler, Roe, and Price (1992), for example, found that observable declines in physical health were reported in one third of the population of grandparents they studied after caregiving began. They also found that more than 51% of their sample complained of joint swelling and stiffness, 41% reported severe back problems, and 25% cited heart trouble. Minkler's (1994) later findings confirmed that grandmothers downplayed the severity of their health problems in an effort to convey that they were up to the task. Further probing revealed that moderate to severe health problems did in fact exist, but there was "not time" for these women to check with their doctors.

Schooling Issues

Grandchildren raised by grandparents may also have emotional, behavioral, and academic difficulties in their school environment (Williams, 2011). This happens because some grandparents are unable to help the children with their school requirements based on a shift in educational requirements. There is also a lack of communication between teachers and grandparents. Teachers and staff need to become aware of the fact that some students are being raised by their grandparents, and teachers should take on the responsibility to come up with resources to help them. However, every situation is different, and this may not prove to be true for every family. Some children may not need additional help, and the student may not struggle in the academic world.

Emotional Benefits

There are four reported benefits to parenting a second time around (Doblin-MacNab, 2006). Most grandmothers experienced a similar emotional bond with their grandchildren as they did with their children. This is most true for raising grandchildren from infancy. Because some parents have children at an early age, where the parents are still, in a sense, children themselves, grandparents found that they never really stopped being a parent. They enjoyed being a parent the first time around and never had to stop. Where parenting the second time around seems like an entirely different situation than before, in this case it is not. Grandparents form the same emotional bond with their grandchildren and get a second chance at parenting. This gives the grandparent a boost in confidence. They report that this opportunity allows them to correct what they perceived as past mistakes with their own children. Grandparents don't necessarily have to use a trial-and-error method because they already know what works best for their family. Because of this, they have expressed a sense of calm and relaxation.

Grandparents no longer have to redevelop parenting skills or assess new ways of parenting. Because of this increased amount of wisdom, they find that it puts less pressure on them to be the perfect parent. They realize that they cannot and will not be perfect so this eliminates some anxiety, which allows them to be less rigid and angry when things don't go exactly how they imagined it. Grandparents report laughing more with grandchildren and enjoying the moment more because they cared less about little details, such as cleaning. The decrease in parenting stress creates a sense of enjoyment and appreciating the time that is spent with grandchildren.

Most grandparents are at an age of retirement when they are called to parent for the second time, creating more time and attention focused on the child or children. Previously, as parents, they were typically raising five other kids or supporting a family with multiple jobs or one job that took up a majority of their time. Now that the grandparents are retired and have more time to focus on grandchildren, they can enjoy things like attending a football game or choral concert for their grandchild that they may have missed with their own children (Doblin-MacNab, 2006).

Support Mechanisms

Guidelines and support can make a big difference in the lives of grandparents and their grandchildren. Grandparents need to acknowledge their feelings, which might include stress and worry, anger or resentment, guilt, and grief. They need to take care of themselves, which includes staying healthy, engaging in hobbies and relaxation, and obtaining help from their grandkids. If grandparents can find support in the form of other people, support groups, and childcare assistance and connect with parents with children, even if they are from a different generation, common bonds can be formed. Also essential is acknowledging the mixed feelings of raising grandkids and creating a stable environment. Encouragement of open and honest communication and encourage the grandchild to maintain contact (if appropriate) with parents will facilitate coping with this major transition (Smith & Segal, 2015).

Religion also plays a key role in parenting a second time around. Caregivers who reported being very religious displayed a much higher relationship quality with their teenage grandchildren, had less angry and defiant youth, better family attachment, and the grandchildren exhibited more protective factors such as improved social relationships (DiSciullo & Duniform, 2012). Guided Practice Exercise 6.5 provides the opportunity to examine the challenges posed by grandparents with primary responsibility for raising a grandchild. Professional counselors will gain insight into this situation, identify challenges posed by this new role, and develop recommendations to alleviate the associated stressors in this life transition.

Guided Practice Exercise 6.5

Many older adults look forward to becoming a grandparent. However, when the grandparent unexpectedly assumes full responsibility for raising a grandchild, the relationship changes in many ways. Many grandparents may feel uncomfortable with this unanticipated role. Interview a grandparent who has parental responsibility for his or her grandchild. Identify the circumstances that led to integrating the grandchild into his or her home. Identify the challenges faced by the grandparents providing care on a daily basis. Make recommendations to alleviate or diminish the challenges experienced.

SUPPORT SYSTEMS

Older adults and their families depend on a multiplicity of supports that extend beyond the health and mental health systems. Patients and caregivers need access to education, support networks, support and self-help groups, respite care, and human services, among others (Scott-Lennox & George, 1996). These services assume heightened importance for older people who are living alone, who are uncomfortable with formal mental health services, or who are inadequately treated in primary care.

Services and supports appear to be instrumental not only for the patient, but also for the family caregiver. Support for family caregivers is crucial for their own health and mental health, as well as for controlling the high costs of institutionalization of the family member in their care. The longer the patient remains home, the lower the total cost of institutional care for those who eventually need it. Family support is often supplemented by enduring long-term relationships between older people and their neighbors and community, including religious, civic, and public organizations (Scott-Lennox & George, 1996). Linkages to these organizations instill a sense of belonging and companionship. Such linkages also provide a safety net, enabling some older people to live independently in spite of functional decline.

Formal Support Systems

Demographic, consumer, and public policy imperatives have propelled tremendous growth in the diversity of settings in which older persons reside and receive care. Care is no longer the strict province of home or a nursing home. The diversity of home settings in suburban and urban communities extends from naturally occurring retirement communities to continuing care retirement communities to newer types of alternative living arrangements. These settings include congregate or senior housing, senior hotels, foster care, group homes, day centers (where people reside during the day), and others. The diversity of institutional settings includes nursing homes, general hospitals (with and without psychiatric units), psychiatric hospitals, and state mental hospitals. In fact, the range of settings and the nature of the services provided within each have blurred the distinction between home and nursing home (Kane, 1995). Table 6.1 identifies housing options for older adults along with newer types of arrangements.

Table 6.1   Housing Options for Older Adults

Type	Description
Board and Care Homes (Personal Care Homes)	Residential setting that provides a basic room, meals, assistance with activities of daily living, arrangements with transportation for appointments, and daily contact with staff
Adult Foster Care Home	Home that provides room, board, and in-home support services in a family setting. More in-home support is provided as compared to a personal care home. Care provided by the staff is based upon the needs of the residents and experience of the staff.
Adult Care Facility (Congregate Housing)	Facilities provide room, board and in-home support services to six or more adults who are unrelated to the operator. Services provided are similar to board and care and adult foster care homes, however they care for more residents. Homes are available to older adults who are no longer able or willing to live completely independently. Residents live in a private apartment and eat in a common dining area independently. They receive assistance with grocery shopping, meal preparation, and housework.
Residential Care Facility	A group residence that provides at a minimum assistance with bathing, dressing, and help with medications on a 24-hour-a-day basis. Facility may provide medical services under certain circumstances.
Assisted Living Facility	Housing option for those who need a wide range of in-home-support services to help them with activities of daily living. Residents do not require level of continuous nursing care. Residents may have private apartments, which are self-contained with their own bedroom, bathroom, small kitchen, and living area. Usually there is a common area for socializing with other residents.
Continuing Care Retirement Communities (CCRC)	Provides a comprehensive, lifetime range of services to include housing, residential services, and nursing care. Residents are required to sign a contract with the provider which contains information on services provided and costs. All housing is located on one campus and residents can live in the type of housing appropriate for their needs and desires. They can move from one level to another while they remain in the CCRC.

(Continued)

Table 6.1 (Continued)

Type	Description
Adult Retirement Communities	Specifically designed for active, independent older people with units to purchase. Occasionally rental units are available. Units may be in the form of single homes, duplexes, condominiums, or garden apartments. Communities provide social and recreational activities and limited services, such as transportation. A manager is responsible for the general maintenance and upkeep of the community. A monthly fee is charged for these services, and residents pay property taxes.
Elder Cottage Housing (ECHO Units)	Small removable modular cottage put on a concrete foundation/slab or treated wood foundation in a back or side yard of a home. This type of arrangement permits an older person to live independently, but close to people who are concerned about them. The cottages vary in size starting with efficiency units. ECHO are units connected to the utilities of the primary dwelling and can be designed to match or complement the main house. The unit is designed to be removed when it is no longer being used.
Village Concept	The village enables active seniors to remain in their own homes without having to rely on family and friends. Villages are membership driven and run mostly by volunteers and, on a limited basis, paid staff. Villages organize access to affordable services to allow older adults to age in place.
Tiny House Movement	An architectural and social movement advocating living simply in small homes. Tiny homes are considered to be a modest 100–400 square feet. Living in a small environment has benefits: less time to clean, less time to maintain, easier to locate lost items, smaller bills, and increased control over the environment.
Nursing Home	A nursing home is the highest level of care for older adults outside of a hospital. They provide assistance with activities of daily living and medical care. A licensed physician supervises each resident's care, and nurses are available 24 hours per day. Rehabilitative services are also available based upon the residents' needs. Personal care services, social services, religious services, and recreational services are available.

There are many community organizations that health care providers can use to help families arrange for services for older adults. Some of the agencies are low cost, no cost, or covered by Medicare or Medicaid. Some of the community service agencies include mobility-impaired transportation services, support groups, adult day services, home health care, churches/synagogues, home delivered meals, hospice care, companion services, respite care, counseling (personal, benefits, financial), and errand assurance programs (Hogstel, 2001).

Across the range of settings, the duration of care can be short term or long term, depending on patients' needs. The phrase "long-term care" has come to refer to a range of services for people with chronic or degenerative illness or disabilities who require support over a prolonged period of time. In the past, long-term care was synonymous with nursing home care or other forms of institutional care, but it now applies to a full complement of institutional or community-based settings.

One important area for an interdisciplinary approach is the extent to which a given setting fosters independent functioning versus dependent functioning, an issue influencing mental health and quality of life. Though certainly not a goal, some settings inadvertently foster dependency rather than independence. Nursing homes and hospitals, for example, are more focused on what individuals cannot do, as opposed to what they can do. Yet their major focus on incapacity (the nursing and health focus) runs the risk of overshadowing function and independence (the home and humanities focus). In other settings, the balance between dependence and independence shifts in the other direction, with the risk of nursing and health needs being inadequately addressed. In recent years, the emphasis has been on "aging in place," at home or in the community, rather than in alternate settings.

The growth of senior centers was boosted by the Older Americans Act of 1975. Title III of the Act directed the development of comprehensive and coordinated services to elders through community-based facilities (Ebersole & Hess, 1990). Senior centers offer a wide variety of services depending on the center and the extent of its funding (state, federal, and private funding). Some of the programs that senior centers may offer are arts and crafts; meal programs; social, recreational, and educational activities; adult day care for the frail elderly; a variety of health-screening services; and various life enrichment activities. These senior centers support older adults in maintaining their independence in the community.

Social Support

Social support refers to help and assistance we give to and receive from others (Novak, 2012). In later life, older people benefit from the support they get from family members and friends. This support takes the form of emotional support, companionship, help with household chores, and a range of other help (Novak, 2012). Older family members also give help to others through financial support and help with childcare. Older adults may also provide a home for unmarried, divorced, or unemployed children. Social support among the elderly represents a main source of personal care and well-being (Litwin & Landau, 2000), and the general context of social support is more critical and amplified by the various problems connected to an aging population.

Aging is a unidirectional process—an individual can never grow younger. There are many older adults who do not want to be identified with a chronological age. These individuals have friends of all ages but also tend to identify with others who are going through the same sequence of roles. An older adult's social relationships, the amount and quality of social roles at a younger age, economic resources to meet changing needs, and capability to perform ADLs are all important considerations in the overall assessment of current and potential future functioning. Regardless of an individual's age, older adults need human interactions to feel needed, appreciated, and useful (Hogstel, 2001). Social support can add quality to the lives of older adults. Case Illustration 6.4 demonstrates a mutually beneficial intergenerational support relationship.

CASE ILLUSTRATION 6.4

Mrs. Gainer was a lively, mentally alert, active older woman until she fell and broke her hip. She received rehabilitation, but she was never the same afterwards. She limited her physical activities, decreased her socialization, and chose to stay inside her one-bedroom apartment. Her family members visited weekly, and a friend occasionally visited as well. She had a friend from a nearby senior adult center visit her; however, due to personal problems, she was unable to continue visiting.

A neighbor within the apartment complex informed Mrs. Gainer that her social worker connected her to an intergenerational program that paired young adults with older adults as companions. Mrs. Gainer agreed to participate in the program. She was paired with a 20-year-old college student who aspires to become a physician. This relationship blossomed over the 4 months in which they interacted with each other. Her companion read stories with her, played games, demonstrated modern dance moves, laughed and joked with her, and did small errands for her. Mrs. Gainer benefited from the companionship, humor, and services provided, and she had the opportunity to provide guidance and impart wisdom to her young friend. Her young companion felt appreciated, learned some life lessons, provided valuable services, and received mentoring and emotional support. Both individuals benefited from this relationship, which initially started off to be one where the young adult was to provide service to Mrs. Gainer. There are many benefits to being a caregiver and many of the benefits are intangible but well deserved.

Measuring Social Relationships

Social support is just one of many concepts used to measure social relationships. Social isolation is the term used to describe a lack of social ties. The concept of social networks refers to the entire range of an individual's relationships and the connections among them. Measures of social integration assess the variety of social ties that an individual has (e.g., spouse, parent, grandparent, friend, volunteer, church member), the number of ties (e.g., number of close friends), or the frequency of interaction with others. Social support measures generally distinguish between perceived and received support and among various types of support. Perceived support is the perception that support is available if needed, whereas received support refers to support that has actually been provided.

Social support is generally categorized into four main types. Instrumental support refers to tangible goods and services such as financial assistance, caregiving, or help with tasks. Emotional support includes the provision of love, caring, sympathy, and other positive feelings. Companionship, or belonging, is often subsumed under emotional support, but some researchers consider it a separate type of support. Informational support is defined as guidance, advice, and problem solving. Appraisal support includes feedback given to individuals to help them in self-evaluation or in appraising situations. The intangible forms of support—emotional, informational, and appraisal support—can be difficult to disentangle.

Satisfaction with the level of support available or received is an additional dimension of support included in some measures. The social resources subscale of the Older Americans and Services Inventory (OARS) provides an example of a social support measure developed specifically for an older population. The subscale includes items on marital status, co-resident individuals, extent and type of contact with others, having a confidant, feeling lonely, satisfaction with interaction with others, and perceived availability of help if sick or disabled (Gallo, Reichel, & Andersen, 1988). Using the OARS social resources measures, Blazer (1982) found that low levels of social interaction and perceived social support increased the risk of mortality.

Benefits of Social Support

Social integration and emotional support provide benefits for overall health. Older individuals who have more interaction with others and who report more available emotional support experience fewer and slower declines in cognitive and physical functioning. Social relationships may help with mortality either by preventing the onset of physical disease or by improving the prognosis of persons with a chronic disease. Studies of the progression of or recovery from physical diseases or injury have produced strong evidence of the benefits of social relationships, as higher levels of social integration and social support are predictive of better health outcomes for those individuals.

Families provide older adults with physical and emotional support that comes in many forms. The family is the greatest source for affection and emotional support, and family members are the primary source of caregiving for disabled or dependent older adults (Hogstel, 2001). Emotional support from children is positively associated with a higher degree of well-being and less distress and cognitive impairments among older people without a spouse (Okabayashi, Liang, Krause, Akiyama, & Sugisawa, 2004). More recent finds emphasize the importance of family and friendship for healthy aging (Thanakwang & Soonthorndhada, 2011) and confirm that chronic stress and loss of functions in older people may be mitigated by informal and formal support (Muramatsu, Yin, & Hedeker, 2010). Family solidarity, in its affective aspect, can be considered a "robust concept" and a fundamental element for social integration in old age (Lowenstein, 2007).

Socialization with others assists in maintaining cognitive status and prevents boredom and depression. Older adults receive the same satisfaction from friends as they do from family members' interactions (Hogstel, 2001). Research has demonstrated that women have more friends than men and seem to fare better as widows than men do. Women have a special relationship with other women, showing affection, spending time with each other, or providing emotional support. Women have traditionally been the caregivers, widows, and single members of society. Men have one or two friends and most consider their spouse as their best friend.

Many elderly report that social involvement contributes to a positive self-attitude and self-acceptance (Reichstadt, Sengupta, Depp, Palinkas, & Jeste, 2010). Shaw, Krause, Liang, and Bennett (2007) note that social support is directly linked to decreased mortality and offers positive health benefits. One reason for this may be that social relationships, as opposed to family, are chosen by the elderly person (Antonucci, Birditt, & Webster, 2010). This allows the individual to surround himself or herself with an effective support system.

Studies have demonstrated that individuals with more social support involvement have high morale and better life satisfaction, personal adjustment, and mental health than those with less involvement. Support systems are influential in helping older adults view life more calmly and relax and focus their minds on important matters. In contrast, a low level of social integration (i.e., social isolation) and loneliness in old age are major risk factors for mortality, independent of traditional biomedical risk factors. In particular, an absence of informal support can have a serious impact on health and quality of life of low-income elderly women living alone, leading to premature institutionalization (Ryser & Halseth, 2011). Greater social vulnerability is associated with mortality in older adults (Andrew, Mitnitski, & Rockwood, 2008).

One stereotype of old age is that older people are lonely and isolated because the later years are characterized by a loss of social ties as adult children leave home, seniors leave the workplace, and friends and spouses die. While some older people are socially isolated, the majority of adults keep up active social roles. The convoy model of social relations describes the way in which individuals purposively work to maintain interpersonal relationships in old age (Antonucci, 2001). Using a life span perspective, the model posits that individuals form convoys of social support in earlier adulthood that they sustain into the later years. These convoys provide a "protective base" that offers both direct benefits and a buffer against stressors. Although some losses do occur, older adults often replace them with new relationships or by intensifying existing ones. Thus, the number of close social ties appears to decline only modestly with age, whereas the types of ties may change.

Social Ties and Demographics

The structure and function of social ties appears to vary somewhat across sociodemographic subgroups. Women provide more and receive more support, and they have a larger number of social ties. Women report greater emotional intensity across their relationships, but they also report more conflict and excessive demands (Shaw et al., 2007). Although older men report fewer social ties than older women, men appear to benefit more from the ties they have (Courtenay, 2000; Shaw et al., 2007). Support provided through the marital relationship is one likely explanation for this gender difference. Older women are more likely to be widowed and thus lack the emotional support of a spouse. In addition, research has shown that men receive greater health benefits from marriage than women (Quadagno, 2002).

The evidence regarding racial and ethnic differences in social relationships suggests minimal variation across groups (Mendes de Leon & Glass, 2004). Older African Americans, Hispanics, and non-Hispanic whites appear to have similar-sized social networks, but minority networks typically include extended family. Minority elders also tend to report closer family ties and more church-based activity. Older non-Hispanic whites, in contrast, may be somewhat more socially active with friends and with volunteer activities and formal organizations.

Data on socioeconomic status differences in social relationships suggest a positive relationship. Higher socioeconomic status individuals tend to report having more support available, providing more support, and including more family and friends in their social networks. Reduced social networks are more frequent among older people with low socioeconomic position (Weyers, Dragano, Mobus, Beck, & Stang, 2008). However, socioeconomic status groups do not differ in their involvement with family. Given that racial and ethnic minority groups fall into different socioeconomic categories, it is not clear to what extent socioeconomic status differences in social ties are confounded with racial and ethnic group differences (Mendes de Leon & Glass, 2004).

There is an aspect of people's lives that healthy traditional cultures have always understood to be of paramount importance to human happiness, well-being, and longevity: Nothing is more important than the quality of human relationships; as individuals and as communities, they are sustained through all kinds of hardships by the boundless commitment they have to support one another, and their complete readiness to provide mutual aid at any time (Robbins, 2007).

Relationships and Health

In the last few decades, there has been an explosion of scientific understanding about the deep connections between interpersonal relationships and health. In Western medicine, there is a great deal of concern about risk factors like high blood pressure, high cholesterol, smoking, and obesity, as they are very often linked to serious disease. But an ever-increasing body of medical research is coming to the conclusion that the quality of relationships with other people is every bit as important to an individual's health as these indicators—if not more so. Chronic loneliness now ranks as one of the most lethal risk factors in determining who will die prematurely in modern industrialized nations (Robbins, 2007). Though the science has been accumulating for the last 30 years, many physicians have been slow to accept the idea that something as intangible as interpersonal relationships could have so much medical significance. They tend to view love as a frill or a luxury, as something that distracts from a rational approach to patient care (Robbins, 2007). Western medicine still often trains physicians and other health professionals to keep emotionally distant from their patients. It's a great loss that even if health professionals are deeply caring people, they receive little approval for their kindness, their gentleness, and their empathy (Robbins, 2007).

The impact of family and social relationships plays an important part in an individual's health and psychosocial well-being. Social interaction and support with spouses, family, and friends can provide one with an acceptance of self and lend to a decrease in mortality (Antonucci et al., 2010). A positive relationship with a spouse can be one of the greatest buffers against physical and psychosocial problems. This relationship has the most impact on one's sense of purpose and mental disposition (Trudel et al., 2008). The Harvard Women's Health Watch (2010) notes that stress levels are decreased for older couples in strong relationships. The sharing of experiences and closeness may have a far greater impact on one's health than previously realized (Gerstorf et al., 2009).

Older adult relationships with children or other family members did not carry the importance of a spousal relationship unless the person is unmarried (Antonucci et al., 2010). Positive interaction with family did not show the decrease in mortality that one might expect. It has been suggested that as people age, their family ties often remain intact as opposed to other relationships since family is thought to be a greater source of support, care, and emotional well-being than a social relationship (Shaw et al., 2007). Antonucci et al. (2010) suggests that families of those nearer to death may choose to hide any troubles and focus on the positive.

It can be difficult for some older adults to develop meaningful relationships late in life. It can be painful and lonely to be old and alone, with no one they knew before. Today, a high percentage of American elders live alone, spending their hours and days watching TV by themselves. Many residents of nursing homes go years without seeing a child. Their only human contact may be other old people and their caregivers. They may feel that they mean nothing to anyone, that no one loves them, and that their love doesn't matter to anyone. Meanwhile, a small but sadly growing number of American children have never met their grandparents (Robbins, 2007). The loneliness of elders in the modern world today is sometimes so profound that they literally die of broken hearts.

Friendships

Older adults need social interaction for their well-being. Emotional care of family and friends helps an older adult maintain and adjust to physiological changes related to aging. Social support is needed on a daily basis, but it is especially important during a crisis. During crisis periods, a single confidante may be enough to maintain an older adult's morale, while the lack of an intimate friend may lead to progressive social withdrawal (Hogstel, 2001).

Friends are important during adulthood in many ways, by serving as companions, sources of affection, and emotional and instrumental supporters. They contribute to psychological well-being, physical health, and longevity. As an older adult, being a friend may be as important as seeing others as friends (Siebert, Mutran, & Reitzes, 1999). In Western societies, friendship is not institutionalized and thus varies considerably in terms of what is expected from a friend. Basic perceptions of what friendship is differ by age, gender, and culture (Adams, Blieszner, & DeVries, 2000). Compared to other relationships, friendship is considered voluntary, although it is influenced by such factors as proximity (who one meets, physical location) and situation (sharing a specific medical doctor). Friends tend to be similar to one another in terms of gender, race, class, and marital status.

Gerontologists have focused on friendship as it affects the psychological and physical well-being of older adults and as a source of social support. For many years, researchers accepted the common perception that as people age, their friendship circles gradually become smaller. More recent research suggests that the relationship between aging and number of friends varies across types of people and contexts. Stevens and Van Tilburg (2011) examined three cohorts of older persons with an average age of 60, 70, and 80 years in 1992 and followed them for 17 years. They found that the younger cohort of adults initially aged 55–64 had friends in their personal networks more often and maintained friendships during the 17 years studied when compared to cohorts who were initially 65–74 and 75–85 (Stevens & van Tilburg, 2011). This stability represents a pattern that clearly differs from the steady decline in having friends found in other studies (Stevens & van Tilburg, 2011). Holmen and Furakawa (2002) found that older adults continued to express high satisfaction with their friendships despite the decrease in the number of friends available to them over time. They found that a loss of satisfaction with contacts, rather than the number of contacts, was associated with feelings of loneliness.

Perception of friendship as an important part of one's life leads to increased positive affect (Siu & Phillips, 2002). Satisfaction with social support and friendship is related to a better ability to take care of the basic ADLs as well as fewer hospitalizations (Ostir, Simonsick, Kasper, & Guralnik, 2002), less cognitive decline (Zunzunegui, Alvarado,

Del Ser, & Otero, 2003), and a better response to rehabilitation (Horowitz, Reinhardt, Boerner, & Travis, 2003; Reinhardt, Boerner, & Benn, 2003). This research has suggested that the improvement of friendships and social support can be a major factor in improving overall quality of life (Stevens, 2001).

Support systems within the same age group are highly regarded as current life tasks are shared. Because older adults have had some similar experiences, they often have common interests. The ease of communication within age groups facilitates mutual support systems. As within other age groups, most older adults feel comfortable with others who have the same values, experiences, and interests. However, this does not preclude the interest in associating with other age groups and family members who are often separated by social and/or physical distance. Sibling relationships are important to older adults even when there is only psychological closeness. These relationships stretch over a lifetime of special and shared experiences with common perceptions of such events as school, religion, parents, home, and growing up. Most sibling relationships are enduring (Hogstel, 2001).

Effective interventions with older clients require the professional counselor to work closely with the family. Aging persons rely heavily on their family members as they age. While many family members perform the caregiving responsibilities, some are taxed because they may be simultaneously raising families and working full or part-time. Should the caregiving role become too much for family members to manage, the formal support system is accessed. Services to maintain elders in the community are initially explored, then more restrictive environments may be sought to enable the aging member to have the supervision necessary for his or her safety.

Grandparents have traditionally provided emotional, financial, and instrumental support to their grandchildren. However, when grandparents assume parental responsibility for their grandchild at this later stage in life, adverse health, financial, and legal responsibilities may be encountered. Counseling professionals will need the knowledge and strategies to assist families and older clients to effectively address all major issues that affect their quality of life. Professional counselors will serve as advocates, work collaboratively with the social services, legal services, and school system to facilitate acquisition of resources. With the increased percentage of older adults, counseling professionals will witness an increased need for their professional services.

KEYSTONES

- The caregiving relationship is a challenging and rewarding experience that allows the caregiver to develop a stronger bond with the elder.
- Caregiver burden is experienced when demands exceed the available resources. This can result in the decline of a caregiver's health.
- Unanticipated parental responsibility for a grandchild poses challenges and opportunities.
- Informal and formal support systems exist to provide assistance to older persons in challenging situations.

ADDITIONAL RESOURCES

Print Based

Fay, J., & Cline, F. (2010). *Grandparenting with love and logic: Practical solutions to today's grandparenting challenges*. Golden, CO: Love and Logic Press.

Feddersen, E. (2009). *Living for the elderly*. Berlin, Germany: Birkhauser Architecture Publishing.

Kornhaber, A. (2002). *The grandparent guide: The definitive guide to coping with the challenges of modern grandparenting*. New York, NY: McGraw-Hill.

Pastalan, L., & Schwarz, B. (2001). *Housing choices and well-being of older adults: Proper fit*. New York, NY: Routledge.

Pynoos, J., Feldman, P., & Ahrens, J. (2005). *Linking houses and services for older adults: Obstacles, options, and opportunities*. New York, NY: Routledge.

Web Based

www.aahsa.org

www.acsu.buffalo.edu/--drstall/hndkO.html

www.aging.state.pa.us/portal/server.pt/community/department_of_aging_home/18206

www.aihw.gov.au/informal-care-ageing/

www.aoa.gov/Aging_Statistics/Profile/2011/6.aspx

www.aoa.gov/aoa_programs/hcltc/caregiver/index.aspx

www.caregiver.com

www.caregiver.org/resources-health-issue-or-condition

www.essentialgrandparent.com/

www.hud.gov

www.grandparenting.org/

www.grandparents.com/

www.mowaa.org/

REFERENCES

Adams, R. G., Blieszner, R., & DeVries, B. (2000). Definitions of friendship in the third age: Age, gender, and study location effects. *Journal of Aging Studies, 14,* 117–133.

Administration on Aging (AOA). (2007). *A profile of older Americans: 2005*. Washington, DC: U.S. Department of Health and Human Services.

Administration on Aging (AOA). (2014). *A profile of older Americans: 2014*. Washington, DC: Administration for Community Living, U.S. Department of Health and Human Services.

American Association of Retired Persons (AARP). (2012). *Understanding the impact of family caregiving on work*. Washington, DC: AARP Policy Institute.

American Association of Retired Persons (AARP). (2015). *Grandfacts*. Retrieved from http://www.aarp.org/relationships/friends-family/grandfacts-sheets/

Andrew, M. K., Mitnitski, A. B., & Rockwood, K. (2008). Social vulnerability, frailty and mortality in elderly people. *PloS One, 3*(5), e2232.

Antonucci, T. C. (2001). Social relations. In J. E. Birren & K. W. Schaie (Eds.), *Handbook of the psychology of aging* (pp. 53–57). San Diego, CA: Academic Press.

Antonucci, T., Birditt, K., & Webster, N. (2010). Social relations and mortality: A more nuanced approach. *Journal of Health Psychology, 15*(5), 649–659.

Aoun, S., & Kristjanson, I. (2005). Challenging the framework for evidence in palliative care research. *Palliative Medicine, 19*(6), 461–465.

Assisted Living Federation of America (ALFA). (2013). *About Assisted Living Federation of America.* Retrieved from www.alfa.org

Bertrand, R. M., Saczynski, J. S., Mezzacappa, C., Hulse, M., Ensrud, K., & Fredman, L. (2012). Caregiving and cognitive function in older women: Evidence for the healthy caregiver hypothesis. *Journal of Aging and Health, 24,* 48–66.

Bhattarai, L. (2013). Reviving the family model of care: Can it be a panacea for the new century? *Indian Journal of Gerontology, 27*(1), 202–218.

Blazer, G. G. (1982). Social support and mortality in an elderly community population. *American Journal of Epidemiology, 115,* 684–694.

Burton, L. C., Zdaniuk, B., Schulz, R., Jackson, S., & Hirsch, C. (2003). Transitions in spousal caregiving. *The Gerontologist, 43,* 230–241.

Calvano, L. (2013). Tug of war: Caring for our elders while remaining productive at work. *Academy of Management Perspectives, 27*(3), 204–218.

Colcombe, S., & Kramer, A. F. (2003). Fitness effects on the cognitive function of older adults: A meta-analytic study. *Psychological Science, 14,* 125–130.

Collins, S. M., Wacker, R. R., & Roberto, K. A. (2013). Considering quality of life for older adults: A view from two countries. *Generations, 37*(1), 80–86.

Coristine, M., Crooks, D., & Grunfeld, E. (2003). Caregiving for women with advanced breast cancer. *Psychooncology, 12*(7), 709–719.

Courtenay, W. (2000). Constructions of masculinity and their influence on men's well-being: A theory of gender and health. *Social Science & Medicine, 50,* 1385–1401.

Crary, D. (2011). Aging in place: A little help can go a long way. *Tallahassee Democrat, 21,* 6.

Doblin-MacNab, M. L. (2006). Just like raising your own? Grandmothers' perceptions of parenting a second time around. *Family Relations, 55*(5), 564–575.

Disciullo, E., & Duniform, R. (2012). *The benefits of parenting a second time around.* Cornell University, College of Human Ecology: Department of Analysis and Management.

Ebersole, P., & Hess, P. (1990). *Toward healthy aging: Human needs and nursing response.* St. Louis, MO: The C. V. Mosby Company.

Eldh, A. C., & Carlsson, E. (2011). Seeking a balance between employment and the care of the aging parent. *Scandinavian Journal of Caring Sciences, 25,* 285–293.

Family Caregiver Alliance. (2005). *Fact sheet: Selected caregiver statistics.* Retrieved from http://www.caregiver .org/caregiver/jsp/contentnode .jsp?nodeid = 439

Family Caregiver Alliance. (2006). *Caregivers assessment: Principles, guidelines and strategies for change. Report from a National Consensus Development Conference. Volume I.* San Francisco, CA: Family Caregiver Alliance.

Feinberg, L., & Choula, R. (2012, October). *Understanding the impact of family caregiving on work [Fact sheet].* Retrieved from http://www.aarp.org/content/dain/aarp/research/public_policy_institute/HC/2012/ understanding-impact-family-caregiving-work-AARP-ppi-Hc.pdf

Fredman, L., Bertrand, R. M., Martire, L. M. Hocheberg, M., & Harris, E. L. (2006). Leisure-time exercise and overall physical activity in older women caregivers and non-caregivers from the Caregiver-SOF study. *Preventive Medicine, 43,* 226–229.

Fredman, L., Cauley, J. A., Satterfield, S., Simonick, E., Spencer, S. M., Ayonayon, H. N., & Harris, T. B. (2008). Caregiving, mortality, and mobility decline. The Health, Aging, and Body Composition (Health ABC) Study. *Archives of Internal Medicine, 168,* 2154–2162.

Gallagher-Thompson, D., & Coon, D. W. (2007). Evidence-based psychological treatments for distress in family caregivers of older adults. *Psychology and Aging, 22*(1), 37–51.

Gallo, J. J., Reichel, W., & Andersen, L. (1988). *Handbook of geriatric assessment.* Rockville, MD: Aspen Publishers.

Gerstorf, D., Hoppmann, C., Kadlec, K., & McArdle, J. (2009). Memory and depressive symptoms dynamically linked among married couples: Longitudinal evidence from the AHEAD study. *Developmental Psychology, 45*(6), 1595–1610.

Grunfeld, E., Janz, T., & Glossop, R. (2004). Family caregiver burden: Results of a longitudinal study of breast cancer patients and their principal caregivers. *CMAJ, 170*(12), 1795–1801.

Hahn, E. A., Kim, G., & Chiroga, D. A. (2011). Acculturation and depressive symptoms among Mexican American elders new to the caregiving role: Results from the Hispanic—EPESE. *Journal of Aging and Health, 23,* 417–432.

Harvard Women's Health Watch. (2010). *The health benefits of strong relationships.* Retrieved from www.health.harvard.edu

Hogstel, M. O. (2001). *Gerontology: Nursing care of the older adult.* New York, NY: Delmar.

Holmen, K., & Furukawa, H. (2002). Loneliness, health and social network among elderly people—a follow-up study. *Archives of Gerontology and Geriatrics, 35,* 261–274.

Horowitz, A., Reinhardt, J. P., Boerner, K., & Travis, L. A. (2003). The influence of health, social support quality and rehabilitation on depression among disabled elders. *Aging and Mental Health, 7,* 342–350.

Jenkins, K. R., Kabeto, M. U., & Langa, K. M. (2009). Does caring for your spouse harm one's health? Evidence from a United States nationally-representative sample of older adults. *Ageing and Society, 29,* 277–293.

Kane, R. A. (1995). Expanding the homecare concept: Blurring distinctions among home care, institutional care, and other long-term-care services. *Milbank Quarterly, 73,* 161–186.

Kiecolt-Glaser, J. K., & Glaser, R. (2001). Stress and immunity: Age enhances the risks. *Current Directions in Psychological Science, 10,* 18–21.

Kozar-Westman, M., Troutman-Jordan, M., & Nies, M. A. (2013). Successful aging among assisted living community older adults. *Journal of Nursing Scholarship, 45*(3), 238–246.

Kropf, N. C., & Cummings, S. M. (2008). Evidence-based interventions with older adults: Concluding thoughts. *Journal of Gerontology, 50*(1), 345–355.

Lachman, M. E., Neupert, S. D., Bertrand, R., & Jette, A. M. (2006). The effects of strength training on memory in older adults. *Journal of Aging and Physical Activity, 14,* 59–73.

Lee, Y., & Tang, F. (2013, November). More caregiving, less working: Caregiving roles and gender differ. *Journal of Applied Gerontology.* Retrieved from Academic One File database,

Lima, J. C., Allen, S. M., Goldsheider, F., & Intrator, O. (2008). Spousal caregiving in late midlife versus older ages: Implications of work and family obligations. *Journal of Gerontology, 63B,* 229–238.

Litwin, H., & Landau, R. (2000). Social network type and social support among the old-old. *Journal of Aging Studies, 14,* 213–228.

Lowenstein, A. (2007). Solidarity-conflict and ambivalence: Testing two conceptual frameworks and their impact on quality of life for older family members. *Journal of Gerontology B: Psychological Sciences and Social Sciences, 62B,* S100–S107.

Mendes de Leon, C. F., & Glass, T. A. (2004). The role of social and personal resources in ethnic disparities in late-life health. In N. P. Anderson, R. A. Rodolfo, & B. Cohen (Eds.), *Critical perspectives on racial and ethnic differences in health in later life* (pp. 353–405). Committee on Population, Division of Behavioral and Social Sciences and Education. Washington, DC: National Academic Press.

Minkler, M. (1994). Grandparents as parents: The American experience. *Aging International, 21,* 24–28.

Minkler, M., Roe, K. M., & Price, M. (1992). The physical and emotional health of grandmothers raising grandchildren in the crack cocaine epidemic. *The Gerontologist, 32,* 5752–5761.

Muramatsu, N., Yin, H., & Hedeker, D. (2010). Functional declines, social support, and mental health in the elderly: Does living in a state supportive of home and community-based services make a difference? *Social Science Medicine, 70,* 1050–1058.

Neugarten, B. L. (1979). Time, age, and the life cycle. *American Journal of Psychiatry, 136*(7), 887–894.

Novak, M. (2012). *Issues in aging* (3rd ed.). New York, NY: Routledge.

Okabayashi, H., Liang, J., Krause, N., Akiyama, H., & Sugisawa, H. (2004). Mental health among older adults in Japan: Do sources of social support and negative interaction make a difference? *Social Science Medicine, 59,* 2259–2270.

O'Reilly, D., Connolly, S., Rosato, M., & Patterson, C. (2008). Is caring associated with an increased risk of mortality? A longitudinal study. *Social Science and Medicine, 67,* 1282–1290.

O'Reilly, E., & Morrison, M. L. (1993). Grandparent-headed families: New therapeutic challenges. *Child Psychiatry and Human Development, 23,* 147–160.

Ostir, G., V., Simonsick, E., Kasper, J. D., & Guralnik, J. M. (2002). Satisfaction with support given and its association with subsequent health status. *Journal of Aging and Health, 14,* 355–369.

Quadagno, J. (2002). *Aging and the life course: An introduction to social gerontology.* New York, NY: McGraw Hill.

Reichstadt, J., Sengupta, G., Depp, C., Palinkas, L., & Jeste, D. (2010). Older adults' perspectives on successful aging qualitative interviews. *American Journal of Geriatric Psychiatry, 18*(7), 567–575.

Reinhardt, J. P., Boerner, K., & Benn, D. (2003). Predicting individual change in support over time among chronically impaired older adults. *Psychology and Aging, 18,* 770–779.

Reinhard, S., Feinberg, F., Choula, R., & Houser, A. (2015). Valuing the invaluable: 2015 update. Washington, DC: AARP Policy Institute.

Robbins, I. (2007). *Healthy at 100.* New York, NY: Ballantine Books.

Ryser, L., & Halseth, G. (2011). Informal support networks of low-income senior women living alone: Evidence from Fort St. John, BC. *Journal of Women and Aging, 23,* 185–202.

Schulz, R., & Beach, S. R. (1999). Caregiving as a risk for mortality: The caregiver health effects study. *The Journal of American Medical Association, 282,* 23.

Scott-Lennox, J. A., & George, L. (1996). Epidemiology of psychiatric disorders and mental health services use among older Americans. In B. L. Levin & J. Petrila (Eds.), *Mental health services: A public health perspective* (pp. 253–289). New York, NY: Oxford University Press.

Shaw, B., Krause, N., Liang, J., & Bennett, J. (2007). Tracking changes in social relations throughout late life. *The Journals of Gerontology, 62B*(2), 890–899.

Siebert, D. C., Mutran, E. L., & Reitzes, D. (1999). Friendship and social support: The importance of role identity to aging adults. *Social Work, 44,* 522–533.

Siu, O., & Phillips, D. R. (2002). A study of family support, friendship and psychological well-being among older women in Hong Kong. *International Journal of Aging and Human Development, 55,* 299–319.

Smith, M., & Segal, J. (2015). Grandparents raising grandchildren: The rewards and challenges of parenting the second time around. Retrieved from http://www.helpguide.org/articles/grandparenting/grandparents-as-parents.htm

Stajduhar, K. I. (2013). Burdens of family caregiving at the end of life. *Clinical and Investigative Medicine, 36*(3), E121–E126.

Stevens, N. (2001). Combating loneliness: A friendship enrichment program for older women. *Ageing and Society, 21,* 183–202.

Stevens, N., & van Tilburg, T. (2011). Cohort differences in having and retaining friends in personal networks in later life. *Journal of Social and Personal Relationships, 28*(1), 24–43.

Strang, V., Koop, P., & Peden, J. (2002). The experience of respite during home-based family caregiving for persons with advanced care. *Journal of Palliative Care, 18*(2), 97–104.

Talley, R. C., & Crews, J. E. (2007). Framing the public health of caregiving. *American Journal of Public Health, 97,* 224–228.

Thanakwang, K., & Soonthorndhada, K. (2011). Mechanisms by which social support networks influence healthy aging among Thai community-dwelling elderly. *Journal of Aging Health, 28,* 1352–1378.

Trudel, G., Bayer, R., Villeneuve, V., Anderson, A., Pilon, G., & Bounader, J. (2008). The marital life and aging well program: Effects of a group preventive intervention on the marital and sexual functioning of the retired couples. *Sexual and Relationship Therapy, 23*(1), 5–23.

Turner, M. J., Killian, T. S., & Cain, R. (2004). Life course transitions and depressive symptoms among women in midlife. *International Journal of Aging and Human Development, 58,* 241–265.

Vitaliano, P. P., Zhang, J., & Scanlan, J. M. (2003). Is caregiving hazardous to one's physical health? A meta-analysis. *Psychological Bulletin, 129,* 946–972.

Weyers, S., Dragano, N., Mobus, S., Beck, E. M., & Stang, A. (2008). Low socio-economic position is associated with poor social networks and social support: Results from the Heinz Nixdorf Recall Study. *International Journal of Equity Health, 7,* 13–19.

Williams, M. N. (2011). The changing roles of grandparents raising grandchildren. *Journal of Human Behavior in the Social Environment, 21*(8), 948–962.

Zunzunegui, M., Alvarado, B. E., Del Ser, T., & Otero, A. (2003). Social networks, social integration, and social engagement determine cognitive decline in community-dwelling Spanish older adults. *Journals of Gerontology: Series B: Psychological Sciences and Social Sciences, 58,* S93–S100.

Loss and Its Effect on Older Adults

"Those who love deeply never grow old; they may die of old age, but they die young."

—Ben Franklin

Learning Objectives

After reading this chapter, you will be able to

1. Analyze the losses experienced by aging persons over the life course
2. Describe the effects of divorce in later life
3. Examine the impact of widowhood in later life
4. Explain the process of death and dying and discuss people's reactions to death

INTRODUCTION

Loss in any form is an inevitable aspect of human existence. However, issues of loss are more common for older adults to experience. With aging comes the natural consequence of many types of losses: people, possessions, status, abilities, and so on. When the emotional pain over the loss of a loved one is not mourned for and dealt with in a healthy manner, it may further constrict an individual's life. Additionally, it can foster a fear of intimacy and an avoidance of emotional attachments and disrupt daily activities.

Cumulative losses can have devastating effects on older persons regardless of whether they are expected or unexpected. These losses may be coped with successfully or unsuccessfully. This chapter will examine the loss of a partner through divorce or widowhood, as well as issues related to death and dying. A basic understanding of the significance of loss as it is perceived by older clients is critical in facilitating any change during the therapeutic encounter. Older clients are resilient, and those in the helping profession can help them to discover or rediscover this positive attribute.

LOSS

Loss is a common theme in later life. Older adults can suffer a great number of losses as they age—physiologically, emotionally, and cognitively, and how they cope with these changes can affect their quality of life. Social definitions of loss are seen as key normative stressors of aging in the context of Kahana and Kahana's (2003) successful aging model. Theorists consider the developmental tasks of minimizing or managing internal losses to be central to notions of successful aging. Therefore, a great deal of research explores the concept of loss.

Research has started to explore the interconnectedness between personal losses such as physical and cognitive decline and social network size in late life (Aartsen, van Tilburg, Smets, & Knipscheer, 2004). Theoretical developments focusing on social loss have pointed to the value of socialization theory for understanding the meaning of loss of friends in later life (deVries & Johnson, 2002). Losses threaten well-being because they often involve permanent and uncontrollable change, which disrupts plans and hopes for the future and challenges assumptions about the self. Whereas functional and physical health after the loss of a loved one does not seem to be affected, consequences in psychological well-being are measureable (D'Epinay, Cavalli, & Spine, 2003).

The dynamics around loss in later life need greater clarification. One pivotal question is why some, in confronting loss, succumb to depression and suicide—which has its highest frequency after age 65—while others respond with adaptive strategies. Research on health promotion also needs to identify ways to prevent adverse reactions and to promote positive responses to loss in later life.

Cognitive Losses

Previous chapters have discussed major cognitive losses that individuals can experience as they age. However, older adults also experience subtle age-related cognitive losses. These declines are a normal aspect of nonpathological aging and can occur in a variety of cognitive domains, including memory, executive functioning, psychomotor ability, and speed of processing (Ball, Wadley, Vance, & Edwards, 2004). Moderate declines in cognitive ability, without dementia, have been shown to impair an older adult's ability to take medications, manage finances, prepare food, shop for groceries, and perform household chores (McGuire, Ford, & Ajani, 2006). All of these issues can affect a person's health, safety, and quality of life.

To prevent or delay these cognitive losses, individuals must work to maintain their cognitive abilities to preserve their everyday functioning. Cognitive remediation training has been shown to improve cognitive abilities in elders (Willis et al., 2006). Each intervention was designed to narrowly target a specific cognitive ability. Memory remediation training (Ball et al., 2002) involved teaching mnemonic strategies (organization, visualization, association) for remembering verbal material. Reasoning remediation training (Ball et al., 2002) involved teaching strategies for finding the pattern in a letter or word series (e.g., acegi . . .) and identifying the next item in the series. Speed of processing remediation training (Ball et al., 2002) involved visual search and divided attention (identifying an object on a computer screen at increasingly brief exposures followed by dividing attention between two search tasks). Decline in cognitive abilities affects all aspects of the functional capacity of older adults, and improvement in cognition may minimize other losses that older persons experience.

Loss of Mobility

As the life expectancy of older Americans continues to increase, of great significance to this demographic is their capacity to live independently and to function well during later life (Katz et al., 1983). This may not always be possible if there is a loss of physical capabilities. Mobility—the ability to walk without assistance—is a critical characteristic for functioning independently. Those who lose mobility have higher rates of morbidity, disability, and mortality (Shumway-Cook et al., 2002). Preserving the ability to walk 400 meters, an excellent distance for community ambulation, is central to maintaining a high quality of life and independence in the community. The Short Physical Performance Battery (SPPB), which includes walking balance and chair stands tests, independently predicts mobility disability and activities of daily living disability. The objective of the Lifestyle Interventions and Independence for Elders (LIFE) pilot study was to assess the effect of a comprehensive physical activity (PA) intervention on the SPPB and other physical performance measures. A total of 424 sedentary persons at risk for disability (70–89 years) were randomized to a moderate-intensity PA intervention or a successful aging (SA) health education intervention and were followed for an average of 12 years. In the LIFE pilot study, subjects showed significant improvements in walking speed and physical performance measures (Pahor et al., 2006) as measured by the SPPB and the 400-meter walk. The LIFE study showed that over 2.6 years of follow-up, the physical activity intervention compared with the health education intervention significantly reduced mobility disability, persistent mobility disability, and the combined outcome of major mobility disability or death. These findings suggest the potential for structured physical activity as a feasible and effective intervention to reduce the burden of disability among vulnerable older persons, in spite of functional decline in later life (Pahor et al., 2006).

Loss of Stability

Older adults who reside in a long-term care setting have an increased and immediate sense of loss. The move to a long-term care setting can be fraught with emotional and psychological turmoil. This includes a fear of losing one's identity, friends, possessions, lifestyle, history, and personal space. Within a long-term care setting, the individual comes into contact with many people who are ill and in their final stage of life, reflecting a "destiny" with which he or she must cope. Case Illustration 7.1 is an example of the cumulative effect of multiple losses in the life of an elderly gentleman. Professional counselors are challenged to address these losses from an individual, family, and institutional system framework.

CASE ILLUSTRATION 7.1

George, an 85-year-old male, had a stroke that has left him unable to ambulate independently or care for himself. His daughter, who lives within the same city, arranged for him to be admitted into a nursing home. This nursing home has only the minimum staff required to meet the regulations for operating a facility and it shows in its quality of care. George would lie in his bed and push the call button numerous times before receiving assistance. His roommate became ill and was transferred to a nearby hospital, where he subsequently died. Since his roommate's death, George has become completely discouraged. His daughter and other family members rarely visit. He has lost all of his possessions and is no longer paying out-of-pocket; therefore, he qualifies for medical assistance. He has lost the will to live and routinely states that he doesn't know how much time he has left. His daughter thought she was doing what was best for her father and that he was receiving excellent care at this 24-hour facility.

This case illustrates loss of physical functioning due to the stroke, loss of a familiar environment, loss of family connection, and loss of a confidante. All of these losses erode the quality of life, and when continuing to live becomes unbearable, then death may be welcomed by the individual. This feeling may also be shared by family members who empathize with their elder and feel helpless to intervene to improve the situation. Caring for a loved one in a dependent state is oftentimes physically and emotionally draining, and obtaining assistance of quality professionals provides a source of relief for family members. Guided Practice Exercise 7.1 provides an opportunity to become familiar with losses associated with the aging process and identify strategies and resources necessary to address them.

Guided Practice Exercise 7.1

Identify losses that older persons experience as they age. How would you address each of the losses you have identified? What resources would you need to assist in this process?

Social Loss

Despite cultural attitudes that older persons can handle bereavement by themselves or with support from family and friends, it is imperative that those who are unable to cope be encouraged to access mental health services. Bereavement is defined as the loss or deprivation that a survivor experiences when a loved one dies. It is not a mental disorder but, if unattended to, has serious mental health and other health consequences.

Rates of widowhood for women are about twice that for men, and rates for both sexes are highest in those aged 85 years and older (72% of women and 35% of men) (Bonanno et al., 2002). Rates of bereavement are higher still. Most widowed people also have lost their parents, many have lost siblings or close friends, and some have lost their children. The death of a loved one is among the most intense stressors anyone can experience. Bereavement brings the deep anguish of grief, often accompanied by a need to reorient one's life. Nevertheless, data suggest that most people cope well with this difficult stressor. The majority of people are resilient following a loss (Bonanno et al., 2002), and intervention is unnecessary and may even worsen outcomes (Jordan & Neimeyer, 2003; Schut, Stroebe, van den Bout, & Terheggen, 2001).

However, it is equally clear that a subgroup of bereaved individuals does suffer bereavement-related health problems, and these can be chronic, serious, and debilitating. Additionally, there is growing consensus that bereavement can lead to a grief-specific condition called "complicated grief" (Lichtenthal, Cruess, & Prigerson, 2004). Complicated grief is prolonged, grief symptoms intensify rather than diminish, disbelief regarding the reality of death lingers, and the loss is not integrated (Worden, 2002). Given the severity of the stress of bereavement, it is not surprising that it is a trigger for mental and physical health problems. Unfortunately, physicians may neglect bereaved family members of elderly people who die (Prigerson & Jacobs, 2001).

Loss stresses include those related to the emotional meaning of the loss and to the need to reconfigure the attachment to the deceased, while restoration stresses focus on doing new things, attending to life changes and tasks, and taking on new roles or identities. These dual processes of coping are thought to proceed in an oscillating manner, and there is some empirical evidence to support this model (Bisconti, Bergeman, & Baker, 2004). Inadequate coping increases the risk for a disorder and/or complicated grief. Factors that may increase the risk of developing complicated grief include: an unexpected or violent death, death of a child, close or dependent relationship to the deceased person, lack of a support system or friendships, past history of depression or other mental health issues, traumatic childhood experiences, and lack of resilience or adaptability to life changes (Mayo Clinic, 2015). Having positive emotions and trait humor have been found to predict better outcomes (Ong, Bergeman, & Bisconti, 2004). Another study found that loss of a spouse, as compared to another significant loss, and more positive caregiving benefits predicted more grief intensity but not higher levels of bereavement-related depression, while caregiver health was related to depression but not grief (Boerner, Schulz, & Horowitz, 2004). Loss of a spouse is one of the most significant losses experienced by older adults, and grief is intensely experienced due to the closeness of the relationship. Caregivers who are most energized by their caregiving role, and who find meaning in what they are doing, often have a difficult time adjusting to the loss. It is suggested that those who are at the greatest risk of distress during the dying process may fare relatively well in the post-loss period.

The high levels of distress related to bereavement in older adults have led some to propose interventions such as support groups as a routine (Gilbar & Ben-Zur, 2002). Some subgroups benefit well from the interventions, and those with high grief intensity and complicated grief appear to benefit most (Jordan & Neimeyer, 2003). Treatment of complicated grief is met with considerable improvement. Interventions like support groups, such as those for widows/widowers (Silverman, 1988), are popular although not well studied. Grief support groups are voluntary non-therapy associations that provide education and emotional support for grieving persons. They offer acceptance, practical information, social connection, and an outlet for altruism. Grief support groups reduce social isolation, decrease disenfranchisement, and promote effective coping. They are offered in many communities through churches and synagogues, hospitals/hospices, funeral homes, and social service and mental health agencies (Humphrey, 2009). Compassionate Friends, Survivors of Suicide, and Parents of Murdered Children are some other support groups arising from national organizations (Humphrey, 2009). Individuals with bereavement-related depression (Zisook, Shuchter, Pedrelli, Sable, & Deaciuc, 2001) should receive standard treatments for these conditions.

It is important to distinguish between depression, posttraumatic stress disorder, and complicated grief because the treatment of these conditions is different. A targeted psychotherapy can produce good results for complicated grief symptoms (Shear et al., 2001), and a randomized control trial has shown this treatment to be superior to interpersonal psychotherapy. An interesting approach to treating bereaved individuals has been developed by studying family functioning in palliative care.

Cultural and social factors play a role in bereavement course and outcomes. There is evidence that those who have strong religious faith can find comfort in their religion, although some who experience a difficult death of a loved one may instead lose faith in religion. There are important cultural differences in bereavement practices as well. For example, one study showed marked differences in coping in China compared to the United States (Bonanno, Papa, Lalande, Zhang, & Noll, 2005). On average, loss of a child has a significantly more prolonged course in the United States than in China, compared to loss of a spouse. Additionally, Chinese individuals use avoidant type coping (avoidance of thinking, talking, and expressing feelings about the deceased) more than U.S. individuals. Cultural considerations are an essential component in addressing loss.

Role Loss

It is important to note that role losses in late life may be counterbalanced by smaller but potentially important role gains such as grandparenthood and volunteer or helping roles. Research emphasizes the importance of sustaining friendships and making new friends for the fastest growing segment of North American society, the oldest-old, who face the risk of outliving their families (DeVries & Johnson, 2002). Such roles may also play a compensatory function relative to other losses. Remarriage after widowhood also represents an important potential for reversing role loss, particularly for older men (Moss & Moss, 1996).

Major Loss

Longitudinal research on major losses (Wortman & Silver, 1990) has documented striking variability in response to loss and suggests that losses that shatter a person's worldview (i.e., death of a loved one) are most likely to result in long-term adverse effects. Existential resources such as personal meaning, choice, and optimism have been found to buffer adverse effects of losses for both community-living and institutionalized older adults (Reker, 2001/2002).

Without successful developmental transitions and effective coping with grief-related concerns, individuals may increasingly develop chronic stress-related symptoms and be susceptible to depression. Through successful coping with challenges, conflicts, and losses, older adults can discover new avenues, opportunities, and a new perspective on life. This, in turn, can foster a renewed vitality, inner strength, and a sense of identity.

Guided Practice Exercise 7.2 provides the opportunity to reflect on loss at a young age and how it can affect someone throughout life.

Guided Practice Exercise 7.2

Older adults experience more losses than other age groups based on their years of lived experiences. Refer to your younger years and identify the first loss you recall experiencing. Was this loss a person, pet, or relocation to a new neighborhood? Recall how you felt and how your family responded to your loss. Were you ever the same afterward, or did your behavior change over time?

DIVORCE

The United States has the highest divorce rate in the world, with roughly 45% of marriages expected to end in divorce (Amato, 2010; Cherlin, 2010). Although divorce has been studied extensively among younger adults, the research to date has essentially ignored divorce that occurs between adults aged 50 and older (Amato, 2010; Cooney & Dunne, 2001; Sweeney, 2010). This omission is notable considering that the United States is an aging society. The proportions ever divorced, currently divorced, and married at least twice are highest among individuals aged 50 and older (Kreider & Ellis, 2011).

Wu and Schimmele (2007) suggested that broad cultural shifts in the meanings of marriage and divorce influence all generations, including older adults. Specifically, the weakening norm of marriage as a lifelong institution coupled with a heightened emphasis on individual fulfillment and satisfaction through marriage may contribute to an increase in divorce among older adults, including those in long-term first marriages. Marriages change and evolve over the life course and thus may no longer meet one's needs at later life stages. Qualitative research indicates that many older couples who divorce have simply grown apart (Bair, 2007). Lifelong marriages are increasingly difficult to sustain in an era of individualism and lengthening life expectancies; older adults are more reluctant now to remain in empty shell marriages (Wu & Schimmele, 2007). However, the empirical evidence on this topic continues to be limited.

Age and Divorce

As divorce has become more accepted in the United States, older couples are often seen as models of how the institution of marriage is supposed to work. There is an assumption that couples that survive the first few decades have accepted their spouses' quirks and problems and are more apt to live out their lives together (Zaslow, 2003). That notion is now being shattered. Guided Practice Exercise 7.3 provides the opportunity to examine feelings about the changes and adaptations required during the process of divorce.

Guided Practice Exercise 7.3

Divorce is a difficult transition for children within the family as well as the couple who are in the process of divorce. Routine activities are disrupted, behavior changes, routines may need readjusted, and a host of emotional and psychological changes are experienced. If you have personal experiences in this area, feel free to share them. If not, identify someone you know who is a child of divorced parents and gain an understanding of what they experienced. Ask them to discuss their personal feelings, interruptions in their routines, changes in family gatherings, and any counseling that was helpful during this process. Finally, locate support services in the community and share with your friend and others who are in need of this information.

Increasingly, middle-aged and older persons are being touched by the experience of divorce, although it continues to be primarily an event that occurs among younger adults. U.S. census data indicate that the median age of the termination of first marriages is age 30 years and 29 years for men and women, respectively (Kreider & Fields, 2011). For second marriages, the median age of divorce is under age 40. Twenty-seven percent of men and 18% of women who divorced during a given year are between the ages of 45 and 64 years, and only 2% of the men and women are older than 65. For men, the probability of future divorce is 23% among 40-year-olds, 8% among 50-year-olds, and 2% among 60-year-olds. For women, the probability decreases from 18% at age 40 to 6% at age 50 to 2% at age 60 (Kreider & Fields, 2011).

The divorce rate among middle-aged and older adults has doubled over the past two decades. This trend is at odds with the overall pattern of divorce for the U.S. population as a whole, which is characterized by stability and perhaps even a slight decline in the rate of divorce (Amato, 2010; Cherlin, 2010). The rise in the rate of divorce among adults aged 50 and over is substantially significant given that half of the married population is aged 50 and older. The doubling of the divorce rate coupled with the aging of the population translates into a considerable share of today's divorces occurring to middle-aged and older adults. In fact, one in four persons who divorced in 2010 was aged 50 or older (Brown & Lin, 2012). More than 600,000 adults aged 50 and older got divorced in 2010 (Brown & Lin, 2012). Although divorce has been studied extensively among younger adults, the research to date has essentially ignored divorce that occurs to adults aged 50 and older (Amato, 2010; Sweeney, 2010). A national study of people who divorced after age 40 found that the women initiated the divorce a majority of the time (American Association of Retired Persons, 2004). Females reported that the most frequent reasons for the divorce were, in order: verbal, physical, and emotional abuse; different values and lifestyles; infidelity; and alcohol or drug abuse. Men reported that the most common reasons were falling out of love; different values and lifestyles; verbal, physical and emotional abuse; and infidelity (Montenegro, 2004).

Factors Affecting Divorce

Divorces are being fueled by longevity, economics, and self-awareness. Seniors are healthier now and don't want to waste two or three decades of the golden years with someone they can no longer stand. More than in previous generations, older women today have careers and their own pensions, so they are less dependent on their husbands. Meanwhile, Viagra may be giving older men new incentives to rediscover passion elsewhere (Zaslow, 2003).

Factors contributing to the boom in breakups among seniors include lack of common purpose (e.g., no kids to raise, interests diverge), boredom (e.g., retired for decades, couples blame each other for tedium), sexual woes (e.g., one partner is uninterested in sex or can't perform), longevity (e.g., healthy couples see long life ahead and don't wish to live it with someone they no longer love), and changing times (e.g., older women are tired of being selfless servants and put their foot down) (Zaslow, 2003).

Divorce and Its Effects

An increasing proportion of people are entering old age already divorced. As the divorce rate in midlife has increased substantially in recent decades, coupled with a decrease in remarriage rates (Shapiro, 2003), cohorts entering later life include a greater proportion of divorced people. The share of the older population that is divorced has increased every decade since 1960 for every age group and for both men and women. In 2010, 11% of women and 9% of men ages 65 and older were divorced (Jacobsen, Mather, Lee, & Kent, 2011). Moreover, the proportion of divorced persons in later life is expected to increase in the future, as more middle-aged cohorts with relatively high percentages of divorced people enter old age.

The rapid rise in divorce during the second half of life has important implications for individuals, their families, and society at large. There is considerable evidence that marital dissolution through widowhood is detrimental to individual well-being (Carr, 2004c; Lee & DeMaris, 2007; Williams, 2004). It is likely that divorce has similar negative consequences, particularly for those who did not want the divorce or who are economically disadvantaged or in poor health.

Parent–Adult Children Relationships

Parent–adult children relationship dynamics often change following parental divorce in mid- and later-life. Divorced older adults no longer have a spouse on whom to rely and are likely to place greater demands on their children for social support, and children may be called on to serve as caregivers in lieu of a spouse. The strain of such intense obligations may weaken intergenerational ties (Shapiro, 2003). Adult children are particularly unlikely to provide care to their divorced fathers (Lin, 2008).

To this point, research has consistently found that divorced older men experience deteriorated relationships with their adult children. They are less likely than married older men to live with an adult child, and they have substantially less contact with their children (Shapiro, 2003). The research on intergenerational relationships of divorced older women is less consistent. Although older mothers' transition to divorce is associated with an increase in at least weekly contact with an adult child, they are at greater risk than married mothers of having at least one child with whom they have little contact (Shapiro, 2003). The research is consistent that the divorce status of older women is not associated with the probability of them co-residing with an adult child (Shapiro, 2003).

The ability of older adults to draw on children for support and care may be constrained in other ways. Some older adults may not have children available nearby to provide care. This situation is likely to be more common in the future with shrinking average family sizes (Hughes & O'Rand, 2004). If later life divorce erodes the health and well-being of older adults, then their needs will only intensify. Furthermore, a decline in economic well-being following divorce would suggest a greater reliance on public rather than private forms of support. One study indicates that unmarried baby boomers are four times as likely to be poor and twice as likely to have disabilities as married boomers (Lin & Brown, 2012). Late-life divorce poses challenges for older adults with limited social supports and financial resources and definitely influences one's emotional and financial well-being.

Economic and Psychological Effects

Marital dissolution generally has negative economic and psychological consequences. Among older women, those who are divorced have dramatically lower incomes and higher poverty rates. Approximately 20% of divorced women aged 65 or older live in poverty, compared with 18% of never-married women and 15% of widowed women (Butrica & Smith, 2012). Differences in poverty rates are even larger at the oldest ages—22% of divorced women aged 80 or older are poor, compared with only 17% of never-married women and 15% of widowed women (Butrica & Smith, 2012). Historically, divorced women have had the highest poverty rates among all aged women in the United States. Higher divorce rates mean that a larger share of future seniors will enter retirement divorced. Absent other changes, this trend could increase poverty rates for future seniors. However, important sociodemographic changes will positively affect the economic well-being of future cohorts of divorced women. The historic increases in female labor force participation and earnings are likely to increase future incomes and reduce future poverty rates for older divorced women (Butrica & Smith, 2012).

While the negative effects of divorce on well-being are well documented in research literature, the large individual differences in psychological adaptation are still not well understood (Amato, 2010). This is especially the case for marital breakup after long-term marriage, which is still a neglected research topic (Pudrovska & Carr, 2008; Sweeney, 2010). This research lags given the increase in divorce rates among adults aged 50 and older. In the United States, divorce rates in this age-group have doubled in the last 20 years (Brown & Lin, 2012), as it did in most European countries. In Switzerland, where the research was conducted, the divorce rate for marriages of a length of more than 20 years has risen from 15% in 1970 to 28% in 2010 (Swiss Federal Office of Statistics, 2011). Demographic and social changes (longer life expectancy and rising expectations for personal fulfillment from marriage) in recent decades are major explanations of this trend. Furthermore, objective barriers to divorce (e.g., economic dependence of women) as well as subjective ones (impact of family values and religious convictions) have been considerably lessened (Wu & Schimmele, 2007).

It is known that the age at which one experiences a critical life event can shape both the nature and context of the event as well as the individual's subsequent adjustment (Pudrovska & Carr, 2008). For middle-aged individuals, divorce may be accompanied by some of the challenges younger persons face but also by a set of distinctive age-related risks as well as resources (Pudrovska & Carr, 2008). Indeed, most people in this age group have to deal with personal changes as well as with multiple and often stressing social roles both professionally and privately (e.g., expectations for help and care from frail elderly parents) (Perrig-Chiello & Hutchison, 2010; Perrig-Chiello, Hutchison, & Hopflinger, 2008).

There is a great body of empirical evidence that associates divorce with symptoms of depression, grief, and anger, which may in turn have detrimental effects on well-being (Amato, 2010; Lorenz, Wickrama, Conger, & Elder, 2006). For most individuals, marital breakup is psychologically stressful and socially destabilizing, but the way adaptation occurs can vary widely. Many individuals adapt rapidly to marital breakup, while others remain vulnerable over a longer period of time, and some do not seem to recover at all. Results from longitudinal studies (Hetherington, 2003) suggest that there are indeed various patterns of adaptation to divorce. Six years after divorce, one-fifth of their study participants were well adjusted to their new situation, whereas 10% were still hopeless and depressed. The others, the large majority, adapted quite well and had average scores for most indicators. Another study conducted by Mancini, Bonanno, and Clark (2011), which examined trajectories of life satisfaction in the years before and after divorce, indicated that the majority of participants showed little change in annual assessments of life satisfaction, while some trajectories diverged sharply from the modal response. The negative feelings that follow divorce, such as loneliness, are mediated by the frequency of contact with children and friends (Pinquart, 2003). Guided Practice Exercise 7.4 examines relationships that are impacted by marital dissolution, which are important considerations in any therapeutic relationship.

Guided Practice Exercise 7.4

High divorce rates among adult children lead to new relationships for older people. A grandmother, for example, may stay in touch with her former daughter-in-law after her son's divorce in order to keep in contact with her grandchildren. She may develop a close friendship with her, and if the former daughter-in-law remarries, the grandmother may develop a relationship with the new family of grandparents. So relationships and the social network expand. Higher incidence of divorce in later years, while still low in comparison to younger persons, poses challenges for the grandparents,

(Continued)

(Continued)

adult children, and grandchildren. The situation becomes more complex if one of the grandparents remarries later in life. This again extends the family network and older persons may find themselves in complex family structures. Knowing this information is helpful, however, navigating through this social web of family ties is sometimes a daunting task. For example, where does your loyalty lie with respect to your original set of grandparents or those of your parent who remarried? Who do you spend holidays with or how do you divide your time so as to give attention to both sets of grandparents? What type of emotions does this scenario evoke within you? How will your life change as a result of divorces and remarriages? These and other issues are brought to therapeutic groups and individual sessions to be discussed and addressed.

Exit strategies are not easy. A divorce can be agonizing and complex for seniors, especially when there are issues involving long-term care and inheritances. Because Medicaid doesn't take effect until a couple's assets are depleted, people who delay a divorce can wind up paying for it financially. Also, dividing assets for heirs becomes complex if a second or third marriage is being dissolved, and there are children from previous marriages (Zaslow, 2003). Attorneys warn seniors to insist that all divorce settlements address health and life insurance, as well as retirement benefits. Divorce can be emotionally and financially devastating in later life. Older persons experiencing this late life transition are encouraged to seek professional services to ensure that all of their needs and concerns are addressed. Guided Practice Exercise 7.5 provides an opportunity to examine the impact of divorce in later life and identify skills required for an effective transition to this new status.

Guided Practice Exercise 7.5

Divorce can occur in later life. What are the ramifications of a divorce in later life if the spouse has never been employed outside of the home? What specific skills would need to be developed to adapt to this unexpected transition?

WIDOWHOOD

The transition to widowhood is a major life event that has implications for the well-being of family members, especially spouses (Carr, 2009; Lee & Carr, 2007). The death of a spouse has been found to be associated with numerous health-related outcomes, including mortality (Elwert & Christakis, 2008; Manzoli, Villari, Pirone, & Boccia, 2007); depressive symptoms (Lee, DeMaris, Bavin, & Sullivan, 2001); functional limitations, chronic conditions, and poor self-reported health (Hughes & Waite, 2009). Utz, Caserta, and Lund (2011) indicate that there is a dynamic relationship between physical and mental health among recently widowed individuals, such that they report poorer self-rated health as they experience higher levels of grief and depressive symptoms. Over time, the mental health trajectories of all widowed individuals become similar, regardless of physical health status.

Widowhood is a stage in the life cycle defined by the loss of one's spouse, but it typically leads to wide-ranging changes in roles, identities, social supports, finances, and living facilities, especially when the transition occurs after many years of marriage. Widowhood is now primarily a late-life phenomenon, as death has become more common among older persons than among young adults. Twenty-four percent of people 65 and older are widowed in the United States (U.S. Census Bureau, 2015). This percentage represents an increase from the 14 million widowed persons in 2012 that included nearly 3 million men and approximately 11 million women (U.S. Census Bureau, 2012). In most countries of the world, older men are more likely to be married and older women are more likely to be widowed (Kinsella & Velkott, 2001). These gender differences in marital status result from several factors, including differences in longevity, women's tendency to marry older men, and widowers' higher remarriage rates. These trends will change, and the ratio of widows to widowers will decrease in the next century as men live longer and marry women closer in age (Kinsella & Velloff, 2001). Guided Practice Exercise 7.6 provides an opportunity to become familiar with the emotions that widows experience and obtain resources to support them in their time of loss.

Guided Practice Exercise 7.6

What are some of the typical responses to the death of a spouse? What do you know regarding the widow's ability to adapt to loss? Identify challenges that are faced by widows after the loss of their spouse. Go online and conduct a search of support groups for widows and share this information with widows and as a resource for your peers.

Effects of Widowhood

The loss of a spouse and subsequent bereavement is the most stressful event that anyone experiences, although it is generally easier later in life than when it occurs "off time" during young adulthood or middle age (Moss, Moss, & Hansson, 2001). However, a large body of research has established that older bereaved spouses have higher rates of mortality and morbidity, weaker immune systems, more depressive symptoms, more chronic conditions, and functional disabilities; a higher number of physician visits and days spent in nursing homes; greater overall health care costs; and higher rates of hospitalization than their married peers (Laditka & Laditka, 2003).

It is notable that research has found no significant differences in the impact of widowhood between African-American and white elderly (Carr, 2004a). Recent research also calls attention to potential posttraumatic growth after loss events, which refers to growth that occurs after a major traumatic event such as losing a spouse. Personal growth resulting from a loss may include changed sense of self, changed relationships, and existential and spiritual growth. Longitudinal research on widowed older persons documented that those who had a high level of dependency on their spouse may benefit from the realization that they are able to cope and live independently (Carr, 2004b).

Mediators of the stressful impact of widowhood and bereavement include income status, social supports, self-esteem (van Baarson, 2002) and religious commitment (Ardelt, 2003), and marital quality (Carr, 2004b). A higher level of social support and religious participation by African Americans compared to whites may explain the lower levels of anger among African Americans after widowhood (Carr, 2004a).

Adaptation and Coping

Contemporary studies of widowhood have challenged many traditional assumptions, including the existence of grief stages, the need for bereaved persons to detach from the deceased and "work through" their grief, and an increase in depression and loneliness during widowhood. More sophisticated research designs have been used with larger samples to control for potentially confounding influences in past research. Longitudinal studies, such as the Changing Lives of Older Couples (CLOC), have yielded innovative findings about how people adjust to widowhood.

It is important to recognize that losses do not have a uniform impact on all older individuals, and research support has not consistently been found for adverse loss effects. Many studies have been completed that demonstrate different strategies that widows and widowers use to adapt to their newfound status. There is also growing recognition of proactive adaptations such as migration to Sunbelt retirement communities, which older adults may undertake to compensate for role losses (Kahana, 2000). Dutch researchers found that the network size of older adults stays mostly stable, as lost relationships are often replaced by new relationships (Aartsen et al., 2004). A decrease in social participation before the death of a spouse has been found to be counterbalanced by increased social participation following the loss (Utz, Carr, Ness, & Wortman, 2002). Furthermore, subjective appraisals of events as losses appear to play an important role in affecting both coping and outcomes subsequent to loss. Cumulative stresses and losses throughout life have been alternatively viewed as leading to negative mental health conditions or to strengthened coping abilities. There is a potentially useful new direction for gerontological research in considering growth opportunities that exist throughout life that may be embedded in losses or after adverse circumstances (Reker, 2001/2002).

Scholars have applied other conceptual approaches beyond that of role theory to examine bereavement and widowhood. Folkman (2001) uses a stress paradigm to examine the adaptive tasks of coping with loss. Stroebe and Schut (2001) propose a Dual Process Model of Bereavement in which bereaved spouses alternate (oscillate) between managing emotional or loss-oriented tasks and practical or restoration-oriented activities. Neimeyer (2001) describes an emerging "new wave" of grief theory that recognizes the complexity and cultural diversity of adjustments to bereavement and widowhood. Neimeyer (2001) has debunked the notion that an invariant sequence of stages of grief occurs among all who experience the death of a loved one and reports that highly individual processes of meaning-making are at the heart of grief dynamics. Neimeyer (2006) has maintained that major losses challenge a person's sense of identity and narrative coherence. Narrative disorganization can range from relatively limited and transient to more sweeping and chronic, depending on the nature of the relationship and the circumstances surrounding the death. According to Neimeyer (2006), a major task of grief involves reorganizing one's life story to restore coherence and maintain continuity between the past and the future. Some experts (Parkes, 2002) have suggested that widowed persons' reactions to loss differ according to their attachment styles.

The majority of widows and widowers are resilient (Bonanno et al., 2002). Almost everyone experiences an initial increase in grief symptoms, but for most people these symptoms subside by 18 months after the loss. Resilient widows and widowers generally are more accepting of death, more extroverted, more emotionally stable, and less dependent on spouses than their non-resilient peers. Resilient grievers also are more likely to have strong social supports from friends, relatives, and children and believe that they could rely on friends and family members for help with housework, house maintenance, finances, and caretaking if they became ill.

Those who grieve chronically have higher levels of interpersonal dependence and dependency on spouses. Widowed persons who are chronically depressed typically have poor coping capacities, low extroversion, poor emotional stability, high interpersonal dependence, and strong feelings about the uncontrollability of life events. In addition, they often have inadequate instrumental supports (Bonnano et al., 2002).

Economic resources are especially important for widows, who often abruptly lose significant income after the death of a spouse. Financial strain is a primary factor affecting widowed women (Umberson, Wortman, & Kessler, 1992). This corroborates data showing that poverty among older widowed women is consistently three to four times higher than for their married peers (McGarry & Schoeni, 2003). In addition, older widows face many more economic disadvantages than older widowers. Older women spend substantial portions of their resources on the health care of a sick or dying spouse, leaving the surviving spouse in a precarious financial situation (McGarry & Schoeni, 2005). Additionally, if the deceased spouse had been employed, the earnings stream from this source will obviously end (McGarry & Schoeni, 2005). This is a global trend, although some widows improve their financial condition by living in multigenerational households (Ofstedal, Reidy, & Knodel, 2004; United Nations, 2002).

Gender differences exist in response to widowhood. There is a general belief that women fare better than men in adapting to widowhood (Bennett, Hughes, & Smith, 2003). Widowed men and women believe this is for three main reasons: Women have better domestic skills, women are socially more capable, and men in the West "bottle-up" their feelings. There is also some marginal evidence that this may be the case at least with respect to emotional responses. Stroebe, Stroebe, and Schut (2001) suggested that men were more emotionally vulnerable than women. Bennett (2007) also suggested that men experienced emotions but were more likely to express them in terms of masculine characteristics such as control and self-sufficiency. Significant gender differences exist in response to widowhood. Investigators report that widows and widowers cope differently with the loss of a spouse.

Widows experienced changes in friendships, were dropped by married friends, however made new friends with other widowed women, and expressed no desire to remarry. Widowers experienced a reduced social network and had to adapt or make new friends and were more likely to remarry. Widowers experienced higher depressive symptoms, lower morale, decreased social engagement, and increased loneliness (Richardson & Balaswamy, 2001). Loss-oriented coping focus on those experiences and behaviors that are associated with a focus on the deceased and was found to influence negative affect (Richardson, 2007). Restoration-oriented coping includes attending to life changes, doing new things, denial/avoidance of grief, new roles/identities/relationships, and distraction from grief and tended to influence positive affect (Richardson, 2007). Engaging in physical activity, hobbies, and other leisure activities, as well as socializing and being involved with others, can provide sources of restoration and respite for the bereaved. Carr (2004c) found that widowed women who had the highest emotional dependence on their spouses had the worst self-esteem while married, but the highest self-esteem and psychological growth during widowhood. Older men, on the other hand, had higher self-esteem while married than in widowhood.

Bereaved spouses must cope with feelings of loss for a lifelong companion, but they must also address concrete matters such as obtaining survivor benefits and maintaining a home. They must perform their former practical chores and those that their deceased spouses once performed. Utz and colleagues (2002) found that older bereaved adults are often overwhelmed when initially confronted with these additional tasks; widows were more troubled by home maintenance chores, while widowers struggled more with household tasks.

Ethnic background and cultural differences affect how widowed persons grieve and how others treat them. Hsu and Khan (2003) found that the adjustments of Taiwanese widows to the loss of a spouse were shaped by the cultural views of a "good death" and "death without suffering" that were based largely on others' interpretations. These widows coped by finding meaning and reconstructing their identities within the Taiwanese cultural context of marriage, death, and bereavement.

Many widowed persons describe their increased social participation as an active method of coping with the loss of their spouses (Utz et al., 2002). Utz and colleagues (2002) found that friends and family members usually assist bereaved persons with instrumental tasks during the early stages of bereavement, and widows tend to receive more support than widowers.

Variability in Response to Widowhood

The circumstances of a spouse's death influence people's bereavement reactions in several ways. Carr and colleagues (2001) found that sudden deaths were associated with elevated levels of intrusive thoughts (unwelcome memories of the deceased or of the events surrounding the death that affect sleeping and concentration) during at least the early months of bereavement. In contrast, prolonged forewarning prior to death (i.e., more than 6 months) increased bereaved persons' anxiety levels after the loss. Sudden violent deaths may be particularly distressing (Kaltman & Bonnano, 2003).

Caring for a spouse often affects a bereaved person's adjustment to widowhood, especially if it continues for many months (Schulz, Barr, & Selman, 2001). The surviving spouse may feel relief when freed from the caregiver role. On the other hand, older widowers who lose contact with friends and family members as a result of caregiving often experience more difficult adjustments to widowhood than those who successfully maintained those relationships (Carr, House, Wortman, Neese, & Kessler, 2001).

The location of a spouse's death and his or her communications about death also influence survivors' initial adjustments to widowhood. When loved ones are in nursing homes, the survivors have already struggled with losses associated with placing their spouses in these institutions; nevertheless, home deaths offer bereaved persons more comfort than when spouses die in hospitals (Richardson & Balaswany, 2001). Survivors may adjust better when the death occurs at home, because a familiar and comfortable setting promotes better communication between spouses. When spouses suffer, however, survivors often experience more negative grief reactions (Carr, 2003; Richardson & Balaswany, 2001). Guided Practice Exercise 7.7 gives the emerging practitioner the opportunity to respect the wishes of a dying person and examine feelings surrounding dying at home versus in another type of environment and supports needed.

Guided Practice Exercise 7.7

Caring for an elderly parent or grandparent can be a rewarding yet challenging experience, but can evoke an array of emotions, especially when the parent or grandparent chooses to die at home. What are your feelings regarding the decision to die at home versus in a hospice, hospital, or nursing home? What changes would need to take place to adjust to this decision? What role do you foresee in this process? What kind of help would you need to respect the wish of your dying parent or grandparent to die in the comfort of his or her home?

These findings underscore the wide variability in people's widowhood experiences and the importance of assessments that allow practitioners to tailor interventions in accordance with death circumstances and to widowed persons' differences, such as gender, economic, and ethnic variations. Widowed persons also vary in the strategies they find most helpful. Some simply appreciate knowing that help is available, whether or not they use it. Others are glad to learn that their feelings are normal and that the acute pain of grief will eventually subside. Most widowed persons indicate that they achieved the most personal growth after the intense grieving period subsided, when they felt ready to reinvest in life through new activities and relationships.

Grief Interventions and Programs

Some federal statutory programs include important provisions for older widowed persons. The Older Americans Act offers a network of services for older bereaved adults. Medicare finances health care and hospice benefits for people over age 65, and the Social Security Act provides economic benefits to retirees, widows, and their dependents. Many communities offer widows and widowers mutual support groups, individual counseling, and programs that assist them with instrumental needs, such as homemaker and chore services, telephone reassurance programs, friendly visitors, repairs, and money manage-ment. Some local area agencies on aging also offer health promotion services, including screening for depression, mental health information, and referrals to psychiatric and psy-chological services.

Most scholars concur that grief interventions work best for those who seek help, but they can be ineffective and create adverse effects when they interfere with normal grieving (Jordan & Neimeyer, 2003; Schut et al., 2001). There is also evidence that treatment is more likely to be successful if it is provided after a delay, preferably between 6 to 18 months after the death (Jordan & Neimeyer, 2003). There is still very little research identifying the spe-cific interventions that work best for different clients under different circumstances. In addition, experts have inadequately evaluated the impact of community interventions such as support services for widows who need assistance with yard work, financial matters, or other instrumental tasks. The efficacy of interventions for widows and widowers increases when clinicians tailor interventions based on clients' gender, ethnic background, and other personal differences.

Importance of Social Engagement

Widowhood engenders a far greater impact on an individual than purely an emotional loss; the transition to widowhood also involves the adjustment to a new role as a single person and the subsequent changes in life that this entails (Carr & Utz, 2002). Relationships with family, friends, and the wider social network take on increased significance following the death of a spouse (Feldman, Byles, & Beaumont, 2000). Social engagement—having close relationships and participation in social activities—strongly influences the ability of the widowed spouse to successfully adapt to widowhood (Bennett, Gibbons, & MacKenzie-Smith, 2010).

Frequency of contact with others has been associated with well-being in widowhood, and a lack of social contact identified as a major risk factor for post-bereavement loneliness (Pinquart, 2003). Friends play a more important role in terms of contact and support later in widowhood (Ha, 2008), which is often centered around social activities (Chambers, 2005).

It is particularly important to understand the social engagement experiences of older widowed men and women because their experiences are likely to be different from those who are widowed at younger ages. Unlike their younger counterparts, the older widowed person is more likely to be dealing with other concurrent stressors such as health concerns, reduced mobility, financial pressures, relocation, cognitive decline, and loss of friends or family members (Carr, 2006). Therefore, concomitant changes relating to aging may also have implications for social engagement, and hence the experience of social engagement during late-life widowhood must be reviewed against this background.

Social activities may also play an important role in the process of adaptation to widow-hood. Social activities are performed with others and, more than any other activity domain, have been associated with physical and emotional well-being (Adams, Leibbrandt, & Moon, 2011). Kreider and colleague (2002) propose that social activities have four different func-tions during negative life events: They may act as a buffer; generate hope for the future, provide continuity, and play a central role in personal transformations. Participation in social activities during widowhood has been associated with lower levels of loneliness, guilt, and sadness; enhanced morale and reduced stress; and better physical and mental health (Janke, Nimrod, & Kleiber, 2008; Pinquart, 2003). Older widowed individuals may be at risk of lower levels of social participation as significant declines in activity levels have been associated with aging (Bennett, 2005), in particular due to reduced financial status, shrinking of social networks owing to deaths of friends, deterioration in physical health, and poorer perceived health status. Guided Practice Exercise 7.8 gives the counselor-trainee an opportunity to examine the impact of losing a spouse in the life of an older client and its impact on her health status.

Guided Practice Exercise 7.8

The death of a spouse has an enormous impact on older women, who on average outlive their spouses. Older women experience an array of emotions that impact their psychological, social, and physical health. The loss of a spouse is defined as a primary loss with resulting secondary losses. Define secondary loss and give three examples of secondary losses. Review the impact of the secondary losses you have identified and develop strategies with your client to begin to address these losses. The grieving process may also be accompanied by physical complaints. Identify your client's perception of her health prior to the loss of her spouse and subsequent to the loss of her spouse. Discuss the differences in her perceptions and develop a strategy to enhance her perceptions of her health and/or actual health status. If you have not been assigned a client, then complete this issue in a role-play scenario.

DYING AND DEATH

Since the post-World War II era, heart disease, cancer, and stroke have become the leading causes of death. The fact that more people than ever before are dying in advanced age of chronic conditions creates unprecedented challenges—for individuals as they confront the dying process of relatives and friends, for the health care delivery system, and for U.S. society as its members struggle to define and implement the idea of a good death.

Dying and death are major categories of the human experience that are culturally determined. Perceptions that dying has begun and the meanings associated with those perceptions are contingent on a range of social and cultural factors, such as the state of biological knowledge; the value of prolonging life or accepting finitude; the relative roles of religion, science, and medicine in creating meaning in everyday life; and personal familiarity with the dying transition. Dying today is shaped by particular notions of therapeutic possibility as well as ideals about approaching the end of life. The distinguishing feature about the process of dying today is that it can be negotiated and controlled depending on the preferences of the dying person, the goals of particular medical specialties, the organizational features of technology-intensive medical settings, and the presence and wishes of family members. Guided Practice Exercise 7.9 provides the opportunity to explore personal feelings about having a limited number of months to live.

Guided Practice Exercise 7.9

What would you do if you were told you only had 6 months to live? What type of ceremony or funeral rituals would you prefer? Why did you choose this particular type of ritual?

The Process of Dying

Dying is the process of decline in body functions that results in death of an organism. It is a complex process that includes physical, intellectual, social, spiritual, and emotional dimensions. Although emotional reactions to dying vary, many people show similar experiences during this process. Much of the knowledge about reactions to dying stems from the work of Elisabeth Kübler-Ross, a pioneer in thanatology, the study of death and dying. Her pioneering work in 1969 was a sensitive analysis of the reactions of terminally ill patients, and it encouraged the development of death education as a discipline and prompted efforts to improve the care of dying patients. She identified five psychological stages that people coping with death often experience (Kübler-Ross & Kessler, 2005).

Denial is the first stage expressed in the process. A person intellectually accepts the impending death but rejects it emotionally and feels a sense of shock and disbelief. The individual is too confused and stunned to comprehend "not being" and thus rejects the idea. The second stage is anger ("why me?"). The person becomes angry at having to face death when others, including loved ones, are healthy and not threatened. The dying person perceives the situation as unfair or senseless and may be hostile to friends, family, physicians, or the world in general. The third stage is bargaining where the dying person may resolve to be a better person in return for an extension of life or may secretly pray for a short reprieve from death to experience a special event, such as a family wedding or birth. Depression is the fourth stage that sets in as vitality diminishes and the person begins to experience symptoms with increasing frequency. Common feelings experienced in this stage include doom, loss, worthlessness, and guilt over the emotional suffering of loved ones and the arduous but seemingly futile efforts of caregivers. Acceptance is the final stage ("I'm ready"). The dying person stops battling with emotions and becomes tired and weak. With acceptance, the person does not give up and become sullen or resentfully resigned to death, but rather becomes passive (Kübler-Ross & Kessler, 2005).

Subsequent research has indicated that the experiences of dying people do not fit easily into specific stages, and patterns vary from person to person. Some people never go through this process and instead remain emotionally calm; others may pass back and forth between the stages. Despite these variations, Kübler-Ross's theory offers valuable insights for those who seek to understand the process of dying. The process of dying is respected and addressed by hospice staff who render care to the patient and family as a unit. Guided Practice Exercise 7.10 provides an opportunity to gain insight into the concept of hospice and how it provides comfort at the end of life.

Guided Practice Exercise 7.10

Hospice provides end-of-life care for persons who have been identified as having 6 months or less left to live. This end-of-life care is comprehensive care provided to the dying person and his or her family. Visit a hospice facility in your local area and identify the types of services offered, types of personnel employed, supportive aftercare services, reimbursement for services, location of facility, and visiting arrangements. What were your overall impressions? Would you consider a hospice for any of your family members? How have your personal views changed regarding caring for persons at the end of life?

Reactions to Grief

The losses resulting from the death of a loved one can be extremely difficult to cope with. The dying person, as well as close family and friends, frequently suffers emotionally and physically from the impending loss of critical relationships and roles. Because relationships vary in type and intensity, reactions to loss also vary. The death of a parent, spouse, sibling, child, friend, or pet will result in different kinds of feelings for different people. For example, the loss of a close relative is typically followed by depressive symptoms, but the loss of a friend is mostly associated with a feeling of loneliness (D'Epinay et al., 2003). Regardless of the type of feeling, the loss of loved ones leaves holes and inevitable changes. Loneliness and despair may envelope the survivor. Understanding of these normal reactions, time, patience, and support from loved ones can help the bereaved heal and move on, even though they will not forget (Corr, Nabe, & Corr, 2008).

Grief occurs in reaction to significant loss, including one's impending death, the death of a loved one, or a quasi-death experience (a loss, such as the end of a relationship or job, that resembles death because it involves separation or change in personal identity). Grief may be experienced as mental, physical, social, or emotional reaction and often includes changes in patterns of eating, sleeping, working, and even thinking. Disenfranchised grief occurs when a person experiences a loss that cannot be openly acknowledged, publicly mourned, or socially supported, and therefore coping may be much more difficult.

Symptoms of grief vary in severity and duration, depending on the situation and the individual. Some of these symptoms are shown in Table 7.1. The bereaved person can benefit from emotional and social support from family, friends, clergy, employees, and traditional support organizations. The larger and stronger the support system, the easier the adjustment is likely to be (Corr, Nabe, & Corr, 2008). Mourning is incorrectly equated

Table 7.1 Symptoms of Grief

Periodic waves of prolonged distress

Feelings of tightness in the throat

Choking and shortness of breath

Frequent need to sigh

Feelings of emptiness

Muscular weakness

Intense anxiety that is physically painful

Insomnia

Memory lapses

Loss of appetite

Difficulty concentrating

Engaging in repetitive or purposeless behavior

Having an "observer" sensation or feeling of unreality

Difficulty in making decisions

Lack of organization

Excessive speech

Social withdrawal or hostility

Feelings of guilt

Preoccupation with image of the deceased

with the word grief; however, mourning refers to culturally prescribed and accepted time periods and behavior patterns for the expression of grief. In Judaism, for example, sitting shiva is a designated mourning period of 7 days that involves prescribed rituals and prayers. Depending on a person's relationship with the deceased, various other rituals may continue for up to a year.

Susceptibility to disease increases with grief and may even be life-threatening in severe and enduring cases. A bereaved person may suffer emotional pain and exhibit a variety of grief responses for many months after the death. The rate of the healing process depends on the amount and quality of grief work that a person does. Grief work is the process of integrating the reality of the loss into everyday life and learning to feel better. Often the bereaved person must deliberately and systematically work in reducing denial and coping with the pain that results from memories of the deceased. This process takes time and requires emotional effort (Worden, 2008).

Case Illustration 7.2 provides an opportunity to examine maladaptive coping mechanisms associated with feelings of loss and bereavement. These behaviors place elders at risk and provide mental health counselors the opportunity to intervene on their older clients' behalf.

CASE ILLUSTRATION 7.2

Ms. Xenith is an 80-year-old female who lives in an apartment in the city. She has resided there since her husband died 10 years ago. Ms. Xenith was once employed at a local car manufacturing company as an assembly worker. She took care of her husband for 4 years before he succumbed to metastatic cancer and describes those 4 years as the hardest of her life.

Ms. Xenith's lifestyle changed slowly after her husband died. She stopped going to football games and socializing with her friends. When asked why, she responds, "I can't bear the thought of living without my husband and I wish I were dead." Her medical history includes hypertension (since 1995), many years of angina, depression from abnormal bereavement (since 2000), and adult onset diabetes. She religiously takes her medications as prescribed by her physician. The most significant lifestyle changes in Ms. Xenith's life are alcohol abuse, social isolation and withdrawal from friends, and physical inactivity. Her dietary habits have changed, increasing in processed and convenience foods and high sodium choices.

Neighbors and friends feel Ms. Xenith has changed and has become a recluse. Although they care, her friends have stopped trying. One neighbor called Ms. Xenith's daughter, who lives 900 miles away, to inform her of the changes and told her to come as soon as possible before she does something to hurt herself, saying "I think she is slowly killing herself." Ms. Xenith has not adjusted to her husband's death. In an attempt to cope with the loss, she is using alcohol. She is at high risk for suicide. Risk factors include being older, living alone, widowhood, and bereavement. The neighbor's call to her daughter may have saved Ms. Xenith's life.

Developmental tasks to complete in the process of grief work have been developed by Worden (2008). Accepting the reality of the loss requires acknowledging and realizing that the person is dead. Traditional rituals, such as the funeral, help many bereaved people move toward acceptance. Working through the pain of grief is another developmental task that must be done or it will manifest itself through other symptoms or behaviors. Adjusting to an environment in which the deceased is missing is a developmental task where the bereaved may feel lonely and uncertain about a new identity without the person who has died. Lastly, the bereaved needs to emotionally relocate the deceased and move on with life. Individuals never lose memories of a significant relationship. However, they may need help in letting go of the emotional energy that used to be invested in the person who has died and finding an appropriate place for the deceased in their emotional lives.

Defining Death

Death eventually comes to everyone, but if individuals live life to the fullest and educate themselves on end-of-life issues, they will be better able to accept the inevitable. To cope effectively with dying, counselors must address the needs of people facing life's final transition. Death can be defined as the "final cessation of the vital functions" and also refers to a state in which these functions are "incapable of being restored" (*The New Shorter Oxford English Dictionary,* 1993). This definition has become more significant as medical advances make it increasingly possible to postpone death.

The concept of brain death, defined as the irreversible cessation of all functions of the entire brainstem, has gained increasing credence. The brainstem is a relay site for sensory and motor pathways and is responsible for such critical body functions as respiration and heart rate. Brain death occurs when the following criteria are met (Ad Hoc Committee of the Harvard Medical School, 1968): unreceptivity and unresponsiveness; no movement for a continuous hour after observation by a physician and no breathing after 3 minutes off a respirator; no reflexes, including brainstem reflexes; a "flat" electroencephalogram for at least 10 minutes; and finally, all of these tests repeated at least 24 hours later with no change and certainty that hypothermia and depression of the central nervous system caused by use of drugs are not responsible for these conditions. Guided Practice Exercise 7.11 provides the opportunity to explore personal feelings regarding death, dying, and death anxiety that will make it easier for the mental health counselor to address these issues.

Guided Practice Exercise 7.11

Many individuals have typically viewed death as a taboo subject; however, it has more recently become a topic of conversation. Many older persons choose to make their wishes known so that they can be adhered to upon death. Young adults vary with respect to the timing of such conversations; some choose to avoid the subject in its entirety. What are your feelings regarding death and the process of dying? Who do you think is more anxious regarding death—young adults, middle-aged adults, or older adults? Go online and conduct research on death anxiety and compare your findings to your answer. What concerns individuals the most with regard to the process of dying or death? What arrangements can you make on an individual level to decrease anxiety for yourself and your family members?

Death and Culture

There is no single attitude or approach toward dying and death among Americans. Cultural diversity has been examined and two themes emerge. First, health workers are trained in particular professional cultures and bring their own experiences to bear on the dying process. Physicians, nurses, social workers, chaplains, and other professionals hold different assumptions about how death should be approached as a result of their professional training, and those sets of assumptions differ from the experiences of patients and families (Koenig, 1997).

Second, the relationships among ethnic identification, religious practices, ways of dying, and beliefs and priorities about care, autonomy, and communication are complex and cannot be neatly organized along ethnic, class, or professional lines. In assessing cultural variation in patient populations, for example, cultural background is only meaningful when it is interpreted in the context of a particular patient's unique history, family constellation, and socioeconomic status. It cannot be assumed that patients' ethnic origins or religious backgrounds will lead them to approach decisions about their death in a culturally speci-fied manner (Koenig & Gates-Williams, 1995).

Denying Death

Attitudes toward death tend to fall on a continuum. At one end, death is viewed as the mortal enemy of humankind. At the other end, death is accepted and even welcomed. For people whose attitudes fall at this end, death is a passage to a better state of being. Most people, however, perceive themselves to be in the middle of this continuum. From this perspective, death is a bewildering mystery that elicits fear and apprehension while pro-foundly influencing beliefs and actions throughout life.

In the United States, a high level of discomfort is associated with death and dying. Those who deny death tend to

- Avoid people who are grieving after the death of a loved one so they won't have to talk about it
- Fail to validate a dying person's frightening situation by talking to the person as though nothing is wrong
- Substitute euphemisms for the word death (e.g., "passing away," "kicking the bucket," "no longer with us," "going to heaven," or "going to a better place")
- Give false reassurances to dying people by saying things like "Everything is going to be okay"
- Silence others who are trying to talk about death
- Avoid touching people who are dying

In an increasingly pluralistic society, there is growing diversity among health care work-ers as well as among patient populations. Especially in urban areas, the cultural back-ground of a health professional is often different from that of a dying patient to whom care is being given. It is impossible and inappropriate to use racial or ethnic background as straightforward predictors of behavior among health care professionals or patients (Kalish & Reynolds, 1976).

Death Anxiety

Advances in life-extending technology, diet, and general lifestyle have improved the longevity of the majority of people, effectively associating death with old age. As a result of these two converging trends, one might assume that older adults, who are statistically "closest" to death, would experience considerable death anxiety. The general trend across studies points to a decrease, rather than an increase, in death anxiety with advancing age, at least through the adult years. Moreover, well-designed survey studies have demonstrated that age is a relatively good predictor of fear of death, accounting for more of the variation in death anxiety than other demographic and social strata variables such as education, income, and ethnicity. However, in later adulthood, death anxiety tends to stabilize. This does not mean that all older people have uniformly low levels of death anxiety, but that as a group they have lower levels of death anxiety than middle-aged people. However, death anxiety does not appear to continue decreasing with age in later life (Kalish & Reynolds, 1976).

Research has shown that the gender difference in death anxiety evident in younger adults—with women reporting more death fears than men—is not present in older adults (Neimeyer, Fortner, & Schulz, 2006). This finding is consistent with research showing that older adults are less differentiated by gender and exhibit a more androgynous gender identity (Neimeyer et al., 2006). Ethnicity has been associated with greater death awareness, with African Americans and Hispanics reporting greater familiarity with death and greater exposure to violence than Caucasians. However, results of studies (Neimeyer et al., 2006) have been mixed regarding whether these ethnic differences are associated with greater anxieties about death among various subgroups. Ethnic variation is an important factor in attitudes and expectations about death, and individual differences within ethnic groups are at least as great as, and often much greater than, differences between ethnic groups (Reynolds, 1976).

The impact of cultural difference on attitudes and practices surrounding death in the United States cannot be denied. The challenge for society is to respect cultural pluralism in the context of an actively interventionist medical system. The challenge for emerging practitioners is to appreciate the diversity in cultural practices and respect personal preferences of family members. Guided Practice Exercise 7.12 provides an opportunity to examine these issues.

Guided Practice Exercise 7.12

Funeral rites vary within states and between various countries. Compare and contrast funeral rites within the United States and two other countries. Compare the unique cultural considerations in the countries identified. Pay particular attention to the types of funerals (e.g., military persons, religious preferences) and memorial services, the duration of mourning, typical type of dress and ornaments worn, types of food served, types of aftercare services, and how the deceased loved ones are remembered. Having conducted your research, do you feel that changes are needed within the United States regarding funeral services? Are you now more comfortable with the prospect of death after conducting your research? Have you made your wishes known to your family regarding how you choose to be treated and the type of arrangements you prefer for your services?

Learning to Honor Death

Some individuals have a particularly hard time accepting death. There may be some people who have overcome this fear, but most are afraid of dying. There is no shame in this, for it is part of human nature. Everyone experiences the desire to push death away and pretend life will go on forever. But still, every day on earth, hundreds of thousands of people die (Robbins, 2007).

The quality of a human life cannot be measured in years; what really matters is how much love, wisdom, and courage was brought to each life that was given. Finding the fountain of youth is not about living forever. It's about allowing life to be guided by the beauty of the soul. It's about finding the fountain of joy and the fountain of life. It's about living so fully that people know they have really lived. It's about loving so fully that they know they have really loved (Robbins, 2007).

Loss and bereavement is natural and inevitable for older adults. Numerous losses occur: loss of status, identity, environment, finances, pets, loved ones, functional ability, cognitive ability, employment, and others. Divorce and widowhood have a major impact on all aspects of one's health and well-being. Death and dying, while important, is only one aspect of the life cycle. Though it is inevitable, a focus on viability and resiliency of older adults is most important. Helping professionals require an understanding of the interplay of loss in various contexts and may need to address fears and uncertainties regarding the process of dying. However, a continued focus on the strengths and resiliency of older persons should be reinforced throughout the counseling sessions.

The experience of loss is a universal experience that can alter the lives of older adults in numerous ways. Mental health counselors need to understand and increase their knowledge of the losses that older persons experience and the subsequent emotional and physical manifestations associated with these losses. For those persons who experience difficulty in coping and adapting to these losses, mental health professionals can utilize their professional skills to assist older clients in transforming and ultimately improving the quality of their lives.

KEYSTONES

- An accumulation of losses is experienced as one ages and require careful examination.
- Many losses experienced by older persons are experienced and managed without professional intervention.
- The prevalence of divorce in later adulthood is increasing and has a number of implications for individuals and their families.
- Widowhood is a major loss that leads to broad changes in roles, social supports, finances, and living situations.
- Professional counselors need increased knowledge and education on issues of widowhood and divorce to work effectively with older clients.
- Counselors working with older clients require knowledge of the dying, death, and bereavement process to assist elderly clients in major life transitions.

ADDITIONAL RESOURCES

Print Based

Aikman, B. (2013). *Saturday night widows: The adventures of six friends remaking their lives.* New York, NY: Broadway Books.

DeSpelder, L., & Strickland, A. (2010). *The last dance: Encountering death and dying.* New York, NY: McGraw-Hill.

Felber, M. (2000). *Finding your way after your spouse dies.* Notre Dame, IN: Ave Maria Press.

Greene, P. (2003). *It must have been moonglow: Reflections on the first fears of widowhood.* New York, NY: Villard Publishing.

Mabry, R. (2006). *The tender scar: Life after the death of a spouse.* Grand Rapids, MI: Kregel Publications.

Neimeyer, R. (2000). *Lessons of loss: A guide to coping.* Memphis, TN: Center for the Study of Loss and Transition.

Russell, L. (2003). Stopping by a cemetery on a snowy morning. *Journal of Grief and Loss, 8,* 221–227.

Web Based

www.ahcpr.gov

www.death-and-dying.org/

www.dyingmatters.org/page/understanding-death-and-dying

www.havenofnova.org/articles/widow_widowers_grief/widowhood.pdf

www.HospiceFoundation.org

www.medicine.jrank.org/pages/1841/Widowhood-consequences-widowhood.html

www.nhpco.org

www.nolo.com/legal-encyclopedia/special-issues-late-life-divorce-32335.html

www.silvercentury.org/polFeatures.cfm?Author_Cnct_Id = 32

www.sisterhoodofwidows.com/

www.totaldivorce.com/news/articles/finance/elderly-couples.aspx

REFERENCES

Aartsen, M., van Tilburg, T., Smets, C., & Knipscheer, K. (2004). A longitudinal study of the impact of physical and cognitive decline on the personal network in old age. *Journal of Personal Relationships, 21*(2), 249–266.

Adams, K. B., Leibbrandt, S., & Moon, H. (2011). A critical review of the literature on social and leisure activity and wellbeing in later life. *Ageing & Society, 31,* 683–712.

Ad Hoc Committee of the Harvard Medical School to Examine the Definition of Brain Death. (1968). A definition of irreversible coma. *Journal of the American Medical Association, 205,* 377.

Amato, P. R. (2010). Research on divorce: Continuing trends and new developments. *Journal of Marriage and Family, 72,* 650–666.

American Association of Retired Persons. (2004). The divorce experience: A study of divorce at midlife and beyond. *AARP, The Magazine.*

Ardelt, M. (2003). Effects of religion and purpose in life on elders' subjective well-being and attitudes toward death. *Journal of Religious Gerontology, 14,* 55–77.

Bair, D. (2007). *Calling it quits: Late-life divorce and starting over.* New York, NY: Random House.

Ball, K., Berch, D. B., Helmers, K. F., Jobe, J. B., Leveck, M. D., & Marsiske, M. (2002). Effect of cognitive training interventions with older adults: A randomized controlled trial. *Journal of the American Medical Association, 288,* 2271–2281.

Ball, K. K., Wadley, V. G., Vance, D. E., & Edwards, J. D. (2004). Cognitive skills: Training, maintenance, and daily usage. *Encyclopedia of Applied Psychology, 1,* 387–392.

Bennett, K. M. (2005). Psychological wellbeing in later life: The longitudinal effects of marriage, widowhood and marital status change. *International Journal of Geriatric Psychiatry, 20,* 280–284.

Bennett, K. M. (2007). "No sissy stuff": Towards a theory of masculinity and emotional expression in older widowed men. *Journal of Aging Studies, 21,* 347–356.

Bennett, K., Hughes, G., & Smith, P. (2003). "I think a woman can take it": Widowed men's views and experiences of gender differences in bereavement. *Ageing International, 28*(4), 408–424.

Bennett, K. M., Gibbons, K., & MacKenzie-Smith, S. (2010). Loss and restoration in later life: An examination of dual process model of coping with bereavement. *Omega, 61,* 315–332

Bisconti, T., Bergeman, C. S., & Baker, S. (2004). Emotional well-being in recently bereaved widows: A dynamical systems approach. *Journal of Gerontology, 59B*(4), 158–167.

Boerner, K., Schulz, R., & Horowitz, A. (2004). Positive aspects of caregiving and adaptation to bereavement. *Psychology and Aging, 19,* 668–675.

Bonanno, G. A., Papa, A., Lalande, K., Zhang, N., & Noll, J. G. (2005). Grief processing and deliberate grief avoidance: A prospective comparison of bereaved spouses and parents in the United States and the People's Republic of China. *Journal of Consulting and Clinical Psychology, 73,* 86–88.

Bonanno, G. A., Wortman, C. B., Lehman, D. R., Tweed, R. G., Haring, M., Sonnega, J., . . . Nesse, R. M. (2002). Resilience to loss and grief: A prospective study from pre-loss to 18-months post-loss. *Journal of Personality and Social Psychology, 83,* 1150–1164.

Brown, S. L., & Lin, I-Fen. (2012). The gray divorce revolution: Rising divorce among middle-aged and older adults, 1990–2010. *Journals of Gerontology Series B: Psychological Sciences and Social Sciences, 67*(6), 731–741.

Butrica, B., & Smith, K. (2012). The retirement prospects of divorced women. *Social Security Bulletin, 72*(1), 11–22.

Carr, D. (2003). A good death for whom? Quality of spouse's death and psychological distress among older widowed persons. *Journal of Health and Social Behavior, 44,* 215–232.

Carr, D. (2004a). Black/white differences in psychological adjustment to spousal loss among older adults. *Research on Aging, 26*(6), 591–622.

Carr, D. (2004b). The desire to date and remarry among older widows and widowers. *Journal of Marriage and Family, 66,* 1051–1068.

Carr, D. (2004c). Gender, preloss marital dependence and older adults' adjustment to widowhood. *Journal of Marriage and the Family, 66,* 220–235.

Carr, D. (2009). Who's to blame? Perceived responsibility for spousal and psychological distress among older widowed persons. *Journal of Health and Social Behavior, 50,* 359–375.

Carr, D., House, J. S., Wortman, C., Neese, R., & Kessler, R. C. (2001). Psychological adjustment to sudden and anticipated loss among older widowed persons. *Journal of Gerontology: Social Science, 56B,* S237–S248.

Carr, D., & Utz, R. (2002). Late-life widowhood in the United States: New directions in research and theory. *Aging International, 27,* 65–86.

Carr, D. (2006). Methodological issues in studying late life bereavement. In D. Carr, R. M. Nesse, & C. B. Wortman (Eds.), *Spousal bereavement in late life* (pp. 19–47). New York, NY: Springer.

Chambers, P. (2005). *Older widows and the lifecourse: Multiple narratives of hidden lives.* Aldershot, UK: Ashgate Publishing.

Cherlin, A. I. (2010). Demographic trends in the United States: A review of research in the 2000s. *Journal of Marriage and Family, 72,* 403–419.

Cooney, T. M., & Dunne, K. (2001). Intimate relationships in later life: Current realities, future prospects. *Journal of Family Issues, 22,* 838–858.

Corr, C., Nabe, C., & Corr, D. (2008). *Death and dying, life and living* (6th ed.). Belmont, CA: Wadsworth.

D'Epinay, C., Cavalli, S., & Spine, D. (2003). The death of a loved one: Impact on health and relationships in very old age. *OMEGA, 47*(3), 265–284.

deVries, B., & Johnson, C. (2002). Multidimensional reactions to the death of a friend in the later years. *Advances in Life-Course Research: New Frontiers in Socialization, 7,* 299–324.

Elwert, F., & Christakis, N. A. (2008). Spousal concordance in health behavior change. *Health Services Research, 43,* 96–116.

Feldman, S., Byles, J. E., & Beaumont, R. (2000). Is anybody listening? The experiences of widowhood for older Australian women. *Journal of Women & Aging, 12,* 155–176.

Folkman, S. (2001). Revised coping theory and the process of bereavement. In M. S. Stroebe, R. W. Hansson, W. Stroebe, & H. Schut (Eds.), *Handbook of bereavement research: Consequences, coping and cure* (pp. 563–584). Washington, DC: American Psychological Association.

Gilbar, O., & Ben-Zur, H. (2002). Bereavement of spouse caregivers of cancer patients. *American Journal of Orthopsychiatry, 72,* 422–432.

Ha, J. H. (2008). Changes in support from confidants: Children and friends following widowhood. *Journal of Marriage and Family, 70,* 306–318.

Hetherington, E. M. (2003). Intimate pathways: Changing patterns in close personal relationships across time. *Family Relations, 52,* 318–331.

Hsu, M., & Khan, D. (2003). Adaptation as meaning construction: A cultural analysis of spousal death in Taiwanese women. *Omega: Journal of Death and Dying, 47,* 169–186.

Hughes, M. F., & O'Rand, A. M. (2004). *The lives and times of the baby boomers.* Washington, DC: Population Reference Bureau.

Hughes, M. E., & Waite, L. J. (2009). Marital biography and health at mid-life. *Journal of Health and Social Behavior, 50,* 344–358.

Humphrey, K. (2009). *Counseling strategies for loss and grief.* Alexandria, VA: American Counseling Association.

Jacobsen, L., Mather, M., Lee, M., & Kent, M. (2011). America's aging population. *Population Bulletin, 66*(1). Washington, DC: Population Reference Bureau.

Janke, M. C., Nimrod, G., & Kleiber, D. A. (2008). Leisure activity and depressive symptoms of widowed and married women in later life. *Journal of Leisure Research, 40*(2), 250–266.

Jordan, J., & Neimeyer, R. A. (2003). Does grief counseling work? *Death Studies, 27,* 765–786.

Kahana, E. (2000). Contextualizing successful aging: New directions in an age-old search. In R. Settersen, Jr. (Ed.), *An invitation to the life course: A new look at old age.* Amityville, NY: Baywood.

Kahana, E., & Kahana, B. (2003). Contextualizing successful aging: New directions in an age-old search. In R. Settersten, Jr. (Ed.), *Invitation to the life course: A new look at old age* (pp. 225–255). Amityville, NY: Baywood.

Kalish, R. A., & Reynolds, D. K. (1976). *Death and ethnicity: A psychocultural study.* New York, NY: Baywood.

Kaltman, S., & Bonanno, G. H. (2003). Trauma and bereavement: Examining the impact of sudden and violent deaths. *Journal of Anxiety Disorders, 17,* 131–147.

Katz, S., Branch. L. G., Branson, M. H., Papsidero, J. H., Beck, J. C., & Greer, D. S. (1983). Active life expectancy. *New England Journal of Medicine, 309*(20), 1218–1224.

Kinsella, K., & Velkoff, V. Z. (2001). *An aging world: 2001.* Washington, DC: U.S. Census Bureau.

Koenig, B. (1997). Cultural diversity in decision making about care at the end of life. In M. Field & C. K. Cassell (Eds.), *Approaching death: Improving care at the end of life* (Appendix E, pp. 363–382). Washington, DC: National Academics Press.

Koenig, B., & Gates-Williams, J. (1995). Understanding cultural difference in caring for dying patients. *Western Journal of Medicine, 163,* 244–249.

Kreider, R. M., & Ellis, R. (2011). Number, timing, and duration of marriages and divorces: 2009. *Current Population Reports* (pp. 70–125). Washington, DC: U.S. Census Bureau.

Kreider, R. M., & Fields, J. M. (2002). Number, timing, and duration of marriages and divorces: 1996. *Current Population Reports* (pp. 70–80). Washington, DC: U.S. Census Bureau.

Kübler-Ross, E., & Kessler, D. (2005). *On grief and grieving: Finding the meaning of grief through the five stages of loss.* New York, NY: Scribner.

Laditka, J. N. L., & Laditka, S. B. (2003). Increased hospitalization risk for recently widowed older women and protective effects of social contracts. *Journal of Women and Aging, 15,* 7–28.

Lee, C. R., & DeMaris, A. (2007). Widowhood, gender, and depression: A longitudinal analysis. *Research on Aging, 29,* 56–72.

Lee, G. R., DeMaris, A., Bavin, S., & Sullivan, R. (2001). Gender differences in the depressive effects of widowhood in later life. *Journal of Gerontology: Social Sciences, 56B,* S56–S61.

Lee, M., & Carr, D. (2007). Does the content of spousal loss affect the physical functioning of older widowhood persons? A longitudinal analysis. *Research on Aging, 29,* 457–587.

Lichtenthal, W. G., Cruess, D. G., & Prigerson, H. G. (2004). A case for establishing complicated grief as a distinct mental disorder in DSM-V. *Clinical Psychology Review, 24,* 637–662.

Lin, I. F. (2008). Consequences of parental divorce for adult-children's support of their frail parents. *Journal of Marriage and Family, 70,* 113–128.

Lin, I. F., & Brown, S. I. (2012). Unmarried boomers confront old age: A national portrait. *The Gerontologist, 52,* 153–165.

Lorenz, F. O., Wickrama, K., Conger, R. D., & Elder, G. H., Jr. (2006). The short-term and decade-long effects of divorce on women's midlife health. *Journal of Health and Social Behavior, 47,* 111–125.

Mancini, A. D., Bonanno, G. A., & Clark, A. E. (2011). Stepping of the hedonic treadmill: Individual differences in response to major life events. *Journal of Individual Differences, 32,* 144–152.

Manzoli, L., Villari, P., Pirone, G. M., & Boccia, A. (2007). Marital status and mortality in the elderly: A systematic review and meta-analysis. *Social Science and Medicine, 64,* 77–94.

Mayo Clinic Staff. (2015). *Complicated grief: Risk factors.* Rochester, MN: Mayo Foundation for Medical Education and Research.

McGarry, K., & Schoeni, R. F. (2003). *Medicare gaps and widow poverty.* Working Paper 2003-065. Ann Arbor: University of Michigan Retirement Research Center.

McGarry, K., & Schoeni, R. (2005). Medicare gaps and widow poverty. *Social Security Bulletin, 66*(1). Retrieved from https://www.questia.com/library/journal/IP3-923906481/medicare-gaps-and-widow-poverty

McGuire, L. C., Ford, E. S., & Ajani, U. A. (2006). Cognitive functioning as a predictor of functional disability in later life. *Journal of Geriatric Psychiatry, 14*(1), 36–42.

Montenegro, X. P. (2004). *The divorce experience: A study of divorce in midlife and beyond.* Washington, DC: AARP.

Moss, M., & Moss, S. (1996). Remarriage of widowed persons: A triadic relationship. In D. Klass & P. Silverman (Eds.), *Continuing bonds: New understandings of grief. Series in death education, aging, and health care* (pp. 163–178). Washington, DC: Taylor & Francis.

Moss, M. S., Moss, S. Z., & Hansson, R. O. (2001). Bereavement and old age. In M. S. Stroebe, R. O. Hansson, W. Stroebe, & H. Schut (Eds.), *Handbook of bereavement research: Consequences of coping and care* (pp. 241–260). Washington, DC: American Psychological Association.

Neimeyer, R., Fortner, B., & Schulz, R. (2006). Death anxiety. In R. Schulz, L. Noelker, K. Rockwood, & R. Sprott (Eds.), *The encyclopedia of aging* (4th Ed.). New York, NY: Springer.

Neimeyer, R. A. (2001). The language of loss: Grief therapy as a process of meaning reconstruction. In R. A. Neimeyer (Ed.), *Meaning reconstruction and the experience of loss* (pp. 261–292). Washington, DC: American Psychological Association.

Neimeyer, R. A. (2006). Widowhood, grief and the quest for meaning: A narrative perspective on resilience. In D. Carr, R. M. Ness, & C. B. Wortman (Eds.), *Spousal bereavement in late life* (pp. 227–252). New York, NY: Springer.

Ofstedal, B. B., Reidy, E., & Knodel, J. (2004). Gender differences in economic support and well-being of older Asians. *Journal of Cross-Cultural Gerontology, 19,* 165–201.

Ong, A. D., Bergeman, C. S., & Bisconti, T. L. (2004). The role of daily positive emotions during conjugal bereavement. *Journal of Gerontology: Psychological Sciences, 59b,* 168–176.

Pahor, M., Blair, S. N., & Espeland, M., Fielding, R., Gill, T. M., Guralnik, J. M., . . . Studenski, S. (2006). Effects of a physical activity intervention on measures of physical performance: Results of the lifestyle interventions and independence for Elders Pilot (LIFE-P) study. *Journal of Gerontology: Biological Science, Medical Science, 61*(11), 1157–1165.

Parkes, C. M. (2002). Grief lessons from the past, visions for the future. *Death Studies, 26,* 367–385.

Perrig-Chiello, P., & Hutchison, S. (2010). Familial caregivers of elderly persons. A differential perspective on stressors, resources, and well-being. *Geropsych: The Journal of Gerontopsychology and Geriatric Psychiatry, 23,* 195–206.

Perrig-Chiello, P., Hutchison, S., & Hopflinger, F. (2008). Role involvement and well-being in middle-aged women. *Women & Health, 48,* 303–323.

Pinquart, M. (2003). Loneliness in married, widowed, divorced, and never-married older adults. *Journal of Social and Personal Relationships, 20,* 31–53.

Prigerson, H. G., & Jacobs, S. C. (2001). Caring for bereaved patients: "All the doctors just suddenly go." *Journal of the American Medical Association, 286,* 1369–1376.

Pudrovska, T., & Carr, D. (2008). Psychological adjustment to divorce and widowhood in mid and later life: Do coping strategies and personality protect against psychological distress? *Advances in Life Course Research, 13,* 283–317.

Reker, G. (2001/2002). Prospective predictors of successful aging in community residing and institutionalized Canadian elderly. *Ageing International, 27*(1), 42–64.

Reynolds, D. K. (1976). Factors influencing death attitudes. In B. Hayslip, Jr. & C. A. Peveto (Eds.), *Cultural changes in attitudes toward death, dying, and bereavement.* New York, NY: Springer.

Richardson, V. E. (2007). A dual process model of grief counseling: Findings from the Changing Lives of Older Couples (CLOC) study. *Omega: Journal of Gerontological Social Work, 48*(3/4), 311–329.

Richardson, V. E., & Balaswamy, S. (2001). Coping with bereavement among elderly widowers. *Omega: Journal of Death and Dying, 43,* 129–144.

Robbins, J. (2007). *Healthy at 100.* New York, NY: Ballantine Books.

Schulz, J. H., Barr, D. J., & Selman, R. I. (2001). The value of a developmental approach to evaluating character education programs: An outstudy study of facing history and ourselves. *Journal of Moral Education, 30,* 3–27.

Schut, H., Stroebe, M. S., van den Bout, J., & Terheggen, M. (2001). In M. S. Stroebe, R. O. Hansson, W. Stroebe, & H. Schut (Eds.), *Handbook of bereavement research* (pp. 705–738). Washington, DC: American Psychological Association.

Shapiro, A. (2003). Later-life divorce and parent–adult child contact and proximity: A longitudinal analysis. *Journal of Family Issues, 24,* 264–285.

Shear, M. K., Frank, E., Foa, E., Cherry, C. Reynolds, C. F. III, Vanderbilt, J., & Masters, S. (2001). Traumatic grief treatment: A pilot study. *American Journal of Psychiatry, 158,* 1506–1508.

Shumway-Cook, A., Patla, A. E., Stewart, A., Ferrucci, L., Ciol, M. A., & Guralnik, J. M. (2002). Environmental demands associated with community mobility in older adults with and without mobility disabilities. *Physical Therapy, 82*(7), 670–681.

Silverman, P. R. (1988). In R. H. Price & E. L. Cowen (Eds.), *Fourteen ounces of prevention: A casebook for practitioners* (pp. 175–186). Washington, DC: American Psychological Association.

Stroebe, M., Stroebe, W., & Schut, H. (2001). Gender differences in adjustment to bereavement: An empirical and theoretical review. *Review of General Psychology, 5*(1), 62–83.

Stroebe, M., & Schut, H. (2001). Meaning making in the dual process model of coping with bereavement. In R. A. Neimeyer (Ed.), *Meaning reconstruction and the appearance of loss* (pp. 55–69). Washington, DC: American Psychological Association.

Sweeney, M. M. (2010). Remarriage and step families: Strategic sites for family scholarship in the 21st century. *Journal of Marriage and Family, 72,* 667–684.

Swiss Federal Office of Statistics. (2011). Bevölkerungsbewegung-detaillierte daten. Scheidung und scheidung-shaüfigkeit. Scheidung nach ehedauer. Retrieved from http://www.bfs.admin.ch/bfs/portal/de/index/themen/01/06/blank/data/03.html

The new shorter Oxford English dictionary. (1993). Oxford, UK: Oxford University Press.

Umberson, D., Wortman, C., & Kessler, R. (1992). Widowhood and depression: Explaining long-term gender differences in vulnerability. *Journal of Health and Social Behavior, 33,* 10–24.

United Nations. (2002). *World population aging: 1950–2050.* Department of Economic and Social Affairs. Population Division. Retrieved from www.un.org/esa/population/publications/worldageing19502050/index.html

U.S. Census Bureau. (2012). America's families and living arrangement: 2010. Washington, DC: Government Printing Office. Retrieved from http://www.census.gov/population/www/soco/emolhh-fam/cps2010.html

U.S. Census Bureau. (2015). *Families and living arrangements.* Retrieved from https://www.census.gov/hhes/families/files/cps2014/tabA1-all.x15]

Utz, R., Carr, D., Ness, R., & Wortman, C. (2002). The effect of widowhood on older adults' social participation: An evaluation of activity, disengagement, and continuity theories. *The Gerontologist, 42*(4), 522–533.

Utz, R. L., Caserta, M., & Lund, D. (2011). Grief, depressive symptoms, and physical health among recently bereaved spouses. *The Gerontologist, 52,* 460–471.

van Baarson, B. (2002). Theories on coping with loss: The impact of social support and self-esteem on adjustment to emotional and social loneliness following a partner's death in later life. *Journals of Gerontology: Series B: Psychological and Social Sciences, 57B*(1), S33–S42.

van Baarson, B., & van Groenou, M. (2001). Partner loss in later life: Gender differences in coping shortly after bereavement. *Journal of Loss and Trauma, 6*(3), 243–262.

Williams, K. (2004). The transition to widowhood and the social regulation of health: Consequences for health and health risk behavior. *Journal of Gerontology Social Sciences, 59B,* S343–S349.

Willis, S. L., Tennstedt, S. L., Marsiske, M., Ball, K., Elias, J., & Koepke, K. M. (2006). Long-term effects of cognitive training on everyday functional outcomes in older adults. *Journal of the American Medical Association, 296*(23), 2805–2814.

Worden, J. W. (2002). *Grief counseling and grief therapy: A handbook for the mental health practitioner* (3rd ed). New York, NY: Springer.

Worden, J. W. (2008). *Grief counseling and grief therapy: A handbook for the mental health practitioner* (4th ed.). New York, NY: Springer.

Wortman, C. B., & Silver, R. C. (1990). Successful mastery of bereavement and widowhood: A life-course perspective. In P. B Baltes & M. M. Baltes (Eds.), *Successful aging: Perspectives from the behavioral sciences.* Cambridge, MA: Cambridge University Press.

Wu, Z., & Schimmele, C. M. (2007). Uncoupling in late life. *Generations, 31*(3), 41–46.

Zaslow, J. (2003, June 17). Will you still need me when I'm . . . 84? *Wall Street Journal.*

Zisook, S., Shuchter, S. R., Pedrelli, P., Sable, J., & Deaciuc, S. C. (2001). Bupropion sustained release for the bereavement: Results of an open trial. *Journal of Clinical Psychiatry, 62,* 227–230.

CHAPTER 8

Opportunities in Later Life

"Never retire. Michelangelo was carving the Rondanini just before he died at 89. Verdi finished his opera Falstaff at 80. And the 80-year-old Spanish artist Goya scrawled on a drawing, 'I am still learning.'"

—Dr. W. Gifford-Jones

Learning Objectives

After reading this chapter, you will be able to

1. Examine the levels of engagement prescribed for older people by the three major psychosocial theories
2. Describe the perceptions of aging in the workplace
3. Analyze the factors impacting the decision to retire and the period of adjustment that accompanies retirement
4. Explain the significance of leisure in the lives of older persons
5. Summarize the benefits of volunteerism on older adults

INTRODUCTION

Adjusting one's lifestyle in older adulthood to enhance personal well-being can be an opportunity for growth. Such adjustments as employment, retirement, leisure, and volunteerism often occur and will be explored in this chapter. Employment in later life gives the older adult more financial resources, more benefits, participation in meaningful work, and opportunities to interact with others to gain knowledge and share ideas. Retirement offers the retiree the opportunity to rediscover various interests, invest in oneself, pursue leisure activities, engage in an encore career, attend to family members, travel, or just relax. Leisure and volunteerism allow opportunities for growth and personal expression, which is often-times unrealized until later life. These activities are recognized as valuable opportunities to be productive and actively engage in meaningful pursuits.

However, not all individuals are able to experience such positive lifestyle changes. There continues to be older persons who must work out of necessity, for whom retirement is not an option. While employment offers many benefits for older workers, they may be challenged by ageism and questions regarding their ability to contribute productively in the work environment. Retirement is a major life transition that is welcomed by most older persons, but sometimes involuntary retirement occurs. Retirement poses opportunities and challenges, and some older persons are now working in retirement for various reasons. Opportunities to engage in leisure and volunteer activities are not a reality for some older adults due to health and financial challenges. An understanding of these major life transitions is beneficial for all practitioners who plan to work or who are currently employed in environments that serve the needs of older adults.

PSYCHOSOCIAL THEORIES RELATED TO ENGAGEMENT

There are numerous elements that factor into successful aging, as the previous chapters have shown. Within the field, three major psychosocial theories outline the ways involvement promotes success: the disengagement theory, the activity theory of aging, and the continuity theory. Each theory adds to the knowledge of the process of aging and the essential role of activity.

Disengagement Theory

The disengagement theory was the first formal theory of aging. Cumming and Henry (1961) argued that normal aging involves a natural and inevitable mutual withdrawal or disengagement, from the society in which they live. Because of the inevitability of death, society and the individual mutually sever their ties in advance so that the death of the individual will not be disruptive to the social system. Either the society or the individual may initiate the disengagement, but once the process is initiated, it becomes circular. Lessening social interaction leads to a weakening of the norms of behavior regarding interaction.

A readiness for disengagement occurs when "the individual becomes sharply aware of the shortness of life and the scarcity of life space as decreasing" (Cumming and Henry, 1961, p. 215). The process is irreversible, universal, and inevitable. Life satisfaction was highest among those who successfully disengaged; however, subsequent research found that some people did disengage but that it was neither universal nor inevitable (Cumming & Henry, 1961). Maddox (1969) criticized disengagement theory by pointing out the distinction between social and psychological disengagement and criticized disengagement for lacking empirical justification. Hochschild (1975) reported that aging was a biological process, while disengagement was primarily a social process, and he described disengagement as a historical artifact when older adults were more likely to feel discarded or abandoned by a society full of negative attitudes. McGuire, Boyd, and Tedrick (2004) suggest that disengagement does not occur but for elders who represent the oldest segment of society. Conger (2015) identified that socialization in old age has positive health benefits more so than social withdrawal. Culture, social conditions, and personality all contribute to variations in aging, and there exist many reasons for disengagement by some older adults. Guided Practice Exercise 8.1 gives the counselor in training the opportunity to explore the positive and negative consequences associated with the disengagement theory.

Guided Practice Exercise 8.1

Think about the disengagement theory. Disengagement was thought to allow older adults to maintain a sense of self-worth through withdrawal to the loss of prior roles. Can you identify any positive consequences associated with disengagement? What are the negative consequences associated with withdrawal from previous roles? Are you familiar with older adults who disengaged from various roles in society and later adopted the same roles as previously held and/or new ones? Explain your response in detail.

Activity Theory of Aging

The activity theory of aging (Havighurst, Neugarten, & Tobin, 1968) argued that the psychological and social needs of the elderly were no different from those of the middle-aged and that it was neither normal nor natural for older people to become isolated and withdrawn. When they do, it is often due to events beyond their control, such as poor health or the loss of close relatives. The person who aged optimally managed to stay active and resist the shrinkage of his or her social world. That meant maintaining the activities of middle age for as long as possible and then finding substitutes for those that had to be relinquished (Havighurst et al., 1968).

Success in aging is active aging. Older people who are engaged in productive activities and have social networks are less likely to be depressed than those who are not engaged (Lennartsson & Silverstein, 2001). Activity theory suggests that older people who take on a large number and variety of activities and roles will have a more positive older age, adjust to aging better, and be more satisfied with their lives (Atchley, 2006; Kart & Kinney, 2001). Utz , Carr, Ness, and Wortman (2002) discovered that it is not the participation in the activities that enhances well-being, but rather the socializing that accompanies engagement in an activity. Activity theory is criticized for being too simplistic in using one variable (activity) as the sole consideration to their explanation of aging (Hochschild, 1975; Quadagno & Street, 1996). The theory also fails to account for variability in personality and environmental factors (Covey, 1981; Estes & Associates, 2001). The activity theory is prescriptive in nature and advises people what to do and what not to do to age well. Levels of activity necessary for positive aging is questionable, as well if the activity is creating satisfaction in or the support a person receives from the role they play in the activity (McGuire et al., 2004).

Continuity Theory

Continuity theory represents a more formal elaboration of activity theory using a life course perspective to define normal aging and distinguish it from pathological aging. Robert Atchley (1989) proposed continuity theory, which analyzed internal and external aging processes. Internal continuity refers to "a remembered inner structure, such as the persistence of a psychic structure of ideas, temperature, affect, experiences, preferences, dispositions, and skills" (Atchley, 1989, p. 184). External continuity is connected to past role performance and can be observed in the continuation of skills, activities, environments, roles, and relationships between middle age and old age. Continuity theory holds that middle-aged and older adults often attempt to preserve ties with their past experiences by substituting new roles that are similar to lost ones (Atchley, 1972, 1989). The theory suggests that people are more satisfied in their older years when their new roles and activities are consistent with previous experiences.

Continuity theory emphasizes that personality plays a major role in adjustment to aging and that adult development is a continuous process. Continuity is an adaptive strategy for successful aging. Continuity of personality means that changes in health, functioning, and social circumstances can be incorporated that still preserve the unique characteristics of the individual. Continuity of activity allows people to prevent, offset, or minimize the effects of aging, and continuity of relationships preserves an individual's social support system (Atchley, 1989). This approach tends to emphasize individual behavior and neglects the societal constraints that deter older people from continuing some activities, but it nevertheless looks positively at continuation of activities such as sports, religion, reading, or teaching.

This theory is useful in many respects. However, it has been criticized because persons with limitations and/or disorders can engage in meaningful experiences (Becker, 1993), and this theory does not focus enough on gender relations or on older women's experiences (Calasanti, 2009). The continuity theory fails to address the unique, non-shared events as instigators of change. It fails to consider people who have unhealthy habits, preferences in middle age, which negatively impacts their health status in later life. The theory assumes that earlier stages of development set the criteria for successful aging. Lastly, the need for continuity may reduce a person's self-esteem when physical or mental declines force a change in lifestyles held earlier. Releasing oneself from former roles can have a freeing effect (McGuire et al., 2004). Resources also vary across socioeconomic groups affecting level of continuity. Case Illustration 8.1 demonstrates the continuity theory and how one elderly gentleman continued to maintain activities enjoyed earlier in life into his later years. This case demonstrates continuing involvement in volunteering, civic engagement, and employment. His basic personality remained intact and, barring any major health crises, this gentleman will slow down but stay engaged in meaningful pursuits.

CASE ILLUSTRATION 8.1

At age 85, Mr. Wilson is as active as he was at age 60. Mr. Wilson believes in activity for pleasure and competitiveness. He developed his competitive nature as a young adult, and it has served him well throughout life. He has competed in marathons, tennis matches, and golf outings and still does. He also plays chess, which he is very good at and reminds others of this on a daily basis. He works with students who require tutoring in math and science, since he was an electrical engineer for 30 years. He really enjoys his volunteer activities and is valued and praised by his students for all of his assistance. He attends church regularly and is also a deacon and chairs the Budget Committee. He feels his religiosity and spirituality has kept him grounded and has enhanced his personal life and his successful career. Although he has officially retired, he is called upon occasionally to serve as a consultant on special projects. Many of his activities started in early adulthood and continue today. Mr. Wilson has no plans to discontinue any of his activities; however, he realizes one day he might have to slow down a little.

EMPLOYMENT

The adult population aged 60 and older by the year 2030 will represent close to 20% of the U.S. population, a significant increase from the 10% this age group represented in 2007 (Administration on Aging, 2008). Similar increases are occurring in the workplace. In 2014, 8.4 million (18.6%) Americans age 65 and over were in the labor force (working or actively seeking work), including 4.6 million men (23%) and 3.8 million women (15.1%). They constituted 5% of the U.S. labor force (Bureau of Labor Statistics, 2014a). The labor force participation of men 65 years and over has been increasing from 16%–18% in 2002 to over 20% in 2014 (Bureau of Labor Statistics, 2014a). The participation rate for women 65 and over started to rise beginning in 2000 from 9.7% to the 2014 level of 14% (Bureau of Labor Statistics, 2014a). The increase in labor force participation of individuals 65 and older can be attributed to changes in economic conditions and retirement policies.

Research by the National Bureau of Economic Research indicates that a large number of individuals who have few economic resources will be forced to retire and will be unable to find new positions, while wealthier individuals will be required to continue working and postpone their retirement (Coile & Levine, 2009). From April to July 2015, the number of employed youth 16 to 24 years old increased by 2.1 million to 20.3 million according to the Bureau of Labor Statistics (2015b). This year, 52.7% of young people were employed in July, little change from a year earlier. The Bureau of Labor Statistics (2015a) projects a 3.3% change in labor force participation between 2012 and 2022 with an annual growth rate of 1.4%. Therefore, the need to retain older workers may also begin to occur. Thus, with more individuals forced into retirement along with workforce retention of older workers, a projected increase in labor force participants is not surprising.

As the population grows older, an increasing share of the workforce will be over the age of 60. Older workers have often been considered less productive than younger ones, raising the issue of whether an aging workforce will also be a less productive one. Burtless (2013) examined this issue and offers evidence that more productive workers stay in the workforce longer than less productive ones. Using a standard measure of worker productivity (hourly wages), workers between 60 and 74 are more productive than younger workers. Compared with workers between 25 and 59 years old, the pay premium for older workers is currently between 10% and 20% of the average wage earned by the young workers. That pay premium has been increasing for a decade. There is little evidence the aging workforce has hurt productivity (Burtless, 2013).

Older workers working full-time has been rising since the mid-1990s. Since 2000, a majority of workers 65 and older have worked full-time. But senior workers are still more likely than their younger counterparts to work part-time. In 2012, workers 55 years of age and over made up 21% of all workers, but 25% of part-time workers (Bureau of Labor Statistics, 2013). The large majority of older part-time workers are employed part-time by choice; few part-time workers prefer full-time employment. Whether more workers would remain at work if they could reduce their hours is not known for certain, but the data suggest they would. About half of older workers with retirement plans express a desire to scale back their hours or otherwise change the type of work they do before or instead of fully retiring; however, those who actually manage to do this are in the minority (Abraham & Houseman, 2004). Few older workers plan on working full-time in retirement (American Association of Retired Persons [AARP], 2003a, 2004).

Older workers seem to prefer phasing into retirement by cutting back the hours they work at their current jobs. Nearly two-thirds of workers aged 50–70 hope for reduced hours or more flexible schedules prior to full retirement, and one-third say they would work longer than planned if a phased retirement arrangement were available (Watson Wyatt Worldwide, 2004). Many cushion the retirement shock as rehired retirees or temporary workers; nonetheless, formal phased retirement programs are rare (Hutchens & Papps, 2004). Bridge work or shared retirement is part of the process of withdrawal from the labor market, which makes the transition to retirement a smoother process.

Some women face a dilemma when performing their workforce role and their role in their families. Thus far, the gender role revolution has focused on rendering men's career paths open to women. Thus, the male career has become the model. Women use it to gauge their experiences, as do their colleagues and bosses. However, the model does not fit, unless women relinquish their traditional family responsibilities as nurturers and caregivers on the domestic front. Increasingly, the model does not fit men's experiences either. Men have been able to follow the conventional career model precisely because (1) they did not have family responsibilities and (2) the employer–employee contract provided internal labor markets and avenues for occupational mobility.

Women in the baby boom generation often deal with a lack of time, which frequently involves women cutting back hours on the job and, often, career prospects. But the larger issue of articulating work life and home life is occurring in an economic climate of reduced opportunity for mobility for all baby boomers, both men and women, and at a time when the male template for success fits ever fewer workers, regardless of gender. The following exercise identifies challenges when women work and assume responsibility for caring for aging parents. Guided Practice Exercise 8.2 will help to develop an appreciation for the challenges in balancing work and caregiving responsibilities and available resources that may prove beneficial to the employee.

Guided Practice Exercise 8.2

Many working women are challenged to maintain their family responsibilities as well as those required by their employers. The demands on their time become even more challenging when caring for aging parents. These women experience an array of emotions, including depression, anxiety, and guilt, which negatively impact their personal well-being. Interview a woman who is working and caring for an aging parent. Investigate the impact of caregiving on her emotional and physical health. Identify aspects of her behavior that have changed to adjust to her caregiving responsibilities, while maintaining her employment. For example, does she have to converse more by phone, leave work early, arrive to work later, and/or call off more frequently than usual? Next, interview the human resources director to ascertain the quantity and quality of available services for employees who care for aging parents.

Ageism in the Workplace

The workplace as a microcosm of society reflects the stereotypes and biases that are part of the national social environment. When age biases negatively affect workplace decisions about employment, termination, retirement, benefits, and training and promotion opportunities, age discrimination is in action. Four types of ageism have been defined in the literature (Anti-Ageism Taskforce, 2006). Personal ageism is an individual's attitudes, ideas, practices, and beliefs that are biased against older people. An example is a health care provider assuming an older patient is not competent to participate in development of his or her medical care when the provider would not make that assumption about a younger patient in the same situation. Institutional ageism refers to established rules, missions, and practices that discriminate against older individuals or groups based on age. Mandatory retirement at a particular age is an example. Intentional ageism refers to attitudes, rules, or practices that are held, implemented, or engaged in with the knowledge that they are biased against older people. Conversely, unintentional ageism is practiced without the perpetrator recognizing the bias (Dennis & Thomas, 2007).

Managers have both positive and negative perceptions about older workers or "senior employees," as substantiated by AARP. Older workers, defined as those age 50 and older, are valued for their experience, knowledge, work habits, attitudes, and commitment to quality as well as their loyalty, punctuality, ability to keep cool in a crisis, and respect for authority (AARP, 1989, 1995; AARP-DYG, Inc. 1992). They are also valued for their solid performance, basic skills, and getting along with coworkers (AARP, 2000). However, negative perceptions are also evident. Older workers can be perceived as inflexible, unwilling to adapt to technology, lacking an aggressive spirit, resistant to new ways, having some physical limitations, costing more for health insurance, and complacent (AARP, 1989, 1995; AARP-DYG, Inc. 1992).

Positive and negative perceptions of older workers also were revealed in a survey of 400 private-sector employers conducted by the Center for Retirement Research at Boston College. The survey focused on employers' evaluation of the relative productivity and cost of white-collared and rank-and-file employees 55 years of age and older (Munnell, Sass, & Soto, 2006). The majority of employers found older managers to be more productive than younger ones. Approximately 40% of the employers indicated the same for older rank-and-file workers. An advantage attributed to the older workers was their ability to interact with customers. The "not so good" news is that employers viewed their older workers as more expensive compared to younger workers. They are usually at the higher end of the pay scale due to years of employment. Also, as the workforce ages the incidence of disability rises (Bruyère, 2006; Kampfe, Wadsworth, Mamboleo, & Schonbrun, 2008). Older people are also more likely to have multiple disabling conditions and to have chronic disabling conditions (Kampfe et al., 2008), which may increase health care costs for employers.

Age-related comments have been presented in court as evidence of age discrimination. The success in winning a case based on statements about age varies. Comments frequently are categorized into "young remarks" such as "We need young blood here," "Let's make room for some MBAs," or "Let's bring in the young guns" (McCann & Giles, 2002, p. 180). The other category is "old remarks" such as "In a forest you have to cut down the old big trees so that the little ones underneath can grow" (McCann & Giles, 2002, p. 181). This statement served as proof of age discrimination in one case. In another, a supervisor's reference to older workers as "alte cockers" ("old fogies" in Yiddish) was considered potentially discriminatory, and terms such as "old fogie," "old and tired," and a "sleepy kind of guy with no pizzazz" have been considered evidence of age bias in others (McCann & Giles, 2002, p. 182). Guided Practice Exercise 8.3 provides the opportunity to examine the significance of work and advocate for the recruitment and training needed to increase participation of older adults in the workforce.

Guided Practice Exercise 8.3

Older adults are increasing their expectations of an active and productive lifestyle, which, for some, means continuing their employment into the later years. You are fully aware of the positive and negative attributes perceived by employers in the field. However, to meet the challenges of the current workplace, it remains essential that older workers retain their employment and for some to return to various types of positions. You are to develop a survey and distribute to a convenient sample of older persons and determine their interest in work. Some of the areas that you can cover include, but are not limited to, types of positions, salary requirements, job search strategies and outcomes, and any other feedback that they voluntarily provide. Compile the results and arrange meetings with at least three organizations to disseminate your findings. Based on your discussions with potential employers, advocate for targeted programming to recruit older persons and the necessity to expand training opportunities.

Changing Practices

Some employers are taking steps to combat ageism in the workplace with specific programs and other approaches. The largest and most acknowledged recognition program is AARP's Best Employers for Workers over 50. It is a national competition that began in 2001 to recognize organizations with the best practices and policies that address the issues of an aging workforce. Companies are judged on their policies and practices for recruitment, education and job training, opportunities for career success, health and financial benefits, alternative work arrangements, and opportunities for retirees. Forty-one employers reported that their managers were evaluated according to "valuing and promoting diversity, including age" (communication with Kathy Brown, AARP, October 10, 2006). These awards are creating a national shift in attitude in recognizing the value of competent older workers and, more importantly, are supported by innovative and effective policies and practices.

Comprehensive training on ageism for all employers and employees in the workplace is needed to combat the oversimplified generalizations regarding the capabilities of the older worker. However, race, gender, and ethnicity are typically the subjects covered in diversity training. This is because these types of discrimination still occur in the workplace, and training is an effective tool in their prevention. Additionally, the Department of Labor requires employers who are federal contractors and subcontractors to report information about the gender, race, and ethnicity of each job applicant and employee but does not require such information on the age of employees or applicants (Department of Labor, 2005). This lack of accountability is a possible reason for the lack of emphasis on age in diversity training. However, age should be included as a significant aspect of diversity training (Department of Labor, 2005).

A relatively new awareness of older workers has emerged as retiring baby boomers take their knowledge and skills with them as they retire. Forward-thinking employers are recognizing the importance of such a loss and are developing policies to avoid it. One approach is to rehire their retirees. Companies such as Monsanto, the Aerospace Corporation, and Cigna Insurance have established formal programs to do just that. CVS does so as well, hiring senior pharmacists as mentors to apprentice pharmacy technicians and high school students in a special internship program to cultivate and reinforce their interests in entering pharmacy careers.

Policy modification is taking place at various levels. To face the possible retirement of the current 15,000 air traffic controllers, federal rules have extended the mandatory retirement age beyond the current 56 years for controllers on a yearly exemption basis. Under the Clinton Administration, U.S. Treasury Department information technology workers were offered a $25,000 bonus to postpone their retirements. The Tennessee Valley Authority (TVA), the largest U.S. power company, having acknowledged that 40% of its workforce would be eligible for retirement within 5 years, surveyed its employees on a volunteer basis to determine if and when they intended to retire. The TVA then used the information to drive workforce planning (DeLong, 2004). Guided Practice Exercise 8.4 provides the opportunity to understand issues pertinent to older workers. Career counseling sessions may be more productive for the professional counselor who is fully aware of the challenges that face older workers.

Guided Practice Exercise 8.4

An older worker is employed in a health care system with few other older adults within his division. He wishes to continue to be of value in the workplace, but full-time employment has become too demanding in his environment. What options are available for this older worker? Do you feel allowances should be made to the environment as a person ages for him or her to remain in a full-time position? What suggestions would you offer to administration to attempt to retain older workers?

Challenges facing older workers who stay past retirement age have broad implications. Delayed retirement may impact the workplace by limiting opportunities for younger workers, posing challenges to younger supervisors in managing older workers, creating corporate culture conflicts, and adding costs to maintain older workers (Bernard, 2013). Counselors must be positioned to assist older workers who remain in the labor force past traditional retirement age in addressing the emotional and psychological stresses that accompany workplace transitions.

RETIREMENT

Most older adults look forward to retirement. The main question is, When is the best time to retire? There are a number of factors that affect this answer, particularly finances and health. Following retirement, retirees go through a period of adaptation, in which they find ways to fill their newfound time. Such activities may include working part-time, participating in new hobbies, or spending time with loved ones.

Factors Affecting the Retirement Decision

Although most older workers eventually retire, there can be great latitude in the timing of this life step. Factors involved in the retirement decision include pension availability, prospects for income security over the long term, job conditions, workplace norms and administrative rules, personal dispositions in regard to work and retirement, family circumstances, and continued ability to perform on the job. Married persons may make mutual decisions, taking the spouse's employment, pension, and health into account. Among these many considerations, wealth and health are of paramount importance as contributing factors in the decision to retire.

Pensions

Few adults can manage to fund retirement from personal savings alone. Thus, pension availability is the necessary condition for retirement because of the need to replace income lost by withdrawal from work. Pension eligibility and age incentives bring various societal, organizational, and personnel objectives to bear on the individual decision

(Ekerdt & Sergeant, 2006). Case Illustration 8.2 highlights the concerns expressed by an older person in the workplace and provides the opportunity to explore ways to diminish his anxiety and examine various resources to facilitate the therapeutic relationship.

CASE ILLUSTRATION 8.2

Mr. Simmons is a 67-year-old gentleman who has a pleasant demeanor, is dedicated to his employer, and works all of the overtime within the factory that is offered. He enjoys his job and expresses that he would like to retire; however, he would not be able to meet his household expenses on his limited pension and Social Security income. His health is deteriorating; however, he is fearful of taking time off, for fear that he'll lose his job. He has a mortgage, expenses for college tuition for two of his children, several personal loans, and a car payment. He also has expenses in traveling to and from work because he lives an hour away from his place of employment. Another concern Mr. Simmons worries about revolves around the rumor of impending layoffs.

As a future mental health counselor, how would you begin to address these issues? Identify areas of immediate concern and those you would work on later in your sessions. What strategies or approaches would you use? How would you investigate the rumor of impending layoffs? What resources would you identify to assist you in working with Mr. Simmons?

About 59 million people received a Social Security benefit in 2014 (Shelton, 2015). Social Security is a key source of retirement income for older Americans, and approximately 23% of people age 65 and older live in families that depend on Social Security benefits for 90% or more of their income (Shelton, 2015). Another 25% receive at least half but less than 90% of their family income from Social Security (Shelton, 2015). Reliance on Social Security increases with age, with nearly one-third of persons aged 80 and older depending on Social Security for 90% or more of family income (Shelton, 2015). Total payments to beneficiaries 65 years of age and older was $929,000 in July, 2015 (Social Security, 2015), which provides evidence for the dependence of older adults on this system.

Employer-Provided Benefits

Employer-provided benefits also guide the timing of retirement. Employers sponsor pensions to serve different objectives: to encourage long tenure, remain competitive in hiring, as an outcome of collective bargaining, as a device to keep promotion lines open to younger staff, or as a means to shed workforces of older personnel who are believed to eventually become less productive or too costly. Pension plans have widely varying characteristics and are unevenly distributed among occupational groups. They are more common and benefit levels more generous in industries characterized by large, highly organized firms and strong labor unions, such as some institutions of higher learning, transportation industry, and some health professionals. Most government workers are covered.

Access to employer-sponsored retirement plans has declined in recent years. Approximately half of workers currently work for employers who sponsor retirement plans, down from 57% in 2000 (Copeland, 2011). Employees at larger establishments have greater access to retirement plans and are more likely to participate when eligible (Bureau of Labor Statistics, 2012). Participation in retirement plans varies with age. The share of all workers participating in an employer-sponsored retirement plan increases with age—but only up to age 64, after which it decreases. In 2011, 50% of all workers age 55–64 participated in a retirement plan, compared to 36% of workers age 25–34 and only 31% of workers age 65 and over (Copeland, 2011).

Defined benefit (DB) plans are becoming less common, though some companies continue to offer them to new hires. A survey of 424 defined benefit sponsors at mid-size and large companies found that 17% still offer defined benefit plans to new hires. These companies reported employee retention as the top reason for continuing such plans (Towers, 2012). In defined benefit plans, employees are promised a steady benefit that can be claimed after meeting an age and length-of-service requirement. Many such plans have early retirement options, and benefit formulas are often structured to encourage retirement at an optimal age beyond which there is little financial advantage to stay on the job. Unlike Social Security, few defined pension benefits are regularly adjusted for increases in cost of living, leaving their projected purchasing power vulnerable to inflation under defined contribution plans, such as the 401(K), in which the employer and/or employee can make contributions of a specified amount to the employee's account. There is no fixed future benefit; retirement income is drawn from the earnings of the account that has been managed or directed by the employee. This shift from corporate paternalism to employee self-reliance puts greater responsibility as well as future risk on the individual, as was made evident during the plunging stock market of 2000 to 2002.

Age incentives for retirement are not a feature of defined contribution plans, yet such savings-style plans increase the feasibility of early retirement, since distributions can begin at age 59. Withdrawals must begin by age 70. Upon taking a distribution, the prospective retiree must decide how to convert his or her investment into a series of periodic income payments to provide a long-term stream of income (Munnel, Lee, & Meme, 2004).

Given a reduction in the expenses associated with working, retirees need to replace 65% to 85% of previous earnings to maintain a comparable standard of living, a goal that nevertheless eludes the majority of retirees if they rely on employer and Social Security pensions alone (Schultz, 2001). Despite employer pensions and efforts to encourage private saving, Social Security remains the major source of income for more than half of all beneficiaries.

Ability to Work

Financial need, coupled with a desire to remain active and productive, may keep older workers in the job longer, but remaining at work may not be as easy as it sounds. Today's workers plan to remain at work considerably longer than today's retirees actually do. Some workers are adjusting some of their expectations about when to retire, perhaps in recognition of the fact that their financial preparations for retirement may be inadequate (Helman, Copeland, & VanDerhei, 2015). Sixteen percent of workers in the 2015 Retirement Confidence Survey say the age at which they expect to retire has changed in the past year, and of those the large majority (81%) report their expected retirement age has increased (Helman et al., 2015). The percentage of workers who expect to retire after age 65 has increased, from 11% in 1991, to 19% in 2000, 24% in 2005, 33% in 2010, and 36% in the 2015 Retirement Confidence Survey. Additionally, 1 in 10 in this survey (10%) say they never plan to retire (Helman et al., 2015). Nevertheless, the median (midpoint) age at which retirees report they retired has remained at age 62 throughout this time. There exists a gap between workers' expected retirement age and retirees' actual age of retirement, which indicates that workers who are not confident about their financial security in retirement plan to retire later, on average, than those who express confidence (Helman et al., 2015).

Some Americans also find themselves retiring unexpectedly. The Retirement Confidence Survey (Helman et al., 2015) found that a large percentage of retirees leave the workforce earlier than planned (50% in 2015) (Helman et al., 2015). Reasons identified for leaving include: health problems or disability (60%), changes at their company, such as downsizing or closure (27%), having to care for a spouse or other family member (22%), changes in the skills required for their job (10%), or other work-related reasons (22%) played a role. Of course, some retirees mentioned positive reasons for retiring early, such as being able to afford an earlier retirement (31%) or wanting to do something else (17%) (Helman et al., 2015).

In general, workers exhibit more control over their retirement decisions to the extent that they have had regular stable employment and enjoy relative social class advantages. However, some workers leaving the labor force trade a history of disability or chronic unemployment for early retirement. Strained financial circumstances cause other workers to forego retirement. Finally, salaried employees in professional positions and the self-employed, having continued employment opportunities and stronger personal investments in their identity as workers, are occupational groups more likely to stretch out their labor force attachment (Ekerdt & Sergeant, 2006).

Adaptation and Adjustment to Retirement

Adaptation is enhanced by a process of anticipating and accepting retirement before it occurs. While few older workers participate or have the opportunity to participate in formal planning programs, financial and lifestyle advice about retirement is widely available (Vitt, 2003). Most preparation for retirement is informal and involves some information seeking and anticipatory rehearsal of the retirement role. Although the role of retired person may never develop the specificity of the work role, there are certain expectations that retirees remain active, independent, self-reliant, and not interfere at their former place of work. The vagueness and flexibility of the retirement role is a particular benefit to retirees whose diminished health and financial resources limit their ability to participate. Overall, the maintenance of personal resources such as income, health, and social networks have a lot to do with the quality of the retirement experience over the longer term (Savishinsky, 2000).

Working in Retirement

The majority of workers plan to work in retirement (AARP, 2002, 2003a, 2004). Reasons for this include being interested in or enjoying what they are doing, wanting to do something productive, wishing to remain active, or the need for income. When asked for the major factor in their decision to work in retirement, the need for money tops the list, followed by the need for health benefits (AARP, 2003a). Case Illustration 8.3 demonstrates the concerns of an elderly female who has plans to reenter the labor force. Mental health counselors will have the opportunity to address the changing workplace landscape, ageism, and appropriate career paths during counseling sessions.

CASE ILLUSTRATION 8.3

Ms. Daniels is a 78-year-old female who raised a family of five children and was married for 30 years until her spouse died several years ago. She earned a master's degree and worked for and retired from the Social Security Administration in an executive capacity. She possesses a high degree of energy and is extremely productive. She volunteered her time while raising her family and continues to volunteer. She's volunteered for the local school conducting fund-raising activities, Girl Scouts, and day care centers just to name a few. She has been increasing her volunteer hours since the death of her spouse several years ago in an attempt to fill the void because she dearly misses him.

Ms. Daniels has recently been feeling that she'd like to return to seek employment in a meaningful and productive capacity. She is concerned regarding stereotypes, ageism, and what type of work she'll be able to find at her age. She feels she does not look her stated age and instead looks as though she is 65. However, she is fully aware of the youth-oriented culture in society and the biases against older adults. She is hoping that her past experience will overshadow any negative preconceptions that employers hold when reviewing applicants who are older. She has sought the services of a counselor who possesses expertise in aging and career development in later life.

Many older workers are interested in working into retirement with a focus on flexible work arrangement such as part-time work and consulting (Anderson, 2015). More than one-third of working Americans age 50–64 (37%) anticipate working for pay past retirement from their current career (Anderson, 2015). Among those who will seek employment post retirement, almost half (44%) will be looking to work in new fields of interest and 23% will stay in the same field, and 33% were undecided (Anderson, 2015). Regardless of the field, respondents were hoping to work part-time (73%), with over half expecting to work for someone else (57%) versus being a contractor (21%) or starting their own business (19%).

Of the retirees who worked for pay in retirement, many gave a positive reason for doing so. Eighty-three percent cited they enjoyed working or wanted to stay active and involved (79%). Financial reasons included wanting money to buy extra items (54%), needing money to cover expenses (52%), a decrease in the value of their savings or investments (38%), or keeping health insurance or other benefits (34%) (Helman et al., 2015). If attractive employment options were available, or if older workers did not face barriers such as age discrimination in their search for employment, more nonworking men and women might convey interest in employment. If more appealing options to continue working but at reduced work hours were also available, greater numbers of older workers might be inclined to postpone the date of full retirement.

New Lifestyles

Depending on their circumstances, retirees exhibit a wide variety of lifestyles. No particular level of leisure participation or social engagement has been shown to be the sole formula for a satisfactory retirement. Recreation, tourism, and travel preoccupy some people, and others use retirement as the opportunity to take up pursuits that they have long deferred, such as further education or skill development, a time-consuming hobby, or even a new line of work. Approximately one-quarter of retirees do some part-time work after retirement.

Other retirees spend a great deal of retirement time by tending relationships with friends and family members. Aside from formal employment, retirees remain productive as they assist their children and grandchildren in various ways, undertake care and support for other relatives, and volunteer their time and skills within their churches and communities. Despite the powerful image of Sunbelt retirement, permanent or seasonal migration to retirement havens or resort communities is undertaken by a relatively small percentage of people. Retirement is a status largely lived out in one's same community, where a continuity of roles, activities, and relationships is available (Ekerdt & Sergeant, 2006).

Despite increased longevity, workers want more than ever to retire, but with flexibility and income security. In the future, they will be more likely to fund retirement with pension and saving devices that place more risk and responsibility on the individual. The proportion of retirees covered by traditional defined benefit plans is shrinking, and even those plans are coming under pressure. Health care costs will continue to outpace the general rate of inflation and complicate the financial feasibility of retirement. Such trends would seem to foretell later retirement, yet decades of pension and Social Security incentives for early retirement have created social norms about the "right time" to retire—expectations that workers may not readily relinquish. Advertisers are strenuously pushing a positive image of retirement to middle-aged and older adults who are a prime market for financial, health, and leisure goods. Such promotions kindle desire for a life stage promising release, self-development, and an active lifestyle (Henretta, 2001).

LEISURE

Leisure fulfills a primary purpose throughout life. With sweeping changes in traditional patterns of employment, timing of retirement, improved and sustained physical well-being, not to mention the quest for meaningful forms of engagement, it is likely the significance of leisure will increase in coming decades. Although work roles have been recognized as central sources of meaning, it may be that changes in the nature of work, constancy of employment, and life-long career ladders will be such that availability of intrinsic rewards wanes and alternative avenues for self-validation and well-being expand. For individuals not engaged in the work world, comparable opportunities for personal confirmation may be sought through leisure (Hendricks & Cutler, 2002).

Definition

Leisure has been defined as nonobligatory time or discretionary activities, including idle reflection, that provide possibilities for self-affirmation, association, and meaning. At one point, leisure was characterized as a residual recuperative realm that one could take part in after the necessities of earning a livelihood and life-maintenance activities were accomplished. In recent years, leisure has been acknowledged as an independent arena of considerable importance. Over the life course, the nature of leisure evolves as a consequence of life stage, family life cycle, other transitions or life events, and the evaluation of interests and abilities, yet leisure pursuits provide normative referents and are a significant source of meaning and of subjective well-being (Hendricks & Cutler, 2002, 2003).

Across the life course, leisure activities reveal focal points relevant to the age of participants. Early in life, leisure reflects activities associated with school and childhood pursuits. Somewhat later it comes to embody family life stages, associations, and children's interests. Later still, leisure encompasses emerging interests and anticipated futures as well as the experience of life's transitions. Some activities or interests are retained, others emerge, and some are dropped, depending on current priorities and abilities. For some, leisure remains an elusive concept because of health and financial challenges that interfere with its pursuit.

Health Benefits

Older adults' participation in leisure activities leads to substantial health benefits, including physical, psychological, cognitive, and social benefits. For example, a strong relationship exists between leisure activities and physical health. Research has demonstrated that increased levels of leisure activity involvement have been associated with a slower rate of motor function decline and a lower risk of developing chronic diseases in older age (Ashe, Miller, Eng, & Noreau, 2009; Bassuk & Manson, 2005; Buchman, Boyle, Wilson, Bienias, & Bennett, 2007).

Whether active or sedentary, engagements in leisure pastimes provide areas for the exercise of personal agency and self-enhancement (Hendricks & Cutler, 2003; Stebbins, 2004). In 2010, older Americans spent on average more than one-quarter of their time in leisure activities. This proportion increased with age: Americans age 75 and over spent 32% of their time in leisure activities, compared with 22% for those age 55–64 (Federal Interagency Forum on Age-Related Statistics, 2012). In 2010, about 11% of people age 65 and over reported participating in leisure-time aerobic and muscle-strengthening activities (Federal Interagency Forum on Age-Related Statistics, 2012). Strength training is recommended as part of a comprehensive physical activity program among older adults and may help to improve balance and decrease risk of falls.

There is no doubt that a busy work ethos continues to underpin much of the analysis of leisure pursuits (Katz, 2000), but arduous activities are not the only ones providing returns to participants. Other forms include sedentary or solitary hobbies, education, religious activities, movies, spectator sports, gardening, reading, cards and board games, travel, meeting friends for meals, journaling/writing, cultural activities, other modes of sociability like visiting, and volunteering—the latter not always included in accounts of leisure engagements. In fact, voluntary memberships and assistance provide not only invaluable service but emerge as a meaningful preoccupation for great numbers of older persons.

Sociodemographic, or compositional factors, including education, income, functionality, health status, age, and gender-based differences, have been recognized by research in the United States, Canada, Asia, and Europe among women and men over age 65 (Chou, Chow, & Chi, 2004; Hendricks & Cutler, 2004; Strain, Grabusic, Searle, & Dunn, 2002). Satariano, Haight, and Tager (2002) found in their cross-sectional analyses of leisure time physical activities of older people that living arrangements and social contacts are predictive of sustained physical activities. In a comparative analysis of time use among older adults in eight European countries and the United States, Gauthier and Smeeding (2003) pointed out that despite cross-national differences, there are marbled similarities in age-patterns of activities engaged in following retirement.

One component of the import of leisure derives from its role as an arena in which intrinsic rewards accrue to participants in the form of affirmation and enhancement of subjective well-being, self-esteem, morale, cognitive, and physical functioning. Leisure provides opportunities to try out alternative self-concepts in the face of social transitions and stands as a significant realm where meanings are created, personal agency expressed, and relationships built or maintained.

Psychological Well-Being

A number of researchers have investigated the contribution of leisure participation on the psychological well-being of older adults (Fernandez-Ballesteros, Zamarron, & Ruiz, 2001; Nimrod, 2007; Thang, 2005). For example, using a qualitative approach in a study of community dwelling older adults, Stathi, Fox, and McKenna (2002) investigated the psychological impact of leisure activities. These participants reported that leisure activities helped them increase their levels of happiness and enjoyment. In a study conducted by Ku Fox, and Chen (2009) in which they used a nationally based representative sample of 3,778 older Taiwanese adults, participation in leisure activities was shown to create a reduced risk of symptoms of depression during the 7-year study.

Other research has shown that older adults participate in leisure activities as a way to experience a sense of belonging to a community as well as create social connections with others (Kerstetter, Yarnal, Son, Yen, & Baker, 2008; Lyons & Dionigi, 2007; Son, Kerstetter, Yarnal, & Baker, 2007). For example, older women members of The Red Hat Society reported that their leisure activities generated a positive environment that fostered a feeling of belonging to a social network (Kerstetter et al., 2008). This feeling, in turn, enhanced the emotional support that they received from their networks. Guided Practice Exercise 8.5

provides an opportunity to explore organizations that provide a sense of community as well as how to develop such an organization, if one does not exist.

Guided Practice Exercise 8.5

The Red Hat Society provides an environment that fosters a sense of community. Investigate the criteria for membership, mission and objectives, and services provided. Within your local community, investigate organizations that have been developed to provide a similar sense of community and social interaction. If no organizations exist, identify the data and information needed to develop one.

Improved Physical and Cognitive Health

Based on the benefits of leisure participation in the lives of older adults, some researchers have explored how different leisure activities have influenced the health of older adults (Chen & Fu, 2011; Dodge et al., 2008; Everard, Lach, Fisher, & Baum, 2000). Everard and colleagues (2000) discovered that in later life, physical leisure activities, such as gardening, walking, and exercising, were associated with increased physical health, while less physical activities such as social or telephone conversations were associated with improved mental health.

Other benefits of leisure participation seemingly range from maintaining quality of life (Silverstein & Parker, 2002) to intellectual functioning (Schooler & Mulatu, 2001) to kinesthetic stability and forestalling other detrimental consequences. Some research has identified intriguing findings implying that leisure activities may be protective against subsequent disabilities, including occurrence of Alzheimer's disease, as well as maintenance of physical and cognitive abilities and perhaps even mortality (Everard et al., 2000; Lennartsson & Silverstein, 2001; Wilson et al., 2002). In one retrospective study of older Swedish twins, extent of leisure activities reported 20 years previously appears to be associated with lowered risk of Alzheimer's disease and other forms of dementia (Crowe, Andel, Pedersen, Johannson, & Gatz, 2003).

Genoe (2010) conceptualized the role of leisure as a tool for fighting dementia. Other studies reported that leisure activities serve as effective tools for improving cognitive functions. In a study of 189 older adults who live in retirement communities, Parisi, Stine-Morrow, Noh, and Morrow (2009) found that the individuals experienced an increase in their cognitive capacities and performances through recreational activities and social engagements. In addition, Dodge et al. (2008) suggested that older adults gain cognitive benefits through leisure activities.

There are many benefits to older adults' participation in leisure activities. Therefore, encouraging older clients to remain active and connected to others through these activities is imperative. Mental health professionals should help their clients to identify pastimes that they may enjoy and find ways to get involved.

VOLUNTEERISM

Although the substantial contributions of America's older volunteers have a long and well-documented history as a vital component to society's overall well-being, volunteerism is changing to reflect the growing diversity of the older population. For many decades now, older adults have willingly provided many types of support when circumstances required their assistance. Often justified as "delayed reciprocity" or as a way of "giving back" to a community, older adults have gradually expanded their volunteer role from one typically perceived as a way to remain active to one with tangible and lasting benefits to the community (Folts, 2006). This expansion has brought with it a new and more positive view of the role of older volunteers.

Older adults are no longer limited to activities such as delivering flowers in local hospitals—although this type of interaction remains a valuable task typically performed by older volunteers. Today's older volunteer is just as likely to be called upon to provide expertise to their local businesses, their governments, or their communities (Folts, 2006). The volunteers associated with the Foster Grandparent Program and Senior Companion Program are personally dedicated to making their social environments a better place. They do this by refusing to abandon children with difficulties in school and older adults who have little or no other contact with the larger community. Guided Practice Exercise 8.6 demonstrates the significance of the volunteer experience to older adults and provides a chance to examine ways to expand volunteer experiences and identify benefits to the volunteer and the organization.

Guided Practice Exercise 8.6

Volunteers are an essential component of many different organizations. Volunteering also provides meaning for older adults. If an older adult wanted to volunteer in a nursing home, how would you determine the tasks appropriate for this volunteer? What benefits would the organization derive from this volunteer experience? What benefits would the older volunteer receive from providing service?

The estimates from the Current Population Survey (Bureau of Labor Statistics, 2014a) indicate that 23.6% of those aged 65 and older volunteer. Cohort analyses indicate that more adults under age 65 volunteer. For example, the Current Population Survey indicated that 28.5% of 45- to 54-year-olds volunteer and 25.9% of 55- to 64-year-olds volunteer (Bureau of Labor Statistics, 2014a). Thus, older age is related to lower rates of volunteering, which is likely because younger adults take on volunteer work related to their children's activities and work settings. Older adults generally have weaker relationships to institutions of work and education, and for adults over age 75, health and disability issues become the primary obstacles (AARP, 2003b). Additionally, younger adults are more likely than older adults to be asked to volunteer, but if asked, older adults are more likely to agree

(Independent Sector, 2000). Once in volunteer roles, older adults devote more time, with a median of 96 hours per year recorded by the Bureau of Labor Statistics in 2014. In 2014, 62.8 million people in the United States population volunteered at least once, accounting for about 7.7 billion hours of service worth $178 billion to American communities (Corporation for National and Community Service, 2015). Volunteering holds significant benefit for the volunteer and for society.

Although older age is related to lower rates of volunteering, the amount of time committed and number of organizations increases until age 75 years (Hendricks & Cutler, 2004). Many studies have documented factors associated with volunteering in later years, and the factor most consistently related to volunteering is education. Accordingly, various measures of socioeconomic status are associated with volunteering. Better health and more social connections have been fairly consistently related to volunteering. Although there is inconsistency in the findings, it is often documented that females, whites, and married older adults are more likely to volunteer. Older adults with more education, income, health, social integration, and religious involvement are more likely to volunteer (Bureau of Labor Statistics, 2014b; Tang, 2006; Zedlewski & Schaner, 2006). There are differential rates of volunteering among ethnic groups, with older adults of color volunteering at lower rates than whites (Bureau of Labor Statistics, 2014b). This may be related to historic segregation, disparities in economic and health resources, as well as structural barriers related to discrimination (McBride, 2007).

Older volunteers are most likely to volunteer for religious and community service organizations, while younger adults are more likely to volunteer for youth and educational organizations, such as schools. Of volunteers age 65 and over, 43.0% did their services mainly through or for a religious organization, compared with 26.1% of volunteers age 16–24 (Bureau of Labor Statistics, 2014b). The type of organizations that attract older and younger volunteers may reflect, among other things, varying motivations for volunteering. There is some empirical support for the idea that older adults have more altruistic motivations to help others or give back to a community, while younger volunteers are seeking to gain employment/educational skills and social relationships (Omoto, Snyder, & Martino, 2000).

Positive Impact on Health

Volunteering is socially valued and recognized as an important role in society. Individuals can engage in volunteering throughout their lives (Kent, 2011). However, volunteering may have a more positive impact on older adults than it has on younger adults (van Willigen, 2000). Specifically, it can contribute to older adults' positive well-being (Windsor, Anstey, & Rodgers, 2008) and increase physical functioning and self-rated health (Luoh & Herzog, 2002; Lum & Lightfoot, 2005). Van Willigen (2000) demonstrated an increase in life satisfaction as a result of increased volunteering. Volunteering is also associated with reduced depressive symptoms (Hong, Morrow-Howell, Fengyan, & Hinterlong, 2009; Musick & Wilson, 2003). Case Illustration 8.4 explores the significance of inclusion of volunteering and leisure pursuits as a means to increase socialization and enhance health quality of life.

CASE ILLUSTRATION 8.4

Ms. Flynn is a 75-year-old proud mother of three sons and grandmother to three lovely granddaughters (who are still very young). Ms. Flynn expected to finish high school, marry a good provider, and raise her family, while maintaining a good home atmosphere. She cared for her husband who had chronic asthma, congestive heart failure, and diabetes and also cared for her mother-in-law for 5 years until she died of cancer. Ms. Flynn never worked outside of the home on a full-time basis; however, she occasionally worked part time to supplement her husband's income. Ms. Flynn's husband died at age 68. Though she received his Social Security check, it was inadequate to meet the needs of her household.

Ms. Flynn was forced to move in with one of her sons and sell her house, which she practically had to give away. She sold most of her possessions but was able to keep a few things that her son allowed her to bring to his home. She has a nice room in the basement with an adjoining powder room. She is invited to all occasions but makes excuses for not attending. She sits in the dark most of the time, watches some television, and constantly worries about money. She is now fearful of going outside and is afraid of being alone. Her son is becoming frustrated with her clinging behavior. He is recommending that she seek help to assist with the temporary adaptation to a new environment, identify leisure pursuits and volunteer activities, and to decrease her anxiety and increase her self-esteem.

Previous research has demonstrated relationships among meaning in life and health, both physical and mental, and volunteerism. Uncovering the impact of physical and mental health and volunteering can predict meaning in life in older adults. Sherman, Michel, Rybak, Randall, and Davidson, (2011) examined the relationship and predictive utility of mental health, physical health, and volunteerism on life regard in a sample of 147 older adults aged 63–98 years. Meaning in life was positively and significantly associated with self-reported satisfaction with health, and individuals who volunteered reported higher life regard. This supports previous research demonstrating a positive relationship between physical health and meaning in life or life satisfaction (Krause, 2007).

There is a growing body of literature that supports a reciprocal relationship between health and volunteering in later life (Morrow-Howell, Hinterlong, Ronzario, & Tang, 2003; Musick, Traphagan, Koenig, & Larson, 2000; Thoits & Hewitt, 2001; van Willigen, 2000). That is, healthier older adults volunteer, and volunteers experience health benefits from their involvement. There exists a positive relationship between volunteering and self-rated health, morbidity, functional ability, mental health, and life satisfaction. The causal mechanisms have not been established, but explanations given include feeling useful, increased self-esteem, increased social connectedness, activity that structures time, role replacement, and role enhancement. Volunteers gain social approval from others, which in turn improves their self-esteem. They have fewer symptoms of anxiety and higher levels of life satisfaction compared with non-volunteers. People who combine paid work with volunteering have even better mental health (Hao, 2008).

Formal Volunteer Programs

Given the multiple benefits associated with volunteering in later life, it makes sense from a public health perspective to maximize involvement of the aging population in volunteer activities. There are few social policies that support volunteerism. Although volunteers can take a tax reduction for uncompensated expenses related to volunteering, federal initiatives primarily support volunteering through the creation of programs, like AmeriCorps, Peace Corps, and Learn and Serve American. However, these programs are biased toward youth. Since the program's founding in 1994, more than 900,000 AmeriCorps members have contributed more than 1.2 billion hours in service across America while tackling pressing problems and mobilizing millions of volunteers for the organizations they serve (Corporation for National and Community Service, 2015). For example, AmeriCorps' volunteers are primarily younger individuals. There have been calls to modify program structures to accommodate the aging population.

Senior Corps connects today's 55 and over with the people and organizations that need them most. They become mentors, coaches, or companions to people in need, or contribute their job skills and expertise to community projects and organizations. Volunteers receive guidance and training so they can make a contribution that suits their talents, interests, and availability (Corporation for National and Community Service, 2015).

The Foster Grandparent Program and Senior Companion Program are large national programs that enable older adults to volunteer. These programs provide small stipends to offset costs, and these volunteers must, in general, be low income and average 20 hours per week of service. Again, advocates call for modification to increase the number of older adults who could contribute to their communities through these programs. There is an increasing body of literature on innovative programs that solicit older adults for their time and talents and target some of society's most pressing issues: failing schools, environmental degradation, and child health. Most financial support comes from foundations and private/corporate contributions, with some partnerships with federal, state, or local governments (Morrow-Howell et al., 2003). For example, Experience Corps engages people 50 years and older in meeting their community's greatest challenges (Morrow-Howell, Johnson-Reid, McCrary, Lee, & Spitznagel, 2009). Two thousand volunteer members tutor and mentor in 19 cities across the country, providing literacy coaching, homework help, consistent role models, and committed, caring attention (AARP Foundation, 2013).

There has been considerable attention devoted to the baby boomers, given the tremendous amount of volunteer resources that they represent in their retirement years. Some survey researchers speculate that future generations are more likely to come forward to serve in large numbers (Peter D. Hart Research Associates, 2002), given the desire for ongoing meaningful involvement. It has been estimated that 50 % of baby boomers will remain involved in the community through work and community service (Peter D. Hart Research Associates, 2002). However, it is not known to what extent caregiving responsibilities will affect longer engagement in work and volunteer roles.

There is evidence that baby boomers may be motivated differently than today's older adults; they may be more interested in social interaction and less likely to volunteer out of religious commitment. It is recommended that because baby boomers are more likely to be currently volunteering, the best way to increase volunteer capacity in future years is to ensure their ongoing involvement (Prisuta, 2004). Nonprofits and government agencies are targeting boomers with skilled-based volunteering opportunities, and in Florida there is a focus on a program called Boomers Experience and Skills Team (BEST) (Forbes, 2013). This program was needed to create something fulfilling and rewarding that builds on the skills and unique talents of baby boomers. BEST will encourage baby boomers to use their job training and life skills to assist unemployed and underemployed residents achieve career success (Forbes, 2013). Guided Practice Exercise 8.7 provides the opportunity to examine feelings, beliefs, and attitudes and to identify modifications necessary to work in a productive capacity with older adults.

Guided Practice Exercise 8.7

As the older population continues to grow, you might find yourself interacting more frequently with older adults. How would this increased interaction affect you in a work environment, civic organization, academic environment, and/or volunteer organization? Are there personal adjustments you would need to make to engage constructively with older adults in these various settings? If so, elaborate on any changes you have identified.

Counseling professionals are in an excellent position to encourage older workers to remain employed, despite pressures and biases that are meant to persuade older persons to prematurely exit the labor force. Counseling professionals will also become excellent allies and advocates against discriminatory policies and practices that impede retention of older workers.

Retirement is an achievable goal for many workers. Professional counselors must examine and facilitate growth in this new identity that will be embraced by many and will be frightening for others. Leisure and volunteerism are valuable from a personal, community, and societal perspective. Older clients may need encouragement to fill a void, engage in meaningful activities, or seek fulfillment. Many have potential and strengths that have not been revealed. The counseling professional can be instrumental in older clients' pursuit of leisure and volunteer roles. Older clients will pose unique challenges to professional counselors due to their extensive life experiences and numerous life transitions. Counseling professionals will be challenged to acquire the knowledge, skills, and positive attitudes to interact effectively with this emerging older client population.

KEYSTONES

- Disengagement theory, the activity theory of aging, and the continuity theory focuses on degrees of engagement in activities in older persons.
- Labor force participation for older men and women indicate an interest in continued employment past traditional retirement age.

- Participation in meaningful employment is sought and maintained by many older workers.
- Retirement is a goal for many older adults, and factors affecting this decision include wealth and health.
- Pursuit of leisure and volunteer activities provides many benefits for older persons and needed services to organizations.
- Increased knowledge of workplace demands, retirement factors, and leisure and volunteer experiences is necessary in counselor preparation programs.

ADDITIONAL RESOURCES

Print Based

Chow, H. (2012). *Physically active leisure among older adults: Measurement, comparison and impact.* Saarbrücken, Germany: AV Akademikerverlag Publishers.

Coile, C., & Devine, P. (2010). *Reconsidering retirement: How losses and layoffs affect older workers.* Washington, DC: Brookings Institution Press.

Harper, M.C., & Shoffner, M. (2004). Counseling for continued career development after retirement: An application of the theory of work adjustment. *The Career Development Quarterly, 52,* 272–284.

Hollis, J. (2005). *Finding meaning in the second half of life: How to finally, really grow up.* New York, NY: Gotham.

Hooyman, N., & Kiyak, H. (2010). *Social gerontology: A multidisciplinary perspective.* Boston, MA: Pearson.

Leitner, M., & Leitner, S. (2012). *Leisure in later life* (4th ed.). Urbana, IL: Sagamore.

Myers, C. (2014). *From empty nest to job success: A simple guidebook for job searching seniors.* Amazon Digital Services.

Nickerson, C. (2014). *Boomerangs: Engaging the aging workforce in America.* Amazon Digital Services.

Patterson, R. (2006). *Growing older: Tourism and leisure behavior of older adults.* Oxfordshire, UK: CAB International Publishing.

Solomon, L. (2000). *Volunteer opportunities for seniors away from home.* Jefferson, NC: McFarland & Company.

Zalinsky, E. (2009). *How to retire happy, wild, and free: Retirement wisdom that you won't get from your financial advisor.* Buckinghamshire, UK: Visions International Publishing.

Web Based

www.aarp.org

www.agingnetworkvolunteercollaborative.org/older-adult-volunteers/

www.employseniors.org/

www.livestrong.com/article/438983-what-are-the-health-benefits-of-leisure-recreation/

www.moneyover55.about.com/od/preretirementplanning/a/NoRetirement.htm

www.nationalservice.gov/pdf/healthbenefits_factsheet.pdf

www.nhs.uk/Livewell/fitness/Pages/activities-for-the-elderly.aspx

www.nia.nih.gov/health/publication/growing-older-america-health-and-retirement-study/chapter-2-work-and-retirement

www.quintcareers.com/working_beyond_retirement.html

www.seniorlivingmag.com/fun-activities-for-senior-citizens

www.transitionsabroad.com/listings/work/volunteer/articles/volunteering-overseas-over-50.shtml
www.urban.org/retirement_policy/older-age-employment.cfm
www.workforce50.com/

REFERENCES

AARP Foundation. (2013). *Experience Corps*. Retrieved from http://www.aarp.org/experience-corps/about-us/

Abraham, K. G., & Houseman, S. N. (2004). Work and retirement plans among older Americans. *Upjohn Institute Staff, Working Paper No. 04-105*. Retrieved from http://www.upjohninstitute.org/publications/wp/04-105.pdf

Administration on Aging (AOA). (2008). *A profile of older Americans: Employment*. Retrieved from http://www.aoa.gov/AoARoot/Aging_Statistics/Profile/2008/12.aspx

American Association of Retired Persons (AARP)—DYG, Inc. (1992). *Employment policy and the older worker in the 1990s*. Washington, DC: Author.

American Association of Retired Persons (AARP). (1989). *Business and older workers-current perception and new directions for the 1990s*. Washington, DC: Author.

American Association of Retired Persons (AARP). (1995). *Business and older workers: A roadmap to the 21st century*. Washington, DC: Author.

American Association of Retired Persons (AARP). (2000). *American business and older employees: A summary of findings*. Washington, DC: Author.

American Association of Retired Persons (AARP). (2002). *Staying ahead of the curve: The AARP Work and Career Study*. Washington, DC: Author.

American Association of Retired Persons (AARP). (2003a). *Staying ahead of the curve 2003: The AARP working in retirement study*. Washington, DC: Author.

American Association of Retired Persons (AARP). (2003b). *A synthesis of member volunteer experience*. Washington, DC: Author.

American Association of Retired Persons (AARP). (2004). *Baby boomers envision retirement II*. Washington, DC: Author.

Anderson, G. (2015). AARP work & jobs study. AARP Research. Retrieved http://www.aarp.org/research/topics/economics/info-2015/1140-post-retirement-career-study

Anti-Ageism Taskforce (2006). *Ageism in America*. New York, NY: International Longevity Center—USA.

Ashe, M. C., Miller, W. C., Eng, J. J., & Noreau, I. (2009). Older adults, chronic disease and leisure time physical activity. *Gerontology, 55,* 64–72.

Atchley, R. C. (1972). *The social forces in later life*. Belmont, CA: Wadsworth.

Atchley, R. C. (1989). A continuity theory of normal aging. *The Gerontologist, 29*(2), 183–190.

Atchley, R. C. (2006). Activity theory. In R. Schulz, L. Noelker, K. Rockwood, & R. Sprott (Eds.), *The encyclopedia of aging* (pp. 9–13). New York, NY: Springer.

Bassuk, S. S., & Manson, J. E. (2005). Epidemiological evidence for the role of physical activity in reducing risk of type 2 diabetes and cardiovascular disease. *Journal of Applied Physiology, 99,* 1193–1204.

Becker, G. (1993). Continuity after a stroke: Implications of life-course disruptions in old age. *The Gerontologist, 33,* 148–158.

Bernard, D. (2013, January 18). The impact of baby boomers working past 65. *U.S. News and World Report*.

Bruyère, S. (2006). Disability management: Key concepts and techniques for an aging workforce. *International Journal of Disability Management Research, 1,* 149–158.

Buchman, A. S., Boyle, P. A., Wilson, R. S., Bienias, J. L., & Bennett, D. A. (2007). Physical activity and motor decline in older persons. *Muscle Nerve, 35*(3), 354–362. Washington, DC: U.S. Department of Labor.

Bureau of Labor Statistics. (2012). *Employee benefits in the U.S. National Compensation Survey.* Retrieved from http://www.bls.gov/news.release/ebs2.nr0.htm

Bureau of Labor Statistics. (2013). Employed and unemployed full- and part-time workers by age, sex, race, and Hispanic or Latino ethnicity. Current population survey. Retrieved from http://www.bls.gov/cps/cpsaat08.htm

Bureau of Labor Statistics. (2014a). *Current population survey.* Retrieved from http://www.bls.gov/cps/htm

Bureau of Labor Statistics. (2014b). Economic News Release: Volunteering in the United States, 2014. Retrieved from http://www.bls.gov/news.release/volun.nr0.htm

Bureau of Labor Statistics. (2015a). *Economic profile of civilian labor force.* Retrieved from http://www.bls.gov/news.release/ecopro.t01.htm

Bureau of Labor Statistics. (2015b). *Employment and unemployment among youth summary.* Retrieved from http://www.bls.gov/news.release/youth.nr0.htm

Burtless, G. (2013). *The impact of population aging and delayed retirement on workforce productivity.* Center for Retirement Research at Boston College. Chestnut Hill, MA: Hovey House.

Calasanti, T. M. (2009). Theorizing feminist gerontology, sexuality and beyond: An intersectional approach. In V. Bengtson, M. Silverstein, & N. Putney, *Handbook of theories of aging* (pp. 487–498). New York, NY: Springer.

Chen, S., & Fu, Y. (2011). Leisure participation and enjoyment among the elderly: Individual characteristics and sociability. *Educational Gerontology, 34,* 871–889.

Chou, K.-L., Chow, N., & Chi, I. (2004). Leisure participation amongst Hong Kong Chinese older adults. *Aging and Society, 24,* 617–629.

Coile, C. C., & Levine, P. B., (2009). *The market crash and mass layoffs: How the current economic crisis may affect retirement* [NBER Working Paper No. 15395]. Cambridge, MA: National Bureau of Economic Research.

Conger, C. (2015). What is disengagement theory? Critiques of the disengagement theory of aging. Retrieved from http://health.howstuffworks.com/wellness/aging/elder-care/disengagement-theory2.htm

Copeland, C. (2011). Employment-based retirement plan participation: Geographic differences and trends. *EBRI Issue Brief,* No. 378. Washington, DC: Employee Benefit Research Institute.

Corporation for National and Community Service. (2015). *Dollar value of volunteering for states: Volunteering in America.* Retrieved from http://www.volunteeringinAmerica.gov/pressroom/value_states.cfm

Covey, H. (1981). A reconceptualization of continuity theory: Some preliminary thoughts. *The Gerontologist, 12,* 628–633.

Crowe, M., Andel, R., Pedersen, N., Johansson, B., & Gatz, M. (2003). Does participation in leisure activities lead to reduced risk of Alzheimer's disease? A prospective study of Swedish twins. *Journal of Gerontology: Psychological Sciences, 58B*, 249–255.

Cumming, E., & Henry, W. (1961). *Growing old.* New York, NY: Basic Books.

DeLong, D. (2004). *Lost knowledge: Confronting the threat of an aging workforce.* Oxford, UK: Oxford University Press.

Dennis, H., & Thomas, K. (2007). Ageism in the workplace. *Generations, XXXI*(1), 84–89.

Department of Labor, Office of Federal Contract Compliance Programs. (2005). *Obligation to solicit race and gender data for agency enforcement purposes.* Office of Federal Contract Compliance Programs, 41CFR Part 60-I, Vol. 70, no. 194, pp. S8945–63. Retrieved from http://www.dol.gov/esa/regs/fedreg/final/2005020176.html

Dodge, H. H., Kita, Y., Takechi, H., Hayakawa, T., Gianguli, M., & Ueshima, H. (2008). Healthy cognitive aging and leisure activities among the oldest old in Japan: Takashima Study. *Journal of Gerontology: Medical Sciences, 63*(11), 1193–1200.

Ekerdt, D. J., & Sergeant, J. F. (2006). Retirement. In R. Schulz, L. Noelker, K. Rockwood, & R. Sprott (Eds.), *The encyclopedia of aging* (4th ed.). New York, NY: Springer.

Estes, C., & Associates. (2001). *Social policy and aging: A critical perspective.* Thousand Oaks, CA: Sage.

Everard, K. M., Lach, H. W., Fisher, E. B., & Baum, C. M. (2000). Relationship of activity and social support to the functional health of older adults. *The Journals of Gerontology Series B: Psychological Sciences and Social Sciences, 55,* S208–S212.

Federal Interagency Forum on Aging-Related Statistics. (2012). Older Americans 2012: *Key indicators of well-being.* Washington, DC: Government Printing Office.

Fernandez-Ballesteros, R., Zamarron, M. D., & Ruiz, M. A. (2001). The contribution of socio-demographic and psychosocial factors to life satisfaction. *Aging and Society, 21,* 25–43.

Folts, W. E. (2006). Introduction to the special issue on elderly volunteerism. *Educational Gerontology, 32,* 309–3+11.

Forbes (2013, April 1). *Why so few baby boomers are volunteering.* Retrieved from http://www.forbes.com/sites

Gauthier, A., & Smeeding, T. (2003). Time use at older ages: Cross-national differences. *Research on Aging, 25,* 247–274.

Genoe, M. R. (2010). Leisure as resistance within the context of dementia. *Leisure Studies, 29*(3), 303–320.

Hao, Y. (2008). Productive activities and psychological well-being among older adults. *Journal of Gerontology, 63B*(2), 564–572.

Havighurst, R. J., Neugarten, B. L., & Tobin, S. S. (1968). Disengagement and patterns of aging. In B. Neugarten (Ed.), *Middle age and aging: A reader in social psychology* (pp. 161–172). Chicago, IL: University of Chicago Press.

Helman, R., Copeland, C., & VanDerhei, J. (2015). The 2015 retirement confidence survey: Having a retirement savings plan, a key factor in Americans' retirement confidence. EBRI Issue Brief No. 413. Washington, DC: Employee Benefits Research Institute.

Hendricks, J., & Cutler, S. (2002). Leisure. In D. Ekerdt (Ed.), *Encyclopedia of aging* (pp. 773–776). New York, NY: MacMillan.

Hendricks, J., & Cutler, S. (2003). Leisure in life-course perspective. In R. Settersten, (Ed.), *Invitation to the life course* (pp. 197–134). Amityville, NY: Baywood.

Hendricks, J. U., & Cutler, S. J. (2004). Volunteerism and socioemotional selectivity in later life. *Journal of Gerontology: Social Sciences, 59B,* S251–S257.

Henretta, J. C. (2001). Work and retirement. In R. H. Binstock & L. K. George (Eds.), *Handbook of aging and the social sciences* (5th ed., pp. 255–271). San Diego, CA: Academic Press.

Hochschild, A. (1975). Disengagement theory: A critique and proposal. *American Sociological Review, 40*(5), 553–569.

Hong, S. I., Morrow-Howell, N., Fengyan, T., & Hinterlong, J. (2009). Engaging older adults in volunteering: Conceptualizing and measuring institutional capacity. *Nonprofit and Voluntary Sector Quarterly, 38,* 200–219.

Hutchens, R., & Papps, K. L. (2004). *Developments in phased retirement.* PRC WP 2004–14. Philadelphia, PA: University of Pennsylvania. The Wharton School, Pension Research Council. Retrieved from http://rider.wharton.upenn.edu/~prc/PRC/WP/WP2004-14.pdf

Independent Sector. (2000). *American senior volunteers.* Washington, DC: Author.

Kampfe, C., Wadsworth, J., Mamboleo, G., & Schonbrun, S. (2008). Aging, disability, and employment. *Work, 31,* 337–344.

Kart, C. S., & Kinney, J. M. (2001). *The realities of aging: An introduction to gerontology.* Boston, MA: Allyn & Bacon.

Katz, S. (2000). Busy bodies: Activity, aging, and the management of everyday life. *Journal of Aging Studies, 14,* 135–152.

Kent, M. (2011). *Today's research on aging: Volunteering and health for aging populations.* Washington, DC: Population Reference Bureau.

Kerstetter, D. L., Yarnal, C. M., Son, J. S., Yen, J., & Baker, B. S. (2008). Functional support associated with belonging to the Red Hat Society, a leisure-based social network. *Journal of Leisure Research, 40*(4), 531–555.

Krause, N. (2007). Stressors arising in highly valued roles, meaning in life among old people. *Journal of Aging and Health, 19,* 792–812.

Ku, P., Fox, K. R., & Chen, L. J. (2009). Physical activity and depressive symptoms in Taiwanese older adults: A seven-year follow-up study. *Preventive Medicine, 48,* 250–255.

Lennartsson, C., & Silverstein, M. (2001). Does engagement with life enhance survival of elderly people in Sweden? The role of social and leisure activities. *Journal of Gerontology: Social Sciences, 56B,* S335–S342.

Lum, T., & Lightfoot, E. (2005). The effects of volunteering on the physical and mental health of older people. *Research on Aging, 27,* 31–55.

Luoh, M. C., & Herzog, A. R. (2002). Individual consequences of volunteer and paid work in old age: Health and Mortality. *Journal of Health and Social Behavior, 43,* 490–509.

Lyons, K., & Dionigi, R. (2007). Transcending emotional community: A qualitative examination of older adults and masters' sports participation. *Leisure Sciences, 29*(4), 375–389.

Maddox, G. (1969). Disengagement theory: A critical evaluation. *Gerontologist, 4,* 80–83.

McBride, A. (2007). Civic engagement, older adults, and inclusion. *Generations,* 66–71.

McCann, R., & Giles, H. (2002). Ageism in the workplace: A communication perspective. In T. Nelson (Ed.), *Ageism: Stereotyping and prejudice against older persons* (pp. 163–199). Cambridge, MA: MIT Press.

McGuire, F., Boyd, R., & Tedrick, R. (2004). *Leisure and aging: Ulyssean living in later life.* Urbana, IL: Sagamore.

Morrow-Howell, N., Hinterlong, J. Ronzario, P., & Tang, F. (2003). Effects of volunteering on the well-being of older adults. *Journal of Gerontology, 58B*(3), S137–S145.

Morrow-Howell, N., Johnson-Reid, M., McCrary, S., Lee, Y., & Spitznagel, F. (2009). *Evaluation of Experience Corps: Student reading outcomes.* Washington University, St. Louis: Center for Social Development.

Munnell, A. H., Lee, J. G., & Meme, K. B. (2004). *An update on pension data.* Issue Brief 20. Chestnut Hill, MA: Center for Retirement Research at Boston College.

Munnell, A. H., Sass, S. A., & Soto, M. (2006). *Employer attitudes towards older workers: Survey results.* Boston, MA: Center for Retirement Research.

Musick, M. A., Traphagan, J. W., Koenig, H. G., & Larson, D. B. (2000). Spirituality in physical health and aging. *Journal of Adult Development, 7,* 73–86.

Musick, M. A., & Wilson, J. (2003). Volunteering and depression: The role of psychological and social resources in different age groups. *Social Science and Medicine, 56,* 259–269.

Nimrod, G. (2007). Expanding, reducing, concentrating and diffusing: Post-retirement leisure behavior and life satisfaction. *Leisure Sciences, 29*(1), 91–111.

Omoto, A. M., Snyder, M., & Martino, S. C. (2000). Volunteerism and the life course: Investigating age-related agendas for action. *Basic and Applied Social Psychology, 22*(3), 181–197.

Parisi, J. M., Stine-Morrow, E. A. L., Noh, S. R., & Morrow, D. G. (2009). Predispositional engagement, activity engagement, and cognition among older adults. *Aging, Neuropsychology and Cognition, 16,* 485–504.

Peter D. Hart Research Associates. (2002). *The new face of retirement: An ongoing survey on Americans' attitudes on aging.* New York, NY: Author.

Prisuta, R. (2004). Enhancing volunteerism among baby boomers. In *Reinventing aging: Baby boomers and civic engagement.* Boston, MA: Harvard School of Public Health, Center for Health Communication.

Quadagno, J., & Street, D. (1996). *Aging for the twenty-first century: Readings in social gerontology.* New York, NY: St. Martin's Press.

Satariano, W., Haight, T., & Tager, I. (2002). Living arrangements and participation in leisure-time physical activities in an older population. *Journal of Aging and Health, 14,* 427–451.

Savishinsky, J. S. (2000). *Breaking the watch: The meanings of retirement in America.* Ithaca, NY: Cornell University Press.

Schooler, C., & Mulatu, M. (2001). The reciprocal effects of leisure time activities and intellectual functioning in older people: A longitudinal analysis. *Psychology and Aging, 16,* 466–482.

Schultz, J. H. (2001). *The economics of aging* (7th ed.). Westport, CT: Auburn House.

Shelton, A. (2015). *Social Security: Who's counting on it?* AARP Public Policy Institute. Retrieved http://www .aarp.org/ppi/info-2015/social-security-who-is-counting-on-it.html

Sherman, N. E., Michel, R., Rybak, G., Randall, G. K., & Davidson, J. (2011). Meaning in life and volunteerism in older adults. *Adultspan Journal, 10*(2), 78–90.

Silverstein, M., & Parker, M. (2002). Leisure activities and quality of life among the oldest old in Sweden. *Research on Aging, 24,* 528–547.

Social Security. (2015). Research, statistics, & policy analysis: Monthly statistical snapshot, July 2015. Retrieved from http://www.ssa.gov/policy/docs/quickfacts/stat_snapshot/

Son, J. S., Kerstetter, D. L., Yarnal, C. M., & Baker, B. L. (2007). Promoting older women's health and well-being through social leisure environments: What we have learned from the Red Hat Society. *Journal of Women and Aging, 19*(3/4), 89–104.

Stathi, A., Fox, K. R., & McKenna, J. (2002). Physical activity and dimensions of subjective well-being in older adults. *Journal of Aging & Physical Activity, 10*(1), 76–92.

Stebbins, R. (2004). *Between work and leisure: The common ground of two separate worlds.* New Brunswick, NJ: Transaction.

Strain, L., Grabusic, C., Searle, M., & Dunn, N. (2002). Continuing and ceasing leisure activities in later life: A longitudinal study. *Gerontologist, 42,* 217–223.

Tang, F. (2006). What resources are needed for volunteerism? A life course perspective. *Journal of Applied Gerontology, 25,* 375–390.

Thang, L. (2005). Experiencing leisure in later life: A study of retirees and activity in Singapore. *Journal of Cross-Cultural Gerontology, 20*(4), 307–318.

Thoits, P. A., & Hewitt, L. N. (2001). Volunteer work and well-being. *Journal of Health and Social Behavior, 42,* 115–131.

Towers, W. (2012). Pensions in transition: Retirement plan changes and employer motivations. *The Aging U.S. Workforce,* Stanford Center on Longevity. Retrieved from http://longevity.stanford.edu/financial-security

Utz, R., Carr, D., Ness, R., & Wortman, C. (2002). The effect of widowhood on older adults' social participation. *The Gerontologist, 42,* 522–533.

van Willigen, M. (2000). Differential benefits of volunteering across the life course. *Journal of Gerontology Series B: Psychological Sciences and Social Sciences, 55,* S308–S318.

Vitt, L. A. (2003). *Encyclopedia of retirement and finance.* Westport, CT: Greenwood Press.

Watson Wyatt Worldwide. (2004). *Phased retirement: Aligning employer programs with worker preferences.* Washington, DC: Author.

Wilson, R., Mendes de Leon, C., Barnes, C., Schneider, L., Bienias, J., Evans, D., & Bennett, D. (2002). Participation in cognitively stimulating activities and risk of incident Alzheimer's disease. *Journal of the American Medical Association, 287,* 742–748.

Windsor, T. D., Anstey, K. J., & Rodgers, B. (2008). Volunteering and psychological well-being among young-old adults: How much is too much? *The Gerontologist, 48,* 59–70.

Zedlewski, S., & Schaner, S. (2006). Older adults engaged as volunteers. *The Retirement Project Perspectives on Productive Aging No. 5.* Washington, DC: The Urban Institute.

Professional Practice in Working With Older Adults

Skills, Attitudes, and Knowledge of Effective Practitioners

"A society's quality and durability can best be measured by the respect, and care given to its elder citizens."

—Arnold Toynbee

Learning Objectives

After reading this chapter, you will be able to

1. Examine the competencies and skills that are needed for counselor preparation and development
2. Analyze the strategies that counselors use when working with older clients

INTRODUCTION

As the aging population continues to grow, the need for counselors trained in gerontological counseling is essential. Older persons are an important population who can benefit from mental-health counseling. As a society, it is critical that we elevate the status of our elders and treat them with respect and dignity, rather than perpetuating negative stereotypes such as believing that they are depressed, unintelligent, neglected, and alone. Gerontological counselors are in a pivotal position to spearhead this process, as they must be appropriately trained to do so.

Development is the common goal of clients in counseling as well as for individuals in the helping professions. Just as with our counseling clients, counselors must build an adequate foundation for future growth. As helpers, they engage in a form of education with your clients. This does not mean counselors "input" information into the clients. Rather, the client creates the information—new thoughts and ideas and new behaviors and feelings. The counselor's task is to provide an encouraging environment that encourages and allows the client to develop at his or her own pace. All individuals are learners who must face new developmental tasks. Even counselors, from beginning to advanced professionals, will always face new challenges and development tasks. These learning opportunities, whether they take the form of a new and challenging client or a complex theory or technique keep counseling alive and exciting.

COUNSELOR PREPARATION AND DEVELOPMENT

Gerontology encompasses the study of dynamic processes of aging as experienced on the social, psychological, and biological levels (Hooyman & Kiyak, 2008). Knowledge of gerontology therefore prepares professional counselors to work more effectively with older clients by facilitating understanding of their worldview. Professional counselors thus are better able to contextualize how aging itself is not the pathology, but rather the context that influences other aspects of the client's life (Mabey, 2011).

Gerontology is an interdisciplinary field (Hill & Edwards, 2004). Having the opportunity to learn information from different perspectives involved in this field will help counselors-in-training consider clients using varying viewpoints. Training within a diversity of classes also serves the student in achieving a deeper conceptualization of the issues involved in working with older adults (Karasik, Maddox, & Wallingford, 2004).

Regardless of the particular model followed, certain areas of information are essential to prepare counselors to work specifically with older persons. This section will explore professional competencies; counselor and relationship skills, attitudes, and values; multicultural issues; ethical issues; and supervision and consultation.

Professional Standards/Competencies

Gerontological competencies for counselors and human development professionals were developed to be used in developing curricula and by practitioners to determine areas of competence for conducting counseling with older persons. Gerontological counselors who specialize in counseling older adults are expected to demonstrate both generic and specialty competencies. Generic competencies are those expected of all counseling students; however, aging specialists acquire additional competencies for the older population.

Essential competencies for gerontological counselors have been identified (Myers, 2010). The competencies are consistent with CACREP (Council for Accreditation of Counseling and Related Educational Programs) standards for professional counseling orientation and ethical practice, social and cultural diversity, human growth and development, career development, counseling and helping relationships, group counseling and group work, assessment and testing, and research and program evaluation (Myers, 2010).

Table 9.1 identifies the essential competencies for gerontological counselors. The CACREP recommends that aging concepts be instilled into existing counselor preparation curricula. According to Myers (2010), there are particular areas relevant to specialty training in gerontological counseling. These areas include normative experience of aging, older persons with impairments, needs and services for older persons, the population and special situations, counseling older persons, and ethics in gerontological counseling.

Aging concepts and gerontological competencies have been established for counselors interested in counseling older adults. Aging concepts are to be infused into existing counselor preparation programs and are closely aligned with CACREP core areas. Counseling students are expected to demonstrate these competencies prior to graduating from his or her counseling program. It must be noted that very few programs exist that offer this specialization; however, this area is viewed as an area of growth for future counselors.

Counseling and Relationship Skills

It is critical for counselors of any specialization to acquire the basic counseling and relationship skills such as empathy, genuineness, and unconditional positive regard, and for counselors who plan to work with older adults, developing a relationship of trust and mutual respect may take additional time. Counselors working with older clients must develop skills in numerous assessments (multicultural, strengths, comprehensive geriatric, cognitive, environmental, functional, career) unique to older persons.

Table 9.1   Competencies for Counseling Older Clients

1. Wellness orientation with genuine respect for the various needs of the older individual and overall aging population.

2. Sensitivity to natural changes as one ages, functional abilities and limitations and environment modifications.

3. Unique considerations in establishing a positive therapeutic relationship with older adults.

4. Knowledge of life span development, theoretical foundations of the aging experience, normative and non-normative changes and behaviors of older persons.

5. Social and cultural diversity issues that recognize the uniqueness of elders and the impact of societal attitudes on independent functioning and family systems.

6. Techniques for facilitating groups with older persons.

7. Lifestyle transitions and career development concerns of older persons.

8. Unique aspects of the appraisal process with older persons including psychological, social, and physical factors that impact the assessment process and ethical considerations.

9. Knowledge of current research regarding older adults and ethical considerations in conducting research on older adults.

10. Familiarity with the formal and informal support system for older adults and comfort in collaborating with multiple professionals in provision of services to elders.

Counselors must also fine tune their communication skills for older adults with cognitive, hearing, visual, or physical impairments and make appropriate adaptations for older clients. They must be particularly resourceful to make appropriate referrals and to facilitate client involvement. They must be skillful with working with resistant clients whose experiences have been remarkably different from the counselor experiences. In addition to these foundational skills, counselors who plan to work with aging persons need additional training programs. Involvement in training programs can occur in a variety of settings located in the community, academic institutions, local agencies, and health care institutions. Counselors and trainees can obtain training in a vast array of topics that include normative age changes, diseases associated with aging, continuum of care, work and retirement issues, medication issues, substance use/abuse, coping with loss, health insurance, social service programs, and a host of topics. Programs can occur through university Life Long Learning Institutes, Alzheimer's Disease Association, Area Agency on Aging, Healthy Aging Institute, Association for Gerontology in Higher Education (AGHE), the Gerontological Association of America (GSA), the National Institute on Aging, and numerous other venues. These programs provide a foundation for knowledge about the older population and the issues that confront these individuals (Damron-Rodriguez, Funderburk, Lee, & Solomon, 2004).

A training program provides counselor trainees or counselors with a supportive climate in which they can explore their personal values, attitudes, and biases about aging and older adults. This exploration can occur in role-play scenarios, completing inventories on aging biases/stereotypes, conducting service-learning activities with older adults, interviewing older persons, exercises identifying older adults (photos) and listing positive and negative characteristics, volunteering with older adults, participation in community events (Alzheimer's, Breast Cancer Awareness), and conducting practicum and internship experiences. A discussion follows all of the intergenerational activities. Counselor trainees have the opportunity to increase their self-awareness and develop appropriate counseling techniques, assessments, treatment plans, and intervention activities.

In addition, skills are needed to understand complex feeling states, as well as to communicate this understanding back to older clients. Counselors will need to discuss issues related to decreased functional ability and must do so in a very supportive manner, while simultaneously emphasizing clients' remaining abilities. Counselors will also need to assist clients with adjusting to an environment that is unfamiliar to them, having had to relocate from their familiar community setting. Counselors in a supportive and affirming manner will educate the client, empower the client to assert him or herself, encourage him or her to participate in activities, and to form relationships with peers. Consequently, counselors should be trained to communicate and present concepts clearly, observe verbal as well as nonverbal client messages, and remain cognizant of client impairments that may interfere with communication. They should also know how to deliver methods in concrete, simple, and understandable ways (Stevens-Roseman & Leung, 2004).

Counselors must be trained to be respectful of older individuals. This can be conveyed by requesting how the older adult wants to be addressed. For example, addressing an older adult with his or her first name only may be viewed as a sign of disrespect. In addition, addressing older persons as "dear" or "hon" can also be viewed as disrespectful and patronizing as well. More time may be required to establish rapport; consequently, more patience is required of counselors in building the relationship and throughout the counseling endeavors.

Counselors working with older clients are encouraged to develop skills specific to older clients. The establishment of the therapeutic relationship cannot be overstated, because this relationship is the foundation necessary for any future treatment options.

Attitudes and Values

There are basic attitudes and values that counselors should be encouraged to examine and challenge (van Zuilen, Rubert, & Silverman, 2001). Positive attitude and respect for older persons is essential. First, counselor-training programs should provide time and space for students to examine their values involving the rights of older clients to develop and work toward their own treatment goals. Valuing older persons as individuals who continue to make positive contributions in society and within their families and communities is central in the counseling process with older clients. Appreciation of a wellness orientation that emphasizes healthy lifestyle and behaviors to prevent the occurrence of a disorder or to minimize the negative impact of a disease is extremely useful when working with older clients. A strengths-oriented perspective that values the strengths brought to the counseling relationship enhances potential coping when confronted with a variety of stressful situations. Also, students need to value life span growth and development, acknowledge many ways to grow old in society, and value the heterogeneity of the older population and their experiences. This examination and challenge of attitudes and values can be accomplished through self-examination, identification of the origin of these values and beliefs (family, community association), and increased opportunities for interaction (senior centers, retirement villages, nursing homes). Second, a gerontological education should teach students that older clients do not attend counseling only to come to terms with life and death. They may have other, more pertinent concerns to be dealt with. Students need to demonstrate a positive attitude and appreciation for the lifetime of experiences. Older adults are keenly aware of their mortality, and students need to appreciate their desire for creative expression, inclusion, and need to be productive and valued in later life. Third, students should be encouraged to examine their roles as gerontological counselors. That is, counselors should learn not to play the role of the client's supportive network. Rather, they should serve as someone who helps, and provides resources to the client to develop another, more appropriate, supportive community. Providing support is important throughout the therapeutic relationship. However, a counselor needs to promote independence and to do this, providing resources and ways to access resources in the community is essential. The therapeutic relationship will be brought to closure at some point; therefore, it is incumbent upon counselors to encourage development of a supportive network in the community that will be the client's support system.

Multicultural Issues in Counseling Older Adults

Older adults represent a rapidly growing and diverse subgroup of the American population. One-fifth of older adults are currently members of racial or ethnic minority groups (8% African-American, 7% Hispanic/Latino, 3% Asian, and 1% American Indians, Native Hawaiian, or pacific Islander) (U.S. Census Bureau, 2011), and it is projected that

40% of the older adult population will be members of racial or ethnic minority groups by 2050 (U.S. Census Bureau, 2012). In addition, older adults may be representative of sexual minorities and identified as lesbian, gay, bisexual, or transgender (LGBT) and also under-represented in the mental health system that minimizes the exposure of professional counselors to this population. This results in the lack of general knowledge regarding older LGBT individuals and lack of preparation to provide professional services for them (Mabey, 2011). Professional counselors are urged to celebrate the diversity that exists within the heterogeneous older adult population and increase exposure to familiarize and become comfortable addressing a myriad of issues in multicultural counseling sessions. Issues of identity, discrimination, stigmatization, lack of support, sexuality, and harassment may be brought to the therapeutic encounter, which may pose a challenge to professional counselors who lack the preparation and sensitivity to address these issues.

Although the importance of multicultural competence is supported in preparatory and ethical standards, current pedagogical practices may be ineffective as graduates of counseling programs frequently report feeling unprepared to effectively work with culturally diverse clients (Bidell, 2005; McBride & Hays, 2012; Rock, Carlson, & McGeorge, 2010). Therefore, counselor educators need to consider how to more effectively meet the challenge and responsibility of cultivating cultural competence for counselor trainees by focusing on increasing skill development (Dickson & Jepsen, 2007; Hays, 2008). Counselors and counselors-in-training must continually engage in learning both in the classroom and outside of the classroom. It is impossible to know everything necessary regarding all cultures and the aging experience; therefore, continued education must occur informally and formally.

Multicultural issues that are common when counseling older adults include issues of chronological age (65–74, 75–84, 85+), ageism, workplace discrimination, double jeopardy (discrimination based on being old and female), triple jeopardy (discrimination based on being old, female, and a member of a minority group), discrimination based on sexual identity (LGBT), society's undervaluing cognitive and functional abilities based on age, socioeconomic issues (poverty, insurance status), cohort differences (Depression era, Recession era), and age gaps (younger counselors with older clients).

Counselors need to be aware of the lifetime of experiences that have shaped the worldviews of their older clients and the timeframe in which they were born. For example, persons born during the Depression grew up during a time of limited resources, a strong work ethic, and a belief in keeping matters within the family. However, the baby boom generation has grown up during a period of prosperity, traveled excessively, have limited savings, and experienced the Great Recession. Counselors must remain aware of the struggles experienced by women, minorities, and persons who do not identify themselves as heterosexuals. These groups have experienced racism, harassment, and social isolation and alienation in many sectors of society (work, education, employment, health care). Counselors must remember that chronological age is a determining factor in our society and may work against older persons. For example, older persons (65+) are encouraged to retire in spite of their ability to continue on their jobs. Older persons are negatively stereotyped as unproductive, lacking motivation, and unintelligent, which influences their interactions and relationships with others. Religious and political affiliation also influences the behavior of older clients. The identified issues are just a few of the issues counselors must be aware of in counseling older clients.

Counselors are faced with an increased challenge to find ways to relate to diverse clients and build strong therapeutic alliances (Owen, Tao, Leach, & Rodolfa, 2011). While it is not feasible for counselors to understand the idiosyncrasies of every culture, it is possible to increase attention to cultural and contextual factors when building the therapeutic alliance (Vasquez, 2007). Successful counseling must include empathic relationships that are culturally sensitive in nature and that employ techniques grounded in mutual empathy (Duffey & Somody, 2011).

Counselors need to address the significance of contextual factors (e.g., socioeconomic status, education, literacy) that may be related to client distress (Comstock et al., 2008). When these factors are overlooked, the counselor and client are at increased risk for perpetuating cultural misunderstandings and negative attitudes toward counseling (Harting, Rosen, Walker, & Jordan, 2004). Failing to attend to contextual factors may lead to disconnection, feelings of being misunderstood, and potential for weakening the therapeutic alliance, which increases the likelihood for treatment withdrawal (Duffey & Somody, 2011). By encouraging counselors and counselors-in-training to pay increased attention to contextual factors and relationships that may be impacting the client, counselors and trainees may gain more insight and ability to empathize with their clients (Comstock, 2005; West, 2005). Acknowledging external relationships and contextual factors may encourage clients to be more engaged in the counseling process, which helps to reinforce the therapeutic alliance (West, 2005).

Counselors and trainees need to increase their knowledge of the cultural and environmental histories of their clients, which gives them an informed view of their older client. Understanding their worldview can be achieved through focused, open-ended questioning combined with significant relationships and power structures (Rodriguez & Walls, 2000). It is also important for practitioners to understand how their multicultural makeup (e.g., race, gender, age) may have a bearing on the counseling relationship due to the client's experiences with these factors outside of counseling, as cultural mistrust has been identified as a barrier to treatment in minority clients (Duncan & Johnson, 2007). Counselors need to pay attention to culturally relevant systemic issues that may affect client functioning, creating constant disconnection due to an effort to assimilate into majority culture (Jordan, 2008). It is important for counselors to be aware of how their role as the counselor and the hierarchal nature of the counselor–client relationship may affect the therapeutic alliance. Through the development of the relationship, clients and counselors work to decrease the hierarchal nature of the relationship.

Counselors must develop mutual empathy, which requires the counselor to allow themselves to be affected by the client because detachment may interfere with therapeutic healing (Duffey & Somody, 2011). Mutual empathy is demonstrated by continuing checking in with the client through empathic exchange, enabling the counselor to better understand the client's worldviews and inviting the client to react to the mutual exchange. The act of mutual empathy can create a more meaningful relationship by encouraging both client and counselor to fully participate in the exchange and feel the impact that each participant has on the other (Freedburg, 2007).

Counselors and counselors-in-training must engage in continued education regarding multicultural issues that impact their older clients. They must obtain the necessary cultural knowledge of the population they are assisting, increase awareness and examine their personal biases and the biases held by their older clients, and appreciate the appropriateness of referral to more culturally competent and experienced practitioners. Counselors must also access experiences to increase their knowledge of multicultural issues through engagement in a mentoring program, involvement in minority and aging sponsored events, attending training sessions on multicultural development, and attendance at conferences focusing on multicultural issues.

Race, ethnicity, gender, and socioeconomic class are determining factors in every segment of American life, including how we age. For example, the aging poor find themselves at a disadvantage with regard to health care and housing. The elderly, as a group, encounter barriers to receiving counseling services. Not surprisingly, there is a correlation between having insurance and using mental health services (Myers & Harper, 2004). An age gap may exist between older clients and younger counselors, which may impede the development of a therapeutic relationship. Older clients may not feel the counselor has the ability to appreciate their long-lived experiences. Additionally, while race should not be a factor that influences the therapeutic relationship, it will have an impact if the client is a member of a minority group (persons of color, women, LGBT). Persons in the minority group may feel a disconnect due to the fact that the counselor may not be able to relate to their experiences of harassment, discrimination, and exclusion. Being old is also a culture of its own. Within that culture, people who are old and healthy live in a different world than those who are old and have a disability. It is helpful to distinguish between two broad categories: the young-old and the old-old, who are different from each other not so much by chronology as by health and self-sufficiency. Counselors need to have a working knowledge of the chronic illnesses and disabilities to which the old-old are especially subject.

Guided Practice Exercise 9.1 engages the future counselor in an examination of characteristics of a culturally competent counselor and self-examination to improve counseling skills in working with multicultural groups.

Guided Practice Exercise 9.1

List the characteristics of a culturally skilled counselor. Now, conduct research on a culturally competent counselor. Compare your list of characteristics to the information obtained from your research. Which characteristics do you possess? What areas do you need to work on to become a more skilled multicultural counselor? What strategies or experiences do you need to increase your skills in this area of counseling? Share your findings with your peers and/or supervisors.

Ethical Issues and Older Persons

It is important to realize that no set of ethical standards can cover every situation that may arise. If counselors are to make appropriate ethical decisions regarding the treatment of older adults, it is important for them to be familiar with models for ethical decision making, specifically, principle ethics and virtue ethics.

Principle Ethics

Principle ethics guide decision making and include fidelity, autonomy, and benefi-cence. Fidelity is the ethical principle that addresses the quality of the relationship between the counselor and the client. It implies that essential elements of the counseling relationship include trust and loyalty. The second principle, autonomy, refers to the right of older adults to make their own choices and decisions regarding matters that affect their lives. This principle implies that counselors must respect their clients' choices and not attempt to force their own values on the client. It further implies that counselors should always seek input on decisions that affect the client, even when the client may have impairment (Myers & Schwiebert, 1996).

Finally, the concept of beneficence dictates that the counselors prevent harm and work toward positive outcomes for the client. Although it is often difficult to ascertain which solution is ultimately most likely to benefit the client, it is incumbent on the counselor to continually strive to keep the client's best interest in the forefront as decisions are evalu-ated (Myers & Schwiebert, 1996). An example of principle ethics in working with older clients would be for the counselor to encourage independent decision making when the older client must relocate to a new environment. The counselor may present resources and examine the appropriateness of the different environments; however, encourage the client to arrive at his or her decision with minimal counselor input.

Guided Practice Exercise 9.2 demonstrates principle ethics of fidelity, autonomy, and beneficence, which if not handled appropriately, may be considered violations of ethical code.

Guided Practice Exercise 9.2

Imagine a group in interaction consisting of the counselor, older adult, and family members. The family has raised the issue that they do not feel their mother should remain in her home because her neighborhood has declined in recent years. As the counselor, is it your obligation to the older client or to the family members? Do you agree or disagree with the family's decision? What additional information do you need to position yourself to make a decision? Is your role to advocate for your older client (who wants to remain independent) or succumb to the desires of the adult children? How would you handle this situation? What ethical principles are you confronted with?

Virtue Ethics

In addition to models of principle ethics, virtue ethics must be considered. Virtue eth-ics complement models of principle ethics and focus on character traits and nonobliga-tory ideals that facilitate the development of ethical individuals. Virtue ethics address how an individual chooses which issue principles to apply to a situation and which principles to follow when two or more principles are in conflict. Virtue ethics address the process by which the individual makes this choice based on his or her own morals and values (Meara, Schmidt, & Day, 1996).

Many older persons are particularly concerned with protecting their rights to privacy. Many are not used to openly discussing sexual behavior, financial problems, and personal inadequacies. In fact, they may consider such talk as inappropriate and embarrassing. Counselors should be trained to work delicately with older persons on such issues, while encouraging the client to talk freely in an environment that is understood to be confidential (Pangman & Sequire, 2000). Having the skills to discuss with the client, values, needs, and fears associated with delicate issues might also be appropriate.

Counselors must also receive training in working with older persons, but also with their family members because they live within a family system. Ethical issues that may arise with older clients might include the decision to place an older client into a nursing home, need to involuntarily commit an older family member into an acute psychiatric facility, obtaining guardianship over their older family member, and many other areas. Counselors working with their older clients and family members will be challenged to provide sensitivity and objectivity simultaneously while remaining focused on what is viewed appropriate for their client. There may exist times when the counselor working with their older client must advocate on behalf of their client, which may produce tension with other family members.

Principle ethics of fidelity, autonomy, and beneficence and virtue ethics guide ethical decision making in the counseling of older adults. Counselors are to be aware of ethical principles and work diligently to adhere to them to avoid violations.

Supervision and Consultation

After obtaining the competencies needed to work with older adults, it is beneficial to professionals to continue growing and learning in their practice. This can be accomplished using supervision and consultation. Supervision is the process of helping both beginning and experienced therapists examine their own clinical and counseling work. Supervision is also a teaching process that is critical to the counselor and therapist development. By consulting with a supervisor or peers, counselors can learn about what they are doing right in work with clients, their developmental blind spots, and their options for further growth and development.

Therapists or counselors who are just starting out will benefit from supervision by professionals in their practice setting and in their college practicum. Those who are advanced in the profession can benefit from peer consultation and supervision from a master therapist or from someone with a different perspective. This process allows all members of the helping professions to learn about the complexities of helping. The most proficient and forward-looking counseling centers, clinics, and agencies incorporate supervision and feedback on clinical interviewing as a matter of course. If students are in agencies which do not provide supervision, then students need to obtain supervision from knowledgeable practitioners in the field, consult with former professors, and attend supervision training sessions within counseling associations. Those counselors or institutions not actively seeking such growth experiences inevitably limit their range as helpers.

Beginning therapists and counselors are motivated to seek out consultation with peers, often forming peer supervision groups on their own. There exists a small, but growing number of helping professionals interested in working with older adults. While they are more numerous in different fields (social work, physical therapy, occupational therapy), they are a small group in the counseling field. Therefore, it may be challenging to locate peers to engage in peer supervision. Some counselors working with a different population (i.e., adult) may choose to access courses to familiarize themselves. They learn through their clients as they age. The Mental Health Counseling Association, American Counseling Association and American Psychological Association are resources, as well as gerontological organizations. One of the most important benefits of a training program is such peer learning. After training, counselors in the work setting often find themselves supervising the work of colleagues and training community volunteers and new students.

Guided Practice Exercise 9.3 gives the counselor-in-training the opportunity to gain feedback from supervisory personnel to improve effectiveness with their older client.

Guided Practice Exercise 9.3

Conduct a 30-minute interviewing session with an older person. Obtain permission to record audio and/or video of this practice session. The goal of this session is to give your client the opportunity to discuss major life transitions while demonstrating attending, active listening, summarizing, and time management skills. Once completed, playback the recording and obtain feedback from your supervisor.

Consultation on a variety of issues related to older clients may occur in a variety of ways. Counselors working with older clients may be working with healthy older clients experiencing a crisis or unanticipated transition or working with older clients who are experiencing chronic mental health issues. These clients may reside at home, in retirement communities, assisted living facilities, or nursing homes or reside with family members. Older clients may be gainfully employed in careers that are rewarding and satisfying or in employment situations where they are facing discrimination due to their age. Therefore, based on the circumstances which the older client may be experiencing, the consultation services will vary. For example, the professional counselor may be contacted to provide group programming for older clients in a nursing home. The counselor may be called upon to provide a psychoeducational lecture series on a mental health topic. The counselor may be consulted by an employer to provide strategies to retain and increase their older adult workforce. A counselor may be called upon to participate in treatment planning meetings (with the consent of their older client) to provide input to better prepare their older client to transition from one environment to another (i.e., from nursing home to assisted living environment).

STRATEGIES TO USE IN COUNSELING OLDER ADULTS

The following section will examine the needs and services for older persons, client empowerment, impairment and adaptations, living arrangements, developmental crises or transitions, and resources. An examination of these areas that affect older adults is very important in preparing clients to work effectively with this population.

Needs and Services for Older Persons

Before discussing the strategies that are typically used in counseling older adults, it is necessary to understand the resources and services that are made available to this group. Many community-based services were established with the Older Americans Act, which was passed in 1965 and amended in 2000.

The act provides for an adequate income in retirement in accordance with the American standard of living and the best possible physical and mental health that science can make available, without regard to economic status. It also places priority on obtaining and maintaining suitable housing that is independently selected, designed, and located with reference to special needs and available at costs that older citizens can afford. The act emphasizes a full array of restorative services for those who require institutional care and a comprehensive selection of community-based, long-term-care services adequate to appropriately sustain older people in their communities and in their homes, including supporting family members and other persons providing voluntary care to older individuals needing long-term-care services (U.S. Code, 2003).

The Older Americans Act also outlines the significance of the opportunity for employment with no discriminatory personnel practices because of age; retirement in health, honor, and dignity; and participation in and contribution to meaningful activity within the widest range of civic, cultural, education and training, and recreational opportunities. Priority is given to efficient community services, including access to low-cost transportation, which provide choices in supported living arrangements and social assistance that are readily available when needed, with an emphasis on maintaining a continuum of care for vulnerable older individuals. Immediate benefit from proven research that can sustain and improve health and happiness is also a component of the act. Finally, the Older Americans Act addresses freedom, independence, and the free exercise of individual initiative in planning and managing his or her own life; full participation in the planning and operation of community-based services and programs provided for his or her benefit; and protection against abuse, neglect, and exploitation (U.S. Code, 2003).

Numerous services are available as resources for older adults. These resources allow clients to maintain their independence within their local communities and enhances their quality of life.

Client Empowerment

Counselors need to believe that older adults are capable of growth and change as they encounter the challenges associated with aging and in life. Counselors must also believe that clients want and need to be active participants in decision making in all aspects of their care.

Client empowerment involves several dimensions: active participation, problem solving, acceptance and responsibility for self-care, informed change, client competency, and perceived control over their health and life. Active participation is essential to client empowerment, and the client must be willing to assume responsibility and participate in goal setting and decision making (Tveiten & Meyer, 2009). Empowerment also involves the client in problem formulation, decision making, and action (Tengland, 2007). Critical thinking and informed decision making about self-care and his or her health is related to empowerment (Anderson & Funnell, 2010). The outcome of empowerment is change in client's performance (Hsueh & Yeh, 2006). Client empowerment is associated with awareness of one's developmental strengths and abilities, evidenced by asserting personal control, feeling more powerful, increased self-esteem and self-worth, inner confidence, enhanced well-being and self-capacity (Shearer, 2007). Finally, client empowerment is a process that enables clients to gain more control over the diverse aspects of his or her life (Lord & Hutchison, 1993).

"Clients create change, not helpers" (Glicken, 2004, p. 5). The role of the counselor is to facilitate the client empowerment process using a strengths-oriented perspective; counselors will assist clients in identifying his or her strengths, resources, and goals. Counselors will also connect clients with personal and community resources to achieve his or her goals. Counselors will also coordinate this process, if necessary.

Examples of client empowerment are assisting clients secure support from family and friends when they have difficult decisions to make (i.e., retirement, relocation to supervised setting). Counselors can also support clients in overcoming their dependence on alcohol, drugs, and/or medications by drawing on their inner strength, faith, and previous coping abilities used in different situations. Clients have overcome numerous challenges in their lives and counselors will draw upon previous coping mechanisms and problem-solving skills to facilitate client empowerment.

Empowering clients to take responsibility for their behavior and involvement in changing maladaptive behaviors is an enlightening process of exploration. Client empowerment is a process that ultimately changes client behavior, which enables the client to engage more fully in all aspects of life.

Empowerment is an important strategy that professionals may need to implement with their clients. Fighting the negative attitudes of society toward the aging process may take a toll on older adults. Such negativity may affect not only elders' feelings of self-worth, but also their lifestyles. Counselors may find it necessary to help some older clients distinguish between the myths or stereotypes and the actual realities of aging. Counselors should develop sensitivity to their own needs and aging process. Consequently, a process around deconstructing such myths should take place within counselor education.

Guided Practice Exercise 9.4 provides a role play that illustrates negative perceptions of aging and how to empower clients to refute negative societal messages.

Guided Practice Exercise 9.4

Engage in a role-play scenario. Person A plays the older client and Person B plays the counselor interviewing the client. The older client expresses disgust with the negative perceptions, ageism, and negative comments made to him or her on a regular basis. The counselor is to convince the client of the positive aspects of aging and empower him or her to be assertive when confronted with negative interactions.

Impairment and Adaptations

There is considerable variation in the aging process, and individual differences must be understood and respected (Serby & Yu, 2003). That is, there are differences between counseling the young and the old. To varying degrees, aging may bring on significant physical changes such as sight, hearing, and memory loss. In such cases, students should be trained to face the client directly, sit close, and speak especially clearly. The counselor should observe how well the older persons can process and digest information. In addition, slower, more distinct, and briefer comments may be necessary. Furthermore, counselors should be trained to note differences between sensory impairments and cognitive deficits (Knight, 2004).

Guided Practice Exercise 9.5 provides the opportunity to conduct a gerontological assessment and modify its use for older clients, while attending to the changes due to aging. The gerontological assessment is a comprehensive assessment of client functioning. There exists specific assessments normed for older adults, and these assessments are administered early in the counseling process. An extensive listing of various assessments is illustrated in Chapter 10. Due to client cognitive and/or physical abilities, modifications may be required.

Guided Practice Exercise 9.5

A comprehensive gerontological assessment provides valuable information that help you better understand and work therapeutically with an older client. This type of assessment is time-consuming and may be exhausting for some older clients. What modifications would you make to complete this assessment with your older clients?

Counselors who choose to work with the elderly population will likely be presented with a plethora of issues outside of that which brought the client initially into treatment. Due to the age of the client, the counselor will need to be aware not only of mental and emotional conditions, but also those which may be of physical concern. Additionally, issues related to cognition may make the therapeutic process more challenging.

There are two main forms of cognition: crystallized and fluid intelligence. Crystallized intelligence is one area of cognition that is often found to increase with age and is defined as the ability to use knowledge that was once acquired earlier in life on later occasions (Vander Zanden, Crandell, & Crandell, 2007). Also one's knowledge base not only remains intact but also continues to grow throughout most of adulthood, only to start declining after age 65 (Cavanaugh & Blanchard-Fields, 2006). A second area of cognition is classified as fluid intelligence and is defined as reasoning ability and a skill not dependent on experience and this tends to peak in young adulthood, only beginning to decline if not regularly used and practiced (Cavanaugh & Blanchard-Fields, 2006). The older client may have difficulty processing new concepts, and as a result, the counselor will have to exhibit more patience and understanding when counseling this population.

The slowing of cognitive processes that occurs with normal aging is noticeable. The impact of slowing in therapy is that conversational flow of each session is usually slower than with younger adults in both the pacing of sentences and the latency between client speech and therapist speech. Speaking quickly leads to communication inaccuracy and the need to repeat information. The therapist working with older clients must be more aware of pacing within sessions and may need to actively resist any internal tendency to speak quickly in response to time pressure, anxiety, or excitement (Knight, 2004).

Changes in the capacity of working memory in later life may require some modification of communication style in the counseling session. Working memory is the active processing capacity of memory, the amount of information that can be actively held in memory and worked on at one time. This limited capacity store may be slightly reduced in later life. If so, it may account for changes in comprehension of speech and in problem-solving abilities. Both of these changes could be compensated for by slowing the pace of speech, simplifying sentence structure, and by presenting problems in smaller pieces. The counselor who tends to use a lot of jargon and make longer and complex interpretations or recommendations will need to modify this style when working with older adults, especially when working the old-old (Knight, 2004).

Life experience is an asset when working with older adults. Older clients often have expertise relevant to the problem that was brought to therapy. Their accumulated knowledge of people and relationships can be brought to bear on current relationship problems. Taking advantage of this expertise can be an adaption for the therapist in a few ways. First, therapists working with younger adults may be more accustomed to encouraging people to explore themselves to discover untapped strengths. Changing that mindset to helping people recall and use already existing strengths is not more difficult, but it is different. Second, working with clients who have more life experience and expertise is also a change of perspective for the therapist. It can be quite exciting for therapists who are open to learning from clients. It may be anxiety-arousing for therapists who are uncertain of their own abilities (Knight, 2004). Guided Practice Exercise 9.6 provides the opportunity to utilize the strengths of an older client to use as a resource within the counseling session.

Guided Practice Exercise 9.6

All clients have something to offer in any therapeutic encounter. Older clients have untapped resources and potentials yet to be discovered. Identify positive resources in your older client and in his or her environment. Identify what your client does extremely well: the positive assets he or she has developed. Once identified, have your older client identify a challenging situation, dilemma, or life transition (widowhood, divorce, relocation, retirement) and how he or she used their strengths and resources to manage or address the situation. End your interaction with strengths identified by your older client. This positive basis can facilitate the treatment planning process.

To establish a relationship conducive to effective counseling, the professional should be skilled in various ways. First, counselors must be able to convey respect for dignity and worth of the older individual. Because some older persons may be reserved and less confident, more time may be needed to establish rapport with them. Asking the client how he or she chooses to be addressed is a sign of respect. In addition, counselors should be trained or have experience employing counseling treatment in flexible settings. For example, some older persons may respond better if served in their homes. Finally, the 50-minute time slot may not be conducive to the client's stamina.

Living Arrangements

Numerous non-institutional living arrangements exist for older persons. They may live with a spouse, alone, with relatives or with persons they are not related to, in homes, condominiums, or apartments that they own or rent. They may also live in subsidized housing, due to low income. They may live in personal care homes, assisted living facilities or in retirement villages. Older persons prefer to reside in their communities and use services to enhance their ability to remain there.

Older persons will also reside in institutional facilities, such as a nursing home. Nursing homes are for those older persons who have difficulty with their activities of daily living and who have medical problems that require supervision and care by nursing personnel. Despite the fact that rehabilitation is a component of their care, most elders view nursing homes as the last resort and would prefer not to be admitted to one.

Guided Practice Exercise 9.7 gives the counselor-in-training the opportunity to conduct research to increase his or her knowledge regarding living environments of various stages of an older clients' life. Knowledge of these resources is essential for a counselor who plans to work with older clients.

Guided Practice Exercise 9.7

As a future counselor who wishes to work effectively with older clients, you must be knowledgeable regarding the continuum of care. Different living environments are required for older persons at different points in their lives based upon a variety of factors. Conduct research on the continuum of care for older persons to understand their structure, eligibility requirements, costs, and locations. Now identify which environments would be acceptable for older adults who are independent and highly functional, those who require some minimal assistance with activities of daily living, and those who have numerous medical problems and require daily supervision. Now identify resources for the older client who has a diagnosis of dementia in the later stages.

Professional counselors are required to understand the types of living arrangements and the impact and interaction between the environment and their older clients. When a fit/congruence does not exist between the older person and his or her environment, it is problematic to the older person and his or her achievement of certain positive outcomes. If there exists an incongruence between the environment and the older adult, then modifications can be made to the environment (rails, better lighting, alarms, walk-in bathtubs), or a referral to a supervised setting may be required, if the elder is unable or unwilling to move in the with residents. For example, continuing to live in one's home with numerous steps in the front and back of the house is incongruent for an elderly person with mobility issues, who has diabetic neuropathy in the lower extremities, or who recently experienced a fall. The professional counselor needs to understand the various environmental arrangements and view this in the context of the needs of their older clients. Better care will be provided if attention is paid to environmental considerations.

Developmental Crises/Transitions

As with individuals of all age groups, older adults often experience developmental crises or transitions. Unlike other age groups, however, the elderly face developmental transitions that frequently require adjustment to loss. While these crises are not experienced by all older persons, nor are they exclusive to the elderly population, they must be faced by many older persons. Consequently, training in working with adjustment issues in general—as well as specific to the elderly population—is imperative.

Guided Practice Exercise 9.8 provides the opportunity to become familiar with the stages of the dying process and its application for dying persons.

Guided Practice Exercise 9.8

Elisabeth Kübler-Ross (1969) identified five stages individuals work through when they face death and dying. The stages are denial, anger, bargaining, depression, and acceptance. Relate how these stages can help you (the counselor) in working with your terminally ill older client and his or her family. What do you view as your role in this situation? Identify issues that arise in each of these stages and ways to address them.

Counselors who choose to work with the elderly population must have significant knowledge of their specific issues, experiences, and concerns that will assist in managing crises/transitions. Oftentimes, when the elderly are referred to a professional in the human service field, they are struggling with emotional, psychological, or physical issues. Depression is a major concern among this age group. Community studies have shown that 25% of elderly persons report having depressive symptoms (Raj, 2004), additionally confirmed by Shirmbeck (2006), with high rates of occurrence (36% to 46%) among those hospitalized (Teresi & Abrams, 2001). According to Erik Erikson's seven stages of human development, elderly individuals would find themselves dealing with the psychosocial crisis of ego integrity versus despair. It is during this stage that the individual evaluates his or her life, accomplishments, and fears. Individuals who fear their own death, feel abandoned or lost due to the loss of loved ones, are experiencing chronic or terminal illness, or feel they have lost the ability to be self-sufficient can find themselves engulfed in a state of despair (Krebs-Carter, 2007; Lewis, 2001). Counselors can help clients examine these crises and develop strategies to address them.

Pervin, Cervone, and Oliver (2005) find that through the progression of Erikson's stages, some individuals are capable of developing a sense of intimacy, an acceptance of life's successes and disappointments, and a sense of continuity throughout the life cycle, a progression that leads to integrity stage in later life. However, other people remain isolated from family and friends, appear to survive on a fixed daily routine, focus on both past disappointments and future death, and are likely to find themselves rooted in despair (Pervin et al., 2005). Counselors will equip clients with the modality necessary to manage this phase.

Older adults are similar to any other population, and they also have certain needs that are often specific for them. Change is a major part of late adulthood, whether it's divorce, retirement, or some other type of change. Older adults are dealing with new experiences and life changes. Regardless of the type of change or time in which it occurs in life, large changes can lead to emotional concerns, like depression or anxiety (Kampfe, 2015).

Despite the fact that many older adults share some concerns with the general population (i.e., divorce, depression, anxiety), there are areas that tend to be more common in late adulthood. For example, many older adults have financial concerns due to being retired, unable to work, or on a fixed income. They might struggle to meet their daily expenses. Increasing health care costs might add to financial troubles older persons face (Kampfe, 2015). Financial issues can lead to many other issues as well. Malnutrition, health care problems, depression, and anxiety are just a few of the concerns older persons face. A counselor working with older adults must pay particular attention to these issues and be prepared to face other issues that result from inadequate finances (Kampfe, 2015). Counselors may need to assist clients with adjusting on a limited budget, explore additional sources of income, and examine the possibility of employment.

Older adults face many problems, and widowhood is more common in late adulthood. As people age, they are more likely to lose their spouse, which can lead to depression and other emotional issues. While widowhood is experienced by both men and women, it is more prevalent among women because they live longer than men. Also, some women have centered their identity on their family, and when children have moved on and their spouse is gone, some women experience a crisis of personality and question their identity. Counselors working with older clients are to pay particular attention to these issues and be prepared to engage in grief counseling with older adults (Kampfe, 2015).

Finally, counselors working with older clients must remember that many older clients face health issues. Even among the healthiest elderly, eyesight, hearing, smell, taste, and mobility decline. Previously identified health conditions of hypertension, stroke, dementia, osteoporosis, arthritis are common concerns for elderly clients, and mental health practitioners must address the emotional, psychological, physical, and social implications of these conditions with older clients. Additionally, older clients may be without a disability; however they may be caring for someone who has a disability. The stress associated with the caregiving role must be addressed by the counselor and teaching stress reduction techniques and other ways to relax may prove valuable in working with older clients (Kampfe, 2015). Assisting clients in securing resources will be helpful during this process.

Resources

One final strategy to help older adults is to enable them to help themselves. Knowledge of formal and informal resources is critical when counseling older clients. Professionals will need to be familiar with the informal support system, which may consist of family, friends, and neighbors and the formal support system, which include private and public organizations, for-profit and not-for-profit systems, continuum of care for living environments, medical, mental health and rehabilitation facilities, social service agencies and programs, plethora of health and mental health professionals. Counselors assisting older clients will serve as referral agents and teach older clients to be resourceful. They will also be required to familiarize themselves with resources specific to the cultural group to whom services are being delivered (i.e., Services and Advocacy for Gay, Lesbian, Bisexual and Transgender Elders [SAGE]). Collaborating with a variety of professionals in multiple settings will increase the likelihood that older clients will receive the services they need.

Myers (1990) reported that the popularity and availability of self-help resources have encouraged younger persons to become more knowledgeable and open to their own feelings and stress responses. On the contrary, older persons may have a limited familiarity with such materials. This contributes to their lack of relevant vocabulary, a smaller array of coping mechanisms, and diminished acceptance and awareness of stress-related concerns and/or symptoms. In such cases, students should become knowledgeable about potential resources that older persons might be inclined to use outside of the counseling office.

Older adults are inclined to use their local senior citizen centers, local aging agencies, local physicians, and health care facilities. Clients in the baby boom generation are more familiar with technology and may choose to browse the Internet for health and mental health resources. Print material may be preferred by older clients who are unfamiliar with technology and/or uncomfortable with its use. Numerous resources are available in local libraries, in academic libraries, local bookstores, and on the Internet. Counselors can encourage older clients to access these resources and teach clients that all information on the Internet is not reliable nor valid. They can obtain resources from the local, state, and government websites as appropriate sites to access health-related information.

There exist extensive resources available in multiple formats for older clients to access. Counselors working with his or her clients will encourage clients to be resourceful in accessing these resources in the community and to become knowledgeable and informed consumers.

KEYSTONES

- Older persons continue to be underrepresented in the mental health system and can benefit from mental health counseling.
- The older population continues to expand and the need for qualified gerontological counselors will continue to rise.

- The American Counseling Association (ACA) has established core competencies for a gerontological counselor.

- Counselor education programs must provide basic counseling preparation and enhance the education with areas that pertain specifically to older adults in an interdisciplinary manner.

- Counselors and counselors-in-training should be prepared to examine their attitudes and values and address multicultural and ethical issues in their work with older adults.

- Supervision and consultation and teaching processes are critical to counselor and therapist development.

- The Older Americans Act, which was passed in 1965 and amended in 2000, established many community-based services that provide for such resources as income in retirement, suitable housing, and long-term health care.

- Strategies that counselors should utilize when working with older adults include client empowerment, being aware of and adapting to physical and cognitive impairments, ensuring that living arrangements align with an older person's capabilities, and training in adjustment issues.

- It is important for counselors to learn about and suggest resources to older persons for use outside of the counseling office.

ADDITIONAL RESOURCES

Print Based

Erford, B. T. (2013). *Assessment for counselors* (2nd ed.). Belmont, CA: Brooks/Cole.

Fuertes, J. N., Spokane, A., & Holloway, E. (2013). *Specialty competencies in counseling psychology*. New York, NY: Oxford University Press.

Geldard, K., & Geldard, D. (2012). *Personal counseling skills: An integrative approach* (Rev. ed.). Springfield, IL: Charles C Thomas.

Giordano, J. A. (2000). Effective communication and counseling with older adults. *International Journal of Aging and Human Development, 51*, 315–324.

Gladding, S. T. (2013). *Counseling: A comprehensive profession* (7th ed.). Boston, MA: Pearson.

Hays, D. G., & Erford, B. T. (Eds.). (2014). *Developing multicultural counseling competence: A systems approach* (2nd ed.). Boston, MA: Pearson.

Huber, R., Nelson, W. H., Netting, F. E., & Borders, K. W. (2008). *Elder advocacy: Essential knowledge and skills across settings*. Belmont, CA: Thomson Brooks/Cole.

Johns, H. (2012). *Personal development in counselor training* (2nd ed.). Thousand Oaks, CA: Sage.

Okun, B. F., & Suyemoto, K. L. (2013). *Conceptualization and treatment planning for effective helping*. Belmont, CA: Brooks/Cole.

Parsons, R. D., & Zhang, N. (2014). *Becoming a skilled counselor*. Thousand Oaks, CA: Sage.

Schwiebert, V., Meyers, J., & Dice, C. (2000). Ethical guidelines for counselors working with older adults. *Journal of Counseling and Development, 78*, 123–129.

Walsh-Burke, K. (2005). *Grief and loss: Theories and skills for helping professionals*. Boston, MA: Allyn & Bacon.

Web Based

www.nhcoa.org/hispanic-aging-network/
www.asaging.org
www.forge-forward.org/aging/
www.cms.hhs.gov
www.ncoa.org
www.dol.gov
www.siecus.org
www.census.gov
www.aoa.gov
www.nimh.nih.gov
www.afar.org
www.aarp.org
www.aghe.org
www.geron.org

REFERENCES

Anderson, R., & Funnell, M. (2010). Patient empowerment: Myths and misconceptions. *Patient Education and Counseling, 79*(3), 277–282.

Bidell, M. (2005). The sexual orientation counselor competency scale: Assessing attitudes, skills, and knowledge of counselors working with lesbian, gay, and bisexual clients. *Counselor Education and Supervision, 44*(4), 267–279.

Cavanaugh, J., & Blanchard-Fields, F. (2006). *Adult development and aging* (5th ed.). Belmont, CA: Wadsworth/Thomson Learning.

Comstock, D. (Ed.). (2005). *Diversity and development: Critical contexts that shape our lives and relationships.* Belmont, CA: Thomson Brooks/Cole.

Comstock, D., Hammer, T., Strentzsch, J., Cannon, K., Parsons, J., & Salazar II, G. (2008). Relational-cultural theory: A framework for bridging relational, multicultural, and social justice competencies. *Journal of Counseling & Development, 86,* 279–287.

Damron-Rodriguez, J., Funderburk, B., Lee, M., & Solomon, S. H. (2004). Undergraduate knowledge of aging: A comparative study of biopsychosocial content. *Gerontology & Geriatrics, 25*(1), 53–71.

Dickson, G., & Jepsen, D. (2007). Multicultural training experiences as predictors of multicultural competencies: Student perspectives. *Counselor Education and Supervision, 47*(2), 76–95.

Duffey, T., & Somody, C. (2011). The role of relational-cultural theory in mental health counseling. *Journal of Mental Health Counseling, 33,* 223–242.

Duncan, L., & Johnson, D. (2007). Black undergraduate students' attitude toward counseling and counselor preference. *College Student Journal, 41,* 696–719.

Freedburg, S. (2007). Re-examining empathy: A relational-feminist point of view. *Social Work, 52,* 251–259.

Glicken, M. (2004). *Using the strengths perspective in social work practice.* Boston, MA: Pearson.

Harting, L., Rosen, W., Walker, M., & Jordan, J. (2004). Shame and humiliation: From isolation to relational transformation. In J. V. Jordan, M. Walker, & L. M. Harting (Eds.), *The complexity of connection: Writings from the Stone Center's Jean Baker Miller Training Institute* (pp. 103–128). New York, NY: Guilford.

Hays, P. (2008). *Achieving cultural complexities in practice: Assessment, diagnosis and therapy*. Washington, DC. American Psychological Association.

Hill, H., & Edwards, N. (2004). Interdisciplinary gerontology education online: A developmental process model. *Gerontology & Geriatrics Education, 24*(4), 23–44.

Hooyman, N., & Kiyak, H. (2008). *Social gerontology: A multidisciplinary perspective* (8th ed.). Boston, MA: Pearson.

Hsueh, M., & Yeh, M. (2006). A conceptual analysis of the process of empowering the elderly at the community level. *Hulizazhi, 53*(2), 5–10.

Jordan, J. (2008). Recent developments in relational-cultural theory. *Women & Therapy, 31,* 1–4.

Kampfe, C. (2015). *Counseling older people: Opportunities and challenges*. Alexandria, VA: American Counseling Association.

Karasik, R. J., Maddox, M., & Wallingford, M. (2004). Intergenerational service-learning across levels and disciplines: One size (does not) fit all. *Gerontology & Geriatrics Education, 25*(1), 1–17.

Knight, B. G. (2004). *Psychotherapy with older adults* (3rd ed.). Thousand Oaks; CA: Sage.

Kübler-Ross, E. (1969). *On death and dying*. New York, NY: The Macmillan Company.

Krebs-Carter, M. (2007). *Ages in stages: An exploration of the life cycle based on Erik Erickson's eight stages of human development*. New Haven, CT: Yale-New Haven Teachers Institute. Retrieved from http://www.yale.edu/ynhti/curriculum/units/1980/1/80.01.04.x.html#d

Lewis, M. (2001). Spirituality, counseling, and elderly: An introduction to the spiritual life review. *Journal of Adult Development, 8*(4), 231–240.

Lord, J., & Hutchison, P. (1993). The process of empowerment: Implications for theory and practice. *Canadian Journal of Community Mental Health, 12*(1), 5–22.

Mabey, J. (2011). Counseling older adults in LGBT communities. *The Professional Counselor: Research and Practice, 1*(1), 57–62.

McBride, R., & Hays, D. (2012). Counselor demographics, ageist attitudes, and multicultural counseling competence among counselors and counselor trainees. *Adultspan Journal, 11*(2), 77–88.

Meara, N., Schmidt, L., & Day, J. (1996). Principles and virtues: A foundation for ethical decisions, policies, and character. *Counseling Psychologist, 24,* 4–74.

Myers, J. (2010). The older persons counseling needs survey. Palo Alto, CA: Mindgarden.

Myers, J. E., & Harper, M. C. (2004). Evidence-based effective practices with older adults. *Journal of Counseling & Development, 82,* 207–218.

Myers, J., & Schwiebert, V. (1996). *Competencies for gerontological counselors*. Alexandria, VA: American Counseling Association.

Owen, J., Tao, K., Leach, M., & Rodolfa, E. (2011). Clients' perceptions of their psychotherapists' multicultural orientation. *Psychotherapy, 48*(3), 254–262.

Pangman, V. V., & Sequire, M. (2000). Seuxality and the chronically ill older adult. A social justice issue. *Sexuality and Disability, 18*(1), 49–59.

Pervin, L., Cervone, D., & Oliver, J. (2005). *Theories of personality* (9th ed.) New Jersey, NJ: John Wiley & Sons.

Raj, A. (2004). Depression in the elderly: Tailoring medical therapy to their special needs. *Postgraduate Medicine Online, 115*(6), 26–42.

Rock, M., Carlson, T., & McGeorge, C. (2010). Does affirmative training matter? Assessing CFT students' beliefs about sexual orientation and their level of affirmative training. *Journal of Marital and Family Therapy, 36*(2), 171–184.

Rodriguez, R., & Walls, E. (2000). Culturally educated questioning: Toward a skills-based approach in multicultural counseling training. *Applied and Preventive Psychology, 9*(2), 89–99.

Serby, M., & Yu, M. (2003). Overview: Depression in the elderly. *Mount Sinai Journal of Medicine, 70*(1), 38–44.

Shearer, N. (2007). Toward a nursing theory of health empowerment in homebound older women. *Journal of Gerontological Nursing, 33*(12), 38–45.

Shirmbeck, P. (2006). Elder issues. [Podcast Recording No. CAS038]. Kent, OH: CounselorAudioSource.net. Retrieved from http://www.counseloraudiosource.net/feeds/cas038.mp3

Stevens-Roseman, E. S., & Leung, P. (2004). Enhancing attitudes, knowledge, and skills of paraprofessional service providers in older care settings. *Gerontology & Geriatrics Education, 25*(1), 73–88.

Tengland, P. (2007). Empowerment: A goal or a means for health promotion? *Medicine, Health Care and Philosophy, 10*(2), 197–207.

Teresi, J., & Abrams, R. (2001). Prevalence of depression and depression recognition in nursing homes. *Social Psychiatry, 36*(12), 613–620.

Tveiten, S., & Meyer, I. (2009). Easier said than done: Empowering dialogues with patients at the pain clinic: The health professional's perspective. *Journal of Nursing Management, 17*(7), 804–812.

U.S. Census Bureau. (2011). 2010 Census Summary File 1: U.S. Census Bureau Projections of the population by race, sex, and Hispanic origin in the United States: 2010–2050 (NP2008-14). Retrieved from http://www.agingstats.gov/main_site/data/2012_Documents/Population.aspx

U.S. Census Bureau. (2012). U.S. Census State and County Quick Facts. Retrieved http://quickfacts.census.gov/qfd/states/00000.html

U.S. Code Online via GPO Access,wais.access.gpo.gov. Laws in effect as of January 7, 2003. Retrieved from http://frwebgate.access.gpc.gov/cgi-bin/getdoc.cgi?dbname = browse_usc&doc.cgi?dbname = browse_usc&docid = Cite:+42USC3001.

van Zuilen, M. H., Rubert, M. P., & Silverman, M. (2001). Medical students' positive and negative misconceptions about the elderly. The impact of training in geriatrics. *Gerontology & Geriatrics Education, 21*(3), 31–40.

Vander Zanden, J., Crandell, T., & Crandell, C. (2007). *Human development: A life-span view* (10th ed.). Boston, MA: McGraw-Hill Education.

Vasquez, M. (2007). Cultural difference and the therapeutic alliance: An evidence-based analysis. *American Psychologist, 62,* 878–885.

West, C. (2005). The map of relational-cultural theory. *Women & Therapy, 28*(3/4), 93–110.

Professional Practice With Goals for Older Adults

"Age is no barrier. It is a limitation you put on your mind."

—Jackie Joyner-Kersee

After reading this chapter, you will be able to

1. Analyze the goals and common approaches of psychosocial interventions
2. Explain the stages of the helping relationship and challenges that may arise
3. Examine common issues that cause clients to seek counseling

INTRODUCTION

The emerging professional practice of gerontological counseling requires highly trained, knowledgeable, and caring practitioners. These practitioners must possess the knowledge, skills, attitudes and behaviors that create an environment that supports the older clients' willingness to divulge intimate life details. A genuine respect and appreciation for older adults and their abilities is a fundamental requirement in initiating dialogue. Counselors must have intangible qualities and a flexibility to perform numerous roles, as well as the ability to work as a member of a multidisciplinary team. Though gerontological counselors are few in number in comparison to other professionals, they are able to provide the interventions to promote and enhance the quality of life for older persons experiencing internal and external challenges.

PSYCHOSOCIAL INTERVENTIONS

An intervention is the introduction of a preventive or therapeutic regimen designed to effect a change in the status of a target individual. It is generally believed that psychosocial interventions recognize the interrelated nature of the physical, psychological, and social dimensions of human behavior and functioning and typically strive to achieve effects in multiple outcome domains. In contrast, many medical interventions (e.g., surgery, pharmacology) are more restricted in their approach and their objectives.

Psychosocial interventions targeted at older adults aim to maintain or enhance their quality of life. Such interventions are commonly an outgrowth of descriptive or correlational research, which has identified factors that significantly impact quality of life and seem to be amenable to change. Psychosocial interventions are increasingly used as an alternative or supplement to surgical or pharmacological approaches because of their general efficacy and relative cost-effectiveness.

Common Goals of Psychosocial Interventions

The vast majority of psychosocial interventions focused on older adults emphasize maintaining or improving physical health, mental health, and social functioning or cognitive functioning, promoting adaptive function, and increasing the likelihood of making healthy life choices that enhance quality of life (Carr, 2009; Sheder, 2010; Wampold, 2010). Of these three goal domains, physical health promotion is the most common, as illustrated by interventions to reduce falls, enhance urinary continence, lower blood pressure, detect prostate cancer, lower cholesterol levels, increase muscle strength, increase peak pulmonary expiration flow rate, increase bone mineral density, enhance self-care behaviors (e.g., medication compliance, exercise), and reduce risky health behaviors (e.g., smoking, alcohol use). Due to the growing number of older adults coping with chronic illnesses that require self-management or that can be prevented to some extent, there are many psychosocial interventions aimed at physical health promotion. From a societal perspective, the ultimate objective of such interventions is to extend the time that the older adult can live independently and thus delay institutionalization.

Guided Practice Exercise 10.1 familiarizes counselors with community services to increase the potential that their older client can remain in their preferred community environments.

Guided Practice Exercise 10.1

Altering the traditional counseling setting is sometimes necessary to reach older potential clients. Many older persons may live in the community but are unable to reach the various mental health centers for services. Visit an older person in his or her home. Assess the individual's needs and strengths to determine the types of services required and what he or she may be willing to accept. This requires the counselor to become familiar with resources in the community, such as Meals-on-Wheels, homemaker services, senior companion and/or phone reassurance services, and other services available in the community. Supportive services will encourage independent living within the community.

Examples of the goals of mental health interventions of older adults include the reduction of anxiety and depressive symptomatology, enhancing sleep quality, and increasing feelings of global or domain-specific satisfaction and perceived control. Some psychosocial interventions are directed at improving quality of life in individuals suffering from or who are at risk for psychiatric illness due to common late-life stressors such as chronic illness, spousal caregiving, and bereavement (refer to Chapters 4–7).

Common goals of psychosocial interventions to support social functioning are enhanced social support, increased recreational or leisure activity, and improved cognitive functioning (e.g., verbal and nonverbal memory, visuospatial ability, overall performance on standardized neuropsychological tests, improved driving skills). Social functioning is important for older adults to live a meaningful life in today's society. It enhances overall well-being, improves self-esteem, encourages the development of meaningful relationships, encourages creative expression, and enhances emotional well-being.

Common Psychosocial Intervention Approaches

Common intervention approaches include behavioral training, physical activity training, peer support for dealing with specific stressors, education, and counseling or psychotherapy (e.g., psychodynamic, cognitive-behavioral, and interpersonal therapies) in an individual or group setting. Educational interventions are perhaps the most general approach, as individuals can be educated on a multitude of issues, such as managing medications, coping with grief, and modifying the home to make it more accessible. In educational interventions, a needs assessment is sometimes conducted with focus groups before developing the intervention content to identify the most important issues faced by the given population.

Because of the high prevalence of physical and psychiatric comorbidity in late life, intervention approaches that treat problems in either of these domains are likely to have effects on both domains. Therefore, multidisciplinary geriatric assessment and treatment programs are becoming more common in health care systems (Devons, 2002; Ward & Reuben, 2015).

There is a history of research on psychosocial interventions aimed at enhancing perceived control, especially with older adults in long-term care settings who have little actual control over their social and physical environment. The increased use of interventions that encourage self-management of health and illness illustrates that there has been a shift toward interventions that focus on the use of various strategies to maintain a sense of control in the face of essentially uncontrollable events.

Other approaches to enhancing quality of life for older adults that are receiving increased attention include reminiscence and life review, preventive health screening, special packaging of medications, pet therapy, music therapy, light therapy, visual stimulation through art, intergenerational programs, adult day care, and cognitive therapy. It is becoming more common to focus on older adults, through changes in their environment, or to focus on multiple individuals simultaneously (e.g., the older adult, informal or formal caregivers, and the physician) during therapeutic interventions.

Psychosocial interventions have been used effectively in the treatment of older adult issues. The ultimate goal of any of the identified psychosocial modalities is to improve the overall well-being of older adults and enhance their quality of life.

STAGES OF THE HELPING RELATIONSHIP

The helping relationship established between the counselor and his or her client is unique. This relationship is built on mutual trust and respect and lays the foundation for all future therapeutic work. Clients are provided with a safe environment to express and explore their innermost thoughts, feelings, fears, and accomplishments. The stages of the helping relationship are similar to counseling other populations; however, the approaches may vary. It remains important to establish rapport, conduct assessments, interview appropriately, set goals, and provide closure. However, unique considerations are required when addressing the needs of older clients. Older clients will vary in their cognitive, physical, social, and functional ability, which require accommodations. Assessment instruments should be those measures normed to older adults. Goal setting will vary due to age-related changes in vision, hearing, cognition, and sight. Environmental adaptations may necessitate wider doors. Counselors will need to examine their feelings and comfort level in discussing delicate issues (i.e., death and dying) with older clients. Therefore, the therapeutic relationship is essential to facilitating the changes required to enhance the well-being and development of older clients.

Creating Therapeutic Relationships

The significance of the therapeutic relationship in effective counseling and psycho-therapy with older adults cannot be overstated. The personal relationship is a key factor in helping older adults. Warren (2001) reports that the relationship between the quality of the patient–therapist relationship and the outcome of treatment has been one of the most consistently cited findings in the empirical search for the basis of psychotherapeutic efficacy with older adults. Writing about the power of the therapeutic relationship, Saleebey (2000) argues that if healers are seen as nonjudgmental, trustworthy, caring, and expert, they have some influential tools at hand, whether they are addressing depression or the disappointments and gains of unemployment. Glicken (2009) identifies the importance of the relationship:

> The relationship is a bond between two strangers. It is formed by an essential trust in the process and a belief that it will lead to change. The counselor's expertise is to facilitate communications, enter into a dialogue with the client about its meaning, and help the client decide the best ways of using the information found in searches for best evidence. (p. 50)

In describing the client-centered approach with older adults, Dacey and Newcomer (2005) report that forming a relationship with the older client requires that we establish rapport, set an agenda for discussion, respect the client's freedom of choice, and by carefully listening to the client, seek to understand and encourage the client to make his or her decisions. Practitioners give advice to their clients as part of the counseling intervention, and this advice should always be given in a nonjudgmental manner.

As practitioners, an understanding of how the client makes sense of his or her world is important. By understanding the client's frame of reference, practitioners are in a better position to facilitate change and life-span development. Being empathic with clients also assists with establishing rapport. If a client does not sense that the counselor understands and appreciates his or her dilemmas, then relationship building is jeopardized. A sensitivity to the tension between the body's physical decline and the simultaneous capacity for growth and maturation is important (Agronin, 2010). Effective listening skills are extremely important, and demonstrating patience to allow clients to express themselves is vital to the interaction. Older clients may need additional time to share their feelings, establish a rapport because traditionally they have underutilized the services of counseling professionals. Establishing rapport is an important initial step in the counseling process, and if this rapport is not established, there exists a strong likelihood that the older adult may not attend future counseling sessions. This is particularly important for counselors working with older adults, given their limited experience with the mental health system and their reluctance to discuss personal issues with outside professionals.

Guided Practice Exercise 10.2 provides experience in establishing rapport through a role-play scenario. The relationship is an essential component of the clients' ability to make progress during treatment sessions.

Guided Practice Exercise 10.2

The goal of this exercise is to establish a rapport with your partner, which is an initial step in relationship bonding. One individual is the speaker, and the other is a listener. Choose a partner unlike yourself in age, gender, and experiences. The speaker relays "who he or she is" to the listener. He or she tells the listener how he or she feels about himself or herself, how he or she feels about the individuals around him or her, and his or her self-views in relation to the important aspects of his or her life. The speaker is practicing self-disclosure and is engaged in personal communications. The listener attempts to accurately repeat what has been conveyed, and the speaker will affirm the accurate remarks. The listener attempts to show concern and respect for the speaker. After 10 minutes, roles are reversed. Once completed, discuss experiences of the exercise and what was learned.

Since therapeutic relationships are the foundation for counseling, there continues to be research on this topic. This allows the development of treatment protocols possible, increasing treatment efficacy, influencing the training of psychotherapists, and providing standard treatment protocols for the purposes of further treatment process research (Warren, 2001).

Therapeutic Relationship and Treatment Outcomes

The adult psychotherapy literature supports the central role of the therapeutic relationship within the psychoanalytic framework, the client is expected to talk freely and be interested in cognitive reflecting on the past as well the current situation (Parsons & Zhang, 2014). American theorists agree on the importance of building a collaborative relationship in which the counselor and client initiate the process of building an egalitarian relationship. Additional phases are investigating the lifestyle, gaining insight, and reorientation (Mosak & Maniacci, 2008; Sweeney, 2009). Existential theory promotes the concept of wellness and living an authentic life (Miars, 2002), and it is developmentally sensitive to life transitions. Central to the practice of existential psychotherapy is the authentic nature of the client–counselor relationship (Parsons & Zhang, 2014). Carl Rogers's client-centered therapy emphasizes the centrality of the relationship between client and therapist as the most important factor in therapy. Rogers (1959) proposed that clients are innately motivated to actualize their potentialities assuming that a psychological climate conducive to growth is provided. The person-centered approach is built on a basic trust in the person (Rogers, 1986) and researchers (Elliott & Freiere, 2010; Wampold, 2001) emphasize the relationship as the factor that makes the greatest contribution to outcome. The Gestalt approach emphasizes that anyone willing to increase his or her awareness can be taught about the cycle of experience and can discover the benefits of increased growth (Melnick & Nevis, 2005). Cognitive-behavioral theories (CBT) principles and constructs are taken from cognitive therapy, which focuses on thoughts, with those of behavioral therapy, which focuses on actions (Parsons & Zhang, 2014). CBT helps clients examine their thinking so they can choose healthy, rational thoughts and beliefs that will result in healthier emotions and behaviors. Behavioral therapists' central assumption is that all behavior, adaptive or maladaptive, is learned. It is therefore believed that maladaptive behavior can be changed through learning (Parsons & Zhang, 2014).

Reality therapy is a present-centered mode of therapy whose goal is to empower clients to take responsibility for their choices as well as learn and implement healthier behaviors and decisions to fulfill universal needs (Scott & Barfield, 2014). Reality therapy is the therapeutic practice based on choice theory (Wubbolding, 2007). Choice theory revolves around the concept of internal control (Glasser, 1998), and other person's reactions and behaviors are simply information that helps us make informed decisions and evaluations about how we behave and what we believe. Solution-focused therapy, rather than focusing on problem formation and resolution, takes an active stance toward helping the client. Solution-focus represents a strengths-based approach in which counselors emphasize the resources their clients possess and how their strengths can be applied to create change (de Shazer, Berg, & Lipchik 1986). Using what clients possess to help them meet their own needs and build satisfactory lives for themselves is a fundamental premise of this approach, and the popularity of this approach lies in its flexibility, collaborative nature, and focus on client strengths (Kim, 2008). Counselors focus on resolving current problems by looking forward rather than backward. The client and counselor work to find solutions with the greatest likelihood of producing change and in co-constructing solutions, clients can find the ones that fit their particular worldview (DeJong & Berg, 2001).

Relational cultural theory (RCT) is guided by the principle that individual growth occurs in and through relationships. The overarching goal of the therapy process is to attain the mutual empowerment that results from increased connection (Miller & Stiver, 1991) and to grow further in relational competence. RCT's emphasis on understanding and evaluating the impact of cultural identity makes it useful for working with diverse cultures and populations. Family systems therapy is used extensively in counseling settings because many clients place great value on their families and need to be considered within the context of the family system for optimal treatment to occur. The family systems approach is beneficial in that it does not place blame for existing problems on either the family or individual members (Corey, 2012). It is understood that each family member and subsystem contributes to overall family dynamics, and no single entity is responsible for all dysfunction within the system.

Many graduate students and early counseling professionals struggle to decide what counseling theories they will use in their counseling sessions. What makes a theory useful to one person and his or her personality will not necessarily be the same for another person. Depending on how to use a specific theory will depend on many factors. The personality and needs of the client, the counselor's personality and knowledge pertaining to a specific theory are just a few of the variables to ponder when choosing a theory (Parsons & Zhang, 2014).

Special Concerns About the Therapeutic Relationship With Older Adults

Despite the strategies and suggestions available for developing a relationship with an older adult, it may not be easy. There are a number of challenges that may be faced in building rapport with members of this population.

Counselors are usually younger than their older adult clients and need to consider how their differences in age and life experience influence the counseling relationship (Myers & Harper, 2004, p. 208). Consequently, more time and sensitivity are required to build rapport with these individuals who may be less comfortable with seeking help, sharing feelings, or asking questions of "authority" figures, particularly in clients who are reluctant to seek help. Younger professionals also need to be prepared to deal nondefensively with older clients who might view them as unable to understand the lived experiences of old age. Older clients may not be familiar with counseling, or they may have problems discussing and dealing with feelings, as is the case with older adults from more traditional cultures and some male clients.

Older persons may view human service workers in the same way they view medical personnel, anticipating that the relationship will be hierarchical and directive, and they may experience some degree of difficulty coping with counselors who ask their opinion or give the client a great deal of personal authority (Myers & Harper, 2004). This can be managed by explaining how the clinician works and why it is so important for the client to have maximum input. Oftentimes, however, older clients are very therapy-savvy, having seen therapy on television and in various films.

Though young-old adults, those aged 65 to 74, tend to have similar concerns as younger persons, the aging process can create complications in treatment planning even for healthy older adults. Physical limitations that affect a client's ability to sit for long periods may require changes in the length of sessions or cognitive or sight impairments may require changes in the assessment process. It may also be wise to focus discussion on a single topic and not let the session flow into other issues, since memory may be impaired and too many subjects may cause confusion.

Other accommodations that may need to be made include lengthening the sessions in individual counseling and increasing the number of sessions for support groups or other group therapy formats, which is more important in reducing relapse for older clients than for younger ones. Psychological treatments should be modified as well. Many traditional counseling approaches can be accommodated to meet the needs of older clients (Gellis & Kenaley, 2008; Kennedy & Tannebaum, 2000).

Client Assessment

The next stage in the helping relationship is assessment. Psychological assessment pervades nearly every aspect of psychotherapeutic work with older people. Thorough evaluation of the psychological status and functioning of an older person is a vitally important but complex process, even for experienced clinicians. The purposes of assessment are to clarify current symptoms and problems, formulate a diagnosis, develop case conceptualization and intervention plans, and evaluate effects of treatment. Some of the major challenges in working with older adults include choosing appropriate tools for the assessment; engaging the right persons in the process; assessing the full range of cognitive, social, functional, and psychological problems; and differentiating disorders from normal aging. Traditional assessment procedures require some modification for older persons. Older adults with less formal education may require a lengthier explanation of any types of assessments administered. For any type of testing (i.e., neuropsychological testing), older adults should be given advanced notice to be prepared with any assistive devices required (i.e., eye glasses, hearing aids). If English is not the native language of the older adults, an interpreter who is bilingual will be needed. While assessments may be given at designated times, flexibility is required for older clients based upon other appointments he or she may have and when they function at their best. Multiple sessions may be required for older clients, especially if they fatigue quickly. Environmental modifications may require wider doors for wheelchair accessibility, enhanced lighting, and positioning client to avoid glare.

Case Illustration 10.1 demonstrates the availability of the counselor to engage with his or her client in a nursing home environment and ascertain appropriate assessments to use in treating a potentially depressed client.

CASE ILLUSTRATION 10.1

A staff member has contacted you (the counselor) to visit a resident who has become withdrawn and complains of lethargy and lack of interest in activities and has a decreased appetite. These behaviors have been observed by the nursing staff for the past 2 weeks. When you visit the resident, she questions her worth, shares that she hopes she doesn't wake up the next morning, and expresses that her family doesn't care about her. As the counselor, how would you interpret her presenting problems? What would your next step be in the process of helping her? Are there assessments or specific appraisals you would use? Is there a need to explore the family dynamics and if so, in what manner?

Clinical Interview

The clinical interview is perhaps the most important and informative strategy during an evaluation of an older person. During the interview, the clinician gathers information about the person's current difficulties, including a history of the problem and attempts at coping. Other topics include an in-depth personal history; mental health history (including interventions); marital, family, social, and work history; and a mental status examination. Collateral interviews with concerned family members or caregivers are a common and very informative component of geriatric assessments.

To facilitate rapport, clinicians should explain clearly the purposes and procedures of the assessment, address any concerns the person may have about the evaluation, and be especially flexible when engaging older persons and their family members. Being generous with warmth, support, and reassurance (when needed) also helps with rapport.

Interviewing older clients requires effective communication, and while effective communication is necessary in counseling all age groups, there are specific recommendations for counselors to enhance their interactions with older clients. Improving interactions with older adults requires recognizing the tendency to stereotype older adults, and it is necessary to conduct an independent assessment and also avoid speech that might be seen as patronizing to an older person (elderspeak) (Williams, Herman, & Gajewski, 2009). Improving face-to-face communication with older adults involves monitoring and controlling nonverbal behavior, minimizing background noise, facing older adults when you speak with them, and paying close attention to sentence structure when conveying critical information. Also use visual aids such as pictures and diagrams to help clarify and reinforce comprehension points and ask open-ended questions and genuinely listen (Duffy, Gordon, & Whelan, 2004; Harwood, 2007; Houts, Doak, & Doak, 2006).

Optimizing interactions between health care professionals and older patients involves many areas. It's important to express understanding and compassion to help older patients manage fear and uncertainty related to the aging process and chronic diseases (Fowler & Nussbaum, 2008). Inquiring regarding an older client's living situation and social contacts is important. When dealing with older adults and their families, remember to always include the older adult in the conversation. Seek information about cultural beliefs and values pertaining to illness and death (Langer, 2008) and engage in shared decision making. The counselor needs to strike an appropriate balance between respecting clients' autonomy and stimulating their active participation in health care (Osborn & Squires, 2012). Avoiding ageist assumptions when providing information and recommendations about preventive care is important (Centers for Disease Control and Prevention [CDC] et al., 2011). Use of direct, concrete, actionable language when talking to older adults, verifying older clients' comprehension, and setting specific goals for client comprehension will enhance the therapeutic encounter (Speer, Reynolds, & Swallow, 2009). Providing quality clinical services is enhanced when the focus remains on the older client. When counseling ethnic minority older clients who are from other cultures, counselors must remember to use humor (which eases tension) and direct communication (preferable in the United States) with caution. This sensitivity to cultural considerations is essential during the counseling process (Pecchioni, Ota, & Sparks, 2004). Providing Internet-savvy older clients with chronic diseases support in locating reputable sources of online support and facilitating collaboration with systems and older clients are also important (Madden, 2010).

Specific recommendations for counselors counseling older adults with dementia involve maintaining a positive communication tone and avoiding speaking slowly to older adults with dementia (Small, Gutman, & Makela, 2003). When communicating with older adults with dementia, simplify sentences and use verbatim repetition or paraphrase sentences to facilitate comprehension in older adults with dementia (Bourgeois, 2002; Savundranayagam, Ryan, & Ana, 2007). Professional counselors provide an unmet need when counseling older clients. Modifications may be required based on the uniqueness of the older client and his or her situation. Specific communication strategies identified will enhance the interview process and potentially facilitate positive outcomes.

The therapeutic relationship is a special bond that exists between the client and the counseling professional. This relationship, if appropriately established, can facilitate the achievement of positive treatment outcomes. However, adaptations or adjustments by the counselor may be required to accommodate the unique needs of older clients.

Comprehensive Geriatric Assessment

Comprehensive geriatric assessment (CGA) is defined as a multidisciplinary diagnostic and treatment process that identifies medical, psychosocial, and functional abilities of an older person in order to develop a coordinated plan to maximize overall health and aging (Devons, 2002). The health care of an older adult extends beyond the traditional medical management of illness. It requires evaluation of multiple issues including physical, cognitive, affective, social, financial, environmental, and spiritual components that influence an older adult's health. CGA is based on the premise that a systematic evaluation of older persons by a team of health professionals may identify a variety of treatable health problems and lead to better health outcomes (Ward & Reuben, 2015). Counselors working with older clients can use this assessment process to identify areas which require intervention for older clients.

Core components of CGA that should be evaluated during the assessment process include functional capacity, fall risk, cognition, mood, polypharmacy, social support, financial concerns, goals of care, and advanced care preferences. Additional components may also include evaluation of nutritional or weight change, urinary continence, sexual function, vision and hearing, dentition, living situation, and spirituality (Ward & Reuben, 2015). Functional status refers to the ability to perform activities necessary or desirable in daily life, and functional status is directly influenced by health conditions, particularly in the context of an elder's environment and social support network. Changes in functional status (e.g., not being able to bathe independently) should prompt further evaluation and intervention. Measurement of functional status can be valuable in monitoring response to treatment and can provide prognostic information that assists in long-term care planning. In addition to measures of activities of daily living (ADLs), gait speed alone has been shown to predict functional decline and early mortality in older adults (Studenski, Perea, & Patel, 2011).

Approximately one-third of community-dwelling persons age 65 years and one-half of those over 80 years of age fall each year (Ward & Reuben, 2015). Persons who have fallen or have a gait or balance problem are at a higher risk of having a subsequent fall and losing independence. An assessment of fall risk should be integrated into the history of all older patients.

The incidence of dementia increases with age, particularly among those over 85 years, yet many patients with cognitive impairment remain undiagnosed (Ward & Reuben, 2015). The value of making an early diagnosis includes the possibility of uncovering treatable conditions. The evaluation of cognitive function can include a thorough history, brief cognition screens, a detailed mental status examination, neuropsychological testing, tests to evaluate medical conditions that may contribute to cognitive impairment (e.g., B12, TSH), depression assessment, and/or radiographic imaging (CT or MRI). It is clear that the extent of assessment and areas of focus of assessment are more extensive for older clients; therefore, counselors must be prepared to make their contributions and make referrals as appropriate.

Depression in the elderly population is a serious health concern leading to unnecessary suffering, impaired functional status, increased mortality, and excessive use of health resources. Depression in the elderly may present atypically and may be masked in patients with cognitive impairment (Arroll, Khin, & Kerse, 2003).

Older people are often prescribed multiple medications by different health care providers, putting them at increased risk for drug-drug interactions and adverse drug events. The counselor should review the patient's medications at each visit. The best method of detecting potential problems with polypharmacy is to have patients bring in all of his or her medications (prescription and nonprescription) in their bottles. Elderly patients should also be asked about alternative therapy (Ward & Reuben, 2015).

The existence of a strong social support network in an elder's life can frequently be the determining factor of whether the client can remain at home or needs placement in an institution. A brief screen of social support includes taking a social history and determining who would be available to the elder to help if he or she becomes ill. Early identification of problems with social support can help planning and timely development of resource referrals. For clients with functional impairment, the counselor should ascertain who the person has available to help with activities of daily living. Caregivers might experience symptoms of depression or caregiver burnout and need referral for counseling or support groups. Elder mistreatment should be considered in any geriatric assessment particularly if the client presents with contusions, burns, bite marks, genital or rectal trauma, pressure ulcers, or malnutrition with no clinical explanation (Ward & Reuben, 2015). The financial situation of a functionally impaired older adult is important to assess, and also elders may qualify for state or local benefits, depending upon their income; therefore, counselors may be asked to assist with securing benefits on behalf of their older clients.

The primary goal of the comprehensive geriatric assessment is promoting wellness and independence. A client's goals in sessions are often positive (e.g., regaining something lost, attending a future event). Frequently, social (e.g., living at home, maintaining social activities) and functional (e.g., completing activities of daily living without help) goals assume priority over health-related goals (e.g., survival) (Reuben & Trinetti, 2012).

Counselors should begin discussions with older clients about preferences for specific treatments while the client still has the cognitive capacity to make these decisions. Clearly timing of this discussion is important because a positive, trusting relationship must be firmly established prior to discussing sensitive issues regarding advanced care planning. These discussions should include choosing an appropriate decision-maker (i.e., appointing a durable power of attorney, also known as a health care proxy, to serve as a surrogate in the event of personal incapacity), clarifying and articulating clients' values over time, and thinking about factors other than the clients' stated preferences in surrogate decision-making (Sudore & Fried, 2010).

Unique Challenges for Assessment

A key issue in assessments of older adults is to select tests that possess evidence of reliability and validity with older adults and furnish age-appropriate norms. Tests developed specifically for older adults, such as the Geriatric Depression Scale, have excellent norms. Likewise, standard intelligence tests now have extensive age norms. Many other psychological and neuropsychological tests did not initially furnish norms for older adults, but researchers have since provided norms for them. However, some psychological tests are still inadequately normed by age or by other relevant characteristics (e.g., gender, ethnicity) for older adults. The Beck Anxiety Scale is brief and easily administered, but results should be viewed with caution in the assessment of frail and less educated older adults. The Rorschach Inkblot Test should only be used with caution in assessing the personality or disordered thinking of older adults, because age-related norms have not been established for the widely used system and psychopathology can easily be over diagnosed by inexperienced examiners testing older adults who are uncomfortable with unstructured tasks. Clinicians and researchers are encouraged to review carefully the technical manual of tests they use to determine if evidence of reliability, validity, and relevant norms for older persons is available. If not, they should be cautious in interpreting scores.

All psychosocial data must be viewed within the context of physical health. Information about medical illnesses is important because many problems, such as thyroid dysfunction, multiple sclerosis, and hypoglycemia, can cause psychiatric conditions (American Psychiatric Association, 2000). Likewise, many medications commonly taken by older adults can cause psychological symptoms. For example, some antihypertensive drugs can induce depressive symptoms, and some analgesics and anticonvulsants can cause anxiety symptoms (American Psychiatric Association, 2000).

Lyness (2004) advises medical and counseling professionals who work with an older population to screen routinely for depression and other mental health issues because mental health concerns can be the underlying cause of many other presenting problems. Due to age-related increases in the frequency of many chronic medical conditions, older adults consume a large amount of prescribed and over-the-counter medications. With increased medication use, older persons are at increased risk for adverse drug effects because of harmful drug interactions and the buildup of medication in the aging body. Diverse drug interactions can cause memory problems that mimic a dementing illness such as Alzheimer's disease. Older adults are encouraged to bring a complete list of medications to the evaluation. It is wise practice to request that the client sign a release as well, so the clinician can communicate with the client's medical providers. Referral for a thorough medical workup is always indicated if the client has not recently been medically evaluated.

Sensory impairments (e.g., hearing and vision) that are also common among older adults complicate assessment. Difficulties perceiving instructions or testing stimuli can have obvious adverse effects on performance. Sensory deterioration is considered a primary cause of reduced performance on cognitive tasks, and even for certain psychiatric disorders such as late-onset paranoia. Physical disabilities similarly complicate assessment by limiting response options (e.g., hand movement or writing, constraining reaction time on speeded tasks), limiting access to test stimuli (e.g., standing to engage in a balance task), or limiting stamina for long evaluation sessions procedures. To ensure the person performs optimally, the environment should be adjusted to reduce the impact of any sensory or physical limitations (e.g., brightly lit testing room, minimal background noise, use of large print versions of tests, multiple short sessions, frequent breaks).

Geriatric Assessment Measures

Table 10.1 identifies selected measurements used in assessing older adults that have been normed for older persons.

The Geriatric Depression Scale consists of a 15-item screening tool for depression in older adults (Sheikh & Yesavage, 1986). Each depressive positive answer receives a one, with a score of 10 or higher indicative of the possibility of depression.

The Mini-Mental State Exam (MMSE) consists of 11 questions that test five areas of cognitive functioning: orientation, registration, attention and calculation, recall, and language (Folstein, Folstein, & McHugh, 1975). The maximum score is 30 (all answers correct) and a score below 23 indicates potential cognitive impairment.

The Clock-Drawing Test (CDT) is a quick assessment of cognitive function that is easy to administer and score in the clinical setting. There are multiple ways to score this test;

Table 10.1 Selected Geriatric Assessment Measures

Measure	Instrument
Depression	Geriatric Depression Scale (GDS)
Cognition	Mini-Mental State Examination (MMSE)
Dementia and Delirium	Clock-Drawing Test (CDT) Confusion Assessment Method (CAM)
Functional/Instrumental Activities of Daily Living (ADLs)	Index of Independence of Daily Living (Katz Index of ADL) Instrumental Activities of Daily Living (IADL) Palliative Performance Scale (PPS)
Caregiver Burden	Burden Interview
Nutrition	Mini Nutrition Assessment (MNA) Nutritional Health Assessment
Alcohol	Short Michigan Alcohol Screening Test (Geriatric Version) (SMAST-G)
Sexuality	PLISSIT Model
Life Strengths	Sources of Life Strengths Measure (SLSAS)

however, the method provided is a 6-point scale from Shulman, Gold, Cohen, and Zucchero (1993). The CDT is often given in conjunction with the Mini-Mental State Examination (MMSE), as the CDT detects impairments in visuoconstructional and executive function, while the MMSE shows orientation, memory, and language functions. Because of the CDT's focus on visuoconstructive ability and cognitive function, it may be more useful than the MMSE in detecting dementia in its early stages. The CDT can be used as a quick assessment for dementia in clinical settings (Kirby, Denihan, & Bruce, 2001; Richardson & Glass, 2002; Shulman et al., 1993).

The Confusion Assessment Method (CAM) assesses for the presence of delirium and was created specifically for clinicians without psychiatric training to use with older patients. It was designed for use in various clinical settings such as in making observations during routine clinical care. The CAM is a simple assessment that can be completed in less than 5 minutes (Inouye et al., 1990).

The Time and Change Test (T&C) was developed as a simple measure for detecting dementia in older patients. It has been used in both hospital and outpatient settings. The T&C Test is easy to use, quick to administer, and highly acceptable to patients. In addition, it has been demonstrated to be useful with ethnically diverse patients across educational levels (Froehlich, Robison, & Inouye, 1998; Inouye, Robinson, Froehlich, & Richardson, 1998).

Measures of function are valuable indicators of the changes experienced by aging and chronically ill patients. The Index of Independence in Activities of Daily Living (Katz Index of ADL) was developed to evaluate changes in these populations, assessing a patient's overall performance of six self-care functions: bathing, dressing, toileting, transferring, continence, and feeding. It can be used to assess the need for care as well as the progression of illness and the effectiveness of treatment and rehabilitation. The Katz Index of ADL has been used in many settings, including clinical practice, nursing homes, and rehabilitation settings (Katz, Downs, Cash, & Grotz, 1970).

The Instrumental Activities of Daily Living (IADL) scale measures eight complex activities related to independent functioning, objectively evaluating a patient's ability to perform the functions and assessing how much assistance he or she requires for each activity, if any. The more these abilities are impaired, the more services will be necessary to maintain a person in the community. The Instrumental Activities of Daily Living (IADL) scale is a brief tool that aids in the formulation, implementation, and evaluation of treatment plans. It is useful in elderly community populations and provides information about a patient's need for support services. It can be completed by obtaining the requested information from either the patient or an informant, such as a family member or other caregiver (Cromwell, Eagar, & Poulos, 2003; Lawton, 1971; Lawton & Brody, 1969; Polisher Research Institute, 2005).

The Palliative Performance Scale (PPS) (Anderson, Downing, & Hill, 1996) was designed to assess the physical and functional status of patients receiving palliative care. It has been used to evaluate progression of disease, symptom management and other care needs, prognosis, and the timing of hospice referral. Scores are given in 10-point increments, ranging from 0 (death) to 100 (full or normal, no disease). Five categories of function are scored, and lower scores indicate greater functional impairment (Moody & McMillan, 2003; Virik & Glare, 2002; Wilner & Arnold, 2004).

The Burden Interview has been specifically designed to reflect the stresses experienced by caregivers of dementia patients. It can be completed by caregivers themselves or as part of an interview. Caregivers are asked to respond to a series of 22 questions about the impact of the patient's abilities on their life. For each item, caregivers are to indicate how often they felt that way (never, rarely, sometimes, quite frequently, or nearly always). The Burden Interview is scored by adding the numbered responses of the individual items, and higher scores indicate greater caregiver stress. Estimates of the degree of burden can be made from the following: little or no burden (0–20), mild to moderate burden (21–40), moderate to severe burden (41–60), and severe burden (61–88). The screening is used to determine if the caregiver needs additional help or respite and to monitor the quality of caregiving (Brown, Potter, & Foster, 1990; Council on Scientific Affairs, American Medical Association, 1993; Cummings, Frank, & Cherry, 2007; Rankin, Haut, Keefover, & Franzen, 1994; Zarit, Reever, & Bach-Peterson 1980).

The Mini Nutritional Assessment (MNA) is a screening tool which is an abbreviated version of the longer version (DETERMINE Checklist) (Nutrition Screening Initiative, 1991). The short version consists of seven questions, and five of the seven questions address mobility, weight loss, food intake, psychological stress, and the presence of neuropsychological problems, such as dementia and depression. The other two questions require objective data in the form of body mass index (BMI) and calf circumference (Bernstein & Munoz, 2016). The benefits of the MNA are that it is designed specifically for older adults; its short form takes less than 5 minutes to administer; it takes into account items such as mobility, depression, and dementia; and finally, it is available in several languages.

The Nutritional Health Assessment (NHA) is a screening tool that is both a patient education tool and a quick, convenient means to identify patients who have risk factors for poor nutritional status. The assessment is a brief, 10-statement form that is completed by the individual and returned to his or her clinician (Nutrition Screening Initiative, 2007).

The Short Michigan Alcohol Screening Test (Geriatric Version) (SMAST-G) is a 10-question screening test for potential alcohol problems in older adults (Blow, 1991). Two or more yes answers warrants further assessment of drinking behavior.

Sexuality assessment for older adults can be conducted with the PLISSIT model, which can assess and manage the sexuality of adults (Annon, 1976). The model includes suggestions for initiating and maintaining the discussion of sexuality with older adults. The PLISSIT model stands for: P—obtaining permission from the client to initiate sexual discussion, LI—providing the limited information needed to function sexually, SS—giving specific suggestions for the individual to proceed with sexual relations, and finally IT—providing intensive therapy surrounding the issues of sexuality for that client. Questions to guide assessment among older adults include: Can you tell me how you express your sexuality? What concerns or questions do you have about fulfilling your continuing sexual needs? In what ways has your sexual relationship with your partner changed as you have aged? What interventions or information can I provide to help you to fulfill your sexuality? (Wallace, 2000).

The older adults' appraisal of their life strengths are at the very basis of older adults' identity development and contribute significantly to their perceptions of empowerment (Aspinwall & Staudinger, 2003; Seligman & Csikszentmihalyi, 2000). The life strengths perspective recognizes that even in the most difficult circumstances, there is reciprocity between older adults' personally constricted views of reality and their social environment (Schlegel & Hicks, 2011; Ungar, 2012). The Sources of Life Strengths Appraisal Scale (SLSAS) consists of nine scaled appraisal measures and is a promising instrument for appraising older adults' sources of life strengths in dealing with stresses of daily life's functioning, and it is a robust measure for predicting outcomes of resiliency, autonomy, and well-being. It is brief, simple, and easy to administer (Fry & Debats, 2014).

Counseling older clients requires a comprehensive approach to examination and identification of strengths, issues, supports, and coping mechanisms. The clinical interview and environment accommodations are essential to this process. Numerous age-appropriate assessment measures have been developed and are useful in the counseling process.

Goal Setting

Counselors and their clients work jointly in devising counseling plans that offer reasonable promise of success and are consistent with the abilities, temperament, developmental level, and circumstances of clients. Counselors and clients regularly review and revise counseling plans to assess their continued viability and effectiveness, respecting clients' freedom of choice (American Counseling Association, 2014). If no agreement can be reached, the counselor should consider referring the client to another professional, rather than continuing a relationship in which a problem exists.

Defining a client's problem is very similar to reflecting content. It requires listening for the central issue to emerge from the elderly client's communications. Many times, however, the older client has multiple problems. Often his or her problem is so complex that many issues and problems arise during the course of discussion. When this occurs, divide the problem into manageable components and ask the client which of those components he or she would like to discuss first. When one problematic situation has been discussed and defined, the counselor and client can move into the next step—clarifying the issues involved in the problem.

Issues may accompany problems, and solutions can become more difficult and complicated. If people's problems were always simple and clear, they would rarely need the help of counselors to solve them. However, once the client's problem has been identified, setting a goal can be a simple matter. Common goals seen in working with older adults include alleviating depressive symptoms; decreasing feelings of anxiety; alleviating pain; improving memory, communication, and sleep patterns; adjusting to the aging process, retirement, and widowhood; decreasing relocation trauma; alleviating guilt over issues of neglect; decreasing perceived caregiver burden; improving functional ability; managing health conditions; navigating the aging network of services; re-entry into the workforce post retirement; engagement in meaningful leisure activities; improving issues related to intimacy; and decreasing pharmacological and substance abuse problems. Goals should be concrete, specific, and easily attainable for clients to feel a sense of accomplishment. Goals should be developed collaboratively between the counselor and the older client. Family members are encouraged to participate in this goal-setting process to reinforce their loved one, and to assist in monitoring their progress. The counselor can turn the problem around and make its solution the goal of the counseling session.

Goal setting is a very important component of the counseling process. Goals are mutually established between the counselor and the client. Goals are specific and worked on in a stepwise succession, and once one goal is achieved, another goal is accomplished.

Intervention and Evaluation

Once the counselor and client have examined the problem and formulated a counseling goal, the next step is to create alternatives, or the steps the client may take to achieve the goal. The counselor may help a client create a method for alternatives by stating the counseling goal and asking the client to list all the possible ways (alternatives) he or she can think of to achieve that goal. After the client has exhausted his or her list of possible alternatives, the counselor can add alternatives that the client omitted. It is preferable to make a written list of the alternatives. One method for examining alternatives is to state the alternative, list positive and negative consequences, and discuss them in depth with the client.

Interventions will be used and will vary based upon the individual client goals. An evaluation of these interventions is required to ensure that the intervention is appropriate for accomplishing client goals. However, interventions will be adjusted if they are observed to be ineffective. The primary goal is for the client to feel a sense of accomplishment, improve his or her self-perceptions, and ultimately enhance his or her physical and emotional well-being.

Termination and Providing Closure

The final stage, termination, involves providing closure and ending the counseling relationship. This stage occurs after the counseling goals have been achieved. Some counseling relationships are short-lived. Many clients have simple, unidimensional problems they wish to explore. Once they explore their problems, they make a decision and do not return for further counseling. It is not unknown for clients to receive the help they require in one session. However, most counseling relationships last for many sessions (McDonald & Haney, 1988).

Ending the counseling relationship is not the same as ending a business partnership. The client has let the counselor into his or her most personal world. It is for that reason that the counselor is a special person to him or her. Counselors terminate a counseling relationship when it becomes reasonably apparent that the client no longer needs assistance, is not likely to benefit, or is being harmed by continued counseling. Counselors may terminate counseling when in jeopardy of harm by the client or by another party with whom the client has a relationship, or when clients do not pay fees as agreed upon. Counselors provide predetermination counseling and recommend other service providers when necessary (ACA, 2014). It may happen that while exploring one problem, several more emerge. The older client may wish to continue the counseling relationship in order to explore the other problems. If the counselor feels that this is beneficial and if he or she wishes to continue, then new goals are defined and the relationship continues. If it happens that the counseling goals are accomplished and both client and counselor agree to terminate the relationship, then the counseling moves into the stage of closure (Parsons & Zhang, 2014).

A guide for the closure process might include tying up loose ends if there is unfinished business. Being sensitive to the feeling of the client about ending the relationship, therefore timing is important. Careful consideration must be given in ending a close relationship that always involves a sense of loss. Referral may be necessary when you feel you have gone as far with a client as is necessary to accomplish the goal(s). Some clients may not appear for a final session, therefore you attempt to reach the client, however without a positive outcome. Speaking with a supervisor and/or professional colleague would be beneficial to process the dynamics of closure with his or her client. After you have terminated a client, it is a thoughtful gesture to follow-up to see how he or she is doing. This thoughtfulness on your part is an indication of your caring.

Providing closure or terminating a client is a delicate process. The counselor and client have engaged in a meaningful relationship that must come to an end. When goals have been attained, there is a sense of accomplishment, however sadness due to a relationship coming to an end.

Alternative Counseling Approach

No particular counseling approach is mandated in working with older clients, therefore counselors choose the approach that best fits their style and their client's needs. Counselors working with older clients help them to adjust successfully to new stages of life. Blando (2011) focuses on the main stages of treatment and allows counselors to alleviate fears and show clients what opportunities await them in old age. Stage 1 is the beginning phase in which the counselor establishes a relationship with the client, identifying their needs and developing an initial analysis and focus for future sessions. For example, an older man might enter the counselor's office reporting feelings of loneliness and boredom. In initial discussions with the man, the counselor might discover these feelings began shortly after he retired from his career. After clearly identifying the source of the client's problem, the gerontological counselor then begins to introduce ideas and solutions. In the case of loneliness stemming from career loss, the counselor might present community resources that allow the client to return to work in some capacity (Blando, 2011).

In Stage 2, Blando (2011) discussed that returning to work for many older adults seems daunting, especially since they had looked forward to retirement. To assist the older gentleman decide on a new plan of action, his counselor might engage in a "pro/con" exercise with him. A pro/con exercise is either a verbal or written exercise that measures the negatives and positives of two options. For example, when constructing a pro/con list about returning to work, a pro might be feelings of accomplishment and self-worth, while a con might be loss of free time. The older adult would continue to add to the list, considering all changes that a return to work might bring to his life.

The final stage of counseling involves reaching a conclusion and acting on it (Blando, 2011). After weighing the pros and cons, the gentleman might reach the conclusion that coming out of retirement isn't the best choice. Unfortunately, this conclusion doesn't solve his initial problem of loneliness, requiring the counselor to consider additional options. For example, while the older client doesn't wish to follow a set work schedule that takes away his free time, many volunteer opportunities exist for older adults. Contacting various senior centers and volunteer groups, his counselor would connect him with organizations in the community, giving him a new sense of purpose, while allowing him to remain flexible with his time. While meeting with clients on an individual basis might increase their personal happiness, gerontological counselors also hope to increase the well-being of older adults on a much wider scale. By reaching out to leaders in the community and beyond, gerontological counselors enact societal changes that have far reaching effects beyond individual counseling sessions.

Counselors working with older clients will approach their concerns on individual, group, family, and community levels. While the encounter may be initiated on an individual basis, at some point during sessions, different modalities that extend beyond the client may be required. Counselors will provide advocacy on behalf of their clients to internal and external systems, link older clients to community organizations, provide resources for their use, consult (as needed) on aging and mental health issues, empower older clients to assert themselves in challenging dilemmas, and educate older clients, family members, and community systems to better serve their older clients. The overall goal in the counselor–client relationship is for the client to leave counseling feeling a sense of accomplishment that has a positive impact on personal well-being.

ISSUES BROUGHT TO THE HELPING RELATIONSHIP

There are several reasons why older clients might seek counseling. Such reasons can include temporary crisis, long-term problems, normal and abnormal transitions, and internal needs. Temporary and long-term problems might include incidences of chronic illnesses or many other biological events. Along with these events are the possibilities of great emotional impacts. Poor sight and, especially, deafness can have negative effects on the client. Both of these physiological impairments can affect the individual's social life. In turn, experiences of isolation or loneliness may prevail. Even in a nursing home, where the older adult's basic needs of food, warmth, and shelter are usually met, the need for safety, broadly defined, is not always satisfied.

Guided Practice Exercise 10.3 provides the opportunity to facilitate a cultural shift in a nursing home that will be beneficial to the staff and older residents.

Guided Practice Exercise 10.3

Residing in a residential setting that limits ones autonomy can be devastating for older persons accustomed to maintaining their independence. Counselors may need to intervene with professionals and paraprofessionals to facilitate culture change that is mutually beneficial for older persons and staff alike. Changing attitudes and ways of communication is essential. Hold a meeting with staff and explore feelings that staff have toward older patients in their setting. Then, examine how patients and family members feel as well. The counselor will collect all of the information and develop a plan to facilitate the cultural shift.

Long-term problems can affect the independence of older persons, as well as their ability to cope with other life changes and transitions. They may feel angry at the body that betrayed them and angry at the society that ignores and strips them of their power and status. Much of this anger may be disguised by depression or other somatic symptoms (Boyd & Bee, 2006). Some estimates of major depression in older people living in the community range from less than 1% to about 5% but rise to 13.5% in those who require home healthcare and to 11.5% in older hospital patients (CDC, 2015).

An abrupt termination of a person's interests and occupation, unless handled carefully, can have disastrous personal effects. The experience of being unwanted, and the loss of incentive and opportunities to continue one's accustomed work may precipitate a restlessness that could lead to depression. Someone who begins retirement at 65, although eagerly anticipating the leisure time, may face lifestyle changes that require a high degree of adjustability. The effects of these lifestyle changes may include a sense of isolation; a lack of focus, productivity, or place in the social structure of society; decreased income; and a lack of stature or status (Serby & Yu, 2003).

Many of the transitions, along with acute and chronic problems, may challenge the very livelihood of older persons. Many mourn the death of significant others and fail to make new contacts and relationships (Kraaij & Garnefski, 2002). Parents and spouses may be long or recently passed on, children may be grown with households of their own, and family members may be great distances away. In addition, retirement from work, loss of prestige, decline of motor and sensory functions, increased loneliness, and increasing physical disabilities may make it difficult for some persons to cope with even the most elementary physical demands of life.

There are a number of population groups vulnerable to social isolation and loneliness, and older adults (as individuals as well as caregivers) have specific vulnerabilities owing to loss of friends, family, loss of mobility or loss of income (Age U.K. Oxfordshire, 2011). Social isolation and loneliness impact quality of life and well-being (Cattan, 2005; Findlay, 2003; Pitkala, 2009), with demonstrable negative health effects (Masi, 2011). Loneliness is associated with depression (either as a cause or a consequence) and higher rates of mortality (Greaves & Farhus, 2006; Mead, 2010; Pitkala, 2009). Negative impact on individuals' health leads to higher health and social service use, while lonely and socially isolated individuals are more likely to have early admission to residential or nursing care (Ollonqvist, 2008; Pitkala, 2009; Savikko, 2010). Counseling interventions used to reduce social isolation or loneliness include one-to-one interventions, group services and wider community engagement (Age U.K. Oxfordshire, 2011; Cattan, 2005; Findlay, 2003). Assisting clients in re-engaging in meaningful social activities and involvement in familial activities will improve their quality of life, while it decreases the isolation and loneliness that lead to negative mental and physical health outcomes. As a defense, they become ego-centered and take refuge in the past. In order to not be seen as incapable or disabled, older persons may withdraw from social engagements and involvement. Similarly, because of social labeling, the effects of ageism, and learned helplessness, older persons may refrain from complaining about their lives. For example, they might refrain from making use of a suicide-prevention telephone center because they do not expect to be saved. In addition, older persons might not talk in depth about their concerns with their physician, as they may assume the physician may not have time to listen to an older person anyway. Approximately 15% of adults aged 60 and over suffer from a mental disorder (WHO, 2015), but this number may be low because older adults tend to underreport behavioral health symptoms.

The topics or themes that are likely to emerge in therapy with older clients are numerous (Frazer, Hinrichson, & Jongsma, 2011). Issues may include issues faced by other age groups and those unique to older adults in the later stage of development. Issues that may emerge include decline in activities of daily living, health issues, which decreases functional ability, anxiety, caregiver distress, communication deficits, decision-making capacity/incapacity, depression, disruptive behaviors of dementia, elder abuse and neglect, falls, unresolved grief and loss, interpersonal disputes, life role transitions, loneliness/isolation, medication issues, memory impairment, nutritional deficits, environmental issues, sexual issues and related disorders, sleep disturbance, emotional distress, substance abuse, employment, leisure, widowhood, volunteerism, retirement, and suicidal ideation (Frazer et al., 2011). Selected issues will be discussed, and Chapters 1–8 highlighted the significance of the extensive list of concerns mentioned above.

Health Concerns

The focus of treatment with some older clients is often on health concerns and this may take different forms. Time is spent on gathering information, explaining, and clarifying. Sometimes the counselor may need to assist the physician who needs help understanding the symptoms the client is presenting and sometimes the client needs help to understand what the physician is recommending. A counselor who has taken on a consulting role with clients will review the physician's recommendations with the client and help the client examine his or her choices. If a client is confused about what the doctor said, consulting with the physician and reviewing a copy of the medical records with the client may take place.

Generally, older clients present themselves as having difficulties being straightforward and identifying which complaints are important. Therefore, clinicians may teach clients strategies to communicate with their doctors. Physicians have been trained to listen for certain types of information; when they do not hear that information or receive too many complaints or digressions, they may not be able to determine the root of the medical issue. Instructing clients on how to present their problems effectively is helpful (Zarit & Zarit, 2011).

Guided Practice Exercise 10.4 allows the counselor to teach the older client how to communicate effectively with his or her physician. This will be accomplished by tasks which will lead to successful accomplishments.

Guided Practice Exercise 10.4

Some older persons may question their self-worth when faced with many of life's challenges. They may lose confidence in themselves and their abilities, leading to decreased self-esteem. They may need help with tasks such as communicating their concerns to their physician. As the counselor, you are to design a series of successful experiences for the client. Keep the ideas manageable and simplistic enough to lead to a success outcome. Identify the tasks and use a simple checklist to record and monitor progress. Once accomplished, review this list with your client in the next session.

Whether illness contributes in a primary or secondary way to psychological distress, psychotherapy can be an effective component of treatment. The emotional consequences of illness and the limitations that the illness has placed on daily life are addressed. Sometimes depression is a barrier to seeking treatment or rehabilitation opportunities that may be helpful. When a problem is not reversible or is life threatening, therapists can help clients sort through the variety of practical decisions they are facing and come to terms with the situation (Zarit & Zarit, 2011).

Acute and chronic illnesses come into play in a direct way. Some clients invariably experience an unexpected illness, such as a heart attack or stroke. The therapist needs to be able to deal with clients' health changes, conveying support during the acute phase of their illness and then helping them maximize their potential for recovery. Therapists working with older people need to be comfortable talking about illness and disability and dealing with problems that sometimes cannot be changed.

Some clients talk excessively about somatic symptoms. It is important to listen to these complaints; however, one needs to find out whether something psychological is leading a client to be so focused on a somatic symptom or whether there might be an authentic health condition. Interestingly, many somaticizing older clients do not think of themselves as frail or vulnerable. Rather, they are not good at identifying which complaints are important. When treating older clients with serious illnesses or disabilities, clinicians sometimes focus on how they would feel in that kind of situation. They may identify the situation as hopeless or overwhelming and so might fail to recognize what the client might be feeling or whether there are realistic alternatives to managing the problem. Learning about the illness and the treatment possibilities, however, can contribute to effective psychotherapeutic interventions (Zarit & Zarit, 2011).

DEALING WITH UNCERTAINTY

Another difference with older clients is the amount of time they dwell on possible risks, or uncertainties. This preoccupation is often found when people do not have many activities or a lot of other things that they are thinking about. They focus on the one event far into the future and worry about all the possible things that can go wrong along the way leading up to that event. As an example, an older woman is planning to move from her house to a condominium because it will be easier for her to manage. Although she wants to make the move, she is spinning a series of "what ifs," in which everything starts to go wrong; for example, her house does not sell soon enough or sells too soon, or she will have difficulty getting movers to deliver her things when she needs them. As a result, she dwells on the thought that the move will turn out badly.

Cognitive interventions for uncertainties are generally possible. Continuing with the example of moving, the therapist can begin by suggesting that it is not possible to solve hypothetical problems that might arise in the future. There are too many unknowns that will come up—for example, when the client's house will sell—before the situation reaches the bad outcome that she is imagining. Instead, the therapist would encourage her to focus on the next steps (e.g., getting the house ready to show to prospective buyers) and not worry about a hypothetical outcome. Taking care of the next steps will create a feeling of being in control and make a positive outcome more likely. Cognitive-behavioral therapy is a highly structured and interactive form of psychotherapy and a relatively short-term treatment that can be administered effectively while the patient and counselor work together to identify and achieve concrete goals for therapy (Chand & Grossberg, 2013; Cox & D'Oyley, 2011). This type of therapy will help the older client identify their automatic thought pattern, and patients are then encouraged to examine the accuracy and usefulness of their thoughts. For example, an exercise might include a thought record in which the patient notes the details of the situation that led to the unpleasant or unwanted emotional reaction itself. The patient then identifies the thinking that might have led to that emotional reaction and examines whether the thought is accurate, appropriate for the context, or useful (Cox & D'Oyley, 2011). In other words, it is possible to help people differentiate between immediate risks that they need to do something about now and far-off risks that are hard to plan for because many other things have to happen along the way to reach that point (Zarit & Zarit, 2011).

Many older people are concerned about what would happen to them if they fell or needed help for other types of emergencies. People who already have lost some functioning are particularly concerned about what will happen to them if they decline further. Probably the biggest "what if" is the fear of going into a nursing home. Finding ways of controlling what might happen reduces feelings of helplessness.

Older clients may express concerns regarding their health, which is interfering with their ability to live independently and causes them distress. Many clients will be preoccupied and may overly focus on one issue to the exclusion of others. It remains the responsibility of the counselor to work constructively with older clients to decrease their anxiety and empower them to manage their health issues to increase their autonomy.

Relationship Issues and Sexuality

Though old age is often a time of losses, it is also a period in life when important relationships continue or even when new relationships form. Older clients may be concerned about resolving problems in a longstanding relationship or developing new relationships. They may want to address conflict with a spouse or child, or they may seek help for family strains that have emerged as the result of recent life changes.

Langer (2009) reported that the greater sexual freedom found among baby boomers encourages an emphasis on maintaining sexual activity throughout the life span, and Jacoby (2005) reported that this generation of older adults is revolutionizing sexuality by focusing on overcoming the physical limitations that accompany age. Although the majority of older adults are engaged in spousal or other intimate relationships and regard sexuality as an important part of life (Langer, 2009), negative stereotypes abound in American culture influencing how older adults are perceived by others and how they perceive themselves (Lindau et al., 2007; Watters & Boyd, 2009). Mental health counselors have a responsibility to acknowledge the stereotypes and validate older adults' experiences, but they must also be able to give them accurate information about normative development so that older adults can base their self-assessments on facts rather than myths or unrealistic expectations (Watters & Boyd, 2009).

Besides fulfilling our responsibility to acknowledge all aspects of older clients' cultural identities, it is essential to consider older adults' needs and desires in all areas of functioning:

physical, emotional, and social or interpersonal. An often overlooked area for older adults is sexuality. Counseling can be used to promote healthy sexuality and sexual expression among older adults and especially among members of ethnic or sexual minority groups because sexual thoughts, feelings, and activity are a vital part of the human experience (Langer, 2009; Muzacz & Akinsulure-Smith, 2013; Watters & Boyd, 2009). The desire to express oneself sexually does not decrease with age (Langer, 2009; Watters & Boyd, 2009). Sexuality in its psychological and social aspects can be a means of communicating intimacy, affection, and esteem (DeLamater & Sill, 2005; Watters & Boyd, 2009).

Sexuality and sexual feelings are not frequently part of treatment, but therapists need to be aware that they can emerge as an important issue. Clinicians can also help their older clients with this issue in a number of ways and must convey acceptance of a discussion of sexual feelings. Because of stereotypes about sexuality and aging, some older people believe that they should not have or discuss these feelings. Therapists must help older clients feel comfortable talking about these issues. They also need to be aware of generational differences in sexual beliefs and practices and the degree of comfort different people have in talking about their sexuality.

Case Illustration 10.2 demonstrates sexual activity on the part of one spouse upsetting the comfortable relationship that has endured for years. The counselor will be challenged to avoid taking sides and show empathy to both parties, while helping them to resolve their intimacy dilemma.

CASE ILLUSTRATION 10.2

Mr. and Mrs. Dennis have been married for 45 years and have become comfortable with their current living arrangement. Mr. Dennis snores, so he sleeps in the bedroom adjacent to his wife. However, recently Mr. Dennis has been much more attentive to his wife and expects her to engage in sexual intercourse several times per week. For the past 10 years, they have enjoyed intimacy, but it did not include direct sexual intercourse. Mrs. Dennis is not interested in sex but does not want her husband to engage in an extramarital affair that would emotionally destroy their relationship. She learned recently that he had a prescription for Viagra and now she understands his sudden interest. She is hoping that you (their counselor) can help her husband realize the ridiculousness of his newfound sexual interest. She also wants you to convince him to get rid of "those pills."

As with other problems of aging, sexual difficulties may have their origins in illnesses and/or medications, as well as in the normal processes of aging (Agronin, 2004). The starting point for treatment is a careful medical assessment to determine the extent to which illness and medication may contribute to sexual difficulties. When obvious physiological factors do not play a major role in sexual difficulties, sex therapy techniques that have proven effective with younger clients can be used with older clients. These techniques include the use of specific procedures and exercises to improve functioning, as well as helping clients recognize and adjust to changes that occur with aging, such as more time needed to become aroused. Although newer medications have shown promise in treatment of erectile dysfunction in men, reports of adverse effects suggest that these medications should be used with caution (Clay, 2012; English & Dean, 2013).

Meaningful relationships add to the quality of life for older adults. Intimacy is expressed in many ways and provides a feeling of closeness to a loved one. Counselors can assist clients in establishing better relationships and work with couples to examine issues that may be problematic within their marriage/union.

Late-Life Transitions

The counseling profession is grounded in a developmental wellness orientation (Locke, Myers, & Herr, 2001); therefore, counselors may be expected to conceptualize client concerns from a nonpathological or wellness orientation. Common late-life transitions include coping with loss, adjusting to retirement and reduced income, grandparenthood, second careers, and creating satisfying leisure lifestyles.

Much of the literature addressing these issues explains the dynamics of and potential problems with late-life transitions and outlines strategies for intervention; however, most recommended strategies are based in theory rather than empirical support. Conclusions from the literature are applied generally rather than specifically to the older population. Brief summaries of the literature on widowhood, caregiving, and grandparenthood provide examples of the types of information available to counselors as a basis for evidence-based practice (Myers & Harper, 2004).

Widowhood

Older women are increasingly represented in today's society and are particularly at risk for a range of chronic health conditions and economic deprivation (Australian Institute of Health and Welfare, 2009). Widowhood is an important, yet common life event that requires a significant amount of adjustment. Despite literature emphasizing the eventual resilience of women (Feldman, Byles, & Beaumont, 2000), where they generally adjust well and continue to live fulfilling lives, there is evidence that the early bereavement period (the first 2 years following death of the husband) carries with it several risks to health, social, and economic well-being (DiGiacomo, Davidson, Byles, & Nolan, 2013). It has been observed that recently bereaved people had increased health risks including increased hospitalization, medication use, changed eating habits, living arrangements, and social relationships (Stroebe, Schut, & Stroebe, 2007). Women are faced with increased health risks and chronic conditions associated not only with bereavement, but also middle and older age. Older women have higher rates of severe disability, and this continues as they age. Increases in depression, anxiety, and loneliness (Onrust & Cuijpers, 2006; Williams, 2005) have also been reported. Many older women live alone upon spousal bereavement (Gustavson & Lee, 2004), an arrangement that may impact on their daily routines, ability to self-manage chronic conditions, as well as economic resources (Angel, Jimenez, & Angel, 2007). These women often have a decreased income upon spousal death, particularly if they had not been in paid employment and have no or little retirement savings. They are more likely to live in poverty than men or their married counterparts, and may suffer from financial and housing insecurity and reduced income despite maintained or increased expenses (Lee, 2003; U.N. Department of Economic and Social Affairs [UNDESA], 2010).

These factors mean that older women may be less equipped to address the challenges of widowhood. Poor physical and psychological health outcomes necessitate the need for counseling professionals, not only to be aware of their circumstances, but also to be responsive to older clients who have recently lost a spouse (Williams, 2005). Providing appropriate, timely bereavement counseling is of critical importance to manage this major life transition.

Lund and Caserta (2001) compared two studies of spousal bereavement, including samples of 192 and 339 men over the age of 50 years. For both samples, support groups were beneficial for facilitating the grieving process, and mixed-gender groups were especially effective. The authors noted that men in their 50s were more effective in coping with spousal loss than were men in their 70s.

Coping with widowhood will be an individual experience for older adults, because no two individuals grieve in exactly the same way. Counselors can encourage their widowed clients to express their feelings in a safe atmosphere. They should allow their clients to reminisce on the good times and share their experiences. Counselors can encourage clients to engage in meaningful activities, develop new interests, and explore new territories. They will assist clients in identifying their strengths during this difficult time and identify their resilient nature. Working through the tasks of mourning will assist clients with the reintegration process, which is required to move forward.

Specific strategies to cope with the loss of a spouse include finding support whether it is a family member or friend, religious institution, support group, or talking to a therapist or grief counselor. Another strategy requires the bereaved to take care of himself or herself because the stress of a major loss can deplete energy and emotional reserves. When grieving, it is important to face your feelings, express your feelings in a tangible or creative way (journal), pay attention to your physical health, refrain from allowing others to tell you how to feel, and plan ahead for major milestones that can awaken memories (anniversaries, holidays) (Smith & Segal, 2015).

Caregiving

Caregiving is a vital role in supporting family members who are sick or persons with disabilities (Singleton, Maung, & Cowie, 2002), and an in-depth understanding of how best to care for those who are dependent and racially diverse is needed (Dilworth-Anderson, Williams, & Gibson, 2002). Without a doubt, the families of those with mental disorders are affected by the condition of their loved ones. Families not only provide practical help and personal care but also give emotional support to his or her relative with a mental disorder. Therefore, the older adult is dependent on the caregiver, and his or her well-being is directly related to the nature and quality of the care provided by the caregiver. These demands can bring significant levels of stress for the caregiver and can affect their overall quality of life including work, socializing, and relationships. Research (Oyebode, 2005) into the impact of caregiving shows that one-third to one-half of caregivers suffers significant psychological distress and experience higher rates of mental ill health than the general population.

Being a caregiver can raise difficult personal issues about duty, responsibility, adequacy, and guilt (Oyebode, 2005). Caring for an individual with a mental health problem is not a static process since the needs of the care recipient alter as their condition changes. The role of the caregiver can be more demanding and difficult if the care recipient's mental disorder is associated with behavioral problems or physical disability (Shah, Wadoo, & Latoo, 2010). Counselors familiar with the caregiving role and the impact it has on the older family member and overall family dynamics are in an excellent position to address the perceived burden experienced by family members caring for aging members. Emotional distress and physical exhaustion are experienced by caregivers and must be managed to continue to provide quality care to older family members.

Ballard, Lowery, Powell, O'Brien, and James (2000) reviewed the literature on dementia and perceived burden and concluded that multiple studies point to the success of cognitive-behavioral interventions in reducing the strain of providing care. Among approximately 5,000 articles written between 1995 and 2002 that deal with caregivers and their mental health concerns (reviewed by Myers, 2003), only a handful tested the efficacy of counseling interventions, psychoeducational support group intervention for midlife caregivers with parent-care responsibilities. Using published measures of knowledge of aging, caregiver burden, and coping resources, they found that a time-limited, structured intervention was successful in reducing participants' perceptions of burden and increasing their coping responses.

Coping strategies for individuals experiencing caregiver burden include respite. Respite care for the loved one gives the caregiver a release from caregiving to engage in other responsibilities. Accessing other family members or friends to provide support is helpful, to decrease the feeling of burden. Joining support groups provides the caregiver the opportunity to feel support from others in similar situations. Paying for care providers, if affordable, decreases the responsibility for caregiving. The caregiver needs to also acknowledge his or her limitations, which might include admission of the love one to a supervised facility. Caregiving burden can also be decreased if the caregiver attends counseling sessions to address their issues and caregiver burden can be decreased if the caregiver gets enough rest, eats a nutritious diet, and makes time to exercise and relax. Latina female caregivers use religion to cope with caring for loved ones with dementia (Coon et al., 2004). Evidence-based psychological treatments used in helping distressed family caregivers of older adults include cognitive-behavioral therapy, individual counseling, and support group attendance (Gallagher-Thompson & Coon, 2007).

Caregiving is an important and necessary role for older adults who require assistance. There are advantages and disadvantages to caregiving, and counselors will seek caregivers when his or her demands exceed their emotional and physical resources. Caregiver burden is addressed by counselors to facilitate better care for their client and a decrease in stress for the caregiver. Improving the mental health of the caregiver will enhance his or her ability to provide the needed care for his or her elder.

Grandparenthood

When parents are unable to raise their children, many grandparents assume this responsibility to avoid their grandchildren being placed in the foster care system. Their plan is to keep the family united; however, oftentimes grandparents are ill-prepared to care for one or more grandchildren. Counselors working with their older clients who are custodial parents will be addressing multiple simultaneously occurring situations that produce stress and diminish the quality of life for their older clients. Counselors will be addressing chronic health problems, decreased social interaction, depression, loneliness, isolation, grieving on several levels, financial and legal dilemmas, coping mechanisms (lack thereof), behavioral issues of the grandchildren, and legal and educational concerns.

Grandparents acknowledge several benefits when raising their grandchildren, and counselors can reinforce these advantages in counseling sessions. These benefits include a sense of purpose, a second chance in life, an opportunity to nurture family relationships, a chance to continue family histories, and receiving love and support (Langosch, 2012). Grandparents also benefit from giving and receiving love (Doblin-MacNab & Keiley, 2009), and perceiving themselves as more effective caregivers (Strom & Strom, 2011). In spite of the benefits, there are real challenges. Brabazon's (2011) study of grandparent-headed families (GHF) in the United States indicate that such families are more economically disadvantaged and have disproportionately high poverty rates, an economic variable strongly associated with poor health outcomes (Longoria, 2009). The economic demands of custodial grandparenting can cause problems with the already compromised health of grandparents as economic support from social service agencies is frequently unavailable or difficult to access. For example, 41% of GHF report having unmet service needs (Yancura, 2013). Counselors will assist their clients in investigating resources for financial support and securing services from social service agencies.

These challenges also extend to one's physical health. Custodial grandparents describe more limitations in performing activities of daily living. Further, caregiving stress may result in exacerbation of health problems (Kelley, Whitley, & Campos, 2010; Williams, 2011). Grandparents in GHF also reported feeling physically tired, having less privacy, and having less time with friends, family, and spouses (Hayslip & Kaminski, 2005). Working with clients who are grandparents raising their grandchildren will require that the counselor work with these clients to alleviate stress that negatively impacts their health.

The challenges faced by caregiving grandparents often influence their emotional and social health (Bundy-Fazioli, Fruhauf, & Miller, 2013). Research has consistently demonstrated that custodial grandparents have high rates of depression (Song & Yan, 2012; Strutton, 2010), with married and older grandmothers experiencing less emotional strain than single or younger grandmothers (Conway, Jones, & Speakes-Lewis, 2011). Custodial grandparents seek health-services less frequently and experience a higher level of distress, emotional problems, clinical depression, and insomnia than grandparents in traditional roles (Song & Yan, 2012). Grandmothers in particular experience higher levels of stress, strain between family members, more severe physical symptoms, and severe depression symptoms (Musil et al., 2011). This is especially true in cases where the grandmother has no high school diploma, is not employed, lives in poverty, and whose grandchildren possess severe behavioral problems (Park, 2009). These grandparents can also experience grief and disappointment over the primary parent's situation, adding to the intense emotional distress (Strom & Strom, 2011). In cases where the primary parent has been incarcerated, used or uses drugs, or suffers from AIDS/HIV, the stress of dealing with the children and the parent's problem can create a tense environment for the custodial grandparent. Additionally, if the child's parent has died, grandparents must simultaneously cope with their own grief as well as that of their grandchild (Sampson & Hertlein, 2015). Providing a safe environment for grandparents to grieve over their losses will be very important in the counseling relationship.

In addition to impaired physical and emotional functions, intergenerational households headed by grandparents may experience social isolation due to the stigma attached to substance abuse, AIDS/HIV, or incarceration of the absent parents (Harris & Kim, 2011). Custodial grandparents can also become isolated from their peers due to caregiving responsibilities. Such responsibilities may put them off time with their peer group (Backhouse & Graham, 2012). The social isolation that grandparents experience may make management of their physical and emotional issues more difficult.

Grandparents assume responsibility for their grandchildren when their parents are unable to care for them. While grandparents provide the best care possible, at times they are challenged physically, emotionally, socially, and financially. Counselors may offer support services, provide bereavement counseling, teach coping strategies to deal with stress, and provide education to increase knowledge of educational, legal, and social services available. They may need to teach assertiveness training, provide referrals, and become a resource to provide linkage to agencies for support. An integrative approach that utilizes a variety of modalities is needed, which might include psychoeducational, family-systems approach, and cognitive-behavioral therapy.

Terminal Illness

People with terminal illnesses often suffer from an inability to find meaning in the last moments of their lives and are unable to deal with significant issues related to family and other loved ones. Often they feel "cast out" because they are no longer healthy or productive and feel as if they are a burden to others because they are unable to care for themselves, in even very basic ways (Hardwig, 2000).

Caffrey (2000) confirms the role of psychotherapy in work with terminal illness. He believes that "palliative" care alone, the reduction of anxiety and depression related to dying, is short-sighted. Glicken (2009) believes that when a patient is approaching death, this can focus and stimulate life forces in a dying person. Kübler-Ross (1969, 1997) identified the "unfinished business" that keeps dying persons temporarily alive. The unfinished business can be simple or complex, but it usually has deep personal roots. The dying person is concerned, not so much about death per se, but about death as a constraint on life matters that need attending to. Terminal illness offers a patient the opportunity for personal growth in the presence of learning to cope with pain and the possibility of death. Greenstein and Breitbart (2000) write that "patients report reordering their priorities, spending more time with family, and experiencing personal growth through the very fact of having had to cope with their traumatic loss or illness" (p. 486). Suffering may lead to empathy and the willingness to reach out to others and the sense of connectedness among people often becomes an overriding positive experience that helps group members cope with painful and distressing conditions in ways that prolong life and add to its meaning.

Counselors working with older clients who are terminally ill can utilize coping strategies with their clients (Livneh, 2000). Problem-focused/solving coping and information seeking refers to resolution of the stress and anxiety of illness through information gathering, focused planning, and direct action taking. Fighting spirit and confrontation refers to strategies described as accepting a serious and perhaps life-threatening diagnosis, while optimistically challenging, tackling, confronting, and recovering from the illness. Focusing on positives utilizing positive restructuring and positive reframing is associated with psychological well-being. Self-restraint is a strategy that refers to personal control to cope with the stresses of a serious or terminal disease and is a predictor of lower emotional distress. Seeking social support and assistance from others has been linked to decreased emotional/psychological distress. Expressing feelings or venting has both positive and negative outcomes. Using humor decreases emotional distress and finding increased life meaning, and this potential is realized in terminally ill patients. High levels of spirituality in dying patients lead to hopefulness that resulted in a more cooperative relationship with helping professionals, improved resolution of long-standing emotional problems, and the desire to live longer (McClain, Rosenfeld, & Breitbart, 2003).

Advance directives provide patients with peace of mind and prevent families the burden of making difficult and emotionally intense decisions at the end of life (Kyba, 2002). Patients who perceive themselves as a burden on others often experience depression and anxiety, which can produce a lower quality of life. To prevent this perceived burden, counselors need to help patients find meaning or purpose in their lives (Tomer, Eliason, & Wong, 2008). Counselors who are aware that patients hold different meanings of life and death can respond to them with understanding and compassion, helping them live their best life until they die (Chibnall, Videen, Duckro, & Miller, 2002). One of the most difficult trials humans must face is loss, and with death comes the loss of oneself. Some terminally ill patients turn to religious and spiritual beliefs in order to understand their experiences and answer difficult existential questions about life and death (Tomer et al., 2008). Counselors who create an accepting environment can use the transpersonal model to help facilitate growth to a higher level of development in patients at the end of life. This approach encourages dying patients to explore the meaning of their death and reach a higher level of consciousness, increasing their knowledge of self.

One challenge for counselors who work with terminally ill patients is helping them to maintain a sense of dignity (Bloche, 2005). Although it can be difficult for patients to achieve dignity when they are facing the challenges of a terminal illness, it is important for counselors to recognize and treat patients who are sick and dying with the same dignity and respect as those who are healthy (Bloche, 2005). Dignity therapy is an intervention that encourages terminally ill patients to address psychosocial and existential issues in two to three counseling sessions (Chochinov et al., 2005). Counselors invite patients to talk about things that matter most to them both in the present and from their past, and for what they want to be remembered for. They ask specific questions to encourage dying patients to tell their stories, and then give patients time to think about and reflect upon their answers. The questions pertain to the patient's life history, emphasizing areas of importance such as roles, accomplishments in life, hopes and dreams, and any advice or information they want to pass on to family and loved ones. Some of the routine questions include (1) Tell me about your life history and the parts you feel are the most important. At that point in your life did you feel you were the most alive? (2) Do you want your family to know specific things about you, and what things do you want them to remember about you? (3) What have you learned about life? (4) What words do you wish to pass onto your loved ones? (Chochinov et al., 2005).

The session is audio recorded then transcribed verbatim by the counselor, who edits the information for clarity, sequencing of life events, and organization of important information. In the next session the counselor reads the document out loud to the patient for accuracy and feedback, allowing him or her to edit any changes (Ando, Morita, Okamoto, & Ninosaka, 2008). When patients hear their words repeated back to them they often become emotional, yet they believe they maintain their dignity, and achieve a better sense of purpose and meaning in life, which can be empowering. Patients also report less anxiety and despair about their impending death after sessions of dignity therapy (Chochinov et al., 2005). Terminally ill patients are able to ensure Erickson's seventh psychosocial state of generativity, where strength comes through care of others and production of something that contributes to the betterment of society, by leaving their created document to family and loved ones as a lasting reminder of who they were and their hopes and dreams for their families' future (Lemay & Wilson, 2008).

Terminally ill patients who desire to avoid further medical treatments have other options than the advance directives for medical care. Suicide and physician-assisted suicide are two choices that have received a great deal of media attention, particularly the physician-assisted suicide cases involving Jack Kevorkian and his suicide machine. The Oregon Death with Dignity Act, first passed in 1994 and went into effect in 1997, allowed a physician to issue a legal prescription to a terminally ill Oregon resident under a very strict set of circumstances (Death with Dignity National Center, 2015). The voters of Washington passed their law in 2008, and it went into effect in 2009. Vermont became the third state with a Death with Dignity law in 2013, and the law went into effect immediately. Montana doesn't currently have a law safe-guarding physician-assisted death. However, in 2009, Montana's Supreme Court ruled nothing in the state law prohibited a physician from honoring a terminally ill, mentally competent patient's request by prescribing medication to hasten the patient's death. Since the ruling, several bills have been introduced to codify or ban the practice, but none of those bills has become law (Death with Dignity National Center, 2015). California's law will take effect 90 days after the state legislature adjourns the special session on health care, which likely will not be until January 2016 at the earliest (ProCon.org, 2015). So currently a total of five states have legalized physician-assisted suicide. Four of these states (California, Oregon, Vermont, and Washington) legalized physician-assisted suicide via legislation and one state (Montana) has legal physician-assisted suicide via court ruling (ProCon.org, 2015).

Counselors, as mental health professionals, may become involved in counseling terminally ill patients, who may express the desire to end their suffering by committing suicide. Assessing suicidal risk in terminally ill patients presents particular challenges; for example, preoccupation with dying or realistic planning for death may not be a true indicator of suicidal intention for terminally ill patients. Many characteristics of terminally ill patients are independent risk factors for suicide in their own right, which include depression, anxiety, delirium, hopelessness, pain and deterioration, and social isolation. Nonjudgmental exploration of the terminally ill patient's suicidal intent is the first step in reducing suicidal risk, and other steps included crises intervention techniques, medication changes focused on reducing physical and emotional discomforts, and advocacy efforts for relieving social and financial stressors.

If the client reveals to the counselor a suicide plan to end his or her pain from a terminal illness, should the client's confidentiality be violated and should the counselor take steps to prevent the client from carrying out the suicide? The ACA Code of Ethics (ACA, 2014) standards expect the counselor to break confidentiality because the client is threatening to harm him or herself. The standard is,

> The general requirement that counselors keep information confidential does not apply when disclosure is required to protect clients or identified others from serious and foreseeable harm or when legal requirements demand that confidential information must be revealed. Counselors consult with other professionals when in doubt as to the validity of an exception. Additional considerations apply when addressing end-of-life issues. (p. 7)

The standard seems clear, but should they apply equally in states with physician-assisted suicide laws? Furthermore, should they apply equally to older adults who have lived long and full lives and who are now making an informed choice to end their lives due to terminal conditions that cause intolerable pain and deterioration? The ACA standards also state that the counselor should endeavor to keep his or her own values from interfering with the counseling relationship. The standard is,

> Counselors are aware of and avoid imposing their own values, attitudes, beliefs, and behaviors. Counselors respect the diversity of clients, trainees, and research participants and seek training in areas in which they are at risk of imposing their values onto clients, especially when the counselor's values are inconsistent with the client's goals or are discriminating in nature. (ACA, 2014, p. 5)

How does the counselor keep his or her values from interfering with a terminally ill person's wish for a right to die?

A very important part of the work of therapists is helping clients negotiate this last transition. Counselors are available to be supportive and to help clients deal with the medical system and any family issues that might arise. In this role, it is very important to stay focused on the quality of life. Most clients do not want their lives artificially prolonged. They reach a point at which they are ready to let go, and the counselor's role is to be an advocate for them. To do that, counselors have to be comfortable talking with them and the people around them about death and with the decision to let them go when it is time (Zarit & Zarit, 2011).

Death and Dying

At the end of life, helping professionals can bring a real advantage to patient care: well-honed communication skills. Patient-centered communication that blends empathic listening with provision of information appears to offer patients the greatest support.

What are the skills helpers need to deliver bad news? It is important to remember that delivering such life-altering news can be very stressful for professionals who are asked to do so. Therefore, awareness of one's own response to dying and understanding of best practices in the area can be useful. Practicing compassion for oneself as well as for clients and their families is a powerful resource. Barclay, Blackhall, and Tulsky (2007) offer a helpful review of key considerations for culturally appropriate communication of difficult information. It's critical for helpers to understand that not everyone wants to hear the same amount of information about prognoses, symptoms and so forth. Sometimes patients' wishes for information are different from those of families. Carefully inquiring about how much information is desired as the dialogue unfolds is a good practice. Sometimes separate conversations are indicated, provided consistent information is delivered. When prognosis is poor, helpers can support realistic expectations by discussing ways to manage symptoms, providing emotional support, and connecting the patient and family with resources rather than offering unrealistic promises.

Cultures differ with respect to how directly bad news should be delivered, and it is essential for helpers to be sensitive to cultural norms in this regard:

> Here the difference is not only about whether to tell the truth, but also about what it means to tell. Learning the truth in a more direct way may be seen as preferable because the ambiguity allows the patient the possibility of hope. (Barclay et al., 2007, p. 963)

In general, prior preparation of advance directives can provide an opportunity for discussing preferences for truth telling while individuals are still healthy. Difficult information should be conveyed with language and pacing that supports patients' understanding. Communication should be caring yet straightforward. It is suggested that the communicator pause to check for comprehension after every three facts. Summarizing the conversation aids understanding as well. Planning for continuing care that includes the patient and/or family can help convey the reality of continuing support through the process (Broderick & Blewitt, 2015).

Counselors work with clients everyday on issues that disrupt the client's life and shake their sense of self. While each symptom or issue is weighed differently within the lives of clients, the issue of death and dying seems to weigh heavily universally with those dealing with death or dying (Kehoe, 2013). As a professional counselor, death and dying is a reality that counselors across all domains and working with every population will encounter. In working with older adults, issues of death and dying arise quite often and present themselves in numerous ways.

There is the loss of loved ones, which increases as individuals age. Lifelong friends, siblings, cousins, and significant others pass away. The impact of losing a loved one is tremendously difficult, while the weight of multiple losses can feel life ending. Counselors help clients understand the grief process, often presented in stages in which the final goal is that of closure and learning to live without the lost loved one. While some clients do not experience the stages (denial, anger, bargaining, depression, and acceptance) in sequence, other individuals may go through a certain stage more than once or enter into another stage simultaneously (Keefer, 2015). A modern approach to grief counseling is re-membering conversations, which has grown out of aspects of narrative therapy and social constructivism theories that deal with death and loss from an entirely different angle than traditional grief counseling. With re-membering conversations, the focus is not on closure rather than gaining an understanding of the client's relationship with the loved one while they were living and helping them to now discover the ways in which their lost loved one can still fit in their lives. In essence, a re-developing of the client's relationship with that lost loved one now that they are no longer physically present. While the physical body may be gone, the relationship with them continues to live on.

A death of a client is inevitable when working with clients who are in the process of dying, and this takes a tremendous toll on all involved. A wide range of reactions include: individuals who want to take advantage of every moment to those who appear to shut down and push people away. It is difficult to find a common approach to working with dying persons (Kehoe, 2013). Family members and health care professionals will share comforting words, which may be unrealistic when a terminal diagnosis has been identified, for example, the doctors don't always know everything. Terminally ill clients want an expression of genuineness when interacting with others and acknowledgement that they are going to die. Family counseling sessions can be very beneficial when a client is near the end of life. Having the family or loved ones present provides the counselor an opportunity to ask the client up front how they want to be remembered or what is it they wish for their loved ones when they are gone. This time can be incredibly healing for the family and friends (Kehoe, 2013).

Older clients, even healthy ones, are often concerned about their own deaths or about deaths of people close to them. Much of the literature on this topic is based on case studies of younger people with illnesses that have predictable trajectories, such as cancer. However, older people can have more varied courses of decline. They also may have different ways of dealing with death. Some older people may feel fear and anxiety about death, but these feelings do not seem as common as among younger individuals. Other older people, while not afraid of dying, are often concerned about the circumstances of their deaths. They do not want to endure painful or unnecessary medical procedures and may want to pass away at home rather than in the hospital. They may question why they have been left behind when others have died or believe they cannot go on with their lives. People may also have unfinished emotional business with their families or issues that they want to resolve before they die. These issues can be value laden for both therapist and client. The most desirable therapeutic stance is one of neutrality, allowing the individual the freedom to express his or her own beliefs and explore the possibilities.

Case Illustration 10.3 demonstrates issues of loss, relocation, delayed grief reaction, and psychiatric illness.

CASE ILLUSTRATION 10.3

Counselors perform various roles but are not specialists in everything; therefore, referrals to other professionals may be warranted. Mrs. Lewis moved from Pennsylvania to Florida and was extremely excited for the first 6 months upon arrival. She had saved her money, sold her house and all of her belongings, and moved after the death of her husband of 45 years. She wanted a fresh start.

(Continued)

(Continued)

However, upon visiting her, Mrs. Lewis's daughter noticed that she cried frequently, had become withdrawn and complained of restlessness, had difficulty sleeping, and was just sad all of the time. She also noticed that her mother was having visual and auditory hallucinations. She thought she was seeing her husband and that he was telling her to move back to Pennsylvania.

Mrs. Lewis has no history of any psychiatric disorders, nor was she on any medications. She only ingests a multivitamin, calcium supplement, and Vitamin D supplement daily. As the counselor, what presenting issues would indicate that you need help in this particular scenario? Identify the professionals who you would consult with. How would you interpret Mrs. Lewis's presenting problem(s)?

Therapists need to be comfortable talking about death and dying and letting clients know they can talk about these issues. Someone who is uncomfortable talking about death and dying will convey that discomfort to clients. Therapists also have to know where they stand personally on end-of-life issues. They need to come to terms with their own beliefs and feelings so that they do not distort or misinterpret what clients say or feel and do not let their own beliefs interfere with clients' making their own decisions.

Therapists must be prepared to lose clients. One of the consequences of empathy is that we get attached to clients. Seeing people who are declining and who will ultimately die is not easy and raises complex feelings in therapists. These losses can feel like the death of a good friend. They come to know clients well and are very involved in their lives. With our older clients, death is not just a loss but can be the culmination of a process that ends suffering or frees them from a life they would not want to live. Therapists may need to obtain professional services to assist with the loss of their clients.

Loss is a major theme associated with aging. Older adults, as they age, based on their longevity, will experience the death of spouses, partners, family members, friends, and neighbors. Their resiliency is a testament to their ability to cope with numerous losses and continue to function. Counselors will address issues related to the dying process, advanced directives, and death rituals. It is extremely important that counselor conduct a self-examination to become comfortable addressing these unavoidable issues related to loss and seek professional counseling services to cope with the loss of his or her clients, if it is necessary.

KEYSTONES

- Older adults can benefit from various psychosocial interventions and will have different goals in comparison to younger or middle-aged clients. Physical health promotion is an important goal for older clients.

- Older persons will access the services of professionals if they are experiencing a crisis, are in a transitional phase of life, and/or if some unmet need interferes with their functioning.

- The personal client-counselor relationship is essential in facilitating progress within the counseling session.

- A multidimensional, comprehensive assessment is necessary to initiate any therapeutic intervention with older adults.

- Physical limitations, health concerns, inadequate appraisal and assessments, and environmental issues pose challenges to the professional counselor.

- In addition to establishing a relationship with clients and assessing them, counselors will help clients set goals and create and carry out an appropriate intervention before terminating the relationship.

- The gerontological counselor performs roles of advocacy, consultant, educator, and coordinator and acts as a referral mechanism for older clients. The counselor helps older clients with topics including health issues, uncertainties, relationship issues and sexuality, late-life transitions, terminal illness, and death and dying.

ADDITIONAL RESOURCES

Print Based

Barry, K. L., Oslin, D. W., & Blow, F. C. (2001). *Alcohol problems in older adults: Prevention and management.* New York, NY: Springer Publishing.

Blando, J. (2011). *Counseling older adults.* New York, NY: Routledge.

Brewington, J. O., & Nassar-McMillan, S. (2000). Older adults: Work-related issues and implication for counseling. *The Career Development Quarterly, 49,* 2–15.

Faber, A. J. (2003). Therapy with the elderly: A collaborative approach. *Journal of Family Psychotherapy, 14,* 1–14.

Harper, M. C., & Shoffner, M. F. (2004). Counseling for continued career development after retirement: An application of the theory of work adjustment. *The Career Development Quarterly, 52,* 272–284.

Hill, A., & Brettle, A. (2006). Counseling older people: What can we learn from research evidence? *Journal of Social Work Practice, 20,* 281–297.

Kottler, J. (2003). *Client and therapist: How each changes the other.* In the gift of therapy (pp. 1–24). San Francisco, CA: Jossey-Bass.

Lee, C. C. (Ed.). (2013). *Multicultural issues in counseling: New approached to diversity* (4th ed.). Alexandria, VA: American Counseling Association.

Lever, K., & Wilson, J. J. (2005). Encore parenting: When grandparents fill the role of primary caregiver. *The Family Journal, 13,* 167–171.

McAuliffe, G. (2013). *Culturally alert counseling: A comprehensive introduction* (2nd ed.). Thousand Oaks, CA: Sage.

Pennick, J. M., & Fallshore, M. (2005). Purpose and meaning in highly active seniors. *Adultspan Journal, 4,* 19–35.

Snyder, B. A. (2005). Aging and spirituality: Reclaiming connection through story-telling. *Adultspan Journal, 4,* 49–55.

Stickle, F., & Onedera, J. (2006). Teaching gerontology in counselor education. *Educational Gerontology, 32,* 247–259.

Sue, D. W., & Sue, D. (2003). Counseling elderly clients. In D. W. Sue & D. Sue, *Counseling the culturally diverse* (4th ed., pp. 393–406). Hoboken, NJ: John Wiley & Sons.

Web Based

www.aca.org
www.nia.nih.gov

REFERENCES

Age U.K. Oxfordshire (2011). *Safeguarding the convoy: A call to action from the campaign to end loneliness.* Oxfordshire, UK: Author.

Agronin, M. E. (2004). Sexual disorders. In D. G. Blazer, D. C. Steffens, & E. W. Busse (Eds.), *Textbook of geriatric psychiatry* (3d ed.). Arlington, VA: American Psychiatric Publishing.

Agronin, M. (2010). *Therapy with older clients: Key strategies for success.* Retrieved from http://www.books .wwnorton.com/books/Therapy-with-Older-Clients/

American Counseling Association (ACA). (2014). *2014 ACA Code of Ethics.* Alexandria, VA: Author.

American Psychiatric Association. (2000). *Diagnostic and statistical manual of mental disorders* (4th ed., Text Revision). Washington, DC: Author.

Anderson, F., Downing, G., & Hill, J. (1996). Palliative Performance Scale (PPS): A new tool. *Journal of Palliative Care, 12*(1), 5–11.

Ando, M., Morita, T., Okamoto, T., & Ninosaka, L. (2008). One-week short-term life review interview can improve spiritual well-being of terminally ill cancer patients. *Journal of Psycho-Oncology, 17,* 885–890.

Angel, J., Jimenez, M., & Angel, R. (2007). The economic consequences of widowhood for older minority women. *Gerontologist, 47*(2), 224–234.

Annon, J. (1976). The PLISSIT Model: A proposed conceptual scheme for the behavioral treatment of sexual problems. *Journal of Sex Education and Therapy, 2*(2), 1–15.

Arroll, B., Khin, N., & Kerse, N. (2003). Screening for depression in primary care with two verbally asked questions cross sectional study. *British Medical Journal, 327*(7424), 1144–1146.

Aspinwall, L., & Staudinger, U. (2003). *A psychology of strengths: Fundamental questions and future directions for a positive psychology.* Washington, DC: American Psychological Association.

Australian Institute of Health and Welfare. (2009). *Australia's Welfare, 9*(117). Canberra: ACT: Author.

Backhouse, J., & Graham, A. (2012). Grandparents raising grandchildren: Negotiating the complexities of role-identity conflict. *Child and Family Social Work, 17*(3), 306–315.

Ballard, C., Lowery, K., Powell, I., O'Brien, J., & James, I. (2000). Impact of behavioral psychological symptoms of dementia on caregivers. *International Psychogeriatrics, 12,* 93–105.

Barclay, J. S., Blackhall, L. J., & Tulsky, J. A. (2007). Communication strategies and cultural issues in the delivery of bad news. *Journal of Palliative Medicine, 10,* 958–977.

Bernstein, M., & Munoz, N. (2016). *Nutrition for the older adult.* Burlington, MA: Jones and Bartlett.

Blando, J. (2011). *Counseling older adults.* New York, NY: Routledge.

Bloche, M. (2005). Managing conflict at the end of life. *New England Journal of Medicine, 23,* 352.

Blow, F. (1991). Short Michigan Alcohol Screening Test—Geriatric Version (SMAST-G). Ann Arbor: University of Michigan Alcohol Research Center.

Bourgeois, M. (2002). The challenge of communicating with persons with dementia. *Alzheimer's Care Quarterly, 3,* 132–144.

Boyd, D., & Bee, H. (2006). *Lifespan development* (4th ed.). Boston, MA: Allyn and Bacon.

Brabazon, K. (2011). Economic challenges faced by grandparents raising grandchildren: Implications for policy development. *Gerontologist, 51,* 175–176.

Broderick, P., & Blewitt, P. (2004). *The life span: Human development for helping professionals* (2nd ed.). Upper Saddle River, NJ: Pearson Merrill Prentice Hall.

Brown, J., Potter, J., & Foster, B. (1990). Caregiver burden can be evaluated during geriatric assessment. *Journal of American Geriatrics Society, 38*(4), 453–460.

Bundy-Fazioli, Fruhauf, C., & Miller, J. (2013). Grandparents caregivers' perceptions of emotional distress and well-being. *Journal of Family Social Work, 16*(5), 447–462.

Caffrey, T. (2000). The whisper of death: Psychotherapy with a dying Vietnam veteran. *American Journal of Psychotherapy, 54*(4), 519–530.

Carr, A. (2009). The effectiveness of family therapy and systemic interventions for adult-focused problems. *Journal of Family Therapy, 31,* 46–74.

Cattan, M. (2005). Preventing social isolation and loneliness among old people: A systematic review of health promotion interventions. *Aging and Society, 25*(1), 41–67.

Centers for Disease Control and Prevention (CDC). (2015). *Depression is not a normal part of growing older.* Retrieved from http://www.cdc.gov/aging/mentalhealth/depression.htm

Centers for Disease Control and Prevention (CDC), Administration on Aging, Agency for Healthcare Research and Quality, and Centers for Medicare and Medicaid Services. (2011). *Enhancing use of clinical preventive services among older adults: Closing the gap.* Washington, DC: AARP. Retrieved from http://www.cdc.gov/features/preventiveservices/clinical_preventive_services_closing_the_gap_report.pdf.

Chand, S., & Grossberg, G. (2013). How to adapt cognitive behavioral therapy for older adults. *Current Psychiatry, 12*(3). Retrieved from http://www.currentpsychiatry.com/index.php?id = 22661&tx_ttnews [tt_news] = 177556

Chibnall, J., Videen, S., Duckro, P., & Miller, D. (2002). Psycho-social-spiritual correlates of death distress in patients with life-threatening medical conditions. *Journal of Palliative Medicine, 16,* 331–338.

Chochinov, H., Hack, T., Hassard, T., Kristjanson, O. L., McClement, S., & Harlos, M. (2005). Dignity therapy: A novel psychotherapeutic intervention for patients near the end of life. *Journal of Clinical Oncology, 23,* 5520–5525.

Clay, R. (2012). Later-life sex. *American Psychological Association, 43*(11), 42.

Conway, F., Jones, S., & Speakes-Lewis, A. (2011). Emotional strain in caregiving among African American grandmothers raising their grandchildren. *Journal of Women and Aging,* 23(2), 113–128.

Coon, D., Rubbert, M., Solano, N., Mausbach, B., Kraemer, H., & Argueles, T. (2004). Well-being, appraisal, and coping in Latina and Caucasian female dementia caregivers: Findings from the REACH Study. *Aging and Mental Health, 8*(4), 330–345.

Corey, G. (2012). *Theory and practice of counseling and psychotherapy* (9th ed.). Belmont, CA: Thomson Brooks/ Cole.

Council on Scientific Affairs, American Medical Association. (1993). Physicians and family caregivers: A model for partnership. Council report. *Journal of American Medical Association, 269*(10), 1282–1284.

Cox, D., & D'Oyley, H. (2011). Cognitive-behavioral therapy with older adults. *British Columbia Medical Journal, 53*(7), 348–352.

Cromwell, D., Eagar, K., & Poulos, R. (2003). The performance of instrumental activities of daily living scale in screening for cognitive impairment in elderly community residents. *Journal of Clinical Epidemiology, 56*(2), 131–137.

Cummings, J., Frank, J., & Cherry, D. (2002). Guidelines for managing Alzheimer's disease: Part I. Assessment. *American Family Physician, 65*(11), 2263–2272.

Dacey, M. L., & Newcomer, R. A. (2005). A client-centered counseling approach for motivating older adults toward physical activity. *Topics in Geriatric Rehabilitation, 21*(3), 194–203.

Death with Dignity National Center. (2015). Death with dignity acts. Retrieved https://www.deathwithdignity.org/learn/death-with-dignity-acts/

DeJong, P., & Berg, I. (2001). Co-constructing cooperation with mandated clients. *Social Work, 46*(4), 361–374.

DeLamater, J., & Sill, M. (2005). Sexual desire in later life. *Journal of Aging and Health, 19,* 921–945.

de Shazer, S., Berg, I., & Lipchik, E. (1986). Brief therapy: Focused solution development. *Family Process, 25,* 207–221.

Devons, C. A. (2002). Comprehensive geriatric assessment: Making the most of the aging years. *Current Opinion Clinical Nutrition Metabolic Care, 5*(19), 19–24.

DiGiacomo, M., Davidson, P., Byles, J., & Nolan, M. (2013). An integrative and social-cultural perspective of health, wealth, and adjustment in widowhood. *Health Care Women International,* 1–17.

Dilworth-Anderson, P., Williams, I., & Gibson, B. (2002). Issues of race, ethnicity, and culture in caregiving research: A 20-year review. *The Gerontologist, 42,* 237–272.

Doblin-MacNab, M., & Keiley, M. (2009). Navigating interdependence: How adolescents raised solely by grand-parents experience their family relationships. *Family Relations, 58,* 162–175.

Duffy, F., Gordon, G., & Whelan, G. (2004). Assessing competence in communication and interpersonal skills: The Kalamazoo II Report. *Academic Medicine, 79,* 495–507.

Elliott, R., & Freiere, E. (2010). The effectiveness of person-centered and experimental therapies: A review of the meta-analyses. In M. Cooper, J. C. Watson, & D. Holldampf (Eds.), *Person-centered and experimental therapies work: A review of the research on counseling, psychotherapy and related practices* (pp. 1–15). Ross-on-Wye, UK: PCCS Books.

English, J., & Dean, W. (2013). *Viagra: Performance, side effects, and safe alternatives.* Retrieved from http://nutritionreview.org/2013/04/viagra-performance-side-effects-safe-alternatives/

Feldman, S., Byles, J., & Beaumont, R. (2000). Is anybody listening? The experiences of widowhood for older Australian women. *Journal of Women & Aging, 12*(3/4), 144–176.

Findlay, R. (2003). Interventions to reduce social isolation amongst older people: Where is the evidence? *Aging and Society, 23*(5), 647–658.

Folstein, M., Folstein, S., & McHugh, P. (1975). Mini mental state: A practical method for grading the cognitive state of patients for the clinician. *Journal of Psychiatric Research, 12,* 189–198.

Fowler, C., & Nussbaum, J. (2008). Communicating with the aging patient. In K. B. Wright & S. D. Moore (Eds.), *Applied Health Communication.* Cresskill, NJ: Hampton Press.

Frazer, D., Hinrichsen, G., & Jongsma, A. (2011). *The older adult psychotherapy: Treatment planner.* Hoboken, NJ: John Wiley & Sons.

Froehlich, T., Robison, J., & Inouye, S. (1998). Screening for dementia in the outpatient setting: The time and change test. *Journal of American Geriatrics Society, 46*(12), 1506–1511.

Fry, P., & Debats, D. (2014). Sources of life strengths appraisal scale: A multidimensional approach to assessing older adults' perceived sources of life strengths. *Journal of Aging Research.* Retrieved from http://www.dx.doi.org/10.1155/2014/783637

Gallagher-Thompson, D., & Coon, D. (2007). Evidence-based psychological treatments for distress in family caregivers of older adults. *Psychology Aging, 22*(1), 37–51.

Gellis, Z. D., & Kenaley, B. (2008). Problem-solving therapy for depression in adults: A systematic review. *Research on Social Work Practice, 18*(2).

Glasser, W. (1998). *Choice therapy.* New York, NY: HarperCollins.

Glicken, M. (2009). *Evidence-based counseling and psychotherapy for an aging population.* Burlington, MA: Elsevier.

Greaves, C., & Farbus, L. (2006). Effects of creative and social activity on the health and well-being of socially isolated older people: Outcomes from a multi-method observational study. *The Journal of the Royal Society for the Promotion of Health, 126*(3), 133–142.

Greenstein, M., & Breitbart, W. (2000). Cancer and the experience of meaning: A group psychotherapy program for people with cancer. *American Journal of Psychotherapy, 54*(4), 486–500.

Gustavson, K., & Lee, C. (2004). Alone and content frail seniors living in their own home compared to those who live with others. *Journal of Women and Aging, 16*(3/4), 3–18.

Hardwig, J. (2000). Spiritual issues at the end of life: A call for discussion. *Hastings Center Report, 30*(2), 28–30.

Harris, L., & Kim, B. (2011). Grandparents raising grandchildren affected by HIV/AIDS in Vietnam: How meaning and context affect coping among skipped generations. *Gerontologist, 51,* 390.

Harwood, J. (2007). *Understanding communication and* aging. Thousand Oaks, CA: Sage.

Hayslip, B., & Kaminski, P. (2005). Grandparents raising grandchildren: A review of the literature and suggestions for practice. *The Gerontologist, 45*(2), 262–269.

Houts, P., Doak, C., & Doak, L. (2006). The role of pictures in improving health communication: A review of research on attention, comprehension, recall and adherence. *Patient Education Counseling, 61,* 176–190.

Inouye, S., Robinson, J., Froehlich, I., & Richardson, E. (1998). The Time and Change Test: A simple screening test for dementia. *Journal of Gerontology, 53A*(4), M281–M286.

Inouye, S., van Dyck, C., Alessi, C., Balkin, S., Siegal, A., & Horowitz, R. (1990). Clarifying confusion: The confusion assessment method. A new method for detection of delirium. *Annals of Internal Medicine, 113*(12), 941–948.

Jacoby, S. (2005). Sex in America. *AARP: The Magazine.* Retrieved from http://www.aarpmagazine.org/lifestyle/relationships/sex_in_america.html

Katz, S., Downs, T., Cash, H., & Grotz, R. (1970). Progress in development of ADL. *Gerontologist, 10*(1), 20–30.

Keefer, A. (2015). *What are the stages of grief counseling in the elderly?* Retrieved from http://www.livestrong.com/article/15-7605-what-are-the-stages-of-grief-counseling-in-the-elderly

Kehoe, L. (2013). *Death, dying, and working with grief with older adults and their families.* Alexandria, VA: American Counseling Association. Retrieved from http://www.counseling.org/news/blog/aca-blog/2013/09/27/death-dying-and-working-with-grief-with-older-adults-and-their-families

Kelley, S., Whitley, D., & Campos, P. (2010). Grandmothers raising grandchildren: Results of an intervention to improve health outcomes. *Journal of Nursing Scholarship, 42*(4), 379–386.

Kennedy, G. J., & Tannebaum, S. (2000). Psychotherapy with older adults. *American Journal of Psychotherapy, 54*(3), 386–407.

Kim, J. (2008). Examining the effectiveness of solution-focused brief therapy: A meta-analysis. *Research in Social Work, 18*(2), 107–116.

Kirby, M., Denihan, A., & Bruce, I. (2001). The Clock Drawing Test in primary care: Sensitivity in dementia detection and specifically against normal and depressed elderly. *International Journal of Geriatric Psychiatry, 16,* 935–940.

Kraaij, V., & Garnefski, N. (2002). Negative life events and depressive symptoms in later life: Buffering effects of parental and partner bonding? *Personal Relationships, 9,* 205–214.

Kübler-Ross, E. (1969, 1997). *On death and dying.* New York, NY: Touchstone.

Kyba, F. (2002). Legal and ethical issues in end-of-life care. *Critical Care Nursing Clinic of North America, 14,* 141–155.

Langosch, D. (2012). Grandparents parenting again: Challenges, strengths, and implications for practice. *Psychoanalytic Inquiry, 32*(2), 163–170.

Langer, N. (2008). Integrating compliance, communication, and culture: Delivering health care to an aging population. *Educational Gerontology, 34,* 385–396.

Langer, N. (2009). Late life love and intimacy. *Educational Gerontology, 35*(8), 752–764.

Lawton, M. (1971). The functional assessment of elderly people. *Journal of the American Geriatrics Society, 19*(6), 465–481.

Lawton, M., & Brody, E. (1969). Assessment of older people: Self-maintaining and instrumental activities of daily living. *Gerontologist, 9*(3), 179–186.

Lee, W. (2003). Women and retirement planning: Towards the "feminization of poverty" in an aging Hong Kong. *Journal of Women and Aging, 15*(1), 31–53.

Lemay, K., & Wilson, K. (2008). Treatment of existential distress in life threatening illness: A review of manualized interventions. *Journal of Psychology Review, 28,* 472–493.

Lindau, S., Schumm, L., Laumann, E., Levinson, W., O'Muircheartaigh, C., & Waite, L. (2007). A study of sexuality and health among older adults in the United States. *New England Journal of Medicine, 357,* 762–774.

Livneh, H. (2000). Psychosocial adaptation to cancer: The role of coping strategies. *Journal of Rehabilitation.* Retrieved from http://www.findarticles.com/p/articles/mi_m0825/is_2_66/ai_62980227/print

Locke, D., Myers, J. E., & Herr, E. H. (Eds.). (2001). *The handbook of counseling.* Thousand Oaks, CA: Sage.

Longoria, R. A. (2009). Grandparents raising grandchildren: Perceived neighborhood risk as a predictor of emotional well-being. *Journal of Human Behavior in the Social Environment, 19*(5), 483–511.

Lund, D. A., & Caserta, M. S. (2001). When the unexpected happens: Husbands coping with the deaths of their wives. In D. A. Lund (Ed.), *Men coping with grief: Death, value, and meaning series* (pp. 147–167). Amityville, NY: Baywood.

Lyness, J. M. (2004). Treatment of depressive conditions in later life: Real-world light for dark (or dim) tunnels. *Journal of the American Medical Association, 291,* 1626–1628.

Madden, M. (2010). *Older adults and social media networking use among those age 50 and older nearly doubled over the past year.* Washington, DC: Pew Research Center.

Masi, C. (2011). A meta-analysis of interventions to reduce loneliness. *Personality and Social Psychology Review, 15*(3), 219–266.

McClain, C., Rosenfeld, B., & Breitbart, W. (2003). *Effect of spiritual well-being on end-of-life despair in terminally-ill cancer patients. Lancet, 361*(9369), 1603–1608.

McDonald, P., & Haney, M. (1988). *Counseling the older adult* (2nd ed.). Lexington, MA: Lexington Books.

Mead, N. (2010). Effects of befriending on depressive symptoms and distress: Systematic review and meta-analysis. *British Journal of Psychiatry, 196*(2), 96–100.

Melnick, J., & Nevis, S. (2005). Gestalt therapy methodology. In A. Woldt & S. Roman (Eds.), *Gestalt therapy: History, theory and practice* (pp. 101–116). Thousand Oaks, CA: Sage.

Miars, R. (2002). Existential authenticity: A foundational value for counseling. *Counseling and Values, 46*(3), 218–225.

Miller, J. & Stiver, I. (1991). *A relational reframing of therapy* (Working Paper No. 52). Wellesley, M: Wellesley Centers for Women.

Moody, L., & McMillan, S. (2003). Dyspnea and quality of life indicators in hospice patients and their caregivers. *Health Quality Life Outcomes, 1*(1), 9.

Mosak, H., & Maniacci, M. (2008). Adlerian psychotherapy. In R. Corsini & D. Wedding (Eds.), *Current psychotherapies* (8th ed., pp. 63–106). Belmont, CA: Thomson Brooks/Cole.

Musil, C., Gordon, N., Warner, C., Zauszniewski, J., Standing, T., & Wykle, M. (2011). Grandmothers and caregiving to grandchildren: Continuity, change, and outcomes over 24 months. *Gerontologist, 51*(1), 86–100.

Muzacz, A., & Akinsulure-Smith, A. (2013). Older adults and sexuality: Implications for counseling ethnic and sexual minority clients. *Journal of Mental Health Counseling, 35*(1).

Myers, J. E. (2003). Coping with caregiving stress: A wellness-oriented, strengths based approach for family counselors. *The Family Journal, 11,* 1–9.

Myers, J. E., & Harper, M. C. (2004). Evidence-based effective practices with older adults. *Journal of Counseling & Development, 82,* 207–218.

Nutrition Screening Initiative. (1991). Report of nutrition screening I: Toward a common view. Washington, DC: Nutrition Screening Initiative. Retrieved from http://www.cdaaa.org

Nutrition Screening Initiative. (2007). Nutritional health assessment. Washington, DC: University of Iowa.

Ollonqvist, K. (2008). Alleviating loneliness among frail older people: Findings from a randomized controlled trial. *International Journal of Mental Health Promotion, 10*(2), 26–34.

Onrust, S., & Cuijpers, P. (2006). Mood and anxiety disorders in widowhood: A systematic review. *Aging and Mental Health, 10*(4), 327–334.

Osborn, R., & Squires, D. (2012). International perspectives on patient engagement results from the 2011 Commonwealth Fund Survey. *Journal of Ambulatory Care Management, 35,* 118–128.

Oyebode, J. (2005). Carers as partners in mental health services for older people. *Advances in Psychiatric Treatment, 11,* 2970–3043.

Park, H. (2009). Factors associated with psychological health of grandparents as primary caregivers: An analysis of gender differences. *Journal of International Relationships, 7,* 191–208.

Parsons, R., & Zhang, N. (2014). *Counseling theory: Guiding reflective practice.* Thousand Oaks, CA: Sage.

Pecchioni, L., Ota, H., & Sparks, L. (2004). Cultural issues in communication and aging. In J. F. Nussbaum & J. Coupland (Eds.), *Handbook of communication and aging research.* Mahwah, NJ: Lawrence Erlbaum.

Pitkala, K. (2009). Effects of psychosocial group rehabilitation on health, use of health care services, and mortality of older persons suffering from loneliness: A randomized, controlled trial. *Journal of Gerontology: Medical Sciences, 64A*(7), 792–800.

Polisher Research Institute. (2005). Instrumental Activities of Daily Living Scale (IADL). Retrieved http://www.abramsoncenter.org/PRI/documents/IADL.pdf

ProCon.org. (2015). *State-by-state guide to physician-assisted suicide.* Retrieved from http://euthanasia.procon.org/view.resource.php?resourceID = 000132

Rankin, E., Haut, M., Keefover, R., & Franzen, M. (1994). The establishments of clinical cutoffs in measuring caregiver burden in dementia. *Gerontologist, 34*(6), 828–832.

Reuben, D., & Trinetti, M. (2012). Goal-oriented patient care: An alternative health outcomes paradigm. *New England Journal of Medicine, 366*(777).

Richardson, H., & Glass, J. (2002). A comparison of scoring protocols on the Clock Drawing Test in relation to ease of use, diagnostic group, and correlations with Mini-Mental State Examination. *Journal of American Geriatrics Society, 50*(1), 169–173.

Rogers, C. (1959). A theory of therapy personality and interpersonal relationships as developed in the client-centered framework. In S. Koch (Ed.), *Psychology: A study of science: Vol. 3. Formulations of the person and the social context* (pp. 184–256). New York, NY: McGraw-Hill.

Rogers, C. (1986). Client-centered therapy. In I. L. Kutash & A. Wolf (Eds.), *Psychotherapist's casebook* (pp. 197–208). San Francisco, CA: Jossey-Bass.

Saleebey, D. (2000). Power to the people: Strength and hope. *Advancements in Social Work, 1*(2), 127–136.

Sampson, D., & Hertlein, K. (2015). The experience of grandparents raising grandchildren. *GrandFamilies: The Contemporary Journal of Research, Practice, and Policy, 2*(1).

Savikko, N. (2010). Psychosocial group rehabilitation for lonely older people: Favorable processes and mediating factors of the intervention leading to alleviated loneliness. *International Journal of Older People Nursing, 5*(1), 16–24.

Savundranayagam, M., Ryan, E., & Anas, A. (2007). Communication and dementia staff perceptions of conversational strategies. *Clinical Gerontologist, 31,* 47–63.

Schlegel, R., & Hicks, A. (2011). The true self and psychological health: Evidence and future directions. *Social and Personality Psychology Compass, 5*(12), 989–1003.

Scott, D., & Barfield, H. (2014). Reality therapy. In R. Parsons & N. Zhang (Eds.), *Counseling theory: Guiding reflective practice.* Thousand Oaks, CA: Sage.

Seligman, M., & Csikszentmihalyi, M. (2000). Positive psychology: An introduction. *The American Psychologist, 55*(1), 5–14.

Serby, M., & Yu, M. (2003). Overview: Depression in the elderly. *Mount Sinai Journal of Medicine, 70*(1), 38–44.

Shah, H., Wadoo, O., & Latoo, J. (2010). Psychological distress in carers of people with mental disorders. *British Journal of Medical Practice, 3*(3), 327. Retrieved from http://www.bjmp.org/content/psychological_distress_carers-people-mental-disorders

Sheder, J. (2010). The efficacy of psychodynamic psychotherapy. *American Psychologist, 65,* 98–109.

Sheikh, J., & Yesavage, H. (1986). Geriatric Depression Scale (GDS): Recent evidence and development of a shorter version. *Clinical Gerontologist, 5,* 154–173.

Shulman, K., Gold, D. P. Cohen, C., & Zucchero, C. (1993). Clock-drawing and dementia in the community: A longitudinal study. *International Journal of Geriatric Psychiatry, 8,* 487–496.

Singleton, J., Maung, N., & Cowie, J. (2002). *Mental health of carers*. London, UK: Office for National Statistics.

Small, J. A., Gutman, G., & Makela, S. (2003). Effectiveness of communication strategies used by caregivers of persons with Alzheimer's disease during activities of daily living. *Journal of Speech, Language, Hearing Research, 46*, 353–367.

Smith, M., & Segal, J. (2015). *Feeling loved: The science of nurturing meaningful connections and building lasting happiness*. Retrieved from http://www.helpguide.org

Song, Y., & Yan, C. (2012). Depressive symptoms among grandparents raising grandchildren: The role of resources. *Australasian Journal of Ageing, 31*, 55.

Speer, N. K., Reynolds, J. R., & Swallow, K. M. (2009). Reading stories activates neural representations of perceptual and motor experiences. *Psychological Science, 20*, 989–999.

Stroebe, M., Schut, H., & Stroebe, W. (2007). Health outcomes in bereavement. *Lancet, 370*(9603), 1960–1973.

Strom, P., & Strom, R. (2011). Grandparent education: Raising grandchildren. *Educational Gerontology, 37*(10), 910–933.

Strutton, J. (2010). *Grandparents raising their grandchildren: A comparative study of depression*. Unpublished Dissertation, Texas A & M University, United States Bureau, U.S. Census Bureau News. Retrieved from http://www.census.gov/newsroom/releases/archives/factsforfeaturesspecial editions/cb/2-ff17.html

Studenski, S., Perera, S., & Patel, K. (2011). Gait speed and survival in older adults. *Journal of American Medical Association, 305*(50).

Sudore, R., & Fried, T. (2010). Redefining the "planning" in advance care planning: Preparing for end-of-life decision making. *Annals of Internal Medicine, 153*(256).

Sweeney, T. (2009). *Adlerian counseling and psychotherapy: A practitioner's approach* (5th ed.). New York, NY: Taylor & Francis.

Tomer, A., Eliason, G., & Wong, P. (2008). *Existential and spiritual issues in death attitudes*. New York, NY: Taylor and Francis Group.

Ungar, M. (2012). *The social ecology of resilience*. New York, NY: Springer.

United Nations Department of Economic and Social Affairs (UNDESA). (2010). *World Population Aging* 2009. New York, NY: United Nations.

Virik, K., & Glare, P. (2002). Validation of the palliative performance scale for inpatients admitted to a palliative care unit in Sydney, Australia. *Journal of Pain Symptom Management, 23*(6), 455–457.

Wallace, M. (2000). Intimacy and sexuality. In A. Lueckenotte (Ed.), *Gerontological Nursing* (Revised ed.). St. Louis, MO: Mosby Year Book, Inc.

Wampold, B. (2010). *The basic of psychotherapy: An introduction to theory and practice*. Washington, DC: American Psychological Association.

Wampold, B. (2001). *The great psychotherapy debate: Models, methods, and findings*. Mahwah, NJ: Lawrence Erlbaum.

Ward, K., & Reuben, D. (2015). *Comprehensive geriatric assessment*. Retrieved from http://www.uptodate.com/contents/comprehensive-geriatric-assessment

Warren, C. S. (2001). Book review of negotiating the therapeutic alliance: A relational treatment guide. *Psychotherapy Research, 11*(3), 357–359.

Watters, Y., & Boyd, T. (2009). Sexuality in later life: Opportunity for reflection for healthcare providers. *Sexual and Relationship Therapy, 24*(3–4), 307–315.

Williams, J. (2005). Depression as a mediator between spousal bereavement and mortality from cardiovascular disease: Appreciating and managing the adverse health consequences of depression in an elderly surviving spouse. *Southern Medical Journal, 98*, 90–95.

Williams, K., Herman, R., & Gajewski, B. (2009). Elderspeak communication: Impact on dementia care. *American Journal of Alzheimer's Disease & Other Dementias, 24*, 11–20.

Williams, M. (2011). The changing roles of grandparents raising grandchildren. *Journal of Human Behavior in the Social Environment, 21*, 948–962.

Wilner, F., & Arnold, R. (2004). The Palliative Performance Scale. Fast facts and concepts #125. End-of-Life Palliative Education Resource Center. Retrieved from http://www.eperc.mcw.edu

World Health Organization (WHO). (2015). *Mental health and older adults.* Retrieved from http://www.who.int/mediacentre/factsheets/fs381/en/

Wubbolding, R. (2007). Reality therapy theory. In D. Capuzzi & D. Gross (Eds.), *Counseling and psychotherapy* (pp. 289–312). Upper Saddle River, NJ: Pearson.

Yancura, R. (2013). Service use and unmet service needs in grandparents raising grandchildren. *Journal of Gerontological Social Work, 56*(b), 473–486.

Zarit, S., Reever, K., & Bach-Peterson, J. (1980). Relatives of the impaired elderly: Correlates of feeling of burden. *Gerontologist, 20*(6), 649–655.

Zarit, S. H., & Zarit, J. M. (2011). *Mental disorders in older adults: Fundamentals of assessment.* New York, NY: Guilford Press.

Therapeutic Approaches and Appropriateness for Older Clients

"It is not by muscle, speed, or physical dexterity that great things are achieved, but by reflection, force of character, and judgment. In these qualities old age is usually not only poorer, but is even richer."

—Cicero

Learning Objectives

After reading this chapter, you will be able to

1. Describe the problem-solving therapy intervention
2. Analyze the use of brief dynamic therapy
3. Examine behavioral therapy approaches
4. Explain cognitive therapy
5. Discuss cognitive-behavioral therapy approaches
6. Summarize the integrative approach
7. Analyze the strengths-based approach
8. Compare and contrast life review and reminiscence therapy
9. Examine the reality orientation philosophy

INTRODUCTION

Professional counselors are in an excellent position to enhance the lives of older clients. Contrary to popular belief, older persons can change and are amenable to psychotherapeutic interventions. Though many of life's transitions are managed effectively without professional help, more older persons are becoming familiar and comfortable with using services of counseling professionals.

The older population is in an advantageous position of having lived a long life and are therefore more knowledgeable and experienced in many areas. Older clients can be introspective, engage in transformation, learn new skills and problem-solving strategies. Recognizing and using their positive attributes serves as a solid foundation in treatment. A sense of mastery can be cultivated in older clients when they build on existing strengths, abilities, and accomplishments. To achieve the clients' goals, numerous interventions have been developed and modified for application to the issues and challenges faced by older adults.

PROBLEM-SOLVING THERAPY

Problem-solving therapy (PST) is a psychological intervention for depression that teaches people a structured method for overcoming problems they feel have either contributed to their depressive state or have become difficult to overcome because of their depression. PST has developed a strong evidence base and has been found to be effective for the treatment of depression in young adults, older adults, medical patients, and adults with disabilities (Rovner & Casten, 2008).

For older adults, deficits in problem-solving skills may be a function of lifelong dysfunction, that is never having developmental opportunity to refine their social problem-solving abilities, or problem-solving deficits may be a function of age-related changes in cognitive processes, in particular deficits in executive functions. Executive functions consist of anticipation, goal setting, planning, initiation, the use of feedback to decrease inappropriate action, and attention shifting—all skills necessary in proper problem solving. As we age, there is a natural loss of some executive capacities, but these age-related declines are normal and generally are compensated for by the use of other brain functions. Although these changes should not significantly affect day-to-day functions, the combination of age-related executive decline and impairments to executive dysfunction conferred by major depression (Reppermund, Ising, Lucae, & Zihl, 2009) present a particular challenge for older adults coping with daily stress. Whatever the cause of problem-solving deficits, whether it is lifelong dysfunction or the combination of age-related declines and deficits associated with major depression, problem-solving therapy is meant to provide for the older depressed patient a compensatory framework, whereby these deficits can be remediated and lead to improvements in functioning and mood. PST was developed as a depression intervention and has since been used in mildly retarded adults, depressed older adults, older adults with mild cognitive impairment, and medically ill populations (Mynors-Wallis, Gath, Day, & Baker, 2000). According to the theory, people most vulnerable to depression are those who either have inadequate problem-solving skills or those whose skills are not being used because they feel unable to change their situation. According to problem-solving theory, the ideal way to intervene in this depressogenic cycle is to teach patients how to mobilize their coping resources and begin tackling the problems in their lives. Once they begin to successfully solve problems, depression lifts and the motivation to face other problems increases.

Guided Practice Exercise 11.1 provides the opportunity to facilitate the acquisition of problem-solving skills for a client.

Guided Practice Exercise 11.1

Your older client is no longer able to ambulate independently and is dependent on her social network to assist with activities of daily living and instrumental activities of daily living. She is depressed by her current situation and constantly states, "I am sorry I am such a burden" and "I really do not know what to do." As her counselor, you are to teach your client how to solve her issues to feel a sense of mastery.

To date, there are two versions of PST, one developed for patients in mental health settings and one developed for primary care patients (PST-PC) (Mynors-Wallis, 1996). The two interventions are similar in content with regard to treating mental illness, but differ in approach. Both versions have further adaptations; for instance, social problem solving therapy (SPST) has been adapted for cancer patients with depression, and PST-PC has been adapted for blind and home bound patients. Both SPST and PST-PC has been adapted and have an evidence base for older adults with depression (Arean, Hegel, & Reynolds, 2001).

Problem-Solving Process

The problem-solving process translates into roughly seven steps that a person must engage in to solve problems. SPST collapses some steps, resulting in a 5-step process, and also includes an initial step that PST-PC does not. The initial step in skill development in SPST is problem orientation, which is not a step in PST-PC. In SPST, problem definition includes goal setting, whereas in PST-PC it is a separate step. Also selecting the solution and development of a plan to implement the solution in PST-PC is collapsed in SPST into solution implementation and evaluation. Table 11.1 illustrates the two approaches.

Both versions of PST teach patients to solve problems by first identifying and defining problems in concrete and objective terms. This step is most important, as it sets the stage for potential solutions. The second step is determining the desired outcome or goal for the problem-solving process, also in concrete and observable terms. After a goal is determined, the client moves to the third step; the creative production of various methods for solving problems and meeting one's goals, while withholding judgment on their effectiveness. The fourth step involves a systematic process to select the best solution for a problem from the list generated by weighing the pros and cons of each solution. The fifth step is to then select the best solution from the generated list based on the thoughtful review of each solution. Once the solution is selected, the next step is to have the client develop a specific plan to implement the solution. The final and seventh step is to evaluate the effectiveness of the plan (once implemented).

Table 11.1   PST-PC and SPST

PST-PC	SPST
Problem identification and definition	Problem orientation
Goal setting	Problem definition
Problem solving methods	Generation of alternative solutions
Examination of pros/cons of solution	Decision-making
Select solution	Solution implementation and evaluation
Plan for implementation of solution	

In SPST, the treatment begins with an initial step called problem orientation, which examines how a client views his or her ability to cope with a problem. This is a cognitive strategy aimed at challenging a person's beliefs regarding his or her ability to solve problems. The second is problem definition, which is concerned with the specific and concrete definition of the problem and setting achievable and definable goals. The third skill, generation of alternatives, involves creating various methods for solving problems and meeting one's goals, while withholding judgment on their effectiveness. The fourth skill, decision making, involves a systematic process to select the best solution for a problem from the list generated. The fifth and final skill in SPST solution implementation and evaluation, involving planning and initiation of solutions and subsequently evaluating the success of the solution (Arean, 2006).

SPST is delivered over 10 to 12 sessions. The first session explains depression and explication of the model. It is important to educate older clients about what depression is and how this therapy works, because so many older adults hold inaccurate ideas about depression and fear psychotherapy. After this introduction, the next five sessions are focused on teaching each of the five skills previously identified. After each step is taught and prescribed, the remaining sessions are spent using the model to solve the person's problems. Guided practice is particularly important in teaching new psychosocial skills. The more opportunities older people have to practice new behavior, the more likely they are to retain the skills and use them in the future (Arean, 2006).

PST-PC is typically six to eight sessions. The first session is one hour long and explains depression and the entire problem-solving model. By the end of the first session, clients have been taught each step in the process, and have at least one problem they will try to solve using the process during the week. Subsequent sessions last 30 minutes and are meant to review the problem-solving steps and continue solving more problems until the person understands and can implement the model with minimal coaching (Arean, 2006).

Although some have speculated as to the relative merits of these two forms of PST (Nezu, 2004), there has been no direct comparison of the two models to determine that one is superior to the other. Further, both versions have their own positive data in support of their efficacy. The decision to use one version over the other may have more to do with the target population than with relative efficacy. PST-PC is an efficient model of psychotherapy that works well within the primary care setting. SPST may be more amenable to mental health settings.

Support for PST and SPST in Older Adults

Arean and colleagues (2010) investigated the efficacy of PST in older patients with major depression and executive dysfunction. Therapists administered both PST and supportive therapy (ST). Results indicated greater improvement in the PST group compared to the ST group. By the end of the 12-week trial more than half of the PST patients met criteria for treatment response and 45% met criteria for remission. Choi and colleagues (2012) found similar responsiveness to PST in a sample with lower socioeconomic status.

Gellis and Bruce (2010) tested the outcomes of a PST intervention for elderly health home care patients with heart disease and mild to moderate depression. Results of this study indicate that PST adapted for home care patients had significant positive effects on older home health care patients with cardiovascular disease.

Gellis and colleagues (2008) tested the outcomes of a PST intervention for medically ill home care patients with minor depression. The control condition was treatment as usual (TAU) augmented with depression education. Results showed significant improvement in depressive symptoms for patients receiving PST, but patients in the TAU conditions did not experience any significant changes on any measure from baseline to post treatment (Gellis et al., 2008). Further analyses indicated that the positive effects of PST were maintained at 3 and 6 months post intervention. There were no significant differences between outcomes at 3 and 6 months for PST participants indicating that depressive symptoms did not begin to rise again after the intervention. PST participants still reported significantly lower depression symptomatology at these follow-up measurements compared to TAU participants (Gellis et al., 2008).

Gellis, McGinty, Horowitz, Bruce, and Misener (2007) tested the outcomes of a home-care-based PST intervention for older adults identified with severe depressive symptoms in an acute home care setting. Forty participants, over 65 and receiving acute home care for medical conditions, participated in the trial and provided baseline, posttreatment, 3-month and 6-month follow-up data. Home care patients in the PST condition reported significantly lower depressive symptoms as compared with the usual care group. Patients in the usual care condition did not experience any significant changes on any measure from baseline to posttreatment. The PST group improved on the Beck Depression Index scores with no advantage for the usual care group reflecting a large effect size. A significant reduction in depressive symptomatology for the PST group was maintained 3 and 6 months after treatment ended (Gellis et al., 2007).

Ciechanowski and colleagues (2004) investigated the efficacy of PST in home-based care with patients with minor depression or dysthymia and with a high level of medical illness. A significant group by time interaction indicated significant group differences in depressive symptoms at 6 and 12 months. Moreover, the odds of a 50% depression treatment response or of complete remission were significantly higher for the PST group at 6 and 12 months. The intervention resulted in significantly lower severity and greater remission of depression compared with usual care at 6 and 12 months. Thirty percent of patients in the intervention group and 12% in the usual care group experienced remission (Ciechanowski et al., 2004).

Problem-solving therapy reduces suicidal ideation in depressed older adults with executive dysfunction (Gustavson et al., 2015). Two hundred and twenty-one participants were 65 years of age and older with a diagnosis of major depression and executive dysfunction as defined by a score of 33 or less on the Initiation—Preservation Score of the Maltis Dementia Rating Scale or Stroop Interference Task score of 25 or less. The suicide item of the Hamilton Rating Scale (HRS) was used as the main outcome measure. Of the 221 participants, 61% reported suicidal ideation (SI). The ST group had a lower rate of improvement in SI after 12 weeks (44.6%) than did the PST group (60.4%). Logistic regression showed significantly greater reductions in SI in elders who received PST at both 12 weeks and 36 weeks after treatment (Gustavson et al., 2015).

Problem-solving therapy for primary care (PST-PC) was compared to community-based psychotherapy in treating late-life major depression and dysthymia. Older adults who received PST-PC had more depression-free days at both 12 and between 12 and 24 months and they had fewer depressive symptoms and better functioning at 12 months than those who received community-based psychotherapy (Arean, Hegel, Vannoy, Fan, & Unuzter, 2008). No differences were found at 24 months. Results suggest that PST-PC as delivered in primary care settings is an effective method for treating late-life depression.

Choi and colleagues (2012) investigated whether passive cognitive coping styles mediated PST treatment outcome in low-income homebound older adults. Both tele-PST and in-person PST were delivered by the same therapists who were trained in PST. Mixed-effects regression analysis was conducted to test the moderating effect of passive coping on the relationship between PST and depressive symptoms at follow-ups. There was a significant main effect of group (PST vs. telephone support call) on reducing depressive symptoms regardless of coping style (Choi et al., 2012).

A study by Williams and colleagues (2000) compared PST to Paxil and placebo in older medical patients with mild depression in several sites throughout the United States. The results indicated that while PST was effective in treating minor depression in older adults, particularly those with greater symptoms of depression, it was not effective in treating dysthmia, and was also subject to site differences in delivery. Another study found that PST-PC, in combination with antidepressant medication, was effective in treating depression in older depressed patients (Haverkamp et al., 2004). Both SPST and PST-PC are efficacious interventions for treating depression in older adults. SPST has more data in support of its efficacy in older adults with major depression and mild cognitive impairments, but PST-PC is fast developing an evidence base for treating both minor and complex depressive disorders in older medical patients (Arean, 2006).

BRIEF DYNAMIC THERAPY

Practitioners of brief psychodynamic therapy believe that some changes can happen through a more rapid process or that an initial short intervention will start an ongoing process of change that does not need the constant involvement of a therapist. A central concept in brief therapy is that there should be one major focus for the therapy rather than the more traditional psychoanalytic practice of allowing the client to associate freely and discuss unconnected issues. In brief therapy, the central focus is developed during the initial evaluation process, occurring during the first session or two. This focus must be agreed on by the client and therapist. The central focus singles out the most important issues and thus creates a structure and identifies a goal for the treatment. In brief therapy, the therapist is expected to be fairly active in keeping the session focused on the main issue. Having a clear focus makes it possible to do interpretive work in a relatively short time because the therapist only addresses the circumscribed problem area (Haggerty, 2013).

Brief dynamic therapy (BDT) is often used with older adults to address issues such as adjustment and traumatic stress disorders, grief issues, and self-concept during aging using a time-limited and focused approach (Kennedy & Tanenbaum, 2000). Techniques typically used in BDT include exploration of unconscious processes, processing of lifetime developmental issues, and facilitating client insight with regard to making life changes. Transference and countertransference are important factors to be aware of when using BDT. Transference refers to redirection of a client's feelings for a significant person to the therapist, whereas countertransference is redirection of a therapist's feelings toward a client (therapist's emotional entanglement with a client) (Etchegoyen, 2005).

The main goals of BDT are to increase awareness and insight into the unconscious processes leading an individual to repeat past experiences and to institute corrective experiences through the interaction between client and therapist. An essential adaptation of BDT for working with older adults includes helping the client regain self-mastery and a positive self-perception, while preventing the development of dependency. Limiting the number of sessions to 15 allows many clients to successfully complete treatment and reduces the development of unhealthy dependency (Kennedy & Tanenbaum, 2000).

Guided Practice Exercise 11.2 gives counselors the opportunity to examine the clients' history and extrapolate strengths and resources to utilize throughout the counseling sessions.

Guided Practice Exercise 11.2

As a counselor, older persons will come to you with issues they view as problematic. Issues may be part of the natural aging process and may include physical changes, such as limitations in functioning and numerous losses. Despite the fact that counseling may be brief, you can examine the breadth of information from your client's expansive life cycle. Counselors need to focus on strengths and resources and help clients view themselves more positively, while acknowledging numerous stressors and transitions. Ask your client questions about the times when he or she felt productive in the past, current situations when he or she feels at his or her best, what will be different when he or she is back to his or her usual self, and how will his or her behavior change once the problems have been resolved.

Arean and Cook (2002) evaluated the use of BDT as a viable therapy and has shown it to be an effective treatment of depression in older adults. Brief dynamic therapy is an effective intervention for late life major depression in healthy and ambulatory elderly adults; however, more research is needed to compare its effectiveness with antidepressant medication.

Brief dynamic therapy (BDT) is a therapeutic intervention particularly appropriate for use in therapeutic sessions with older adults. It is advantageous in that it addresses issues of adjustment, stressful disorders, grief, and self-concept issues, which are routinely experienced by older adults. The brief nature of this approach reduces the potential dependency, which may occur in a longer form of therapy.

BEHAVIORAL THERAPY

Behavioral therapy is focused on helping an individual understand how changing their behavior can lead to changes in how they are feeling. The goal of behavior therapy is usually focused on increasing the person's engagement in positive or socially reinforcing activities. Behavioral therapy is a structured approach that carefully measures what the person is doing and then seeks to increase chances for positive experience (Herkov, 2013a).

Common techniques include self-monitoring, which is the first stage of treatment in which the person is asked to keep a detailed log of all of their activities during the day. By examining the list at the next session, the therapist can see exactly what the person is doing. A schedule of weekly activities is where the patient and therapist work together to develop new activities that will provide the patient with chances for positive experience. Role playing is used to help the person develop new skills and anticipate issues that may come up in social interactions. Behavior modification is a technique used in which the patient will receive a reward for engaging in positive behavior (Herkov, 2013a).

Behavioral approaches, such as relaxation, desensitization, and shaping new responses, have many potential applications with elderly persons. Behavioral treatments are effective with insomnia, depression, and anxiety and in helping families manage problems related to dementia and other chronic medical and mental illnesses (Rusin & Lawson, 2001; Smith et al., 2002; Teri et al., 2003). Many behavioral interventions have been conducted in institutional settings. The targets of these programs have included increasing social participation, increasing exercise, improving self-care activities, managing incontinence, training social skills, and particularly, controlling problems such as wandering and agitation.

Behavioral therapy is valuable with older clients as much for its basic concepts and approaches as for specific techniques. The overriding emphasis in behavioral therapy is observation: observing the specific behaviors, thoughts, or feelings that are problematic for a client, their frequency (or absence), and the circumstances in which problems occur. This direct approach to problems appeals to the practical side of many older people. As with the use of empathy, careful observation challenges therapists to go beyond cultural stereotypes about aging. The focus on overt behavior in particular also helps therapists and clients move beyond incorrect attributions of problems. Clients, for example, may mislabel problems or may describe a problem as occurring more or less than it actually does. By obtaining the specific details of the problem and when and how it occurs, the clinician gains valuable information for planning treatment (Zarit & Zarit, 2011).

Behavioral therapy provides a simple framework for helping clients understand and learn to handle their problems. Through discussion of findings from behavioral assessments, therapists demonstrate the A-B-C (antecedent-behavior-consequence) model of behavior (Teri Logsdon, & Uomoto, 1997). Behaviors have antecedents, that is, specific events that trigger them, as well as consequences or events that occur to reinforce the problem. This approach helps clients understand that problems do not emerge out of the blue and that they have some control over the situation. This type of concrete framework works well with clients who are not well educated and for whom more cognitively demanding approaches might be problematic (Zarit & Zarit, 2011).

Another approach that is especially useful with older clients is to emphasize implementing new behavior in specific, graduated steps. Rather than instructing a client to carry out a complex set of behaviors, the therapist breaks down tasks into steps or components that are easy to master and remember. In many instances, clients agree to carry out new behaviors but delay or put off actually doing anything new. Behavioral approaches address this problem with schedules for specific behaviors and reinforcements for carrying them out. The detailed, concrete steps involved in planning and scheduling new behaviors are often critical in helping depressed or dependent clients break out of a cycle of passiveness and inaction. In a broader sense, behavioral approaches encourage clients to take an active role in treatment, which is especially useful for older clients who feel helpless or overwhelmed. The strong educational component helps clients understand why they are having problems and how new behaviors can help them overcome those problems (Zarit & Zarit, 2011).

Probably the most useful feature of a behavioral orientation is its emphasis on evaluating the outcome of treatment. Health care professionals, family members, and older clients themselves are often pessimistic about the possibilities for change. An effective way to counter this skepticism about the value of treatment is to demonstrate that there have been measurable improvements. A detailed assessment, which is the first step in behavioral treatment, provides a clear baseline against which outcomes can be evaluated. By obtaining concrete evidence of progress, clinicians can reassure clients about the capacity to improve or to benefit from psychotherapy.

COGNITIVE THERAPY

Cognitive therapy is based on the theory that much of how we feel is determined by what we think. Disorders, such as depression, are believed to be the result of faulty thoughts and beliefs. By correcting these inaccurate beliefs, the person's perception of events and emotional state improve (Herkov, 2013b). Research on depression has shown that people with depression often have inaccurate beliefs about themselves, their situation, and the world (Herkov, 2013b). Common cognitive errors include personalization, which is relating negative events to oneself when there is no basis. Dichotomous thinking is seeing things as black and white, or all or none. This is usually detected when a person can generate only two choices in a situation. Selective abstraction is focusing on certain aspects of a situation, usually the most negative. Magnification-minimization is distorting the importance of particular events (Herkov, 2013b). Cognitive therapists work with the person to challenge thinking errors and by pointing out alternative ways of viewing a situation, the person's view of life, and ultimately their mood will improve. Cognitive therapy can be as effective as medication in the long-term treatment of depression (Herkov, 2013b), which is prevalent in older adults.

In cognitive therapy, older clients learn to look at their thoughts objectively (distancing), re-evaluate thoughts rather than automatically accepting and reacting to them, and reframe problems and expectations of themselves and their world. By becoming aware of the rules and assumptions they use to experience their world, clients are more easily able to change maladaptive cognitions. With increased awareness of their basic assumptions and by re-evaluating their life rules, older adults can begin to free themselves from debilitating expectations that result in depression or other forms of pathology.

Guided Practice Exercise 11.3 encourages the counselor to examine faulty thinking and reframe cognitions in more positive and productive ways.

Guided Practice Exercise 11.3

As a counselor, you will need to address issues of client dependency, feeling a burden on family members, feelings of worthlessness and expressions of hopelessness. Using a cognitive approach, identify strategies to address these cognitions. How will you attempt to restructure or reframe your client's negative perceptions and expressions? Be sure to incorporate the clients' strengths in your analysis.

Global and specific issues related to loss, coping, and depression can be effectively addressed through cognitive therapy with older clients. In working with issues of depression, the clinician's task is to challenge negative schemas and decrease the arousal associated between schemas and current life experiences (Hyer et al., 1990). The reported positive effects of cognitive therapy in dealing with issues of self-concept and feelings of hopelessness, two primary concerns of older adults, make the treatments particularly useful for older adults who are depressed and/or trying to cope with significant bio-psychosocial issues (Rush, Beck, Kovacs, Weissenberger, & Hollon, 1982).

Cognitive therapy has several distinct advantages for older adult patients. For one, the practical emphasis on dealing with present problems that counteracts the common belief among older adults that it is too late to manage issues from earlier in life. Similarly, the underlying assumption that a person can change his or her mood by simply changing his or her thinking is likely to have more appeal than models that imply that substantial changes to personality or relationships are required. Finally, compared to the models in which the therapist is viewed as the all-knowing expert, the collaborative aspect of cognitive therapy affords a greater opportunity for typically younger psychotherapists to give credit to older patients for their experiences and their knowledge acquired with age. Conversely, cognitive therapy may not be ideal for older patients who have some age-related cognitive deficits, due to the heavy emphasis on learning new concepts and homework assignments (Rybarczyk, 2006).

Cognitive therapy is an effective psychotherapeutic intervention that shows promise in treatment of older clients. Its emphasis on identification of inaccurate thoughts and systematically reframing these cognitions is appropriate for cognitively intact older adults.

COGNITIVE-BEHAVIORAL THERAPY

What older people believe about themselves and their experiences and how they typically appraise events in their lives is a major focus of treatment. CBT is based on a cognitive model of the relationship among cognition, emotion, and behavior. Mood and behavior are viewed as determined by a person's perception and interpretation of events, which manifest as a stream of automatically generated thoughts. These automatic thoughts have their origins in an underlying network of beliefs or schema. The therapeutic process consists of helping the patient become aware of his or her internal stream of thoughts when distressed and to identify and modify the dysfunctional thoughts. Behavioral techniques are used to bring about functional changes in behavior, regulate emotion, and help the cognitive restructuring process. Modifying the patient's underlying dysfunctional beliefs leads to lasting improvements. In this structured therapy, the therapist and patient work collaboratively to use an approach that features reality testing and experimentation (Chand & Grossberg, 2013).

Core principles of CBT remain unchanged when treating older adults; however, many CBT programs for older adults explicitly address physical health as well as spiritual and religious beliefs and behavior in the treatment (Paukert, Phillips, & Cully, 2009). A number of practical issues may limit the effectiveness of CBT for a specific patient, including patient beliefs about the usefulness of therapy compared with medication, financial considerations, active health issues, sensory impairment, mobility, transportation issues, and cognitive changes. Consideration should be given to these factors when delivering CBT to older adults (Cox & D'Oyley, 2011). A modification to the standard CBT manual is necessary for older adults, which includes increasing type size to account for visual impairment and also increasing the number of sessions to provide for added summary and review, or explicit learning and memory tools may be incorporated (Cox & D'Oyley, 2011).

Several features of cognitive-behavioral therapy make it well suited for work with older people who are cognitively intact, open to change, and believe in nonpharmacological treatments. First, as with behavioral approaches, there is a strong psychoeducational component. Clients learn about how their thought processes affect behavior and emotions, as well as learning to identify the thoughts they are having that trigger emotions. As in behavioral therapy, the techniques are applied to everyday situations. The detailed process of planning and scheduling intervention helps overcome a client's passivity. Other features that cognitive approaches have in common with behavior therapy are the emphasis on identifying when, how often, and in what context problems occur and on evaluating the outcomes of specific interventions (Zarit & Zarit, 2011).

The heart of cognitive therapy is identifying what people think about themselves and their circumstances. There are so many negative stereotypes about elderly people that clients readily incorporate these stereotypical beliefs into their self-concepts. The issues older people raise often have a basis in reality but are also somewhat exaggerated. One of the most complex issues that therapists see in older adults is differentiating between a reasonable sense of sadness or grief over loss and an overgeneralized and excessive preoccupation with it. Clients who have experienced losses often believe that life is not worth living or that they will never be happy again. The cognitive-behavioral therapist can discuss the appropriateness of being sad over a loss while challenging the exaggerated belief that the client will never again be happy.

When therapists use cognitive-behavioral approaches with younger clients, they can readily identify which beliefs are excessive or exaggerated. If a college student proclaims that her life is over because her boyfriend has broken up with her, the therapist recognizes the exaggeration right away. He or she knows that the client will have more relationships in her life and can feel secure in challenging this negative belief. When an older client makes a similar generalization following the death of a spouse, clinicians may accept it uncritically. The death of a spouse is, of course, more serious than breaking up with a boyfriend or girlfriend, and a period of grieving is normal. But when grief persists long after the spouse's death, it is usually due to exaggerated beliefs that make the loss worse than it needs to be (Zarit & Zarit, 2011).

In order to differentiate the realistic and reasonable consequences of loss from exaggeration, the therapist engages clients in a gentle process of questioning and challenging beliefs. Clients learn to identify overgeneralizations or other distortions in their self-appraisals and the events in their lives and to activate more realistic appraisals of themselves. This questioning process must always be embedded with empathy. It should never become harsh or argumentative, even when the therapist is directing clients to examine critically the assumptions they have been making (Zarit & Zarit, 2011).

Guided Practice Exercise 11.4 provides the opportunity to explore the dynamics of major life transitions and a maladaptive response and address a client's issues.

Guided Practice Exercise 11.4

Mr. James worked his entire life and retired from the railroad at the age of 68. He has sufficient financial resources and planned well for his retirement from a financial perspective. He is healthy and takes only one medication for hypertension. He never had time for hobbies and has been widowed for 10 years with no desire for an intimate relationship. He is bored, lonely, and unsure of what to do with himself, so he began drinking heavily. He has initiated counseling because he is aware he has a drinking problem. As a counselor, define his problem(s), identify the issues, create questions to ask Mr. James, and determine alternatives that need to be explored to assist him in better understanding his pattern of drinking.

Stanley and Novy (2000) report positive results with anxious older clients using cognitive-behavioral therapy and relaxation training. Lang and Stein (2001) recommend that treatment of anxiety in older adults should be tailored to the individual needs and cognitive abilities of the client. Some older clients resent advice given by professionals younger than they are. They may find relaxation approaches inappropriate or childish. Systematic desensitization may be seen as unrelated to their situation or to the origins of their anxiety, and they may view changes in the way they are told to perceive life events as dangerous to their survival since long-held beliefs and behaviors have often served them well in the past. Being asked to view a situation with clarity and rationality may suggest to the older adult that counselors believe they are lying about an event. Older adults may discount psychological explanations for their anxiety and prefer to think that it has a physical origin. All of these cautionary suggestions should be taken into account when working with anxious older adults or the counselor runs the risk of having psychological treatments dismissed completely (Glicken, 2009; Lang & Stein, 2001). A suggestion to encourage better acceptance of any intervention is to give clients reading materials to help them understand the origins of their anxiety and the approach most likely to help relieve their symptoms.

Cognitive-behavioral approaches are another form of short-term treatment where clients are taught to overcome addiction to alcohol. In cognitive-behavioral approaches, the client is taught to identify the situations that lead to drinking and to rethink those situations in more positive and rational ways. Perceptions of stressful events are important, and clients are taught to logically rethink the situation and to reduce the stressful impact that may bring with it alcohol abuse (Glicken, 2009).

Both cognitive therapy and behavioral therapy, the two components of CBT have a significantly better effect than placebo on outcome measures of depression (Cox & D'Oyley, 2011). CBT and behavioral therapy are recommended interventions for the treatment of unipolar major depressive disorder with clear data on efficacy. The data suggest that in older adults, the combination of CBT with antidepressants results in a greater response rate than treatment with medication alone (Canadian Coalition for Seniors' Mental Health, 2006). Simon, Cordas, and Bottino (2014) investigated CBTs in improving depressive symptoms, disability, and cognition in older adults with depression and cognitive deficits. They found that older adults with depression and cognitive deficits can benefit from CBTs. Improvements in mood and disability were more consistent than changes in cognition. CBT has also demonstrated efficacy in the treatment of generalized anxiety disorder (GAD) in older adults (Laidlaw, Thompson, & Dick-Siskin, 2003; Thorpe, Ayers, & Nuevo, 2009) and may have a role to play in the prevention of other clinically significant anxiety disorders in older adults followed in primary care for one year (vant Veer-Tazelaar, van Marwijk, & van Oppen, 2009).

Cognitive-behavioral therapy has been shown to be effective in addressing issues of self-concept, depression, loss, anxiety, and substance abuse in older adults. The collaborative nature of this approach engages older clients in the process of examining his or her cognitions, emotions, and behaviors.

INTEGRATIVE APPROACH

Clinicians have used a number of ways to integrate the various counseling theories or psychotherapy, including technical eclecticism, theoretical integration, assimilative integration, common factors, multitheoretical psychotherapy, and helping skills integration (Norcross & Goldfried, 2005).

The first route to integration is called common factors and "seeks to determine the core ingredients that different therapies share in common" (Norcross, 2005, p. 9). The advantage of a common factors approach is the emphasis on therapeutic actions that have been demonstrated to be effective. The disadvantage is that common factors may overlook specific techniques that have been developed within different theories. Common factors theory asserts it is precisely the factors common to most psychotherapies that make any psychotherapy successful.

The second route to integration is technical eclecticism, which is designed "to improve our ability to select the best treatment for the person and the problem . . . guided primarily by data on what has worked best for others in the past" (Norcross, 2005, p. 8). The advantage of technical eclecticism is that it encourages the use of diverse strategies without being hindered by theoretical differences. A disadvantage is that there may not be a clear conceptual framework describing how techniques drawn from divergent theories might fit together.

The third route to integration commonly recognized is theoretical integration in which "two or more therapies are integrated in the hope that the result will be better than the constituent therapies alone" (Norcross, 2005, p. 8). Some models of theoretical integration focus on combining and synthesizing a small number of theories at a deep level, whereas others describe the relationship between several systems of psychotherapy.

Assimilative integration is the fourth route and acknowledges that most psychotherapists select a theoretical orientation that serves as their foundation but, with experience, incorporate ideas and strategies from other sources into their practice. This mode of integration favors a firm grounding in any one system of psychotherapy, but with a willingness to incorporate or assimilate, in a considered fashion, perspectives or practices from other schools. Increasingly, integrationists are acknowledging that most counselors prefer the security of one foundational theory as they begin the process of integrative exploration. Formal models of assimilative integration has been described based on a psychodynamic foundation (Stricker & Gold, 2005) and based on cognitive-behavioral therapy (Castonguay, Newman, Borkovec, Holtforth, & Maramba, 2005).

Other newer models that combine aspects of the traditional routes have been developed. Clara E. Hill's (2014) three-stage model of helping skills encourages counselors to emphasize skills from different theories during different stages of helping. The first stage is exploration and is based on client-centered therapy. The second stage is entitled insight, and interventions used in this stage are based on psycho-analytic therapy. The last stage is the action stage and is based on behavioral therapy. Good and Beitman (2006) described an integrative approach highlighting both core components of effective therapy and specific techniques designed to target clients' particular areas of concern. This approach can be described as an integration of common factors and technical eclecticism. Multitheoretical psychotherapy (Brooks-Harris, 2008) is a new integrative model that combines elements of technical eclecticism and theoretical integration. Therapists are encouraged to make intentional choices about combining theories and intervention strategies. An approach called integral psychotherapy (Forman, 2010; Ingersoll & Zeitler, 2010) is grounded in the work of theoretical psychologist and philosopher Ken Wilber (2000), who integrates insights from contemplative and meditative traditions. Integral theory is a meta-theory that recognizes that reality can be organized from four major perspectives: subjective, intersubjective, objective, and interobjective.

Various psychotherapies typically ground themselves in one of these four foundational perspectives, often minimizing the others. Integral psychotherapy includes all four. For example, psychotherapeutic integration using this mode would include subjective approaches (cognitive, existential), intersubjective approaches (interpersonal, object relations, multicultural), objective approaches (behavioral, pharmacological), and interobjective approaches (systems science). By understanding that each of these four basic perspectives all simultaneously co-occur, each can be seen as essential to a comprehensive view of the life of the client. Integral theory also includes a stage model that suggests that various psychotherapies seek to address issues arising from different stages of psychological development (Wilber, 2000). Finally, integrative psychotherapy can be described as any multimodal approach that combines therapies.

The development of Contextual Cohort-Based Maturity Specific-Challenge (CCMSC) model can be understood as a first step toward applying integrative therapy principles to older adults. The CCMSC model is an alternative to the loss-deficit model of aging (Knight, 2004). This model recognizes that multiple coexisting factors contribute to the experiences of aging. Approaching psychotherapy with older adults with this recognition in mind brings a more comprehensive understanding to life changes, and respects the diverse and specific nature of experiences influencing a client's reality.

The CCMSC model acknowledges that over time, the body's decreased capacity for repair can accumulate as damage and increased susceptibility to disease. However, decline is not synonymous with getting older. Knight (2004) addresses the psychological consequences of aging, yet emphasizes the positive aspects within the life development process, challenging the stereotypical frame through which older adults are commonly viewed and see themselves.

In this model, older adults are seen as more mature than younger ones in certain important ways but also are recognized to be facing some of the hardest challenges that life presents to adults, including adjusting to chronic illness and disability, grieving for loved ones, and caregiving. The special social context of older adults and the fact that they are members of earlier born cohorts raised in different sociocultural circumstances may require adaptations that are not dictated by the developmental processes of aging (Knight, 2004).

Specific challenges in later life use different techniques that are rooted in differing therapeutic traditions for each specific challenge. Grief work is virtually a therapeutic approach in its own right, therapy in chronic illness and disability primarily uses cognitive-behavioral strategies, life review draws on psychodynamic techniques and principles, and therapy dealing with caregiving relies on stress and coping models and draws from family systems therapy and cognitive-behavioral interventions. In this sense, the CCMSC model can be seen as a form of eclecticism, applied to common problems of later life (Knight, 2004).

Case Illustration 11.1 provides the opportunity to utilize an eclectic approach to address the clients' terminal diagnosis, stages of the grieving process, family dynamics, and unfinished business, while giving the client as much control as possible.

CASE ILLUSTRATION 11.1

Dr. Hobbs was a 74-year-old physician who developed prostate cancer that was localized. After he had his prostate removed, he continued to work and felt fine. However, he started experiencing pain in his hips and legs and had some difficulty with ambulation. He took over-the-counter medications to be able to continue working, which was extremely important to him. At the insistence of his son, he returned to his oncologist. After a series of scans, he was diagnosed with metastatic cancer that permeated his bones. He was given numerous doses of chemotherapy, however without success. He was informed that he was being transferred to a nearby hospice because it was projected that he had only 3 to 4 weeks to live. Dr. Hobbs was angry and upset because he had patients who needed him and could not understand why this happened to him. He did not believe in counseling and thought it was for persons who could not handle their problems.

His family consulted the counselor to help Dr. Hobbs decrease his anger so that they could assist him in his dying process. The counselor used a strengths-oriented approach, which ultimately helped Dr. Hobbs realize his accomplishments, take care of his unfinished business, and spend quality time with his loved ones. He never arrived at the level of acceptance, but he felt good about his accomplishments, which included a thriving medical practice, providing a good quality of life for his family, paying for the education of all of his children, and being an excellent role model. The counselor also assisted Dr. Hobbs with updating his will, developing his advanced directives, and communicating with friends who he had planned to visit in the future. Building on his accomplishments and achievements enhanced his quality of life and allowed him to be more comfortable in the dying process.

Puentes (2003) integrated two distinct psychotherapeutic approaches into one mental health nursing intervention for the treatment of affective symptoms in older adults. Cognitive therapy was integrated with life review techniques. The life review techniques were used to enhance the outcomes of cognitive therapy experience for older adults enrolled in outpatient psychotherapy treatment for acute adjustment disorder with an affective component (Puentes, 2003). There may exist situations in which one psychotherapeutic approach is inadequate to address the issues presented in counseling sessions with older clients. An integrative approach that draws upon several different therapeutic approaches may be indicated.

STRENGTHS-BASED APPROACH

Older clients have overcome tremendous adversity within their lives, and they have used their strengths and resiliency to adjust to life transitions and crises. Strengths-based approach utilizes the client's strengths as a central focus to facilitate growth within the counseling relationship. Specific assessment tools utilized include Care-Receiver Efficacy Scale (CRES), Functional-Age Model of Intergenerational Treatment, Vital Involvement

Practice (VIP), Improving Mood-Promoting Access to Collaborative Treatment (IMPACT), Program to Encourage Active Rewarding Lives of Seniors (PEARLS), and Identifying Depression Empowering Activities for Seniors (IDEAS).

Strengths-based approaches share some commonalities, including client resources, collaborative client–helper relationship, causality and effectiveness, and anti-ageist perspective. These approaches assume that clients enter therapy with many skills, capacities, and resources (personal and environmental), which are acknowledged and reinforced. The primary therapeutic endeavor is to elicit and channel appropriate and relevant client skills toward the achievement of the client's goals.

A collaborative client–helper relationship is important when using a strengths-based approach. In contrast, in pathology or deficit-based approaches, the relationship between client and helper tends to be hierarchical, with the therapist or other clinician acting as a benevolent expert with the responsibility of teaching the client new skills and knowing what is best for him or her. In contrast, strengths-based approaches emphasize collaborative client–helper relationships in which the client and helper together seek to discover which client capabilities will prove useful for developing solutions in line with the goals and outcomes that are important to the client (Ronch & Goldfield, 2003).

Causality and effectiveness are an essential component of strengths-based approaches as well. These models focus on building healthy tendencies that already exist within the client's life. This type of process allows therapy to be efficient in terms of time as well as other resources. In comparison, deficits or pathology models tend to spend a great deal of time in attempting to understand how unhealthy tendencies develop or maintain themselves.

An anti-ageist perspective is critical and interwoven throughout the process. This perspective recognizes the contributions and accomplishments of individuals as they age. It acknowledges the struggles, challenges, and hardships that older persons have endured while simultaneously acknowledging the various ways older adults have been able to overcome the adversities in their life. It is a perspective that is unbiased and recognizes the abilities and various roles which they have performed within their families, communities, and the larger society. Viewing older adults from a wider lens enables the clinician to appreciate the diversity and heterogeneity that exists and to draw upon their strengths and empower their clients to facilitate change.

The aspects of the strengths-based approach are of special benefit to therapists working with older clients because these processes prevent therapists from limiting the scope of their thinking and actions (in assessing or intervening) in terms of generalizations based on age or diagnostic categories. Older clients who have the ability to communicate and remain actively involved in this process will benefit. Therapists instead are able to notice subtle possibilities and abilities in their clients that otherwise might have been missed. The principles of these strengths-based approaches also benefit older clients because these individuals are not forced to take on new roles based on societal myths about the deficits presumed to be intrinsic to aging in order to resolve their problems (Ronch & Goldfield, 2003).

A strengths-based approach is a manner of working with individuals, families, and organizations grounded in the principles that individuals have existing competencies and resources and are capable of learning new skills and problem solving; can use existing competencies to identify and address their own concerns; and can be involved in the process of healing and self-health (Hirst, Lane, & Navenec, 2011). A strengths-based approach is more than a set of hard and fast rules. It is a perspective. It strives to lead with the positive and values trust, respect, intentionality, and optimism. It is based on the idea that people and environments interact and change each other in the process. Each has the ability to build the other's capacity (Hirst et al., 2011), and it is an alternative to the historical deficit approach found in the fields of mental health and social services where deficits, problem behaviors, and pathologies are the focus (Trout, Ryan, La Vigne, & Epstein, 2003). Rather than focusing on individual weaknesses or deficits, strengths-based practitioners collaborate with adults to discover individual functioning and strengths.

Health care and human service professionals may utilize a strengths-based perspective in their work with individuals. While they do not explicitly follow a particular model, they view and define individuals "by their values, strengths, hopes, aspiration, and capacities, regardless of the stressful or burdensome nature of the situation around them" (Peacock, 2010, pp. 642–643). This perspective guides their work as they seek to balance problems with the strengths of individuals and their environments (Chapin & Cox, 2001; Rashid, 2009) and form plans of care to fit individuals and families (Kivnick & Stoffel, 2005).

A strengths-based perspective is collaborative and reduces the power differential between professionals and individuals/families (Anuradha, 2004; Rashid & Osterman, 2009). A strengths-based perspective includes guiding concepts such as empowerment and social justice (Anuradha, 2004; Chapin & Cox, 2004). While practitioners utilizing a strengths-based perspective may refer to the influence of solution focused therapy, positive psychology or health and human care professionals' emphasis upon individual strengths, their descriptions suggest that they are influenced by such approaches, rather than by actually utilizing the models (Hirst et al., 2011).

Strengths-based assessment tools provide practitioners with positive methods to assess strengths and competencies and thereby develop a strengths-based intervention plan. One such strengths-based tool is the Care-Receiver Efficacy Scale (CRES) (Cox, Green, Seo, Inaba, & Quillen, 2006). The CRES assesses self-efficacy in older adults who are care receivers. This scale was developed in order to fill the need for assessment of self-efficacy of older adults, and also to assist in the measurement of empowerment and strength-oriented approaches that are designed to increase self-efficacy in older adults receiving care. The CRES was tested on older adults (177) 55 years of age and older who required at least 6 hours of care per week and were cognitively able to participate (mean of age participants was 78.4 years). The scale has five subscales: (1) self-care performances, (2) relational coping with caregivers, (3) perceptions of dependence, (4) performance-related quality of life, and (5) accepting help.

Strengths-based interventions are designed to enhance the strengths of particular populations. Functional-Age Model of Intergenerational Treatment is a strength-based assessment and intervention that focuses on the older adult's functional capacities and looks at how older adults can meet the demands of the environment. This approach can be used to assess the older adult's environment and to assess the interdependence between family members (Greene, 2000). In assessing functional age, the professional examines three aspects of capacity: biological, psychological, and sociocultural. Vital involvement practice (VIP) is a strengths-based intervention for working with older, frail adults (Kivnick & Stoffel,

2005). The intervention involves tailoring individual care plans to systematic identification of individual strengths and assets, including the environment and consideration of strengths in relation to individual and environmental challenges. Improving mood-promoting access to collaborative treatment (IMPACT) is a program for older adults who have a major depression or dysthymic disorder (Centers for Disease Control and Prevention & National Association of Chronic Disease Directors, 2009). Program to Encourage Active Rewarding Lives for Seniors (PEARLS) is a brief, time-limited, and participant-driven program that teaches depression management to older adults with depression. It is home based (Center for Disease Control and Prevention & National Association of Chronic Disease Directors, 2009). Identifying Depression, Empowering Activities for Seniors (IDEAS) is a community depression program that is focused at the detection of depressive symptoms in older adults in order to reduce their intensity (Center for Disease Control and Prevention & National Association of Chronic Disease Directors, 2009).

Strengths-based approaches are effective in illuminating the strengths that older clients have used to manage their personal issues throughout life. This approach is essential in working with older clients at a time in which many are experiencing the consequences of aging, hardships, and losses. This approach capitalizes on the resources that older clients have used in the past and bring to the counseling relationship.

REMINISCENCE THERAPY AND LIFE REVIEW

Reminiscence Therapy

Reminiscence therapy (RT) was developed to use with older adults as they reflect on their lives in positive and negative ways. RT is based on Erikson's (1950) theory of psychosocial development, and use of this therapy is seen as a way of regaining balance in an older adult struggling with his or her search for meaning, mastery over life, and self-esteem (Kettell, 2001).

Life review (LR) is the main focus of RT as individuals work on resolving past issues in order to find meaning in the present and promote ego integrity (Kennedy & Tanenbaum, 2000; Pinquart & Sorensen, 2001). RT is a psychosocial intervention that improves self-esteem and provides older patients with a sense of fulfillment and comfort as they look back at their lives (Jones, 2003). Although reminiscing involves recalling past events, it encourages older patients to communicate and interact with a listener in the present (The Benevolent Society, 2005). Reminiscence sessions may be formal, informal, one-on-one, or in a group setting (Klever, 2013).

Reminiscence therapy is all about engaging older patients throughout the day with positive interactions during meal and bed times, bath/shower times, when assisting with walking, or when giving medications. Reminiscing takes minimal skill, but following some guidelines can maximize a reminiscence session. The open-ended question is the most important tool (The Benevolent Society, 2005): How are you getting along today? How long have you and your husband been married? Other helpful tools include active listening, responding positively, asking follow-up questions, and allowing time for silence and emotion. If appropriate, share your own experiences as an offer of support (Klever, 2013).

Many memories spring from mementos, keepsakes, souvenirs, and photographs. Using objects as prompts for memories is especially helpful for patients with dementia.

Chiang and colleagues (2010) examined the effects of reminiscence therapy on psychological well-being, depression, and loneliness among institutionalized elderly people. In an experimental study design, 92 institutionalized elderly people aged 65 years and over were recruited and randomly assigned to two groups. Those participants in the experiential group received reminiscence therapy eight times during 2 months to examine the effects of this therapy on their psychological well-being. After providing the reminiscence therapy to the elderly in the experimental group, a significant positive short-term effect (3 months follow-up) on depression, psychological well-being, and loneliness, as compared to those in the comparison group was found (Chiang et al., 2010). Reminiscence therapy in this study sample improved socialization, induced feelings of accomplishment in participants, and assisted to ameliorate depression.

Melendez-Moral, Charco-Ruiz, Mayordoma-Rodriguez, and Sales-Galan (2013) examined a reminiscence program among institutionalized elderly adults. Institutionalization during old age requires tremendous adaptability. Among the main consequences of the difficulty of adapting to the institutional context are prevalent depressive symptoms and low well-being. Reminiscence has proven to be among the most effective at minimizing these outcomes. Following a group format, the intervention lasted eight sessions and compared a treatment group and a control group, using pre-post measures and a single-blind design. Significant results were obtained, including a drop in depressive symptoms and improved self-esteem, satisfaction, and psychological well-being (Melendez-Moral et al., 2013).

Reminiscence therapy has been proposed as a potentially effective strategy to improve quality of life and psychological well-being for elderly nursing home residents (McKee et al., 2005). This approach involves the recollection, review, and re-evaluation of personally experienced past events. It is believed that reminiscence therapy can help elderly individuals by increasing self-acceptance, providing perspective, and enabling the resolution of past conflicts (Coleman, 1994). The first approach works best with older adults who have relatively good mental health and involves the simple recollection of positive autobiographical events, with the goal of fostering positive emotions. The structure and format of reminiscence interventions also vary considerably across studies. Generally, reminiscence treatments last 6 weeks or longer, and include at least one or two sessions per week, each session lasting between 1 and 2 hours. Moreover, reminiscence activities can be performed either one-to-one or in groups. Reminiscence groups include between six and eight participants and are usually managed by institutional care workers or psychologists (Gaggioli et al., 2014).

The effectiveness of reminiscence therapy has been investigated by several meta-analyses (Bohlmeijer, Roemer, Cuijpers, & Smit, 2007; Forsman, Schierenbeck, & Wahlbeck, 2011; Peng, Huang, Chen, & Lu, 2009; Pinquart, Duberstein, & Lyness, 2007; Pinquart & Forstmeir, 2012). Pinquart and colleagues (2007) analyzed 57 controlled studies, of which eight compared reminiscence with a control condition. Reminiscence was associated with a large effect size, comparable with CBT. These findings lead the authors to conclude that reminiscence and CBT are effective modalities of treatment for depression in older adults. A more recent review by Pinquart and Forstmeier (2012) aggregated results of 128 selected studies. Findings showed that reminiscence interventions produced small to moderate improvements of depressive symptoms and of other indicators of mental health, such as ego integrity, purpose in life, and death preparation. In addition, it was found that improvements of depression were greater than improvements of positive mental health and cognitive performance. Findings suggest that reminiscence therapy is a promising nonpharmacological approach to improve mental health in elderly individuals (Gaggioli et al., 2014). RT specifically tends to be less structured compared with life review therapies in general.

Life Review Therapy

Many older people enjoy sharing their life stories, and this seems to be a pleasurable experience for them. Storytelling not only serves as a means to pass information from one generation to the next, but also to uplift the older persons' status within the community (Haber, 2006). Reviewing one's life allows the older person to preserve his or her identity while shaping and evaluating it in a new way. Life review is a psychoanalytically based intervention which critically analyses one's life history and aims to achieve ego integrity of the participant (Haber, 2006). Life review (LR) is commonly used to provide emotional and spiritual support for older people and the older person who is facing the end of life (Jenko, Gonzalez, & Seymour, 2007). It is also regarded as an important developmental task of an individual throughout the life span (Pasupathi, Weeks, & Rice, 2006; Webster, 2002).

Given that life review is grounded in the life-stage developmental theory of Erikson, it is not surprising that the outcome variables of related studies are usually related to ego integrity and despair. Some studies revealed that life review interventions promoted ego integrity (Haight, Michel, & Hendrix, 2000) and enhanced psychological well-being in older people (Bohlmeijer et al., 2007). These studies showed that life review improved personal meaning (Westerhof, Bohlmeijer, van Beljouw, & Pot, 2010), increased life satisfaction (Bohlmeijer et al., 2007; Chiang, Lu, Chu, Chang, & Chou, 2008; Haight et al., 2000), increased self-esteem (Chiang et al., 2008), and promoted adaptation of older people (Chiang et al., 2008). In addition, studies also revealed that life review interventions prevented despair in older people (Haight et al., 2000), alleviated depressive symptoms (Bohlmeijer, Smit, & Cuijpers, 2003; Hanaoka & O'Kamura, 2004); decreased anxiety (Ando, Morita, Akechi, & Okamoto, 2010), death anxiety (DePaola, Griffin, Young, & Neimeyer, 2003), and hopelessness in older people (Ando et al., 2010; Hanaoka & Okamura, 2004).

Korte, Bohlmeijer, Cappeliez, Smit, and Westerhof (2012) investigated life review therapy in a multisite pragmatic randomized controlled trial (RCT) with older adults with moderate depressive symptomatology. Life review therapy was compared with care as usual. Results indicated that compared with care as usual, life review therapy was effective in reducing depressive symptoms, at post-treatment, at 3-month follow-up, and for the intervention also at 9-month follow-up. Small significant effects were found for symptoms of anxiety and positive mental health.

There are numerous designs of life review interventions conducted to achieve ego integrity of older persons. Besides reviewing one's life along each developmental stage, life review can also be structured around one or more life themes, such as family themes (Haber, 2006; Haight & Haight, 2007). Life review can be conducted in either dyad or group format. Dyad life review is on a one-to-one basis, with one reviewer and one therapeutic listener (Haight & Burnside, 1993). This is easier to access and poses less complicated confidentiality issues. Group life review consists of a therapeutic listener and a group of reviewers. This may raise more complicated confidentiality issues, yet adds the benefit of helping the reviewers establish peer relationships.

There are also different designs of life review interventions with respect to number, duration, and frequency of sessions. The number of sessions may range from 30 minutes to 2 hours, with 1-week interval or more (Ando, Morita, Ahn, Marquez-Wong, & Ide, 2009; Ando et al., 2010; Hanaoka & Okamura, 2004). Some researchers use the Life Review and Experiencing Form (LREF) to guide life reviews (Haight & Haight, 2007), while some use special designed programs, such as the "looking for meaning" program to frame the reviews (Westerhof et al., 2010). Some memorabilia, like scrapbooks, family photo albums, letters, and cherished possessions were involved as catalysts to inspire memories during the life review process (Ando et al., 2010). Advantages to life review include its flexibility to accommodate many topics; application to older adults with diverse backgrounds; and use in individual, family, or group counseling settings.

Guided Practice Exercise 11.5 provides the opportunity to engage in the life review process with an older client utilizing familiar artifacts.

Guided Practice Exercise 11.5

Develop a list of topics that will assist older persons in beginning the life review process. Be sure to include major milestones, health, intimacy, experiences with loss, crises experienced, spiritual development, and career. Now identify how you would structure the sessions, time requirements, material required, and ending the session. Finally, have family members provide family photos, scrapbooks, and other personal items to utilize in this life review process.

LR therapy is indicated for older clients coping with stressful life events or the realization of their own mortality. Techniques that are used in RT and LR therapies are homework assignments that involve finding mementos, photos, journals, autobiographies, and other memorabilia from one's life to share with the therapist in an effort to resolve past issues and gain tolerance of present conflicts (Kennedy & Tanenbaum, 2000).

In working with older adults, especially those who are survivors of traumatizing life events (e.g., Vietnam War's prisoners), LR therapists demonstrate a commitment to listen and understand what the client is experiencing while reviewing his or her past. During this process, clients experience a myriad of emotions, including rage, resentment, and distrust, all of which may affect their engagement in treatment. The therapist's listening attitude and the development of a meaningful degree of understanding between both parties play a critical role in the client's coping response to current life-threatening illnesses, losses, or nursing home placement, which may trigger memories of catastrophic events (Kennedy & Tanenbaum, 2000).

Reminiscence and life review therapies are effective interventions used with older adults to facilitate personal growth in a variety of settings. These interventions engage the clients in a personal exploration of life events that impact their current psychological state. Overall well-being, self-esteem, and personal growth have been achieved utilizing reminiscence and life review therapy.

FAMILY SYSTEMS APPROACH

Family members are frequently involved in treatment of older adults. The substance of treatment frequently involves family issues as well. Therapists must make complex judgments about what actually may be occurring within a family and when to bring in other family members to gather information or involve them in treatment. Treatment usually does not involve family therapy in a traditional sense; it is not what older people or their families seek, nor is it usually necessary in addressing the presenting problems. Rather, a family systems perspective is applied to understand how the family functions and focuses on the features that are most relevant to the stability of the system (Zarit & Zarit, 2011).

Family problem-solving models have been shown to be effective with depressed older adults in methadone maintenance treatment (Rosen, Morse, & Reynolds, 2011). Psychoeducation family interventions have generally been applied in the field of mental health and utilized to support and educate family members about their loved one's illness (Evans, Turner, & Trotter, 2012). Magliano and colleagues (2005) conducted a 1-year follow-up study on the implementation and effectiveness of a psychoeducational family intervention in six European countries. The authors report the psychoeducational intervention was associated with a statistically significant improvement in patients' symptoms and social functioning as well as in family burden and coping strategies (Magliano et al., 2005).

Family as the Therapeutic Unit

Many older adults face multiple biopsychosocial challenges as they age, which include changes in physical and cognitive abilities; barriers to accessing comprehensive, affordable, and high-quality health and mental/behavioral health care; decreased economic security; lack of affordable, accessible housing; increased vulnerability to abuse and exploitation; and loss of meaningful social roles and opportunities to remain engaged in society (National Association of Social Workers, 2010). These challenges often affect entire families who struggle to provide physical, emotional, financial, and practical support to their aging members. Therefore, the family is considered a therapeutic unit and affects the mental health of older adults.

Family Stresses in Later Life

Older adult family members can be considered beneficial to the therapeutic process, but usually only when they are called upon to discuss a younger adult client. The parent(s) of an adult client, for example, might be asked to participate in therapy in order to strike a new balance in the family relationship (Headley, 1977). Although the older parent might benefit from such an experience, it generally is not his or her psychological distress that has called attention to the dysfunction of the family system. However, there are a number of psychological difficulties that older adults face that can best be treated by family therapy, including marital counseling. Marital status and marital disruptions such as the death of a spouse or divorce have a major impact on family relations, especially intergenerational relations, and therefore on support for and from children (Gaymu, Ekamper, & Beets, 2008). Divorce and separation result in fewer contacts and support from (former) family members and children. Adult children may feel less obligated and are less likely to provide support, for example, care and financial support, to divorced or remarried parents. Divorced fathers in particular have a higher risk of losing the support of and contact with their children (Haberkern, Schmid, Neuberger, & Grignon, 2012).

Family counseling can address issues related to caregiving. Adult children provide care to their parents and also increasingly manage care arrangements and ensure that someone looks after their aging parents. Children are an important care resource to cope with the care demands of their parents; however, care of older persons by their children is likely to decline (Pickard, 2013). The availability of children to provide this care and also the willingness to provide remains an issue (Pickard, 2013). These issues and the challenges associated with caregiving are stressors that can be addressed in family counseling sessions.

Retirement may bring similar stress to the family system. The readjustment of the traditional spouse's daily schedule to accommodate a full-time husband is not the only difficulty. It is becoming more frequent that both marriage partners have pursued lifetime careers. In many cases the husband, maybe being somewhat older than the wife, retires first. He may find that his daily life is disrupted when the wife subsequently retires. In either instance, the couple may experience stress as they adjust to the impact of the loss of the work role and its concomitant rewards for one or both of the members of the system.

Although it is generally believed that sexual desires decrease with age, sexual desires, thoughts, and actions continue throughout all decades of life (Wallace, 2012). Human touch and healthy sex lives evoke sentiments of joy, romance, affection, passion, and intimacy, whereas despondency and depression can result from an inability to express one's sexuality (Wallace, 2012). Counselors can play an important role in assessing and facilitating change to enhance the sexual health of older clients. The sexual components of the marital relationship may also require therapeutic intervention in later life. This aspect is often ignored because of negative attitudes about sexuality in later life. Society, counselors, and older couples themselves may be subject to such attitudes.

Counselors are in a position to educate clients on sexual issues, but they often lack knowledge and comfort in discussing sexual issues with older adults (Gott, Hinchliff, & Galena, 2004). However, for counselors who are comfortable and educated in gerontological issues, counselors can educate clients on medical conditions associated with poor sexual health and function (Morley & Tariq, 2003). Other issues that impact sexual functioning include medications (Montejo, Llorca, Izquierdo, & Rico-Villademoros, 2001); normal aging changes (Kessenich & Cichon, 2001; Lobo, 2007); and environmental barriers (Hajjar & Kamel, 2004). Family counseling sessions will include education, client assessment, and compensation for normal changes of aging and environmental adaptations (Freedman, Kaunitz, Reape, Hart, & Shu, 2009; Wallace, 2008; Wespes et al., 2007).

Case Illustration 11.2 illustrates family dynamics, marital discord, sexual issues, the impact of retirement, anger management issues, and communication challenges operating simultaneously.

CASE ILLUSTRATION 11.2

Mrs. Thomas is a highly functional and active 75-year-old female who attended the initial counseling session at her daughter's request. Mrs. Thomas complains of being anxious, constantly worrying about even the smallest things, which is unusual for her. Her husband recently retired after 40 years on the job and is now at home all day long. Mrs. Thomas was a traditional wife and is accustomed to managing her home in the way she chose until her husband's recent retirement. Now he bothers her all of the time, trying to plan her days; insisting on specific meals (never did this before), and is micromanaging everything. When she carries out her activities, she is scolded for the slightest mistakes, and she just complies with her husband's requests. She has grown accustomed to direct sexual intimacy 1 to 2 times per week, at best. However, now he insists on 5 to 6 times weekly. She stays up late at night, hoping that he'll fall asleep. She has only revealed a limited amount of information to her children; however, she is contemplating a legal separation and subsequent divorce.

As the counselor, what are some of the questions you would pose to Mr. Thomas? How would you define the problem? What issues are involved in this case? Is the presenting problem the only problem? What methods would you employ in managing this case?

Families of older people come in all different shapes and sizes. There is no single "dynamic" of an older family or of children's relationship with their elderly parents, such as role reversal, that influences interactions. Rather, the variations in family structure and relationships are considerable. Each family has its own history, structure, and rules, many of which are implicit. Shared memories and unresolved grievances color how family members deal with one another. Interactions from childhood may continue to affect relationships in the present between parents and children and among siblings, but so may the ongoing exchanges that have taken place since children reached adulthood.

Many parents provide considerable emotional and tangible support to children well into their adult years, whereas others may use their resources to manipulate children or place demands on children for attention. From the children's perspective, some learn to appreciate and relate to parents as adults, whereas others persist in psychological struggles that were established in childhood—for example, to gain recognition or acceptance from a withholding parent. The clinician must encounter each family with an open mind about what the psychological issues might be in order to intervene effectively (Zarit & Zarit, 2011).

Working with families demands a different perspective and set of skills than are used with individual clients. One of the biggest mistakes that inexperienced therapists make is to assume that family members can easily get focus and address a current problem in a rational and straightforward way. A family systems perspective goes beyond a focus on the individual and instead looks at patterns of interactions among family members and the roles that each person has within the family (Haley, 1976; Herr & Weakland, 1979). This perspective helps guide the therapist in considering when and how to intervene.

The starting point is gathering information about how a particular family functions. It is important to consider who is influential or powerful within the family; who makes decisions; who is viewed positively by other family members; and who is seen as weak, needy, or problematic. How family members communicate with each other is also relevant. Building on these observations, it is possible to conceptualize problems as caused by interactions rather than by the behavior of one person. Viewing problems in this way opens up more possibilities for intervention. When working with a couple or a family, formulating problems as interactions can break the cycle of accusations and help them try new ways of relating with one another. In many of the situations that involve families—such as when someone is suffering from dementia or chronic psychiatric problems—the patient cannot change. Nevertheless, it is possible to change the interactions others have with that person and with one another, thereby lessening strain on the family as a whole (Zarit & Zarit, 2011).

One of the most important elements of a family systems approach is that the therapist does not take sides, assign blame, or support one person against another. Clinicians are often caught up in tense family situations rife with disagreement about what is best for an older client. The issue of whether an older person should move to an institutional setting is likely to produce disagreements. Therapists in this situation may reflexively take sides with the family member they most identify with: the older person, his or her spouse, or one of the children. Whoever that might be, that person has a role in the family and elicits certain reactions from everyone else. By taking that person's side in the discussion, the therapists either will produce the same reactions from other family members that this person usually provokes or will fail to bring the family together on a course of action.

Families are not always involved in treatment, nor should they always be involved. But when the older client wants others' involvement or is dependent on them, they need to be included, at least to some extent. Even when the family is not included in treatment, a systems perspective is useful for understanding an older client's relationships with them. Family therapy views a person's symptoms as taking place in the larger context of the family. Family therapy is a style where cognitive, behavior, or interpersonal therapy may be employed. However, it is most often used with interpersonal therapy (Herkov, 2013c). Some special techniques of family therapy include genogram, which is a family tree constructed by the therapist, and it looks at past relationships and events and what impact these have on the person's current emotional state. Systemic interpretation may view a disease (i.e., depression) as a symptom of a problem in the larger family. Communication training examines dysfunctional communication patterns within the family and identifies and corrects them, and individuals are taught how to listen, ask questions, and respond nondefensively (Herkov, 2013c). Family systems approach is particularly appropriate for addressing elderly client and family issues in therapeutic sessions.

Guided Practice Exercise 11.6 examines family dynamics within a dysfunctional system to provide for a growth opportunity for the client, while providing empathy for the loss of loved ones in the network of family relationships.

Guided Practice Exercise 11.6

There exist many challenges within the family when caring for an aging parent while simultaneously experiencing the pain of losing loved ones. Family members may cease to communicate effectively and fail to carry out their responsibilities and may not function as a cohesive unit. These families may, for a brief period of time, be viewed as dysfunctional. This deterioration in the family system will be one reason to seek professional counseling. Despite problematic challenges in the family system, the counselor is still able to encourage emotional growth for the aging client while grieving the loss of family members. Examine issues that cause problems for family members in caring for an aging parent. Identify perceived emotions on the part of the older client and different family members. How would you express support and empathy to both parties? Describe how you might maximize growth for older clients while identifying contributions of family members?

REALITY ORIENTATION

Reality orientation (RO) is a general philosophy of inpatient treatment for reducing confusion in geriatric patients. According to the RO philosophy, confusion results from understimulation of the patient, care providers' lack of insistence or expectation that the patient perform normal behaviors, and care providers' nonreinforcement of desired behaviors when they are performed (Folsom, 1968; Taulbee & Folsom, 1966). Therefore, confusion can be reduced using mental stimulation, social interaction, and adjustment of behavioral contingencies.

The following theoretical assumptions underlie this psychosocial-behavior model of treatment:

1. Most behavior is learned and can be changed.
2. Behavior brought about by organic changes in the individual can also be modified.
3. The logical place for new behaviors to be learned is a social environment where new expectations and different social interactions elicit new behavior.
4. Environments can be created to provide the opportunity for and the reinforcement of desired behavioral changes.
5. The individual has some capacity for new growth and the assuming of responsibility for behavior. (Taulbee & Wright, 1971, p. 61)

Reality orientation is an effective intervention for older adults who are cognitive impaired. The treatment approach and advantages of this approach will be examined in the next section.

Treatment Approach

The primary goal of RO is to reduce confusion in older adults within their environments. In its initial conceptualization, RO was believed to accomplish the goal through three components. The first component was staff maintenance of a specific attitude toward the patient, usually one of "active" or "passive" friendliness (Folsom, 1968). This component has been referred to as attitude therapy. The second component involved staff's presentation of basic orienting information during their interactions with confused patients (e.g., reminding patients of who and where they are), and staff involvement of patients in the environment, by commenting on what was happening in the environment and by reinforcing the individuals' awareness of and interest in their environment.

The third component entails the use of basic and advanced classes in orientation. These classes were used in addition to the second component. The use of props or environmental cues was encouraged, including signs, clocks, calendars, RO boards (information about location, date, day, weather, holidays), newspapers, televisions, pictures, and personal belongings. Classes were run in small groups with an optimal size of three to six individuals meeting with one or two staff members (Lynch & Aspnes, 2004). The second and third components make up, respectively, what is now known as 24-hour Reality Orientation and Classroom Orientation.

Since its conception, RO's therapeutic goals have been elaborated and its techniques more clearly defined (Drummond, Kirchhoff, & Scarbrough, 1978) and documented (Holden & Woods, 1988). Certain aspects of the philosophy have proliferated, for example, use of calendars and other orienting material can be found in almost all long-term care facilities. The evolution of RO programs also has often resulted in the rise of Classroom RO without 24-hour RO, despite the assertion that classroom RO will not be effective on its own (Folsom, 1968). This modification de-emphasizes the focus on social interaction with others in the environment that, increasingly, appears to be the most beneficial aspect of RO (Kasi-Godley, 2006).

Use in Individuals With Dementia

RO was developed for reducing confusion in institutionalized individuals. The source of confusion may stem from a variety of conditions, such as stroke, dementia, or psychiatric disorder. However, little consideration has been given regarding whether there should be differences in RO according to the reasons for confusion. In practice, RO is used most commonly with patients with dementia, but few attempts have been made to explain the way in which dementia might influence the individual's ability to benefit from RO (Kasi-Godley, 2006).

Guided Practice Exercise 11.7 provides the opportunity to administer the mini-mental state examination while acknowledging that the results obtained are just one component of the assessment process.

Guided Practice Exercise 11.7

Many older clients may be afraid they are losing their memory. As a counselor, you choose to administer a mini-mental state examination. Ask your older client the following questions: Where are you now? Where are you located? What is today's date? What is the month? What day of the week is it? What year are we in? When were you born? In what month were you born? How old are you? Who is the president of the United States? Who am I? What is my role? Have you ever seen me before? Where were you last night? Make sure that your client answers the questions, not family members. Also make sure you are aware of any medications your client was on when he or she complained of memory problems. Score the first 10 questions according to the following scale:

0–2: no or minimal brain syndrome

3–5: mild to moderate brain syndrome

6–8: at least moderate brain syndrome

9–10: severe organic brain syndrome

What does your client's score indicate? What additional information do you feel you need to work with this client?

RO permits the individual with dementia to build competency (e.g., re-learning information), thereby reducing feelings of helplessness engendered by repeated failing at simple tasks that can no longer be accomplished because of progressive impairment. However, feelings of competence are contingent on the use of activities that are appropriate to the ability level and needs of the individual (Woods, 1979). Environmental adaptations that reduce the need to remember and external aids, such as reminders to do something or of how to do something, of where an item is located, or even what something is (i.e., diaries, memory wallets, and word-orientation procedures), are effective (Douglas, Ames, & Ballard, 2004). There exists a need for provider input to draw attention to the aid.

Another strategy is rehearsal, which involves adjusting the retrieval period during learning, one item at a time, according to whether the item was successfully recalled on the previous trial; however, this technique is circumscribed and time intensive for the caregiver, and the effort required may exceed the gains achieved. In fact, some of the most effective memory interventions are more comprehensive, such as cognitive remediation programs that focus on exercising remaining abilities or re-learning of skills within an interpersonal context. These types of programs often entail multiple components that aim to enhance memory functioning through problem-solving exercises and increase social interaction through communication skills. Individuals with dementia participating in comprehensive cognitive skills remediation programs have shown maintained cognitive and behavioral functioning as well as improved mood and coping responses (Quayhagen, Quayhagen, Corbeil, Roth, & Rodgers, 1995), although gains tend to be most likely in mildly impaired individuals.

Reality orientation therapy has been associated with significant improvements in cognition and behavior and with a reduced risk of admission to care among people with Alzheimer's disease (Metitieri, Zanetti, & Geroldi, 2001; Spector et al., 2003). A meta-analysis of six controlled trials concluded that reality orientation should be considered as part of dementia care programs (Spector, Orrell, & Davies, 2000). However, baseline cognitive function may influence response to reality orientation therapy (Zanetti, Oriani, & Geroldi, 2002).

Patton (2006) investigated the use of reality orientation and the perception of its effectiveness in older persons' mental health care. Six psychiatric nurses practicing in an older person mental health care inpatient unit took part in in-depth semistructured interviews. Upon analysis, interview data yielded five themes. Reality orientation means interacting with patients about the patient's current environment and issues in his or her predicament. The sampled nurses used reality orientation frequently in their nursing work, most frequently used in morning and evenings. Reality orientation is implemented through interacting with the patient. It may also be implemented as part of other approaches, such as occupational therapy. Reality orientation is an approach that can be used to help older persons experiencing mental health problems cope with not being able to comprehend and recognize their environment, and it may hold some benefit for older disorientated persons, such as facilitating a greater level of orientation (Patton, 2006).

Due to interest in the promise of cognitive stimulation or rehabilitation programs for cognitively impaired adults, there has been renewed interest in RO, albeit a version that more approximates cognitive stimulation programs (Woods, 2002). This new wave of RO research focuses more on the means of improving cognitive functioning through additional interpersonal functioning and communication targets (Savorani et al., 2004; Spector et al., 2003). Reality orientation has, until more recently, experienced a decline in popularity over the years, especially in comparison to validation therapy because of concern about people applying the theory without taking into account the person's emotions and mental health (Heerema, 2014). Validation therapy emphasizes the feelings behind the behaviors or statements. It encourages the person to talk about the reality they're in and postulates that by processing those perhaps unresolved issues, they'll eventually be able to be more at peace (Heerema, 2014).

Reality orientation (RO) is an approach where the environment, including dates, locations, and current surroundings, is frequently pointed out and woven into the conversations with the person who has dementia. Strategies for reality orientation include talking about the time of the day, the date, and the season; use the person's name frequently; discuss current events; refer to clocks and calendars; place signs and labels on doors and cupboards and ask questions about photos or other decorations (Heerema, 2014). Reality orientation continues to be used in settings to decrease confusion with cognitively impaired patients in institutional settings.

KEYSTONES

- Numerous therapeutic interventions exist for counselors working with older clients.
- Problem-solving therapy holds potential for treating older persons with depressive disorders.

- Brief dynamic therapy is an effective intervention for clients with adjustment disorders, grief, and traumatic stress.

- Relaxation, desensitization, and shaping new responses are behavioral approaches used with older persons.

- Cognitive therapy aims to alter the clients' irrational beliefs and holds enormous promise for older persons.

- Exaggerated beliefs are effectively challenged within the cognitive-behavioral approach.

- Integrated therapy is a more recent intervention which holds promise with working with older clients due to its eclectic nature.

- Retrieving past memories and resolving conflicts can be achieved in life review and reminiscence therapy.

- Older adults live within a family unit, and the family systems approach emphasizes the dynamics of the family system.

- Reality orientation therapy is an established philosophy used extensively with older persons with memory deficits.

ADDITIONAL RESOURCES

Print Based

Balk, D. E. (Ed.). (2007). *Handbook of thanatology*. Northbrook, IL: Association for Death Education and Counseling, The Thanatology Association.

Folstein, M. F., Folstein, S. E., & McHugh, P. R. (1975). Mini-mental state: A practical method for grading the cognitive state of patients for the clinician. *Journal of Psychiatric Research, 12*(3), 189–198.

Gibson, F. (2006). *Reminiscence and recall* (3rd ed.). London, UK: Age Concern.

Morgan, A. (2003). Psychodynamic psychotherapy with older adults. *Psychiatric Services, 54*(12), 1592–1595.

Qualls, S. H., & Knight, B. G. (Eds.). (2006). *Psychotherapy for depression in older adults*. Hoboken, NJ: John Wiley & Sons.

Web Based

www.aamft.org/iMIS15/AAMFT
www.apa.org/pi/aging/resources/guides/psychotherapy.aspx
www.encyclopedia.com/topic/Reality_Orientation.aspx
www.iagp.com/
www.agpa.org/
www.minddisorders.com/Flu-Inv/Interpersonal-therapy.html

REFERENCES

Anuradha, K. (2004). Empowering families with mentally ill members: A strengths perspective. *International Journal for the Advancement of Counseling, 26,* 383–391.

Ando, M., Morita, T., Akechi, T., & Okamoto, T. (2010). Japanese task force for spiritual care efficacy of short term review interviews on the spiritual well-being of terminally-ill cancer patients. *Journal of Pain Symptom Management, 39*(6), 993–1002.

Ando, M., Morita, T., Ahn, S., Marquez-Wong, F., & Ide, S. (2009). International comparison study on the primary concerns of terminally ill cancer patients in short-term life review interviews among Japanese, Koreans, and Americans. *Palliative Supportive Care, 7*(3), 349–355.

Arean, P. A. (2006). Depression treatment preferences in older primary care patients. *Gerontologist, 46*(1), 14–22.

Arean, P. A., & Cook, B. L. (2002). Psychotherapy and combined psychotherapy/pharmacotherapy for late-life depression. *Biological Psychiatry, 5*(3), 293–303.

Arean, P. A., Hegel, M. T., & Reynolds, C. F. (2001). Treating depression in older medical patients with psychotherapy. *Journal of Clinical Geropsychology, 7,* 93–104.

Arean, P., Hegel, M., Vannoy, S., Fan, M-Y., & Unuzter, J. (2008). Effectiveness of problem-solving therapy for older, primary care patients with depression: Results from the IMPACT project. *The Gerontologist, 48*(3), 311–323.

Arean, P., Raue, P., Mackin, R., Kanellopoulos, D., McCulloch, C., & Alexopoulos, G. (2010). Problem-solving therapy and supportive therapy in older adults with major depression and executive dysfunction. *American Journal of Psychiatry, 167*(11), 1391–1398.

The Benevolent Society (2005). Reminiscing manual version. Retrieved from http://www.scribd.com/doc/28526151/Reminiscing-Handbook-For-Those-Workiing-With-Older-Adults

Bohlmeijer, E., Roemer, M., Cuijpers, P., & Smit, F. (2007). The effects of reminiscence on psychological well-being in older adults: A meta-analysis. *Aging and Mental Health, 11*(3), 291–300.

Bohlmeijer, E., Smit, F., & Cuijpers, P. (2003). The effects of reminiscence and life review on late-life depression. A meta-analysis. *International Journal of Geriatric Psychiatry, 18*(12), 1088–1094.

Brooks-Harris, J. (2008). *Integrative multi-theoretical psychotherapy.* Boston, MA: Houghton-Mifflin.

Canadian Coalition for Seniors' Mental Health, 2006. *National Guidelines for Seniors Mental Health: The assessment and treatment of depression.* Toronto, ON: CCSMH. Retrieved www.ccsmh.ca.

Castonguay, L., Newman, M., Borkovec, T., Holtforth, J., & Maramba, G. (2005). Cognitive-behavioral assimilative integrative. In J. C. Norcross & M. R. Goldfried (Eds.), *Handbook of psychotherapy integration* (2nd ed., pp. 241–260). New York, NY: Oxford.

Centers for Disease Control and Prevention & National Association of Chronic Disease Directors. (2009). *The state of mental health and aging in America.* Issue Brief 2: Addressing depression in older adults: Selected evidence-based programs. Retrieved from http://apps.nccd.cdc.gov/MAHA/MahaHome.aspx

Chand, S., & Grossberg, G. (2013). How to adapt cognitive-behavioral therapy for older adults. *Current Psychiatry, 12*(3). Retrieved http://www.currentpsychiatry.com/home/article/how-to-adapt-cognitive-behavioral-therapy-for-older-adults/99ca3dc03cddedc62b20b672dcc4e56c.html

Chapin, R., & Cox, E. (2001). Changing the paradigm: Strengths-based and empowerment-oriented social work with frail elders. *Gerontological Social Work Practice: Issues, Challenges, and Potential, 36,* 165–179.

Chiang, K., Chu, H., Chang, H., Chung, M., Chen, C., Chiou, H., & Chou, K. (2010). The effects of reminiscence therapy on psychological well-being, depression, and loneliness among the institutionalized aged. *International Journal of Geriatric Psychiatry, 25*(4), 380–388.

Chiang, K., Lu R., Chu, H., Chang, Y., & Chou, K. (2008). Evaluation of the effect of a life review group program on self-esteem and life satisfaction in the elderly. *International Journal of Geriatric Psychiatry, 23*(1), 7–10.

Choi, N., Hegel, M., Marinucci, M., Sirrianni, L., & Bruce, M. (2012). Association between participant-identified problems and depression severity in problem-solving therapy for low-income homebound older adults. *International Journal of Geriatric Psychiatry, 27*(5), 491–499.

Ciechanowski, P., Wagner, E., Schmalig, K., Schwartz, S., Williams, B., Diehr, P., & LoGerlo, J. (2004). Community-integrated home-based depression treatment in older adults: A randomized controlled trial. *Journal of the American Medical Association, 291*(13), 1569–1577.

Coleman, P. (1994). Reminiscence within the study of ageing. In J. Bornat (Ed.) *Reminiscence reviewed: Perspectives, evaluations, achievements.* Buckingham, UK: Open University Press.

Cox, D., & D'Oyley, H. (2011). Cognitive-behavioral therapy with older adults. *British Columbia Medical Journal, 53*(7), 348–352.

Cox, E., Green, K., Seo, H., Inaba, M., & Quillen, A. (2006). Coping with late-life challenges: Development and validation of the Care-Receiver Efficacy Scale. *The Gerontologist, 46*(5), 640–649.

DePaola, S., Griffin, M., Young, J., & Neimeyer, R. (2003). Death anxiety and attitudes towards the elderly among older adults: The role of gender and ethnicity. *Death Studies, 27,* 33–354.

Douglas, S., James, I., & Ballard, C. (2004). Non-pharmacological interventions in dementia. *Advance Psychiatric Treatment, 10,* 171–177.

Drummond, L., Kirchhoff, L., & Scarbrough, D. (1978). A practical guide to reality orientation: A treatment approach for confusion and disorientation. *The Gerontologist, 18,* 568–573.

Erikson, E. (1950). *Childhood and society.* New York, NY: W.W. Norton and Company.

Etchegoyen, H. (2005). *The fundamentals of psychoanalytic technique.* London, UK: Karnac Books.

Evans, P., Turner, S., & Trotter, C. (2012). *The effectiveness of family and relationship therapy: A review of the literature.* Melbourne, Australia: PACFA.

Folsom, J. C. (1968). Reality orientation for the elderly mental patient. *Journal of Geriatric Psychiatry, 1,* 291–307.

Forman, M. (2010). *A guide to integral psychotherapy: Complexity, integration, and spirituality in practice.* Albany, NY: SUNY Press.

Forsman, A., Schierenbeck, I., & Wahlbeck, K. (2011). Psychosocial intervention for the prevention of depression in older adults: Systematic review and meta-analysis. *Journal of Aging Health, 23,* 387–416.

Freedman, M., Kaunitz, A., Reape, K., Hart, H., & Shu, H. (2009). Twice-weekly synthetic conjugated estrogens vaginal cream for the treatment of vaginal atrophy. *Menopause, 16*(4), 735–741.

Gaggioli, A., Scaratti, C., Morganti, L., Stramba-Badiale, M., Agostoni, M., Spatola, C., . . . Riva, G. (2014). *Trials, 15,* 408.

Gaymu, J., Ekamper, P., & Beets, G. (2007). Who will be caring for Europe's dependent elders in 2030? *Population, 62*(4), 675–706.

Gellis, Z., & Bruce, M. (2010). Problem-solving therapy for subthreshold depression in home healthcare patients with cardiovascular disease. *The American Journal of Geriatric Psychiatry, 18*(6), 464–474.

Gellis, Z., McGinty, J., Tierney, L., Jordan, C., Burton, J., & Misener, E. (2008). Randomized controlled trial of problem-solving therapy for minor depression in home care. *Research on Social Work Practice, 18*(6), 596–606.

Gellis, Z., McGinty, J., Horowitz, A., Bruce, J., & Misener, E. (2007). Problem-solving therapy for late-life depression in home care: A randomized field trial. *The American Journal of Geriatric Psychiatry, 15*(11), 968–978.

Glicken, M. (2009). *Evidence-based counseling and psychotherapy for an aging population.* Burlington, MA: Academic Press.

Good, G., & Beitman, B. (2006). *Counseling and psychotherapy essentials: Integrating theories, skills, and practices.* New York: W.W. Norton.

Gott, M., Hinchliff, S., & Galena, E. (2004). General practitioner attitudes to discussing sexual health issues with older people. *Social Science & Medicine, 58*(11), 2093–2103.

Greene, R. (2000). Serving the aged and their families in the 21st century: Using a revised practice model. *Journal of Gerontological Social Work*, 34(1), 43–62.

Gustavson, K., Alexopoulos, G., Niu, G., McCulloch, C., Meade, T., & Arean, P. (2015). Problem-solving therapy reduces suicidal ideation in depressed older adults with executive dysfunction. *The American Journal of Geriatric Psychiatry*. Retrieved from http://www.dx.doi.org/101016/iiaqp.2015.07.010

Haberkern, F., Schmid, T., Neuberger, F., & Grignon, M. (2012). The role of the elderly as providers and recipients of care. In *The Future of Families to 2030* (pp. 189–257). Paris, France: OECD Publishing.

Haber, D. (2006). Life review: Implementation theory, research and therapy. *International Journal of Aging and Human Development, 63*(2), 153–171.

Haggerty, J. (2013). *Psychodynamic therapy*. Psych Central. Retrieved from http://www.psychcentral.com/lib/psychodynamictherapy/

Haight, B. K., & Burnside, I. (1993). Reminiscence and life review: Explaining the differences. *Archive of Psychiatric Nursing, 7*(2), 91–98.

Haight, B. K., & Haight, B. S. (2007). *The handbook of structured life review*. Baltimore, MD: Health Professions Press.

Haight, B. K., Michel, Y., & Hendrix, S. (2000). The extended effects of the life review in nursing homes residents. *International Journal of Aging and Human Development, 50*(2), 151–168.

Hajjar, R., & Kamel, H. (2004). Sexuality in the nursing home, part I: Attitudes and barriers to sexual expression. *Journal of the American Medical Directors Association, 5*(2), S42–S47.

Haley, J. (1976). *Problem-solving therapy*. San Francisco, CA: Jossey-Bass.

Hanaoka, H., & Okamura, H. (2004). Study on effects of life review activities on the quality of life of the elderly: A randomized controlled trial. *Psychotherapy Psychosomatic, 73*(5), 302–311.

Haverkamp, K., Arean, P., Hegel, M. T., & Unutzer, J. (2004). Problem-solving treatment for complicated depression in late life: A case study in primary care. *Perspectives in Psychiatric Care, 40*(2), 45–52.

Headley, L. (1977). *Adults and their parents in family therapy: A new direction in treatment*. New York, NY: Plenum Press.

Heerema, E. (2014). Using reality orientation in the treatment of people with Alzheimer's disease. Retrieved from http://alzheimers.about.com/od/treatmentofalzheimers/a/Using-Reality-Orientation-In-The-Treatment-Of-People-With-Alzheimer's-Disease

Herkov, M. (2013a). *About behavior therapy*. Psych Central. Retrieved from http://psychcentral.com/lib/about-behavior-therapy/

Herkov, M. (2013b). *About cognitive psychotherapy*. Psych Central. Retrieved from http://psychcentral.com/lib/about-cognitive-psychotherapy/

Herkov, M. (2013c). *About family therapy*. Psych Central. Retrieved from http://psychcentral.com/lib/about-family-therapy/

Herr, J. J., & Weakland, J. H. (1979). *Counseling elders and their families: Practical techniques for applied gerontology*. New York, NY: Springer.

Hill, C. E. (2014). *Helping skills: Facilitating exploration, insight and action* (4th ed.). Washington, DC: American Psychological Association.

Hirst, S., Lane, A., & Navenec, C. (2011). Strength-based approaches for mental wellness in seniors and adults with disabilities: Final report. *Alberta Health Services—Addiction and Mental Health*.

Holden, U., & Woods, R. (1988). *Reality orientation: Psychological approaches to the confused elderly* (2nd ed.). Edinburgh, UK: Churchill Livingstone.

Hyer, L., Swanson, G., Lefkowitz, R., Hillesland, D., Davis, H., & Woods, M. G. (1990). The application of the cognitive behavioral model to two older stressor groups. *Clinical Gerontologist, 9*(3–4), 145–190.

Ingersoll, E., & Zeitler, D. (2010). *Integral psychotherapy: Inside out/outside in*. Albany, NY: SUNY Press.

Jenko, M., Gonzalez, L., & Seymour, M. (2007). Life review with terminally ill. *Journal of Hospice & Palliative Nursing, 9*(3), 168–169.

Jones, E. D. (2003). Reminiscence therapy for older women with depression. Effects of nursing intervention classification in assisted-living long-term care. *Journal of Gerontological Nursing, 29*(7), 26–33.

Kasi-Godley, J. (2006). Reality orientation. In R. Schultz, L. S., Noelker, K. Rockwood, & R. L. Sprott (Eds.), *Encyclopedia of aging* (4th ed.). New York, NY: Springer.

Kennedy, G. J., & Tannebaum, S. (2000). Psychotherapy with older adults. *American Journal of Psychotherapy, 54*(3), 386–407.

Kessenich, C., & Cichon, M. (2001). Hormonal decline in elderly men and male menopause. *Geriatric Nursing, 22*(1), 24–27.

Kettell, M. (2001). Reminiscence and the late life search for ego integrity: Ingmar Bergman's *Wild Strawberries*. *Journal of Geriatric Psychiatry, 34,* 9–41.

Kivnick, H., & Stoffel, S. (2005). Vital involvement practice: Strengths as more than tools for solving problems. *Journal of Gerontological Social Work, 46,* 85–116.

Klever, S. (2013). Reminiscence therapy: Finding meaning in memories. *Nursing, 43*(4), 36–37.

Knight, B. G. (2004). *Psychotherapy with older adults* (3rd ed.). Thousand Oaks, CA: Sage.

Korte, J., Bohlmeijer, E., Cappeliez, P., Smit, F., & Westerhof, G. (2010). Life review therapy for older adults with moderate depressive symptomatology: A pragmatic randomized controlled trial. *Psychological Medicine, 42*(6), 1163–1173.

Laidlaw, K., Thompson, L., & Dick-Siskin, L. (2003). *Cognitive behavioral therapy with older people.* Chichester, UK: John Wiley & Sons.

Lang, A., & Stein, M. (2001). Anxiety disorders. *Geriatrics, 56*(5), 24–30.

Lobo, R. (2007). Menopause: Endocrinology, consequences of estrogen deficiencies, effects of hormone replacement therapy treatment regimens. In V. L. Katz, G. M. Lentz, R. A. Lobo, & D. M. Gershenson (Eds.), *Comprehensive gynecology* (5th ed.). Philadelphia, PA: Mosby Elsevier.

Lynch, T., & Aspnes, A. (2004). Individual and group psychotherapy. In D. Blazer, D. Steffens, & E. Busse (Eds.), *Textbook of Geriatric Psychiatry* (3rd ed., pp. 443–458). Washington, DC: American Psychiatric Publishing.

Magliano, L., Fiorillo, A., Fadden, G., Gair, F., Economou, M., Kallert, T., . . . Maj, M. (2005). Effectiveness of a psychoeducational intervention for families of patients with schizophrenia: Preliminary results of a study funded by the European Commission. *World Psychiatry, 4*(1), 45–49.

McKee, K., Wilson, F., Chung, M., Hinchliff, S., Goudie, F., Elford, H., & Mitchell, C. (2005). Reminiscence, regrets and activity in older people in residential care: Associations with psychological health. *British Journal of Clinical Psychology, 44,* 543–561.

Melendez-Moral, J., Charco-Ruiz, L., Mayordoma-Rodriguez, T., & Sales-Galan, A. (2013). Effects of a reminiscence program among institutionalized elderly adults. *Psicothema, 25*(3), 319–323.

Metitieri, T., Zanetti, O., & Geroldi, C. (2001). Reality orientation therapy to delay outcome of progression in patients with dementia: A retrospective study. *Clinical Rehabilitation, 15,* 471–478.

Montejo, A., Llorca, G., Izquierdo, J., & Rico-Villademoros, F. (2001). Incidence of sexual dysfunction associated with antidepressant agents: A prospective multicenter study of 1,022 outpatients. Spanish working group for the study of psychotropic-related sexual dysfunction. *The Journal of Clinical Psychiatry, 62*(3), 10–21.

Morley, J., & Tariq, S. (2003). Sexuality and disease. *Clinics in Geriatric Medicine, 19*(3), 563–573.

Mynors-Wallis, L. (1996). Problem-solving treatment: Evidence for effectiveness and feasibility in primary care. *International Journal of Psychiatry in Medicine, 26*(3), 249–262.

Mynors-Wallis, L. M., Gath, D. H., Day, A., & Baker, F. (2000). Randomized controlled trial of problem-solving treatment, antidepressant medication and combined treatment for major depression in primary care. *British Medical Journal, 320*(7226), 26–30.

National Association of Social Workers (NASW). (2010). *Family caregivers of older adults.* Washington, DC: Author.

Nezu, A. M. (2004). Problem solving and behavior therapy revisited. *Behavior Therapy, 35*(1), 1–33.

Norcross, J. (2005). A primer on psychotherapy integration. In J. C. Norcross & M. R. Goldfried (Eds.), *Handbook of psychotherapy integration* (2nd ed., pp. 3–23). New York, NY: Oxford University Press.

Norcross, J., & Goldfried, M. (2005). *Handbook of psychotherapy integration* (2nd ed.). New York, NY: Oxford.

Patton, D. (2006). Reality orientation: Its use and effectiveness within older person mental health care. *Journal of Clinical Nursing, 15*(11), 1440–1449.

Pasupathi, M., Weeks, T., & Rice, C. (2006). Remembering as a major process in adult development. *Journal of Language and Social Psychology, 25*(3), 244–263.

Paukert, A, Phillips, L., & Cully, J. (2009). Integration of religion into cognitive-behavioral therapy for geriatric anxiety and depression. *Journal of Psychiatric Practice, 15,* 103–112.

Peacock, S. (2010). The positive aspects of the caregiving journey with dementia: Using a strengths-based perspective to reveal opportunities. *Journal of Applied Gerontology, 29,* 640–659.

Peng, X., Huang, C., Chen, L., & Lu, Z. (2009). Cognitive behavioral therapy and reminiscence techniques for the treatment of depression in the elderly: A systematic review. *Journal of Internal Medicine Research, 37,* 975–982.

Pickard, L. (2013). A growing care gap? The supply of unpaid care for older people by their adult children in England to 2032. *Ageing and Society,* 1–28.

Pinquart, M., & Sorenson, S. (2001). How effective are psychotherapeutic and other psychosocial interventions with older adults? A meta-analysis. *Journal of Mental Health and Aging, 7,* 207–243.

Pinquart, M., & Forstmeier, S. (2012). Effects of reminiscence intervention on psychosocial outcomes: A meta-analysis. *Aging and Mental Health, 16,* 541–558.

Pinquart, M., Duberstein, P. R., & Lyness, J. M. Effects of psychotherapy and other behavioral interventions on clinically depressed older adults: A meta-analysis. *Aging and Mental Health, 11*(6), 645–657.

Puentes, W. (2003). Cognitive therapy integrated with life review techniques: An eclectic treatment approach for affective symptoms in older adults. *Journal of Clinical Nursing, 13,* 84–89.

Quayhagen, M. P., Quayhagen, M., Corbeil, R. R., Roth, P. A., & Rodgers, J. A. (1995). A dyadic remediation program for care-recipients with dementia. *Nursing Research, 44*(3), 153–159.

Rashid, T. (2009). Positive interventions in clinical practice. *Journal of Clinical Psychology, 65,* 461–466.

Rashid, T., & Ostermann, R. (2009). Strength based assessment in clinical practice. *Journal of Clinical Psychology: In Session, 65,* 488–498.

Reppermund, S., Ising, M., Lucae, S., & Zihl, J. (2009). Cognitive impairment in unipolar depression is persistent and non-specific: Further evidence for the final common pathway disorder hypothesis. *Psychological Medicine, 39*(4), 603–614.

Ronch, J., & Goldfield, J. (2003). *Mental wellness in aging: Strengths-based approaches.* Baltimore, MD: Health Professions Press.

Rosen, D., Morse, J., & Reynolds, C. (2011). Adapting problem-solving therapy for depressed older adults in methadone maintenance treatment. *Journal for Substance Abuse Treatment, 40*(2), 132–141.

Rovner, B., & Casten, R. (2008). Preventing late-life depression in age-related macular degeneration. *American Journal of Geriatric Psychiatry, 16*(6), 459.

Rush, A. J., Beck, A. T., Kovacs, M., Weissenburger, J., & Hollon, S. D. (1982). Comparison of the effects of cognitive therapy and pharmacotherapy on hopelessness and self-concept. *American Journal of Psychiatry, 139,* 862–866.

Rusin, M. J., & Lawson, J. J. (2001). Behavioral interventions and families: A medical rehabilitation perspective. *Journal of Clinical Geropsychology, 7*(4), 255–269.

Rybarczyk, B. (2006). Cognitive therapy. In R. Schultz, L. S. Noelker, K. Rockwood, & R. Sprott (Eds.), *Encyclopedia of aging* (4th ed.). New York, NY: Springer.

Savorani, G., Chattat, R., Capelli, E., Vaienti, F., Giannini, R., Bacci, M., . . . Ravaglia, G. (2004). Immediate effectiveness of the "New Identity" reality orientation therapy (ROT) for people with dementia in a geriatric day hospital. *Archives of Gerontology and Geriatrics, 38* (Suppl. 9), 359–364.

Simon, S., Cordas, T., & Bottino, C. (2015). Cognitive behavioral therapies in older adults with depression and cognitive deficits: A systematic review. *International Journal of Geriatric Psychiatry, 30*(3), 223–233.

Smith, M. T., Perlis, M. L., Park, A., Smith, M. S., Pennington, J., & Giles, D. E. (2002). Comparative meta-analysis of pharmacotherapy and behavior therapy for persistent insomnia. *American Journal of Psychiatry, 159*(1), 5–11.

Spector, A., Orrell, M., & Davies, S. (2000). *Reality orientation for dementia. Cochrane database of systematic reviews* (Issue 4). Oxford, UK: Update Software.

Spector, A., Thorgrimsen, L., Woods, B., Royan, L., Davies, S., & Butterworth, M. (2003). Efficacy of an evidence-based cognitive stimulation therapy programme for people with dementia: Randomised controlled trial. *British Journal of Psychiatry, 183,* 248–254.

Stanley, M., & Novy, D. (2000). Cognitive-behavior therapy for generalized anxiety in late life: An evaluative overview. *Journal of Anxiety Disorders, 14*(2), 191–207.

Stricker, G., & Gold, J. (2005). Assimilative psychodynamic psychotherapy. In J. C. Norcross & M. R. Goldfried (Eds.), *Handbook of psychotherapy integration* (2nd ed., pp. 221–240). New York, NY: Oxford.

Taulbee, L. R., & Folsom, J. C. (1966). Reality orientation for geriatric patients. *Hospital and Community Psychiatry, 17*(5), 133–135.

Taulbee, L. R., & Wright, H. W. (1971). A psychosocial-behavioral model for therapy. In C. W. Spielberger (Ed.), *Current topics in clinical and community psychology* (Vol. 3, p. 61). New York, NY: Academic Press.

Teri, L., Gibbons, L. E., McCurry, S. M., Logsdon, R. G., Buchner, D. M., & Barlow, W. E. (2003). Exercise plus behavioral management in patients with Alzheimer's disease: A randomized controlled trial. *Journal of the American Medical Association, 290*(15), 2015–2022.

Teri, L., Logsdon, R., & Uomoto, J. (1997). Behavioral treatment of depression in dementia patients: A controlled clinical trial. *Journal of Gerontology B: Psychological Science, Social Science, 52*(4), 159–166.

Thorpe, S., Ayers, C., & Nuevo, R. (2009). Meta-analysis comparing different behavioral treatments for late-life anxiety. *American Journal of Geriatric Psychiatry, 17,* 105–115.

Trout, A., Ryan, J., La Vigne, S., & Epstein, M. (2003). Behavioral and emotional rating scale: Two studies of convergent validity. *Journal of Child and Family Studies, 12,* 399–410.

vant Veer-Tazelaar, P., van Marwijk, H., & van Oppen, P. (2009). Stepped-care prevention of anxiety and depression in late life: A randomized control trial. *Archives of General Psychiatry, 66,* 297–304.

Wallace, M. (2008). How to try this: Sexuality assessment. *American Journal of Nursing, 108*(7), 40–48.

Wallace, M. (2012). *Issues regarding sexuality: Sexuality in the older adult.* Retrieved from http://consultgerirn.org/topics/sexuality_issues_in_the-older_adult

Webster, J. (2002). Reminiscence functions in adulthood: Age, race and family dynamics correlates. In J. D. Webster & B. K. Haight (Eds.), *Critical advances in reminiscence work: From theory to application.* New York, NY: Springer.

Wespes, E., Moncada, I., Schmitt, H., Jungwirth, A., Chan, M., & Varanese, L. (2007). The influence of age on treatment outcomes in men with erectile dysfunction treated with two regimes of tadalafil: Results of the SURE Study. *BJU International, 99*(1), 121–126.

Westerhof, G., Bohlmeijer, E., van Beljouw, I., & Pot, A. (2010). Improvement in personal meaning mediates the effects of a life review intervention on depressive symptoms: In a randomized controlled trial. *Gerontologist, 50*(4), 541–549.

Wilber, K. (2000). *Integral psychology: Consciousness, spirit, psychology, therapy.* Boston, MA: Shambhala.

Williams, J. W. Jr., Barrett, J., Oxman, T., Frank, E., Katon, W., Sullivan, M., . . . Sengupta, A. (2000). Treatment of dysthymia and major depression in primary care: A randomized control trial in older adults. *Journal of the American Medical Association, 284*(12), 1519–1526.

Woods, B. (1979). Reality orientation and staff attention: A controlled study. *British Journal of Psychiatry, 134,* 502–507.

Woods, B. (2002): Reality orientation: A welcome return? *Age and Aging, 31,* 155–156.

Zanetti, O., Oriani, M., & Geroldi, C. (2002). Predictors of cognitive improvement after reality orientation in Alzheimer's disease. *Age and Ageing, 31,* 193–196.

Zarit, S. H., & Zarit, J. M. (2011). *Mental disorders in older adults: Fundamentals of assessment.* New York, NY: Guilford Press.

Future Trends

"There will come a time when you believe everything is finished. That will be the beginning."

—Louis L'Amour

Learning Objectives

After reading this chapter, you will be able to

1. Describe the issues that counselors must address to help older adults age successfully
2. Analyze challenges that face older adults in health care
3. Discuss future issues regarding employment and retirement for older adults
4. Examine the needs and challenges of gerontological counseling

INTRODUCTION

Counseling older adults will necessitate an emphasis on building upon the strengths and resiliency of older clients and a focus on a promotion of a healthy lifestyle. Health issues and the health care delivery system will continue to be a major concern for older adults as they attempt to address their health and mental health needs in later life. This heterogeneous population will require counselors who are academically prepared to address late-life transitions and who are resourceful, as well as those who can be advocates and work in a multidisciplinary team. These counselors need to be comfortable working with older clients in nontraditional counseling venues, while utilizing multiple psychotherapeutic approaches to enhance the wellness of their clients.

POSITIVE AGING

Numerous researchers have identified terms to attribute positive attributes to the aging population. Terms such as *productive aging, successful aging,* and *comfortable aging* are used to remove the negative connotation of the aging experience, which has historically diminished the self-esteem and lowered the status of aging persons. Regardless of what terms are used, many older persons are living longer and healthier lives and successful aging is a necessity. Therefore, counselors who provide services to older adults are in unique positions to facilitate their growth and development, making the aging experience more positive.

Counselors are challenged to understand and apply the knowledge of aging and build upon the strengths, wisdom, and experiences of older clients as they address their issues during therapeutic sessions. An increased number of professionals in the future will begin to interact with older adults and empower them to manage their issues in various ways.

Exercise, nutrition, stress reduction, and healthy behaviors will continue to be central to enhancing mental and physical well-being. Therefore, it's incumbent upon future professionals to become comfortable crossing disciplines and interacting and communicating within a multidisciplinary framework. It is inevitable that older persons will need to manage numerous physical and psychological issues, which are normative changes that accompany the aging process. However, the goals should be acknowledging disease processes, making the necessary modifications while simultaneously continuing to build on the older person's abilities versus disabilities. A holistic approach will become more routine in the lives of older persons, which emphasizes all domains operating simultaneously. Counselors will become proficient in recommending techniques to reduce stress, teaching stress reduction techniques and educating older clients on the significance of healthy behaviors to manage life transitions.

HEALTH CARE

Future issues revolve around availability of services, accessibility to services, and coordination of health care services. These issues continue to plague the health care and mental health care delivery system. For example, some regions have greater availability to services than other areas; major metropolitan areas have more health care centers, technology, and professional schools than rural areas.

Accessibility to services continues to present challenges because fundamental to accessibility is whether older persons can get the services that exist. There continues to exist, today and into the future, barriers to accessing health and mental health services. Barriers include transportation, cost, geographical location, availability of support systems, language issues (if English is not the first language), distance issues, lack of insurance, weather considerations, and hours of operation. Until all of these barriers are addressed in depth in all communities, accessibility will remain problematic in the future.

Coordination of services will ultimately become the responsibility of family members. Family members will become the coordinators of their loved one's health, mental health, and social needs. Currently, coordination of care is assumed to be the responsibility of the primary care physician. However, with the continued increased demands on physicians' time and the limited amount of time spent with older persons, these factors may impede their roles as care coordinators. With aging persons, it is essential that someone acts as the coordinator of services to ensure that all needs are met, services are provided, and that the older adults do not obtain the services they need. Lack of coordination will subject older persons to unnecessary hospitalizations, unmet health and mental health services, inadequate or limited attention to their numerous concerns, and ultimately decreases their quality of life.

EMPLOYMENT AND RETIREMENT

Many older persons today are more educated and healthier than previous generations. As such, there is an expectation for some to continue employment into their later years and for others to retire when they feel it is appropriate, which, for many, extends beyond age 65. Due to personal reasons, health considerations, financial assets (or lack thereof), and a desire for a particular lifestyle, retirement and work decisions will occur at different points in time for each older person.

Older workers will remain at companies that value their contributions and pay them accordingly. Companies can offer incentives to remain in the workforce, offer various training and educational opportunities; flexible scheduling; or opportunities for part-time work, consulting, or contract positions or bridge jobs. Older workers will continue to be needed in the future to train, educate, mentor younger, and/or new workers. They will act as role models as they are today and will provide this role in the future. This can only exist if companies decrease their biases and stereotypes of the capabilities of older workers and value their contributions.

Retirement will continue to be a reality for many Americans and a fantasy for others. Older adults who have invested in retirement plans, whether they are defined contribution plans or defined benefit plans have some financial resources during their retirement years. They may also have assets in the form of real estate, stocks, bonds, coin collections, art collections, stamp collections, and savings. Additionally, these retirees will benefit from Social Security payments, which will be at the higher end of the income scale. With proper management of assets and continued good health, these older adults will be able to enjoy numerous leisure pursuits and other endeavors.

However, for older persons who are working and expect to continue to work into their later years, out of necessity, retirement remains an elusive concept. These older persons may disregard a traditional retirement age due to financial necessity. They may be forced to retire due to health concerns or a downturn in the economic conditions. Their assets will be minimal, they are renters versus home owners, many do not have pension plans, and if so, they are inadequate. Their primary source of income is Social Security, and they receive small payments. There is a push by many organizations, both public and private, to move away from defined benefit plans to defined contribution plans where the employee assumes more risk versus the employer. This trend will continue to exist.

Companies are slow in addressing the need to retain older workers; however, there are some that value older workers, and there is an expectation that more companies will join this movement (Chou, 2012). Continued education and training is needed to educate persons in key administrative positions who make the ultimate decision regarding the strategic direction of their companies. Social Security will continue to be a debated topic, as the age for benefits may continue to rise, and decreasing benefits to accommodate a growing older population is also a strong possibility. However, Social Security will continue to provide full and/or partial benefits in the future for retirees. Older workers will work longer and continue to pay into Social Security, benefitting the system and the economy.

COUNSELING CONSIDERATIONS

It has been clearly illustrated that there exists an inadequate number of gerontological counselors today, and there is an expectation that the numbers will grow at a slow, but gradual pace. Barriers continue to exist, which impede older persons' access to mental health services and particularly services provided by professional counselors. With the aging of the baby boomers, who are growing up in a more relaxed and open culture, more older persons will access the services of professional counselors. However, this access may occur more for older persons with financial means because coverage for mental health services is limited, at best. The push to provide more coverage in this area will continue, as well as the push for licensed professional counselors to be reimbursed under Medicare for mental health services for older persons. Though this issue continues to be a struggle, it remains a possibility.

Continued advocacy is necessary on behalf of older persons in general and also specifically for older persons with special needs. This advocacy will occur at the local, regional, state, and federal levels. Advocacy is necessary, and activism is also indicated. Through advocacy and activism, policies, procedures, and laws can be developed to address the needs of older clients.

Education continues to expand in the field of gerontology, and there is an expectation that this will continue. Educational opportunities are formal and informal in nature. More education and consistent updating of content is necessary for counselors who work with older clients as well as for other health care personnel and the general public. This education for the masses can occur at very early stages of development and throughout the life span. Ageism can be diminished if all collective bodies become more educated on the strengths and contributions of older persons versus a focus on the frailties, disabilities, and negative connotations associated with the aging process. Counselors can lead this effort for their clients and become a primary resource for peers and lay persons in the community.

Older adults do not live in isolation, and most exist within a family system. A family systems approach will become more essential when working with older clients. Counselors must learn to become more comfortable working with families while maintaining the older person as their primary client. No longer is it appropriate for other caring persons to make decisions on behalf of the older client. The older client, unless deemed to be legally incompetent, should continue to be the decision maker in his or her treatment. In the future, counselors will need to become better communicators, negotiators, and mediators to assist in resolving family conflict.

Numerous therapeutic modalities will continue to be utilized in treating older clients. For instance, counselors will use the comprehensive psychosocial geriatric assessment to gather valuable information. Therapeutic modalities will continue to be tailored to meet the unique needs of older clients. An eclectic approach will be emphasized in the future, or one which is considered integrative in nature. The heterogeneity of the aging population offers challenges and opportunities in clinical work. More research will be conducted on the therapeutic modalities in the future.

The older population is a population that has many unmet needs. They experience major transitions related to loss, employment, retirement, relocation, health issues, and numerous other transitions. Counselors are positioned to work effectively with this population once they have acquired the knowledge, skills, and attitudes that are essential. Counselor education programs have the unique opportunity to prepare counselors in gerontological counseling and propel this group of professionals into the future.

KEYSTONES

- Accessing the strength and resiliency of older clients is essential in the counseling relationship.
- Promoting healthy behaviors enhances emotional and physical well-being of older adults.
- Availability, accessibility, and coordination of health and mental health services remains challenging.
- Older workers can be a valued resource; however, more attention is needed in internal and external employment settings.
- Retirement is a realistic possibility for some older persons, while it remains a challenge for many who need to work into later years.
- Numerous challenges exist in counseling older clients; however, many opportunities exist to increase gerontological counselors to meet the increased needs of an aging population

ADDITIONAL RESOURCES

Print Based

Bandura, A. (2009). Social cognitive theory of mass communications. In J. Bryant & M. B. Oliver (Eds.), *Media effects: Advancements in theory and research* (2nd ed., pp. 99–124). Mahwah, NJ: Lawrence Erlbaum.

Bowling, A., & Iliffe, S. (2011). Psychological approach to successful ageing predicts future quality of life in older adults. *Health and Quality of Life Outcomes, 9,* 13.

Brownell, P., & Kelly, J. (2013). *Ageism and mistreatment of older workers: Current reality, future solutions.* New York, NY: Springer.

Cornwell, E., & Waite, L. (2009). Social disconnectedness, perceived isolation, and health among older adults. *Journal of Health and Social Behavior, 50,* 31–38.

Flamez, B., Smith, R., Devlin, J., Richard, R., & Luther, M. (2008). Learning styles and instructional preferences: A comparison of an online and traditional counseling course. *Journal of Technology in Counseling, 5*(1).

Kampfe, C. (2015). *Counseling older people: Opportunities and challenges.* Hoboken, NJ: John Wiley & Sons.

Martin, L. G. (2009). Interventions to improve late life. *Population and Development Review, 35*(2), 331–340.

Renfro-Michel, E., O'Halloran, K., & Delaney, M. (2010). Using technology to enhance adult learning in the counselor education classroom. *Adultspan Journal, 9*(1), 14–25.

Web Based

www.cdc.gov/aging
www.counseling.org
www.census.gov
www.nutrition.tufts.edu
www.healthinaging.org
www.chronicdisease.org
www.mentalhealthamerica.net
www.humanservices.edu.org/counseling.html

REFERENCE

Chou, R. J. (2012). Discrimination against older workers: Current knowledge, future research directions and implications for social work. *Indian Journal of Gerontology, 26*(1), 25–49.

Index

Cases and tables are indicated by c or t following the page number.

About the Author

Adelle M. Williams is a native of Baltimore, Maryland, and currently resides with her family in Pittsburgh, Pennsylvania. She earned her PhD and Master's in Education in Rehabilitation Counseling and her undergraduate degree in Sociology from the University of Pittsburgh. She later obtained a Master's in Business Administration from Robert Morris College. Throughout her academic pursuits she has focused on aging and aging-related issues.

Currently, Dr. Williams is the Gerontology Coordinator and Professor within the Public Health and Social Work department within Slippery Rock University of Pennsylvania since June 2015. She teaches graduate counseling courses and undergraduate gerontology courses and is described as a dynamic professor who inspires students to advocate for the interests of our elders. Prior to this appointment, Dr. Williams was a Professor and Gerontology Coordinator within the Clinical Mental Health Counseling Program within the Counseling and Development and responsible for the newly created Aging specialization. Other positions held within the University include Professor and Gerontology Coordinator within the Health and Safety Management department, Assistant to the Dean for the College of Health, Environment and Science, Director of the Health Services Administration Program, Co-developer of the Long Term Care Administration specialization, Adjunct Professor within the Department of Allied Health and Faculty Liaison to Queen Margaret College in Edinburgh, Scotland.

Dr. Williams's research interests include aging, health and mental health, cultural diversity, women's issues, and administration. She has published articles in the Gerontologist, Protective Services Quarterly, The Afrocentric Scholar, The Journal of Allied Health, American Journal of Occupational Therapy, The Journal of Long Term Care Administration, Physical Therapy Education, The Journal of Health Administration Education, and the Pennsylvania Journal of Health, Physical Education, Recreation and Dance.

Dr. Williams has presented at the local, state, national, and international levels. She has been invited to present and invited to deliver the keynote address at several commencement ceremonies. She has attained grants and managed the grant application process. Dr. Williams has conducted many program reviews and interviewed by the media.

Clinical positions in the private sector included clinician, clinical supervisor, admissions administration, and research program coordinator within the Geriatric Psychiatry and Behavioral Neurology Unit of Western Psychiatric Institute and Clinic. She conducted individual, family, and group sessions, lead reminiscence groups, interpreted various assessments, and connected older adults with community services while operating within a multidisciplinary team. She also served in a consultant capacity for the Center for Aging and Research Program Director at the Mercy Hospital of Pittsburgh within the Geriatrics Division. Her clinical, research, and administrative experiences have proven valuable in teaching students to appreciate the challenges and opportunities inherent in the aging process and professional work with older adults.